Contributions to Management Science

More information about this series at
http://www.springer.com/series/1505

Ioan Constantin Dima • Mariana Man

Modelling and Simulation in Management

Econometric Models Used in the Management of Organizations

Springer

Ioan Constantin Dima
"Valahia" University of Targoviste
Dambovita
Romania

Mariana Man
University of Petrosani
Petrosani
Hunedoara
Romania

ISSN 1431-1941 ISSN 2197-716X (electronic)
Contributions to Management Science
ISBN 978-3-319-16591-2 ISBN 978-3-319-16592-9 (eBook)
DOI 10.1007/978-3-319-16592-9

Library of Congress Control Number: 2015938760

Springer Cham Heidelberg New York Dordrecht London

Printed on acid-free paper

Springer International Publishing AG Switzerland is part of Springer Science+Business Media (www.springer.com)

Never regard study as duty but as an enviable opportunity to learn to know the liberating influence of beauty in the realm of the spirit for your own personal joy and to the profit of the community to which your later work belongs.

Albert Einstein

Foreword

The globalisation we face nowadays derives from the fact that, by starting from the technological and economical development, a significant number of human activities are situated on such a large scale and scope that they exceed the national borders within the limits of which the sovereign states exercise their right to govern. The enhancement of current globalisation represents the fundamental feature of world economy at the beginning of the twenty-first century and is characterised by emphasising the trend to reduce and remove the barriers between the national economies and enhancing the connections between these economies.

The diversity and flexibility, the ability to adapt and respond to changes in the environment and the focus on customer needs satisfaction are key categories in the future management. Rapidly changing business environment in the economic, social and technological areas poses new challenges for the creation of effective management tools. Because of the complexity and volume of information and knowledge affecting the organisation functioning, contemporary organisations operate inefficiently because of the old, rigid and hierarchical decision-making system. Companies operating in such a dynamic environment are looking for management models based on the knowledge that allows them for intensive utilisation of the development of science, technology, organisation and management and the whole range of specific skills and dynamically developing competence.

The current management models insufficiently apply the knowledge and skills of employees and their undoubted advantages as a willingness to create new solutions, taking initiative and responsibility, which can in effect create a competitive advantage.

Moreover, it is well-known maxim *"You can't manage what you don't measure. It is an old management adage that is accurate today. Unless you measure something you don't know if it is getting better or worse. You can't manage for improvement if you don't measure to see what is getting better and what isn't."* In this context, the consideration included by I.C. Dima in the book "Econometric Models Used in the Management of Organisational Entities" based on econometrics methods' usage seems to be very useful for business practice and important for knowledge development.

The importance of a systemic approach in a market economy, which is the basis of the solutions proposed by the authors in this book, is the result of rapidly increasing flow of material and information flows. International cooperation has been expanded, which increases the corporate links that directly impact on enterprise systems. New relationships within the organisation are formed and new generations of system solutions also created causes that require a thorough knowledge of the functioning of the solutions and mechanisms for the development of management systems of economic organisation. Today, the need of reevaluation of current methods of management and search for solutions based on real econometrics foundations is clear. In this context, the consideration proposed by authors is perfect and ready for introduction.

This book is recommended to the reader by dealing with three research sub-themes in a unitary concept, which are together the research achieved by publishing this book. It is a matter of organisational entities dealt with in terms of systems theory, theoretical aspects of the econometric research and all the models used by econometrics to study the organisational management.

In the first research sub-theme, considering that the general theory of systems—cybernetics—and the current stage of the scientific research enable their approach at a more systematic scientific level, this book highlights some aspects of the genesis and development of hierarchical systems related to the hierarchy of the movement forms, matter and society, as well as that of the level of organisation. The evolution of the natural systems, in general, along with the physical, chemical, economic, political and managerial phenomena, presents unitary cybernetic aspects based on admitting the adjustments and associating the structures with invariants. Studying these aspects, the book introduces trans-disciplinary principles of epistemological level, which provide an axiomatising basis to elaborate the genesis and development of systems on all organisational levels. In this respect, the following area dealt with elements of systems theory, theory of organisations and organisational entities in the globalised market economy.

The second research sub-theme deals with econometrics as being that branch of economic sciences which studies the relations between the economic variables, as they appear postulated in an abstract model. It is operated with the distinction between *econometrics broadly*—which does not limit a priori the scope of usable methods and models and makes use of all structural and quantitative techniques—and *econometrics narrowly*—which limits a priori this scope to all the statistical methods and therefore appears as a set of applications of statistics in economic modelling. The connection between variables is obvious in both cases, through an abstract model of econometric relations. In essence, notions of model, object, relation, function, simulation, modelling, trend, input–output, etc., are accessed.

The last part of the book—through the third research sub-theme—provides the reader with elements of econometric modelling, which currently and frequently make use of the probabilistic mathematics and random analysis. The refusal to accept the uncertainty at the model level normally results in the difficulty to introduce the design of the evolution of economic processes into analysis, if one does not take into account the information, without which the uncertainty cannot be studied. Therefore, the abstract model in econometrics is a support and a reference point of reasoning in general and in particular a generator of a certain conceptualisation of the central idea of connection between the variables describing the evolution within the system. The book presents econometric models focused particularly on the functions of organisational entities, but not only. I also give special interest to modelling the production quality, modelling the costs, modelling the innovative activity, etc.

When addressing the complex issues dealt with in the book, the authors enter into dialogue with the opinions presented by a rich classical and contemporary bibliography, as well as with the opinions presented in the communications delivered at international scientific conferences and with those existing in the papers published in journals with a high scientific impact.This study is the result of many years of author's experience expanded through international collaboration with researchers from universities in many countries and business management practices including large transnational corporations.

This book is addressed to both theoreticians and practitioners in the field of operative management of industrial production. This equally concerns those who study—students, graduates and doctoral students, those who have experience in this field—researchers and professors, as well as those who actually work in production—engineers, technicians, economists, developers, logisticians, company managers, presidents of the administrative board, etc.

It was personally a great pleasure to collaborate with the authors and we are pleased that this book is an important milestone forward in econometrics methods introduction in management. We hope that you too feel the same after reading this book, and we are sure, it can be inspiring for discussion and managerial solutions improvement.

Poland
September 2014

Maria Nowicka-Skowron
Janusz K. Grabara
Sebastian Kot

Preface

About the Subject

The enhancement of current globalisation represents the fundamental feature of world economy at the beginning of the twenty-first century and is characterised by emphasising the trend to reduce and remove the barriers between the national economies and enhancing the connections between these economies. Although it is one of the most used terms in the literature, it cannot be said there is a generally accepted definition. One of the best known definitions given to globalisation is that of the World Bank, which considers that over the last years, an increasingly larger part of the global economic activity takes place between people and companies from different countries.

The globalisation we face nowadays derives from the fact that, by starting from the technological and economical development, a significant number of human activities are situated on such a large scale and scope that they exceed the national borders within the limits of which the sovereign states exercise their right to govern. The new actors had to cope with the challenge caused by the monopoly-type governance. Multinational corporations, global financial markets, non-governmental organisations as well as criminal organisations and international terrorist networks appeared. Their activity is not covered by international laws which are based on formal agreements between the nation-states, for they have not been able so far to find a common ground for agreements aiming at the issue of globalisation.

In this context, this book is the result of an interdisciplinary scientific research in economy, mathematics, statistics and systems theory. By using such knowledge, modelling and simulation become successful managerial techniques that are based on broad mathematical knowledge applied in the management of organisational entities dealt with in terms of systems theory.

The theoretical elements have been used to conduct the scientific research focused on three directions:

- applying the systems theory in the study of organisational entities;
- using the theoretical knowledge of mathematics for the cybernetic approach of economic phenomena and processes;
- using the econometric models by the management of organisational entities.

All three directions emphasise the systemic approach of the research issues from this book and also the feedback relation characteristic to cybernetic systems, which are a special class of systems.

Organisation of the Book

The book deals with the problem of scientific research carried out in 16 chapters forming its content.

The 16 chapters are grouped into three parts, namely:

- System of Organisational Entities
- Problems on the Econometric Theory
- Econometric Models Used in Management

Taking into account the scientific theory elements used in this research, each part includes a corresponding number of chapters, which are the result of the research performed.

Thus, Part I, System of Organisational Entities, is structured into three chapters dealing with notions on the systems theory (concept, techniques and methods, automatic adjustment systems, systems risk, etc.) and theoretic problems on the use of systems theory when dealing with the organisational entities (definition of the organisational entities, cybernetic system of the organisational entities, functions of the organisational entities, operating cycle, etc.).

Part II of the book, Some Problems on the Econometric Theory, is structured in three chapters and presents the main theoretical problems of econometrics underlying the development of econometric models used in management. Problems are dealt with, such as the relationship between econometrics and scientific management (defining the econometrics, contradictions in econometrics, econometric research, object-signal and model in econometrics, the econometric functions, etc.); dealing with the simulation and modelling as econometric techniques (the model, modelling, simulation, matrix calculus of the models, the input–output model, the IT technique used in modelling, etc.); presenting the production functions used in econometrics (building the production functions, calculating the production functions, difficulties in calculating the production functions, the Cobb–Douglas functions, the Leontieff Model, etc.).

Section III, called "Econometric Models Used in Management", which is also the last one of the book, is of special importance as in its ten chapters it deals with the application of econometrics, meaning the use of econometric models in the management of organisational entities.

The problems dealt with in the chapters of this part refer to the use of linear programming to elaborate the econometric models (the technique of linear programming, the Simplex algorithm, convergence, dual Simplex algorithm, re-optimisation, parameterisation, etc.); the use of dynamic programming to create econometric models used in management (time, trend, discrete dynamic programming, stationary dynamic programming, graphs used to interpret dynamic programming, etc.); graphs used to elaborate econometric models of management (graph elements, oriented graph, transport network graph, critical path, Hamiltonian circuit, etc.); the use of the queuing string theory to create the econometric models used in organisational management (queuing networks, fundamental elements of the queuing networks, service stations, service factor, populations serviced, etc.); the use of game theory to elaborate econometric management models (game theory, use of the game theory, managerial decision-making, application of the decisions based on the game theory, etc.); the use of econometric models in the management of stocks (definition of stocks, characteristics of stocks, stochastic equations, the inverse of a matrix of the stochastic equation, heuristic models of stocks, etc.); use of econometric research to model the replacement of fixed assets from the organisational entities (the definition of fixed assets and their classification, the fixed wear and obsolescence of fixed assets, models for making the decisions to replace the fixed assets, models for making the decisions to modernise fixed assets, etc.); modelling the production cost by using econometric techniques (production cost, matrix of production cost, primary production expenses, system of organisational entities, matrix model of the production cost, etc.); the use of the budgeting technique in elaborating models of the unit production cost (definition of the budget, types of budgets, budgeting activity, budgeting types, structural elements of the unit production cost, etc.); and the elaboration of econometric models for the production quality management, in general, and of total production quality, in particular (the concept of production quality, the concept of production non-quality, continuous improvement of the quality of products, concept of total quality management, Taguchi technique used in the production quality management, etc.).

The complexity of the scientific research presented in this book is the result of a systemic and interdisciplinary approach of the knowledge in the field of economy, management, technology, systems science, mathematics and statistics.

Target Audience

This book is addressed to both theoreticians and practitioners in the field of operative management of industrial production. This equally concerns those who study—students, graduates, doctoral students, those who have experience in this field—researchers, professors, as well as those who actually work in production—engineers, technicians, economists, developers, logisticians, company managers, presidents of the administrative boards, etc. The intention of this book is to create a challenge regarding the debate of the theoretical and practical problems the operative management of industrial production is facing.

Targoviste, Romania Ioan Constantin Dima
Petrosani, Romania Mariana Man

Acknowledgement

It is indeed our pleasure and honour to acknowledge those who have helped to make this book possible.

We would first like to thank Mr. Christian Rauscher, Senior Editor, Business/Economics, and Ms. Barbara Bethke, Business/Economics. We also thank Mr. Thomas Hempfling, Editorial Director/Asset Management, and Mr. Heinz Weinheimer, Executive Vice President... at Springer for their professional support in editing this book.

We are grateful to all who decided to participate in this publication project as the members of Editorial Advisory Board, contributors and reviewers. Also we are thankful to most of the authors who were willing to simultaneously serve as reviewers for chapters written by other authors.

The chapters have been written in the authors' native language and translated into English by Ms. Elvira Magdalena Tanasescu. Editing and page layout have been performed by Ms. Camelia Alexandrescu.

Electronic preparation of this book to be made available to the publisher Springer has been possible with the company laboratories Arves of Craiova, manager engineer Sorin Matei.

The authors appreciate the services rendered by Ms. Elvira Magdalena Tanasescu, Ms. Camelia Alexandrescu and Mr. Sorin Matei.

As neither of them is an English native speaker, there may be some minor grammar errors.

Last but not least, we would like to express our sincere thanks to our families for their understanding and patience during the editing of the book.

Ioan Constantin Dima

About the Authors

Ioan Constantin Dima is a graduate of the Faculty of Economic Science, University of Craiova, Romania. He obtained his doctorate in Economic Science, in 1988, from the University of Craiova. From 1994, he is a Scientific Coordinator of PhD in Economics in the field of management at the Doctoral School of the "Lucian Blaga" University of Sibiu and "Valahia" University of Targoviste, visiting professor at the Faculty of Management, University of Czestochowa, Poland, associate professor at Technical University of Kosice, economist at CIMAE Craiova, TCI Craiova, university professor (assistant, lecturer, professor), University of Craiova, University of Petroşani, "Constantin Brâncuşi" University of Târgu-Jiu, University of Piteşti, "Lucian Blaga" University of Sibiu, ARTIFEX University of Bucharest, "Valahia" University of Târgovişte, Dean, Manager of Department, Head of Department at "Constantin Brâncuşi" University of Târgu-Jiu, University of Petroşani, University of Piteşti, ARTIFEX University, "Valahia" University of Târgovişte, Manager of the Territorial Branch of CRUFOC financed by a programme of the European Union, Manager at SC G.M.C. SRL Craiova, Expert Assessor at ARACIS, Assessor at CNCSIS—MEdCTS, Member of CNATDCU—MEdCTS Commission of Contestation Assessment regarding the confirmation of didactic titles, scientific titles and professional degrees in MEdCTS, member of AGER, member of AROMAR, member of FIMAN, member of CECAR, member of the Scientific Committee of the Publishing House "Cursuri Universitare"—the Polytechnic University of Bucharest, member of the Editorial Board of the Scientific Bulletin—The Series Economical Sciences of University of Piteşti, member of the Editorial Board of the Annals of the "Valahia" University of Târgovişte, Economical Series, member of the Editorial Board of the Annals of the University of Petroşani, member of the Editorial Board of ANCOM—Bucharest, member of the Board "THE ANNALS OF THE UNIVERSITY OF LUXEMBOURG, member of the Scientific Editorial Board of "Vyrobne Inginierstvo", the Technical University of Kosice, Faculty of Industrial Engineering, Presov, Slovakia, member of the Scientific Editorial Board of "Polish Journal of Management", Technological University of Czestochowa, Faculty of Management, Poland, member of Editorial Board of Journal of Reviews on Global Economics, Associate Editor of Topclass

Journal of Business Management, Member of Editorial Board of "Organization Review", Poland, Member of Editorial Board of IJTEMT, which is a non-profit educational organisation working for expansion of research in the field of Economics Management and Technology, Scientific secretary at AGIR Publishing House, founder member of the "Scrisul Românesc" Foundation, founder member of the International Conference of Cooperation in the Basin of the Black Sea (Varna 1994, non-governmental organisation), member of the European Conference of the Deans of Scientific Faculties (Paris 1994), member of the Comisia of Curricular Reform for higher Economical Education, member of the Catalogue—Director of the didactic personnel in the field of economics for the inter-university exchange of courses, member of the National Consortium of Economic Business Schools, member of the CEDIMES INSTITUTE, member of the Academic Society of Management in Romania, member of the Royal Economic Society, etc. He is author or coauthor of 53 professional books and of 380 scientific papers in Romania and international journals and in proceedings of international seminars and conferences.

Mariana Man is a graduate of the Bucharest University of Economic Studies, Romania—Faculty of Planning and Economic Cybernetics. She obtained her doctorate in Economic Science, in 1998, from the Bucharest University of Economic Studies. Between 2000 and 2008, Professor MARIANA MAN was the deputy dean of the Faculty of Sciences at the University of Petroşani and from 2008 is manager of the "Center of Economic and Social Researches for Regional Development" of the University of Petroşani, Romania. From 2000, she is publisher-in-chief of the international publication "Annals of the University of Petroşani—Economics", is a valuable specialist and experienced researcher with numerous documentations in country and abroad and has a rich practical activity in superior economic education, being a professor in many universities. Her main activities and responsibilities include courses and seminars, scientific research—doctorate coordinator (at the Valahia University of Târgovişte, Romania), academic administration, coordination of scientific publications, consultant and trainer in the financial and accounting field. She has a sustained scientific activity. She is author or co-author of 15 professional books published in the United States of America by IGI Global, in Germany by LAP LAMBERT Academic Publishing, in Croatia by InTech, She is author or co-author of 15 specialised books published by prestigious publishing houses from: Croatia, Germany, Poland, Romania, Slovakia and the United States of America. She is a member of different professional-scientific structures and committees: expert accountant—member of The Body of Licensed Accountants and Accounting Experts in Romania—and permanent expert evaluator—member of Romanian Agency for Quality Assurance in Higher Education. For her scientific and organisational work, she received a number of awards and distinctions, among others, individual and collective awards conferred by universities from Romania.

Contents

Part I
System of Organisational Entities

Chapter 1
Considerations on Systems Theory

1.1 Views on the Concept of a System

The knowledge acquired about the environment, human (as rational being) and society have allowed the development of some theses and generalisations determining the transitions of systematic thinking from the scope of theory into that of practical activity. This has allowed that the notion of system—initially used only in the technical field—would become a basic tool for the economic research and analysis and contribute to solving the abstract—and sometimes sensitive—issues which the theory of systems is currently facing.

Thus, by actually approaching the problem, any phenomenon, activity, process—even the beings—can be considered as systems of a certain type—more complex or less complex—characterised by two categories of environment and namely: environment outside the system, meaning the area where the system occurs and the environment inside the system, expressed by relations between its components and usually considered variable sizes. Hypothetically, under this aspect, when both the connections of the system with the outside and those between the components are zero—meaning null—the system is isolated.

If we referred to the systems created by humans or to the natural ones, the previously mentioned connections are not null, because such systems receive and give information to the environment, which arises the requirement that in the analysis of social systems, especially to start from the atomic—dissipative structures and from the utility of systems. In such situations, the extension of the parameters taken into account, combined with the high degree of difficulty regarding the quantifications, makes mathematicians' mission difficult in creating a system of equations appropriate to the studied system. This difficulty amplifies if we consider that, in order to surprise any evolution, abstract behaviours must be taken into account (such as: information, activities, etc.), as well as actual behaviours (meaning: the number of jobs, number of employees, assets such as fixed assets) of the system. Such a concept ensures the measurement and determination of

I.C. Dima, M. Man, *Modelling and Simulation in Management*, Contributions to Management Science, DOI 10.1007/978-3-319-16592-9_1

the particularities in the case of timeless systems, temporal systems and social systems.

Regardless of the form of organisation, size or purpose of action, any natural or artificial product can be represented by a conventional model. If we consider a physical good "F" which we associate a set of commeasurable characteristic to (volume, weight, speed, etc.) as some injective functions at the time t, taking into account the number of characteristics, the set "M_F" may be created:

$$\text{“}M_F\text{”} = \{f_1(t),\ f_2(t)\ldots f_n(t)\} \tag{1.1}$$

Mathematically speaking, a set of the input–output pairs can be created, ordered in time as follows:

$$(x(t_0, t_1), y(t_0, t_1)) \in F \tag{1.2}$$

with the condition of positive sequence:

$$t_1 < t_2 < \ldots < t_n \tag{1.3}$$

Analytically, the set "F" may have the following form:

$$F = \{(x, y)\} \tag{1.4}$$

and the sets:

$$I(F) = \{x/(x/y)A\} \tag{1.5}$$

$$E(F) = \{y/(x/y)A\} \tag{1.6}$$

represent the set of input segments and respectively the set of the output sets of the system, meaning the quantitative commeasure of those input and output sizes (Fig. 1.1).

Based on the previous specifications, the system is designed as a structure that involves the takeover at a time t_0 of some input sizes from the outside environment, their transformation into others—which are usually different from the input ones and their render at another time t_1 as products and/or services (Fig. 1.2).

Therefore, any output y of the system depends not only on the state of the input x, but also on the state of the system Z_F, which in its turn depends on the input, meaning:

$$Y_F = f(Z_F, X) \tag{1.7}$$

If we define the input as being all the elements needed for the operation of a system, and the output as being all the resulted elements, then we define the state Z_F as the assembly of variables the values of which at a time t fully determines (along with the current values of the sizes inputted from the outside) the subsequent

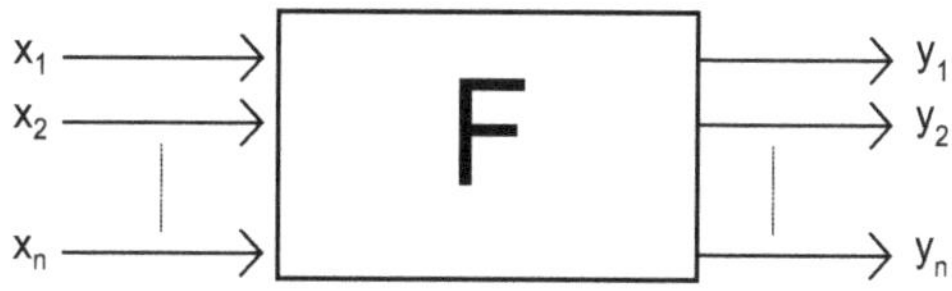

Fig. 1.1 The abstract model of the physical good "F"

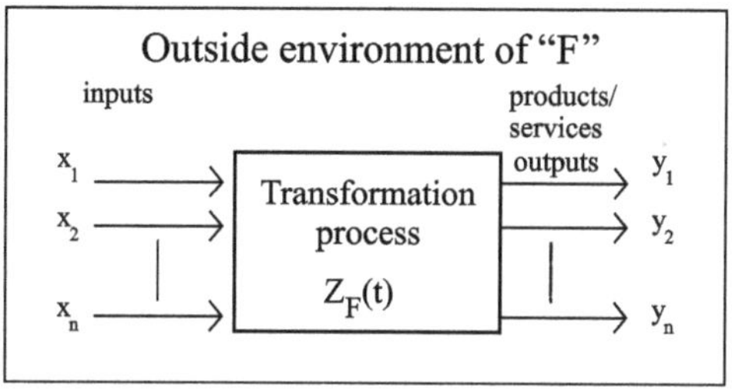

Fig. 1.2 The inputs and outputs from the system

behaviour of the system. Therefore, in a certain sense, the state expresses the past evolution of the subsystem. In this regard, the unique values of the inputs, outputs and states correspond to the time t, the hypothesis of simultaneity of several values being excluded, and knowing the structure of a system involves the determination of the dependence of the input states.

$$Z_F(t) = \Phi(x_t) \tag{1.8}$$

Therefore, the concept of system has a double determination, meaning it includes both the analysed "F" physical good, and the representation of its structure and causality by the relation:

$$\text{input}\ldots.. > \text{state}\ldots. > \text{output} \tag{1.9}$$

Thus, in such an acceptation, the concept of system also has the following elements: set of interrelated objectives; orderly action; organised whole of knowledge; sizes and concepts; environment wherein a set of information is inserted that is processed and delivered to the output; framework where performers, machines and workstations, computer electronic equipment work together.

There are mainly two large classes of systems: natural systems and systems created by humans, and their analysis must take into account: the driven system, meaning that reunion of subsystems that is co-ordinately guided, taking into account their interaction; the structure of the system, which contains reaction loops, information points, data processing centres, decision points, places to complete the actions triggered by decisions; the component subsystems, which have their own areas for the input–output data and have self-driving processes in their structure; the driving system defines that reunion of subsystems guiding the driven system.

Because all elements of the system contribute in transforming the inputs into outputs, its operation at a given time t is given by the amount of the operations performed during that period and is influenced by the action of the outside

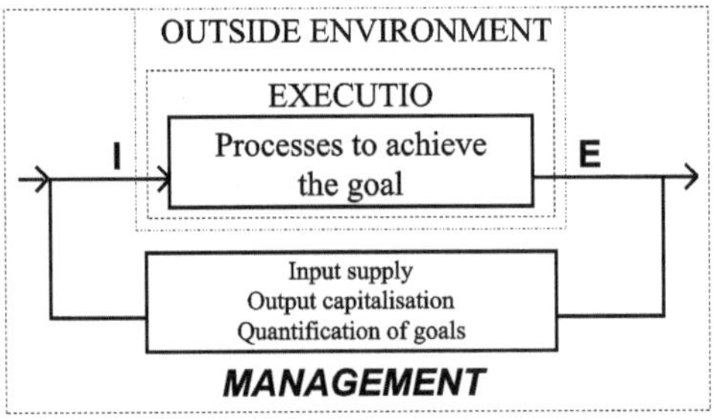

Fig. 1.3 The operation of the system

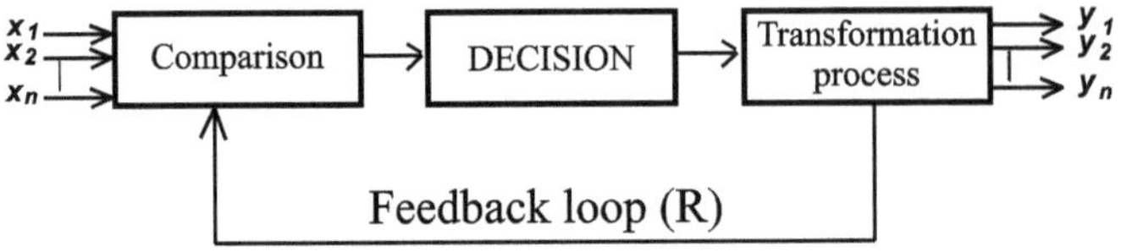

Fig. 1.4 Cybernetic system

environment, exerted both on the driven system (also called execution system) and on the driving one (also called control system) (Fig. 1.3).

The performances of the system depend on the quality of the driving system, the capacity to remove or prevent the possible perturbations, meaning factors that make the outputs deviate from the original value. In this respect, there is a class of—self-adjusting—systems, which are able to maintain their self-control for certain periods of time, in achieving the final goal. The cybernetic system is part of this category, characterised by the occurrence of the feed-back, the function "R" between input and output (Fig. 1.4).

In such a system, the input-output analysis can be formulated in two forms: explicit analysis, where the sets are defined by their characteristic functions, equal to the unit for each input-output pair belonging to a certain component of the system and zero for those which do not belong to it; the implicit analysis, where the component systems are defined by the input-output relations and not by the characteristic functions.

By means of this theoretic thoroughness, some major problems of the theory of systems can be answered to, regarding both the components, meaning the subsystems, and the behaviour of the system understood as being an invariant relation, specific to the group of sizes and a given level of resolution, having values of the same structure. The amount of the relations that determine the behaviour of the system represents its organisation, the part of organisation that remains constant is its structure, and the variable portion of the organisation defines the program of the system.

If we consider the relation between the generant (G) of the system and the resistance (R) of the system, in terms of the behaviour of the system, we distinguish the following states of behaviours, namely: system the behaviour of which is attached by the balance state (G = R); system the behaviour of which is displayed by its evolving state (G > R); system the behaviour of which is displayed by its regressive state (G < R).

Based on such theoretical specifications, the operation of the economic systems takes into account general goals, the achievement of which is possible by preparing and programming the allocation of some material, human and financial resources, their processing by technological procedures and guiding them to the desired finality, meaning products and services.

1.2 Techniques and Methods Used in Systems Theory

Modelling and simulating any system are conditioned by knowing its structure and functionality. Cognitively, such an approach is generically called the system analysis.

Taking concepts characteristic to some disciplines—IT, cybernetics, operational researches, etc.—the analysis of the systems has however created its own methodology, characterised to be both ameliorative (starting from the existing situation, one aims at the improvement of the studied system), and constructive (the information and decision in various phases of the operation of the studied system shall serve to design a better one). The methodology of the analysis of systems has several stages, and namely: knowing the system, when the general information about the outside environment of the studied system is, intensifying the basic informational and decisional information; the critical evaluation of the system state, meaning the detection of imperfections and their remedy according to the relevance, efficiency, rationality criteria, etc.; designing the new system, as a response to the one studied initially; the implementation of the new designed system.

Although the pioneering of the automated algorithmic techniques is the technical systems, one can currently speak of their evolution and refinement, getting to the creation of the expert systems in the social-economic field. This, although the statistical approximation does not provide a pertinent analysis of the systems, but the observation, experiment, deduction and analogy provide the information and tools needed to grasp the relevant and characteristic sizes which shall underlie the project of the new system as being counterweight of the studied system. Starting from these theoretical considerations, any company "system" is an assembly of material, financial and human resources which it has at a given time, in order to achieve the basic and predetermined objective, which the entire activity performed within the company gravitates around.

In order to achieve this goal, it is necessary to perform certain processes (all operations performed to transform the inputs into outputs) conditioned by certain precise rules (normative acts and stipulations, technological requirements, etc.), which be both requirement and restrictions (Fig. 1.5).

In this regard, amending the existing conditions and resources leads to acquiring some results which, combined, are not always identical to the amount of components of the objective. Therefore, the results become the basic factor of achieving or

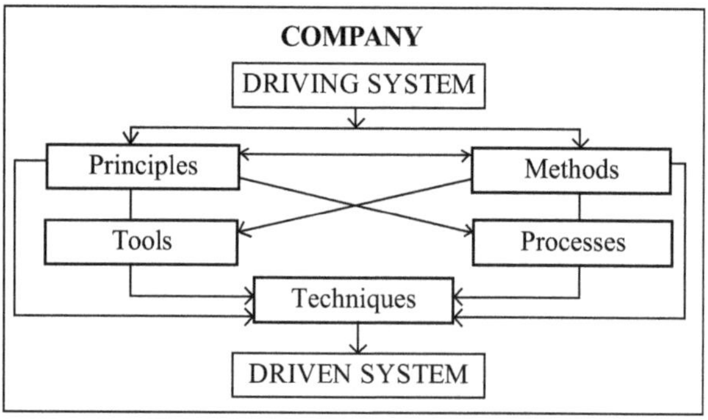

Fig. 1.5 Analysis of the "Company" system

not achieving the objective. Concluding, we may affirm that should it be relatively simple to identify the objective, measuring it has many difficulties essentially determined by the requirement to achieve a consistency between its components and the results of performing the processes in the system.

The complex nature of the analysis of systems is determined by the weight of identifying the processes performed to achieve the goals and aims at amending the content and volume of the resources; by the weight of supplying the resources which would represent inputs for the transformation processes; by the difficulties of capitalising the outputs from the transformation processes. Besides knowing the structure and functionality, the system analysis also aims at determining the properties of the given system, its controllability and observability.

If the system analysis can be done only on an existing system—to identify the structure, functionality and properties of the studied system—diametrically opposed to it, the synthesis of systems is a difficult, abstract operation, which aims at determining the structure of a system with initially defined functions and properties. It means the synthesis is done by starting from the function to be achieved, the objectives proposed and existing resources, designing the system aiming to identify its structure.

If in the field of technical systems, the design methodology (considered as tool) has made great progresses in elaborating the methods (meaning the way to be followed within the system to transform the inputs into outputs), in the field of the "company" system, the techniques (means used inside the "company" system to perform certain operations) have evolved to such an extent as they represent the common denominator of the synthesis of systems.

Because in terms of the theory of systems, the physical nature of the system characteristic sizes can be ignored, the synthesis provides the opportunity to physically achieve a class of systems and determines the achievement of certain performances (minimum or maximum, depending on the requirements), meaning a certain relation between inputs, states and outputs which does not belong to the given system. In this case, the system optimality is done if the input function determines extreme values and if the system is thus designed as for any input the performance would be extreme, being applicable especially in technique.

In this context, the analysis and synthesis of systems are in reverse connection relation and underlie the development of models by means of which the operation of systems is simulated.

Modelling is integral part of the family of structural (complex) methods, having yet a series of peculiarities.

The analogies model—reality are important, sometimes indispensable tools for knowing the systems regardless of their nature. Therefore, modelling is a process of mediated knowledge of the reality with some representations called models, meaning an artificial, more simple system is used by modelling, the model which the behaviour of a real system it represents is studied with.

The model is a multiple representation of reality, subordinated to the purpose of research, without this simplification distorting the essential characteristics of the studied system. To be functional, any model must meet two conditions, namely: the condition of isomorphism (the model to operate similarly, analogically with the real system which it represents) and the condition of homomorphism (the model is similar to the real system concerning the essential elements).

The model describes the connections that are established between inputs, outputs and states and is the object of applying the modelling activity. The application of system modelling is done in several stages, namely: specifying the field to investigate by accepting the correct information and rejecting the false one; quantitatively developing the mathematical model, taking into account the new information in qualitative terms; forecasting the future development of the system based on the solution of the mathematical model; correcting the errors which appear in the decisional process based on repeated experiments; influencing the environment outside the system with decisions in complete form.

Taking into account the complexity of systems, there is a variety of the classes of models, among which: Physical models or templates of the original system which in their turn are subdivided into linear models and non-linear models, into stationary models and dynamic models into deterministic models and probabilistic models and with discrete structure; numerical (mathematical) models of the initial system which are subdivided as physical models; hybrid (numerical and physical) models having the same subdivisions as the previous ones.

Pursuing the behaviour of systems in time is done by means of information files from the data banks. If deviations occur in reality in the system management in relation to the solutions of the mathematical model, then the sizes disrupting the system operation shall be modified, and one shall attempt the optimal system development in time by successive tests.

To optimise the structure of the systems, one operates with models to simulate the system structure and aims at determining the optimum decisions which the driving system must take regarding the driven system, normally using the economic-mathematic model. This is the result of a process where the subject achieves a similitude (an isomorphism) between object and model, having at the base a theory of the researched subject This is why, the model as carrier of a certain information about the researched system is shown only by the information which the subject has, and modelling as an informational process subordinated to the purpose of the research.

The theoretic basis of the economic-mathematic model consists of a logical system of universal statements (hypotheses, premises) of which, by precise rules, final sentences are deducted (theorems, conclusions), and the empirical basis consists of statements of limited feature in time and space, which must be verified by experiment in order to assess the validation degree of the model.

The economic-mathematical models have the purpose to provide optimum, possible variants for the development and reorganisation of the established systems, under the conditions and by complying with the restrictions given. This is possible only by simulation, which studies the behaviour of a real system by means of a replacement system (simulator). Simulation thus allows the detailed analysis of the alternatives for the future development of systems and provides the possibility of a prediction in their evolution.

1.3 Use of Automatic Adjustment Systems in Management

The cybernetic approach of the automatic adjustment systems involves the existence of a structure generically called driving systems.

One cannot speak about the automatic adjustment of a system without defining the following terms: to adjust is the verb defining the action to achieve or restore the state of a system the characteristic sizes of which have been subject to deviations from the restrictions imposed; the adjustment defines the action to adjust and its action; automatic adjustment is that adjustment of the system which leads to the adjustment without the direct intervention of the human performer in the system.

In this context, the automatic adjustment of a system is provided through those technical and informational structures called driving systems. Within the latter, the adjusted system is called driven subsystem, generically called driven process, and its driving is done by a second subsystem, the driving subsystem, called automation device.

In their development, the system driving the processes has been divided into closed circuit driving systems and open circuit driving systems.

In principle, within the driving systems, the component phenomena of the automation device experience a much lower energetic state compared to those in the driven subsystem or driven process, where significant energies are circulated. Therefore, in this respect, the two subsystems are well defined, so that it is recommended that for the automation device the operation—therein—with low power energetic signals, both for technical and economic considerations, and ecological and human protection considerations.

In terms of the sizes that technically and information-wise characterise the driving systems, more precisely the driving subsystem in relation to the driven subsystem, the following are known: the control size of the driven process which represents the output size of the automation device and input size for the driven subsystem (the driven process)—by means of which the automation device performs the automatic driving of the driven subsystem (driven process); the disturbing size of the driven process is that input size for the driven subsystem (the driven process), which changes independently of the action of the automation device and represents the input size for the driving system; the disturbing size of the driven process is an output size for the driving system, and its levels and variations in time reflect the technical-economic performances of the size recorded by the driving system. It is thus allowed to assess the satisfaction degree of the conditions and restrictions imposed to the driven subsystem (driven process) by the driving subsystem; the measurement output of the driven process is that internal size for the closed circuit driving system by means of which the information of the automation device is provided regarding the state of the driven subsystem (driven process); the reference size which may be both internal size and external size of the automation device and input size for the driving system as information, is that size prescribing the desired state of the driven subsystem (driven process) or its operating mode.

Knowing the component sizes of the systems and correlating with the relations that may occur between them, the following situations exist in the practical operation of the driving systems: the driven subsystem (driven process) is stable and unaffected by disturbances, in which case both the closed circuit driving systems and the closed circuit driving systems are able to adjust the driven subsystem (driven process) by providing a certain state to it and/or a certain type of changing the state of the driven subsystem (driven process); the driven subsystem (driven process) is unstable and/or affected by disturbances, in which case only the closed circuit driving systems are able to adjust the driven subsystem (driven process) by providing certain categories of its states and/or certain ways to change the state of the driven subsystem (driven process) in time.

By generalising the content of such situations, the automatic adjustment system can be defined as being that closed circuit driving system equipped with the adjustment function, meaning able to perform the activity of adjustment of the driven subsystem (driven process). This definition highlights the broader scope to cover the closed circuit driving systems compared to the automatic adjustment systems, the relationship between them being from the whole to the part.

The automatic adjustment system performs the adjustment function by permanently changing the action of the automation device on the driven subsystem (driven process) in accordance with the deviation of its state from the conditions imposed, the change being always guided into the direction of reducing the deviations assessed by measurement.

The adjustment is done automatically and requires three operations to be done, in the following logic: measuring the state of the driven subsystem (driven process) by means of the measurement outputs and transmission of the result observed by means of the reaction on the automation device; assessing the process state, assessing the quality size called size adjusted from the measurement outputs and comparing it to the prescribed quality size; establishing and preparing the control size according to the deviation of the quality size from the prescribed value, thus taking into account the adjustment error, meaning the difference between the prescribed value and the real one of the quality size.

When in the closed circuit driving systems the action of the automation device on the driven subsystem (driven process) does not logically cover the three operations, those systems are not automatic adjustment systems, and when they are partially covered, those systems are generically defined as being automatic driving systems.

For the smooth operation of the automatic adjustment systems, they must be designed as such as to intervene whenever disturbances occur in the operation of the closed circuit driving systems, disturbances which, in terms of their origin, they can be external disturbances (exogenous to the system) and internal disturbances (endogenous to the system).

Taking into account the manner of operating these disturbances, we distinguish: load-type external disturbances corresponding to the variable loads which the driven subsystem (driven process) work with; parasitic-type external disturbances which refer to the external factors acting on the automatic adjustment system and which can be detected by actual or equivalent signals; parametric external disturbances which originate from the action of internal factors which result in changing the characteristic parameters of the dependencies; parasitic internal disturbances which are caused by the action of the internal factors acting on the automatic adjustment systems and which can be detected both by actual and equivalent signals; parametric internal disturbances which are caused by the action of internal factors which determine the change in the characteristic parameters of the dependencies; structure internal disturbances which are caused by the action of internal factors which determine the change in type of dependencies.

Neither the load-type disturbances or the parasitic ones influence the informational behaviour way of the driven subsystem (driven process) or of the automatic adjustment system, because they do not change the type of the various dependencies.

If the perseverance of disturbances in time is taken into account, we distinguish the persistent-type disturbances and non-persistent disturbances.

Taking into account the way of variation in the driving or reference size, the automatic adjustment systems are divided into two broad categories: constant reference automatic adjustment systems for which the disturbing size of the driven process is constant in time, intended to provide a constant value of the assessment output. For these reasons, they are also called disturbance rejection systems; time-variable reference automatic adjustment systems, systems where the disturbing size of the driven process is variable in time, having to ensure the monitoring of the changes over time by the adjusted size, which is why they are also called monitoring systems or servo-systems.

In their turn, the monitoring systems can also be: with an a priori known reference also called programmed reference automatic adjustment systems, when the automation device is done analogically (when the reference is provided by a programmable reference element) or numerically (when the reference is done by a software dedicated to this purpose) and with an a priori unknown reference also called actual monitoring systems, in which case the driving size does not originate from the automation device, but from a source outside of it. The rejection of the disturbances and monitoring the references may be provided accordingly—in this second case—based on the availabilities of some models of the sizes exogenous to the automatic adjustment system. This means the actual or principle existence of a copy of the model of exogenous sizes within the automatic adjustment system called internal model. Only thus an automatic adjustment system can be achieved, which would provide the purposes of adjusting the driven subsystem (driven process) under the action of some input sizes subject to some persistent disturbances.

If the control size, driven process variation over time is taken into account, we distinguish: continuous control size automatic adjustment systems, characterised by the control size continuous variation over time, which takes values within a compact range, which is why they are also called adjustment systems with continuous action. In this case, the continuous control sizes originate from the analogical automation devices; discontinuous control size automatic adjustment systems (also called with discontinuous action) are characterised by a discontinuity of the control size, which can be: Discontinuity over time, when it changes its value only in discrete moments, on various time sub-ranges, taking constant values and discontinuity in amplitude, when this can only take certain discrete values. In the case of this group of systems, the most common ones are: The two-step, three-step automatic adjustment systems and numerical automatic adjustment systems.

The classifications of the previously presented automatic adjustment systems highlight that they should by designed as such as to normally ensure the automatic performance of the driven subsystem adjustment process by the automation device and not to highlight just the importance of the adjustment function.

The adjustment processes performed by means of the automatic adjustment systems are not characteristic only to the technical field, their distribution area being extended. Generally, in the technical field, such systems are used to drive the technological plants in various industrial fields, in order to drive a variable multitude of processes, starting from the simple processes to the complex ones, from the processes technically characterised by broad tolerances to those characterised by severe adjustment restrictions, from the processes that occur in pilot stations, meters and control devices to the processes which actually occur within the technological plants, etc. Except for the technical field, the automatic adjustment systems are encountered in the field of biosystems, economic and social phenomena, the hybrid human-beings-machine manufacturing systems, etc.

The comparative analysis of the automatic adjustment systems used in the technical field to those used in the other fields of activity enables the achievement of some useful analogies both for understanding certain biological, economic or social phenomena, and for the continuous improvement and elevation of the automatic adjustment systems in principle. With all the importance given to technology, the human being has the great merit to have discovered the first the principle of automatic adjustment common to all categories of systems.

The application of using the automatic adjustment systems into the industrial practice must take into account certain technical-economic aspects and namely: the complexity and particularities of the driven subsystem (driven process); the performances required to the automatic driving system (materialised into: the size of the driven process; the complexity of the interactions within the driven process; the importance of the driven process within the technical-economical process; the nature of the disturbances acting within the system; the estimated service life of the process; the degree of detailing the system knowledge; the level of equipping with devices other than transducers and execution devices, etc.); the existence of several types of automation equipment, of which the way of placing their measurement and protection elements can be chosen, in relation to the disturbances within the system; the placement location of the automation device so that it would ensure the transmission of the signals without disturbances between them and the execution element on the one hand and between the transducer and the device on the other hand; choosing and distributing the power supply of the system elements over time; the possibility to use existing operators, as well as the need to replace them when the operating situation requires it.

In practice—complying with the technical and economical aspects leads to achieving the economic performances of operation imposed to the automatic driving system. They refer to: the quality of driving (it is decisive for the option of using the automatic adjustment systems); constant quality of products; rational use of the factors of the production process (creating better working conditions for the performer); lowering the production costs both following the more rational exploitation of the production factors and following the increase of the production volume determined by the use of the automatic adjustment systems in the production management; simple detection of the inappropriate operation of the system and increase of safety in operating the systems; providing a low power consumption in the driving process; making the automatic adjustment systems with as low investments as possible and with as short recovery deadline as possible.

In order to achieve these performances, an appropriate activity is necessary to elaborate the automatic adjustment systems used in developing the driving systems for industrial processes.

Elaborating the automatic adjustment systems is a logical process that goes through several stages and namely: preparing the feasibility study, aimed at substantiating the investment needed to make the driving system and mainly aiming to achieve an economic efficiency of the driving system, at maximum level; the system analysis aims to identify the problems that must be solved by the automatic driving system, to establish the loads of the system and meet the automation function of the system adjustment device; the elaboration itself of the execution project for the driven process automatic adjustment system materialises in preparing a project that is the result of both designing the equipment (dimensional-constructive design) and of algorithmic design. The dimensional-constructive design stage has a different content when equipment existing in an automation system or from several compatible systems are used for making the automatic driving system—a case where the design comes down to adapting its configuration based on combining certain basic models that are manufactured in series, taking the elements established in the system analysis phase as starting point and materialised both in the principle block diagram and in the functional block diagram, compared to the situation where got technical and economical considerations new modules are needed—in which case the dimensional-constructive design increases its duration by the time needed to design and homologate the new modules.

The algorithmic design phase provides the design of the automatic driving algorithms, especially of automatic and adaptive control and optimal adjustment.

When the prior experience in the analytical approach of an automatic adjustment system is missing, the development is done sequentially by following the following steps: the analysis of the driven process that consists of a mathematical model of the driven process appropriate to the design (the complex model increases the duration to develop the order and the simple model is less accurate and affects the accuracy to achieve the system functions), the transformation of the objectives of process driving from technical-economical terms into qualitative and quantitative mathematical terms, the specification of the model properties (stability, observability, controllability, etc.); the synthesis of the system informational structure, in order to establish an informational structure which could provide the imposed automation functions; designing the driving algorithms, meaning determining the algorithms related to the adjustment, control, monitoring functions, etc. for the structure of the automation device designed in the previous phase. It begins by establishing an adjustment rule, meaning the specification of their general mathematical aspect, it continues with determining the values of the parameters by experimentally applying the adjustment rule, including the correlation of the values thus calculated and it ends by assessing the performances of the driving system, meaning the comparison of the performances established by designing the system to those imposed by the specifications; the implementation of the driving system consists of the actual installation of the automation equipment, respectively testing and commissioning the automatic adjustment system for driving the process.

The correct operation and with maximum results of an automatic adjustment system for driving a process requires a good knowledge by the human factor, both of the driven process and of the automation device, in terms of the components and phenomena that occur within the driven process. This is why it is necessary to know and exactly meet the operation documentation for an automatic adjustment system, including the human factor training by the company manufacturing the automatic adjustment system which an extended operation practice of the human operator must be added to. Simultaneously with the increase of the sizes of systems and problems related to their design, implementation and operation, the maintenance problem for such systems and for providing their security in operation acutely arises. This is because the equipment and machines are increasingly more sophisticated technically and constructively, and the system operator must solve all problems specific to the engineering of systems so that their maintenance would be done with minimum costs, under the conditions of ensuring a high level of reliability in operation.

1.4 Information in Systems Management

The management of systems essentially involves finding the sequences of inputs that guide a given system on a certain trajectory. Any problem in the management of systems involves two aspects: knowing the culture and system operation manner, which requires a prior system analysis and the achievement of the preset system dynamics, which makes it also get a synthesis character. The management of systems uses several methods, namely: simulation (it uses a model of the system in order to simulate the effects of the decisions before they would be applied to the system itself); prognosis (it simulates the behaviour of a system for a future period of time, with the purpose to achieve some predictions on the evolution of its states and outputs); optimisation (reaching the maximisation or minimisation performance, as applicable). Taking into account the nature and level where the problems should be solved, two large groups are distinguished in the management of systems, as follows: problems solved directly by the driving system (analysis of deviations, decision making, fulfilment of an action plan, the control of fulfilling the action plan, etc.) and problems solved by formative driving systems (system development, planning the effort for performing the changes needed in the system, etc.)

Therefore, studying the management of systems is objectively needed, taking into account the particularities of systems, operating limits regarding the knowledge of inputs and outputs, delimiting the components, etc.

The process of system management considered as a cycle of analyses, decisions and actions intended to transform the inputs into outputs must necessarily be subject to the operating procedure rules, understood as all the regulations set forth from the input to the output and which express the specific conditions to exercise the operations, as well as the requirements imposed to the performance of the process. It uses both the principle notion understood as thesis or universal sentence serving as starting point, and the procedure notion, understood as the sequence of the operations needed to collect, process and transmit the information, which consist of routines and decisions and refer to inputs concerning the information.

According to the opinions in literature, the management of systems must meet a series of principles, such as: the principle of complexity, which results from the interdisciplinary character itself of the management science, principle of transitivity from simple to complex, whereby approaching a problem is done inductively; the principle of historical approach, meaning the study of managerial relations in the lawlike context of the development process; the principle of systemic approach, which involves taking into account all structural and functional elements of the driven system in their interdependence; the principle of structural approach requires to correctly deal with any theoretical problem under the aspect of implications it determines mainly on the existing structures.

Meeting these and other principles determines several ways of approaching the management of systems, as follows: functional approach, which requires that optimising the activities and adjusting the processes cannot be done unitary for several managerial stages; the logical approach, which starts from strictly meeting

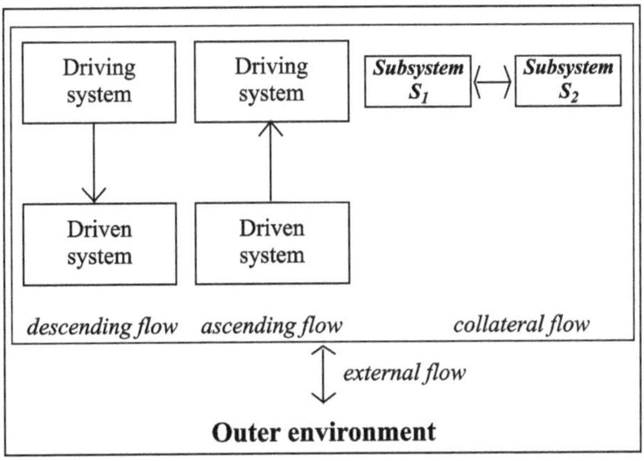

Fig. 1.6 Types of informational flow

the nature of the natural relations and logical sequence of actions that lead to achieving the objective, systematic approach, which implies that the system is a complex of structural elements interconnected through relation and connection type links.

The management of systems requires collecting, processing and transmitting a large quantity of data concerning the internal state of the system and its relations with the environment. All these data, along with the technical means for collecting, processing and transmitting it form the structure of the informational flow.

This may be: descending flow (it achieves the connection between the driving system and driven system); ascending flow (it achieves the connection between the driven system and driving system); collateral flow (it achieves an exchange of information between the subsystems of the system); external flow (it achieves the connection with its outer environment) (Fig. 1.6).

In any system, two flows circulate, the technological flow and informational flow, where no gaps should exist. Avoiding the gaps is done by optimising the correlations between the technological and informational flow, by means of determining and probabilistic mathematical models, prepared under the operation of that system.

The informational flow is designed as an assembly of processes and means of collection-processing, storage and transmission of data from the driven system to the driving system and vice versa, in order to optimally guide the operation of the driven system. Based on such a flow, the driving system knows the actual activity of the driven system, critically examines the situations, adopts decision to guide the system as a whole towards the objective.

This is done when the informational flow is rational, meaning: it is flexible under the aspect of the operating mechanism of the informational content; it has a high qualitative level regarding the accuracy, flexibility and age of information, minimum response time of the action triggered; it is operative, continuous and efficient; it is surprising, selective and accessible, it provides a maximum efficiency with a minimum cost.

The informational flow is rational when its organisation is modern, which involves meeting the following principles: the achievement of the unit between the technological flow and the informational one; the correlation between the organisational structure and modern informational flow of the system; the achievement of a direct dependence between the processing level and information efficiency; concordance between the information transmitted and the received one; the achievement of a dependence between the hierarchic level and information level.

The analysis of the informational flow in order to characterise it is a phased process that includes: the analysis and synthesis of the information flow; the rationalisation of the data strings and agglomeration of the processing sequences; designing the data collection, processing and transmission equipment; the implementation of the new informational flow; establishing the efficiency of the new informational flow operation.

The purpose of the informational flow analysis consists in knowing the current state of the system and adopting a set of decisions concerning the optimum management of the input and output states of the system.

1.5 The Risk in Systems Management

In order to address the risk in systems management, the following aspects are taken into account:

Dealing with the Risk in the Theory of Decision

For the conventional theory of decision, choice involves a compromise between risk and hoped output. Those who make the decision and who are a little adventurous prefer to minimise risks being prepared to scarify part of the hoped output in order to reduce the range of the possible results. On the contrary, those who have the taste of risk shall consent to a reduction of hoped output in order to increase this range. In theory, decision makers begin by assessing the risks before making a choice between the various possible risk-output combinations.

Obviously, it is not always how this is done in practice. It happens that decision makers deny the existence of a risk or consider it to be negligible. This negation often associates an acceptance of the risk actuarial reality to a refusal to integrate this reality. Without being psychological or pathological, this refusal may mean a philosophical rejection of probabilistic judgement applied to a unique case, or the trust in the casualty of events.

Various experiments have enabled emphasising in certain people the tendency to see a casualty in the random events and therefore a possibility to master them, as well as a tendency to establish connections from the cause to effect between events which were established to be purely accidental.

Managers' Definition of Risks

Managers' view of risk is different than the one existing in the theory of decision, particularly being less accurate. Managers rarely measure the risk of an option according to the variation of distributing the probabilities of possible results. There appear at least three characteristic features: most managers do not consider the uncertainty of a positive output to be an important aspect of risk. The possibilities to win have an essential importance in assessing the attraction of an option, and the idea of "risk" is related to a negative result; for managers, risk is not a probabilistic concept. Most managers consider the uncertainty to be a risk factor, and the amplitude of possibly bad results an outstanding element. There is the possibility to define the risk in terms which would define what could be lost and not the moments of distributing the results ("I assume high risks to probabilities but not to total amounts", "I do not look at the probability of a success or of a failure, but the amplitude of risk"). This tendency to ignore or minimise the probability of a loss after its moment reveals more repugnancy to loss than to risk. It is obvious that managers assess the risk they assume more depending on a few key values and not depending on the support provided by the computer or probability theory; most managers do not want to reduce the risk to a single figure element, although they seek a certain accuracy in assessing the risk based on numerical calculations ("Nobody needs a ciphered assessment", "Do not cipher the risk, you must be capable to discern it"). Aware of the multiple aspects of risk, managers say that risk cannot be expressed by a single figure or by a statistical series, and quantifying the risk by a single figure is almost impossible, because risk is a multidimensional phenomenon.

Managers' Attitude Towards Risk

Managers' tendency to assume risks varies depending on individuals and contexts. Individual behaviour variations originate from experience and existing context. Thus, certain individuals like risk less than others, and certain motivation elements related to risk are integral part of a certain personality. These differences from one individual to another are however less important compared to those resulting from the incentive measures and from the managerial behaviour standards.

According to certain studies, the average staff has the tendency to say "the more they climb hierarchically, the less people are willing to assume risks", and senior staff believe that new managers able to assume risks must be trained.

Managers admit that risk assumption is also a need and a pleasure in leading positions, observing it is rather a personal motivation than an incentive measure. There are three essential motivations in assuming calculated risks, namely: risk assumption is essential to the success of the decisions made; risk assumption is for managers rather a matter of professional obligation than a personal incline; manager's risk assumption has an emotional content due to anxiety, fear, excitement and joy, due to the danger of providing delicate chills.

Variations attributable to the context differences can be added to these three essential motivations. Thus, managers' attitude in relation to risk is that of the staff in general, it can vary according to the conditions, meaning that risk assumption depends on the relation between the position at a given moment and certain critical reference points, such as: profit level, size of liquidities and sales at a reference level, current position of the organisation and its possible disappearance, etc.

Managers' Risk Management

The first studies about managers' behaviour concluded they avoid the risk rather than to accept it. They do this by short-term reaction to short-term information, instead of anticipating the future events. They avoid the risk which an unsafe environment represents, by negotiating contracts that pay off the insecurity.

More recently, MacCrimmon and Wehrung have done the same observations and observed that managers avoid taking risks, by delaying their decisions and delegating others. Other studies show that managers avoid facing the risk, considering it as something that can be controlled. They do not accept the idea that the risks they face are inherent to their situation. On the contrary, they are convinced they can limit them, by dominating the dangers, thanks to their capabilities. Keyes showed how people with the spirit of enterprise and taste for risk aim to dominate the uncertainties of destiny, instead of accepting they must assume some risks. Adler establishes a distinction between the managers avoiding the risks, between those who assume them and those who dominate them. The latter are not content to assume the risks, but try to dominate and change them.

Should a given option promise a pretty good efficiency, but it represents an unacceptable risk, managers try to find methods to reduce the danger, by simultaneously maintaining the gain. They sometimes start by refusing the assessments. But mostly, they try to overturn the situation. Managers consider they assume risks, but only do it if they have sufficiently changed the conditions, to be sure of the success. Before any decision, they prepare a risk control strategy.

Most managers believe that they can do better than expected, even after reviewing the estimates. This tactic, also called "adjustment", is considered as a classical reaction of managers towards risk, based on their trust in the ability to reduce the risk, taking into account how their experience is interpreted. Beyond their previous decisions, most staffs believe they knew to increase their chances of success. If they accept the risk it is partly because they greatly hope they shall not need to bear the consequences.

1.6 The Attitude of Managers on Risk Taking in Organisational Entities

The study of the casuistry of managers' attitude highlights three managerial attitudes which differ from the traditional risk conceptions that thus enable to better understand the process of making the managerial decision.

Low Credibility in Probabilistic Estimates

The studies developed in recent years highlight managers' distrust in the accurate assessments in terms of probability, which they just do not understand or simply do not use. A rough determination of probability serves as an excuse to exclude certain possibilities beyond the preliminary calculations of decisions. The possible results the probability of which is very low are ignored, without taking into account their possible evolution. Or, when an initially low probability is combined with important consequences, as in the case of major unforeseen catastrophes or large unexpected discoveries, not taking into account the events with a very low probability can change everything. In a world where the very unlikely events, but full of consequences are however a rule, it is not known how a system could reasonably take them all into account. As it is probably the case, if some of these events shall be generated for sure, the system that is in trouble in this type of events of low probability is prepared for an inexistent environment. This attitude leads to many systems being taken by surprise permanently by events the probability of which was a priori very low and which they were not prepared for at all. But the non-permeability of assessments exceeds the frame of very low probabilities and it seems it would be more equal to the volume of the result that defines the risk for managers and not to the weight of this volume by its probability. This is obvious in using phrases like "maximum risk", "an occasion you that you feel", "in the best or worst of the cases". Such behaviour is not without consequences. It favours the trend in assuming greater risks, if the distribution of probabilities of possible outcomes gets an almost rectangular shape. Compared to the situation in digits, this shape is oval.

Such behaviour can appear that is less intelligent than an actual consideration of the probability variations. However, we have to admit that managers' confusions in terms of risk are to reflect the ambiguities maintained in all literature that deals with the engineering of choices. According to the decision theory, the term "risk" refers to the probabilistic incertitude of the outcomes of a choice. In recent papers dealing with the assessment and management of risks, this term is no longer applied to the unpredictability of results, but to their cost, especially in terms of mortality or illness. According to this last terminology, the interest centre has shifted from variability towards establishing a compromise between a special "risk" and other costs (for example, between the frequency and gravity of accidents and monetary cost of the security measures). The most frequent attitude consists of taking into account the expected value of distributing the probabilities of unfavourable outcomes compared to other peak moments. Thus, the "risk" becomes "hazard", it does not cover the variability of a possible result, but its expected value. Therefore, the substantial contribution of the theory of taking the decision and need to taken into account the distribution of possible outcomes as a whole.

Managers' tightness to the assessments of probabilities also reflect the terminological imprecision of risk theoreticians and decision making. It can also be explained by a certain number of practices of decision making that are often omitted by the theoriticians of rational choices. It is always difficult to estimate the probabilities of a result, as well as the desired output, and the subjective value that could be assigned to the output achieved is far from being obvious. The information is disturbed by conflicts of interests arising between the information source and recipient.

As these difficulties are particularly sensitive in the field of estimating the probabilities, it is absolutely normal for a manager to grant less credibility to the probability assessments than to the assessments of the value of a result. Relative attention that is given to them depends on the relative credibility.

The Importance of Managerial Preferences in Risk Assumption

Empirical studies regarding the risk assumption show that preferences in terms of risk vary depending on the context. For example, the decision maker's choice of risky operation depends on the one hand on the relation between the dangers and opportunities the option represents and, on the other hand, on certain critical objectives which he/she has set, on the other hand. From a behavioural point of view, this modality of assuming the risk according to the context would be generated less by a coherent risk preference than by a change of priorities inside an assembly of contradictory and ambiguous preferences. Following a change of situation or objectives, the decision maker's attention is not directed on the dangers of an option but rather on the advantages which it represents.

All those who studied the human activity in problem solving have observed this managers' trend to assess the keys of the problem. Thus, the behaviour of choice is not just dictated as it is usually deemed by their preferences and changes, but it can also be interpreted in terms of attention. In order to understand a behaviour in the situation of a complete information, it is probably preferred that it would refer to the notion of attention rather than to that of decision. There are certain theories which emphasise the sequential consideration of a small number of options, other s show how the leeway ("slack") extends or contracts according to the comparison between the results and aspirations, and some theories highlight the importance of the presentation order and composition of the agenda.

Many of these theories consider that the decision maker focuses his/her attention on one critical value, for example, the threshold that separates the subject success from the subjective failure. Recent remarks seem to confirm the importance of two critical values. The values quoted most frequently are a result target-threshold (for example the blind spot) and a survival level. These two reference points consist of three possible states: success, failure, disappearance. Adding a critical value related to the disappearance changes a little the forecasts concerning the attention (or preferences in terms of risk).

Generally, for that which is above the result threshold, the main objective is to avoid any action that would risk to go below the threshold. The attention focused on the danger, the earning opportunities switch to the secondary plan. A relative aversion for risk for managers who succeed arises from here and particularly for those who remain right above the threshold. The more symmetrical the distribution of results is, the more covariant dangers and opportunities are and once the focus is on dangers, the opportunities have less importance in choosing. The results should be significantly higher than the objective for managers to inquire the opportunities and assume the risks.

For the decision makers who did not (or foresee they shall not) achieve their goal, the desire to reach the goal generally leads them to assuming the risks. Their attention is then focused on opportunities rather than on dangers, besides when it is very close to the survival threshold. If the results are higher than this threshold, the choice shall be directed towards relatively increased variance options and therefore towards assuming risks. If they are close to the survival threshold, choosing this type of options shall be tempered by a more acute awareness of the dangers they represent.

How Managers Assume Risks

Managers react vividly to the subject of risk assumption. They care about their reputation in this field and only want to speak about their peers' deficiencies or about the fact that their organisation is not able to encourage them to make risky decisions wisely. On the other hand, they provide value to risk assumption, which they consider essential for innovation and success. But at the same time, they make the difference between "assuming risks" and "wining a bet". For the, the good manager is that who "assumes risks", not that who "plays". But for those who study the theory of statistical decision, this distinction may seem misleading, because the theory presents decision making under risk conditions, and not under bet conditions, either against nature, or against other strategic actors. From this point of view, choosing a special strategy in the professional field depends on the same general considerations as a poker game strategy. The pertinence of this parallel was admitted by the decision theoreticians whom tried, without much success, to promote a criterion for evaluating managers that privileges "good decisions" rather that "good results". According to them, elaborating a choice related to the happy denouement (due to hazard) of a risky situation.

In our opinion, if managers establish a distinction between assuming the risk and the game of hazard, it is first because the company that assesses them does the same and then because their experience makes them believe they can control destiny. The company values risk assumption, but not the game and by "game", it understands an assumption of the risk that took a bad turn. In this company which values good management, managers must obtain and keep the reputation of taking "good" risks (meaning those that result in a success) and avoid "bad" risks (resulted in failures), under (perhaps inevitable) conditions of incertitude.

It happens that managers exaggerate more or less consciously, the risky features of certain successful actions. This attempt to get themselves an image of adventurers is not of great importance. With the help of history, it is not difficult to distinguish those who were brilliant adventurers of those who behaved as imprudent players, even though the difference was not perceptible at the time of their decision. The posterior reconstruction enables telling the history, by minimising the role of "hazard", in the sense of the complete probabilistic phenomenon or with inexplicable variation. The risky choices that took an ugly turn are therefore considered to be errors. The warning signals that have been neglected are more obvious than they were at the time of the decision.

History is not content to separate decision makers into winners and losers, but it assigns this actual state to the judgement and capacity differences. Neither the company and especially the manager that succeeds has a reason to doubt the following statement: good managers are able to choose the good risks and remove the bad ones, therefore they can solve the apparent inconsistency of social norms that also require risk assumption and ensured success. Taking into account managers' experience, they believe they can influence the hazard and control a process that apparently seems to be subject to the laws of probabilities, which incites them to accept even better the risks which they would have not thought of.

Assuming risks is also part of the manager's role. He/she is that causing the changes and assuming the (good) risks. Hence, managers' behaviour directed towards change, because everybody expected the same type of behaviour from them. Not without some vanity, managers believe it is possible to make the difference at the time of the decision, between the risks the resolution of which shall be favourable and the unfavourable ones. They are also proud they can control risks and can increase their chances to succeed. These illusions are perfectly consistent with the certainty that their decisions shall certainly have a positive result.

Under current conditions, we can deem that the decision maker does not follow the canons of traditional theory of decision and classical concepts of risk, which emphasise the character differences between individuals, which does not represent a basis suitable for studying managers' behaviour. In their majority, they consider the assessments of probabilities to be slightly reliable and likely to be controlled after making the decision. The elements which they take into account in their decisions and actions that result from here closely depend on their current preoccupation. Instead of assessing and accepting the risks, managers are looking for the options which they can control in order to achieve their objectives. Although not all have the tendency to assume risks, the differences fade through their confidence to master destiny, through the sentiments of risk encouragement and from the context where their choice runs. These factors are the origin of the thesis that affirms that assuming a risk is essential for those who want to be a manager.

This managerial approach of risk is important not only to understand well the decision-making process, but also for assuming the risk and risk management. Therefore, if we want to encourage or hinder managers' risk assumption, we should first adapt to the interventions of their thinking manner. For example, it could be more efficient to change their reflective patterns and illusions about themselves than to determine them to change their opinion about the probability of events.

References

Blackburn WR (2007) The sustainability handbook. Environmental Law Institute, London
Boulding KE (1956) General systems theory: the skeleton of science. Manage Sci 2:197–208
Daft R (2004) Management. Dryden, New York, NY
Davis K (2010) Human organizational behaviours. McGraw Hill, New York, NY
Forlan M, Kenney V (2008) Corporate information systems. Irwin, Boston, MA
Kreitner R (2008) Management. Houghten Hifflin, Boston, MA
Landon K, Landon PJ (2004) Management information systems. Mac Millan, New York, NY
Lesca N (1996) Gestion de l'information. Litec, Paris
Lucey T (1991) Management information systems, 6th edn. D.P. Publications, London
Mintzberg H (2004) The risk and fall of strategic planning. Prentice Hall, New York, NY
Robins S (2001) Management, 3rd edn. Prentice Hall, New York, NY
Stoner I, Freeman E (2009) Management. Prentice Hall, Englewood Cliffs, NJ

Chapter 2
Addressing the Organisational Entities by Using the Systems Theory

2.1 Theoretical Aspects on Organisational Entities

The overall systems theory developed during the last half century is based on the works of Ludwig von Bertalanffy, who made a first draft of the overall systems theory used in the study of open systems that continuously exchange matter and energy with the outer environment. In the 1950–1970s, other researchers dealt with the mathematical logical—conceptual device of the overall systems theory, which was required both as a way of overcoming the false "mechanism—organicism" alternative in the field of biology, as well as a focused expression of the theoretical innovations generated by the current study of sciences, with profound philosophical incidences.

The main consequence of the overall systems theory is the introduction of a new scientific view (called "systemic"), thanks to the methodological virtues of the conceptual triad "system-structure-function" in the research of totalities (organised assemblies). In general, the system can be defined as a set of interconnected elements, which actively or potentially interact and can be identified in any physical, social or conceptual area.

The systems are universally presented in cosmos, in the physical-biological reality and in the social life, and social systems usually consist of organisational entities, which are a system in their turn, however without any social system being an organisational entity in itself.

The study of organisational entities based on systemic theory is based on the following concepts: structuring according to the geographical criteria achieved when its size requires the establishment of some distinct subunits in different places; the formalisation indicates the degree according to which an organisational entity is mainly formal or informal. Normally, the larger the organisational entity, the stronger its formalisation, in order to guarantee the preservation and consistency of activity; the administrative intensity provides the support between the activities of administrative (executive) nature and those of (decision and control)

I.C. Dima, M. Man, *Modelling and Simulation in Management*, Contributions to Management Science, DOI 10.1007/978-3-319-16592-9_2

management. Thus, no organisational entities with mainly (most of) administrative or mainly (normally political) management structures can exist; the centralisation considers the nature of the process of adopting the decisions to focus the power on the top of the hierarchy (centralised structures) or on its lower levels (decentralised structures); the size of the organisational entity refers to the number of its members, which is an extremely important aspect that could generate an "organisational dilemma" (to what extent can increase its number of members without lowering its functionality?) An optimal universally valid structure of the organisational entity does not exist. The structural optimum is determined by its purposes, environmental influences, particularity of the activity, and ultimately by the actual conditions of achieving its essential processes: production—making the specific "products"; support—providing the "inputs" and "outputs"; maintenance—ensuring the internal functionality; adaptation—through the feedback between the "outputs" and "inputs" and management. In other words, this involves a distinct form of correlation between people and goals, as well as between people and structures—as the latter, of essential part defining the systems; the organisational purpose is the very reason of the establishment and existence of the organisational entity. The mere existence of the purpose, which is extremely necessary, is not sufficient. Stating the purpose, its enunciation, the construction of an even achievable purpose is only a first momentum. For this, it should be noted that any organisational purpose is a general purpose whose transformation into final practical results requires: the guarantee of the existence of some significant joint parts between the individual goals, between the interests and aspirations of those individuals forming the organisational entity. It is a matter of the ways to actually achieve the correspondence between the general purpose and the individual goals (in this sense, it is necessary to formulate the general purpose and "translate" it into forms that are accessible to the individuals within the organisational entity. In this way, by keeping its essence, the general purpose multiplies in specific goals, accessible to all members of the organisational entity. Simultaneously, each of its members faces the need to understand and appropriately formulate their own interests, own purposes, as a basis for the actual communication of the specific purposes and for a conscious and responsible assumption of the general purpose).

The organisational entity is an open, adaptive system, taking into account that it is a components of some larger systems with which it has harmonised connections through the management process. At the same time, it also has its own degree of autonomy, an independent operation. The organisational entity can be understood only by seeing it as an open system whose internal processes are interrelated with the environment. The open system is a hypothetical construction which does not exist and cannot exist in reality. The organisational entity will probably never exist as a fully closed system, because its components are always influenced by forces outside the system. Therefore, it should be analysed contextually and, in this sense, we may speak of "degrees of permeability" to environmental influences, but not of a closed system.

The organisational entity is a social system of activity that reunites people (human resources) and material resources by means of which it achieves the purpose which it has been created for: products, works, services, according to the social order. Whatever the organisational economic entity, people built it consciously and deliberately to produce something that the society needs. Its objective (purpose) is the basis underlying its emergence and, at the same time, it is the motivation for maintaining it further. Even though the purpose changed in time and the current one does not coincide anymore with that which it has been created for, it still remains if it has a purpose, if it satisfies a need.

The organisational entity is a dynamic system, meaning that its evolution and viability are determined by the changes produced within the system, in its relations with the environment.

The organisational entity is also a probabilistic and relatively stable system, because it is a reunion of joint components through many connections, subject to some disturbing factors, yet able to maintain its operation within some limits that define the way of behaviour.

The organisational entity is a self-adjustable and self-organised system, as it is able to cope with the various influences from outside and inside, by means of management, through decisions. As self-adjustable system, it acts according to a set of rules and values and it adjusts itself depending on several elements, namely: human elements in mutual interaction; the fact that it has the freedom of choice of means and ways of action, as well as of how to formulate future goals, meaning it has flexibility; the variable activity of people, which is closely related to motivation and conviction, to satisfaction and moral status, to the complex behaviour, to the communication and information systems, to the models adopted in the decision-making process and their performance.

Self-organisation expresses the ability of the organisational entity to restore the balance of its behaviours in relation to the occurred perturbations, and self-training reflects the ability which it has to use the previous experiences in order to optimise its own activity.

The organisational entity is a hierarchically-arranged system, where a precise division of the work operates, and the individuals have clearly defined statuses. One of its basic features is the existence of a hierarchic structure of the management, respectively of a collective or some "teams" operating with leading managers located on various hierarchic levels.

But, to get a more complete image of the organisational entity, it is necessary to emphasise it must be seen both as a system and as "supra-system". As a system, it is included into the global society, and as supra-system, it incorporates other systems. At the same time, it includes several sub-systems, each having a specific function. D. Katz and R. Kahn have recorded an operational classification of the systems (sub-systems) participating in the internal "life" of the organisational entity, which indicates five generic types of its subsystems, namely: the production subsystem—service provision that is the most important, as transformations based on processing the "inputs" into the system therein and thus obtaining the "outputs"; the supporting subsystem acquires the "inputs" from the environment (people, materials, energies), places the "outputs" and achieves the connections of the organisational entity with the external environment; the maintaining subsystem equipping its interior with what is necessary to the achievement under the best conditions of the activity, mechanisms for labour force recruitment and training, for request and motivation being included according to its rules, for application and positive or negative sanctions to achieve the goals suggested by it; the adaptive subsystem, which develops corrective actions to adapt the system after receiving the influences from the environment; the management subsystem that includes the activities performed in order to control, coordinate and conduct the many subsystems of its structure, having adjustment mechanisms and being invested with structural authority on several levels. It is the one adopting the decisions needed to coordinate and conduct all the other subsystems.

The need to organise the human activity and establish the organisational economic entity arises from the human cooperation imperative, because by cooperation, people can do together things they cannot achieve by themselves therein. Man knows in order to transform. Man causes changes in nature, in the environment in order to facilitate the living conditions. Homo sapiens intertwines with homo faber; in their most general expression, man is a social being. Man, as entity, as individual, lives and can only live together with their fellows.

Therefore, the basis of the emergence and existence of organisational entities consists both in their characteristic to achieve the individual goals more rapidly and more efficiently than by isolated action, and in their ability to respond to some fundamental human needs.

The entire structure and all organisational processes result from people's, groups' and leaders' combination and relationship. Each of the three categories of elements is a vital subsystem thereof—the individual subsystem, the group subsystem and the managerial subsystem, which in their turn are featured by specific processes resulting from the input stimulus and are expressed by output behaviours.

Thus, one may speak of the following subsystems: the individual subsystem that includes the following characteristic processes—the motivation (nature and intensity of the interest of presence and action therein), development (professional and human evolution), adaptation (the ability to deal with new stimuli, including to act under intense stress); the group subsystem includes processes occurring on three strongly interfering planes—the intra-group plane (inside the group), extra-group (outside the group) and inter-group (at the level of the supports between the groups). The characteristic processes are the interaction between individuals, socialisation of individuals (inside each group), the competition and cooperation at the level of relations between groups; the managerial subsystem involves processes such as—influence (of individuals and group/groups under the leader's authority), adoption of the decision and coordination of its implementation (management itself), communication with individuals and groups inside the authority area, achievement of management not only under normal conditions of stability, but also under conditions of change, including "exceptional" situations of stress.

An analytical picture of the organisational entities' study based on the systemic theory is achieved by classifying them according to some criteria. Their classification enables better understanding the integration of individuals into the organisational entities and their efficient operation. The simplest and most suggestive classification is based on their structuring degree, distinguishing two types: informal organisational entities and formal organisational entities.

It should be noted from the very beginning that their pure, informal or formal forms are difficult to detect virtually, each organisational entity including both forms of organisation in variable proportions. Therefore, it is advisable to separately analyse: the informal plane of an organisational entity consisting of spontaneous undefined or poorly defined relations between its members. Its norms, rules are spontaneously accepted and by so doing, not being imposed, the acceptance is intense, the adhesion degree being high; its formal plane aims at its official structure, which is clearly defined by describing the rules of construction and behaviour, the roles and (power, authority and responsibility) relations between its members, by indicating the leaders, the hierarchy, by stating the conditions of access, evolution and output from the organisational entity.

Beyond the formal plane, existing in any organisational entity, those approaching most to the formal type are the bureaucratic ones.

Other classification methods take into account the purpose, the benefit of the activity or nature of its members' behaviour. Thus, in the specialised American literature, five different types of organisational entities are identified, which are characteristic to the contemporary society differentiated based on the general purpose of each one of them: volunteer associations, religious, scientific ones; military organisations; philanthropic (charity), spiritual, social assistance organisations; corporate-type (industrial, financial, etc.) organisations; family business organisations: small businesses, as well as the Mafia. Also in the U.S., it is operated with a classification chart based on the principle "who benefits from the specific organisational activity", which classifies them into four types: mutually beneficial organisations, whose first beneficiary are the members and those registered who hold a rank (political parties, unions, clubs, etc.); business organisations, which have as primary beneficiary the owners and managers (industrial companies, banks, insurance companies, retail and wholesale shops); organisations performing services and have as primary beneficiary the customers (employment agencies; hospitals, schools, mental health clinics); public organisations the large public benefits from (statistics at state level, military service, police and fire departments, National Guard).

Considering three types of power: coercive, remunerative and normative power, A. Etzioni classifies the organisational entities according to the confrontation types and sets three types of dual structures (between the rulers and the ruled) therein: coercive organisations (concentration camps, prisons, asylums, prisoner-of-war camps, labour camps, coercive unions); utility organisations (industrial enterprises, research institutes, business unions, farmers' organisations, military organisations in peacetime); normative organisations (religious organisations, political and ideological organisations, hospitals, colleges and universities, voluntary associations, schools, professional organisations).

There are also dual structures to be established in the following combinations: normative-coercive, such as combat units; utility-normative, which include most of the organisational entities; utility-coercive—agricultural and traditional industrial exploitations.

The alert dynamics of the information society determines the organisational entities of any type to continually adapt to an environment undergoing permanent change. Under these conditions, the bureaucratic entity, stated as "mechanic type" entity that proved its efficiency and rationality in a relatively stable and predictable environment will be able to adapt to radical social and technological changes or, will eventually disappear? The question is one of the most important ones.

As A. Toffler (1973) stated, "each age gives rise to a form of organisation suited to its rhythm". In order to survive the modern society's accelerated rhythm of change, the bureaucracies will need to find new, more flexible forms of organisations.

W. Bennis, one of the most respected theorists of organisational entities, in the analysis he operates on the bureaucratic organisation, considers that its mechanisms are rather rigid and inertial, having a slow ability to change and adapt, which made him state, since 1964, that "in the next 25–50 years" we will all witness the "end of bureaucracy". His anticipations have not yet come true, but the bureaucratic organisational entity, as it was conceived by M. Weber and founded as a dominant form of human organisation, has experienced a continuous evolution and adjustment, the current characteristics and forms of organisation which it takes being slightly different.

W. Bennis presents a number of features of the future's organisations, characteristics that the bureaucracy has incorporated one by one, from the need to continuously adapt to changes. The typology that H. Mintzberg did to bureaucratic organisations captures this evolution.

In the classification H. Mintzberg achieves, he captures the various forms the bureaucratic organisation has taken in the continuous attempt to adapt its organisational structure to the individual's needs to affiliate and manifest to the environmental dynamics.

The five basic structures which he identifies are: the simple structure characterised by the increasingly stronger pressure into the direction of centralisation exerted by the strategic (management) peak. It has little or no technical structure, low number of supporting staff, minimum differentiation between departments and a hierarchy with few steps. The coordination is done from the top to the bottom, by direct control from the strategic peak. Also, the peak domination is increasingly more perceived as paternalistic and autocratic, inconsistent with the modern types; the mechanistic bureaucracy does not depend on one person (being safer from this point of view). The strongest pressure comes from the technical structure, from those in fields like the planning, financial, production fields and from others in the same category. The pressure is exerted in the direction of standardisation. Control becomes almost an obsessions, making managers' work more difficult, who spend much energy trying to coordinate all elements of the structure. This is efficient in repetitive work, but it is subject to the conflicts between the peak and the base and between departments; the professional bureaucracy is a form of expression and evolution of bureaucracy that begins to correspond more to the characteristics of the modern organisational entities described by Bennis, meaning it emphasises promoting people according to their professional knowledge, not to the rank and enables their free grouping depending on the issues that must be solved; the divisional form of bureaucracy is widespread in private industrial corporations, but can also be encountered in universities with several campuses or in the medical administration that controls several hospitals and generally in all centralised economic systems where the governmental courts control a large number of organisational economic entities. This structure is "above" the mechanistic bureaucracy, because it operates as a "general headquarter" that controls several such mechanistic bureaucracies. Although the divisional form is the most modern one, Mintzberg considers that out of the five structure, this could be the most vulnerable on to legislative and social changes; adhocracy is the last of the bureaucratic-type organisational structures described by Mintzberg, which, in the language used by Mintzberg, it is at the junction of decentralisation with the organic form of organisation. This type of organisation is also suggested by A. Toffler, which responds best to future's requirements, rapidly adapting to the environmental changes due their main feature of being innovative. They are young organisational entities that are based on research and must be innovative. The key-element in an adhocracy is the research-development supporting staff, but the operating core is also key-element, that is the experts the innovation depends upon. There are two variants of adhocracy: operating, which works directly with customers, such as an advertising agency; administrative, which serves itself, such as NASA, in the field of American space exploration.

The new type of adhocracy, characterised by temporality, intra- and inter-group great mobility, due to the groups of specialists formed depending on the problem to be solved, automatically forms another type of organisational man. Unlike the type of the traditional bureaucratic type which, in order to protect its economic security, it must meet the hierarchy, identifying itself with the performable duties of the job to dehumanisation, in modern bureaucracy, the organisational man is that to whom the initiative and free speech are facilitated, the high flexibility feature being absolutely indispensable to the associative man, who must adapt and rapidly reintegrate into the various groups of which they are called to join.

However, as Toffler warned, "increasing the level of organisations' adaptability reduces the degree of people's adaptability". In other words, the temporality of the associative man's organisational relations (therefore, the acceleration of the flow of organisational relations they must establish), the need to adapt to rapid changes (therefore, the continuous learning of the "rules of the game") many times lead to social and psychological tensions, the individual being deprived of the security of an affiliation and of a stable state that would provide them with a certain balance, a situation which may become frustrating and tiring at some point.

Although it presents many difficulties and the predictable forms that can be identified stray more or less from the initial features, the bureaucratic organisations are still maintained. In conclusion, one may state that the pragmatic rationality, achieved in an organisational control and efficiency of operation, provided by the bureaucratic mechanisms are the two attributes required for any social operation, which determined the perpetuation of the bureaucratic organisation, regardless of what forms it will take in its continuous adaptation to social changes.

2.2 Organisational Entities: A Cybernetic System

In essence, by company (organisation), we define a group of people, organised according to certain legal, economical, technological requirements, which frame and develop a complex of working processes, by using certain means of labour, ultimately resulting in obtaining products and services in order to make an income or a profit as high as possible.

The company must be analysed as a whole consisting in several parts, meaning this will be systemically approached, which provides the following features to it: socio-economic system, as it reunites manufacturing factors and labour force, by means of which it accomplishes its functionality according to the set aims, which result from the social need. The employees' action onto the production means has as basic component, their potential of knowing and volume of knowledge, which determines their motivated behaviour in the process of accomplishing the economical and social aims set forth for the company; dynamic system, meaning that the changes made within the company or in its relations with the environment determine a certain track in the company's evolution, which defines the company's viability or non-viability; complex system, as the company represents a reunion of elements, labour force and production factors, and multiple and deep links are set forth in between them, allowing the action of the "company" system. These elements are not simple passive components, as some of them act in adequate ways for achieving certain aimed objectives; probability system, meaning that the company's action as a whole is subject to the influence of some random factors which permanently tend to disturb its balance; open system, as any company is a component of the bigger systems represented by economy and society; self-adjustable and self-organising system, as the company performs its activity as link of the national economy, in order to accomplish certain aims converging the national interests.

Deemed as a system characterised by the aforementioned features, the company has an operating mechanism defined by the following features: the company is a legal unit assembly, with a certain functional autonomy; the company is formed of subsystems behaving semi-independently, because their operation is subordinated and integrated to the operation of the assembly directed towards achieving the objectives which it has been created for; the company has the specific input parameters, which correspond to its profile and which it transforms within the processing procedure into outputs necessary to the environment where the company operates; the company is able to self-adjust its activity by its own management, which based on the information gathered from the company's operating environment, properly processed and capitalised are used in taking the needed managerial decisions.

In this context, any company approached through the theory of the systems includes two categories of functions and namely: Random functions, which reunite the basic elements of the production and form the physical process of transforming the inputs into outputs; directing functions, which consist in fixing the action programs of the random functions, when trying to accomplish these programs and fixing the correlations necessary to the permanent orientation of its activity towards accomplishing the set objectives.

2.3 System of Organisational Entities Functions

Taking into account the company's systemic approach, it is a matter of an independent system of the company's functions, but which may be deemed as a subsystem compared to the "company" system it generates.

The functions of each company may be represented in three states and namely: potential or virtual (it is not manifested during a certain period of time due to certain reasons—normally of efficiency), integrated (when certain specific activities are performed within the company and others at a higher level), real or effective (the assembly of the specific activities is performed within the company).

The company's function is a component of the process organisation of the company and represents the assembly of the homogenous and/or complementary activities, performed by a person or group of people of a certain specialty, by using specific methods and techniques, in order to accomplish the first degree derived aims.

The following functions of the company are known: the function of research-development represents the assembly of the activities that are performed within the company in order to accomplish the aims in the domain of creating new ideas and transforming these ideas into novelties useful to the company's future development; the activities forming this function are the scientific research, technological engineering and introduction of the technical progress (it includes the assembly of the company's attributions for accomplishing the aims in the domain of applicative research, consisting in discovering new ideas or practically implanting new knowledge), the activity of investments-constructions (the assembly of the company's attributions referring to the transformation of the material, financial and human resources into fixed assets, accomplishing new production capacities, modernising, developing, reconstructing and renewing the existing ones), the organisation of the production and work (creative-innovative attributions in the domain of introducing some methods, techniques and tools for organising and directing the productive activities); the function of production represents the assembly of the basic, auxiliary and connected activities, by means of which the aims are obtained in the domain of manufacturing products, performing works or services by the company. The following activities are mainly included: the fabrication or utilisation (transformation of the production material factors into products, works and services forming the basic objective of the company's activity), the technical quality control (it aims the production factors, the fabrication flow and finished products, maintenance and repair of machines, equipment and plants) takes into account their maintenance in an operational state, preventing and highlighting as much as possible the effects of their obsolescence and physical wear), auxiliary production (for providing the conditions necessary for a good progress of the basic production in the company); the commercial function states the totality of the activities meant to concur in accomplishing the aims in the domain of setting the company's connections with its environment in order to procure the production factors and in providing the manufacture (sale) of products, works and services that are the objective of the company's activity. Three main activities are distinguished, thusly: the activity of technical-material supply (it fully, complexly and duly provides the production factors for performing the production process continuously and in good conditions), the activity of sale (it refers to delivering products, performing works or services and collecting their equivalent value, it therefore refers to passing them from the production field into the circulation field), the activity of marketing (it has the aim of creating and discovering the consumers' needs in order to direct the specific production towards satisfying the real and potential consumers' requirements); the financial-accounting function includes the assembly of the activities by means of which the objectives regarding the procurement and use of the financial means necessary to the company, as well as the value registration and expression evidence of its patrimony. This function includes two categories of activities and namely the financial activity (obtaining and rationally using the financial means necessary to the company) and the accounting activity (value expression registration and evidence of the company's patrimony); the function of personnel includes the assembly of activities performed within a company for accomplishing the objectives in the domain of providing and developing the human potential it needs. The main activities included in this function are planning, recruitment, selection, enclosure, formation, improvement, motivation, promotion, remuneration and protection of the hired personnel; the function of logistics includes the assembly of activities having as aim the release of a quantity of a product at the lowest price, at the location and moment where there is an effective demand for that respective product. This function uses logistical systems which do not only distribute goods and services for satisfying the material needs and desires, also propagating the ideas related to cultural, social and economical progress.

This function is in an interdependency connection with the function of research-development, the function of production, commercial function, the financial-accounting function and function of personnel receiving and offering in its turn valuable information.

This function is done through the activity of the logistical operators, logistical providers and logistics manager.

The totality of the company's functions forms a system of dynamic character representing internal interdependency connections depleting all component activities concurring in fulfilling the activity objective of the "company" system.

2.4 Economy of Organisational Entities: A Micro-economic Cybernetic System

The achievements obtained till present in the field of cumulating and systematization the knowledge about environment, people and society allowed the passing of systematic thinking from the theoretical sphere into the practice of different fields of activity. This fact makes the concept of system-initially used only in technique—to become a basic instrument in the economic research and analysis. It thus contributes to solving abstract and sensible problems of the problems.

In this way the practical approach of the problem leads to the fact that any phenomena activity or process can be considered as systems of a certain type—more or less complex. They are characterized by two categories of environment, namely: external environment of the system, meaning the area in which the area manifests and the internal environment of the system, expressed through the relations established between its compound elements and considered variable measures. Hypothetically, the system is isolated when its connections both with the exterior as well as the connections between its component elements are zero.

If we refer to artificial or natural systems the connections mentioned above are not zero because these kinds of systems receive and give the surrounding environment information. This leads to the necessity of starting from atomic-dissipate structures and from the utility of systems, especially in the social systems. In such cases the cybernetic system in economy has a special place. The cybernetic system in economy is defined as the assembly of interacting elements. It comprises people, objects and means of labor, in which the activities of manipulation, manufacturing and control of materials, information and human actions focus on the accomplishment of an established program determined by the an leading effort based on feed-back.

According to this definition both the economy of the firm and of the economic branches as well as national economy can be considered as a micro, respectively macro economic cybernetic systems. For instance the cybernetic system of the firms can be represented through the following flow-process chart (Fig. 2.1).

The input E in the process mainly regards the factors of production: material, human and financial. By their nature the input components are made up of: production materials and raw materials, fuel, exogenous power for production, labor force etc.

In the specialized literature such a grouping of the input components of the process is known as the grouping of primary elements. For the input in the process decomposed in primary elements, the following notation is considered:

$$E_i = E_1, E_2 \ldots, E_i \ldots, E_I \tag{2.1}$$

The output of P from the process generally materializes in finished, semi-fabricated products etc.

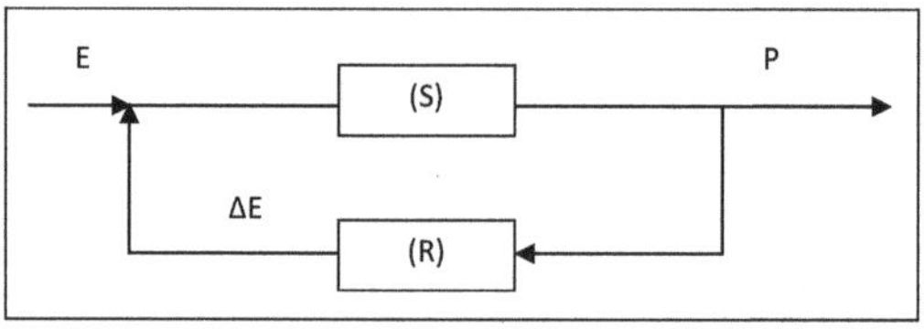

Fig. 2.1 Flow-process chart representation of the firm. (S)—developed process; (S)—the operator which the developed process (S) has; (R)—the regulator of the process; (R)—the operator that the process regulator (R) has; E—the input in the process; P—the output from the process; ΔE—the correction made to the input E in order to maintain the equilibrium of the process

Assuming that the output from the process is decomposed in J groups of product on the following assortments:

$$P_j = P_1, P_2 \ldots, P_j \ldots, P_J \tag{2.2}$$

The achievement of these in a certain period of time t takes place in the following quantities:

$$\begin{array}{l} N_1 \text{ units from the group of the products } P_1, \\ N_2 \text{ units from the group of the products } P_2 \\ \ldots\ldots\ldots\ldots\ldots\ldots\ldots\ldots\ldots\ldots \\ N_j \text{ units from the group of the products } P_j \\ \ldots\ldots\ldots\ldots\ldots\ldots\ldots\ldots\ldots\ldots \\ N_J \text{ units from the group of the products } P_J \end{array} \tag{2.3}$$

In the case of the firms that produce a single product from a certain quantity (thousands tones), in order to achieve it a certain consumption of material, financial and human factors of production takes place. Thus certain expenses are done in the respective process of production with each of the input components $E_1, E_2 \ldots, E_i \ldots, E_I$. The consumption of the factors of production expressed in monetary units represents the manufacturing costs and the production cannot take place without this consumption. All the expenses met for the quantities from the components $E_1, E_2 \ldots, E_i \ldots, E_I$ consumed during production for the achievement of a certain output level, define the conversion costs realized by the firm in that period.

A similar grouping of the manufacturing expenses on primary elements corresponds to the input grouping of factors of production. In the firm this similar grouping comprises the following: the expenses met for the raw materials and the materials consumed in production, fuel expenses, power expenses, the redemption of the consumed fixed means, personnel wages for production etc.

The achievement of the finished products in a firm is conditioned by a certain organization of the production process. Generally the organization of the production process develops on production sections and as part of these it takes place on operations. According to the role that the production sections have in achieving the products of the firm, they are main sections or auxiliary sections. Main or basic sections represent the center of the basic activities of a firm, namely the main places of production. All the operations necessary for the achievement of the finished product are done in the basic sections. The activity from the basic sections is doubled by a whole range of auxiliary activities that are done by auxiliary sections (mechanic, electric workshops etc.). The auxiliary sections are meant to ensure those conditions necessary for the developing the operations of production that take place in the basic sections.

Both the basic activity developed in the main production sections and the secondary activities developed in the auxiliary sections are very important for the achievement of products. Certain relations are established between these. Certain exchanges of activities and information take place, the section influence each other and they finally tend to achieve a self-adjustment process. As a result the firm can be seen as a complex microeconomic cybernetic system and the sections where the process of production takes place represent the subsystems. The connection of the production sections, as subsystems of the complex microeconomic system, can be parallel, serial and mixed.

For the input in the process (S) of the system decomposed into sections, the classification on groups of primary elements is preserved: E_1, E_2..., E_i..., E_I. This decomposed input is at the same time the input for the subsystems of the system, respectively for the main and the auxiliary sections. Due to the role of the auxiliary sections, namely that of serving the main sections in the development of the production process, the input in a main sector may also contain components that represent the outputs of the auxiliary sections. This means that the input in of a certain primary element E_i $\left(i = \overline{1,I}\right)$ in a main sector is made up of the share of the E_i element input in the system meant for the auxiliary sections and contained in their output towards the respective section.

If the notion of primary own input is introduced for the firs component of the input from element E_i and the notion of transferred primary input for the second component then the input from the primary element E_i $\left(i = \overline{1,I}\right)$ in any main sector is made up of its own and transferred input. Obviously this decomposition is also preserved if the input E_i $\left(i = \overline{1,I}\right)$ takes place in an auxiliary section.

The primary input E_i, own or transferred, in a certain main sector of production suffers some transformation operations in order to achieve the commended output from the process (S).

If the output from the process (S) is considered as being made up of a range of products distributed in J groups on the assortments P_1, P_2..., P_J then, the achievement of any product from the P_J group implies the performance of the following operations upon the components of own primary input:

$$\begin{array}{l} OM_{j1} \text{ operations in the main sector 1} \\ OM_{j2} \text{ operations in the main sector 2} \\ \cdots\cdots\cdots\cdots\cdots\cdots\cdots\cdots \\ OM_{jS*} \text{ operations in the main sector } S* \end{array} \tag{2.4}$$

where: S* is the number of the main sections.

The operations that are necessary to be done in the case of the components of own primary input in the first $S^* < S$ sections of production, respectively in the main sections, so that the output from the process (S) makes part of the P_J products group, can be represented in the following matrix:

$$O = \begin{vmatrix} O_{j11} & O_{j12} & \cdots & O_{j1M_{j1}} \\ O_{j21} & O_{j22} & \cdots & O_{j2M_{j2}} \\ \cdots & \cdots & \cdots & \cdots \\ O_{jS^*1} & O_{jS^*2} & \cdots & O_{jS^*M_{jS^*}} \end{vmatrix} \tag{2.5}$$

where: $O_{jSU_{js}}$ represents the operation number; $u_{js}\left(u = \overline{1, M_{jS}}\right)$ done in the main section; $s\left(s = \overline{1, S^*}\right)$ related to any of the products from group $P_j\left(j = \overline{1, j}\right)$

If the output from the process (S) is heterogeneous and composed of J groups of products, then the number of matrixes of the type (2.3) is equal with J and represents the difference between the technologies of the products that belong to different groups. The J matrixes are identical if the output is homogenous.

While the components of primary input that takes place in the main sections focus on the transformations presented in the matrix (2.5), the components of primary input transferred in the same sections focus on the insurance of the conditions necessary for the performance of these operations and thus they focus on the achievement of the final goal—the commanded output of the system, which is made up of J groups of products.

The primary input in a main sector whose consumption per operations and products can be measured, is called primary input directly measurable and in the opposite situation it is called primary input that is not directly measurable. Obviously, a part of the component of owned primary input is directly measurable and the other is not (for example: the worker's labor consumption, respectively that of the sector chief). Any primary input directly measurable in a sector is necessarily own while a primary input that cannot be directly measurable is own or transferred.

Considering the primary input $E_i\left(i = \overline{1, I}\right)$ its directly measurable component is marked by E_{i0}, while the component that cannot be directly measured is marked by E_{i1}. In its turn, this component decomposes in its components:

$$E_{i10} \text{ and } E_{i11},\ E_{i1} = E_{i10} + E_{i11} \tag{2.6}$$

where: E_{i10}—represents the own component, E_{i11}—transferred component.

For the primary input directly measurable E_{i0}, it is not necessary the use of a third index, because it is always:

$$E_{i0} = E_{i0} \tag{2.7}$$

Starting from the destination held by our own or transferred input component that cannot be measured directly, in relation to the production process of a sector, the following classification can be done for E_{i10} and E_{i11}:

E_{i101}, E_{i111}—the component of the primary input E_{i10} and E_{i11} meant for the maintenance and functioning of the equipment of the sector;
E_{i102}, E_{i112}—the component of the primary input E_{i10} and E_{i11} meant for leading the process in a main sector;
E_{i102}, E_{i112}—the component of the primary input E_{i10} and E_{i11} in a main sector and meant for leading the whole process.

As a result of these classifications, the primary input $E_I\left(i = \overline{1, I}\right)$ in a main production sector is made up of the following components:

E_{i0}—the component of the primary input E_i, directly measurable;
E_{i101}—the component of the primary input E_i, directly unmeasurable, own, meant for the maintenance and functioning of the equipment in a main sector;
E_{i102}—the component of the primary input E_i, unmeasurable directly, own, meant for leading the activity in a main sector, namely the component of the primary input E_{i10} that represents the information of the command of the regulator (R) towards the process (S) from the section $s = \overline{1, S^*}$, information of own local command;
E_{i103}—the component of the primary input E_i, unmeasurable directly, meant for leading the whole process. It belongs to a main sector of production, namely it is that component of the primary input E_{i10} in a main sector, representing the command information of the regulator (R) of the process (S) towards a main sector of production $s = \overline{1, S^*}$, information of own central command;
E_{i111}—component of the primary input E_i, unmeasurable directly, transferred meant to the maintenance and functioning of the equipment in the sector from which it derives;
E_{i112}—component of the primary input E_i, unmeasurable directly, transferred and meant for leading the sector from which it derives, namely that component of the input E_{i11} in a main sector, representing command information of the regulator of an auxiliary sector $s = S^*, S^* + 1, \ldots, S$ towards the own process—information of local transferred command;
E_{i112}—component of the primary input E_i, unmeasurable directly transferred and meant for leading the whole process, namely that component of the input E_{i11} in a main section, representing the command information of the regulator (R) of the process (S) towards an auxiliary section $s = S^*, S^* + 1, \ldots S$—the information of central transferred command.

Thus, the firm can be seen as a microeconomic cybernetic complex system in which the following aspects are present: the process (S) is the result of the serial, parallel or mixed connecting of the production sections and these ones are cybernetic systems with feedback; the regulator of the process (S) is the element (R)—the running of the film-together with the leadership of the sections and their components; the input in the process (S) is made up of the primary elements E_i; the input E_i in each section is characterized through the following components: $E_{i10}, E_{i101}, E_{i102}, E_{i103}, E_{i111}, E_{i112}, E_{i113}$ $\left(i = \overline{1,I}\right)$ and through the operations from the matrix (2.5) that lead to the achievement of the P_J output.

2.5 The Complex Cycle of Organisational Entities Operation

Developing a theory of the operation of organisations, which is based on these premises, requires knowing very well the informational possibilities provided by the organisation, of those to use the information, the constraints, which influence the operation of organisations, including the convictions of the members within the organisation. In this context, a better understanding of the factors affecting the operation of organisations based only on experience is not important just to improve the activity within the organisation but also it is absolutely necessary to develop a theory to adapt the organisation to its environmental operating conditions.

Just like the individual intelligence, the intelligence of the organisation as a whole, without which the decisional process cannot be designed in a full operating cycle of the organisation is based on: rationality of organisation operation, based on the use of forecasts regarding the future consequences for selecting the development options of the organisation; the use of experience in operating the organisation, by turning the knowledge gained from experience, necessary to make a choice between various options possible. This is done in the activity of the organisation by experimentation, assessment, estimation, control, etc. The two previously mentioned features highlight the complexity of the complete cycle of operation of the organisation and requires the following problems to be dealt with:

- establishing the complete cycle of the operation of the organisation and its analysis, which assumes that: At some point, certain members of the organisation find out a deviation between the world as they imagine it (being given the possibilities and restrictions of the moment) and the world as it is in reality. Such a deviation causes a certain behaviour of the organisation or certain choices of its team. The outside world responds to these choices in a well-defined manner, which changes the individual evaluations, according to the state of the external world and efficiency of the organisation actions. Designing thusly the complete cycle of the organisation operation involves the existence of several elements in countered in a successive chaining, such as: the cognitive features and preferences of individuals that influence their behaviour; individuals' behaviour influences the preparation of the organisation; the preparation of the organisation involves a certain reaction of the environment; this reaction of the environment changes the cognitive features and individual preferences (Fig. 2.2).

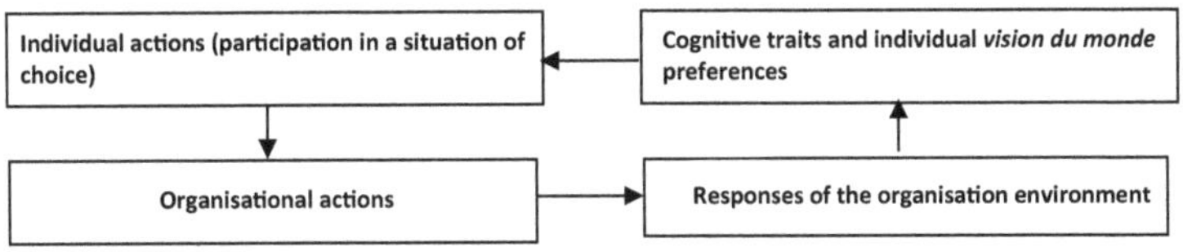

Fig. 2.2 The complete cycle of organisation operation

The complete cycle of organisation operation therefore contains four simple relations, but each of them is sufficiently complex, which is why the good operation of the complete cycle of the organisation cannot be imagined otherwise. In its turn, this complexity of the cycle to prepare the organisation is what gives rise to some limitations of the theory in the field, which cannot be ignored;

– identifying the individual convictions and actions of the members of the organisation and studying them. Adopting the decision within the organisation is based on the interest of its members and is generally appealing to the extent where the resources assigned for such an action are important. However, the study will literature in the field shows that the members of the organisation do not have a stable level of activity in relation to the inputs and outputs of the organisation. The attention of the members of the organisation on its problem varies considerably, as level and form, from one person to another and from one period to another, for the same individual. This variation and its connection with the individual convictions and attitudes is understood better if it is taken into account that the time and energy of the individual and organisation do not overlap.

The involvement of the members of the organisation into the process of decision making is not an appealing activity for everyone, in all situations and at any time, because the ability to have convictions, attitudes and concerns is greater than the ability to act. Thus, one can perceive a choosing situation as being pertinent, but not have the time or energy necessary to act in this respect. In this case, certain convictions or values of the individual are noticed, not without their behavioural implications. Even if time or energy do not represent an inconvenience, there are other situations that should be taken into account and allow the individual to express their concerns. The distribution of their attention shall not depend on the content of a single choice, not on the range of possible situations of choice. It would be an error to believe that a set of convictions and preferences of the individual and organisation are always materialised through a certain behaviour in all situations of choice, independently of the cases brought to attention;

– identifying and studying the individual actions within the complete cycle of organisation operation. It is generally considered that the operation of the organisation is based on the individual actions of its members. Thus, a decisional process transforms the individual behaviours into an organisational activity. The economic literature abounds with attempts to express the nature of this visible hand. The process is sometimes translated through deductive images (objectives, sub-objectives and derivatives of the organisation, efficiency, etc.), and at other times through images of the default conflict (markets, bureaucracy, etc.). In this concept, the operation of the organisation is considered to be a consequence of the individual action, and the organisations are all the elements of which these are formed of. In this context, the connection between the action of a member and that of an organisation is of weak intensity. The operation of the organisation in a complete cycle must take into account the relation between two aspects such as: An aspect that takes into account the calendar of the changes within the organisation and the other aspect, which takes into account the change of the context of the occurrence of each change within the organisation however as independent element;

- approaching the operation of the organisation, taking into account the influence of its exterior environment. The complete operating cycle of the organisation provides a connection between the actions of the organisation and the actions that take place in the environment where it operates, which are deemed to be natural reactions of the environment to the operation of the organisation. The way in which the environment reacts to the operation of the organisation must be understood as being the nature of the relations between events, factors and structures of the environment and not as an answer to what the organisation does. The same action of the organisation could therefore determine different environmental reactions to various moments and various actions. This is because the organisations act under the conditions of the restrictions imposed by the environment. There are few cases where these restrictions are not observed and the environment reacts unambiguously. But, most of the time, the operating range is relatively tight, and inside of it only a very low part of it can be assigned to the actions taken by the organisation;
- identifying the reactions of the environment to the individual convictions of the members of the organisation and their analysis. The classical theory of the operation of the organisation proposes two hypotheses of the relationship between the environment and individual convictions of the members of the organisation, as follows: in the first hypothesis, the problem is silenced, meaning that the decision-makers are informed perfectly about the different options and their consequences, the complete cycle of the operation being perfectly understood before any individual action within the organisation; in the second hypothesis, the relation is designed according to a model of the rational individual adaptation, meaning that the convictions and representations of the world are correlated with the reality, through experience, and the individual identifies their convictions and behaviour, according to their experience, observations which they make on the events.

The changes of the organisation environment, both internally and externally, leads to a certain reflection on the cross is to prepare the com fiction is of the members within the organisation. In many cases, the interpretation of an organisation operating process is just as important as the actual and immediate action, which is generally studied less. The individuals, as well as the organisations develop their own myths, fictions, legends and illusions, but which they are often in conflict with. Therefore, models to prepare the convictions are needed, which do not necessarily include as hypothesis the domination of events or of objective realities.

The actions and events observed in the environment are often ambiguous and it is not known very well what is going on there and why. This ambiguity can be inherent in the events that occur or it can result from the difficulties which the organisation must deal with. The complexity of the environment and its changes often exceed the cognitive abilities of the individuals. Our interpretations are also seldom based only on own observations and are greatly supported on those of others, and the individual's trust in an interpretation depends very much on their trust in its author.

If the classical theory of the complete cycle of the organisation operation is taken into account, which states that the members of an organisation participate in its activity and decision-making and it is admitted that they are encountered in the context of a more complex world, less stable and less comprehensible, being placed in a world where the possibilities to control are very limited, then it may be concluded that all relations of the complete cycle of the organisation operation can be interrupted or changed in depth, with the consequence to change the organisation as a whole.

Moreover, the complete cycle of the organisation operation is often disturbed by exogenous factors that avoid the internal control, because the complete cycle of the organisation is embedded into a larger organisational system. The external factors may dictate the individual action, without reference to the individual training of the organisation members, as well as the action of the environment, without reference to that of the organisation or finally, the individual training, without reference to the action of the environment. For these considerations, a theory of the organisation operation is necessary, in a complete cycle that would respond to all these observations, a theory which shall be characterised through the following features, as follows: it is a theory of the organisation operation, both contextually and structurally. Contextually in that it will take into account that the relations of the complete cycle of operation are changed by the exogenous events, the calendar of the events, fluctuations of the participation of the organisation members and structurally in that it shall deal with the stability possibilities of a system in a clearly contextual way; it is a theory of the organisational attention dealing with the distribution of attention between the potential participants at the operation of the organisation; it is a theory of the operation of the organisation under ambiguity, which it implicitly includes the complete cycle of the organisation operation.

2.6 The Control Process in Organisational Entities

The control of the organisation is a complex process that depends on a number of variables, wherein interaction connections are established, as follows: the structure of the organisation; the culture of the organisation members; the social, economic and political environment where the organisation operates, etc. These variables are in ambiguous and complex relations, both with the control process and with the mechanisms of the organisation.

In small organisations, characterised by the continuity of the production process, the entrepreneur or the senior management can personally and systematically observe, monitor and control the activity of the subordinates. In large organisations, where the division of labour is well developed, the discontinuity of tasks and hierarchy of responsibilities, the policy and objectives of the organisation are established or at least ratified by senior managers and are communicated to the employees placed on lower positions, whom responsibilities are assigned to afterwards, in order to act accordingly. Determining the fulfilment of objectives and, in case of failing to fulfil them, taking the most important actions, represent the appanage of the senior management. This is the process of control.

Without controlling what the employees do in the organisation, there is a danger of some tendencies for the organisation to develop centrifugally, meaning that the employees begin, intentionally or not, to do their job working for their own interest and personal goals. In order to counteract the tendencies created by the process of differentiation and in order to provide what is called the congruence of the employees' goals, it is necessary to create centripetal forces within the organisation, which shall control and integrate its members' varied activities, which could theoretically be done by designing and implementing the control systems and processes, developed according to the goals of the organisation. Thus, the type of former and intentional control appears, which refers first of all to the ways in which certain employees are made to ensure the behaviour of others, so as to achieve the fulfilment of goals as the organisations want.

Even though both Hopwood and Dalton use a different terminology, they identify three categories of control, which are encountered in an interaction. Thus, the categories of the administrative and production control, social control and self-control of Hopwood correspond more or less with Dalton's concepts of organisational, informational and individual control.

The formally modelled administrative control is socially constructed, meaning it has numerous assumptions, beliefs and values included into the model and operation manner. It is involved in a social context mediating its operation, especially in that it faces spontaneous social controls, developed to adjust the behaviour of members. The social and administrative controls are finally implemented by means of the individual self-control. Therefore, the situation of the control in any organisation may be entirely understood and explained only through the interaction of these three variants.

The administrative and production control is a category of control referring to those mechanisms, techniques and processes which have been consciously and intentionally modelled, in order to try to control the organisational behaviour of certain individuals, groups and organisations. Apparently, they aim to create a situation where the employees are more likely to behave in those ways that lead to achieving the organisational objectives, which have been presumably decided by certain conditions of the employees or have been established for the organisation by the interested and powerful parties. In this regard, the model of Mintzberg of what is called the mechanism of coordination can be seen as a taxonomy of the different types of administrative and production control, even if this helps, it tends to ignore those things caused by the impact of social control and self-control.

The most common form of administrative and production control is the use of formal rules and procedures, which Mintzberg catalogued as an attempt to standardise the process of labour. The largest organisations use such standards, regulating the behaviour of its employees. By creating a bunch of rules and procedures, based on some important means of monitoring the subsequent behaviour of members and by using the sanctions, in order to ensure the satisfaction of the employees, this type of control serves to specify what should and should not be done by the employees of the organisation in certain situations. Thus, the rules constrain the employees' behavioural limit, increase the predictability of their actions and the likelihood that the observation of the organisation's requirements would dominate these behaviour.

According to the opinions of Max Weber, such a framework of the rules established intentionally and impersonally to govern the performance was one of the most important and special characteristics of the bureaucratic administrative system. For Weber, this process of bureaucratisation meant increasing the subordination of the employees by the accurate calculations of the means by which certain goals can be achieved and which have imprisoned people in an iron cage. First of all, the bureaucracy may cause unpredictable malfunctions, meaning that the strict observation of rules can become an end in itself, and this is why it often undermines the initial goals which the rules intended to protect. Second of all, it is also clear that, as a result of some of the basic features of the work done, it is not always possible to predict or calculate the means by which the goals can be achieved, to pre-programme them, by creating certain rules and procedures, what, where and when the employees are to do. As Perrow pointed out in his analysis about the impact of technology in organisations, they are two aspects of the attempts, which influence the extension towards those attempts that can be pre-programmed. The first one is the number of exceptional cases, new events, situations and problems encountered in the process of work and perceived as abnormal. The second aspect is the nature of the process of searching, taken by the employees when these exceptions occur. This search can be analysed, so that the problems are solved in a way that involves logical, analytical steps. But, if the problems are vague and poorly designed, the process of searching is basically irresolvable, and the problems can be solved only by using the residues of the irresolvable experience and intuition.

Where the tasks are complex and unpredictable, it is impossible to create preset rules, in order to regulate the behaviour of employees. Indeed, for many of the organisation's activities, it can be crucial to allow employees to express their freedom of action. As long as it focuses on the posterior effects of the behaviour rather than on the behaviour in itself, the administrative and production control can ensure the control, leaving the fulfilment of daily tasks up to the employees' wisdom and freedom of action. Where this control is used, it should be possible to measure the consequences of the behaviour, meaning what has been achieved by fulfilling the tasks.

This type of control can give freedom of action in fulfilling the tasks, by applying certain processes and mechanisms. First of all, the objectives (or standards) must be decided by stating the results obtained by the personnel after fulfilling the tasks. Second of all, there must be certain objectives by which real, performed, obtained tasks can be observed and measured, in relation with those objectives, thus being possible to compare the actual performance with the purpose, target. It is not necessary to know how the tasks have been fulfilled, in the sense of control, but accurate and reliable measurements should be available for the inspection. It should also be possible to analyse and explain the deviations concerning the achievement of initial objectives and thus, if needed, appropriate measures should be taken to correct the execution of the tasks. Where the initial objectives have been reached, a rewarding strategy should exist, designed to refresh and encourage the employees' behaviour.

The development of rules, procedures and the anticipated description of the different and various types of control can be seen as crucial attempts to provide at work behaviour of the subordinates, dominated by the objectives and priorities of hierarchic superiors. This is often called the congruence of purposes. However, these obvious forms of control cannot entirely reach the purpose to regulate the behaviour of the subordinates in order to achieve the congruence of purposes. Moreover, where production cannot be measured in the actual sense and where the tasks are unpredictable, any form of this control shall be inadequate.

The social control mainly involves the process of socialisation, by which the employees send to each other certain cultures within the organisation which they are part of. In order to understand the notion of socialisation, it is important that in the case of moving an employee from an organisational context, or from ones status to another, the image about self, the set of values, beliefs and options, adapted to a set of social relations which provide stability and continuity, this idea may change as the group also changes. This idea has been suggested for the first time by Mead, who argued that, if the employees anticipated and planned the actions and activities and if they think on and learn from their own previous behaviour, they should be able to look at themselves in the same way in which they look at those they may know According to Mead, this human capacity of self-awareness depends on each individual's ability to absorb and adopt others' attitudes. According to Mead, our understanding of ourselves is a reflection of the views of others, important people and which means something in our lives. Shibutani defines a group of reference as a group whose presumptive perspectives are used by an actor, as a reference frame for their perceptual field.

Thus, a reference group has the role of being a source of ways of thinking, feeling, perceiving and assessing and as an auditorium that can be mentally present or absent in any interaction, but whose behaviour the actor shall guide.

The subjective world of an employee may be influenced harder by the social interaction, by certain employees, whom become a reference group which the employees are increasingly guided and which is used for personal assessment. Van Maanen proves the importance in the socialisation of these social networks and highlights the connection between accepting certain cultures by an employee and the latter's involvement in the social networks. However, the direct involvement of the employee into a certain social network does not mean that network automatically becomes a reference group for about the employee. Therefore, in a community with accepted attitudes, the individuals acquire these attitudes to the extent where the community serves as a positive reference point.

However, it is important to highlight that the reference groups shall not necessarily transmit the norms and values which are consistent with those of a certain culture adhered by the coalition of the superior hierarchy. Indeed, the researchers on employees' behaviour provide numerous examples of the value of employees and norms reflected in daily practice. Even in managerial hierarchies of an organisation there is evidence suggesting the diversity of cultures, some of them being antagonistic.

Dalton observes the tendency of affiliations to develop around their own interests, which are many times in antithesis with those of others. Burns affirms that these affiliations, with standards and values contrary to management, can develop around older managers, whom have not been promoted and need to act defensively. Burns contrasts these coalitions with those developed around young managers, whose own interests are met in accordance with the culture of senior management. Thus, by establishing the social relations with colleagues (hierarchically superior or subordinates) and by expressing their sympathy and appreciation, the individuals can become sociable, by accepting certain predominant standards and values in the social network. Maintaining these relations does not depend just on the personal knowledge shown and on accepting the culture of the social group, thus proving they are competent members, but these relations are also transmitted to them.

As long as beauty is in one's own eyes, despite the various social informational pressures, one can imagine that groups strive to make the members conform to their standards, beliefs and practices, the individuals deviate from the culture of their group, by identifying to the alternative group or to that which they aspire to, which they do not share the same community with. By informally transmitting certain values, beliefs, attitudes and expectations, this social control is not exercised just horizontally, but it can also occur vertically, between the hierarchical superiors and subordinates.

In any direction, the control is not achieved only by formal means, but also by pressures exercised by the individuals on each other. This is why, in any situation, the controllers and those who can be controlled have social relations with each other. The personal reasons, hopes and relations of all members of the organisation exercise a significant effect on the process of control of the results.

Self-control is necessary because the administrative and production control as well as the social one have influences on the organisational behaviour of the employees. These must be expressed through the personal actions and attitudes of the managers and employees. They must act as self-controllers, the control which people exercise on their own behaviour. For this to happen, the standards included in the administrative or social control must be directly or indirectly... internalised by the personnel of an enterprise and operate as personal control on attitudes and behaviour. Hopwood continues to highlight that, for this to happen, the administrative and production control, as well as the social one in question must express the reward to personal values and desires.

References

Askin RM, Standridge CR (1993) Modeling and analysis of manufacturing systems, 1st edn. Wiley, New York, NY

Blackburn WR (2007) The sustainability handbook. Environmental Law Institute, London

Bovel L (2003) Management. McGraw Hill, New York, NY

Certo S (2004) Modern management. Allyn & Bacon, Boston, MA

Daft R (2004) Management. Dryden, New York, MA

Dima IC, Man M (2013) Budgeting and management control in industrial companies. Lambert Academic, Saarbrucken

Gordon B (2007) Management information systems. McGraw-Hill, New York, NY

Grifiin R (2008) Management. Houghton Mifflin, Boston, MA

Hall RH (2007) Organizations: structures, processes and outcomes. Prentice-Hall, Englewood Cliffs, NJ

Kotter J (2002) The general manages. Free Press, New York, NY

March JG, Simon HA (1993) Organizations, 2nd edn. Wiley, New York, NY

Robins S (2001) Management, 3rd edn. Prentice Hall, New York, NY

Chapter 3
Organisational Entities Under the Conditions of Market Economy Globalisation

3.1 Market Economy Globalisation

Market economy is the economy that is organised and functions on the basis of the mechanisms of the market in a liberalised system in all its aspects. The main moments of reproduction are limited only by a series of general rules, such as the public order or the sanitary norms. The main dimension of this economy is the market and the basis of its functioning is the market mechanism. This mechanism consists mainly in the movement of prices, according to the ratio between supply and demand on the competitive market. Economic agents (producers and consumers, sellers and purchasers, offerers and petitioners of economic resources) freely confront, namely without state interference. Thus, economic structures and behaviors that are based on the mechanism of the market and behaviors confrontation allow the working of the market. The total absence or the minimum presence of governmental regulations is therefore a requirement of market economy. Market economy synthetically comprises three major categories of goods: products and services achieved by firms, production factors and the coin. Therefore economic activity comprises a flux of firms, goods and services towards the consumers. This one is doubled by a monetary flux in an opposite direction. Economic activity also comprises a flux of services provided by the possessors of the factors of production. This flux is doubled by a monetary flux that represents the incomes of those who sell their productive services to firms. In this way economic circuits are formed.

Market economy can be defined as an economy of goods that have reached a certain level of development in which goods and services are merchandises whose price is formed on the market according to the demand-supply ratio. Firms desire cost minimization and income maximization, enjoy administrative autonomy, freedom of choice for their own activity and they have access to credits for completing their own capital or for purchasing goods in installments and paying interests for them.

I.C. Dima, M. Man, *Modelling and Simulation in Management*, Contributions to Management Science, DOI 10.1007/978-3-319-16592-9_3

The following features define the actual form of market economy: it is multipolar economy in the sense that it comprises a variety of distinct centers of decision, economic activity and administration representing production agents who offer factors of production as well as consumers; it is a decentralised economy, meaning that the decisions are taken by independent economic agents whose actions are spontaneously and automatically coordinated by means of the market, monetary fluxes but in this economy a series of macrodecisions interfere; it is a firm economy, meaning that the microeconomic space is fundamental for the activity unfolding. The firm is the economic unity of production ensuring the connection between products and service markets and factor markets in which the entrepreneur is the central figure of economy; it is an economy of monetary calculations, meaning that money, because it facilitates the quantification and evaluation of costs and results, represent the connection between past, present and future and it also serves as a common denominator of economic agents activities; it is an economy in which the state has an indirect and global intervention; it is an economy in which the profit is the mobile of the economic agents and the central objective of the firm and for its achievement the firms are limited only by their own capacities and by respecting the other economic agents rights; it is based on the domination of the competitive markets mechanisms, meaning that these represent the supreme arbiter of economic decisions; the state represents a component of the market economy function mechanism, but the market forces and private decisional centers remain essential.

The market and the market economy have evolved in time. At the end of the ninteenth century they were the closest to the ideal model of functioning but even then their form was not pure. Different regulations that have established restrictions or privileges for certain persons or certain groups have existed in certain forms and in a certain measure.

The globalisation we face nowadays derives from the fact that, by starting from the technological and economical development, a significant number of human activities is situated on such a large scale and scope that they exceeded the national borders within the limits of which the sovereign states exercise their right to govern. The new actors had to cope with the challenge caused by the monopoly-type governance. Multinational corporations, global financial markets, non-governmental organisations as well as criminal organisations and international terrorist networks appeared. Their activity is not covered by international laws which are based on formal agreements between the nation-states, for they have not been able so far to find a common ground for agreements aiming the issue of globalisation.

Among the most invoked causes of the current globalisation, we list the following: the internet (technology) which is in many ways the emblem of globalisation because the globalisation of financial markets, the transfer of some very large amounts around the world in just a few seconds would not be possible without this technology, or the organisation of integrated production at trans-national level; rapid decrease of transportation costs is due to the very large boom trade and logistic activity have undergone. Thus, the merchandises can be transported much faster; the end of the Cold War is also one of the causes of globalisation. If in the conflict between the East and the West the world was divided into two sides which maintained few relationships between them, in 1989/1990 this delimitation known as the "Iron Curtain" collapsed. Those states that belonged to the "Eastern block" opened into the direction of world market, the global issues have a particularly important place, especially at consciousness level, an evidence being not just the "One World"-type shops in the industrialised and ultra-developed states. However, the global issues also need an internationalisation of the politics, stimulating the development of a global consciousness. Thus, organisations such as Greenpeace or Amnesty International are committed to certain global themes such as the environment or human rights, becoming "Global Players". Thus, the beginnings of some new global companies appear clearly; without liberating the world trade within GATT, respectively of OMC, this globalisation could not have been really possible. Those who criticise the globalisation such as the ATTAC network increasingly draw the attention on the fact that globalisation is not an inevitable process, but rather a result of deregulation policy of the US started at the end of the Second World War.

The sizes of current globalisation are closely interlinked. Among these, we list the following: economical size which refers to the enormous increase of trade and direct investments, the globalisation of financial markets, production integrated at trans-national level, trans-national corporations, local competition; the size of "environment" takes into account certain global issues, such as atmospheric warming, the ozone hole or cutting down of rainforests which most impressively illustrate the phenomenon of globalisation because in this case it is certainly a matter about global issues which need a global approach; the social size refers to the fact that the world has become a "global village", innovative remote communication networks (chat, e-mail) adding to the traditional communities such as family or neighbourhood, which cannot however replace these traditional communication scopes; the cultural size meaning that Hollywood productions can be viewed everywhere around the world, and the "Americanisation" of world culture is an undeniable fact. However, regional and local cultures do not disappear because of this. On the contrary: informing about these cultures is one of the secondary phenomena of globalisation; the political size takes into account that politics faces major issues. The globalisation and competition at a local level limits the area of acting for national politics, many issues being able to be solved accordingly only at an international, respectively global level. Therefore, new political forms must be found. In this sense, the European integration is seen as a successful response to the challenges of globalisation. The regional and national politics suffered and still suffers from the delimited and dematerialised economy increasingly practiced at an international and global level.

The consequences of the current globalisation directly affect us all. In this context, a prudent assessment of the opportunities and risks of globalisation plays an important role, distancing us from the current trends of demonisation or rather of glorification of the consequences of this phenomenon.

The following can be listed as consequences of globalisation: erosion of the national statute meaning it does not disappear or become useless, as it suggests in many comments, but it erodes. Thus, certain additional levels appear where the issues can be solved—both superior and inferior to the national statute; the social dumping refers to the fact that the increase of competition capacity within the global competition at the local level and implicit drop of assumed expenses with social insurance payment is seen as a necessity, especially by the industry, while the unions warn on the danger resulted from the so-called social dumping; the emphasise of the gap between the poor and the rich due to the fact that those enterprises with a significant threat potential could threaten to move into "cheaper countries" regarding the workforce. These existed far before having started the discussions about globalisation, but worsened due to globalisation. The movement of those protesting against globalisation try to draw our attention on this and they managed to attract in the meantime a significant number of supporters; "Global Governance" aims to (re-)tame the "tiger", meaning the capitalism released by "globalisation". When the issues start to get an increasingly more global feature, their political solution must also become "global". In this sense, there are various projects, which inclusively aim to form a global state. For this purpose, the concept of "global governance" was invented, which means: a management of the world without a global leadership system, an internal policy at world level, a policy of the new world order, the politics in the twenty-first century, a concept opposed to neo-liberalism, a response to globalisation. The global governance aims to fill the resulted void, the regulatory deficit, by cooperating at the international level—the state however keeping its own regulatory functions, but also by forming some new political forms.

The international production, including the production of trans-national companies, branches and other companies linked to the multinational companies, by agreements and alliances, without capital participation has known a strong development. The old scheme of manufacturing in a country and selling in another country has given room to the international manufacturing operations. The technologic progress allows the decomposition and desegregation of production processes. Companies choose the place that meets the most favourable production factors for each of the stages of the production process. Consequently, the export does not represent often the sale of a national product to a foreign buyer, but it results from the different national localisations of those companies that participate in crating the same product. The multinational companies can contribute in stimulating the economic development in the implantation countries, in strengthening their technological abilities, in creating their human resources, in facilitating the access to new markets.

In this context, the logistic functioning of the company with ist other functions essentially includes all activities of the specialized personnel (director of logistic and logistics operators) which aim to offer the customer the necessary product when needed, where needed, in the quantity needed and with a correct price-quality ratio.

The approach of a new domain of company's management, the logistical one, imposes the knowledge of own aims and methods of study. But, in order to facilitate the implementation, its main components must be prevalently set forth. Impelled by the change in the structure of potential clients, suppliers have performed ground changes in their distribution. The institution of the method of "just times" has imposed special rules even within the company for supply and transfer of products, semi-finished goods and pieces in between workshops, with consequences over suppliers too, whom needed to rethink the distribution logistics depending on clients' new data.

3.2 The Production System: Component of the "Organisational Entities" System

The production system, through its characteristics can be placed in the category of opened systems. This is the result of its behaviour, characterized through receiving the material, financial and labour resources from the outside environment (thus inputs). These ones are then transformed in finished products and services (thus outputs) and they are transmitted to the external environment.

The essence of the definition of the cybernetic system is that this one is a reunion of systems aiming at the achievement of a mutual transfer of information between the component subsystems and between these ones and the environment so that on a certain period of time the self-adjustment process of the whole reunion to be ensured. If we take into account this definition, the production system can be placed in the category of the cybernetic systems (closed, with feedback).

The component elements of the production system are in fact internal subsystems between which material and informational relations are established. The material relation results most of the time in the transformation of raw materials and power that take place in the technological and economic process. The informational relation refers to the information present between the subsystems of the production system regarding the following aspects: What finished product must be obtained?, What raw materials will be used?, What technology will be used? etc. In this category there are also included the informational relations of the production system with the external environment. These relations offer the managers the necessary information for the decision making process. Their influence should not be minimized.

The production can achieve its objective—the achievement of products, the carrying out of services, the execution of works—only when it is in a continuous correlation, from an informational point of view, with the other systems of the firm, for example: the commercial system (which through its components offers information about market requirements, consumer's' preferences, the supply graphic with raw materials and materials, the volume of the previous sales and its forecast in the future etc.); the human resources system (which offers information about the volume and the structure of labour, the promoting of labour, the motivating of labour etc.); the technical system (which offers information about the consumption norms, the types of machines and installations that are used or will be used, the hours of accidental cease etc.).

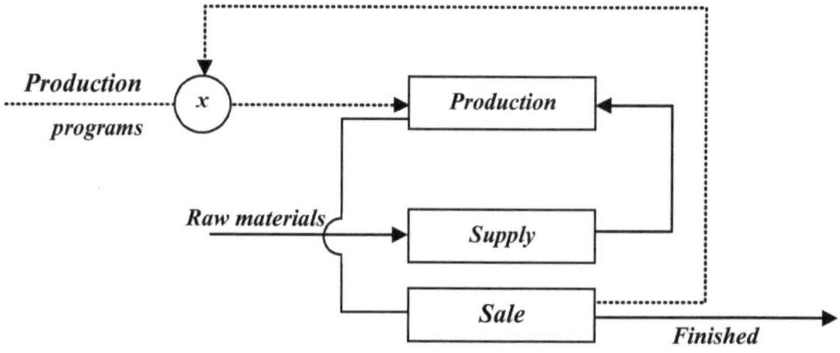

Fig. 3.1 The relation production system-commercial system

The informational relations that highlight the communication between the production system and the exo-system determine the dynamic nature of the relations in the production system, which is in a continuous change. This modification leads to the change of the structure of the production system and when this modification takes place according to a certain objective, the system self-adjusts.

In Fig. 3.1 it can be noticed that the outputs from the production system, namely the finished products are in fact inputs for the commercial system (the sale activity). At the same time, the outputs from the commercial system (the provision with raw materials and materials, the information about the market etc.) together with the production program lead to inputs for the production system.

In this way a mutual condition appears between the two systems, namely: a direct connection (production plan-finished products-products sale) and an inverted connection (the requirements of market-the sale plan-the modification of the production plan).

If there were no inverted connections, then a certain disturbance of the production plan would lead to a disturbance of the product sale, without any possibility of reducing or eliminating the disturbances from the output. But the signaling of these disturbances permits in fact the gradual decrease of the output at the pre-established values. The emergence of the inverted connection permits thus the self-adjustment of the production system functioning, namely the modification of the input (qualitative and quantitative) so that it permits the achievement of the desired output.

The self-adjustment of production is based on its structuring in controlling system and controlled system (carry out) between which mutual relations of interdependency are established (Fig. 3.2).

3.3 Some Theories on the Structure of Current Organisational Entities

The best known specialised opinions on the formal and informal structure of organisational entities refer to:

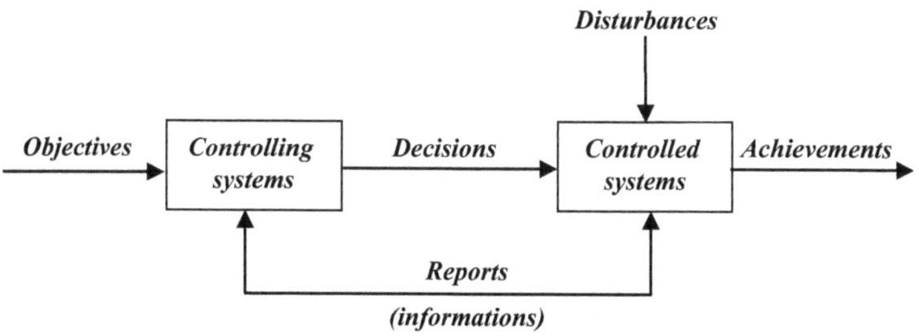

Fig. 3.2 The structure of the production system

The Theory Versus Classical Theory

The first studies on the organisational structure have tried to determine general guidelines about the (real) efficient managerial practice, originating from the practical experience of the authors. For example, starting with Fayol's papers, authors like Gulick and Urwick have tried to teach lessons from their own experience as managers or officers, where they extracted a bundle of Fayol's principles and rules from, recognised truths that are considered to be proven, which can be universally applied, in any kind of organisation, regardless of its context and purposes. This group of authors is usually called the classical school, as long as their recommendations have usually pursued the architectural and literary style which underlined the formalism, symmetry and rigidity. These principles included the scaling concept, the principle of the control unit and opening the concept of control. Combined, these principles prescribe a hierarchy in which all members are placed into a single pyramidal structure of relations, with the authority descending from the top to the bottom, so that the subordinates receive orders from more than just one hierarchic superior who, in turn, does not have more subordinates than what one can effectively supervise. Although Urwick gives a formula to determine the size of this opening of control, no agreement has been reached regarding how big this should be. Other principles suggested by the classical school included matters like: division of work by specialisation and delegation of the routine tasks to subordinates, under the control of hierarchic superiors.

As Fayol's statements show, regarding the esprit de corps, the human element is not fully ignored, but these theoreticians generally assume they have been first of all motivated by the economic reward. This rational assumption, together with the total lack of attention to the behavioural problems has led to the commentators describing the classical theory as a metaphorical machine, as long as it treats the members of the organisation as mechanisms of a well lubricated machine, which actually creates the concept of the organisation without people.

Although the popularity of the classical school must not be underestimated, its generalisations about the organisation itself are sufficiently supported by an empirical evidence. Indeed, by examining all their recommendations, Simon characterises them as being vague, fundamentally ambiguous and totally useless.

The Theory Contingentation

Subsequently, the empirical researches suggest that the recommendations supported by the classical school have not been as incorrect as they were actually delimited by condition and application. As Burns and Stalker reflect, the beginning of administrative wisdom is to understand that there is no optimal management system. At various levels, these authors have approached this topic, implicitly or explicitly referring to a direction towards the open system, based on an organic analogy or a metaphor. This has led to the focus on the interaction between organisation and its wider environment, the organisation being seen as importer of energy and environmental resources, which it converts into various goods, services and secondary products, which are exported to the organisation, thus changing the circumstances of the environment where the organisation operates. This idea has led to many researches of various subsystems and interfaces needed to achieve these processes, especially regarding how an organisation is affected and is, from many points of view, dependent on its environment.

The concerns focused on how the organisations needed to adapt to the requirements of the environment (if they wanted to survive), as well to those of the biological organisms. For our purposes, one of the most important results of this approach is to lead to a clear rupture from the universal recommendations of classical theoreticians, by creating the known theory such as the theory if.... then.... (of contingentation).

The first research for using the term of theory of contingentation belonged to Lawrecence and Lorsch, who tried to reproduce one previous study of Burns and Stalker. They discovered that, finding the appropriate organisational forms depended on particular environmental imperatives. For example, the mechanistic organisations were defined as being characterised by situations where the problems and tasks were divided by specialisations. Everyone pursues their task is something different from real tasks, as general concerns, as if it were the subject of a subcontract. Somebody at the top is responsible to supervise their fulfilment. The technical methods, duties and authority assigned to each functional role (each function) are distributed precisely. The interactions within the management tend to be vertical. In relatively stable environments, especially when the organisation uses the same technology and working methods, these mechanistic structures were considered to be suitable.

One may observe the similarity between the anatomy of mechanistic organisation of Burns and Stalker and many of the classical theory recommendations.

The theory of contingentation does not suggest that classical theory is not good, or is appropriate, or inappropriate, depending on the particular circumstances of the organisation.

In contrast, where an organisation must face a high level of insecurity, caused by the new unpredictable tasks, created by the demands of a rapidly changing environment, an organic organisational structure is considered to be more appropriate.

The organic systems are adapted to the unstable conditions, when the problems and requirements of actions cannot be divided and distributed into a well defined hierarchy, among the responsibilities of specialists, whom must meet their tasks in the light of knowing the duties of the company as a whole. The positions lose much of their formal definition regarding the methods, responsibilities and authorities, which must be permanently redefined, with the interaction with other participants in meeting certain tasks. The interaction extends both sideways and vertically in an equal manner. Communication between people of various ranks tends to resemble a lateral consultation rather than a vertical command.

The Matrix Structure

An example of this type of organisation is the matrix. While the horizontal lines show functional specialisations of the team where the members come from, the vertical lines represent the teams where the specialists combine the takeover of tasks or projects. Therefore, formal communication and the channels of the authority are simultaneously both lateral and vertical, ignoring the recommendations of classical theorists regarding the hierarchy and control unit. The matrix also shows the various combinations of the members within the multifunctional teams with discontinuous activity, in order to deal with the current problems and projects. Thus, the matrix provides the possibility to more broadly deal with the flexibility in the manner in which these teams are formed, disbanded and reconstructed, as they appear or is it is responded to various problems and tasks.

There are problems with the matrix organisations. These may give rise to conflicts between functions and ambiguities between the members of various teams, especially since they mast deal with some situations where there is dual authority. Moreover the matrix highlights people and available technical resources, as soon as new projects appear. Where the human and material resources are scarce or difficult to obtain, it can lead to internal conflicts against which projects should be supported. On the other hand, besides the fact that it allows an increased flexibility, a matrix structure can lead to high technical standards are, as teams of specialists interact with the members in their functional specialisation also in other fields of knowledge and expertise. Each member can continue their personal improvement by enhancing their own experience. The various advantages and disadvantages of the matrix structure mean it is vital to identify the circumstances were such organic structures are the most advantageous.

Organic Structure

Based on the Burns' findings, Lawrence and Lorsch have developed the organic structure, highlighting the complexities which arise from the interaction between organisational elements and the restrictions in acquiring the different structural models, Lawrence and Lorsch especially amplifies how the different parts of an organisation interact with the various environments and that should be thus structured in the various ways, in order to cope with the different demands. For example, in some organisations, the research and development department can interact with the very uncertain and rapidly changing environment, compared to that which the production department is facing. Therefore, these shall need various types of structures, in order to cope with these demands. Therefore, the general structure of the organisation may involve certain combinations consisting of various forms of organic structure and mechanisms between them.

Even if these recommendations for the best choice have been improved and developed in the meantime, the allusion of this concept remains generally unchanged. A predominant theme was that certain organisational arrangements are more efficient than others in coping with the uncertainties. The level of the experienced incertitude may be seen as a function of the gap between the volume of information needed for the test performance and for the volume available for processing. The contextual factors taken into consideration in increasing such an incertitude includes the dynamism and complexity of the environment, which makes the forecasts on it difficult and, in conclusion, planning appeal events that shall occur within the environment, as well as the task and technological complexity, which make it difficult to mention early what should be done, by whom, how, where and when.

It appears that the organic structure allows higher performances in certain circumstances. It does not provide only increased flexibility to the organisation and consequently, it allows the rapid adaptation to the unexpected requirements, but it creates a higher capacity to process the information, as long as it allows the development of lateral connections within the organisation, as average in attempting to cope with the incertitude and complexity. But the whole problem is further complicated by the existence of other contextual factors that also impose specific requirements in choosing the organisational arrangement.

Some of these requirements are best met by the flexibility given by any organic structure. This is because such a structure is designed to encourage the creativity, to assume the risks and creativity, being even more motivating to reward the intrinsic work. However, other contextual requirements, such as the size, stability of the environment and predictability may be better treated by the features created by a more mechanised structure.

3.4 The Ambiguous Environment for the Development of Organisational Entities and Its Influence on Managerial Decisions

An expert system can be defined as being a "set of programs composed to skilfully (cleverly) judge a real condition á propos of the concerns thought to require a considerable human expertise."

If this definition does not allow to precisely delimit the range of expert systems in relation to that of conventional programming, it has less merit to outline the objectives of expert systems; it is neither more or less than attempting to replace or assist the human in the fields where a human expertise is practiced. It remains to define this ability which we agree to call expertise of "that whom, through experience, has a great ability in a profession or in something" (Littre). The field of expert generally has at least three features, and namely: it is insufficiently structured to give room to sufficiently defining algorithms, models or methods to solve, to be directly programmed; it is presented as a relatively independent or autonomous form. They are "entities", "granules" of knowledge; it is a developing subject. The expertise requires a constant updated through review and complement.

The expert systems must therefore deal with scattered knowledge, divided into plots, to make the know (how) to run experiments. Everything is insufficiently classified, ordered or structure to be formalised as algorithms.

The exposure to know—to make of the expert is a problem in itself. It can only be presented in "disorder". The number of rules is very large. Following the circumstances, these rules can be totally or partially contradictory. They cannot be complete and are in a continuous evolution.

Approaching the "expert system" must be therefore radically different from that of conventional programming. That to know—to make (the base of knowledge) must be completely independent from its exploitation. The ideal was that it would be captured and seized in the machine as "granules", a little different that the data. Then this knowledge shall not be dealt with anymore, but shall be consulted closely through an associative access. The declarative knowledge was opposed to procedural knowledge.

Finally, the facial composite of a good expert system may be characterised by the following features: knowledge and their exploitation are independent; the knowledge shall be exploited in a non-determinist manner; the reasoning performed by the machine shall be drawn; the language used in the human-machine interface shall be as close as possible to natural language; the representation formalism of the rules shall coincide with the expert's expression; the qualitative, uncertain, imprecise quota of knowledge shall be taken into account; the rules (knowledge) shall be combined and ramify in order to form new rules and therefore new knowledge; the inferences of knowledge or conclusions cannot be drawn; it shall be easy to make changes as additions, deletions or revisions to the already inserted rules and their links.

The architecture of the expert systems is organised in order to be able to respond as best as possible to the aforementioned features and generally involves four parts: a knowledge base containing facts and rules relating to the object of the system; and inference engine equipped with the combination of facts and rules in order to get a result; a dialogue interface to assist the user at that moment of the system operation; a module to acquire the knowledge to facilitate entering the data, facts and rules of exploitation.

The whole expert system operates basically following some logics, namely: the knowledge base contains facts and rules. The facts are the assembly of the affirmative knowledge necessary to treat the domain dealt with; the rules act on the facts just like the operating knowledge. They are "granules" of expertise. They trigger either actions, or facts, or both of them simultaneously. Theoretically, it should not have been possible for the rules to be entered in a certain order and they should have been independent from the inference mechanism that exploits them. In reality, the inference engine often enters many contradictory things; the inference engine represents the program of the expert system. But, compared to conventional programming which only knows one treatment cycle, by transaction or registration, this can have there several cycles. The machine starts by researching the rules likely to be triggered. Every selected rule is then executed, which eventually involves changing the base of facts, more rarely the induction of a rule. In the latter case, we say that the system is equipped with a capacity of habit.

The cycles succeed each other until the exhaustion of the rules that can be triggered or until finding a stopping condition (getting a result, for example).

The operation mode of the engine naturally depends on that who designed it. Some people prefer to work "extensively", and others work "thoroughly". Finally, if five rules were applied for example, which one should we start with? The way of execution of the rules forms the control strategies of the inference. The starting engine is programmed to react according to these strategies. The users must take this into account.

There are equally several possibilities to assess the errors or invocation modes. It is generally a matter of the previous connection or the posterior one. In the previous connection, the resolution is done upwardly, following the data. If a rule is triggered, then it is performed even if its conclusion does is not of any interest for the beginning of the research. This has the disadvantage of requiring the machine to load all the facts and trigger the execution of rules without interest. In the posterior connection, the process is different. The objective may be to know if something is achieved. For this, one shall work in cycles.

The posterior connection is therefore driven by the objective that must be achieved. It is a matter of a descending resolution. The questions are asked only when needed. Only interesting rules are executed. It is the most appropriate way to solve the diagnostic problems.

Certain expert systems authorise a mixed function. In this case, the facts are considered as if they were established or in the course of being established. The rules can simultaneously behave according to the facts of one or another type.

The connections between the ambiguity of information and adopting the decision are frequent in the researches of the behaviour of organisations and establish the existence of some influences that take into account both the features of the individuals and those of organisations.

One may speak of the existence of some consequences and namely: consequences of the environment ambiguity on the decision makers' activity. When approaching the consequences concerning the decision makers' activity, three ways are distinguished and namely: The first consists in adapting the system to the observed features of human beings. Instead of a supporting system in decision making, disconnected from the world, as decision makers want it and however they do not use, the system may be designed to provide them with the information in a familiar and useful form. The main difficulty of this system consists in understanding the users' demands and in adapting the system to these demands; the second approach consists in modifying how decision makers adopt the decisions and their attitude in relation to information. During its evolution, management and operational research theory operated significant changes in the field of adopting decisions in modern organisations. Recent researches regarding the decision behaviour have been related to the strategies of improving the capacities of information processing by the human brain. Decades of efforts for determining the decision makers to adopt a behaviour closer to the decision theory precepts have proven that this is not an easy duty because the prejudices, a priori reasoning and decision makers' wisdom are resistant to decision theory influences and modern statistics; the third approach consists in replacing human beings with machines, mainly computers accompanied by logicians in expert systems. Replacing the information electronic and mechanic processing by human processing is frequent nowadays, as phrases like artificial intelligence, knowledge engineering and expert systems are too. Even if the speed at which this process occurs was all the time exaggerated enough, progresses have been achieved for situations where the problems can be decomposed into hierarchical structures or into situations where the amount of available pertinent information exceeds the human memory operation capacities. The perspectives of improving man's decision adoption through a form of computer software are promising in the case where a decision involves the storage and operation of a large number of data or in the case of modelling the complex organisational processes if the structure of the organisation allows this. We should also emphasise the problem of capacities of storage and data processing which the modern computer-based information systems have available. Contemporary researches in the field of data processing show that the exploratory analysis of the data collected, without reference to a precise use, clearly progresses to prior formulation of the needs for information. This verifies the arguments according to which future information systems give up the idea of a close connection between the collection of information and anticipation of its use; consequences of the environment ambiguity on the decision theory. Theoretic researches on adopting the decision have shown that individuals and organisations make decisions, which are in contradiction most of the time with the ethical principles, partly putting this contradiction on the account of theory limits and not on the limits of human behaviour. For example, a rigid connection between the information and decision is not useful in ambiguous situations where preferences, causal structures and meanings are vague and changeable. In practice, this type of situation is frequent, determining that numerous decision problems of contemporary organisations would enter without difficulty within the decision theory, being suitable to its laws. However, the most interesting of the practical decision problems, most of them do not fall within this framework.

The difficulties arose from the ambiguity of decision environment, preferences, pertinence, intelligence can be illustrated by a reflection on some aphorisms suggested by decision theory applied in an ambiguous organisational environment and namely: never start an action unknowingly. To the extent where it is operated inside the anticipative and consequential framework of rationality, it is important to know what is desired before acting. However, it is obvious that intelligent decision makers often behaved as if they would not believe in this need. They see in action a way to discover and elaborate preferences, rather than a modality to operate based on them; refrain yourself under ignorance. One of the axioms of the theory of decision rational choices is that actions are justified by understanding and anticipating their consequences. Even if it is admitted that this understanding of consequences cannot be total, however the optimal amplitude of ignorance is determined by its expected consequences.

Do not ask a question if its answer cannot change your decision; in the decision theory optics, the value of an information is related to the capacity of reducing the uncertainties which surround choice, although the essence regarding the information collected, purchased or communicated does not emphasise a direct pertinence for decisions. It is possible to create a background of knowledge and meanings, usable for possible actions or to explain the experience. The participants understand the collection of information as an investment into a collection of knowledge and as an aid to define and choose preferences and options; do not speak before knowing what you want to say. Certain communication theoreticians say that a message must be fully understood by its issuer before being sent, as accurately as possible, to its addressee. But a large part of the effective communication in organisations as in daily life overcomes ambiguous formulations and leads to answers representing the message and seeks its possible meanings. In this context, an information system must be designed based on a static and precise decision structure that would allow the resolution of some elementary problems in organisations. Under conditions of ambiguity however, it is necessary to design a system for imprecise decision structures and which would be of a dynamic character.

3.5 Development of Organisational Entities "in Waves"

The acknowledgement of human society's development "in waves", according to Alvin Toffler's concept proposed in his work The Third Wave (1980) implies the analysis of the firm's evolution (industrial unit, corporation), in the same context, but taking into account the characteristics of the changes in every wave.

The following waves can be distinguished in the human society's development: the First Wave of human society development is characterized by the agricultural revolution, which created the necessary conditions for the passing on a superior level of development of the human society; the Second Wave which is in fact the same with industrialization covered a large geographical area and it is still continuing in nowadays. Its origins are represented by the materialism and human supremacy. This leads to the focus on competition, self-preservation and consumption, which were the results of some pollution problems, the solid wastes elimination, multiple forms of criminality etc. In this stage of development we are separated and we have to compete; the Third Wave or/and the postindustrial wave has a great impact within modern industrial nations and it focuses more and more on the balance and on the maintenance power of the society. During its development, the members of the society become more sensitive to the preservation problems, to life s sanctity and cooperation. Thus, we are connected and we must co-operate; the Forth Wave has its beginnings in the end of The Third Wave, and the integration of all life dimensions and responsibilities in the whole becomes the central point of human society. The recognition of the identity of all live systems will lead to the appearance of some new conditioning and interconditioning relations. They are useful both for the human factor as well as for other factors of production. In this stage of development we are oneand the same and we choose to co-create.

In the context of the structural modifications of human society, the modifications of the role of the firm's activity also take place. The firm has the role of gross serving, namely it should not only do business in the intrinsic meaning of the word. In the last decades business has become the dominant institution in world's culture in the detriment of the other institutions of society (political, social, etc.), but which have a decreasing capacity of offering effective leadership possibilities. This is the reason why business must assume their responsibilities of the whole.

Most of the present firms remained from The Second Wave are centralized, hierarchical and focused on some values such as: profit, efficiency, size and development The derivation of The Second Wave has its origins in the military model of development adopted (namely: survival, self-preservation, the defeat of competition, victory) in which success is calculated trough summing up (the achievement of the profits). The temporal horizons of future development are between 5 and 10 years.

The field of activity of the firm manly focuses on business, technologic and economic problems and the general managers' answer only towards the shareholders. The attitudes and the policies of these firms reflect the nationalist concerns in which globalization is considered as an economic investing process of the foreign country. Nowadays their activity should become more responsible and it should have more varied objectives.

The transition to The Third Wave requires the firm to consider itself a creator of values. In this way its philosophy of making business suffers an essential change, in the sense that the firm will focus its activity on finding solutions trough which it can satisfy first of all its shareholders needs and then the needs of production itself. This thing happens on the grounds that there is a mutual relation between the firm on one hand and the employees, employers, shareholders and customers on the other hand. The strategy of the firm focuses on the anticipation of the future needs that are independent of it and the businesses become a vehicle trough which people can develop and serve their fellows. Thus there are certain concerns upon the following aspects: knowing the customers' needs, wining the sales markets, offering some services of a certain structure and of an adequate level etc. But, all these need a fundamental change in the human consciousness, from fear to trust, from the need of controlling towards the giving up control, from rigidity to a culture of learning etc. Thus the premises for the passing to the society of the third millennium will be created.

The firm of The Fourth Wave will be aware of its roles of serving the society as well as of delivering the products, doing services and executing works for a mass of private consumers. The firm will transform its self-image from that focused on manufacturing to a serving conception in the firs place and it will act as a leader in approaching the mass problems of society, focusing on the ones that have a positive influence. In this way the serving-manager model imposed by Robert K. Greenleaf will become the corporatist ethos of The Forth Wave.

The activity of the firm can now acquire a leading role in the global responsibility and citizenship if: it is achieved the intellectual transfer from the defeat the competition to the serving of citizens; the main objective of the firm's activity becomes the identification of the real needs of the consumer citizens; it becomes aware of the advantages of mass organization and it invests in order to achieve such advantages; it begins to think at global level why it acts locally; it admits that it is an assembly of individuals—with their own characteristics, but within the formal and informal structure of the firm.

As the firms evolve—within the cyclic modifications from the structure of human society—it is necessary to think twice the way of defining its assets. In this redefinition of the firm's assets the following accounting techniques should be taken into account: the generalization of capital property; the becoming international of social and ambient costs of doing business which are considered external; investments in natural resources trough pollution credits that the firms, in the 3R cycle, transform their competence in salable patrimonial goods; individual capital of creativity insertion in the assets of the firm—as forms of wealth that depend on the people.

In fact the approach of the assets (wealth) of the firm depends on the characteristics of each Wave of development and on the place this one has in the structure of that Wave of development.

Thus: in the firm of the Second Wave, the assets derive from the achievement of a positive final result, which satisfies the employees and creates a good impression on the beneficiaries of the firm. It is due to the profit and it focuses less on the social elements; in the Third Wave, the assets of the firm focus more on the social elements and on resources, thus a change in the system of fundamental values takes place; the firm of the Forth Wave will have an universal heritage according to the community ethos that will dominate then and which in its turn will be significantly important in the structural organization and in its management.

Simultaneously with the modifications in the approach of firm's heritage, some modifications occur in the organizational structure of the firm. These modifications focus on a certain evolution tendency of the formal and informal structure of the firm.

The criticisms upon the present organizational structure of the firm emphasize the fact that the model from the Second Wave—characterized by hierarchy and authoritative administration—is inflexible and this fact makes the firm incapable of promptly reacting to the changes of the external environment. In this Wave the following variants of hierarchical formal organization have been met: matrix organization shares the loyalties of the employees thus dividing the decision making process and this leads to the inefficiency and low level of trust. Thus any stimulus is eliminated so that the manager does not approach the traditional role, which insists on him being the boss. In the informational revolution of the last 10 years such a conception—of being the boss—it is not only out of date but also destructive; the structural decentralized organization on business centers gives a lot of credit to autonomy, unified loyalty, unique aim and flexibility. This fact protects the firm of implosion (collapse trough itself).

The former organization of a firm of the Third Wave is done according to the values-team model that aims at the achievement of values. It is based on the collaboration between employees and between these and the customers of the firm. It is a democratic structure, all the members of the team are equal, including the managers (chosen by the members of their team) who are in fact the interface with other groups. It is a very flexible structure that gives the firm the ability of responding to the continuously changing needs and tendencies of the market.

The firm of the Forth Wave will be structured according to a commentary model, which is based on a change in the consciousness of all individuals. Its structure is democratic, participate and which permits the action of the firm to be focused on its customer's satisfaction. It will be doubled by a common vision and it will act both trough intuitive processes and techniques as well as through the logical and rational methods that are familiar to the present management. According to this organizational structure the firm acts locally as a responsible member of its external community. This action takes place in two ways: as a group of people and as a way of being that unites the members of the group. The first way of action is due to the fact that the people gather together, in a certain place and time with the help of the formal structure of the firm. The second way of action is due to the fact that through the functioning of the firm the barriers between people are eliminated as a result of the existence of the former structure.

The firm of the third millennium will function in ambient conditions, in which environment protection will not be a problem anymore and ecology will not be against economy. The management of the firm of the Forth Wave will be done in the bio-politics epoch due to the recent progresses from biotechnology, due to environment crisis and to the global democratization. Bio-politics will comprise entire nations and gradual evolutionist changes and it will lead to great changes for the entire human kind. The collapse of private wealth will take place when the conventional distinction between public and private will disappear as private values will be extremely important for the public welfare. In this way in a bio-political environment no one will declare as apolitical.

In this context the firm of the third millennium—the new corporation—will have the following characteristic features: it is an example for the other institutions of society; its employees act locally and at the same time think globally; it profoundly modifies its assets focusing on the social accounting and on the accounting of the resources; it becomes an organization meant to serve, being conscious of its being a producer of moral effects; it is transformed in a community of welfare, being conscious of the complete and varies structure of its shareholders; it is a model of environmental concern; it develops breaking new ground actions in the field of advanced technologies with real tendencies towards the technological evaluations; it has in its leading staff bio-politicians fully conscious of their responsibility of fulfilling people's destiny in a modern society.

References

Betbeze JP (2000) Economie de l'enterprise contemporaine. Nathan, Paris
Bovel L (2003) Management. McGraw Hill, New York, NY
Brilman J (1998) Les meilleurs pratiques de management. Éditions d'Organisation, Paris
Burgh J (2006) Enterpreneurship. Wiley, New York, NY
Daniels J, Radebaungh H (2009) International business. Addison-Weslley, Reading, MA
Dima IC, St V (2012) Persuasion elements used in logistical negotiation. Lambert Academic, Saarbrucken
Ghild J (2004) Organization: a guide to problems and practices. Harper & Row, London
Hall RH (2007) Organizations: structures, processes and outcomes. Prentice-Hall, Englewood Cliffs, NJ
Kipnis D (1990) Technology and power. Springer, New York, NY
Merchant KA (2007) Control in business organizations. Pitman, Boston, MA
Schroeder RG (2007) Operations management. McGraw-Hill, New York, NY
Toffler A (1996a) Al treilea val. Editura Z, Bucureşti
Toffler A (1995) Corporaţia adaptabilă. Ed. Antet, Bucureşti
Toffler A (1996b) Previziuni. Premise. Antet, Bucureşti
Toffler A (1996c) Spasmul economic. Ed. Antet, Bucureşti
Wren DA (2007) Evolution of management thought. Wiley, New York, NY

Part II
Some Problems on the Econometric Theory

Chapter 4
Econometrics and Scientific Management

4.1 Econometrics and Its Contradictions

Usually, the term "econometrics" is given to a concept the scope of which refers to a very complex scientific discipline, emerged in the mathematics, statistics and economics interference areas.

Its object of study is of course the economics, but under a particular given aspect, namely the quantitative one, it has as extreme limits the political economy in the most general sense. In fact, the object of study consists in analysing the connections between the set of the national economy and its components, respectively their behaviour, thus removing the enterprise economy, the quantitative aspects of which are studied by the operational research.

Concerning the quantitative aspects, it should be noted that the methods used by econometrics in its object study is not exhaustive.

The field of econometrics is defined by the economy mathematical models it uses, which transpose the problems of economy into the language of mathematics, to handle more easily the complex system of concepts of the political economy and disciplines derives from it. *Econometrics seeks numerical values for the parameters of the mathematical economy models.* It deals with the measurement of the economic objects, having the mathematical-economic models as analogous equivalents.

The method of econometrics is provided by the mathematical statistics, but there is a significant delimitation between econometrics and the quantitative economy in general. Not all data acquired by measurements and not all quantitative information must or can be provided by mathematical statistics. In the mathematical economy models, values derived from engineering amounts (technical data), from intuitive assessments or directly from primary statistical records can also be used, which can be very good and very useful. However, sometimes the technical data are missing or corrupted by various factors, and the statistical data acquired by direct observations do not correspond to the true structure of the phenomenon which it reflects only

I.C. Dima, M. Man, *Modelling and Simulation in Management*, Contributions to Management Science, DOI 10.1007/978-3-319-16592-9_4

apparently. In this case, the mathematical statistics will seek the link between the data derived from observations, so that it would reveal the true structural or causal relation studied in the economic object where from these data derive.

Let us assume we make "T" observations on "n" processes. We shall thus record series of "T" elements each from the variables "x_{1t}, x_{2t},. . ...., x_{nt}", corresponding to the observed processes. We simultaneously perform "T" "y_t" observations on a parallel process. We know or decide, with some reason, that the "y" values are determined by the "x" values in a certain way. Thus, in reality, the "x"-s are converted into "y"-s and there is a certain mechanism for the conversion from "x" to "y". The purpose of econometrics is precisely the discovery of this conversion mechanism that consists in formulating several rational hypotheses for this mechanism as mathematical models, and then, in adapting them, the discovery of the necessary data of our observations, choosing that model which will provide maximum likelihood as the "true" one.

This definition of econometrics requires certain additional explanations, namely:

- *econometrics is not to be confused with the mathematical statistics*, but it uses part of its apparatus. In general, anything can be used in econometrics from the mathematical statistics. But so far, in practice, those methods postulating the normal distribution (Gauss-Laplace) of the observed values errors of the studied variable have been applied mostly. This is not an exclusive specification, but it is rather the observation of an actual situation. The reasons result from the very treatment of econometric methods;
- *econometrics is not the only method to quantitatively research the economic relations*. A number of structural features of economy may also be researched with methods other than what classifies in the definition given to econometrics. To illustrate these differences, we can exemplify with the most common method of non-econometric quantitative economy, namely the input-output method of W. Leontief.

This is based on a relatively simple mathematical and theoretically easy to handle model of the links between the branches of national economy. It is assumed here that between the production branches, there is a system of interdependencies that may be represented as a system of linear equations. The value (numeric expression) of the system coefficients can be determined based on direct statistical records, which reproduce a ratio between the deliveries of "intermediate" goods from one branch to another and the total production of the branches. If these equations now serve as predictive tools based on these coefficients calculated as such, this is another issue. One thing is clear, namely that the model satisfactorily represents the structure of the system of branches at the moment which statistical data refer to (if they were correct). Here, at least in a primary phase of the quantitative research, no statistical-mathematical (probabilistic) methods are used, the direct data fitting quite well in the postulated mathematical model. Thus, one starts from a clear model of the "mechanism of transformation" of the intermediate productions (productive consumptions) into total production, and by direct measurement, a mathematical-quantitative model is obtained.

However, we do not always have such a clear and acceptable a priori model of the various mechanisms of transformation of a set of variables into another. Among these, econometrics sets and verifies the hypotheses with probabilistic feature. In this context, it is obvious that econometrics particularly uses part of the statistical methodology.

The difference between the statistical methods used by natural sciences, particularly the experimental ones and the econometrics can be best understood by following the examples of contradictions between statistical data (observation data) and the structure it generates.

If the economic science would be an experimental science, then its problems and difficulties, which are ultimately problems of dynamic series, would be solved otherwise than by statistical methods.

For the Cobb-Douglas functions—the experimental solution is the one described by Malinvaud in the chapter of his treaty on econometric statistics, as follows: "if we imposed the enterprise "i" to engage the randomly chosen quantities "N_i" and "K_i" and if we saw what production "Q" it gets". It is precisely the laboratory method by means of which: one of the factors is successively modified for constant values of the other—and vice versa. In such cases, we record the "pure effect" of each factor on the production level. Of course, this is not possible in practice and even if such an experiment would be effectively organised, the result could not be guaranteed due to the vitiation which the experiments with humans are exposed to.

In the case of the experimented demand/price curves the "experiments", the situation analysed in "laboratory conditions" could be imagined by the question: "how much would you buy of the product "i" if the price would be successively "$p_{i1,}$ p_{i2} .... p_{in}"?" Only that this assumes that the person questioned would have previously built the demand curve for oneself. This is a vicious circle. Not only that the feed-back effects on the demand statistics are not thus removed, but other similar effects generated by some peculiarities of the human behaviour are also inserted.

The justified question that appears is: in natural sciences, can a concordance always be set between the signal (observation data) and the model parameters?

The concordance is more easily achievable as the rational models of natural sciences cannot originate from subjective experiences, in experiences and introspections such as the demand/price models. Thus, even if there is a contradiction between the model and reality, we shall not know it unless it will also be affirmed as a contradiction between the model and observation data. In natural sciences, we have no other information about "reality" than the observation data, so that they must be concordant with the model. In the sciences on the human, there is also other information than those of the observations (subjective experiences, emotions), which can lead to challenging a model based on observation data. Natural sciences are absolved of this. As long as the observation data have a certain regularity, the model that adapts immediately to them will be recognised as to reflect the truth. It is as if a demand/price function with the first derivative would reflect the truth.

However, a difference appears as soon as predictions are done based on the empirical economic models. But this does not mean that many models in the natural sciences are "truer" in relation to the "thing itself" which they reflect, but only that the observations of the prediction come from the same source as the initial observations, meaning it they involve the same deformations. In economics, the observations of the research period and those of the forecast period can easily come from different sources, which is why our desire to identify the underlying structure common to the signals from both sources is also so strong. This is also the reason why, compared to natural sciences, the economic sciences must use the same sources. This is why econometrics must be interested in the "estimation systems" and in "minimum squares in two stages". These methods, commonly designated with the term identification methods, are specific and distinctive for econometrics. At the same time, econometrics emphasises less some statistical methods which, in natural sciences, have a considerable role, as is the correlation method. The reason lies in the different way of identification of the mechanism for converting some variables into others, and also in establishing the connections between them.

The peculiarities of the statistics used in econometrics implies both a definition of the limits of quantitative methods used in economics, and an emphasis of the boundaries of all quantitative empirical methods, but which are not the limits of the rational mathematical methods. The significance and utility of these methods exceed the strict range of quantitative researches. Mathematics dealt with as scientific language, in general, and as language of the economist, in particular, transcends the limits of quantitative-empirical knowledge and is generally the tool we use to go beyond the implicit restrictions of the empirical knowledge, to the extent where the human reasoning is capable of it.

Because the econometric research is primarily based on quantitative methods, some contradictions occur, namely:

- *the contradiction between structural and phenomenological.* The measurements (quantitative, statistical observations) do not always refer to the actual structure whereon an economic object is built. The data (as accurate and correct our observations would be) can reflect superficial aspects that are very far from the essence of the phenomenon investigated, so that the connection we establish between them would have nothing in common with the structural connection which is at their origin;
- *the contradiction between causal and stochastic* is largely a consequence of the first contradiction, because we must admit probabilistic hypotheses in many cases, regarding the connection between the variables observed simply because we are ignorant concerning the "complete" causal relations. In fact, this ignorance gives essence to econometrics. If we directly knew the structural connections sought, we would also distinguish the system of causal relations that act between them. However, as the statistics only refers to phenomena, this road must be travelled by means of the probabilistic calculation;
- *the contradiction between rational and empirical.* The deductive models often come in conflict with the results of empirical research. At first glance, we must give in to favour of the empirical results. However, knowing the changes that

may occur, it will be clear that we cannot and are not allowed to give up on our strictly theoretical deductions, under any circumstance.

Knowing these contradictions provides more clarity regarding the distinction between mathematical economics and econometrics. The first one rationally deals with the structural and causal aspects of economy, and the second one, along with other quantitative methods, empirically deals with the phenomenological and statistical aspects of the economic object. But the phrased contradictions cannot be solved by a single quantitative method, and thus econometrics uses a system of methods to find the solution.

At the same time, there may be an absolute resolution of the aforementioned contradictions on a strictly quantitative plan, because the very quantitative methods and, therefore, the econometrics have their internal unsolvable contradictions. These are not limits of knowledge, but limits of the method. As method of knowing, econometrics has its limits. But knowing must go up to these limits in order to exceed them through other methods. Often, exceeding these limits cannot be done with quantitative methods, but only through rational and intuitive methods. For these reasons, the econometric knowledge of economic phenomena is a phase or stage in the process of knowing. Even though in many cases this method does not solve, but rather creates or more precisely discovers contradictions and cracks in our knowledge, it thus provides enormously much to us. The works appears before the economist in a completely different way than before and after the study of econometrics (as of any other methods or mathematical economy). Therefore, we distinguish a knowledge of the pre- and meta-econometric economy, and the distinction of these two stages justifies precisely the study of econometrics.

4.2 Considerations on the Object–Signal–Model Relation in Econometric Research

Mathematical economics deals with adapting the mathematical methods to building the models of the micro- and macro-economic processes and structures. In a first phase of building the model, the empirical data are not taken directly into account. Problems and contradictions arise however when we try to reconstruct the structure we represented in purely rational ways from statistical data, through a mathematical-economic model. Here, the usual statistical methods are no longer useful. The experience of quantitative research in economics shows us that there are several stages in the dialectic process of building an empirical model from a rational model.

At first, there is the object or the investigated process which we represent in a more or less aggregated or detailed way, through several mathematical models. Then we note the signals which the investigated "object" emits. This is achieved through the economic statistics.

A very common—yet erroneous—practice consists in shifting from statistics to directly building some numerical models, possibly using even various statistical techniques to estimate equations (the method of least squares). The results thus obtained can easily contradict the rational mathematical representations. Sometimes, in such a confrontation, the statistical model simplistically prevails to the prejudice of the rational one.

This kind of quantitative study merely establishes links between statistical data and not to ideally reconstruct the mechanism the signals of which are precisely these data. For they are only signals, which can hide a complicated mechanism with reverse connections, possibly correctly represented in strictly rational, non-empirical models.

Econometrics exceeds this simplistic way of approaching the quantitative economic analysis, characterised by the simple correlation with the standard methods of some statistical data. It starts from the idea that the statistics we have are generated by mechanisms which are more complicated than the direct relations they evince. Therefore, it primarily starts from the mathematical economy that builds models of the possible. Thus, for the researcher, several rationally represented variants of mechanisms are generators of statistics. In other words, econometrics deals with the models of mathematical economics as mechanisms generating statistics, choosing afterwards the model that can be plausibly considered as its generator, for a given statistics. This involves some complicated processing of statistical data, so that sometimes, by the time one gets to choose the most likely model, a whole range of very different models must be experienced. Econometrics is a method of experimentation on mathematical models—the only kind of experiment which economic sciences are capable of, since their research subject cannot fit into any research retort. This is the disadvantage of a non-experimental science, which develops and improves its knowledge in these ways of a spare quantitative analysis.

Both the advantages and the limitations of the econometric method appear gradually, if we study it in terms of the contradictions between the signal and the model, which is the main manifestation of what is the contradiction between the rational and the empirical. Understanding this contradiction is crucial for the use of econometric methods by the economist.

The main purpose of presenting the object-signal-model relationship is that, when listing various computational techniques, it is shown that there is no real regression, but only convenient regression. The convenience is defined—not very rigorously—as a minimum deviation of the econometric model from the assumed mathematical-economic model of structure. Thus, we make the distinction between two levels of knowing the objects researched, namely: the theoretically structural one and the econometric one. The theoretically structural model has itself a complex origin, relying both on empirical researches, including previous econometric researches, and on deductive reasoning. The econometric model must be completed with the theoretical model on two levels: structural and quantitative. Should there appear a contradiction between these two variants, then we know that the structural model is not necessarily the incorrect one. The deformations inherent to econometric methods to build the economic equations and functions are those which warn us on the fact that an inconsistency between the "model" and the "measurement" does not yet mean also a deficiency of the theory or of the strictly rational (therefore not empirical) models that correspond to it.

Thus, the aim of econometrics is to ensure a correspondence between the reality and the observation by way of mutual researches between theoretical and empirical models is difficult to achieve, due to some inconsistencies. Indeed, during the econometric assessments, some unexpected curiosities may arise.

Some of them yet appeared in the researches before the First World War, but their serious analysis was done only in 1930–1945. Also during this period, some methods were also found, to reduce the undesirable effects of these difficulties. But the analysis of the systems of equations, of the regression in several stages or several "movements" is recent and it is currently continued to perform promising researches in this field.

The origin of the difficulties may be sought in the contradiction between the structure of the observation data and the objective structure of the researched object, from the observation of which we obtained these data. The problem is not as severe as in natural sciences, due to the invariant feature of the structures which they research. Therefore, the results of quantitative researches in economics are also more frail than in natural sciences. The main causes that determine such difficulties occur both in the case of estimating the equations, and in the case of applying them to predictions.

In the case of assessments, the main causes that diminish the value of the results are: the collinearity of variables; non-reversibility of functions obtained; sub- and supra-identification; the autocorrelation of the residue in the case of auto-regression.

In the case of projections, the causes consist in the structural mutations that cause the main inconveniences.

All these difficulties arise when studying some special problems of quantitative economic analysis. For each particular case, the solution was sought by starting not only from the general methodological principles, but also from the specificity of the case of the methods adopted and according to the researcher's flair.

4.3 Expressing the Economic Relations by Econometric Functions and Equations

Building econometric features and equations that characterise some actual processes and structures is done only by generating some real systems. Thus, the laws of objectively-random errors and those of the artificially-random ones will converge in building the econometric models. For this, it is required to adjust a statistical function, because any analysis of statistical data starts from an a priori hypothesis formulated in the scientific theory.

If between the two sets of statistical data (variables of a phenomenon) there is or there is not a causality or association (functional parallelism) connection, this does never result directly from the data. Certain meta-empirical deductions will be those that will give the explanation sought. However, if a connection is admitted even only once as hypothesis, then the form of this dependency must be established.

Let us consider two sets of data:

$$\begin{matrix} y_1, y_2 \ldots\ldots y_n \\ x_1, x_2 \ldots\ldots x_{n.} \end{matrix} \tag{4.1}$$

We assume that between each (y_i,x_i) pair, there is a relation that may be described (but not necessarily explained) by a certain function. The function must be as "economic" as possible, meaning it should describe the relation sought, with maximum simplicity. In principle, no matter how bizarre the distribution of some points (y, x) on a Cartesian diagram would be, a function of one kind or another, of some greater or lesser complexity can always be thought or imagined. Of course, it is always a problem whether the development of some very complicated functions is worthwhile such effort. Typically, certain simpler, easy-to-formulate types of functions will give a reasonable idea to the sought relation.

The mathematical simplification of the relation yet also involves changing the value of one of the variables.

Thus, if a function

$$y_i = f_1(x_i), \tag{4.2}$$

which for all values "x_i" would give exactly the values "y_i" observed, is too complicated, then we shall need to admit another function:

$$Y_i = f_2(x_i), \tag{4.3}$$

wherein the dependent variable "Y_k" for any "x_k" will be different from "y_k" corresponding to the same "x_k" in the range of observed data.

The new simplified function will then generate the following pair:

$$\begin{matrix} Y_1, Y_2, \ldots\ldots Y_n \\ x_1, x_2, \ldots\ldots x_{n.} \end{matrix} \tag{4.4}$$

The previous formulas show that the calculated function must be thus adjusted to the statistical data so that the difference $y_i - Y_i$ would be as low as possible. This requirement will need to be explained more fully.

Typically, it is considered that the difference $u_i = y_i - Y_i$ is a random variable and certain hypotheses are issued about the distribution of its values. This hypothesis determines a whole string of possible hypotheses, among which the most important one is that the variable "Y_i" is in fact the actual measure of the observed phenomenon, which is certainly determined by the pair-size "x_i"; the difference up to the empirical figure "y_t" resulting from a random deviation. This hypothesis is, indeed, artificial, but indispensable. Artificial, for the function does nothing but to describe the probability of an indispensable relation, because it is the best thing we can do. As long as the relation between two variables can only be explained by a vague theory, we need to use the most likely function.

To explain the relation between two empirical variables, we have several methods.

The simplest relation between two variables is the linear one:

$$Y = a + bx, \tag{4.5}$$

(a and b being constant).

Let us assume that we have two empirical data sets:

$$\begin{matrix} y_1 y_2 \ldots\ldots y_n \\ x_1 x_2 \ldots\ldots x_n \end{matrix} \tag{4.6}$$

and enter each pair (y_i, x_i) by a point in a system of coordinates. If we observe, for example, that the points placed in a diagram are around a straight line, we can hypothesise a linear relation. It thus remains to establish "exactly" the values of the two constants of the straight line that describes the relation. Defining the straight line must be done by reducing to the minimum the differences $y_i - Y_i$, and the value sought is obtained by minimising the sum of the squared deviations between the empirical variable and the calculated one. Ultimately the variation of the actual data from the expected ones will be minimised.

The actual data are not the data of our observations. Most of the calculated values are considered to be expected or probable, in virtue of a meta-empirical reasoning.

Thus, we shall calculate:

$$\min \sum_i (y_i - \overline{Y})^2 \tag{4.7}$$

If we assume that the function that determines our expectations is linear, then:

$$\sum_i (y_i - Y_i)^2 = \sum_i (y_i - a - bx_i)^2 \tag{4.8}$$

The data (values) of the expression (4.8) are the components of the empirical sets (observations) of "x_i" and "y_i", following to find an "a" and a "b" which would minimise it.

Therefore, the following system of equations must be solved:

$$\begin{aligned}\left(\sum y_i\right) &= na + b\left(\sum x_i\right)\\ \left(\sum x_i y_i\right) &= a\left(\sum x_i\right) + b\left(\sum x_i^2\right)\end{aligned} \tag{4.9}$$

where "n" and the expressions between the brackets are known.

From the point of view of the calculation rules, we shall need to take into account that a single pair (x, y) of data does not provide any information about the form of the relation between the variables. Indeed, if we had only one pair of (x, y), we would have for:

$$\min(y - a - bx)^2 \tag{4.10}$$

the equations

$$\begin{aligned}\frac{\partial \sigma^2}{\partial a} &= -y + a + bx = 0\\ \frac{\partial \sigma^2}{\partial b} &= -yx + ax + bx^2 = 0\end{aligned} \tag{4.11}$$

The two equations being proportional in "x_k", there is no solution for "a" and "b".

Intuitively, the problem can be better understood in geometrical terms. A pair of "dependent" data is a point. Or, an infinity of straight lines can go through one point, its coordinates not being sufficient in order to determine the parameters of any of them. The definition of the function being sought in a space with two dimensions, at least two pairs of data will be needed in order to geometrically, but not statistically define a straight line. To know the form of the relation between two stochastic variables, it is necessary to know a sufficiently large number of their values.

The process shown above fully refers to linear functions or to non-linear functions that become linear by logarithmation.

For example, the function:

$$y_i = a\prod_{i-1}^{n} x_i^{\alpha_i} \tag{4.12}$$

(where "α_i" is the exponent of the "i"th independent variable and "a" is a constant), can be transformed into a linear function through logarithms:

$$(\log y_i) = (\log a) + \sum_i (x_i \log x_i) \tag{4.13}$$

Also, the function:

$$y_i = y_0 e^{\lambda x_i} \tag{4.14}$$

(where "e" is the base of the natural logarithm and "λ" is a constant) can be transcribed into natural logarithms as a linear function:

$$(\ln y_i) = (\ln y_0) + \lambda x_i. \tag{4.15}$$

These functions have a very special significance in econometrics. Most of the econometric models known nowadays use these types of logarithmic-linear functions.

The more complex economic relations cannot be estimated by a single equation, this being clear even if we use the simplest methods of the mathematical economy. The estimation of some more complicated dependencies however implies methods and reasoning that are more complicated than that which the estimation of a single equation relation is based upon.

The purpose of estimating or adjusting some econometric functions or equations is ultimately to obtain an efficient forecasting tool. Achieving the desideratum of the expected efficiency is however a function of the degree of concordance between the econometric model (the specified numerical mathematical-economical model) and the structure underlying the statistical data, the observation data. However, the correspondence sought is not limited only by the sometimes very serious contradiction between the structure of the object investigated and the signals it sends to us and are reflected in statistical data, but also by the simplifying hypotheses we impose ourselves to the econometric construction itself. They refer to the type and characteristics of the errors in econometric models. The econometric experience has however shown that these hypotheses are the most acceptable ones, saving us from additional deformations from those which, in one way or another, are implicit to our observations. This is precisely why econometrics will use the models the errors of which are characterised by the Gauss-Laplace ("normal") distribution law. Knowing now how econometric models are actually built, they can be explained mathematically.

It has been shown that the "ideal" is the normal distribution of the error generated by a model. This ideal somewhat also corresponds to common sense, since the normal distribution of an error means its concentration around the expected value of the error, which is zero.

If, for a set of relations:

$$\begin{aligned} y_1 - a - bx_1 &= u_1 \\ y_2 - a - bx_2 &= u_2 \\ &\cdots\cdots\cdots\cdots \\ &\cdots\cdots\cdots\cdots \\ y_n - a - bx_n &= u_n \end{aligned} \tag{4.16}$$

we shall alternate several pairs of values "a" and "b", for after a number of attempts, an estimated set would result:

$$\hat{u}_1, \hat{u}_2, \ldots\ldots\ldots\hat{u}_n, \tag{4.17}$$

so that the condition to be *a normal distribution* would be satisfied, then we shall obtain a model of *maximum likelihood.*

In terms of forecasts, this means that the probability of forecast errors must correspond to normal distribution:

$$p(u_1,\ u_2,\ \ldots,\ u_n) = \frac{1}{\left(\sigma_u^2 \cdot 2\pi\right)^{\frac{n}{2}}}\exp\left(-\frac{1}{2\sigma_u^2}\sum_i u_i^2\right)du_1 du_2 \ldots du_n \tag{4.18}$$

If we admit that:

$$u_i^{\,2} = (y_i - a - bx_i)^2, \tag{4.19}$$

then the function of likelihood L will be:

$$L = \frac{1}{\left(\sigma_u^2 \cdot 2\pi\right)^{\frac{n}{2}}}\exp\left[-\frac{1}{2\sigma_u^2}\sum (y_i - a - bx_i)^2\right] \tag{4.20}$$

By noting in natural logarithms:

$$\ln L = -\frac{n}{2}\ln 2\pi - \frac{n}{2}\ln\sigma_u^2 - \frac{1}{2\sigma_u^2}\sum_i (y_i - a - bx_i)^2 \tag{4.21}$$

Maximising the likelihood of the function (4.21) requires the cancellation of its derivatives:

$$\begin{aligned}
\frac{\partial(\ln L)}{\partial a} &= \frac{1}{\sigma_u^2}\sum_i (y_i - a - bx_i) = 0 \\
\frac{\partial(\ln L)}{\partial b} &= \frac{1}{\sigma_u^2}\sum_i x_i(y_i - a - bx_i) = 0 \\
\frac{\partial(\ln L)}{\partial \sigma_u^2} &= -\frac{1}{2\sigma_u^2} + \frac{1}{2\sigma_u^4}\sum_i (y_i - a - bx_i)^2 = 0
\end{aligned} \tag{4.22}$$

The reasoning from (4.20) to (4.22) can be expressed as follows:

- to start with, a function “L” is described, the value of which is given by the variables which only one thing is known about, namely that they are normally distributed;
- then, we want to maximise the value of the function “L”, meaning the “likelihood” of our model. “L” will be maximum when the errors $(y_i - a - bx_i)$ will be subject to the law involved precisely by the form of “L”;
- to maximise the function “L”, it is necessary to cancel the partial derivatives.

The first two of the three equations obtained are known and they are the familiar equations of regression:

$$\begin{aligned} \Sigma y_i &= na + b\,\Sigma x_i \\ \Sigma x_i y_i &= a\Sigma x_i + b\,\Sigma {x_i}^2. \end{aligned} \qquad (4.23)$$

The values of "a" and "b" must however be subject to a restriction given by the third equation which requires that:

$$\frac{1}{2\sigma_u^4}\sum (y_i - a - bx_i)^2 = \frac{n}{2\sigma_u^2} \qquad (4.24)$$

meaning

$$\frac{1}{n}\sum (y_i - a - bx_i)^2 = \sigma_u^2, \qquad (4.25)$$

and namely *the squared average deviation of the error is also its estimation with maximum likelihood.* Or, the system (4.23) is also obtained by minimising this deviation and thus the first two equations in (4.22) are compatible with the third one.

A fact of great significance for econometrics results from here. If in the case of the regression analysis, we seek the best model to represent the mechanism of transforming some variables "x" and "y", in the case of the maximum likelihood analysis, we seek to transform the random errors normally distributed in "y". But the two transformations are compatible with one another and they are the essence of econometrics, as it is known to this day. In this respect, the emphasis on the models with distributed normal errors must also be interpreted and we may thus say that *econometrics is the estimation technique according to the principle of maximum likelihood of the methods of economic mathematics.*

Such an interpretation is not normative nor exclusive, but it is the crystallisation of an experience and also reflects a certain convention. In fact, the various quantitative methods in the economic analysis such as the inter-industry analysis, the operational researches, econometrics, etc., each have their unifying principle justifying their establishment as disciplines. Thus, those methods established based on the principle of maximum likelihood have been called econometrics, although in the current language, the term is sometimes widely used.

Although there are several types of econometric functions that express various more important relations are as follows:

- functions expressing technical relations known before performing the statistical calculation. One example would be the technical (engineering) functions between the volume of a certain production and the technological consumptions corresponding thereof. We distinguish cases where we know the mathematical form of the function, but without also knowing the value of the parameters, as well as cases where these elements are also given to us. The Leontief-type production functions are an example for this category of functions. The problem here consists either in evaluating the size of the parameters, or in evaluating only the random deviations from these sizes;

- functions expressing dependencies clarified in national terms, but without a precise mathematical definition. For instance, the demand-income relation calculated based on the Engel budgets can be an example in this respect. Indeed, no one can doubt that such a relation exists, but its form cannot be defined in advance, as it has no technical feature. The econometrics is left with the task to find a suitable function, which then the economist would take "for granted". It is clear that if we establish that the production of branch "i" ("x_i") absorbs from the branch "j" a quantity "x_{ij}" of semi-finished goods, then in the function:

$$x_i = \frac{1}{a_{ij}} x_{ij} \tag{4.26}$$

the parameter "a_{ij}" can be interpreted in a material-technical sense and is the measure of a quantity in the production of branch "i". But instead, if we establish that the demand "c_i" for the product "i" is a function of the income "v" in the form:

$$c_i = av^b \text{ or } c_i = \frac{v}{1 + \exp(a + bv)}, \tag{4.27}$$

then neither "a", nor "b" or "k" will have a previously known *material* correspondent to represent;

- functions expressing an assumed relation, which is however insufficiently clarified from a theoretical point of view. The relation between the variables on the extremities of a complicated chain of dependencies are included into this category. Situations of this kind may be covered only by highly aggregated "surrogate" functions, which do not always give very significant results in the case of single equation assessments. A typical example would be the Cobb-Douglas type production functions, where the national income—being itself a "metaphysical" indicator is linked to the labour force and fixed funds. Basically, to the point where the wide variety of fixed funds combined with the wide variety of labour forces results into what we call the "national income", many highly complicated transformations occur, which could be described—if data existed—only just as complicated functions. Therefore we use to brief information provided to us by an aggregate model.

The types of functions shown above are econometrically acceptable. For the first types, the well and then correctly evaluated functions can provide a good approximation of the mechanism for transforming the independent variables into dependent result-variables. Even in the latter case, when the sought underlying structure has a certain stability, we may admit, within certain limits, a transformation of one form or another.

However, any of these functions can be seriously influenced by factors that are not directly observable. Such negative influences are the collinearity, respectively the irreversibility of the regression function.

4.4 Connections of Econometrics to Management Science

To have an overview of the economy as object of the operational research is useful to analyse the history of management, as well as the links between these scientific disciplines.

Management is perceived differently by those exerting it, certain specialists do not give due consideration to the history of management occurrence and development and to the management theory, starting from the assumption that theory is abstract, not having practical utility, and history has no relevance for the contemporary society. However, this idea is incorrect because management, as any scientific discipline, cannot be assimilated, and the current managerial problems cannot be solved without studying the history of management, its evolution from the embryo form to the current one.

The evolutionary approach of the managerial field shows that, although management has crystallised as a science only in the twentieth century, the managerial practices and thinking occurred thousands of years ago, with the establishment of the first human communities. Along with the development of the human society, changes within the management activity have been recorded, under the influence of social, economic and political factors, so that the genesis and development of management as a science is related to a certain economic, social and industrialisation stage of the society. The transition from one economic system to another was possible both due to a higher qualitative level of the productive activity, and to the existence of a managerial activity with better functional and structural characteristics.

The seeds of the management process appear in the primitive commune by the crystallisation of the early forms of the management activity, of the one-man management based on rules and regulations. The main form of macro-social management emerges with the emergence of the state. Thus, Egyptians applied the management functions to build the pyramids, Sumerians used rules and regulations of governance, Greeks used various systems of governance, Babylonians possessed an extensive set of laws and policies of governance, Romans used delegations of authority. In feudalism, the management system is diversified, predominating the authoritarian-type management, and the information system develops due to the emergence of paper and printing.

However, only in the twentieth century, in capitalism, one can speak of a scientific approach to management. Scientific management emerged in the U.S.A. in the first decade of the twentieth century, based on the idea of maximising

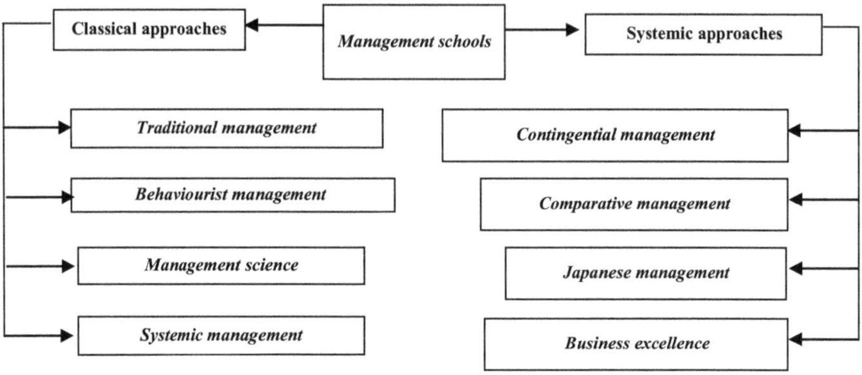

Fig. 4.1 Management schools

the results of the industrial activity with minimum efforts by efficiently using the labour force, which requires finding some new management methods.

The process of outlining and asserting the management science is structured in different approaches, originally having theories and concepts collected in thinking ways. Studying the literature reveals the existence of many management schools (Fig. 4.1).

The study of thinking and managerial practice should start from the traditional (classical) management initiated by F. Taylor and H. Fayol, represented by H. Koontz, C. O' Donnel, M. Weber. In his basic paper, Taylor stated the management concept as that type of management that guides the businesses by using standards established based on facts and truths resulted from observation, experiments and systemic reasoning, focusing on issues related to the growth of the labour productivity by improving the management of the productive activity within operational workshops. Fayol expands the scientific management in the whole company, formulating the functions and principles of the company's management. The special merits of this trend consist in the fact that the managerial tools and methods developed by its representatives significantly contribute to the formation of management science, as well as to the impregnation of an economic optics to management, corresponding to the economic finality based on which the company's creation and expansion are based. The criticism on classical management aims at the simplistic deal and mechanistic view on the human being, the contradictory feature of some principles, the complete ignorance of the motivations of the human factor.

Correcting such shortcomings of the traditional management were later the focus of the behaviourist management representatives. A. Maslow, R. Lickert, D. McGregor, E. Dale, G. Fiedmann, E. Mayo focused on the study of human relations, motivation, behaviour and way of entering the people community. Thus, E. Mayo states that the individuals who form a workshop are a group wherein relations between the individuals and their leaders are developed, which become habits. A. Maslow, founder of the motivation theory, considers that productive human relations cannot occur in the absence of motivation, and managers must be aware of the existence of several levels of motivation. D. McGregor have developed the X and Y theories on human qualities, in the X theory, having a negative view of the human being, and within the Y theory positively addressing man, considering them able of self-management and accepting the responsibilities. The behaviourist approach achieves the shift of the focus from the formal relations to the informal ones, placing the human factor in the forefront within the management process and emphasises the need to diversify the labour, using sociological and psychological concepts and methods. The criticism on this trend aims at the overvaluation of the organisational climate role as motivational element, the focus being exclusively on the human factor within the company.

If the scientific management initiated by Taylor expects the resolution of management problems by applying some specific procedures based on the analysis of each actual situation, the management science (quantitative approach) shows that managers are able to achieve essential improvements of the organisation, by using accurate methods and a modern mathematical device represented by operational researches. The exponents of this concept are E. Turban, J. Meredith, C.W. Churchman, R. Raiffa, S. Beer, J. Lesourne. The authors Turban and Meredith define the management science as the application of the scientific method to the analysis and resolution of the managerial decision problems, the operational researches being a term used almost inter-changeably with the management science. The merits of the quantitative approach consists in scientifically underlying the economic decisions, using and adapting the mathematical and statistical tools to the social practice requirements. The criticism aims at the quantitative reductionism of the suggested methods and techniques, disregarding the human qualitative elements, which leads to inadequately dealing with the management functions.

A higher level of the evolution of theoretical thinking in the managerial field was the occurrence of systemic management that starts from the general systems theory, founded by Ludwig von Bertalanffy. He observes that, in order to understand and organise the whole, it is necessary to know both the parties, and the relations between them. The systemic approach, represented by P. Drucker, F. Kant, M. Porter, C. Popov, H. Simon, deals with the phenomena and processes in their interdependence, introducing the concept of hierarchical, closed and open systems. This movement takes into account all previous approaches and theories in solving the decisional problems, taking over a number of elements it deals with in an integrating vision and, starting from the goal of the organisation as a system, it determines its requirements against components it integrates into the structure of the assembly. The interdisciplinary feature of systemic management results from the fact that the conceptual and methodological arsenal specific to various disciplines in a balanced approach of the management relations, paying a relatively equal attention to its five functions (prediction, organisation, coordination, training and evaluation), placing the economic finality of the organisation in the forefront, in a forecasting and scientifically well grounded vision.

Contingential management provides management with a new dimension against the systemic approach, starting from the idea that the decisional process is strongly conditioned by all the circumstances in which it is performed, therefore, when adopting the decisions, one must take into account the system as such and the situation in which it evolves. In the literature, presentations of how employees participate in the decisional process are often encountered. S. Robbins shows that attracting employees in the decision-making process is sometimes a preferred style of management, but not all the time, there being situations where leaders must take autocratic decisions. The promoters of this approach have identified more than 100 contingential variables, the most common being: the dimension and objectives of the organisation, the route of the operational technology, environmental uncertainty, individual differentiation. Contingential approach is however criticised because it creates the environmental image of a captive organisation, but in reality, its evolution is marked by the interaction between the environmental factors and management techniques.

Contingential management has been improved by the representatives of comparative management (R.N. Farmer, B.M. Richman), who proved that the organisation's outside environment significantly influences the managerial practices, speaking of educational, socio-cultural, political, economic, legislative variables. Studies conducted in this field emphasise many variables of the outside environment, which influence the organisational management characteristics: the emphasises innovative feature of the activity, liberal economy, high dynamism and intense competition for North American organisations, the limited intervention of the state in the economy, government orientation towards the social problems, the modest dynamics of the activity for West European organisations, orientation towards the long-term economic growth, the proliferation of creative organisations, the focus on productivity for Japanese organisations.

Enhancing the efficiency requirements and increasing the role of the human factor within the organisation have determined the outline of two new approaches: Japanese management and business excellence, considered as the modern versions of behaviourist management.

Japanese management has contributed to the substantial improvement of management, introducing a number of specific methods and techniques: the Kaizen, a philosophy that involves ongoing efforts to increase the quality and reduce the production costs; the Kanban method, a process to organise the interrelations between the workplaces integrated into the just in time delivery system, by which written, standard forms are aborted; the Just in Time system, a method of delivering the components when they are necessary, causing the avoidance of stocks. The American professor of Japanese origin, William Ouchi, has proposed a hybrid that combines the philosophy of the American management with the Japanese one, called the Organisation corresponding to theory Z (Table 4.1). He considers that forming Z-type organisations will enable the Western to cope with the Japanese competition, and the Japanese to cope with the competition on the markets wherein they operate.

Business excellence is the contribution of some Americans in management, T. Peters and R. Waterman who, in the paper called In Search of Excellence (1982), they conduct a research on the causes that ensured the success of US

Table 4.1 Forming the Z-type organisations

No.	Types of organisations		
	Japanese organisations	American organisations	Z-type organisations
1.	Lifetime employment	Limited term employment	Long term employment
2.	Assessment and slow promotion	Assessment and rapid promotion	Assessment and rapid promotion
3.	Non-specialised careers	Specialised careers	Specialised careers
4.	Implicit control mechanisms (self-control)	Explicit control mechanisms (special rules)	Mixed control mechanisms
5.	Collective elaboration of decisions	Individual elaboration of decisions	Elaboration of decisions by (participatory) consensus
6.	Collective responsibility	Individual responsibility	Individual responsibility
7.	Holistic spirit	Segmental attitude	Holistic attitude in terms of employees

companies, by using certain performance indicators: rate of innovation, growth of share capital, average rate of recovering the capital. The conclusions of the research have been summarised in a set of eight attributes of excellence (Table 4.2). However, a number of criticisms were brought on them, related to the inclination towards human and behavioural relations and ignoring the principles formulated in contingential management.

In Romania, the first concerns related to management have been either in the form of Taylorist concepts, or in the form of original elaborations: public meetings formed (1831), collective assemblies of the Convention in 1858, the bicameral system introduced in Romania in 1866, the work of E.I. Nechifor (Act of Nechifor—1838). In the twentieth century, original ideas and scientific competence in the field of management were proved by G. Bariţiu, B.P. Haşdeu, A.D. Xenopol, D. Cantemir, N. Bălcescu, N. Iorga, and the beginning of the twentieth century is characterised by the intensification of the concerns about related to placing the labour, production and management on scientific bases.

A theoretically and practically unceasing action was to establish in 1927 the Romanian Institute of Scientific Organisation of Labour on the initiative of a few scientists (V. Madgearu, G. Marinescu, G. Ţiţeica, D. Gusti, C.D. Buşilă, G. Ionescu-Siseşi). Following the establishment of communism in Romania, a decline in management has been recorded for two decades. A revival was felt in 1966 when Romania has shown a slight opening to the West.

Studies have been conducted regarding the management of companies (Management and industrial interruption economy, the Dictionary of management and organisation, the Encyclopaedia of undertaking management) and bodies were established, with duties in management training (Centre for the improvement of training the management officials in undertakings, the Institute for Production Management and Organisation within the Ministry of Labour, the Council for the Economic-social Organisation Problems). As a result of the constraints imposed by the external environment of organisations, the period prior to 1989 was characterised by substantial differentiations in the scope of management in relation

Table 4.2 The eight attributes of business excellence formulated by Peters and Waterman in 1982

No.	Excellence attributions	Description of attributes
1.	Inclination towards action	– Small-scale experiments, easy to organise, with the purpose to generate knowledge, interest and commitment – Managers are openly manifested, getting involved in any field
2.	As close as possible to the customer	– Satisfying the customer is obsessive for the organisation – Customers' requirements are taken into account throughout the design-production-marketing cycle
3.	Entrepreneurship and autonomy	– Taking the risk is encouraged and failures are tolerated – Innovators are encouraged to defend their projects – The flexible structure enables the inventive employees to organise themselves in small groups that can implement various projects
4.	Productivity through people	– The individuals are treated respectfully and worthily – Enthusiasm, trust and sense of family are cultivated
5.	Competence—the engine of values	– The company's clear philosophy is propagated and fully complied with – Personal values are openly recognised
6.	Adhesion	– Attaching the manager to the business they know best – The focus is on internal development
7.	Simple structure, with minimum staff	– The authority is decentralised as much as possible – The top staff is minimal, the talents are stimulated to manifest freely
8.	Coexistence of tolerance with exigency	– A close strategic and financial report is balanced by autonomy, decentralisation of the authority, opportunities for creativity

to the management concepts and practices specific to the countries with market economy.

Radical changes in the management field occurred after 1990, when the concepts and managerial tools at organisation level were reconsidered in terms of the market economic conditions. The fundamental changes that occurred determined the creation of an environment resulted from legislative changes, changes in the system of economic levers, liberalisation of prices, mutations in the employees' mentality, leading to the manifestation of some managerial behaviours specific to the period of transition from the market economy.

Thus, we may speak of: management paralysis, characterised by an expectancy attitude as a result of permanent transformation of the organisations' environment; inertial management marked by the tendency to return to the management systems and methods have previously proved their viability; the management of change, resulted from applying many restructuring variants, often with disastrous consequences; pragmatic management, which has enabled the design of viable survival; strategies for short periods of time; adaptive management, specific to recent years, which aim at radical structural transformation.

Management science, therefore the management as a science, has emerged relatively recently as a result of the contribution brought in this area by a large number of specialists from all over the world, although in a rudimentary form, it exists since the beginning of the organised life of human community. The term management has a particularly complex meaning, being determined by its multiple meanings: management is a science, an organised and coherent set of knowledge by which the phenomena and processes produced in the organisation's management; it is an art that reflects its pragmatic side and consists in the manager's skill to apply the scientific knowledge to the realities of various situations; it is a specific state of mind, reflected by a certain way of seeing, desiring, seeking and accepting the progress.

The definitions of pragmatic management are encountered particularly in the North-American literature. Pringle and Longenecker consider the management as the process of acquiring and combining the human, physical and financial resources in order to meet the primary purpose of the organisation—obtaining products and services desired by a certain segment of the society. Reece and O'Grady define management as being the process of coordinating the human, information, physical and financial resources, in order to achieve the organisation's purposes. The Russian professors Popova and Krasnopoiasa consider that the science of management deals with the laws of general management and synthetic laws of its components. According to Professor O. Nicolescu, management means to study the management processes and relations in order to discover the regularities that govern them and design new management systems, methods and techniques that would ensure the increase of competitiveness.

According to contemporary definitions, management is the process undertaken by one / several individuals in order to coordinate the activities of other people, to obtain results which they would not have if they acted individually; it is a process of efficiently performing the activity through other people, achieving the organisation's goals by working with people and using the other organisational resources.

The essence of management science is the study of the management relations and processes, which result in discovering principles, regularities and the other elements that explain the content and dynamics of management. As a science, management takes the information on the management processes and undergoes them to some analysis procedures, in order to improve the existing management methods and complete them with new ones.

Management places the human being in all its complexity at the centre of its investigations, both as subject and as object of management, also having an applicative character, resulted from the fact that an important place within management science is occupied by designing new systems, methods, techniques and procedures that form the tools made available to managers in order to achieve the organisation's objectives.

The importance of management science results from the fact that it provides rules for improving the managerial decisions, enables the manager to recognise the economic consequences of managerial behaviour and the effects caused to the organisation by the actions of economic factors. The utility of management science can be statistically proven meaning that those organisations that use several scientific management tools are more viable than those that are based on a intuitive management. To support this affirmation, Kreitner suggests a formula for the managerial success: $S = A \cdot M \cdot O$, where S (success) is the product between A (managerial ability), M (motivation to manage) and O (opportunity of management), showing that, if one of the three terms is zero, the managerial success becomes void.

As practical science, management is very sensitive to the changes caused in the society by various factors. The most significant evolutions and directions in contemporary management take into account: increasing the interdisciplinary character of the management activity; emphasising the anticipative character of management; strengthening the global vision, integrating the management; emphasising the motivational side that reflects changes regarding the approach of the human factor by the management; emphasising the national and sectoral character of management, parallel with increasing its universality; increasing the importance of the management of change and management of conflicts; developing the concept of reengineering.

According to P. Drucker, the current and future condition of management is negatively defined by the new postulates of management: management is general, standing out in all economic and social areas; development of the spirit of innovation is the essential feature of modern management; the management is engrafted on the cultural, social and political traditions of each country, on the historical conditions of its development; management is oriented towards the continuous increase of intellectual and physical work productivity; management is the main factor to increase the efficiency of the activity performed; management is the main "animator" of economic development.

If the science of management is that which reveals principles, rules, requirements that reflect the essence of the management relations and processes, designing methods and techniques applicable in practice, the scientific management is that which provides their use in various actual conditions, depending on the objectives to be achieved, being a dynamic and perfection activity, achieved by the means provided by science. It therefore results that scientific management is all the processes by which the theoretic-methodological elements provided by the science of management are operational in social practice. In fact, scientific management is the daily work done by the manager of a company, being a system of rules and actions that ensure the achievement of objectives in conditions of efficiency of the economic objectives. With a strong practical and applicative feature, scientific management takes into account the that part of managers' activity that is based on knowing the theoretical-methodological elements provided by science and their implementation in order to acquire the maximum result with low efforts.

The other part of the managerial work refers to the empirical management based on intuition, common sense, experience, imagination, responsiveness, mental state and the talent of that that decision-maker. Empirical management includes the evolution of the society until the late nineteenth century and early twentieth century, assuming the resolution of problems according to the personal qualities of managers without prior analyses. This type of management exclusively formed the content of the management activity within all social areas before the emergence of scientific management, a fundamental requirement of the contemporary period.

Scientific management requires a rational and systemic activity, a creative contribution from the manager in order to adopt the tools provided by science under the actual conditions involved by each individual situation. Therefore, we can say that scientific management has certain characteristic features: it promotes the creative thinking and effort, being a rational way of solving the problems within the organisation; it is a concept characterised by the diversity and heterogeneity of the content and expression; it customises the management work, fully manifesting in the decisions and actions of managers; it provides the enhancement of profitable businesses, assuming a work of selecting the values by scientific criteria.

Considering the scientific management as a set of processes by which the theoretical and methodological elements serve the social practice by their operationalisation, the entire personnel of an organisation must have a minimum of managerial knowledge, so that they can beneficially participate to increasing the efficiency of that organisation.

Manager's work requires multiple, theoretical knowledge and practical detachments that enable them to understand the theoretical bases of the managerial activity, to create a fund of specialised documentation, to outline their performance limits, behaviour and ethical criteria.

In the current conditions of a competitive market economy, the empirical management based only on personal qualities and manager's intuition, without any prior analyses, is not sufficient to ensure a modern and efficient management. The management work requires intensive creative imagination, based on the new conquests of science, in order to solve the various complex situations that occur in an organisation. Thus, the management science is not so much of interest for the economic activity, but rather, through the contribution it has in solving many problems the organisations face in today's world.

It results that the correlative approach of the management science and scientific management of the organisation is not only possible, but absolutely necessary, starting from the idea that management, as rational and systemic activity is based on knowing the specific principles and using the appropriate methodologies provided by science.

The scientific management of the organisation starts from the logic assembly of ordered activities, rules and principles, by means of which the entire activity of the organisation is oriented towards the achievement of the objectives set. However, scientific management is not limited only to the mere application of theoretical-methodological elements provided by management science, but it requires creative effort, an adaptation and a combination of the techniques provided by scientific knowledge.

The interrelation between the management science and scientific management is increasingly more intensive in the current period, being determined by several factors. Thus, the fact the science has become a force of production determines an increase of conditioning the quality of management to apply the elements provided by management science, the economic practice needing to take into account increasingly more the management science—scientific management—competitiveness trinomial. Increasing the level of training of the organisation's personnel, the ability of employees to embrace and use the methodologies provided by the management science is another factor that determines the enhancement of the scientific management—management science interdependence. The proliferation of participatory management within the organisation adds to all these, which contributes to the amplification of this report.

Scientific management, consisting in the application of the principles and rules formulated by the management science in actual conditions, outlined based on the goals to be achieved, is clearly in an interdependence relation to management science, the relationship set between the two elements however exceeds the classical environment of the theory-practice relationship. This is because management is operationalised through the practical involvement of the entire personnel within the organisation and not only of a certain group of specialists. Thus, considering the scientific management as a set of processes by which the theoretical and methodological elements serve the operationalisation of the social practice, the entire personnel of an organisation must have a minimum of managerial knowledge, so that their involvement in the participatory management would complete and welcomed for increasing the organisation's efficiency.

Since the fifth decade of our century, a phenomenon emerges that promotes the information and decision among the essential elements of our times, a phenomenon determined primarily by the extraordinary growth of the structural and functional complexity of enterprises. The merger-integration processes, the emergence of organisational structures with productive activities by very large geographical areas and also with multiple problems related to marketing the products, raising the tech level of the facilities and appropriately sharp specialisation of the labour force are only some of the aspects of this complexity of the modern enterprise.

As a consequence of this situation, an extraordinary increase in the amount of information held and handled in enterprises along with formulating some more severe business conditions in terms of information quality emerges (its relevance and efficiency). In addition to the production of goods, an increasingly more important production of information also appears. The information becomes even a product or a commodity that can be negotiated, ending to be an object of activity of some specialized organizations, along with services.

Regarding the decision-making processes, it is the first time when the problem of finding some optimal or nearly optimal solutions is raised, in the wide diversity of managerial problems.

The main subjects regarding the managerial activity that occurred at this stage are: operational research, cybernetics, informatics, psycho-sociology of organisation and general systems theory.

Operational research, which may be briefly defined as a discipline of optimising the decisions by means of mathematical modelling emerged during the Second World War.

Considered by some to represent the mathematical school of scientific management, operational research is characterised primarily by the process of preparing the normally mathematised models that describe the economic processes for which decisions will be made, which will be as profitable as possible.

Cybernetics is the science that deals with the management and adjustment of complex systems.

Among the most characteristic attempts to improve the methods used in recent decades in the management science, along with the massive use of mathematical procedures and electronic computers, there is also the systemic-cybernetic concept.

The system can be defined as any section of reality wherein a set of phenomena, objects, processes, beings or groups interconnected through a set of mutual relations, including the environment are identified and which act together to achieve some well-defined objectives. The set of elements and their relationships, as well as the relationships between components and assemblies form the structure of the system. At a given time, the set of the features of a system determines its structure.

For the analysis of the systems behaviour, the concept of black box was proposed globally, which is the system seen as a whole, irrespective of its internal processes. The black box receives impulses from the environment, which are called inputs into the system and, by processing these impulses, it turns them into actions on the environment, which are called outputs from the system.

The systems can be classified:

- according to their nature into: Natural systems;
- elaborate systems such as the technical, economical, conceptual ones;
- according to the operation mode, there are: Open systems wherein the outputs do not influence the inputs; closed systems wherein the inputs are influenced by the outputs;
- according to the behaviour, the following are distinguished: Deterministic systems with a high degree of knowledge; probabilistic systems with a high degree of uncertainty.

The mechanism of transforming the inputs into outputs can be described by means of the transfer functions that have particular forms, depending on the nature of the system.

The system becomes a cybernetic system when adjustment occurs (reverse connection, feedback), meaning the intervention on the inputs to maintain the outputs at the level of desired objective parameters.

Thus, the analytical expression of the transfer functions and of the adjustment mechanism leads to very diverse and often very complex mathematical forms.

The whole economy can be viewed as a system whose components (social-economic organisations of different sizes) are interlinked by material and information flows and have a behaviour oriented towards achieving specific objectives. In their turn, the organisations, which are components of the system as a whole, can be considered systems, and the division can continue to the identification of some elementary and indivisible components. The purpose of the cybernetic-systemic research applied to the social-economic reality is to surprise the behaviour of the systems, and one of the ways to describe this behaviour is to find the expression of the transfer functions and adjustment mechanism.

Adopting the cybernetic-economic perspective in socio-economic sciences is an outstanding theoretical gain and it is very likely that in the next few years, complete and unitary systemic cybernetic theories will appear, widely applied to the socio-economic reality widely.

Informatics can be defined as the discipline of data processing by means of electronic computing equipment.

The main problems that can be considered as belonging to informatics are: data collection, data preparation, their coding, their transmission, data processing by means of electronic computing equipment, their storage and preservation.

The problem of the explosive development of informatics and its role in economy, administration, space researches, military strategy, science, education, etc. is well known. Thus, from only a few electronic computers and a few specialists in informatics in 1945, hundred of millions of computers and millions of specialists have been reached nowadays.

The psycho-sociology of organization has emerged as a new trend in the disciplines of management around 1950, when St. Mareh, F. Simon and other representatives of the so-called psycho-sociological school mainly approach the problem of the psychological and sociological factors on the decisional department of the human resource. In the concept of this school, decision making is not only based on rational criteria, but it is also based on how the stimuli are perceived and depends on the position of the decision maker and their relations with other group members.

In other words, no matter how much methods and high finesse and technicality equipment are used to solve managerial problems, it is people who ultimately and greatly influence the efficient operation of the system, therefore, the individual reactions and relations between individuals in the system must be studied.

Closely related to cybernetics, the general systems theory (GST) proposes a perspective that would systematise the viable ideas of the various orientations in management science.

The basic ideas of the general systems theory have been formulated by J. Forrester in his paper Industrial Dynamics and namely:

- any system consists of interdependent elements (parts), jointly acting under a common purpose;
- all links between the system elements, as well as all links with the whole form the system structure;
- the complexity of the systems depends more on the system structure than on the nature of its components;
- two systems with (partially) identical structures are called homomorphous (the simpler system will be a model of the more complex homomorphous system);
- two homomorphous systems will have a similar result, wherefrom it results the possibility to study the properties of the actual systems by using stimulation systems;
- the (static) structure of a system pre-exists to its behaviour (system dynamics);
- the movements in a system are done by actual and continuous flows;

- in an economic body, all categories of movement can be grouped into the following types of interconnected flows: Material flows; flows of orders; money flows; human flows; equipment flows; information flows;
- the information flow has a central role in the operation of systems;
- the decisional processes are considered to have a central role in the mechanism of systems and are proposed as discontinuous;
- adjustment is an element characteristic to the operation of systems;
- the processes that occur in the economic systems are normally non-linear.

Based on these premises, Forrester creates a method to describe the behaviour of an enterprise, which uses cybernetic, information, psycho-sociological methods, as well as mathematical modelling processes. Physical and technical analogies are also used, and simulation is used as a basic process to describe the behaviour of the systems.

Broadly, in Industrial Dynamic, it is aimed to understand the state of a system by means of equations that describe in time the inputs, transformations and outputs from the system, for the six types of flows mentioned above. Based on this mathematical description, simulations can be done on the computer, by means of which the evolution of the system can be forecasted.

The GST ideas and methods, impressive by their complexity, are undergoing methodological sedimentation and practical experimentation.

The vast majority of the sentences listed above that underlie the theory of Forrester can be explicitly or implicitly found at the base of the practical methodologies of systematic analysis. The concepts of information flow and decision-making process are also dominant in the systemic analysis just like in the GST, and tracking the mechanism of transformation of the inputs into outputs is the main object of the system analysis just like that of the GST. However, the procedure used by the systemic analysis is not mathematical anymore, but it is based on the explicit qualitative description of the information-decision processes. Moreover, in the practice of the system analysis, along with designing the information processes and particularly decisional ones, it is aimed to improve them, therefore, optimum criteria are taken into account. In the action of efficient design of the information-decisional process, the systemic analysis often fully calls on processes of the operational research and informatics techniques.

References

Allen RGD (1991) Mathematical economics. Mac Millan, London

Chase RB (2004) Operations management for competitive advantage, 10th edn. McGraw-Hill, Boston, MA

Christ C (1996) Econometric models and methods. Wiley, New York, NY

Dima IC (2013) Organisational strategies – a systemic approach – on the example of the automotive industry. Lambert Academic, Saarbrucken

Fisher DC (2010) Leading a sustainable organization. ASQ Press, Milwaukee

Goldberger A (2001) Econometric theory. Wiley, New York, NY
Johnston J (1993) Econometric methods. McGraw-Hill, New York, NY
Klein LR (1992) An introduction to econometrics. Prentice-Hall, Eglewood-Cliff, NJ
Lange O (1991) Wster de econometrii. PWN, Warszawa
Schatteles T (1971) Metode econometrice moderne. Ed. Ştiinţifică, Bucureşti
Tinberjen J (1952) Einführung in die Őkonometrie. Humboldt Verlag, Wien-Stuttgart
Valavanis St (1999) Econometrics, an introduction to maximum likllihood methods. McGraw-Hill, New York, NY

Chapter 5
Simulation and Modelling: Econometric Technique

5.1 The Model and Modelling in Econometrics

The concept of model, used so much in modern science, is relatively new, but the method of modelling is just as old as the concerns of people for scientific knowledge.

The model is an isomorphic representation of reality, which, by providing an intuitive and yet rigorous image, in the sense of the logical structure, of the studied phenomenon, it facilitates the discovery of links and laws impossible or very hard to find in other ways.

When elaborating the economical-mathematical patterns, the economical theory has an especially important role as it formulates categories, the objective concepts and laws of the economical reality. The mathematical patterns can faithfully represent the economical phenomena only based on the economical theory.

As tool of scientific knowledge, the model is used in very many theoretical and practical disciplines. Although there are many types of models, they can be: verbal-descriptive patterns, mathematical patterns, physical patterns, physical-analogical patterns (of the static or dynamic model type), graphic patterns etc.

In economic sciences, particularly in management, the models are used in all their diversity of types. During the last decades, the tendency of mainly using the mathematical patterns has emerged increasingly more, particularly because of their capacity to rigorously concentrate the essence, as well as their possibility to be programmed by means of electronic computers, forming together a tool of scientific investigation, a prodigious extension of human intelligence.

A methodological systematisation of mathematical models used in management is risky given the recent continuous and spectacular changes, it would have a purely scholastic feature, without real theoretical or practical utility.

I.C. Dima, M. Man, *Modelling and Simulation in Management*, Contributions to Management Science, DOI 10.1007/978-3-319-16592-9_5

After extending the studied context, the main types of mathematical models known in this area may include: the macroeconomic models, those relating to the national economy, to the branch (sub-branch) or to the economy of a large territory (a county, a certain industrial, agricultural area, etc.); microeconomic models, at the level of enterprise, trust, combined, etc.

The cybernetic-economic models study the relationship between the inputs and outputs in an economic body, by highlighting the adjustment phenomena that determine the smooth operation of the system. Most of the cybernetic-economic models are macroeconomic models.

The econometric models describe the behaviour of the economic bodies by means of some systems of equations wherein the numerical elements are determined statistically. These models are usually also macroeconomic models.

The simulation models try to establish how some macro- or microeconomic bodies operate, by providing some combinations of random values to the independent variables that write the processes. By reading the values the dependent variables receive therein, significant sizes are achieved in the studied process.

The systemic models aim to capture all aspects from an economic body (for example, in Forrester's models, it is considered that by identifying the six characteristic flows, the behaviour of the system as a whole can be known).

The models of operational research are characterized by adopting an optimum or nearly optimum solution for the studied phenomenon. The models of operational research are based on a great variety of mathematical processes and have applications at macro- level but particularly at the microeconomic level. The are the main tool in optimising the decisions in the analysis of systems.

The aforementioned typology is very relative, because there are frequent similarities and overlaps between the aforementioned groups. Thus, the econometric models are often of cybernetic type, the simulation is used in almost all mathematical models, the models of operational research can be used to systematically describe a body, etc.

To be efficient, the modelling activity is always performed in the system analysis, and namely as a moment of the stage to design a new system. A number of phases that occur during the system analysis before this moment has a preparatory feature for performing the modelling and others, further to it, are necessary for implementing the models developed.

The main stages of elaborating a mathematical model to solve a management problem are:

- the first phase of modelling has a preparatory feature and consists in knowing the reality in the studies body, in order to improve the information-decision mechanism. Describing the logic of the decisional processes, along with considering the objectives of the future system, are the main elements of knowledge of the reality required for modelling;
- the second stage of modelling is to actually construct the model. In most cases in practice, this consists in applying a classical tool of modelling chosen from the extremely wide range which the theory of operational research makes it

available. In such situations, the analyst's ability consists in establishing the correspondence between the reality and the modelling tool known from the literature. There are also cases when such a correspondence cannot be established, the analyst having to elaborate new models, which can be combinations of classical models from the theory field;
- new actual models. In the first case, it all comes down to knowing the reality and the theory well, which a dose of skill in combining the methods should be added to. In the second case, it is a matter of original creation. Preparing an actually original mathematical model requires a very solid mathematical culture, imagination and talent, besides deeply knowing the reality that is to be modelled. There is a great diversity in the mathematical and logical structure of models, from very simple, non-axiomatised models, such as those from linear programming to the combinatory models in problems of graph theory, analysis of the critical route and operative production programming and to the high finesse models shown in an axiomatised way, such as those of utility or group decisions. Obviously, elaborating a model in an aximatised form is a higher stage in the process of modelling, which cannot however be always achieved in practice.

An axiomatised (axiomatic system) model includes: the axioms of the system, representing propositions expressed in mathematical form, usually very few, which include some truths of great generality regarding the phenomenon that is modelled, so general that all specific and particular observations will be deducted from the general ones; interference rules, representing rigorous prescriptions, the only ones admitted in the system, by means of which it is passed from axioms to theorems or from already demonstrated theorems to new ones; theorems, meaning more or less particular, mathematically expressed sentences, deducted step by step by interference rules from axioms and which have properties of the modelled phenomenon.

When the axiomatic modelling process exhaustively explains the concepts that are to be used, meaning a list of notions and mathematical operations admitted in the system is given since the beginning, a higher form of axiomatic system is achieved, which is called formal system.

Formal systems are used yet very little in science and even less in management.

Axiomatisation and, in the final analysis, formalisation is the future in mathematical modelling, due to the exceptional rigour it introduces to the considerable reduction of intuition and arbitrary elements, which although they are much less than in non-mathematical models, they are still present in mathematised modelling;

- the third stage of modelling is to face the model with the reality and eventually with its experimentation. This stage is done during the system implementation, which can be considered the fourth and last stage of modelling.

One of the main features of all methods of operational research is that some problems of the operational research can be viewed from the merely theoretical perspective, as a mere mathematical problem, but for management, the operational research methods will be treated in close connection with practical problems.

From the historical point of view, it is true that some of the operational research problems arose especially in a merely mathematical aspect, long before the organised activity and the name of operational research appeared. Thus, some notions of graph theory are known for over a century, the queuing theory having its origin in some works of Erlang in the second decade of our twentieth Century, and the inventory theory appears near 1930. As an independent discipline, operational research however appeared during the Second World War, by establishing some complex teams (mathematicians, engineers, economists, biologists, psychologists, etc.), with the task to optimise the decisions concerning preparatory actions for military operations. After the war, the teams so formed rapidly turned to peaceful activities.

Spectacularly developing in the last three decades, the theoretical and particularly the practical concerns in the field of operational research have come to globally drive today hundreds of thousands of professionals.

Modelling is a component of the structural (complex) methods, having yet a series of peculiarities, which justify their establishment in a distinct category.

The model—reality analogies are important, sometimes indispensable tools for knowing the actual phenomena and processes. Therefore, modelling is a process of knowing the reality in a mediated way, by means of representations called models. In other words, an artificial, more simple system is used by modelling, by means of which the behaviour of a real system it represents is studied.

The model is a simplified (material or symbolic) representation of the reality and is subordinated to the purpose of the research, however, without this simplification distorting the essential characteristics of the studied phenomenon or process.

To be functional, any model must meet the following conditions:

- to be isomorphic, meaning the model should operate similarly (analogy) with the system it represents;
- to be homomorphous, meaning that the model is similar to the reality in terms of the essential elements, yet being able to neglect the secondary properties in terms of the research purpose.

Provided that the essential characteristics are met, this very simplification of some complex systems favours turning to models, otherwise the research is done directly on the real systems.

In terms of the economic-mathematical modelling, it is a method of researching and knowing the phenomena and complex processes of economy, judged in an abstract manner, turning to logical and mathematical formalisation.

The economic-mathematical model (M) is the result of a process where the subject (S) achieves a similitude (an isomorphism) between the object and the model, having at the base a theory (T) of the researched object (O). This is why, the model as carrier of a certain information (I) about the researched system is shown only by the information which the subject has, and modelling is an informational process subordinated to the purpose of the research.

The theoretic basis of the economic-mathematic model consists of a logical system of universal statements (hypotheses, premises) of which, by precise rules, final sentences are deducted (theorems, conclusions), and the empirical basis consists of statements of limited feature in time and space, which must be verified by experiment in order to assess the validity degree of the model. The set of initial propositions describes the behaviour of the factors of the economic activity that occur in a space-time environment bounded by a given institutional order and technological structure, therefore by an economic specified mechanism.

The economic-mathematical models have the purpose to provide possible variants to develop and structure the future economic-social activity, in order to choose the most convenient solutions that ensure meeting the major goals set out under the conditions of and by complying with the restrictions of that stage.

I the management of economic-social activities, various types of economic-mathematical models are used.

Their classification involves their approach from several points of view:

- according to the elaboration technique, the following are distinguished: models based on production functions (where the results of the production activity are quantitatively conditioned by a number of factors, and the relationship between these variables is expressed as an equation that intercepts the causal connection and the multiple correlations between the dependent variable and the independent variables); models of optimization, each having an objective function (optimisation criterion) under the conditions of data restrictions, by resolution aiming at maximising or minimising the indicator chosen as function—objective; simulation models, created from a number of chained equations that enable the combination of different variables in a certain sequence, based on the input information and optional (decision) parameters, as well as depending on the functional interdependence between all these elements in the economic mechanism; inter-branches models (input–output) of analysing and designing the structure of production costs and distribution of social production based on the complex mutual relations between the components of the production process;
- according to their aggregation degree, these can be: aggregated models with a small number of variables, representing the analysed economic systems (subsystems) in a concentrated form; disaggregated models, where the areas analysed are structured by components (e.g.: the national economy is addressed by branches);
- according to the time factor, the following are known: Static models, used to represent some phenomena or economic processes at a given time; dynamic models, which show the evolution in time of the phenomena or economic processes taken into account.

Between the different categories of models mentioned herein, there are many links, any model can circumscribe characteristics belonging to several classification criteria.

The economic-mathematical modelling is a complex process involving a certain sequence of works, grouped into three stages, namely:

- stating the model, which includes: Choosing the area that is subject to modelling (national economy, a branch, a county, etc.); establishing the time scope (long, medium or short-term); doing a retrospective analysis and a diagnosis on the actual system, identifying the propositions $p^1(0), \ldots, p^n(0)$, which form the description;

$$\{p_1(0)\}_{j=1}^{n} \rightarrow \left\{p_j(M)\right\}_{j=1}^{n} \tag{5.1}$$

- testing the model refers to: Specifying the statistical period that is considered conclusive for the retrospective analysis and for testing the model; collecting the statistical data for the chosen variables, ensuring the comparability regarding the inclusion scope and the prices in which they are expressed; elaborating the model diagram (geometrical representation); writing the relations of the model; calculating the size of optional parameters for the statistical period and, based on this, setting the optional parameters for the scope of the forecast; testing the model with data from the past period and highlighting the deviations from the statistical data;
- applying the model to the actual management problem, it is a matter of: Using the model for the management problem, taking as base the last available statistical data, thus acquiring new information and properties; the analysis and interpretation of the results obtained, as well as their validation in terms of accuracy of the calculations and plausibility of the solution provided to the decision-makers.

$$\left\{p_j(M)\right\}_{j=n+1}^{n+m} \tag{5.2}$$

This category of models uses quantitative relations that can be achieved for the entire national economy, for its branches or for other economic components (should they include a sub-branch of the industry).

5.2 Using the Matrix Calculus to Study the Models

Besides the advantages of a radiograph of the problem, transcribing the regression problem with matrix operators also provides the possibility to go better into the model structure.

Let us note the hypothetical relation:

$$y_i = a_0 + a_1x_1 + a_2x_2 + \ldots. + a_0x_0 + u_i \tag{5.3}$$

in matrix terms so that:

a) The set of "k" values taken for each of the "n" variables can be noted with a vector of "k" elements (k>n)

$$Y = \begin{vmatrix} y_1 \\ y_2 \\ \vdots \\ y_k \end{vmatrix} \quad X_i = \begin{vmatrix} x_{i1} \\ x_{i2} \\ \vdots \\ x_{ik} \end{vmatrix} \tag{5.4}$$

b) The constants of the equation to form a vector of "n+1" elements

$$A = \begin{vmatrix} a_0 \\ a_1 \\ \vdots \\ a_n \end{vmatrix} \tag{5.5}$$

c) a unitary vector of "k" elements and those "n" vectors "X_i" to be reunited in a matrix of "k" rows and "(n+1)" columns

$$X = \begin{vmatrix} 1 & x_{11} & x_{21} & \ldots & x_{n1} \\ 1 & x_{12} & x_{22} & \ldots & x_{n2} \\ \vdots & \vdots & \vdots & & \vdots \\ 1 & x_{1k} & x_{2k} & \ldots & x_{nk} \end{vmatrix} \tag{5.6}$$

d) one vector of "k" elements to include the values taken by the random variable

$$u = \begin{vmatrix} u_1 \\ u_2 \\ \vdots \\ u_n \end{vmatrix} \tag{5.7}$$

The "k" hypothetical equations are written as matrix:

$$Y = AX + u. \tag{5.8}$$

We need to obtain:

$$\min u'u = (Y - AX)'(Y - AX) = Y'Y - 2A'X'Y + A'X'XA, \tag{5.9}$$

where $A'X'Y \equiv Y'XA$ = one scalar.

The minimum of the squared deviations is obtained solving the system:

$$\frac{\partial(u/u)}{\partial A} = -2\,X'Y + 2\,X'XA = 0. \tag{5.10}$$

If we consider that:

$$X'Y = X'XA_i \tag{5.11}$$

then we obtain

$$A = (X'X)^{-1}X'Y, \tag{5.12}$$

where

$$X'X \equiv \left|\sum x_{ij}\right|$$

5.3 The Input-Output Model and Its Characteristics

The input-output model or—as it is also called—the Leontief model of the inter-industrial relations is one of the most efficient methods of the quantitative economic analysis, taking into account the fact that in a broader usual sense, the term econometrics refers to the method and the *input-output model.* However, there is not any econometrics treaty where at least one single chapter would be dedicated to this method (except for the paper of Oscar Lange). This is fully justified if we take into account the particularities of the specific methods of econometrics. However, the outstanding contribution of Leontief (also called the method of the "balance of the relationships between branches") is worth mentioning as a prototype for the quantitative structural analysis techniques which have been developed with great success, along with the econometric methods that have different features. Some of their problems are common because a certain methodological "superstructure" of the inter-industrial analysis techniques is convergent with econometrics.

Distinctions should be made between the structure inter-industrial analysis and econometrics. To start with, a set of the measurement results is done: "$n \cdot n$" elements "x_{ij}", "n" elements "y_i" and "n" elements "x_i". By a simple division, "$n \cdot n$" elements result the elements "a_{ij}", which are the constants of the system. One may thus observe that all the data of the model come from the direct measurement of the *structure* of the interdependence of branches.

Let us consider that the researched "object" is shown as it has been outlined by Leontief, meaning a system of linear equations that can accurately represent any technical relation between the branches of national economy. Although there is this system, there is no possibility to directly "photograph" the networks of streams, which is why it is required to use statistics that would give us spare data on the sets of data "x_i" (total production) and "y_i" (final demand) for each branch of activity and for several moments.

Starting from the hypothesis that:

$$x_i = f(y_i, x_1, x_2, \ldots x_n) \tag{5.13}$$

and

$$(x_i - y_i) = z_i = F(x_1, x_2, \ldots x_n) \quad (5.14)$$

and taking into account that the relations (5.13) and (5.14) are linear, a number "n·n" of coefficients "a_{ij}" must be found. If there are "n·n" statistics "x_{ij}" available, the work would be pretty simple. But this is not possible. For this reason, we start by "guessing" the constants "a_{ij}", meaning they would be assessed without having a well established method. This is in conflict with econometrics which has a study method, because it issues certain hypotheses about the researched function and only then it chooses the function parameters. This is done by estimating the parameters so that they would correspond with *maximum likelihood* to the hypotheses issued regarding their characteristics.

In the same context, the Cobb-Douglas function can be a macroeconomic model according to the mathematical economy definitions, but it has some serious infirmity, not only in terms of the problematic feature of its calculation, but also even in terms of the *econometric idea* requirements. Beyond statistics, the goal of the econometric researches themselves is to discover the underlying mechanism that transforms a category of economic objects the recorded signals of which are a set of data in another category of economic objects the observed signals of which form another set of data. However, the production functions, although fully interpretable in terms of economics, show only the simultaneity of the movement of three sets of variables, plus the trend that is embedded therein, but not the mechanism that transforms the "work" and the "investment" into "national income".

Complex mathematical models can be designed and have even been built, which satisfactorily represent such a mechanism with all its circuits and feedbacks, in a principled way. The Leontief model is a more modest form of such a representation—and also the most popular one. But schematically, besides the fact that they are limited strictly to the production apparatus of the national economy, the equations of the input-output relations also have the shortcoming that their constant components result from an instantaneous recording of a single datum. Indeed, there is no guarantee and certitude for the fact that the ratio $a_{ij} = x_{ij}/x_j$ is true in *general* and not only for the values given by "x_{ij}" and "x_j". If for each "square" of the input-output table there was a function from engineering sources instead of a number, then more complicated and "truer" equations can be done. Of course, by completing the model also with future predictions on the evolution of the technology of various branches.

In the ideal form set forth herein, no planning body in the world shall ever have a balance of the relations between branches. Serious additions and improvements to the numerical values included in a Leontief model can however be done by using the methods of econometrics, reaching the point of convergence of all quantitative methods in the economic analysis.

Econometrics can serve in two ways to the structure quantitative models based on instantaneous records, namely: it contributes to the assessment of the parameters of the models or to the correction of their statistically obtained value; it provides the data that result from the econometric analysis as addition elements, by incorporating them into the model, besides the data of instantaneous records.

5.4 Optimisation Models

Any model optimisation model is a mathematical construction operating with a system of variables subject to some restrictions by which it is aimed to set the best solutions, seen in the light of the chosen function—objective (to minimise or maximise the value of an indicator). In some cases, optimisation involves the use of several objective—functions, related to the same restrictions, leading to a function—purpose (which implies to simultaneously minimise or maximise the objective functions in a correlated manner, by synthesis).

The optimisation models used in the management activity involve the anticipation, as a first approximation, of the levels of variables that are restrictions of the system, and then their combination so as to achieve the (minimum and maximum) extremal solution that is the objective function.

The mathematical programming problems are classified into this category, which are able to intercept the set of production factors, activities and economic relations, under the conditions of the limited character of the resources, which leads to taking into account several possible variants, of which one is the optimum.

Such an economic system represented by the set of activities ($a_1, a_2, \ldots, a_n$) and resources ($R_1, R_2, \ldots R_m$), through the vector of the efficiency vector and the state vector of the economic system can be represented by a linear programming model:

$$\text{optimal}\,[f(x)] \tag{5.15}$$

In the conditions of:

$$g_i(x) \leq\geq b_i \qquad i = 1, 2, \ldots, m \tag{5.16}$$

$$x \geq 0 \tag{5.17}$$

The relation (5.15) is the criterion of optimising the problem, and the relations (5.16) and (5.17) are the functional restrictions of the problem, namely the direct ones. By the nature of the functions f(x) and $g_i(x)$, the model can be of static or dynamic programming, etc.

The method used to obtain the optimal solution for a problem of optimal depends on the actual form of the model, meaning the form of the objective function, the nature of the model (certain, uncertain) parameters and restrictions.

For the overall optimum problem defined by the mathematical programming model (5.15 and 5.17), its optimal solution is a vector X that maximises or minimises the objective function while satisfying the functional and the direct restrictions.

The problem of linear programming is a particular case of the general optimal problem, consisting only of linear relations and has the following structure:

$$\max(\min)[f(x)] = C'x \tag{5.18}$$

In the conditions of:

$$A \times x \leq\geq b \tag{5.19}$$

$$X \geq 0 \tag{5.20}$$

$C' = (c_1, c_2, \ldots c_n)$ the line vector of the efficiency coefficients for the activities a_j, $(j = 1, 2, \ldots, n)$ that form the actual system;

X=the column vector with the components $x_1, x_2, \ldots, x_n$, which is the level of activities;

A=the matrix consisting of technical coefficients a_{ij} (i =1. 2, . . ., m; j=1, 2, . . ., n), which is specific consumptions from the resource i for a unit x_j (in the case of resources), or the contribution of the activity a_j to achieving the characteristic i of quality (in the case of>= type restrictions);

b=a column vector of components b_i $(i = 1, 2, \ldots, m)$ that represents the quantities available from the resource i or the minimum level imposed on the quality characteristic i.

The linear programming models are widely used both in macroeconomic modelling and in the microeconomic one. Besides the applied valences, by including it into the theory of economic optimum, linear programming has brought many contributions to the development of the economic analysis and scientific substantiation of the decision.

The stochastic programming is a model of form (5.18)–(5.20) wherein one or more coefficients from the sets A, B or C are random variables.

The flexible programming is a linear programming problem wherein it is operated with fuzzy sets which it is characteristic for them that the membership of variables to a certain class of values (or a domain) is not defined accurately.

In multi-criteria programming, it is aimed to achieve the solution X that would simultaneously satisfy several objective functions $f_i(X)$.

The problem of the size for the national social—economic system can be overcome by decomposing the large systems into blocks and by using appropriate methods to achieve the best solution. The fact that the economy is organisationally structured into components underlies this method, and they can be represented more easily with mathematical programming models, and the optimal solution of the aggregate system can be reached by successively improving the partial optimums by using the technique of re-optimisation. The models shown so far deal with different aspects of the managerial activity, providing partial information, which cannot cover all aspects. One way to correct this shortcoming is to elaborate and use an integrated system of models that incorporate both the strategic and tactical problems, and aspects regarding the aggregation and disaggregation of components, also providing the possibility to verify the solutions by comparing the variants.

5.5 Production Models

The econometric study of the—micro- or macroeconomic—production mechanisms requires the early creation of some mathematical, non-empirical rational models. For the economist, the statistical-econometric research is equivalent to the laboratory research in the field of other sciences. This has something in common with them regarding the research technique, namely the construction prior to the empirical research of some mathematical models. In this context, it should be mentioned that *not all production models of the mathematical economics are suitable for econometric treatment*, because in the case of the production models, between the econometric ones and those with other features, there is no report of superiority-inferiority, they are complementary, but each having its place in the quantitative research.

The study of the micro or macro production mechanisms requires the early creation of some mathematical, non-empirical rational models. Thus, the statistical, econometric research equals the laboratory research in the field of other sciences and if it has something in common with them regarding the research technique, then this consists precisely of the prior construction of the empirical research of some mathematical models.

By means of the production activity, one is to understand the transformation of primary factors into a production result. There are mathematical models for various production activities, with very special characteristics. Such models are not always suitable for an operational research and nor do they imply this. Operational research intervenes where only a few very general, yet essential features are known for the studied structure. In such cases, the model must also be very general in order to adapt to the very different production features. Theoretical expectations of this nature are possible because there are certain characteristics of production that can be designed and are true even though we do not have sufficient empirical evidence on them. Naturally, such problems of epistemology are far from the concern of operational research, but the merits of the aforementioned statement can be demonstrated on an example of the inverse case: an absurd situation of production can be designed, but not achieved. Let us assume that in an enterprise the production of which is y_t, at the time t, various combinations between the work forces x_{1t} and x_{2t} can be done, which lead to this production.

A very general model of the process is as follows:

$$y_t = f(x_{1t}, x_{2t}) \tag{5.21}$$

It could be hard to object against such a general, practically all-inclusive function. A certain set of statistical data leads to explicating the relation in linear form (5.21):

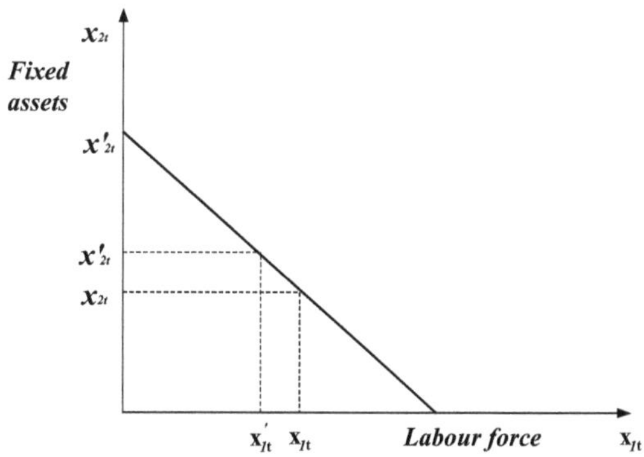

Fig. 5.1 Graphical representation of the equation (5.22)

$$y_t = a_1 \cdot x_{1t} + a_2 \cdot x_{2t} \tag{5.22}$$

The absurdity and irrationality of such as function is obvious taking into account the definitions given to x_{1t} and x_{2t}. According to the mathematical structure of (5.22), it would mean that there is the possibility to simultaneously have:

$$\begin{aligned} x_{1t} &= 0 \\ x_{2t} &> 0 \\ y_t &< 0 \end{aligned} \tag{5.23}$$

That is, nobody to work ($x_{1t} = 0$), the mean of production to be present in a certain quantity ($x_{2t}>0$) and yet production to be achieved ($y_t < 0$). Obviously, this does not exist in reality. Of course, some combinations between the labour force and the fixed assets can be imagined, but they are probably very limited.

Graphically, the equation (5.22) is represented in Fig. 5.1. Here, one and the same amount of production (y_t=const) can be achieved by different combinations of x_1 and x_2. For example, if the labour force employed is reduced from x_{1t} to x'_{1t}, then it is necessary to multiply the means of production used in production, from x_{2t} to x'_{2t}.

But how far will these transformations be done? In no event fixed assets can be produced with x_{2t}, when the labour force was reduced to 0, as it would result from the transformation limit. Therefore, even if such substitutions can be done between factor, they are either limited or are approximations.

In the first case, the production model would be completed with additional restrictions.

$$y_t = a_1 \cdot x_{1t} + a_1 \cdot x_{2t} \tag{5.24}$$

$$x_{1t}^{(2)} \geq x_{1t} \geq x_{1t}^{(1)} \quad \text{si} \quad x_{2t}^{(2)} \geq x_{1t} \geq x_{1t}^{(1)} \tag{5.25}$$

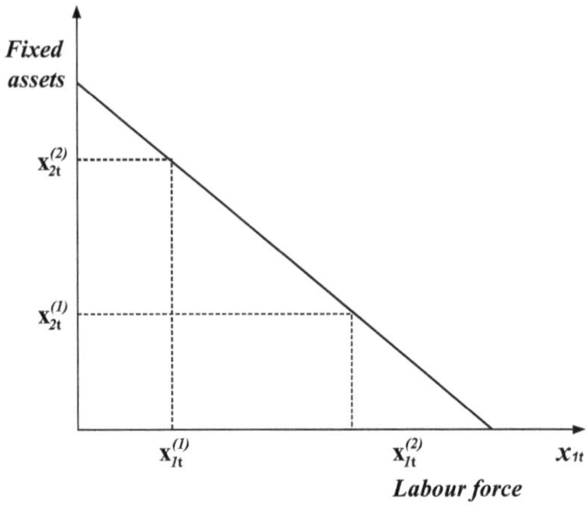

Fig. 5.2 Graphical representation of the equations (5.24) and (5.25)

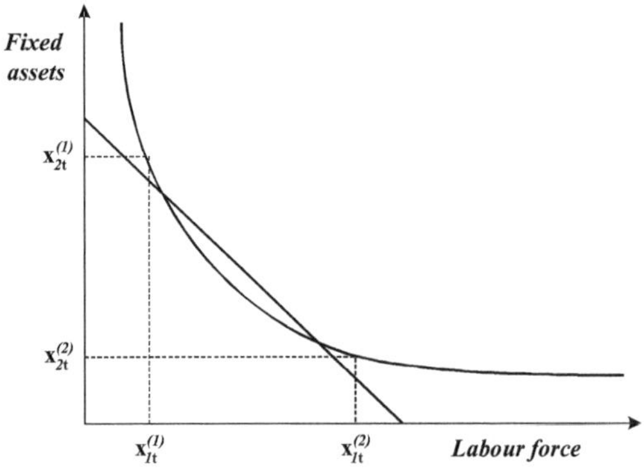

Fig. 5.3 Graphical representation of the equation (5.21)

The case is shown in Fig. 5.2:

The second case (5.21) can be represented by a transformation curve, the interpretation of which is much more convenient and has more generality. Thus, in Fig. 5.3, the range $x_{1t}^{(1)} - x_{1t}^{(2)}$ wherein we eventually accept the existence of a linear relation can be indeed tolerably approximated by a straight line. Here, the absurd case, shown by the values $x_{2t} > 0,\ x_{1t} = 0,\ y_t > 0$, has been avoided as follows: a transformation function has been introduced for a certain level y_t of the production between the two considered factors, so that no factor could ever be reduced to 0, hither and beyond the limits $x_{1t}^{(1)}$ and $x_{1t}^{(2)}$, one of the factors increasing too much (or to infinity), the production will not use it.

Transformation curves, and respectively transformation functions of this type may be accepted whenever we postulate the substitutability of the production factors. They will also be called substitution curves or functions. For the case with non-substitutable factors, another type of models will be adopted and then one will see what the possible connections are between the two types of production functions. For different levels of production, there will be an appropriate number of

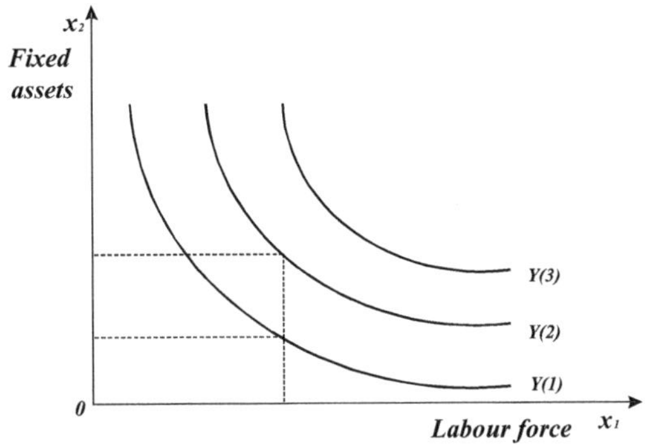

Fig. 5.4 Graphical representation of the various production levels

production curves like those shown in Fig. 5.3, and namely, as they are represented in Fig. 5.4. Here, Y(i) is different production levels.

In a three-dimensional space, the entire production function can be represented.

$$y = f(x_1, x_2) \tag{5.26}$$

Of course, in principle, the more general production functions are of interest

$$y = (x_1, x_2, \ldots, x_n) \tag{5.27}$$

The differential or marginal increase in the production function (also called the marginal efficiency) being for the n factors:

$$\frac{\partial y}{\partial x_1}, \frac{\partial y}{\partial x_2}, \quad \ldots, \quad \frac{\partial y}{\partial x_n} \tag{5.28}$$

The differential (marginal) substitution between two factors I and j will be represented by the ratio:

$$\frac{\partial y}{x_i} \bigg/ \frac{\partial y}{\partial x_j} = \frac{\partial x_j}{\partial x_i} \tag{5.29}$$

The following four general types of functions are distinguished:

– with constant yield when any further increase in a factor will determine an increase in the production result, at a constant ratio:

$$\frac{\partial y}{\partial x_i} > 0; \quad \frac{\partial^2 y}{\partial x_i^2} = 0 \tag{5.30}$$

– with increasing yield:

$$\frac{\partial y}{\partial x_i} > 0; \quad \frac{\partial^2 y}{\partial x_i^2} > 0 \tag{5.31}$$

– with decreasing yield:

$$\frac{\partial y}{\partial x_i} > 0; \quad \frac{\partial^2 y}{\partial x_i^2} < 0 \tag{5.32}$$

– with a maximum extreme:

$$y_i\text{max, when} \frac{\partial y}{\partial x_1} = \frac{\partial y}{\partial x_2} = \ldots = \frac{\partial y}{\partial x_n} = 0 \tag{5.33}$$

These functions have a technical feature. In terms of economy, they are related to the idea of an optimum. For example, such a combination of the production factors, which would lead to a kind of economic optimum, such as maximum yield, minimum cost, etc.

For illustration, let us consider the case with the two factors. If the unit cost of the two factors is respectively p_1 and p_2, then the straight line:

$$C = p_1 \cdot x_1 + p_2 \cdot x_2 \tag{5.34}$$

will be the isoquant that shows the possible combinations of x_1 and x_2 at the same cost (budget) of production C.

In fact, a system of coordinates (Fig. 5.5) is densely populated with such isoquants.

If a manufacturer now has a budget C, which they want to distribute between the two factors so as to achieve a maximum production with it, then they will insert the appropriate isoquant into a graph (Fig. 5.6) including the transformation functions and will choose that which provides a maximum y at a given C.

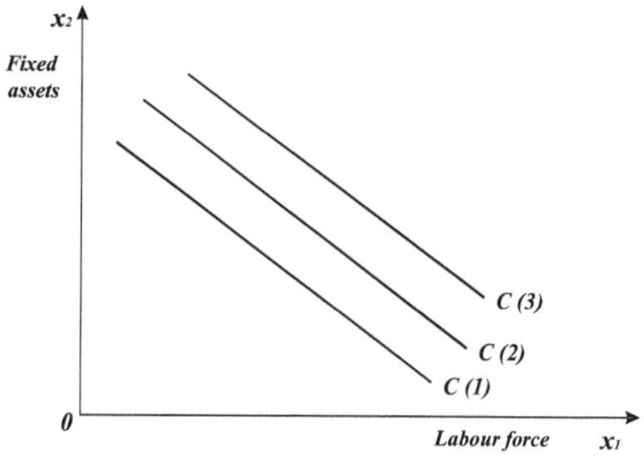

Fig. 5.5 Graphical representation with two production factors

Fig. 5.6 Representation with two production factors under the conditions of a maximum dependence

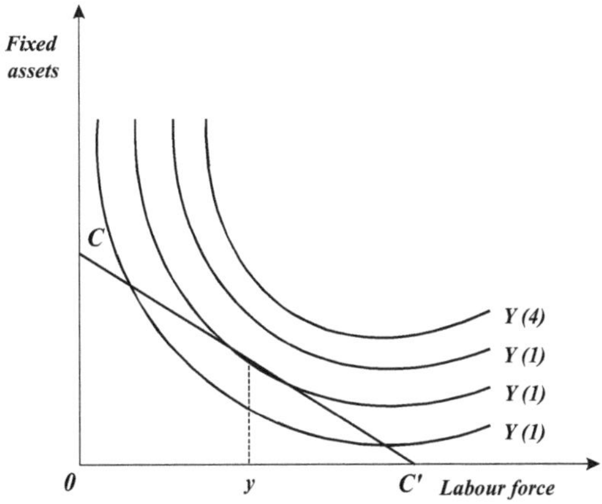

In the example shown in Fig. 5.6, the maximum production will be at a cost C, of y(2). Mathematically and generally, we say that at a given budget, the maximum production will be defined by that transformation curve to which the isoquant of costs is tangential. This necessary condition is mathematically formulated by the relations:

$$\frac{\partial y}{\partial x_1}\Big/ p_1 = \frac{\partial y}{\partial x_2}\Big/ p2 \quad \text{sau} \quad \frac{\partial x_2}{\partial x_1} = -\frac{p_2}{p_1}, \tag{5.35}$$

This implies a certain characteristic of the production function, which we will accept as being given, namely: to be convex to the origin and continuously derivable. The reverse is also true: at a pre-indicated level of production, the minimum costs will be given by the cost isoquant tangential to the transformation function, corresponding to this production.

In this group of models, a special case is that of the models with non-substitutable factors used for substitutable processes, because the *hypothesis of substitutability* of factors may be related to some cases and to some rather limited intervals, as a rational, tolerable approximation.

A more analytical presentation of the possible structures in the economic activity however shows that the *hypothesis of non-substitutability* of factors and components of the production processes are rather more suitable for most of the cases. However, there are many possible connections between the two hypotheses, which refer to complementary situations or rather to complementary aspects of the same situation. It is precisely this quality they have that provides them with general validity also in the econometric analysis.

A production process is assumed, which at facility level uses constant quantities "m_1" and "k_1" of labour force and fixed funds. At any level "x_1" of the production, the consumption of factors will be "(m_1,x_1)" and "(k_1,x_1)" *simultaneously and non-substitutably*. For one and the same product there is also a second production process where at facility level, "m_2"($\neq$"m_1") and "k_2"($\neq$"k_1") are consumed. If the two processes the consumptions of which will be noted by vectors are driven at the level of “x_1” and “x_2”, the total consumption will be:

$$x_1\begin{vmatrix} m_1 \\ k_1 \end{vmatrix} + x_2\begin{vmatrix} m_2 \\ k_2 \end{vmatrix} = \begin{vmatrix} M \\ K \end{vmatrix} \tag{5.36}$$

It is also implied that there is a limit $x_1+x_2=X$ given for the production level, then there will be an infinity of possible combinations between the two processes, between the extremes ($x_1=X$; $x_2=0$) and ($x_1=0$; $x_2=X$). And here, the substitution between factors has become possible again on the set of the two processes, by relatively changing the share of the two processes. This representation yet also involves the impossibility of substitution until the cancellation of the consumption of one of the factors.

Thus, for example, if:

$$m_1 > m_2$$
and
$$k_1 < k_2$$

the productive consumption of “K”, can be reduced, but only as a function of increasing “x_1” and therefore the substitution is relative.

Thus, it is switched from the *substitution of factors* to the *substitution of activities* represented by vectors. A specialised discipline deals with such situations, a discipline conventionally called activity analysis. If the relations between them are linear, replacing and continuing the activities are dealt with by the method of linear programming, usually classified in the activity analysis. Linear programming is not econometrics, but its basic concepts are used to build and interpret the econometric models.

5.6 Simulation in Econometrics

Modelling based on simulation is an increasingly more widespread method for analysing the complex phenomena hard or impossible to study directly and immediately. Basically, it consists of the construction of mathematical structures that represent by analogy the essential characteristics of the phenomenon or the process being investigated, which enables testing of an infinite number of variants by changing some (optional) parameters of decision until the most plausible and more convenient solution is achieved.

The simulation model is based on capitalising some (exogenous) input variables and on designing some optional parameters in different variants, as well as of some random factors (for planned works under risk and uncertainty), and a number of chained equations results from their combination, wherefrom output (resulting, endogenous) variables are obtained, which become elements for calculating some new conditions.

As the number of initial input variables and optional parameters increases, more all-inclusive simulation models are done.

It is recommended that some initial variables and optional parameters would be predicted with other methods, including the optimisation models, which strengthens since the beginning the plausibility of the simulated system (Fig. 5.7).

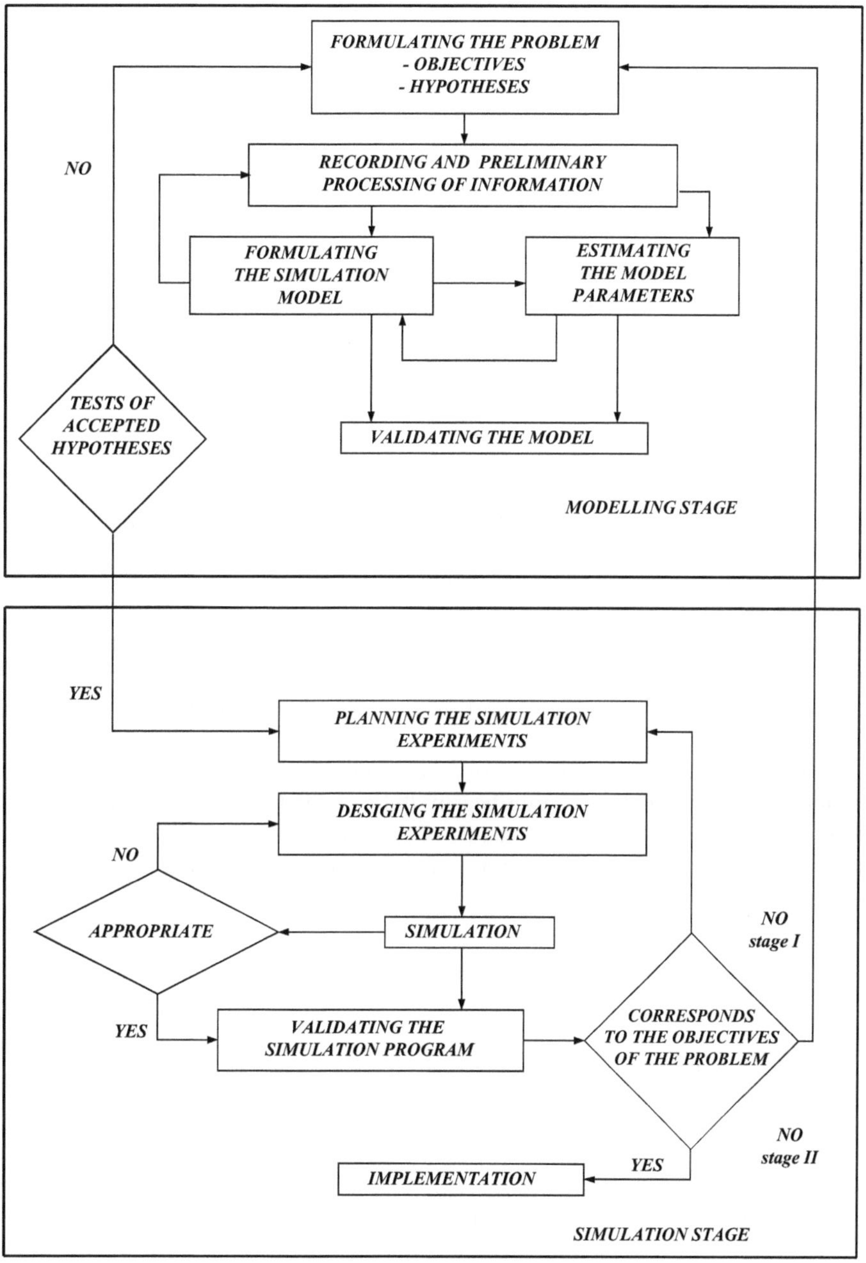

Fig. 5.7 The stages of the simulation process

The game type simulation consists in experimenting on the model, by giving some arbitrary values to the input variables, monitoring the effect on the state and output variables, and on the objective function or functions. The input variables can be deterministic or stochastic. The deterministic ones are taken by the computer from an outside environment (magnetic, perforated tapes, etc.) or determined based on an algorithm imposed by the subject, and the stochastic ones are generated by the computer through appropriate procedures.

The dependence between the input variables and the state or output ones is determined by the logical structure of the model and the computer simulation and requires the transcription of the simulation model into an algorithmic form, illustrated by a logical chart, specifying the dependencies, the logical conditionings and the arithmetic operations required.

The analysis of the simulation model solutions is the final stage that consists in processing the simulated data, calculating the statistics to validate the results through appropriate significance tests, choosing the most efficient solution in relation to the performance criterion (criteria).

5.7 Industrial Production Simulation Model

The activity of stimulation of production systems (systems with discrete events) is made according to Fig. 5.8, which mentions that this activity has two phases: modelling and simulation.

According to the terminology used in system theory, the model of a production system is made up of *objects* or *entities* (parts to be manufactured, machines, tools etc.) and *relations* between these objects (e.g. the "likelihood" that a part be passed on to a certain processing machine).

An object is characterised by one or several *attributes* for which values may be awarded; in fact, objects are described by these attributes. Attributes are of two types: fixed attributes, defining the nature of the object (car type objects, type of car etc.) and their features (the dimensions of a tool, its cost, the value of the losses generated by an accident etc.); variable attributes which *evolve* in time (such as the

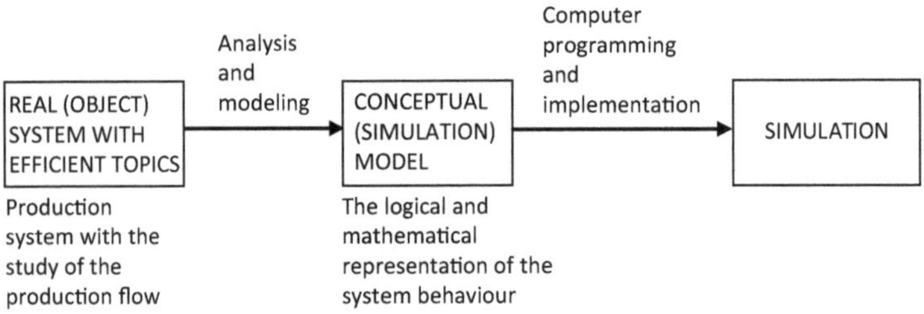

Fig. 5.8 The graphical representation of the simulation of production systems

situation of loading a car, the operating state of a car, the *position* of a part in a workshop or within the manufacture flow).

Objects of the same nature may be regrouped into *classes*, mentioning the number of elements for each class. Likewise, relations are described by fixed (*relational*) attributes which mention certain characteristics of the relation (performance times for each part and each machine etc.). Relations can only have fixed attributes if the object (modelled) system remains the same for the entire time interval considered. These standard definitions result in the concept of *state* (as given by industrial dynamics or continuous automatics); *the state* of an object at a given moment is the sum of the values of all the variable attributes of that object, at that moment. The instantaneous state of the system is the multitude of the states of all the objects in the system, at a given moment. Previously introduced concepts only allow the description of the multitude of possible states of the system. Moreover, complete models contain *operational rules*, which allow the description of the evolution of the system (its trajectory), from a state to another.

If these state changes occur in a continuous manner, we get a *continuous model*. If changes can only occur at certain moments and discontinuously, we have a *discrete event model*. This is, basically, the case of models where we are only interested in the initial and end dates of a multitude of activities (production tasks). In automatic production issues, discrete event models are generally used. In the discrete case, for the entire interval of time when the state of an object does not change, it is supposed that the object is involved in a certain activity (which can only be rest, i.e. the wait before the transition to a processing phase). If the state of an object varies (changes), it is said that this is an *event*. An event is, therefore, a change in the state of an object, which initiates an activity which was not developing before. Generally, events are *casual*, i.e. the circumstance of their apparition depends on the evolution of the system and, therefore, on other previous events. However, so-called *determined* events may also exist: those which occur at certain moments, predefined through a *time generator* (clock), such as the beginning and end of shifts in production workshops. According to these definitions, we notice the duality between event and activity. Any activity is *marked* upon its beginning and end (which is the beginning of another activity), by an event. Therefore, any event marks the beginning of an activity (which can also have a zero duration).

When, in a model, we often find sequences of similar events or activities for a type of object, we may define what we call a *process*. The process is the finite succession of states of an object, i.e. the succession made up of one or several activities referring to that object. The relationship between the process, events and activities may be represented in a very simple way, through the scheme in Fig. 5.9.

The previously presented terminology is meaningful not only for establishing the scheduling model itself (through mathematical presentation), but especially for correctly using simulation languages and for programming simulation on basis of the logics of state change.

The description of the instantaneous state (through instantaneous models) has been presented up to this phase. Subsequently, we must analyse the methods for describing the dynamics of states, i.e. the state change mechanism (through

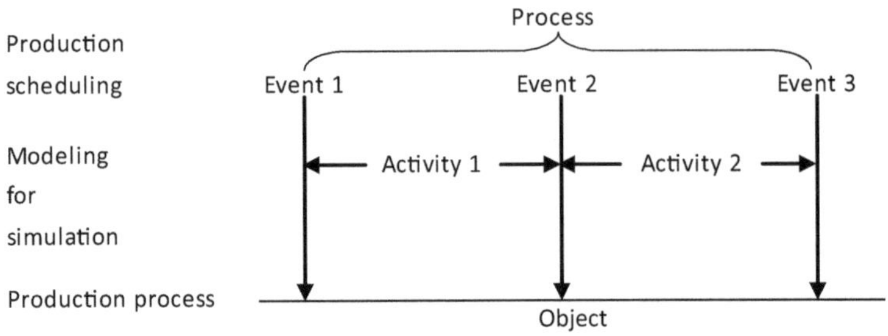

Fig. 5.9 The relationship between the process, events and activities

dynamic models). To this purpose, for each event, we must define the activities undertaken by the various objects *issued* by such event (at the end of the previous activity). *Precedence restrictions* between various activities are thus defined. *Trajectories*, i.e. the sequences of activities undertaken by the objects, must meet these restrictions, which—therefore—must determine a multitude of possible *transitions* between the states of the system.

The characteristics of dynamic models (the *logics* of state dynamics) are the following: the parallelism of activities and the use of synchronisation elements (various activities may occur at the same time, that is in parallel, but an activity can only start when all the objects it refers to are free); non-determinism, as some state changes can only be done by adding decision rules into the model.

For automatic production systems, the state change mechanism is of two types: one is determined by technological restrictions (e.g.: types and dimensions of part sets, tool ranges, processing tolerances etc.), which cannot be changed in the model and which are related to *operational rules*; the other one is not known a priori and is determined by *management* and *steering rules*. Within this model, the *choice* shall determine the performance of the system (such as productivity), through a better control of the production flow.

Operational rules limit the multitude of possible transitions between states and require the definition of another precedence chart between activities. Management and steering rules allow to choose the transition to make at a certain moment and define the *trajectories* of objects.

The various types of models may be obtained according to the model opening the state change mechanism (logics): networks with waiting wires, potential charts with charges, diodes, PERT charts etc.

The diversity of the simulation models for planning and scheduling, in their concrete form of presentation is, obviously, determined by the particulars of the apparition as well.

Production simulation consists in reproducing, step by step, event by event, the evolution of the system state in time, as determined by the logic (mechanism) of state change, using the system model (i.e. a mathematical representation of the relations between the original/object system). Therefore, the real system is replaced by a mathematical representation reproducing the original with a certain approximation. For this reason, the state change logic must be described by algorithms or procedures, as developed and complex as required for a *good* representation of real operation. In this context, the attribute of *good* refers to the original model approximation, assessed on an isomorphic basis, as the effect obtained by simulation, considering that the model leads, by simulation, to a result (an *assessment*, a *conclusion*, a decision), which satisfies us, according to the evolution of the original, in terms of a certain performance index. This *suppleness* in description (representation) allows us to model the system with the degree of details (approximation) required within the issue to be solved, with no *excesses* resulting in useless expenses, in terms of materials and time. Therefore, *an evolutional and structured approximation* of modelling within the various study phases may be conceived.

There are various forms of logical description of state change, as *things are seen*. Thus, according to G. Bel, from the point of view of our description of the original system—through the events occurred, through the activities to be taken or the processes encountered—we may use three different approximations, which we shall briefly present in the following.

We May Have

- *the approximation by events*. This is the basic approximation, the most popular and the most frequently used. We must remember that: the analysis of the system, accomplished according to its way of operation, allows us to record the various types of events (state changes) which may occur during the *life* of the system; it is modelled under a logical algorithm form, according to the state change corresponding to these types of events, so that, in case of occurrence of fortuitous events (circumstances depending on the state) we may clearly separate the *conditions* on the state of the system (at the moment of the event), from the corresponding *state changes*. For this modelling, we may use a graphical representation called *event chart*. After this phase of modelling, the study of the dynamic compartment of the system consists in the chronological execution of the state change mechanism, associating the occurrence date to each event. The most frequently used method, in this type of modelling, for time increase, is *the method of the next event*. Because occurrence times of fortuitous events are accessible and because it is known that no change state shall occur outside such events, time advance is made by jumping from an event date to the date of the next event. Therefore, event dates are ordered in a *timeline*. This order shall be, eventually, re-established after each apparition and processing of an event. Timelines are handled and maintained by means of a group of programmes and data structures, named *synchronisation nucleus*, included in the simulation programme;
- *the approximation by activities*. Within this approximation, dual to the previous one, we use system analysis for recording, not the events, but the various types of activities which may be encountered in the operation of the system. State change modelling is made specifying the conditions of the system state for each of the different cases of activities. In order to accomplish this model, we may resort to the representation through *activity cycles*, similar to representation through

PERT charts. The procedure used herein for time advance consists in using a clock and a time pace, through which we make time increase. For every time increase, we examine whether the conditions for beginning or ending an activity are met. If all the prerequisites are met, the state change determined by this activity is not done. Examining the multitude of all the activities for each time increase by a pace, we shall be sure that all possibilities are investigated and, thus, that all interactions are considered. There is a combined approximation of the production system (activity-event), named the *three-phase method*, but it is, however, more laborious;

– *the approximation by processes*. In this approximation, frequently found in the simulation languages most used nowadays for scheduling automated production, instead of defining the logic (mechanism) of state change related to each event or each beginning of activity, this logic is separately opened for certain sequences of predetermined event or "processes", through the combination events-activities-processes (Fig. 5.10).

Of course, the sequences (processes) which are reproduced many times in various moments for various objects are chosen. For instance, the sequence of events corresponding to the displacement of an object in a waiting wire of a service station (workshop) may be represented through a process, because – for this object—starting from the event of arrival in the waiting wire, the change logic shall always be the same for the entire succession of events, up to the event *end of service in station*.

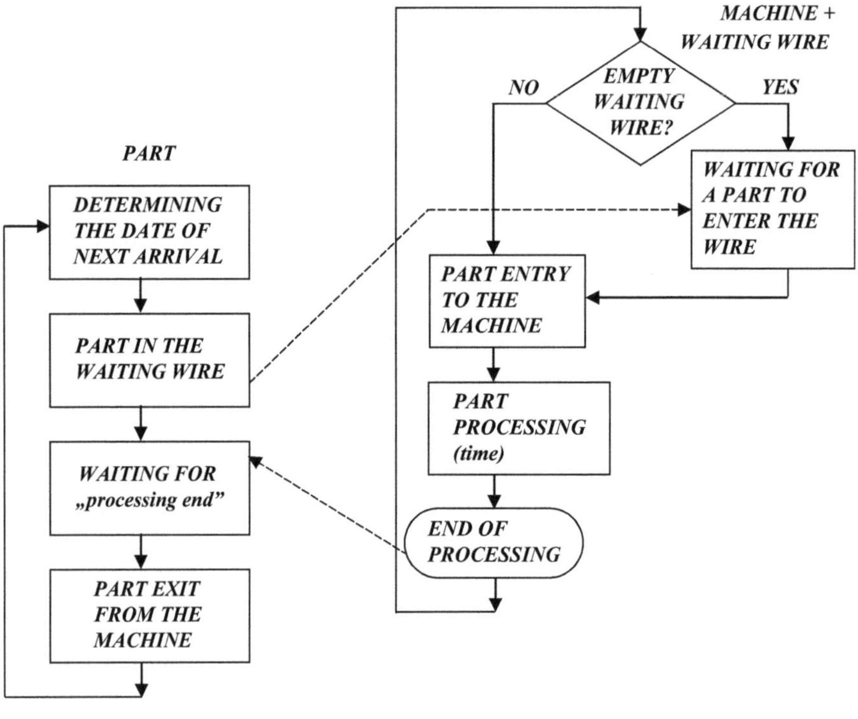

Fig. 5.10 The graphical representation of the machine+waiting wire process

Modelling by process requires, in the first time, the definition of the processes encountered in a system. For each of these processes we must then describe the logic of the state change associated to this succession of events, from the process incoming event to the process outgoing event. Conflicts or synchronisation between processes are considered by using a rule of the type *wait until another event outer to the process*. Thus, each process may be interrupted, may have subordinated sub-processes, may be *preserved*, may be determined to wait for other processes until certain conditions are met etc. Fig. 5.10 presents, as an example, a possible description for two processes: $car + waiting\ wire$ and *part*. On the scheme, we marked by dashed lines the interaction between the two processes, given by the instruction *wait until*, which allows for the synchronisation of the two processes, by means of messages. The full description of system operation is made by specifying the various interactions between processes. For production systems, part-type processes generally interact with all the others, which is seen in the trajectories (displacements) of parts along the system. Modelling is then made in a fully natural way, simply describing the *displacement* of parts. Within their process of processing, from a machine to another one, in management, from a record method to another, within the decisional process, from a control point to another etc. Thus, we get models whose (formal) structure is close enough to the (physical) structure of the object system.

Currently, research in the field of production system modelling are oriented towards the inclusion of human relations, representing the connections with the *intelligent* part of the system (steering rules, operative management, management and scheduling rules). As for the production simulation model (by event, by activities, through the three-phase method, by processes etc.), it is made depending on the amplitude of the system, the existing means of simulation (equipment systems and programming systems), the expenses involved by simulation and the informational effects of the use of the modelling time. For two of the previously described models, these effects are presented in Fig. 5.11:

Assessment criterion	Model type	
	by events	by process
- results of the simulation	*detailed*	*average*
- implementation of the simulation	*slow*	*quick*
- performance of the simulation	*slow*	*quick*
- use of simulation programmes	*easy*	*complicated*

Fig. 5.11 Criteria—effects correlation

Irrespective of the model used, all the operations required for performing the simulation are made sequentially and, therefore, they may be opened with a classical programming language (as an algorithm and at the user's level). In particular, this is valid for the numerous simulations of scheduling in workshops, performed electronically. In fact, this is true for most simulations specialised for a production system and a given issue.

Simulation languages may be placed between *highly* specialised oriented simulation programmes and very general programming languages. They are obtained because, during the simulation process, a wide range of concepts and operations required for the accomplishment of any simulation (common to all particular applications) may be derived, which may be programmed once and for all and then directly used for programming a new case. Examples of common operations: the maintenance of a time marking (generating) system (a *clock*), the management of the event timeline, the generation of aleatory numbers, time *handling* etc. Starting from the seventh decade, a certain number of languages specially adapted for simulation through events have begun being developed pursuant to the high number of applications performed. Through reiteration in various applications, these languages were gradually improved, enforced and extended, until including a wide range of simulation applications (through the same language). There was thus obtained what we nowadays call simulation languages, which may be classified according to the type of approximation through production simulation models which they use or whose application is more advantageous.

Production simulation may be based on a model through the hierarchized approximation of production planning in the case of an industrial company. The end products delivered to beneficiaries are called *items* and shall be marked with the index k (k = 1, 2, … K). Planning is made for a horizon T, long enough to consider the possible seasonality of the demand for the products (items) concerned.

Within each company, production planning consists in dividing the production, which the company must achieve within a horizon T (also named *plan charge*, which, more often, refers to a period of 1 year), by various time intervals (specific to technological cycles) and beneficiaries (depending on the demands in contracts).

Then, the horizon T is divided into t periods, (t = 1, 2, … T), and, for each of the periods, we must determine the Z_{kt} amount to be manufactured for the k item so as to meet the requirements of $\overline{d}_{kt}$ beneficiaries (known from the contracts), considering the limits regarding production capacities and other available means. Moreover, this production must be made by minimising global production costs (Fig. 5.12).

Thus, the production planning issue in an industrial company may be formally represented through the following global model:

$$\min\left[\sum_{k=1}^{K} 1\sum_{t=1}^{T}\left(c_{kt}Z_{kt}h_{kt}\overline{S}_{kt}\right)+\sum_{t=1}^{T}\left(r_tB_t+s_tS_t\right)\right] \tag{5.37}$$

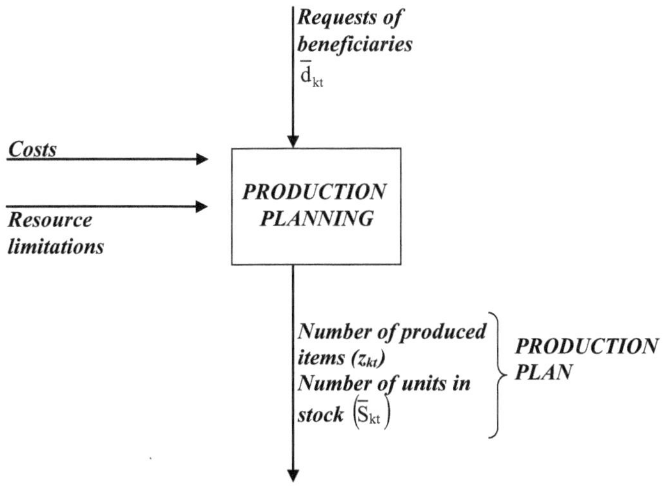

Fig. 5.12 The graphical representation of the minimisation of production costs

$$\overline{s}_{kt-1} + Z - \overline{s}_{kt} = \overline{d}_{re} \quad k = 1, 2, \ldots T \tag{5.38}$$

$$k = 1, \ m_k Z_{kt} \langle S_t + R_t, \quad t = 1, 2, \ldots T \tag{5.39}$$

$$R_t \leq (rm)_t, \quad t = 1, 2, \ldots T \tag{5.40}$$

$$S_t \leq (sm)_t, \quad t = 1, 2, \ldots T \tag{5.41}$$

$$Z_{kt}, \ \overline{s}_{kt} \geq 0, \quad k = 1, 2, \ldots T \tag{5.42}$$

$$R_t, \ S_T \geq 0, \quad t = 1, 2, \ldots T \tag{5.43}$$

The decision variables are: Z_{kt}—the number of k items to be manufactured during the period t; $\overline{s}_{kt}$-the number of k items in stock at the end of the period t; R_t, S_t-the duration of regular manufacture and, respectively, the additional duration, both in hours, during the period t.

The parameters of the model are: c_{kt}—production cost by k item (product) unit in the period t (no labour); h_{kt}—the cost of storage of a k item unit during the period t; $r_t s_t$—labour (lei/h) for the rhythmical (normal) and, respectively, additional manufacture during the period t; $(rm)_t$, $(sm)_t$,—maximum available values in normal hours and, respectively, in additional hours during the period t; m_k—the inverse value of the penalties for the accomplishment of work productivity for item k and d—demands from beneficiaries for the k item during the period t.

Restriction (5.38) represents the S state equation of the model. Relations (5.39, 5.40, 5.41) and (5.43) introduce limitations on the available means. The relations (5.42) and (5.38) introduce the requirements that demands (orders) should always be satisfied (no delay) and (5.37) is the goal function.

Generally, the implementation of this type of issue is "dynamic", as it uses the notion of gliding horizon, which allows for the consideration of data fluctuation. We shall finally notice that effectively applied decisions only refer to the amounts Z_{kt} (k = 1, 2, ... K) associated to the first period (t = 1) of the considered T horizon.

The high number of variables and restrictions (due, among other factors, to the variety of items, i.e. products) restrains the possibilities to use the model (5.37), (5.38), ... (5.43). Moreover, this modelling implies knowledge of the orders (including requests for exportation) referring to items, for all the periods of the horizon. The effect of the errors in the prediction of detailed orders, especially in the case of long terms, render extremely difficult the application of the model (5.37), ... (5.43).

All these considerations made some authors abandon the model (5.37), ... (5.43), which accomplishes a *global approximation* of production, preferring a *hierarchised approximation.*

In order to accomplish this modelling, a two-layered structure is used. This structure is obtained by regrouping into the same type (marked as *i*) the multitude of items with common manufacture characteristics, such as: the same production and storage cost; the same penalties for not meeting the require productivity; similar seasonal demands (requests) etc. We shall mark by *K(i)* the multitude of items *k* belonging to type *i*. Then, the sum $\sum_{i=1}^{1} K(i)$ represents the multitude of all items.

Planning is made in two steps, as follows:

Planning at a higher level (called aggregate level). In this step, only *high* aggregates, i.e. those referring to types *i* are considered and we determine:

X_a which represents the number of *i* product units during the period *t*;

S_a—the number of *i* units in stock at the end of the period *t* (what we shall name *aggregate stock*), so as to meet the demand regarding types (marked as D_{it}), considering the company's available means. The goal of this planning level is still the minimisation of production costs (Fig. 5.13).

The problem to be solved at this level is, hence, analog to the global issue (5.38), ... (5.43), with the formal difference that *k* items are replaced by *i* types. We obtain the following *aggregate model*:

$$\min\left[\sum_{i=1}^{r}\sum_{i=1}^{i}(C_aX_a + h_aS_a) + \sum_{i=1}^{r}(r_tR_t + s_tS_t)\right] \tag{5.44}$$

$$S_{t\text{-}1} + N_a - S_a = D_a, \quad i = 1,2, \ldots I, \ t = 1,2, \ldots T \tag{5.45}$$

$$\sum_{i=1}^{t} m_aX_a \le S_t + R_t, \quad t = 1,2, \ldots T \tag{5.46}$$

$$R_t \le (rm)_t, \ t = 1,2, \ldots T \tag{5.47}$$

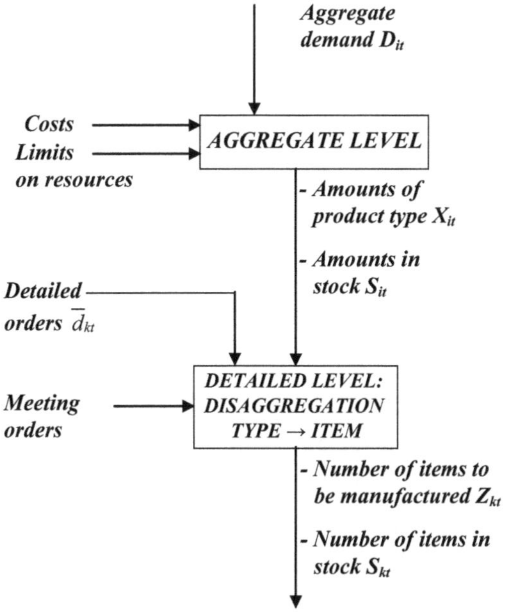

Fig. 5.13 The minimisation of production costs at an aggregate level

$$S_t \leq (sm)_t, \quad t = 1, 2, \ldots T \tag{5.48}$$

$$X_a, S_a \geq 0, \; i = 1, 2, \ldots I, \; t = 1, 2, \ldots T \tag{5.49}$$

$$R_t, S_t \geq 0, \; t = 1, 2, \ldots T \tag{5.50}$$

Planning at a lower level, called "detailed level" (Fig. 5.13). The decision variables of this level are Z_{kt} and s_{kt}. In fact, this level marks the disaggregation of the upper level, i.e. the production X_{it} is allocated between the items representing these types:

$$\sum_{k \in K(t)} Z_{kt} = X_a, \; t = 1, 2, \ldots T, \; i = 1, 2, \ldots I \tag{5.51}$$

$$\sum_{k \in K(t)} s_{kt} = S_a, \; t = 1, 2, \ldots I \tag{5.52}$$

We must notice that this model introduces effective demand and the effective stock, marked as D_a and S_a, respectively, according to formula (5.45) and formula (5.49), for types i, not the request and aggregate real stock, marked as $\overline{D}_a$ and $\overline{S}_a$.

At this detailed level the following formulae are also introduced:

$$s_{kt-1} + Z_{kt} - s_{kt} = d_{kt},\ k = 1, 2, \ldots K,\ t = 1, 2, \ldots T \quad (5.53)$$

$$Z_{kt}, s_{kt} \geq 0,\ k = 1, 2, \ldots K,\ t = 1, 2, \ldots T \quad (5.54)$$

Restrictions (5.51) and (5.52) are the so-called *disaggregation coherence restrictions*. The detailed plan resulting from the disaggregation is achievable if the restrictions (5.53) and (5.54) are met. This demonstrates the equivalence between formulae (5.53) and (5.54) and:

$$\sum_{i=1}^{t} Z_{k1} \geq \max\left(0, \sum_{i=1}^{t} \overline{d}_{k1} - \overline{s}_{t0}\right), \quad (5.55)$$
$$k = 1, 2, \ldots K\ t = 1, 2, \ldots T$$

where $\overline{s}_{t0}$ represents the initial stock of the real item *k*.

Formula (5.55) is a necessary and sufficient condition for the achievability of the detailed plan.

Therefore, this hierarchised approximation decomposes a complex (complicated!) issue into sub-issues with a simpler solution, but the global coherence of this approximation should always be considered and observed. Thus, the decisions made in every step must be consistent, as these decision must not generate non-achievability during the following periods.

5.8 Expert Systems Used in Industrial Production Models

In the conditions of computing the human society, the operational management activities can be improved by using artificial intelligence. Therefore, an expert system is proposed, for the metallurgical industry, for the casting activity for parts necessary in mining industry.

The efficient operation of the integral production systems is based on artificial reasoning, as condition for simulating the human reasoning and supplying the expert's essential role in an actual domain. The expert system represents a major component of *artificial intelligence*, by means of which the knowledge of some experts in that domain are stored and, by means of a declarative approach, can be then dynamically exploited by an artificial mechanism, simulator of natural rationing triggered at the level of the human brain. The phrase *expert system* generally evokes the new techniques of management in various activity domains and which are currently assimilated through the notion "*contents of a database management*".

The notion of "expert system" refers to a software that uses all knowledge specific to the various activity domains during the process of elaborating a resolution for each problem that may intervene within a well defined domain. Therefore, the expert system *Aims at gathering the experience and rationing of a human expert for replacing it*. This accumulation represents the formation foundation of the knowledge base, which is one of the basic components of these systems (Benchimol, Levine & Pomerol, 1990).

The expert system is an intelligent system based on the symbolic representation of knowing, implemented on a hardware structure specific to the application, which processes a lot of knowledge for solving special issues about activities that are difficult to examine.

Regardless of the definition of the expert system, there are four features which classifies a software as expert system. It works at the expert level of competence; it uses an inference mechanism for accomplishing deduction; the expertise performed is based on knowledge specially gained; programming such systems involves the presentation of the knowledge of some experts in the domain, this knowledge could be kept in the database for future use.

The architecture of any expert system must contain at least three main modules, which determine the so-called *essential system*, in Fig. 5.14, an expert system is represented, adapted to the necessities connected to the operational management.

The main modules of the expert system are:

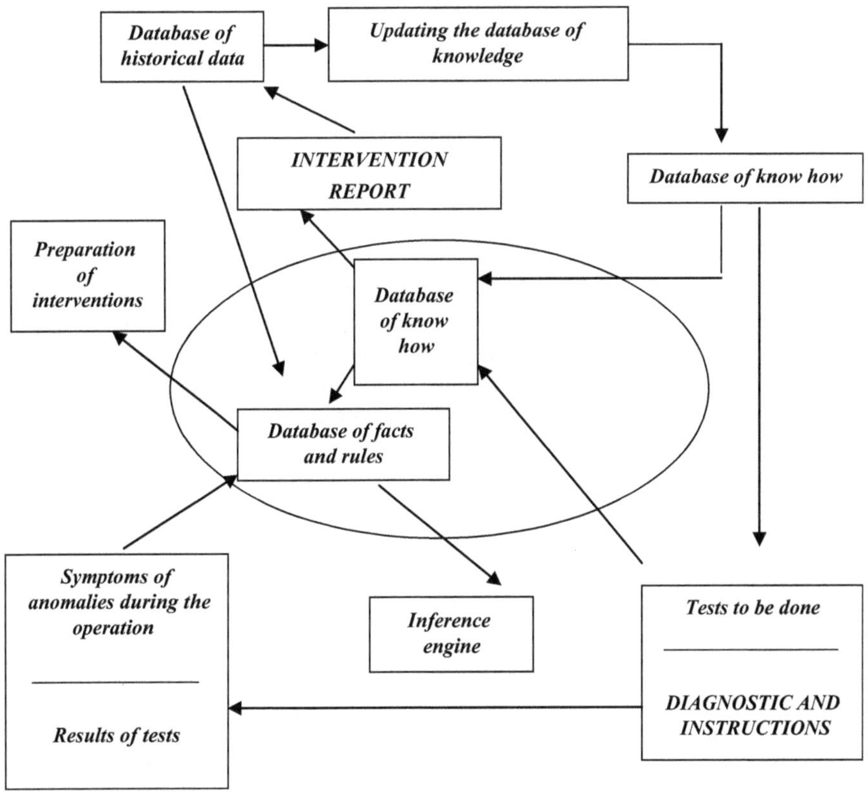

Fig. 5.14 The schematic representation of an expert system for the operational management

- *the knowledge database*—represents the component which stores the system's permanent specialised knowledge, provided by the expert in that respective domain. The knowledge database is formed by the *database of facts* and *the database of rules*, integrating the knowledge related to solving a problem in a given domain, the knowledge consisting of facts (assembly of data related to the problem) and rules (laws, methods and elements of rationing applicable to facts) treated by means of an engine of inferences with the aim to accomplish an objective requested through the problem dealt with;
- *the knowledge purchase module* allows the formation of a system's knowledge database. Usually, the knowledge specific to the domain is taken over from human experts by means of a specialist in the engineering of knowing. Another modality of getting knowledge specific to the domain is to automatically generate this knowledge using various methods of learning;
- *the database of rules and the database of facts* are elementary components of the knowledge database. *The database of rules* is formed by the manifold of relations representing the expert's knowledge and fulfils the following meanings: it consists of the rules which the connections between facts are specified by; the rules use initial (known) facts for deducting new facts based on inductive and deductive processes (in the situation where the rules may provide the direction and control of the manner which other rules are applied, the concept of *metarules* is highlighted). *The database of facts* consists of all facts which the creator of the expert system has enclosed in it or which are deducted during the rationing (of the inference process). The database of facts consists of an assembly of structures of complex data charged with a certain meaning, generically called "*facts*", related to a particular problem which a resolution is requested for through the system of a database of knowledge. The facts represent the assembly of the affirmative knowledge necessary to treat the domain dealt with;
- *the inference engine* is destined to exploiting the assembly of knowledge for solving the problems and it represents the actual processing element in the expert systems, which activates the corresponding knowledge in the knowledge database, starting from facts (problem input data), thusly forming rationing which lead to new fact called output facts. in conclusion, the interference engine is a software implementing algorithms of ratiocinations of *deductive* (directed by facts), *inductive* (directed by aims) and *mixed* (featured by the course of an inductive ratiocination, followed by a deductive ratiocination) types, but which does not depend on the knowledge database;
- *the inference mechanism* is the executive part of the expert system that uses the codified knowledge from the database of knowledge for creating inferences and drawing conclusions. It is a software which allows: exploiting the know-how database, coordinating the ratiocination for deducting new facts which would represent the new know-how database of the system, dynamically creating and explaining ratiocination, adopting resolutions on rules that must be triggered and on order where they are applied, procuring new knowledge. In fact, the inference mechanism is the core of an expert system which performs deductions in the

process of solving a problem, by covering and eventually changing and adjusting the elements from the know-how database.

Regardless of the ratiocination mode used, *the basic cycle* of an engine of interferences carries four stages: *the selection* extracts from the database of rules and from the one of facts all information characteristic to the subdomain of solving the problem; the *filter* consists in comparing the premises, the rules previously selected to the facts featuring the issue to be solved, for determining the submanifold of applicable rules and on must be chosen for being performed; *the execution itself* of a rule consists in adding one or more facts into the database. It is also possible that at this stage, external procedures would apply, respectively to have access to the database, to processors of tables or to questions asked to the user.

The occurrence of IT equipment and efficient software, which may be purchased for low prices, allow each manager of an industrial company to take into account the use of IT use, without incurring too big of a financial risk.

In practice, there are several modalities of choosing and using an expert system. Thusly, a first choice must follow the possibility of the expert system to cover the time gap "t" that exists between the duration necessary to getting an answer and the duration necessary to forming knowledge at the time when it is questioned.

The starting point for such a step was to know the main features of the casting technology, as first modality of getting familiar with the process itself of performing the operations necessary to the cast items in the finished form, for costs as low as possible and in the conditions of minimising the risks of there occurring damages.

Thusly, *casting represents the technological process of making parts for mining machines, by solidifying the molten material in the cavity of a mold.*

Compared to other technologies, casting represents the following advantages: the possibility to obtain the parts with complex configuration, with a shape as close as possible to the finished one; the small amount of processing addition; the use of machines of simple and cheap construction, reusing the waste of materials by melting, which have resulted during the technological process or partial recovery of the value of scraps, lower unitary costs of the cast parts than of those made by other procedures etc. between the disadvantages associated to this technological process, the most frequent are: high probabilities of obtaining parts with defects; probabilities of lower resistance compared to the wrought parts; the use of some considerable amounts of materials for obtaining the parts etc.

Making the shapes represents the printing operation of the foundry pattern in the formation mixture. After extracting it, the pattern remains, where the melted metal is poured in order to obtain the parts. This is the main operation in the technological process of obtaining the cast parts and decisively conditions their quality parameters. Making the shapes can be performed *manually* (in frames, in soil or by patterns) or *mechanised* (by throwing, by pressing with a membrane, by shaking and pressing, by blasting etc.).

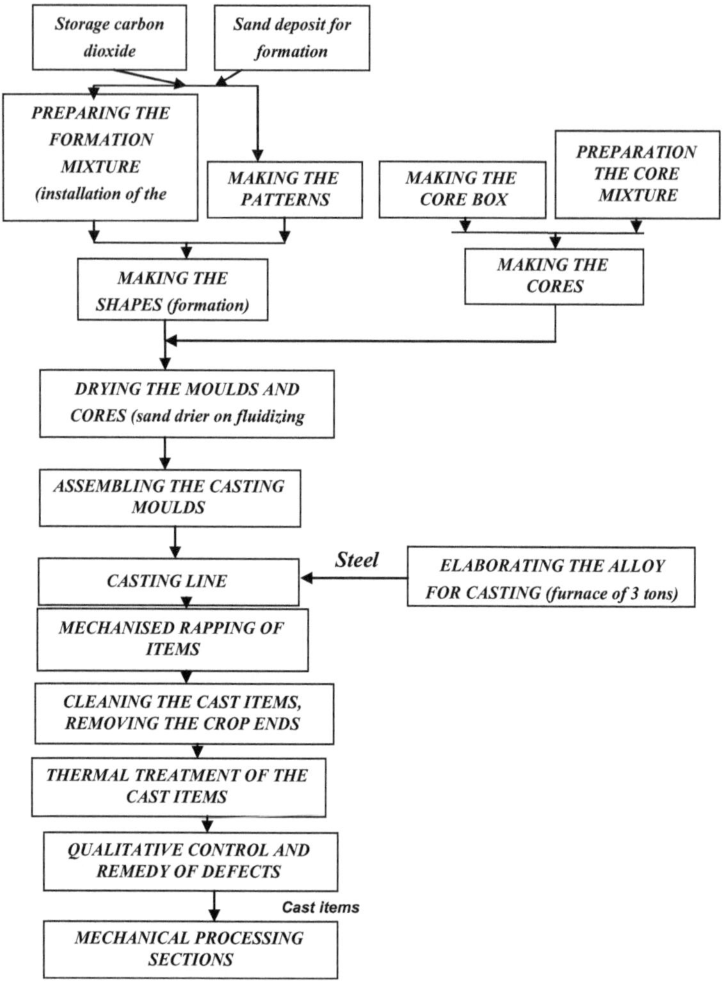

Fig. 5.15 The diagram of the technological process for obtaining the parts cast at a firm

At a firm, the classical method is used, that of manual formation in frames, featured by low costs related to the documentation, shaping materials and tools under the conditions of low accuracy and quality of the cast surfaces (Fig. 5.15).

Drying the shapes and cores represents the operation by means of which they are subject to heating in order to remove the water from the formation mixtures and to increase the bonding capacity of the binders. By drying, a considerable increase of the mechanical resistance of the formation mixture is performed, as well as the decrease of permeability and limitation of the gas amount which develop in the moulds during casting. At a firm, the sand dryer on fluidising bed is used for drying the cores, as well as for drying the moulds.

Assembling the moulds for casting consists in assembling the semi-moulds and cores into a single system. The cores and mould cavity are supported by means of stamps, and when these are missing or are too long, it is done by means of wood supports. After assembling the moulds and elaborating the alloys, then follows the *casting itself* into moulds. The melted metal is taken from the casting pot and directed into the cavity of the mould, by means of the *casting line.*

Rapping is the operation by means of which the item is taken out from the shaping frame and most of the formation mixture is removed from the outside and the core mixture from the inner cavities of the items. Rapping the mould is done after the metal has solidified and cooled down at a temperature where no more defect dangers can occur, by cooling the item more rapidly in the air.

Cleaning is the operation of removing the formation mixture adherent to the cast items. Usually, cleaning is done in several stages: *superficial cleaning* done for removing the waste heads; *preliminary cleaning* consisting in removing as much as possible the formation mixture from the item; *final cleaning* which is done after the thermal treatments applied and consists in removing all materials which are still on the surface of the item (formation mixture remained or oxides formed during the thermal treatment). Final mechanised cleaning is done at a firm by means of the *sandblast machines*, which direct an abrasive jet over the items which are to be subject to this process.

Removing the waste heads represents the operation of cleaning away the crop ends and the casting network from item A.

Removing burrs from the cast item implies the cleaning of the excess of material which appears on the plane of shape saturation.

Thermal treatments are applied to the cast items, with the following aims: removing the internal strains occurred when casting; relieving the processing by chip removal; improving some mechanical properties when no other thermal treatments are performed anymore or when the structure is to be prepared for obtaining some better properties for future thermal treatments.

The probability of there occurring defects in foundry is higher than in other activity sectors, reason for which the qualitative control must be run more intensely. Taking into account all of these, qualitative control in foundries is of two types: *preliminary control* applied on materials used and operations before casting the item, in order to eliminate the possibilities of defects to occur, respectively the *final control*, which is done on the cast item and must be performed in two stages. During the last stage, the item is monitored, starting from rapping and going through all other operations, in order to find out potential defects and for adopting as quickly as possible the adequate measures. During the second stage, the control of the items is done, after all operations for obtaining the gross cast item have finished, in order to retain those cast items which do not correspond to mechanical processing, respectively, to future use.

Taking into account all of the above, an *expert system is elaborated below for managing the casting technological process for metals at a firm*

Frame-software preceding the elaboration of the expert system for managing the technological process of casting the metals at a firm.

I. Stating the components which will form the expert system base of rules and base of facts.

Step 1. Defining the arguments that will be used by the predicates of the expert system and namely: the type of the date used by the system from the data list will define economical categories, such as: existence (is), attributions (has), making the pattern (is_in), preparation of the moulding compound (is_on), moulding sand deposit (is_by), costs (cost) and needs (needs).

Step 2. Defining the predicates, meaning the calculation rules and questions taking into account the definitions from step 1.

Step 3. Stating the standards to fulfil for the operation of the base of rules and base of facts for the expert system. These standards can be schematically represented in the following logical diagram (Fig. 5.16):

Question 1: Is the preparation of the moulding compound unsatisfactory?
It displays: Is x unsatisfactory?
Question 2: Is it in the moulding sand deposit?
It displays: Is x in the moulding sand deposit?
Question 3: Is the pattern made?
It displays: Is x made?
Question 4: Is the pattern good?
It displays: Is x good?
Question 5: Is the cost greater than 100?

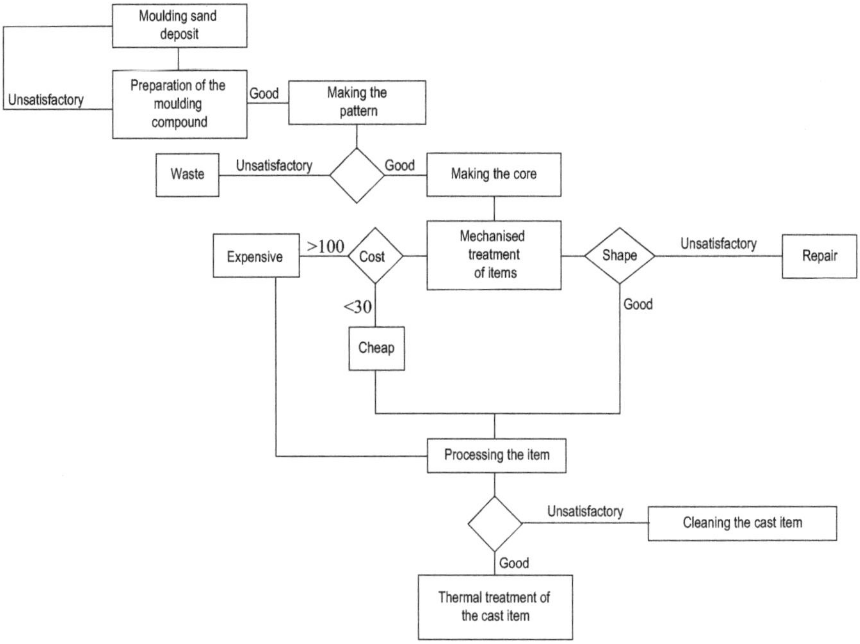

Fig. 5.16 Logical diagram

It displays: Is the cost x greater than 100?
Question 6: Is the cost lower than 30?
It displays: Is the cost x lower than 30?
Question 7: Must it be repaired?
It displays: Must x be repaired?
Question 8: Is x treated mechanised?
It displays: Is x treated mechanised?
Question 9: Is x subject to thermal treatment?
It displays: Is x subject to thermal treatment?
Question 10: Is it at the melting limit?
It displays: Is x at the melting limit?
Question 11: Is it well processed?
It displays: Is x good for processing?

II. Stating the components of the inference motor and user interface.

Step 1. Defining the arguments that will be used by the predicate of the expert system and namely: using entirely the files from the database (of facts).

Step 2. Defining the predicates, meaning the rules according to which the expert system inference motor works, taking into account the definitions from step 1 and namely: defining the process (proc_user), triggering the technological process (start_exp), reading the characters defining the technological process (read_char), defining the interference (interference), complying with the rules of the technological process (process_rule), stating whether the rules of the process are or are not complied with (getresponse), validating the received response (validresponse), fulfilling the first stage of the process (get_first), deleting the data (delete), verifying the response (check_ans), making the base of facts (add_fact), verifying the facts (check_fact), analysing the process (process_why), displayed rule (display_rule), clearing the base of facts (clear_facts), performing the iterative process for checking the fulfilment of all stages of the technological process of making the finished product (moulded item) (repeat), converting the results obtained from checking the stages of the technological process into data (convert) that will be used at the next stage regarding the analysis of the degree of fulfilling the standards featuring the technological process.

Step 3. Stating the standards to fulfil for the operation of the inference engine of the expert system and presenting them in a logical diagram.

start_exp:
Displaying the text "Expert system" in a user window
It displays: "i-init, a-add facts"
nl—predicate returning true and which has as effect the transition to a new line
It displays: "q-quit, r-run", nl
It displays: "Enter your option: (i/a/q/r)"
It reads the entered character
If the character entered is q then the process ends.
If the character entered is i
It displays: "Does it delete all facts?"

It reads the character and if it is y, it deletes all facts.
If the character entered is a
It displays: "Enter a fact:"
It reads S
It converts S into T, it adds T to the base of facts.
If the character entered is r
It displays: "What is your query?"
It reads the question
It converts the query into Term.

Clearing the base of facts
Adding a fact T or, if not, adding the clause
It displays: "The fact already exists", nl

It converts S into T:
It opens the file "convt.dat" for writing
It displays S, it closes the destination file
It opens the file "convt.dat" for reading
It reads the destination file
It closes the destination file, it reads from the keyboard.

Process (Question):

Interference
It displays: "Was your query verified with probability?"

Process (Question):

It displays: "Your query cannot be verified"

Interference:
It verifies whether the fact complies with the rules of the technological process
Interference:

It verifies whether the fact complies with the rules of the technological process
If yes, it is added to base of facts, if not, it is deleted
Complying with the rules of the technological process
If the first stage is fulfilled
Interference

Response R:

It reads Ask
It compares Ask to Rep
R=Rep

Anonymous response:

It displays: "Please try another response"
Response R

Verifying the response
Verifying the action:

It displays: "The action used is Fact"

Verifying the action:

Question
Reception of the response
Verifying the response

If the response is Y, the action is added into the base of facts
Verifying the response

Analysing the process
Verifying the action

Analysing the process
Analysing the process end-to-end

Analysing the end process
Rule displayed peak

Rule displayed peak:

It displays: "Analysing the process:"

It adds to the base of facts
Fulfilling the first stage of the process (peak)
Deletion end-to-end
It deletes the sign end-to-end
It deletes the last sign (end)
Repetition

Repetition

The expert system for improving the operational management related to the cast items is especially destined to assisting the exploitation and maintenance personnel when diagnosing the complex defects which may occur during the course of this process and for the efficiency of the technical measures that must be taken after the occurrence of those respective disfunctionalities. This system has the advantage of exploiting the memory of the past events and the experience of more experts whom participated at founding the system's database of know how, without comprising them into an expert system, such knowledge cannot be transmitted to those who ensure the use of the system forward.

The complex mutations that occur in the current industrial context have determined companies to revolutionise their strategies, to search permanent innovation for keeping and/or winning some new market segments. All these occur during a period of *"explosion"* of the IT systems, highlighting the need of integrating all company's activities by means of the computer. As *strategic option* in the domain of operational management, *computing the activity by using the expert systems* represents a pragmatic modality of improvement, which must be explored thenceforth at a firm, due to some incontestable advantages such as: *performance*—the expert systems do not lose their knowledge as time passes by, being capable of continuously working; *the possibility of being multiplied*—many copies of an expert system may be easily done, while creating new human experts represents a long and expensive process; *efficiency*—implies low costs compared to performing the expertises by the human specialists; *consistency*—similar actions are processed and treated in the same manner; *objectivity*—the system is not accessible as opposed to human experts whom can be subjective; *documentation*—an expert system may provide a permanent documentation of the decision process; high *working speed* etc.

References

Arrow KJ (1989) Time series analysis of interindustry demands. North-Holland, Amsterdam
Askin RM, Standridge CR (1993) Modeling and analysis of manufacturing systems, 1st edn. John Wiley, New York
Barnett H (1994) Specific industry output projections. Princeton University Press, Princeton
Benchimol G (1990) Expert systems in enterprise. Edition Hermes, Paris
Breton B (1999) Systemes experts en gestione. Les Editions D'organisation, Paris
Hood WC (1983) Studies in econometric method. John Wiley, New York
Klein LR (1995) Econometrics models in United States. North-Holland, Amsterdam
Koopmans TC (2001) Statistical inference in dynamic economic models. John Wiley, New York
Lesca N (1996) Gestion de l'information. LITEC, Paris
Middelhoek AJ (2002) Tests of the marginal stability of input-output coefficients in applications of input-output analysis. North-Holland, Amsterdam
Schatteles T (1971) Metode econometrice moderne. Ed. Ştiinţifică, Bucureşti
Stone R (2006) Mathematics in the social sciences and other essays. Chapman and Hall Ltd, London

Chapter 6
Use of Production Functions in Econometrics

6.1 Creation and Motivation of Production Functions

Highlighting the connection between factors and the results of production is one of the difficult problems of econometrics. Although the input-output type models highlight many of the structural characteristics of the relation between factors and the results of production, they are serious reasons as to the long-term veracity of such connections, if the records were done once. Because the usual input-output models do not allow substitutability between the production processes, it is only assumed that a product made in a process is as a vector with invariant elements, which excludes any possibility of substitution between factors However, in reality, such replacements are possible and occur, both between raw materials and matters fully consumed to make the new product, and between its primary factors, understanding that they are those which are in their material form do not come into the composition of the new product and are not lost in the technological process (e.g.: fixed funds, labour force, land and other natural factors).

Partial substitutability between primary factors exists in reality and is reflected by a Cobb–Douglas (CD) type function with two independent variables:

$$Y = AM^{\alpha}F^{\beta}, \tag{6.1}$$

where:

Y is the national income;
M—the productive man-hours consumed;
F—fixed funds incurred in production.

In this context, we may conclude the following:

- the CD function has a sufficiently general form for the economic analysis, any other type of substitution function can be ultimately transformed into a CD function;

I.C. Dima, M. Man, *Modelling and Simulation in Management*, Contributions to Management Science, DOI 10.1007/978-3-319-16592-9_6

- if we represented the relation $Y = f(M, F)$ by a linear function, this would mean that by reducing one of the two factors to "0", production could continue, which would not make economic sense. In the CD case, cancelling one of the factors—for example F, cancels the very production process;
- the fact that, usually $\alpha + \beta = 1$ and $(\alpha, \beta) > 0$, it is a guarantee that a single factor cannot increase however much, because the efficiency is decreasing for the two factors and their substitutability is limited within the economic process.

There is no doubt that such a limitation excludes the technical progress, which is why it was necessary for the function to be improved and completed.

The purpose of such statistical functions is to evaluate the relative efficiency of the primary factors in the national economy and the possibility of substituting them.

In general form, such a function is noted as follows:

$$y = A\prod_{i=1}^{n} x_i^{\alpha_i}, \tag{6.2}$$

where:

y is an indicator of the production result;
x_i—the variable corresponding to the "i"th factor;
A, α_i—constants.

It may be said that the Cobb-Douglas function is a generic model of any simple manufacturing activity, in the sense that the limitations (restrictions) of some activities have not been taken into account.

Let us however analyse the Cobb-Douglas function characteristics, starting from its classic form of three variables. In this sense, "the result of production" will be noted with "Y" and will represent the national income, the total social product or the production of the enterprise, taking into account that the objective of the "M" research will be the wage-fund, the number of workers in the most desirable case, the productive man-hours provided, and "F" will be the fixed funds available or, possibly, an adjusted set of investments. In this context, "M" could be the overall increase of the wage-fund, and "Y" the increase of the national income.

The statistical relation between these variables is expressed as follows:

$$Y = AM^{\alpha}F^{\beta}u, \tag{6.3}$$

where:

u is a random variable.

By logarithmation, we obtain:

$$\log Y = \log A + \alpha \log M + \beta \log F + \log u \tag{6.4}$$

equality, which serves to calculate the parameters “A”, “α”, “β” by the method of the least squares.

The parameters “α” and “β”, whose estimation based on the series of “Y”, “M” and “F”, are actually elasticities of the two factors taken into account. This means that during the period which the research refers to, the increase by averagely 1 % of the current wage-fund has determined an increase by α% in the result of the production activity. For the fixed funds, “β” has a similar interpretation.

The demonstration can be easily done by means of the differential efficiency (partial derivative) of the two factors involved in the producing the national income. Thus, in absolute terms, differential growths of “M” and “F” cause the changes:

$$\frac{\partial Y}{\partial M} = \alpha A M^{(\alpha-1)} F^{\beta} \tag{6.5}$$

and

$$\frac{\partial Y}{\partial F} = \beta A M^{\alpha} F^{(\beta-1)} \tag{6.6}$$

concerning the value of “Y”.

The percentage expression of the relations (6.5) and (6.6) enables the calculation of the elasticity coefficients “α” and “β”:

$$\frac{\partial Y}{\partial M} \cdot \frac{M}{Y} = \frac{\alpha A M^{\alpha} \cdot F^{\beta}}{A M^{\alpha} \cdot F^{\beta}} = \alpha \tag{6.7}$$

$$\frac{\partial Y}{\partial F} \cdot \frac{F}{Y} = \frac{\beta A M^{\alpha} \cdot F^{\beta}}{A M^{\alpha} \cdot F^{\beta}} = \beta \tag{6.8}$$

Typically, the CD functions are calculated based on indices when it comes to complex categories, such as the national income, fixed funds, labour force, etc.

Between the elasticities “α” and “β” ($\alpha>0$ and $\beta>0$), there can normally be the following relation:

$$\alpha + \beta = 1. \tag{6.9}$$

Under normal circumstances, this would mean an increase of the production proportionally to the total increase of fixed funds and wage-fund, the proportion being given by the coefficient “A”.

When

$$\alpha + \beta < 1, \tag{6.10}$$

we have a decreasing efficiency of the sum of factors used. In other words, a simultaneous increase by 1 % of the volume used of the two factors will cause a smaller increase of the national income of less than 1 %.

In the case where:

$$\alpha + \beta > 1, \tag{6.11}$$

the situation is characterised by an increasing efficiency in the simultaneous increase of the factors.

In the actual situations concerning the development of national economy or of an enterprise when the conditions are very rarely "normal", because technical progress always intervenes, the increase of the labour productivity cannot be expressed permanently by an equality as $\alpha+\beta=1$ in a CD type model.

The total elasticity (sum of partial elasticities) of the primary factors in the Cobb-Douglas models can be expressed in a particular form. We start from the very realistic hypothesis that the simple change in the volume of a factor cannot change its function of efficiency and that a factor external thereof must intervene—the technical progress or an increase of labour productivity—in order to change it. Thus, this condition also occurs in the case of regular Cobb-Douglas functions, in the sense that if nothing changes on the "outside", then they are not allowed to change the values of "α" and "β" either and, consequently, nor the ratio between these elasticities. Thus, certain mathematical characteristics are assigned to the function, which in their turn have an economic interpretation. In this sense, the characteristic of the homogeneity of the production function will be here at the heart of researcher's concerns.

For the general case, be the function:

$$y = f(x_1, x_2, \ldots x_n) \tag{6.12}$$

Let us multiply the variables by a constant "K". If the function has such a structure, so that by multiplying the entire function with the same constant, the result is invariable, we say that the function is homogeneous of degree 0.

Meaning, if:

$$f(Kx_1, Kx_2, \ldots Kx_n) = f(x_1, x_2, \ldots x_n), \tag{6.13}$$

this means that

$$f(x_1, x_2, \ldots x_n) = K)\, f(x_1, x_2, \ldots x_n), \tag{6.14}$$

where $K=1$.

In such a case, the multiplication of the variables does not change the value of the function. Obviously, a *production function*, involving in opposition also the idea of *non-production* cannot have such a feature.

If, instead,

$$f(Kx_1, Kx_2, \ldots Kx_n) = K^r f(x_1, x_2, \ldots x_n), \tag{6.15}$$

then we have a homogenous function of degree "r" (r≠0), which means that multiplying the function with a "K" constant raised to the power of "r" is equivalent to the multiplication of each variable of the function by this constant.

Let us consider the case of the generalised production function:

$$y = f(x_1, x_2, \ldots, x_n) = ax_1^{\alpha_1} x_2^{\alpha_2} \ldots x_n^{\alpha_n} \tag{6.16}$$

If we multiply each variable by "K" and if the new relation is

$$K^r y = K^r(x_1, x_2, \ldots, x_n) = a(Kx_1)^{\alpha_1} \cdot (Kx_2)^{\alpha_2} \ldots (Kx_n)^{\alpha_n}, \tag{6.17}$$

because

$$K^r y = K^{(\alpha_1+\alpha_2+\ldots+\alpha_n)} \cdot a{x_1}^{\alpha_1} {x_2}^{\alpha_2} \ldots {x_n}^{\alpha_n}, \tag{6.18}$$

where

$$\alpha_1 + \alpha_2 + \ldots + \alpha_n = r = 1 \tag{6.19}$$

then this is a homogenous function of degree 1 also called linear homogeneous function. It is precisely the case of the Cobb-Douglas function with the sum of elasticities equal to 1. The value of the function multiplied by a constant is equal to the value of the function when each independent variable is multiplied by the same constant.

This undoubtedly means that the total elasticity of factors is equal to the unit. Precisely this hypothesis underlies the simple static production functions.

6.2 The Trend in Production Functions

The hypothesis of total elasticity is not always valid. In general, one can easily imagine a situation where we multiply the two factors of the Cobb-Douglas function by the same constant, for example, increasing each primary factor by 50 % and yet the value of the function to increase by 2. This means that a positive change has intervened in the efficiency of factors, which in mathematical terms means that a *neutral technical progress* has been registered. Thus, although the volume of differential efficiency of each factor changes positively, $\frac{\partial Y}{\partial M}$ respectively $\frac{\partial Y}{\partial F}$, the ratio $\frac{\partial M}{\partial F}$ remains invariable. This justifies the insertion of a trend factor into the function:

$$Y = A(t) \cdot (M \cdot F), \tag{6.20}$$

where:

A(t) is an indicator of the technical progress, if it has a constant rhythm and can be defined as:

$$A(t) = e^{\lambda t}, \tag{6.21}$$

where:

"λ" is the indicator of technical progress and shows by how many percentages "Y" grows over what is determined by the increase of the volume of "M" and "F".

For example, if "M" and "F" have increased by 10 % each, while "Y" has increased by 15 %, then $\lambda = 0.05$, and the function may be noted as:

$$Y = {x_1}^{\alpha_1} {x_2}^{\alpha_2} e^{0.05t} (x_1 + x_2 = 1) \tag{6.22}$$

in the case where each year a gain of the same order of the technical progress would be achieved. That is why a statistical estimate that is to have meaning must be take into account such a more generalised production function. Usually, the more general formula proposed by Tinbergen is applied.

$$Y(t) = B \cdot M^{\alpha}(t) \cdot F(t)^{(1-\alpha)} \cdot e^{\lambda t}, \tag{6.23}$$

where "B" is a constant representing the production/factors relation

$$\frac{Y}{M^{\alpha} \cdot F^{(1-\alpha)}} \tag{6.24}$$

at the initial time ($t=0$).

The estimation of the parameters of (6.22) type function is the main object, but independent from the technical features on which we focus in particular, it is interesting to see what considerations Robert Solow does on its veracity. In fact, the inclusion of the trend factor into the production function and a range of other technical innovations to develop some more complicated production functions are thanks to Solow.

Regarding the trend function, he shows that: "If the aggregate production function (6.22) is estimated by dynamic series for *developed countries*, "λ" is always around 0.015, and "α" is about 0.75. An important conclusion results from here, namely that the possibility to accelerate the economic growth through faster accumulation of the capital is extremely limited. This results from the fact that (6.22) involves:

$$\frac{1}{Y} \cdot \frac{dY}{dt} = \lambda + \alpha \frac{1}{M} \cdot \frac{dM}{dt} + (1 - \alpha) \frac{1}{F} \cdot \frac{dF}{dt}. \tag{6.25}$$

If we take into account the aforementioned numerical values and assume that the labour force increases by 1 % per year, and that the capital/production ratio is equal to 3, the production will increase by about 3 % per year if 10 % of the national income is invested. If the investment quota is doubled from 10 % to 20 %, then the growth rate remains slightly below 4 %, which seems to be a reward …".

There are some reserves that Solow's numbers can be accepted today for what he calls "developed countries".

On the contrary, we know that in the last decade, in some more developed countries, a λ=0.02–0.04 has been calculated, which considerably improves the numbers that indicate the result of accumulation. *Technically*, it is obvious that the size of "λ" and the ratio $\alpha/(1-t)$ are the main indicators, being determined for an efficient accumulation. This problem however has to do with the theory of economic growth.

The insertion of a *trend* variable is justified by means of a function of labour productivity deducted from the Cobb-Douglas function.

If we admit the restriction

$$\alpha + \beta = \alpha + (1 - \alpha) = 1 \tag{6.26}$$

then the function (1) will be transposed as follows:

$$Y = AM^{\alpha}F^{(1-,\alpha)} \tag{6.27}$$

If the labour productivity is noted by the ratio

$$\frac{Y}{M} = A\left(\frac{F}{M}\right)^{\alpha} \tag{6.28}$$

solving the system

$$\begin{cases} \sum \log\left(\frac{Y}{M}\right) = n\log A + \alpha \sum \log\left(\frac{F}{M}\right) \\ \sum \log\left(\frac{Y}{M}\right) \cdot \log\frac{F}{M} = \log A \sum \log\left(\frac{F}{M}\right) + \alpha \sum \log\left(\frac{F}{M}\right) \end{cases} \tag{6.29}$$

will enable us to calculate the parameters of the Cobb-Douglas function.

The study of the aforementioned production function highlights some deficiencies that result from the its very structure. Here, a Y/M ratio is expressed as a function of another F/M ratio, which means that a change in the labour productivity expressed by the Y/M ratio is regarded as the result of changing the ratio between fixed funds and the labour forces employed, which in its turn is one of the indicators of "technical endowment".

This is why additions to the existing formula are necessary, also including a variable on the technical progress, which is generally represented by an element of *trend*. In this case, the most common form for the case with two variables is that proposed by Solow

$$Y(t) = M^{\alpha}F^{\beta}e^{\lambda t} \tag{6.30}$$

or in logarithmic form

$$\ln Y(t) = \alpha \ln M + \beta \ln F + \lambda t \tag{6.31}$$

where:

t is the time;
λ—a parameter representing the speed of the technical progress.

In general form, this can be written:

$$Y = e^{\lambda t}\prod_{i=1}^{n} x_i^{\alpha_i} \tag{6.32}$$

The formula of labour productivity can be deduced from (30) and we get:

$$\frac{Y}{M} = e^{\lambda t}\left(\frac{F}{M}\right)^{\beta} \tag{6.33}$$

or

$$\ln\left(\frac{Y}{M}\right) = \lambda t + \beta \ln\left(\frac{F}{M}\right) \tag{6.34}$$

It is clear that in (6.32) or (6.33) an increase in labour productivity, even under the conditions of a constant F/M ratio could be interpreted as a result of the technical progress. Of course, an open problem remains, whether this technical progress comes from the improvement of the machinery and aggregates or it is rather the result of a better organisation, qualification, etc. It is a very important action to determine to what extent the endowment with fixed funds from different periods contributes to the technical progress. One answer to this complicated question was given by Solow in one of his papers on the production functions, but so far it has not led to conclusive results.

6.3 Techniques to Calculate Production Functions. Difficulties and Methods to Overcome Them

The study of calculation techniques takes into account the classical form with three variables of the production function, although, the generalised form is that which can be of both applicative and analytical importance. However, for this variant, usually there are insufficient data, while for the "classical" type functions, the data of any statistical yearbook are satisfactory and the economist thus has the option to undertake a number of studies. For these reasons, there occur are many technical calculation problems, due to some difficulties.

If we consider a simple production function:

$$y = Ax_1^{\alpha}\ x_2^{\beta}, \tag{6.35}$$

where:

y = national income or total product—in industry (indices)
x_1 = the manpower or the provided man-hours—in industry (indices)
x_2 = fixed funds or productive investments—in industry (indices)

then the values of "α" and "β" should be found, solving for logA, "α" and "β", the system:

$$\begin{cases} \sum \log y = N\log A + \alpha \sum \log x_1 + \beta \sum \log x_2 \\ \sum \log y \cdot \log x_1 = \log A \sum \log x_1 + \alpha \sum (\log x_1)^2 + \beta \sum \log x_1 \log x_2 \\ \sum \log y \cdot \log x_2 = \log A \sum \log x_2 + \alpha \sum \log x_1 \log x_2 + \beta \sum (\log x_2)^2 \end{cases} \tag{6.36}$$

So far, everything seems as simple as possible, only that the usual method of adjusting the functions by using the method of least squares involves certain difficulties which cannot be so overcome so simply.

As it results from a range of researches, it is not a matter of simple coincidence here, but of something much more serious, because the phenomenon is repeated many times, in many cases. The first time, the difficulties resulted from here have been discovered by Mendreshausen, who assigned them to collinearity or multicollinearity among the independent variables. Taking into account the high frequency at which this problem occurs in the case of calculating some CD functions, the multicollinearity should be analysed, which occurs when the relation between the independent variables is so close, so that it becomes impossible for us to explain the extent to which it influences the dependent variable.

Thus, if within a function

$$Y_1 = f(x_{1t}, x_{2t}) \tag{6.37}$$

we shall observe that there is such a relation between "x_{1t}" and "x_{2t}" which can be expressed for each moment "t" of the series by

$$x_{1t} = kx_{2t} \tag{6.38}$$

then we have the equality,

$$\begin{vmatrix} \sum_t x_{1t}^2 & \sum_t x_{1t} \cdot x_{2t} \\ \sum_t x_{1t} \cdot x_{2t} & \sum_t x_{2t}^2 \end{vmatrix} = \sum x_{2t}^2 \begin{vmatrix} k^2 & k \\ k & 1 \end{vmatrix} = |0| \tag{6.39}$$

The solution of overcoming such difficulties arises from the very characteristics of the function, where the focus is primarily on elasticities. It can be seen that there are indirect ways to obtain the elasticities "α" and "β". If for a 1 % increase in the variable "x_1", the value of "y" increases by "α" percentages, then for an increase by "Δx_1", we have:

$$\frac{\Delta y}{y} = \alpha \frac{\Delta x_1}{x_1}. \tag{6.40}$$

The same is for "β"; and the complete equation for the percentage increases will be:

$$\frac{\Delta y}{y} = \alpha \frac{\Delta x_1}{x_1} + \beta \frac{\Delta x_2}{x_2}, \tag{6.41}$$

for "Δy", "Δx_1", "Δx_2" approaching the limit.

For the dynamic series, the percentages can be considered in relation to time.

$$p = \alpha m + \beta k, \tag{6.42}$$

where:

$$p = \frac{dy}{dt} \cdot \frac{1}{y}; \; m = \frac{dx_1}{dt} \cdot \frac{1}{x_1}; \; k = \frac{dx_2}{dt} \cdot \frac{1}{x_2}. \tag{6.43}$$

For the variant $y = x_1^{\alpha} \cdot x_2^{\beta} \cdot e^{\lambda t}$, the following equation is considered:

$$p = \alpha m + \beta k + \lambda, \tag{6.44}$$

in which case, the optimal adjustment will be done normally with the method of least squares.

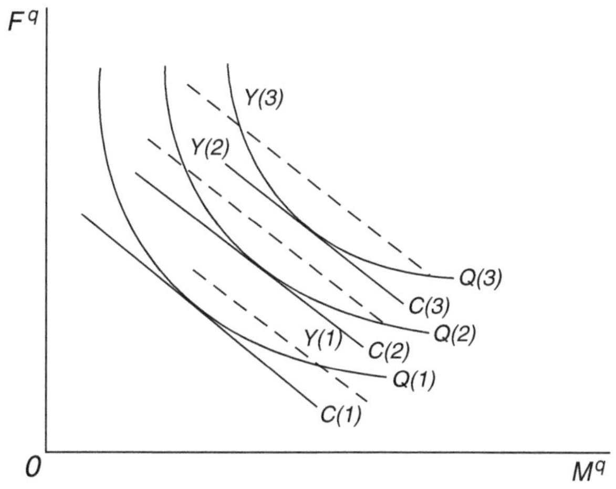

Fig. 6.1 Graphical representation of the factor-result relation

Apparently, the problem has been solved, however this variant also involves difficulties in some cases, but they are totally different.

The difficulties arise from the fact that the original data of the series do not reflect any real relation between them. It is worth studying the situation where statistical data reflect one of the possible relations between factors and the result, by virtue of the production function by which it is defined, which is however insufficient to draw conclusions on the values of the actual function parameters.

Now, we see that the data may not relate to anything Fig. 6.1 shows such a case.

The cost and transformation functions are interpreted as before. It happens here that the three production levels are achieved through a combination of factors which differs from the one determined by the situation where the slope of "C" is equal to the tangent of "Q". Theoretically, we can say that the production was uneconomical, although so many factors could have caused such an "inefficient" production. In this case, there may be many examples: natural disasters which led to the destruction or removal of a factor; the defence needs that may require saving a factor; long-term economic strategy which requires some manipulation of resources; bad management, which in some cases has entirely statistically unexplainable circumstances. Whatever the reason, whether justified or unjustified, the statistical data do not help us get too close to the actual form of the sought structure of the production functions.

All these possibilities must be known and understood if we want to also know the degree of trust we can give to econometric production functions.

6.4 Econometric Form of the Leontief Model

An equation from a Leontief system has an extremely appealing form for those who study the regression analysis:

$$y_i = (1 - a_{ii})x_i \sum_{i}^{j \neq i} a_{ij}x_j \;\; (i = 1, 2, \; \ldots\ldots n) \tag{6.45}$$

Thus, the sought "a_{ij}" coefficients can be obtained by linear regression from a series of "T" elements "y_i" and series of "T" elements "x_i" ($T > n$) and an econometric Leontief model can be successfully used for forecasts. But this is not possible first of all due to the identification difficulties. Because the relation depends on several equations, it is unlikely for something useful to result by direct regression. The problem of the degrees of freedom is the second major barrier in the way of "direct econometrics" of the Leontief models. It is known that the series of data on which evaluations must be done are to be of "n +1" elements, if the desired number of sought parameters is "n". This is a strictly mathematical condition, but we know it is good for the quality of acquired data, if the degrees of freedom are greater than 1. If we now consider that the most modest Leontief system itself has at least 25 equations, each having 25 coefficients, we observe it quite easily that the evaluations based on a series of 26–35 years are not conclusive.

In return, the Leontief method is actually "zero degrees of assessment", because the "series" consist of a single element and the assessments are always done for a single parameter. The known procedure is: $a_{ij} = x_{ij}/x_j$.

Is there a useful synthesis way between the two insufficient methods?

The main objective consists in improving the quality of the prediction of coefficients "a_{ij}". If we have the input-output balance over several successive years, one part achieved by instantaneous records and another one by technical-engineering adjustments, we can move to the regression analysis of the technological coefficients. The fundamental hypothesis of this analysis is that in reality not the theoretical condition:

$$x_{ij}(t) = a_{ij}x_j(t), \tag{6.46}$$

is valid for any "t", but the stochastic relation:

$$x_{ij}(t) = a_{ij}x_j(t) + u_{ij}, \tag{6.47}$$

where u_{ij} is a random variable with the average 0 and normal distribution.

Conversely, we must obtain such a value for "a_{ij}" in (6.45), which would satisfy the usual conditions:

$$\sum_{i} u_{ij}(t) = 0, \ \sum_{i} u_{ij}^2(t) = \min, \tag{6.48}$$

and, at the same time, to be normally distributed.

Any equation of the Leontief system will have a new form:

$$x_i = \sum_{i=1}^{n} a_{ij} x_j + y_i + u_i, \tag{6.49}$$

where

$$u_i = \sum_{i=1}^{n} u_{ij}. \tag{6.50}$$

The question to be asked is: how can we get random variables?

Let us suppose that we have all the technological coefficients for one "base year" and we note them with "$\bar{a}_{ij}$". For any other year, by knowing the total productions of the branches "x_i" and the final productions "y_i", we can do some assessments of the term "u_i".

At any time "t", we shall have:

$$r_i(t) = x_i(t) - \sum_{j=1}^{n} \bar{a}_{ij} x_j(t) + y_i(t), \tag{6.51}$$

where:

$r_i(t)$ is an estimate of $u_i(t)$.

But this is not satisfactory, because we need to know the components of "r_i", namely each "u_{ij}", which are the only information that can be useful. Or, they cannot be directly deduced from the formula (6.49).

One solution that provides valuable results, which are interesting in principle but basically unsatisfactory, was proposed by Arrow and Hoffenberg. Improvements and adaptations of this model will serve in various circumstances, as applicable. One statistical condition must however be met, meaning that: sufficiently long series of "x_i" and "y_i" should exist for all branches taken into account. The method implicitly involves a fairly high degree of aggregation, meaning to consider relatively few input-output branches. At the same time however, it is not the system (6.45) to be estimated by regression, but a more complicated system of mathematical form. Here are the essential trends of this procedure.

First of all, the coefficients "a_{ij}" will be dealt with as being dependent on several variables specified, as well as on a trend variable.

In the case of the Arrow-Hoffenberg analysis, for USA, it is shown that:

$$a_{ij}(t) = b_{ij} + c_{ij}t + d_{ij}w(t) + e_{ij}V(t) + F_{ij}\left[v_j(t)/x_j(t)\right]. \tag{6.52}$$

where:

w is the ratio of military expenses to the "total civil production". During the years analysed by the authors, this factor had special significance, because an input-output branch is always an aggregate, which is why for a change in the internal composition of the aggregate also determines changes in the value of the coefficient. The authors of the model admit that in every branch, the share of military production influences in one way or another, the size of "a_{ij}". The insertion of the variable "*w*" must respond to the requirement to thus take into account the involvement of the aggregate determined by the war production;

V = the "actually available" income per capita. In the case of this variable, the focus is also on the aggregate structure. If the actual personal income increases, a shift of production is determined within the aggregate, towards the goods of higher quality;

x_j = the volume of total production in the branch "j";

v_j is a variable that requires certain explanation. It is the so-called "learning variable". When the production of a certain branch increases rapidly, a certain waste of raw materials is possible, which may lead to an increase in the input coefficients "a_{ij}". Therefore, we suppose that a production that exceeds the level of a "peak" from previous years may have such an effect. The variable v_j is the phenomenon and is defined as *an excess of the previous maximum production, in a year "t"*. If the current year "t" and the "previous maximum" were analysed in the year $\hat{s} < t$, then:

$$\begin{aligned} v_j(t) &= 0, \text{ dac } x_j(t) < x_j(s) \\ v_j(t) &= x_j(t) - \max x_j(s) \end{aligned} \tag{6.53}$$

Wherefrom it results that, in the case of $x_j(t) < x_j(s)$, the ratio $[v_j(t)/x_j(t)]$ will be null;

t = the trend variable, with all its meanings about time.

By inserting now (6.50) into (6.47), we get the relation:

$$\begin{aligned} x_j(t) = &\sum_{j=1}^{n} b_{ij}x_j(t) + \sum_{j=1}^{n} c_{ij}x_j(t)t + \sum_{j=1}^{n} d_{ij}x_j(t)w(t) + \sum_{j=1}^{n} e_{ij}x_j(t)V(t) + \\ &+ \sum_{j=1}^{n} f_{ij}v_j(t) + y_i(t) + u_i(t) \ (i = 1, 2, \ldots, n) \end{aligned} \tag{6.54}$$

The system (6.52) is not yet very encouraging for regression estimations, but for now, it is only the start, meaning we started from the idea that some value can be *predetermined*, meaning they are previously known. They are null values. For example, in an input-output balance, there are empty "squares". This reduces the number of variables of the equation, in some cases on only a few connections. Thus one can find series with sufficient "degrees of freedom" and coefficients may be found for the "smaller" equations, applying all kinds of artifices for the others. The initial model is however significant because it explains many aspects of the econometric dependence of the variables "a_{ij}" by a number of variables outside the balance.

The simple estimates according to Leontief procedure are not satisfactory in themselves. This is why, the coefficients "a_{ij}" must be verified with econometric methods. There is not a single method of this kind, but various methods will apply in order to get a most likely Leontief projection matrix, as applicable. One of these methods is the regression to dynamic series of "$a_{ij}(t)$" according to a model similar to (6.50). Such dynamic series can be created for some products from direct statistical data or selectively on the specific consumptions. Not all dynamic series are however suitable for such an adjustment. In some cases, however, even a simple average can be helpful to us.

In other cases, we may benefit from our knowledge regarding the "predetermined variables", meaning those cases when the distribution row of a branch has many elements $x_{ij}=0$. In these cases, efficient Arrow and Hoffenberg estimates can also be provided. In this regard, the *triangulation method* of the Leontief tables is very helpful, by means of which some "short" equations may be discovered, for which sufficiently long dynamic series exist.

6.5 Cobb-Douglas Functions, Leontief Function and Their Economic Interpretation

In the production functions, the Cobb-Douglas functions and the Leontief function have a special place among them.

Let us make a comparison within the transformation functions between the Leontief production function factors. Among others, one branch "j" receives the inputs from the branches "i" and "k". In a production, the inputs are "x_{ij}" and "x_{kj}", the transformation coefficients being:

$$a_{ij} = \frac{x_{ij}}{x_j} \text{ and } a_{kj} = \frac{x_{kj}}{x_j} \tag{6.55}$$

It results from (6.53) that:

$$\frac{a_{ij}}{a_{kj}} = \frac{x_{ij}}{x_{kj}}, \tag{6.56}$$

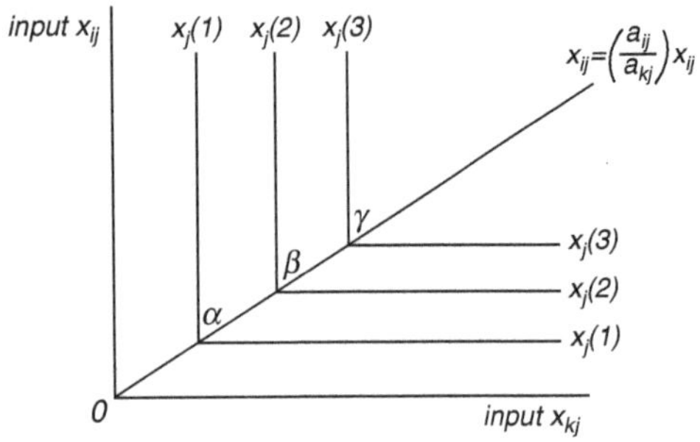

Fig. 6.2 Graphic representation of the Leontief function

which leads to the function:

$$x_{ij} = \left(\frac{a_{ij}}{a_{kj}}\right) x_{kj}, \qquad (6.57)$$

which is the *constant relation between the inputs*. This condition remains valid fro all *input* factors under the conditions where the postulates of the Leontief model maintain their validity.

Figure 6.2 clearly shows the impossibility of substituting the factors in a Leontief model.

The points "α", "β" and "γ" indicate the quantities "i" and "k" absorbed into the production of branch "j" at three successive production levels: $x_j(1)$, $x_j(2)$ and $x_j(3)$. If we move from the point "α", for example, to the right, increasing the quantity of "x_{kj}" along the isoquant "$x_j(1)$", production may continue to be maintained, only if "x_{ij}" remained constant. Therefore, any increase in the amount of "x_{kj}", at the same quantity of "$x_j(1)$" is unnecessary and therefore not economical, and does not contribute in any way to reducing (saving) the other input factor.

In the case of CD functions (Fig. 6.3), things are however different.

Here, an increase of a factor from "M_1" to "M_2" enables a reduction of the consumption of the other factor from "F_1" to "F_2", further providing the same production quantity (national income) "Y(1)". Thus, in the case of the Cobb-Douglas functions, there is the possibility to substitute the various production factors.

Figure 6.3 corresponds to a theoretical rational scheme, which "believes" in the existence of an analogous situation and in reality. It is very likely for this to be the case, because this model is accepted as prerequisite for the studies regarding the production functions. However, statistical data interpose between "reality" and "reason", "structure" and "model". They are series of "Y", "M" and "F", which do not always reflect the sought correspondence, but which we cannot say that they exist however. All values "Y", "M" and "F" are done in a certain physical quantity and at a price based on which they are assessed. If, for example, we note the number of man-hours provided in industry with "M^q" and the wage with "p_1" and if the

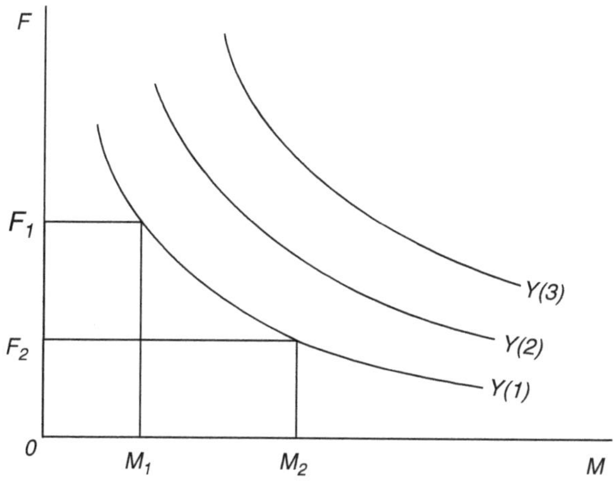

Fig. 6.3 Imaginary graphic representation of the Cobb-Douglas function

physical volume of production means "F^q" requires a unit investment of "p_2", then the cost of producing the national income can be noted by means of the expression:

$$M^q p_1 + F^q p_2 = C, \tag{6.58}$$

and

$$M = M^q p_1 \text{ and } F = F^q p_2. \tag{6.59}$$

If now the "physical volume" of the national income is noted with "Q", we can represent in Fig. 6.4 what happens in reality, compared to Fig. 6.3 where the reality was reflected by an imaginary thinking.

In this figure, "Q (1)", "Q (2)", etc. are the factor transformation functions on successive production levels of the national income. At the same time, "C(1)", "C (2)" are the isoquants of costs under the conditions where "p_1" and "p_2" changed over time, reflected by the different slope p_1/p_2 of the straight lines.

The lowest costs being provided at the point where the slope of the cost straight line is equal to the tangent of the "Q" transformation curve. On this spot, the value volume "Y" of the national income is defined, which is:

$$A(M^q p_1 + F^q p_2) \equiv Y, \tag{6.60}$$

where:

A is the multiplication factor similar to the reverse of the "investment/product" ratio.

In the case shown in Fig. 6.4, the statistics will provide us with series from the data "Y(1)" and "Y(2)", etc., and not "Q(1)", "Q(2)" etc., which have no real correspondent. But "Y(t)" is an aggregate indicator which creates quite a lot of difficulties. However, in the case shown so far, the situation seems to be pretty

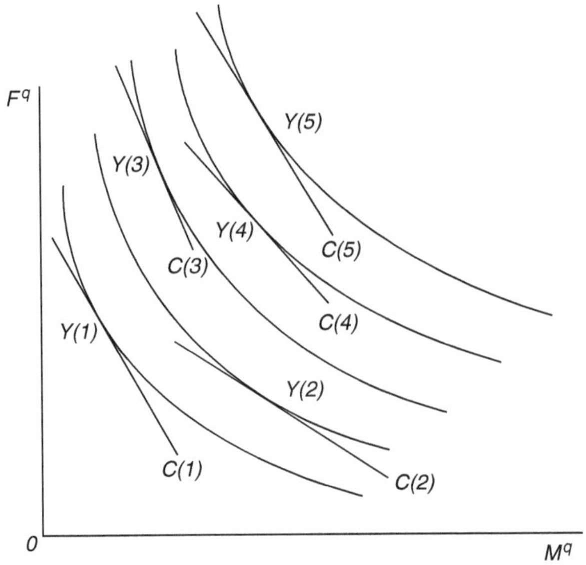

Fig. 6.4 Real representation of the Cobb-Douglas function

advantageous for the specialist in econometrics. All points "Y" are on the same rate of curves and this their regression to "F" and "M" leads to reasonable estimates of "α" and "β" or "1 − α". Unfortunately, the trends reflected in statistics can sometimes be considerably different, rather resembling those cases shown in Figs. 6.5 and 6.6.

In both cases, for all "recorded" levels of production, the same ratio between "F" and "M" appears. Therefore, each "Y" is placed on the same straight line, their substitution would be technically be possible, but it would be uneconomical and thus, de facto, throughout the observation period, it is a constant ratio between the two factors. In the situation shown in Fig. 6.5, the allure of the production function does not change and the cost function remained the same. In Fig. 6.6, a change in the allure of both functions occurred, but so that to maintain a constant F^q/M^q ratio.

These graphs show the inconclusiveness of the data in the series "y (1)", "y (2)" etc., in order to determine the real production function by regression.

Thus, a paradoxical situation occurs, where the statistics "from" CD type curves provide information wherefrom Leontief type relations can be deduced. The example in Fig. 6.5 shows such a case reduced now to the level of "branch" (as opposed to that at the level of "national economy").

The production of the branch-example is measured in quantities "Q" and sold at the price "p_3", using only two factors: "M^q" at the price "p_1" and "F^q" at the price "p_2". All productive enterprises in the branch have the same Cobb-Douglas type function. The transformation and cost functions noted are those in Fig. 6.5. Here, the p_1/p_2 ratio is constant, meaning all isoquants have the same slope.

All this is not known. What is known from statistics are however the series:

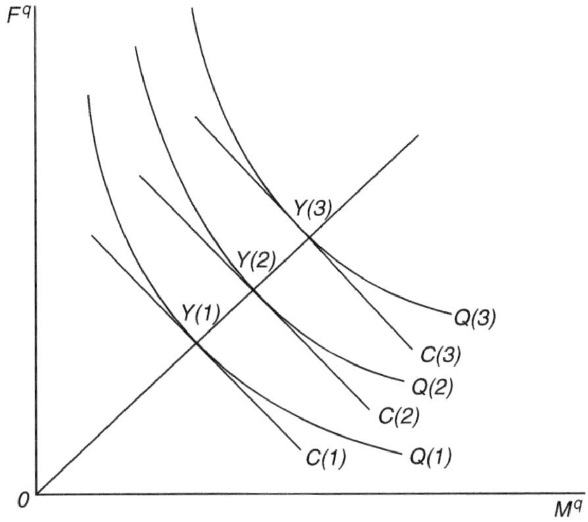

Fig. 6.5 De facto representation of the Cobb-Douglas function

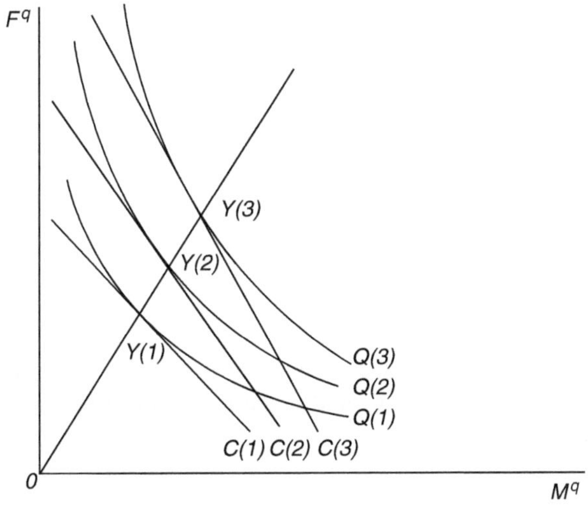

Fig. 6.6 Graphical representation of the change in the production function and cost function

$$
\begin{aligned}
&Y(1) \equiv p_3Q(1),\ Y(2) \equiv p_3Q(2), \ldots\ldots \\
&M(1) \equiv p_1M^q{}_1,\ M(2) \equiv p_1M^q{}_2 \ldots\ldots\ldots \\
&F(1) \equiv p_2F^q{}_1,\ F(2) \equiv p_2F^q{}_2 \ldots\ldots\ldots\ldots
\end{aligned} \tag{6.61}
$$

Thus, one may observe that between the consumed factors and the branch product there is a constant ratio over time:

$$\alpha_m = \frac{M(1)}{Y(1)} = \frac{M(2)}{Y(2)}$$
$$\alpha_f = \frac{F(1)}{Y(1)} = \frac{F(2)}{Y(2)} \tag{6.62}$$

Otherwise noted:

$$\alpha_m = \frac{p_1 M^q}{p_3 Q}$$
$$\alpha_f = \frac{p_2 F^q}{p_3 Q} \tag{6.63}$$

These ratios are not however technical relations. They are economic relations, determined by the level of prices, technically representing only on possible point on the transformation functions. The statistics do not reflect this and thus it appears that there are Leontief production functions in the studied branch, when actually the relations are of the Cobb-Douglas type. Typically, when the statistics is not represented in this form, it will be impossible to directly deduce a CD function. Instead, it may be observed that there is a constant ratio between the two factors:

$$\frac{\alpha_m}{\alpha_f} = \frac{p_1 M^q}{p_2 F^q} \tag{6.64}$$

and thus the straight line:

$$p_1 M^q = \left(\frac{\alpha_m}{\alpha_f}\right) p_3 F^q \tag{6.65}$$

will serve as forecasting tool according to the principles of the Leontief model.

For this to also be valid in the future, one of the two conditions must surely be met:

- the p_1/p_2 and M^q/F^q ratios remain constant at the same time, which means maintaining the ratio of prices and the same CD function;
- if p_1/p_2 changes, technical changes must also occur in the CD function so that the corresponding M^q/F^q ratio would change reversely with the changes in the ratio of prices.

If such statistics are used to estimate the production functions of the branch, then this will be done for the observation period, by a function of only two variables and not three, as is the case with the CD function. In general, the function is noted as follows:

$$y = \frac{1}{\alpha_m} M \text{ or } Y = \frac{1}{\alpha_f} F. \tag{6.66}$$

By linear regression of "Y", once to "M" and then to "F", we can get the sought coefficients.

The analysed situation is frequently reflected in statistical data, but in no case it is more difficult. If the price ratio remains constant for a long time, then a regular shift of the production function can still be corrected by a trend element.

The linear dependence between the independent factors of a production function is less difficult than the linear connection of their logarithms.

In reality, the CD function analyses a fact that has already happened, a past evolution and therefore any prediction based on this includes an lower or higher hazard element. In addition, the function is not directly based on technical structure data and is therefore it is normal that the use of CD functions is done in conjunction with the structural models.

The exponential production function has an analytical feature. Of course, at the same time, it serves in making the economic policy decisions, but only indicatively. This cannot be directly used, because an arbitrary extrapolation based on this could lead to absurd results, due to several reasons, namely:

- direct extrapolation based on a CD would mean that any of the independent variables can be increased however much, without modifying the value of the other and yet "Y" to grow. For example, any increase in the volume of fixed funds, without an increase in the labour force used, should increase the national income. But this is an absurdity. Although in some cases (automation under "ideal" conditions), even a reduction in using the labour force could lead to an increase in the national income. In general, an independent increase of "M" and "F" can only be admitted within certain limits.

According to Euler's formula, it results that:

$$\frac{\partial Y}{\partial M} \cdot M + \frac{\partial Y}{\partial F} \cdot F = Y, \tag{6.67}$$

and so that "M" and "F" can also independently determine an increase of "Y". This would be true only if there was an absolute substitutability between "M" and "F". Or, "M" and "F" are substitutable only to a certain extent and within certain limits. If the calculated parameters "α" and "β" refer to a period when a technique has been gradually inserted, which changed the M/F ratio, then indeed an independent increase in one of the factors is still possible, until the new technique will be generalised. If things are not so, then "M" and "F" are complementary;

- besides the partial complementarity of the factors "M" and "F", there are also other reasons that limit the conclusiveness of extrapolation based on the CD function, related to how the available factors have been used. Thus, it is possible that during the analysed period, an inefficient combination of "M" and "F" may have been used and thus the parameters obtained would reflect a suboptimal use, which must not be maintained in the future.

For all these reasons, the predictive role of the CD function is dependently narrow by its use combined with a number of other indicators.

However, assuming that a satisfactory CD function has been estimated, verified with statistical data, the functions thus obtained may be very helpful in determining the growth rate of the investments, labour force, national income, in the context where certain types of production functions remain valid.

We must observe that we are facing a phenomenon of under-utilisation of a research means, which is so good and subtle as the production functions are, namely simply because no systematic efforts were done, of corresponding proportions to research the national economy, by using this tool. In order to get sufficiently conclusive functions, a simple regression calculation is not enough and, undoubtedly, a coordinated plan of parallel researches is required.

It is well known that so far, the best results have been done in Cobb-Douglas researches at enterprise level. This is because many of those problems the industrial enterprises face are not as complex as those the econometrics faces at the level of the national economy, which requires a more complicated mathematical apparatus to solve them.

References

Behr B (1965) Messmethoden der Volksuwirtschaftlichen Productivitütsentwicklung mit Hilfe oggregierter Productionsfunktionen. Akademie, Berlin

Carter AP (1990) Contribution to input-output analysis. North Holland, Amsterdam

Goldberger A (2001) Econometric theory. Wiley, New York, NY

Halabuk L (1987) Das ungarische experimentelle makromodell in matematiek und kybernetik in der Őkonomie. Academie, Berlin

Hannan EJ (2002) Time series analysis. Methnen, London

Johnston J (1993) Econometrics methods. McGraw Hill, New York, NY

Klein LR (1992) An introduction to econometrics. Englewood Cliff, NJ

Leontieff W (1953a) The structure of the American-economy 1919–1939. Oxford University Press, New York, NY

Leontieff W (1953b) Studies in the structure of the American economy. Oxford University Press, New York, NY

Leontieff W (1966) Input-output economies. Oxford University Press, New York, NY

Nerlove M (1995) Estimation and identification of Cobb-Douglas function. North Holland, Amsterdam

Schatteles T (1971) Metode econometrice moderne. Ed. Ştiinţifică, Bucureşti

Theiss E (1965) Statistiche Bestimmung der Parameter von Macromodellen. Akademie, Berlin

Tinter G (1990) Handbuch der Őkonometrie. Springer, Berlin

Part III
Econometric Models Used in Management

Chapter 7
Models Based on Linear Programming

7.1 Theoretical Foundation of Linear Programming

The linear programming mathematical model used to represent an economic system consists of a set of linear relations, of which one reflects the objective pursued and the others include the economic or technological restrictions.

To better understand the mathematical model of a linear programming problem, in its general form, we shall first analyse a simple example, namely: distribution of production tasks between enterprises in the case of a single product.

A number *m* of enterprises that manufacture the same product must supply *n* beneficiaries. In Table 7.1, we note the quantities $a_i (1 \leq i \leq m)$ achieved by the *m* enterprises, the quantities $b_j (1 \leq j \leq n)$ which the *n* beneficiaries need, the transportation costs of a product unit from the enterprise $A_i (1 \leq i \leq m)$ to the beneficiary $B_j (1 \leq j \leq n)$ which we noted with c_{ij}, as well as the production costp_i of a unit of the product of enterprise A_i.

To determine the optimal repair of the production tasks by enterprises, so that the transportation expenses and production cost for the whole manufactured and transported quantity would be minimum.

If we note with x_{ij} the quantity of the production of enterprise A_i that is to be delivered to the beneficiary $B_j (1 \leq i \leq m\ ,\ \ 1 \leq j \leq n)$, then the relations:

$$\begin{aligned} & x_{11} + x_{12} + \ldots + x_{1n} = a_1 \\ & x_{21} + x_{22} + \ldots + x_{2n} = a_2 \\ & \ldots\ldots\ldots\ldots\ldots\ldots\ldots\ldots \\ & x_{m1} + x_{m2} + \ldots + x_{mn} = a_m \end{aligned} \tag{7.1}$$

express the fact that the sum of the quantities delivered to the n beneficiaries by the manufacturer A_i must be equal to the quantity manufactured in this enterprise $(1 \leq i \leq m)$.

I.C. Dima, M. Man, *Modelling and Simulation in Management*, Contributions to Management Science, DOI 10.1007/978-3-319-16592-9_7

Table 7.1 The relation m suppliers, n beneficiaries

Beneficiary / Enterprise	B_1 B_2 ... B_i ... B_n	Available	Unit cost
A_1	c_{11} c_{12} ... c_{1j} ... c_{1n}	a_1	p_1
A_2	c_{21} c_{22} ... c_{2j} ... c_{2n}	a_2	p_2
→	→	→	→
A_i	c_{i1} c_{i2} ... c_{ij} ... c_{in}	a_i	p_i
→	→	→	→
A_m	c_{m1} c_{m2} ... c_{mj} ... c_{mn}	a_m	p_m
Demand	b_1 b_2 ... b_i ... b_n	–	–

Taking into account that each beneficiary must receive from the *n* manufacturers a quantity equal to their demand, it means that the following relations must also be met:

$$\begin{aligned} x_{11} + x_{21} + \ldots + x_{m1} &= b_1 \\ x_{12} + x_{22} + \ldots + x_{m2} &= b_2 \\ \ldots\ldots\ldots\ldots\ldots\ldots\ldots\ldots \\ x_{1n} + x_{2n} + \ldots + x_{mn} &= b_m \end{aligned} \tag{7.2}$$

The nature of the problem obviously requires that all quantities x_{ij} are not negative:

$$x_{ij} \geq 0 \ (1 \leq i \leq m, \ 1 \leq j \leq n) \tag{7.3}$$

The problem that needs to be solved requires that the quantities x_{ij} are determined, which meet the above conditions, so that the total expenses are minimum, meaning the function:

$$Z(x_{11}, x_{12}, \ldots, x_{1n}, x_{21}, x_{22}, \ldots, x_{2n}, x_{m1}, x_{m2}, \ldots, x_{mn}) = (p_1 + c_{11}) \cdot x_{11} + (p_1 + c_{12}) \cdot x_{12} + \ldots + (p_m + c_{m1}) \cdot x_{m1} + \ldots + (p_m + c_{mn}) \cdot x_{mn} \tag{7.4}$$

would have the minimum value.

Therefore, the mathematical model consists of:

1. *the function to be minimised*

$$\min Z(x_{11}, x_{12}, \ldots, x_{m1}, x_{m2}, \ldots, x_{mn}) = \min \sum_{i=1}^{m} \sum_{j=1}^{n} (p_i + c_{ij}) \cdot x_{ij} \tag{7.5}$$

2. *the restrictions*

$$\sum_{j=1}^{n} x_{ij} = a_i \qquad 1 \le i \le m \qquad (\text{m equalities})$$
$$\sum_{i=1}^{m} x_{ij} = b_i \qquad 1 \le j \le n \qquad (\text{n equalities}) \tag{7.6}$$

3. the condition of negativity of the variables

$$x_{ij} \ge 0 \; (1 \le i \le m \;,\; 1 \le j \le n) \; (m, n \text{ variables}) \tag{7.7}$$

By analysing the example shown, it results that in a linear programming problem restrictions can occur written as inequalities (such $\le$ as or $\ge$) or equalities. The optimisation criterion chosen also requires in some cases to maximise the objective function, and in other cases, its minimisation.

To study and interpret the solutions of a linear programming problem, the economic forms and its standard form are of special interest.

Definition 1 One problem of linear programming is given as standard form if all restrictions are equations (equalities) and the non-negativity conditions are imposed to all variables.

The standard form of a linear programming problem has been defined from the beginning, as any linear programming problem needs to be first brought to the standard form in order to be solved by means of the *Simplex algorithm* (or dual *Simplex*).

Thus, the problem:

$$\begin{aligned} &\max[Z(x)] = 3 \cdot x_1 + 4 \cdot x_2 + x_3 \\ &x_1 + x_4 + x_5 = 6 \\ &x_2 - 2x_4 + x_5 = 0 \\ &x_3 + x_4 + 3x_5 = 2 \\ &x_j \ge 0; \quad 1 \le j \le 5 \end{aligned} \tag{7.8}$$

is a linear programming problem given as standard form.

If we insert the notations:

$$A = \begin{pmatrix} 1 & 0 & 0 & 1 & 1 \\ 0 & 1 & 0 & -2 & 1 \\ 0 & 0 & 1 & 1 & 3 \end{pmatrix}; \; b = \begin{pmatrix} 6 \\ 0 \\ 2 \end{pmatrix}; \; C = \begin{pmatrix} 3 \\ 4 \\ 1 \\ 0 \\ 0 \end{pmatrix}; \; X = \begin{pmatrix} x_1 \\ x_2 \\ x_3 \\ x_4 \\ x_5 \end{pmatrix} \tag{7.9}$$

then the problem taken into account can be written as matriceal form, as follows:

$$\max[Z(x)] = (3 \quad 4 \quad 1 \quad 0 \quad 0) \cdot \begin{pmatrix} x_1 \\ x_2 \\ x_3 \\ x_4 \\ x_5 \end{pmatrix}$$
$$\begin{pmatrix} 1 & 0 & 0 & 1 & 1 \\ 0 & 1 & 0 & -2 & 1 \\ 0 & 0 & 1 & 1 & 3 \end{pmatrix} \cdot \begin{pmatrix} x_1 \\ x_2 \\ x_3 \\ x_4 \\ x_5 \end{pmatrix} = \begin{pmatrix} 6 \\ 0 \\ 2 \end{pmatrix}, \begin{pmatrix} x_1 \\ x_2 \\ x_3 \\ x_4 \\ x_5 \end{pmatrix} \geq 0 \tag{7.10}$$

By generalisation, the mathematical model of a linear programming problem given as standard form is as follows:

$$\begin{aligned} \min(\max)[Z(x)] &= C' \cdot X \\ A \cdot X &= b \\ X &\geq 0 \end{aligned} \tag{7.11}$$

Thus, A is a matrix with m lines and n columns called the matrix of the technological coefficients, X is a column vector with n components called the vector of activities, b a column vector with m components that we shall further call the vector of *resources*, and C a column vector with n components called the vector of *costs*. The scalar product of the vectors C' and X was noted with $C'X$.

$$\begin{aligned} C'X &= \sum_{j=1}^{n} c_j \cdot x_j \\ C' &= (c_1, c_2, \ldots, c_n); \qquad X = (x_1, x_2, \ldots, x_n) \end{aligned} \tag{7.12}$$

Definition 2 One problem of linear programming is given as canonical form if all restrictions are inequalities of the same sign and the non-negativity conditions are imposed to all variables. If the sign of the restrictions is $\geq$, then the objective function must be minimised, and if the sign of the restrictions is $\leq$, the objective function must be maximised.

In both cases, the restrictions of these problems are called concordances. If the above definition is expressed in as concisely as possible of a mathematical form, the form *I* or *II* of a linear programming problem results, as follows:

$$\begin{array}{ll} \min[Z(x)] = C' \cdot X & \max[Z(x)] = C' \cdot X \\ A \cdot X \geq b & A \cdot X \leq b \\ \text{(I)} \ X \geq 0 & \text{(II)} X \geq 0 \\ I & II \end{array} \tag{7.13}$$

It should be stated that in practical applications, situations where the model simultaneously includes restrictions of all types occur frequently. Restrictions of the form $\geq$ are unconditioned for problems that require the maximisation of the objective function, and those of the type $\leq$ are inconsistent for the problems which the minimisation of the objective function is required for. But any linear programming problem can be brought to the standard form or the canonical form by means of some elementary transformations performed on the variables or (and) restrictions as well as by means of the operator applied to the objective function.

These transformations are:

- *Transforming the maximum operator into minimum (or vice-versa) and is based on the equality:*

$$\max_{x \in X} [Z(x)] = -\min_{x \in X} \{-Z(x)\} \tag{7.14}$$

true for any set *X* and any real function defined on *X*.

Particularly:

$$\max C' \cdot X = -\min(-C)' \cdot X \tag{7.15}$$

- *Transforming the sign of an inequality is done by also multiplying by* -1;
- *A variable x to which no sign restrictions are required is replaced by the difference of two negative variables:*

$$x = x_1 - x_2; \qquad x_1 \geq 0 \ , \ x_2 \geq 0 \tag{7.16}$$

- *The equations are transformed into inequations based on the fact that a'x is equivalent to the following inequations of contrary sign:*

$$a' \cdot x \geq b \ ; \ a' \cdot x \leq b \tag{7.17}$$

- *The inequations are transformed into equations, taking into account the fact that the inequation a'x≤b can be written as an equation* $a' \cdot x + y = b$ *inserting gap variables (or compensation variables)* $y \geq 0$*. Analogously, an inequation in the form* $a'x \geq b$ *is transformed into the equation* $a' \cdot x - y = b$ *by subtracting the gap variable* $y \geq 0$*. We need to mention that the gap variables do not appear in the objective function, or in other words, they appear in the objective function with the coefficients* $c_j^e = 0$ (c_j^e, *which correspond to the gap variables).*

The aforementioned transformations enable the acquirement of the standard or canonical form equivalent to any linear programming problem. The importance of using these transformations does not only consist in establishing the equivalence which was mentioned above. They will occur more specifically when questioning the use of the Simplex algorithm to solve a problem or when the dual problems of the linear programming problems will be considered.

Theorem 1 If the linear programming problem

$$\begin{aligned} \min(\max)[Z(x)] &= C' \cdot X \\ A \cdot X &= b \\ X &\geq 0 \end{aligned} \tag{7.18}$$

admits a program (admissible solution) when it has at least one basic program (admissible solution).

Demonstration: be $X = (x_1, x_2, \ldots, x_k, 0, \ldots, 0)'$ a program of the programming problem considered, where we placed the positive components on the first k places in the vector *X*, *k=0, 1, 2,…, n*, (this does not restrict the generality by anything).

If $k=0$ the demonstration is complete, because $X=0$ is by definition a basic program.

Therefore, be $k>0$.

Then two situations are possible:

- *the vectors* $a_1, a_2, \ldots, a_k$ *(the column vectors in the matrix A corresponding to the positive components* $(x_1, x_2, \ldots, x_k)$ *are linearly independent. In this case, X is a basic program.*

  We can now also specify the basis *B* corresponding to this program. However, if $k=m$ then the basis $B = (a_1, a_2, \ldots, a_m)$ is obvious. However, if $k<m$ then, because $\text{rang}A = m$ was assumed, there are the independent linear vectors $a_{i_{k+1}}, a_{i_{k+2}}, \ldots, a_{i_m}$, which along with the vectors $a_1, a_2, \ldots, a_k$ form a base and therefore, in this case, the base related to the basic program taken into account is not unique;
- *the vectors* $a_1, a_2, \ldots, a_k$ *are linearly independent, which means that there is one vector* $Y \in R^n$, $Y = (y_1, y_2, \ldots, y_k, 0, \ldots, 0)$, $y \neq 0$ *for which* $A \cdot Y = 0$.

  We may assume that at least one component $y_i < 0$ (otherwise, we reason with the vector $Z=-Y$).

  In this case, the following can be written:

$$A \cdot X + \lambda \cdot A \cdot Y = A \cdot (X + \lambda \cdot Y) = b \tag{7.19}$$

and, therefore $X + \lambda \cdot Y$ will be program of the linear programming problem taken into account, if $\lambda \geq 0$ is chosen so that:

$$X + \lambda \cdot Y \geq 0$$

Particularly for:

$$\lambda = \lambda = \min_{i,\, y_i < 0} \left\{ \frac{x_i}{-y_i} \right\} \tag{7.20}$$

we obtain the program $X + \lambda_0 \cdot Y$ which has $k-1$ strictly positive components at the most.

The columns corresponding to these components are either linearly independent and then we obtained a basic program, or are linearly dependent and then we resume the reasoning made in this regard. After a finite number of steps, we reach the case *a)*, and therefore we get a basic program.

Theorem 2 If the linear programming problem

$$\begin{aligned} \min(\max)[Z(x)] &= C^{'} \cdot X \\ A \cdot X &= b \\ X &\geq 0 \end{aligned} \tag{7.21}$$

admits an optimal program, then it has an optimal basic program.

Demonstration: Be $X = (x_1, x_2, \ldots, x_k, 0, \ldots, 0)^{'}$ an optimal program (where it has been assumed so far that the first *k* components are strictly positive).

If $k=0$ the demonstration is complete;

If $k>0$, two situations are possible:

- *the vectors* $a_1, a_2, \ldots, a_k$*are independently linear and then X is an optimal basic program:*
- *the vectors* $a_1, a_2, \ldots, a_k$*are dependently linear and the following exists* $Y = (y_1, y_2, \ldots, y_k, 0, \ldots, 0)^{'} \in R^n$ *so that* $A \cdot Y=0$. *and therefore there is the program* $X + \lambda \cdot Y$ *for the chosen convenient program* λ, *meaning of* $\lambda \in [\lambda_1, \lambda_2]$ *where*:

$$\lambda_1 = \begin{cases} \underset{\frac{i}{y_i} > 0}{\max} \left\{ -\frac{x_i}{y_i} \right\} \\ -\infty \quad \text{if all } y_i \leq 0 \end{cases} \qquad \lambda_2 = \begin{cases} \underset{\frac{i}{y_i} < 0}{\min} \left\{ -\frac{x_i}{y_i} \right\} \\ +\infty \quad \text{if all } y_i \geq 0 \end{cases} \tag{7.22}$$

From the fact that *X* is an optimal program and $X + \lambda \cdot Y$ is program, it results that $C^{'}Y = 0$, because otherwise, by choosing on λ of a sign contrary to the value $C'Y$, we shall have:

$$C^{'} \cdot (X + \lambda \cdot Y) = C^{'} \cdot X + \lambda \cdot C^{'} \cdot Y < C^{'} \cdot X \tag{7.23}$$

which would contradict the fact that *X* is an optimal program. Therefore, $C^{'} \cdot (X + \lambda \cdot Y) = C^{'} \cdot X$ meaning $X + \lambda \cdot Y$ is an optimal program.

No, we can choose $\lambda_0 = \lambda_1$ or $\lambda_0 = \lambda_2$, so that the optimal program would have $k-1$ strictly positive components at the most.

The remaining *k* − *1* vectors can be linearly independent and then the theorem is demonstrated or they can be linearly independent and then the reasoning done is repeated.

Theorem 3 The set of admissible solutions for a linear programming problem is a convex set.

Demonstration: Let us assume that the problem is given in the standard form. (It is proceeded in this analogous way if the problem is given in canonical form).

$$(\min)\max[Z(x)] = C' \cdot X \tag{7.24}$$

The set of admissible solutions is:

$$\{X \in R^n : A \cdot X = b \ , \ X \geq 0\}$$

Be X_1, X_2, two such solutions. Then, for $\lambda \in [0, 1]$,

$$X = \lambda \cdot X_1 + (1 - \lambda) \cdot X_2 \geq 0$$

and moreover:

$$\begin{aligned} A \cdot X = A \cdot [\lambda \cdot X_1 + (1 - \lambda) \cdot X_2] = \lambda \cdot A \cdot X_1 + (1 - \lambda) \cdot X_2 \\ = \lambda \cdot b + (1 - \lambda) \cdot b = b \end{aligned} \tag{7.25}$$

which proves the statement.

Theorem 4 The objective function of a linear programming problem receives the optimal value in an extreme point of the convex set *D* of all admissible solutions of the problem.

Demonstration: To be fixed, we assume it is required to minimise the objective function and note with $\widetilde{D} = \{X_i, i \in I\}$ the set of extreme points of *D*.

Be X_1 an extreme point (or one of them if there are several) for which

$$C' \cdot X_1 = \min_{i \in I} \left\{ C' \cdot X_i \right\} = \overline{Z}_1 \tag{7.26}$$

We assume it would not be true, therefore the following would exist: $X_0 \in D - \widetilde{D}$ so that

$$C' \cdot X_0 = \overline{Z}_0 < \overline{Z}_1 \tag{7.27}$$

Because X_0 is not extreme, it means it can be expressed as follows:

$$X_0 = \sum_{i \in I} \lambda_i \cdot X_i \quad , \quad \lambda_i \geq 0 \quad , \quad \sum_{i \in I} \lambda_i = 1 \tag{7.28}$$

But:

$$\overline{Z}_0 = C' \cdot X_0 = \sum_{i \in I} \lambda_i \cdot C' \cdot X_i \geq \sum_{i \in I} \lambda_i \cdot C' \cdot X_1 = C' \cdot X_1 = \overline{Z}_1 \tag{7.29}$$

which is a contradiction. Therefore, X_1 is an optimal program.

Consequence. If the objective function receives the same optimal value in several extreme points, then any convex linear combination thereof is the optimal solution of the linear programming problem.

Demonstration: Indeed, be $X_1, X_2, \ldots, X_k$ extreme points for which

$$C' \cdot X_1 = C' \cdot X_2 = \ldots = C' \cdot X_k = \min_{i \in I} \left\{ C' \cdot X_i \right\} = \overline{Z} \tag{7.30}$$

and be the convex linear combination $\sum_{i=1}^{k} \lambda_i \cdot X_i = X$.

Then X is still an admissible solution, and the objective function has the value

$$C' \cdot X = \sum_{i=1}^{k} \lambda_i \cdot C' \cdot X_i = \overline{Z} \sum_{i=1}^{k} \lambda_i = \overline{Z}. \tag{7.31}$$

To understand the previously presented theorems and the technique to solve a linear programming problem, the geometrical interpretation in the space of their activity is required (R^n). Therefore, in the most general case, we have a linear programming problem given as standard form:

$$\begin{aligned} \max[Z(x)] &= C' \cdot X \\ A \cdot X &= b \\ (\text{II}) X &\geq 0 \end{aligned} \tag{7.32}$$

by choosing any base B, we can write:

$$\begin{aligned} &\max[Z(x)] = \left(C^B\right)' \cdot X^B + \left(C^S\right)' \cdot X^S \\ &(B, S) \cdot \begin{pmatrix} X^B \\ X^S \end{pmatrix} = b \\ &\begin{pmatrix} X^B \\ X^S \end{pmatrix} \geq 0 \end{aligned} \tag{7.33}$$

$$\begin{aligned} & \max[Z(x)] = \left(C^B\right)' \cdot X^B + \left(C^S\right)' \cdot X^S \\ \text{meaning} \quad & B.X^S + S.X^S = b \\ & X \geq 0 \end{aligned} \tag{7.34}$$

or by multiplying on the left the restriction system by B^{-1} and by doing the required replacements, we get:

$$\begin{aligned} & \max[Z(x)] = \left(C^B\right)' \cdot \left[B^{-1} \cdot b - B^{-1} \cdot S \cdot X^S\right] + \left(C^S\right) \cdot X^S \\ & X^B = B^{-1} \cdot b - B^{-1} \cdot S \cdot X^S \\ & X^B \geq 0, \ X^S \geq 0 \end{aligned} \tag{7.35}$$

which leads to the following linear programming problem in economical form, equivalent to the given one:

$$\begin{aligned} & \max[Z(x)] = \left[\left(C^S\right)' - \left(C^B\right)' \cdot B^{-1} \cdot S\right] \cdot X^S \\ & B^{-1} \cdot S \cdot X^S \leq B^{-1} \cdot b \\ & X^S \geq 0 \end{aligned} \tag{7.36}$$

It results from here that the set of possible solutions of a linear programming problem can be interpreted either as an intersection of hyperplanes in the space of R^n activities, or as a section in the R^{n-m} space (the space of secondary variables X^S).

Definition. The intersection of a finite number of semi-spaces $a' \cdot x \leq b_i$, $i \in M = \{1, 2, \ldots, m\}$ is called a section.

Therefore, the section is the set of the solutions of a system of linear inequations. A bordered section is called convex polyhedron.

7.2 Using the Simplex Algorithm in Linear Programming

According to what has been shown in the previous paragraphs, a possibility to solve the linear programming problems is to determine all bases B in matrix A. From the set of basic solutions (corresponding to the set of bases), we retain the subset of the solutions for which $B^{-1} \cdot b \geq 0$, meaning the subset of the possible basic solutions and we choose from them that or those that minimise (or maximise) the objective function. Although this method may be applicable, practically it is entirely inefficient, because even in the case of some linear programming problems of small size, it is necessary to investigate a number of C_n^m bases.

Sometimes, these calculations could be unnecessary or when the optimum is infinite, only considering the basic programs does not highlight this situation.

In order to remove this shortcoming, a systematic and efficient method to exploit the basic programs is used, which is called the Simplex algorithm and provides the possibility to sequentially move from one basic program to another, so that the value of the objective function would decrease, when the objective function is minimised or to increase when the objective function is maximised.

Moreover, the Simplex algorithm provides basic criteria, based on which we can decide whether the linear programming problem has no optimal solution or has an infinite optimum.

To show the Simplex algorithm, the standard form of a linear programming problem will be used, meaning:

$$\begin{aligned} \min(\max)[Z(x)] &= C' \cdot X \\ A \cdot X &= b \\ X &\geq 0 \end{aligned} \tag{7.37}$$

If *B* is a base (we shall assume that $B^{-1}, b \geq 0$) then the system $A \cdot X = b$ can be written as follows:

$$X^B = B^{-1} \cdot b - B^{-1} \cdot S \cdot X^S \tag{7.38}$$

Inserting the notations $\overline{X}^B = B^{-1} \cdot b$ and $y_j^B = B^{-1} \cdot a_j$, where a_j is the column *j* in matrix *A* corresponding to the secondary variables $(j \in I_s)$ where I_s is the set $\{j : a_j \in S\}$, then the above equality becomes:

$$X^B = \overline{X}^B - \sum_{j \in I_s} y_j^B \cdot x_j \tag{7.39}$$

or

$$x_i^B = \overline{x}_i^B - \sum_{j \in I_s} y_{ij}^B \cdot x_j \quad (j \in I_B)$$

where $J_B = \{i : a_i \in B\}$.

Let us see now how we can express the objective function by using the secondary variables X^S.

For this, we start from the expression of the objective function and make successive replacements based on the above notations:

$$Z = C' \cdot X = \sum_{j=1}^{m} c_j \cdot x_j = \sum_{i \in J_B} c_i \cdot x_i + \sum_{j \in J_S} c_j \cdot x_j = \sum_{i \in J_B} c_i \cdot \left(\overline{x}_i^B - \sum_{i \in J_B} y_{ij}^B \cdot x_j \right) + \sum_{j \in J_S} c_j \cdot x_j = \\ \sum_{i \in J_B} c_i \cdot \overline{x}_i^B - \sum_{j \in J_S} \left(\sum_{i \in J_B} c_i \cdot y_{ij}^B - c_j \right) \cdot x_j \tag{7.40}$$

If we use the notations:

$$Z^B = \sum_{i \in J_B} c_i \cdot x_i^B = C_B' \cdot \overline{X}^B \tag{7.41}$$

and

$$Z_j^B = \sum_{i \in J_B} c_i \cdot y_{ij}^B = C_B' \cdot y_j^B$$

we get the relation:

$$Z = Z^B - \sum_{j \in J_S} \left(z_j^B - c_j \right) \cdot x_j \tag{7.42}$$

Below, we shall use the *minimum* operator for the objective function, following to see what happens when it moves to the maximum.

To highlight the Simplex algorithm, it is necessary to present some propositions, which will be the foundations of the optimal solution calculation algorithm.

Proposition 1 If $z_j - c_j \leq 0$ for any $j \in I_s$, then the admissible solution corresponding to the base $B\left(X^B = B^{-1} \cdot b\right),\ X^S = 0$ is optimal.

Demonstration: Let us note with *Z* the value of the objective function corresponding to this basic admissible solution. For any admissible solution, from the fact that $x_j \geq 0$ results $\sum_{j \in J_S} \left(x_j - c_j\right) \cdot x_j \leq 0$ and therefore if we note with *Z* the value corresponding to the objective function, we get $Z = Z - \sum_{j \in J_S} \left(x_j - c_j\right) \cdot x_j \geq Z$ of which the affirmation is justified.

Proposition 2 If $k \in I_s$ exists so that $z_k - c_k > 0$ then the admissible solution related to base *B* is not optimal (except for the degenerated solution) and can be improved if x_k takes positive values.

Demonstration: Indeed, if the value of the secondary variable created to the value $x_k' > 0$ is given, then we get a new program with the value of the objective function:

$$Z^0 = Z - \sum (z_k - c_k) \cdot x_k^0 < Z \tag{7.43}$$

meaning a better program (should it give a smaller value to the objective function).

The new program produced is not a basic program, as it has *m+1* strictly positive components $x_i, (i \in I_B)$ and x_k.

Of course, when x_k increases, it is possible not to stay anymore in the section of programs. Then the question is how much x_k can increase to still remain in the section of programs. What can be noticed immediately is that with increasing the x_k, the values of the basic variables also change according to the relation.

$$x_i^B = \overline{x}_i^B - y_{ik}^B \cdot x_k \qquad i \in I_B \tag{7.44}$$

Proposition 3 If $k \in I_s$ exists so that $z_k - c_k > 0$ and all $y_{ik} \leq 0$ for all $i \in I_B$, then the problem has an infinite optimum.

Demonstration: If all $y_{ik} \leq 0$ then the relation (7.44) shows that variable x_k can increase as much as possible without any of the basic variables becoming negative. Or, in this case, the objective function:

$$\begin{aligned} Z^0 = Z - (z_k - c_k) \cdot x_k &\to -\infty \\ x_k &\to +\infty \end{aligned} \tag{7.45}$$

therefore the objective function tends to $-\infty$ along the range.

$$\begin{aligned} &x_i = \overline{x}_i - y_{ik}^B \cdot x_k \qquad && i \in I_B \\ &x_j = 0 && i \in I_S - \{k\} \ ; \ x_k \geq 0 \end{aligned} \tag{7.46}$$

Proposition 4 If $z_k - c_k > 0$ and $y_{ik} > 0$ exists, then the value of the variable x_k can increase until it reaches the value θ_l:

$$\theta_l = \frac{\overline{x}_l}{y_{l_k}} = \min_{i \in I_B} \left(\frac{\overline{x}_i}{y_{i_k}} \right) \qquad y_{jk} > 0 \tag{7.47}$$

in which case a new basic program is obtained, related to the base $\widetilde{B}$ deducted from *B* by replacing the vector a_k with the vector a_l.

Demonstration: If $y_{ik} > 0$, then, in order to have $x_i = \overline{x}_i - y_{ik}^B, x_k > 0$ for all $i \in I_B$ the following must:

$$x_k \leq \frac{x_i}{y_{ik}} \tag{7.48}$$

for all $i \in I_B$, $y_{ik} > 0$.

Let us assume that the value of the variable x_k can increase only to the value resulted from (7.47) and that this minimum is reached for the index $l \in I_B$. For this value x_l is cancelled and therefore we get a new basic program where the basic variables are x_k and $x_i, (i \in I_B)$ (meaning a basic program) corresponding to the base $\widetilde{B}$ obtained from *B* by replacing the vector a_l with the vector a_k. From the fact that $y_{ik} \neq 0$, it results that the column vectors from the matrix $\widetilde{B}$ are linearly independent.

Therefore, x_k cannot increase more than the value resulted from (7.47), as the value of the variable x_l would then become negative. Corresponding to this increase, the value of the objective function decreases by the amount:

$$\frac{x_l}{y_{l_k}} \cdot (z_k - c_k)$$

Let us observe that there may be several indicators for which $z_j - c_j > 0$. Of these, it is preferable to choose that which maximises the expression $\frac{x_l}{y_{l_j}} \cdot (z_j - c_j)$ as the fastest decrease of the objective function is provided and will lead to a smaller number of iterations in the Simplex algorithm.

In practice, a simpler criterion is however used, which is handled more easily, namely: that index *k* is chosen, for which $z_j - c_j$ is maximum, meaning $z_k - c_k = \max(z_j - c_j)$.

Therefore, applying the Simplex algorithm to solving a linear programming problem consists in the following stages:

- *an initial base B is determined and for this base, the following sizes are calculated:* $x_i^B, Z^B, z_j^B - c_j, y_{ij}^B$;
- *the differences* $z_j - c_j$ are analysed having the base input criterion; if all differences $z_j - c_j \leq 0$, the program is optimal; if there is at least one index j $\in I_S$ so that $z_j - c_j > 0$ is determined $k \in I_S$ for which $z_k - c_k = \max(z_j - c_j)$;
- *the vector that is to exit the base is determined*, having the base output criterion; if all $y_{ik} \leq 0$ the problem has an infinite optimum; if there is $y_{ik} > 0$ the index 1 is determined, so that the relation (7.47) is satisfied;
- *the vector* a_l *is replaced in the original base B with the vector* a_k *obtaining a new base* $\widetilde{B}$, which means sizes $\overline{x}_i, \overline{Z}, z_j - c_j, y_{ij}^B$ are transformed, according to the relations:

$$x_k^{\widetilde{B}} = \frac{x_l}{y_{l_k}}; \quad y_{kj}^{\widetilde{B}} = \frac{y_{l_j}}{y_{l_k}} \tag{7.49}$$

$$x_i^{\widetilde{B}} = x_i - y_{ik} \cdot \frac{\overline{x}_l}{y_{l_k}}; \quad y_{ij}^{\widetilde{B}} = y_{ij} - y_{ik} \cdot \frac{y_{l_j}}{y_{l_k}}, \quad c \neq 1 \tag{7.50}$$

$$Z^{\widetilde{B}} = Z^B - (z_k - c_k) \cdot \frac{\overline{x}_l}{y_{l_k}}; \quad z_j^{\widetilde{B}} - c_j = (z_j - c_j) - (z_k - c_k) \cdot \frac{y_{l_j}}{y_{l_k}} \tag{7.51}$$

Before proceeding, let us justify the relations (7.49), (7.50) and (7.51) from above.

From (7.39) we get for $i = l$

$$x_l = \overline{x}_l - \sum_{j \in I_S - \{k\}} y_{l_j} \cdot x_j - y_{l_k} \cdot x_k$$

The following is determined from this relation:

$$x_k = \frac{1}{y_{l_k}} \cdot \left[\overline{x}_l - \sum_{j \in I_S - \{k\}} y_{l_j} \cdot x_j - x_l \right] = x_k^{\widetilde{B}} - \sum_{j \in I_S} y_{k_j}^{\widetilde{B}} \cdot x_j \tag{7.52}$$

Where we noted:

$$I_{\widetilde{S}} = I_S - \{k\} + \{l\}, \quad x_k^{\widetilde{B}} = \frac{\overline{x}_l}{y_{l_k}}, \quad y_{k_j}^{\widetilde{B}} = \frac{y_{l_j}}{y_{l_k}} \cdot (y_{l_l} - 1)$$

The components of the relation (7.52) identical to the terms defined are the new elements of the line i = 1 expressed on the base *B*.

To express now the other basic variables x_i, $\left(i \in I_{\widetilde{B}}\right)$ according to the secondary variables x_j, $\left(j \in I_{\widetilde{S}}\right)$ we replace x_k obtained above in the other relations that give us x_i, $\left(i \in I_{\widetilde{B}} - \{l\}\right)$

We therefore have:

$$x_i = \overline{x}_i - \sum_{j \in I_S - \{k\}} y_{ij} \cdot x_j - y_{ik} \cdot x_k = \overline{x}_i - \sum_{j \in I_S - \{k\}} y_{ij} \cdot x_j - \frac{y_{l_j}}{y_{l_k}} \cdot \left(\overline{x}_l - \sum_{j \in I_S - \{k\}} y_{l_j} \cdot x_j - x_l \right) =$$
$$\left(\overline{x}_i - y_{ik} \cdot \frac{\overline{x}_l}{y_{l_k}} \right) - \sum_{j \in I_S - \{k\}} \left(y_{ij} - y_{ik} \cdot \frac{y_{l_j}}{y_{l_k}} \right) \cdot x_j + \frac{y_{ik}}{y_{l_k}} \cdot x_l = \overline{x}_i^{\widetilde{B}}$$
$$= \overline{x}_i^{\widetilde{B}} - \sum_{j \in I_S - \{k\}} y_{ij}^{\widetilde{B}} \cdot x_j \tag{7.53}$$

Where:

$$\overline{x}_i^{\widetilde{B}} = \overline{x}_i - y_{ik} \cdot \frac{\overline{x}_l}{y_{l_k}} \quad \text{şi} \quad y_{ij}^{\widetilde{B}} = y_{ij} - y_{ik} \cdot \frac{y_{l_j}}{y_{l_k}} \quad (i \neq 1) \tag{7.54}$$

The terms of this relation are precisely those defined by (7.50).

Finally, if we start from the equation (7.42) and replace with the new secondary variables, we get:

$$Z = \overline{Z} - \sum_{j \in I_S - \{k\}} (x_j - c_j) \cdot x_j - (x_k - c_k) \cdot x_k = \overline{Z} - \sum_{j \in I_S - \{k\}} (z_j - c_j) \cdot x_j - (z_k - c_k) \cdot \frac{1}{y_{l_k}} \cdot$$
$$\left[\overline{x}_l - \sum_{j \in I_S - \{k\}} y_{l_j} \cdot x_j - x_l \right] = \overline{Z}^{\widetilde{B}} - \sum_{j \in I_S} \left(z_j^{\widetilde{B}} - c_j \right) \cdot x_j$$

where we noted by:

$$I_{\tilde{S}} = I_S - \{k\} + \{l\}, \quad \widetilde{\overline{Z}}^B = \overline{Z}^B - (x_k - c_k) \cdot \frac{x_l}{y_{l_k}}$$

$$\widetilde{Z}_j^B - c_j = x_j - c_j - (x_k - c_k) \cdot \frac{y_{l_j}}{y_{l_k}} \tag{7.55}$$

The relation obtained justifies the formulas (7.51), the element located at the intersection of the line l with the column k is called pivot.

For a problem where the maximisation of the function $Z(x)$ is required in the statement of the Simplex algorithm, only the base input criterion is changed, namely: if all differences $z_j - c_j \geq 0$ then the program is optimal: if there is at least one index $j \in I_{\tilde{S}}$ so that $z_j - c_j < 0$, k is determined, so that $z_k - c_k = \min(z_j - c_j)$.

The elements required to apply the Simplex algorithm are noted in a table called Simplex table. To simplify the writing, let us assume that the base B consists of the first m columns of the matrix A and that is why the original Simplex table has the form shown in Table 7.2.

If for a problem of minimum there are differences $\Delta z_j = z_j - c_j > 0$ (and for the maximum ones $\Delta z_j = z_j - c_j < 0$) the solution $X^B = (\overline{x}_1, \overline{x}_2, \ldots, x_k, 0, \ldots, 0)$ is not optimal and will enter the vector a_k into the base, a vector determined by means of the input criterion $\Delta z_k = \max|z_j - c_j|$. The vector a_k will enter instead of vector a_l set forth by applying the base output criterion.

Table 7.2 Table of pivot calculation

			c_1	c_2	…	c_l	…	c_m	c_{m+1}	…	c_k	…	c_n	
B	C_B	$\overline{x}^B$	a_1	a_2	…	a_l	…	a_m	a_{m+1}	…	a_k	…	a_n	θ_i
a_1	c_1	$\overline{x}_1$	1	0	…	0	…	0	$a_{1,m+1}$	…	a_{1k}	…	a_{1n}	$\frac{\overline{x}_1}{a_{1k}}$
a_2	c_2	$\overline{x}_2$	0	1	…	0	…	0	$a_{2,m+1}$	…	a_{2k}	…	a_{2n}	$\frac{\overline{x}_2}{a_{2k}}$
⋮	⋮	⋮	⋮		⋮		⋮		⋮		⋮			
a_l	c_l	$\overline{x}_l$.	0	0	…	1	…	0	$a_{l,m+1}$	…	a_{lk}	…	a_{ln}	$\frac{\overline{x}_l}{a_{lk}}$
⋮	⋮	⋮	⋮		⋮		⋮		⋮		⋮			
a_m	c_m	$\overline{x}_m$	0	0	…	0	…	1	$a_{m,m+1}$	…	a_{km}	…	a_{mn}	$\frac{\overline{x}_m}{a_{mk}}$
z_j		$\overline{Z}$	c_1	c_2	…	c_l	…	c_n	z_{m+1}	…	z_k	…	z_n	–
Δz_j		–	0	0	…	0	…	0	Δz_{m+1}	…	Δz_k	…	Δz_n	–

$$\theta_l = \min_{i \in I_B} \left(\frac{\overline{x}_i}{y_{i_k}} \right) = \frac{\overline{x}_i}{y_{l_k}} \qquad y_{jk} > 0 \tag{7.56}$$

We note that in the initial Simplex table $y_{ij} = a_{ij}$ and therefore the pivot is the element a_{l_k}.

The next step of the Simplex algorithm consists in applying the relations (7.49), (7.50), (7.51) by means of which we calculate the elements of the Simplex table corresponding to the base $\widetilde{B}$. All aforementioned calculations, required to obtain a new base, are an iteration of the Simplex algorithm.

7.3 The Convergence of the Simplex Algorithm

By applying the Simplex algorithm, in a finite number of not more than C_n^m iterations, we get the solution of the linear programming problem that can be a finite or infinite optimum.

Before discussing the aspects related to the use of the Simplex algorithm for the degenerated problems, we shall analyse the degeneration cases and their consequences on the linear programming model.

Degenerated programs can arise in the following situations:

- *if the vector of the free terms has some null components, which means it is placed in the plane determined by some of the vectors a_j, then when applying the base output criterion, the ratio $\theta_l = \min(\theta_1, \theta_2, \ldots, \theta_m)$ is not uniquely determined;*
- *where the vector of the free terms is not linearly independent to any system consisting of $(m-1)$ column vectors in matrix A (this means that vector $a_0$passes through a tip of the convex polyhedron defined by the restrictions of the problem), when applying the base output criterion the ratio $\theta_l$is not uniquely determined.*

For a problem having at least one degenerated program, there is the possibility for the looping phenomenon to appear, besides the aforementioned consequences, phenomenon consisting in the return to one of the bases corresponding to a previous iteration. In this situation, the value of the objective function remains unchanged during some iterations and therefore the iterative process continues indefinitely.

It should be however noted that degeneration does not necessarily lead to the looping phenomenon and that in the practical problems solved so far no occurrence of looping was observed.

In order to eliminate the degeneration, the technique of perturbation is used, which consists in replacing the system of restrictions, the linear programming problem given in standard form with the system:

$$A \cdot x = b + \sum_{j=1}^{n} a_j \cdot \varepsilon^j \tag{7.57}$$

where a_j the column vectors of the matrix A, and $\varepsilon > 0$ is a sufficiently arbitrary number.

Without restraining the generality, we can assume that we have the base $B = (a_1, a_2, \ldots a_m)$. By multiplying the relation (7.57) on the left to B^{-1} we get the solution corresponding to this base:

$$\overline{x}_i^B(\varepsilon) = \overline{x}_i^B + \varepsilon^i + \sum_{j=m+1}^{n} y_{ij}^B \cdot \varepsilon^j \quad (i = 1, 2, \ldots m) \tag{7.58}$$

or

$$\overline{x}_i^B(\varepsilon) = \overline{x}_i^B + \sum_{j=1}^{n} y_{ij}^B \cdot \varepsilon^j \quad (i = 1, 2, \ldots m) \tag{7.59}$$

The two relations are equivalent, because $y_{ij} = 0$, and the other elements of the line i, $y_{ij} = 0$ for all $j \in B$.

Due to the perturbation of the vector of free terms, the base output criterion changes, the vector that is to be removed being determined by the relation:

$$\min_{i(y_{ik}>0)} \left(\frac{x_i^B(\varepsilon)}{y_{ik}^B} \right) = \min_{i,\, y>0_{ik}} \left(\frac{\overline{x}_i}{y_{ik}} + \frac{y_{i1}}{y_{ik}} \cdot \varepsilon + \frac{y_{i2}}{y_{ik}} \cdot \varepsilon^2 + \ldots + \frac{y_{in}}{y_{ik}} \cdot \varepsilon^n \right) \tag{7.60}$$

thus, the perturbed problem is not longer degenerated.

Based on the above relation, the following practical rule to eliminate the degeneration can be formulated:

– *first, the relations* $\frac{\overline{x}_i}{y_{ik}}$ *are compared, which also provide the size order of the relations and the following are determined: the minimum*

$$\frac{x_i^B(\varepsilon)}{y_{ik}} \quad i = 1, 2, \ldots \tag{7.61}$$

If the minimum is not unique and is done on a set of indices I_0 which compare the relations:

$$\frac{y_{i1}}{y_{ik}} \quad i \in I_0 \tag{7.62}$$

corresponding to the first power of ε.

– *if this minimum is not unique and is done for a set of indices I_1, the relations are compared:*

$$\frac{y_{i1}}{y_{ik}} \quad i \in I_1 \subset I_0 \tag{7.63}$$

which are the coefficients of ε^2.

The procedure continues as such until a unique minimum is obtained. In the worst case, the minimum of the relations:

$$\frac{y_{im}}{y_{ik}} \quad i \in I_{m-1} \subset I_{m-2} \tag{7.64}$$

must be unique and therefore the variable that comes out of the base is unequivocally defined.

Therefore, if the initially given Simplex algorithm changes with the results obtained here, the convergence of the Simplex algorithm will also be provided (in other words, the optimal solution is obtained after a finite number of iterations).

7.4 The Basic Program in the Simplex Algorithm

In order to apply the Simplex algorithm, it is necessary to know a basic program.

If the mathematical model of the linear programming problem is:

$$\begin{aligned} &\max\left[C'X\right] \\ &A \cdot X = b \\ &X \geq 0 \end{aligned} \tag{7.65}$$

By bringing it to the standard form, a basic program always appears, namely the program corresponding to the base consisting of auxiliary vectors. As not all problems that occur in practice are in this form, it results it is necessary to know the overall methods to determine an initial basic program.

Given that the Simplex algorithm applies as standard, we will consider the linear programming problem given as:

$$\begin{aligned} &\min(\max)[Z \cdot (x)] = C'X \\ &A \cdot X = b \\ &X \geq 0 \end{aligned} \tag{7.66}$$

In order to determine a basic program that would be the starting point of the Simplex algorithm, the following models can be used:

– *the method of the two phases*, which implies that matrix A of the linear programming problem (7.66) does not contain any unitary vector and that $b \geq 0$ (otherwise, we only have to multiply by -1 the restrictions for which $b_i \langle 0$).

If to each equation (restriction) i an "artificial variable" is added to, $x_i^a \geq 0$ the following is obtained:

$$\begin{aligned} & A \cdot X + I \cdot X^a = b \\ & X \geq 0,\ X^a \geq 0 \end{aligned} \tag{7.67}$$

where I is the unit matrix of the $m \times m$ type. It may immediately observed that the problem (7.66) has a solution if and only if the system (7.67) as solutions of the form $(X, X^a) \geq 0$ with $X^a = 0$.

If we get such a basic solution with $X^a = 0$, then the vector X is an initial basic solution for the problem (7.66).

Therefore, in order to obtain a solution of the system (7.67) with $X^a = 0$, we solve the linear programming problem, by using the usual Simplex algorithm:

$$\begin{aligned} & \min W = \min\left(\sum_{i=1}^{m} x_i^a\right) \\ & A \cdot X + I \cdot X^a = b \\ & X \geq 0,\ \ X^a \geq 0 \end{aligned} \tag{7.68}$$

This is phase I of the method and aims to remove the artificial variables.

For this linear programming problem, as it may be easily noticed, we have the initial basic solution $X=0$, $X^a = b$ corresponding to the base defined by the matrix I attached to the system of restrictions. Because $x_i^a \geq 0$, it results that: $\sum_{i=1}^{m} x_i^a \geq 0$ and therefore also $\min \sum_{i=1}^{m} x_i^a \geq 0$.

Two situations are possible: or minimum $W>0$ and then the problem (7.66) has no solutions, as not all artificial variables were removed from the base; all artificial variables have been removed from the base, then minimum $W=0$ and then we obtained a solution with $x_i^a = 0\ (1 \leq i \leq m)$, therefore a basic program of the problem (7.66) and with this basic program, it is proceeded to solving the problem $\min[C'X]$, which is the second phase of the method (we focused on the minimum to the objective function).

$$A \cdot X = b,\ \ X \geq 0 \tag{7.69}$$

If in problem (7.66) there is a variable x_j which appears in one equation i with coefficient $a_j = 1$, which means that matrix A contains a unitary vector, then it is no longer necessary to add an artificial variable into that equation, as the variable x_j can be taken into the initial base.

It is understood that in the situation where there are k such variables, we will insert only $m-k$ artificial variables, and the more this shortens the first phase, the higher is k;

- *the method of the artificial base with penalty coefficients* starts from the fact that the previous methods make it possible to artificially build a starting point to be able to apply afterwards the Simplex algorithm.

Let us assume that we have the linear programming problem given.

$$\begin{aligned} & \mathrm{A} \cdot \mathrm{X} = \mathrm{b} \\ & \mathrm{X} \geq 0 \\ & \min(\max)[\mathrm{Z} \cdot (\mathrm{x})] = \mathrm{C}' \mathrm{X} \end{aligned} \tag{7.70}$$

Where the matrix of the technological coefficients A is of the $m \times m$ $m<n$ type and we have no information on the rank of matrix A and therefore we cannot emphasise a base.

Creating an initial starting base in the version of their penalty consists of the following:

The given problem is replaced with a modified problem or the *extended problem* and namely: the situation where min $W=0$ may occur, but in the base, only the artificial variables $x_i^a = 0$ remained in the base. In this case, the solution is degenerated and, in order to obtain a basic solution of the problem (7.66), the process to remove the artificial variables is continued.

$$\begin{aligned} & min[Z(x)] = C'X + \Lambda' X^a \\ & A \cdot X + I \cdot X^a = b, \ \mathrm{X} \geq 0; \ \mathrm{X}^a \geq 0 \end{aligned} \tag{7.71}$$

$\Lambda = (\lambda, \lambda, \ldots, \lambda)$ is the vector of penalties having m components, all equal to λ, a sufficiently large positive number. If the objective function must be maximised, then the extended problem has the form:

$$\begin{aligned} & \mathrm{A} \cdot \mathrm{X} + \mathrm{I} \cdot \mathrm{X}^a = \mathrm{b}, \ \mathrm{X} \geq 0, \ \mathrm{X}^a \geq 0 \\ & \max[\mathrm{Z}(\mathrm{x})] = \mathrm{C}'\mathrm{X} - \Lambda'\mathrm{X}^a \end{aligned} \tag{7.72}$$

with the same notations we mentioned.

If the initial problem has the finite optimal solution, it will also be optimal solution for the extended problem.

Mutually, any optimal solution of the exiting problem that does not have any strictly positive artificial variable is an optimal solution of the initial problem.

If the initial problem has the objective function unbounded (corresponding to its optimum category) and the extended problem will have the objective function unbounded; the converse is also true.

This is why it is sufficient to solve the extended problem, where a possible basic solution was emphasised, in order to determine the optimal solution of the initial problem.

In the first stage, the extended problem for which there is the obvious initial base which the basic solution corresponds to:

$$X^a = b, \; \left(x_1^a = b_1; x_2^a = b_2, \ldots, x_m^a = b_m\right) \tag{7.73}$$

In order to determine the vector that enters into the base, that difference $z_j - c_j$ containing the term λ with the greatest positive coefficient is chosen (i sit is a problem of minimum) or the lowest negative coefficient (if it is a problem of maximum).

If an artificial vector has been removed from the base, we can calculate further its components in the new base.

The first stage ends when after applying the Simplex algorithm we encounter one of the following situations: all artificial vectors were removed from the base.

Thus, an initial basic solution of the initial problem was determined, by means of which we pass to the second stage when the initial problem is solved: not all the artificial vectors were determined from the base, but the unknowns corresponding to the artificial vectors remained in the base are null and the optimum conditions are verified. We thus obtained a possible basic degenerated solution of the initial problem; at least one artificial vector remained in the base, which a strictly positive variable corresponds to and the negativity (or positivity) conditions of the differences $z_j - c_j$ are verified.

In this case, the initial problem does not have the basic possible solution and therefore it does not have the optimal solution.

In the second stage, the application of the Simplex algorithm with the basic solution obtained on the first stage is continued, until all quantities $z_j - c_j$ are negative (respectively positive) or it is shown that the problem does not admit an optimal solution.

7.5 The Dual Simplex Algorithm

Be it a base *B* for the primal problem of minimum so that the conditions $z_j - c_j \leq 0$, $(z_j - c_j \geq 0)$ are verified, if it is a problem of maximum.

The vector $C_B' \cdot B^{-1}$ is a dual program for the main problem and in the case of a problem to minimise, we shall have:

$$C_B' \cdot B^{-1} \cdot a_j = Z_j \leq C_j \quad (j = 1, 2, \ldots, n) \tag{7.74}$$

The corresponding vector X^B is called as such after we have seen the basic achievable dual program (solution).

If in addition $X^B \geq 0$, meaning it is a primal program achievable, then the base B is optimal for the primal problem and therefore $C_B' \cdot B^{-1}$ is an optimal program of the dual.

The dual Simplex algorithm starts from a dually achievable solution, but which is not achievable (for the primal problem) and aims to remove the negative variables from the base, by maintaining the optimality criterion verified in each iteration.

Let us assume that by starting with the primal problem:

$$\min[Z(x)] = C' \cdot X, \;\; A \cdot X = b, \;\; X \geq 0 \tag{7.75}$$

the dual of which is:

$$\max[G(u)] = b' \cdot U, \; U' \cdot A \leq C', \; U \text{ any} \tag{7.76}$$

It may be immediately observed that for any couple (X,U) of primal dual programs, we have:

$$\overline{U}' \cdot b \leq C' \cdot \overline{X} \tag{7.77}$$

Let us assume that a base B is known for the primal problem:

$$\left(B = \left(a_{j1}, a_{j2}, \ldots, a_s, \ldots, a_{jm}\right)\right), \; \{j_1, j_2, \ldots, j_s, \ldots, j_m\} \in \bar{J}_B \tag{7.78}$$

so that $U' = C_B' \cdot B^{-1}$ is a dual program, meaning:

$$\widetilde{U}' \cdot a_j \leq c_j, \; (j \in J_B), \tag{7.79}$$

or written otherwise

$$z_j - c_j \leq 0, \; (j \in J_s) \tag{7.80}$$

We assume that the basic primal solution $\overline{X}^B = B^{-1} \cdot b$ is dually achievable.

If U is not optimal solution, then $\overline{X}^B$ is not a program for the primal problem, meaning there is at least one index s so that $\overline{x}_b \leq 0$.

Conversely, if there is $\overline{x}_l \langle 0$ then we can find another solution $\tilde{U}$, better than $\bar{U}$.

Be ρ_l the limit of index l of the matrix B^{-1} and let us note $\widetilde{U}' = \overline{U}' - \theta \cdot \beta_l$

By multiplying to the right by b, we get:

$$\widetilde{U}' \cdot b = \overline{U}' \cdot b - \theta \cdot \beta_l \cdot b = \overline{U}' \cdot b - \theta \cdot \overline{x}_l \tag{7.81}$$

It results from here that for any $\theta > 0$ we get $U' \cdot b > \overline{U}' \cdot b$ (meaning a better value of the objective function).

On the other hand:

$$\widetilde{U}' \cdot a_j = \overline{U} \cdot a_j - \theta \cdot \beta_l \cdot a_j \cdot (j = 1, 2, \ldots, n) \tag{7.82}$$

Meaning: $\widetilde{U}' \cdot a_j = \overline{U} \cdot a_j - \theta \cdot y_{lj} = z_j - \theta \cdot y_{lj},\ j \in J_s$

$$\begin{aligned} \widetilde{U}' \cdot a_s &= \overline{U} \cdot a_s = z_s = c_s,\ s \in J_s - \{l\} \\ \widetilde{U}' \cdot a_l &= \overline{U} \cdot a_l - \theta = z_l - \theta = c_l - \theta \end{aligned} \tag{7.83}$$

Now, two cases are possible:

- $y_{lj} \geq 0,\ j \in J_s$

  In this case, U' is a dual program whatever $\theta > 0$ may be and if we make $\theta \to \infty$ in the relation $U' \cdot b = \overline{U}' \cdot b - \theta \cdot x_l$ it results that the dual does not admit a maximum.

  Therefore, in this case, the primal problem does not admit an optimal solution;
- $y_{lj} < 0$ For at least one index $j \in J_s$

  In this case, U' remains a dual program only and only if $z_j - \theta \cdot y_{lj} \leq c_j,\ _{(j \in J_s)}$, therefore for:

$$\theta \leq \min_{j / y_{lj} \langle 0} \left[\frac{z_j - c_j}{y_{lj}} \right],\ j \in J_s \tag{7.84}$$

If we take:

$$\theta = \frac{z_k - c_k}{y_{lk}} = \min_{j / y_{lj} \langle 0} \left[\frac{z_j - c_j}{y_{lj}} \right],\ j \in J_s \tag{7.85}$$

then:

$$U' \cdot a_k = z_k - \theta \cdot y_{lk} = z_k - \frac{z_k - c_k}{y_{lk}} \cdot y_{lk} = c_k \tag{7.86}$$

Let us consider the matrix *B* deduced from *B* by replacing the vector a_l with the vector a_k.

Because $Y_{lk} \neq 0$, it results that $\widetilde{B}$ is a base with the set of the indices of the column vectors $\left\{ Y_{\widetilde{B}} = Y_B - \{l\} + \{k\} \right\}$ then $\widetilde{U}' \widetilde{B} = C'_{\widetilde{B}}$ and thus $\widetilde{U}' = C\widetilde{B}' \cdot \widetilde{B}$

Let us note $\widetilde{X}^{\widetilde{B}} = \widetilde{B}^{-1} \cdot b$ the new basic solution.

If $\widetilde{\widetilde{X}}_S^B \geq 0$ this basic solution will be an optimal basic program of the dual problem.

If $\widetilde{\widetilde{X}}_S^B < 0$ for at least one index $s \in J_{\widetilde{B}}$, the iterative process is continued, obtaining a new dual solution $\widetilde{\widetilde{U}}$ of better decision.

At each iteration, if the case when $\theta=0$ is (temporarily) removed, the value of the objective function of the dual [G(u)] is strictly increasing and therefore no base can be repeated.

On the other hand, in order to start applying the algorithm, we must know a dual program, which excludes the possibility that the primal problem would not have a minimum finite. As the number of bases is obtained after a finite number of iterations, we necessarily reach (at the latest when we have gone through all the bases) one of the following situations:

$\overline{X}^B \geq 0$ and therefore the program is optimal.

Or $\overline{x}_l^B < 0 \ (l \in J_B)$ and $Y_{lj} \geq 0 (j \in J_s)$ and the primal problem does not have a solution.

To obtain in each iteration the maximum increase of the objective function of the dual form, we must determine the index l so that:

$$\overline{x}_l \left(\frac{Z_k - C_k}{Y_{lk}} \right) \tag{7.87}$$

would be maximum.

However, just as it was also done for the primal Simplex algorithm, in practice this condition is replaced by a simpler one:

$$\begin{aligned} &\overline{x}_l = \min\{\overline{x}_s\} \quad s \in J_B \\ &s/\overline{x}_s < 0 \end{aligned} \tag{7.88}$$

In each iteration, the value of the objective function of the dual premium increases and therefore also that of the dual problem.

The steps of the dual simplex algorithm are:

- *a base of the primal problem is determined, so that* $Z_j - C_j \leq 0$ *(or* $Z_j - C_j \geq 0$ *in the case of the problem of maximum)*;
- *the optimal solution* $\overline{X}^B = B^{-1} \cdot b$ *is tested.* If $\overline{X}^B \geq 0$, the program is optimal. Otherwise, be $I_l^B = \{s \in J_B : \overline{x}_s < 0\}$
- $Y_{sj}(s \in I_l^B, j \in J_s)$ *is tested.* If $Y_{sj} \geq 0$ for at least one $s \in I_l^B$ and any $j \in J_s$ the primal problem has no programs.

If there is $Y_{sj} < 0$ for at least one $j \in J_s$ and any $s \in I_l^B$ l of the relation is determined:

$$\overline{x}_l = \min_{s \in I_l}\{x_s\} \tag{7.89}$$

Which is the criterion of base output and then the k index from the following relation is determined:

$$\frac{x_k - c_k}{Y_{lk}} = \left[\frac{z_j - c_j}{Y_{lj}}\right]_{j/Y_{lj<0}} \tag{7.90}$$

which is the criterion of base input. In the case of the problems of maximum, the ratio with maximum value is chosen:

– *a new base* $\widetilde{B}$ *deduced through B by replacing the vector* a_n*with the vector* a_k*and the new Simplex table is calculated, according to the rule known, to the primal Simplex algorithm.*

The algorithm is repeated from step b until the optimal solution is obtained.

In the case of the problems of maximum, the operation of minimum is replaced with that of maximum in the relation that defines the criterion of base input.

This algorithm will be used in application for *Parametric programming*.

7.6 Re-optimisation and Parameterisation in Linear Programming

Besides the variables x_j the level of which must be determined, the linear programming problems also contain a number of constant sizes materialised in the components of the vectors *b*, *C* and from the matrix *A*. It is obvious that the practical value of the optimal solution depends on the accuracy by which the level of these constants has been determined. The previously analysed methods of linear programming are static models, they do not capture the dynamic aspects of the economic phenomena. But in the practical activity, frequent changes of the conditions underlying the linear programming model appear.

Therefore, the need to develop some mathematical methods appeared, which would enable the dynamic approach of the economic phenomena.

The re-optimisation and parameterisation of the linear programming problems only deal with the aspects related to the variation of elements, *constants* of the models attached to the economic phenomena.

The *re-optimisation* or post-optimisation consist in recalculating the optimal solutions of a linear programming problem in the case where the axes between the initial conditions change.

Through the *parameterisation* of a linear programming problem, it is aimed to determine the possible variants of optimal solutions in the case where some of the *constants* of the model vary linearly or non-linearly according to one or several given parameters.

It is known that during the execution of production, there may occur a number of changes of some elements that are the informational support of the linear programming models, against the optimal program determined based on some preset economic and technical conditions.

Thus, the components of the vector of free terms may change compared to their level preset following the change of the capacity of the means of production, the availability of labour force or raw materials, the change of the level required to some economic or technical indicators that characterise the *quality* of an optimal program.

Changing the manufacturing technology has direct effects on the production costs and on the specific consumptions of resources. If these changes have not been directly anticipated, the solution of the linear programming model used to optimise the production program does not correspond to the actual conditions in which the economic process is performed.

If during the planning period a product is assimilated in the linear programming model, a new variable must be inserted and therefore, the matrix A will include a new column vector. Replacing a source of energy with another, a material with another etc. involves the inclusion of some additional restrictions into the model.

In such situations, the question arises whether the optimal solution obtained based on the initial conditions still maintains its optimality feature after their change. In order to answer the question, we will need to verify the solution in the new conditions. If, by verification, we reached the conclusion that the solution is no longer optimal, then a new problem arises, that of finding methods to re-optimise the solution, methods that would use the previous results, for thus the volume of calculations would decrease as much as possible, even if they are done on an electronic computer.

Therefore, the purpose of re-optimisation is to study the changes that occur in the optimal solution of a linear problem when the data of the problem change. The importance of such a study lies in the economy of work that can be done, by using the information we already have, meaning the optimal solution known.

In the process of re-optimisation, the following aspects will be addressed separately: changing the vector of *free terms;* changing the vector of *costs* C; changing a column vector of the matrix A; changing a line vector from A; changing the number of the system restrictions; changing the number of variables.

In order to re-optimise a linear programming problem, it is necessary to go through the following stages:

- *verifying the optimality of the solution under the conditions of changing the data of the problem;*
- *determining the optimal solution of the modified problem (if the solution of the initial problem is no longer optimal).*

As the re-optimisation refers to the optimal solution $\left(\overline{X}^B\right)$ of the problem:

$$\begin{aligned} \min(\max)[Z(x)] &= C' \cdot X \\ A \cdot X &= b \\ X &\geq 0 \end{aligned} \tag{7.91}$$

We shall further deal with all cases of re-optimisation based on the standard form of the linear programming problem and namely:

- *modifying the vector of the free terms*, assuming that the vector b is replaced by $\widetilde{b} = b + \delta b$ then the optimal solution $\left(\overline{X}^B\right)$ changes as follows:

$$\widetilde{X}^B = B^{-1} \cdot \widetilde{b} = B^{-1} \cdot (b + \delta b) = \overline{X}^B + B^{-1} \cdot \delta b \tag{7.92}$$

  As the differences $\Delta Z = C'_B \cdot B^{-1} \cdot A - C'$ are independent of the vector b, the new solution $\left(\overline{X}^B\right)$ is: optimal if all components of the solution are positive $\left(\overline{X}^B \geq 0\right)$; dually achievable if the vector $\left(\overline{X}^B\right)$ also has negative components.

  In the second case, in order to find the optimal solution, the vector $\left(\overline{X}^B\right)$ is inserted in the column of free terms in the final Simplex table of the initial problem and the dual Simplex algorithm is applied;
- *modifying the coefficients of the objective function*, if after solving the initial problem the vector of the coefficients of the objective function becomes $\widetilde{C}' = C' + \delta C'$, then the solution $\overline{X}^B = B^{-1} \cdot b$ remains unchanged, but the differences ΔZ_j

$$\begin{aligned} \widetilde{z}_j + \widetilde{c}_j &= \widetilde{C}'_B \cdot B^{-1} \cdot a_j - \widetilde{c}_j \\ &= C'_B \cdot B^{-1} \cdot a_j + \left(\delta C'\right)_B \cdot B^{-1} \cdot a_j - \left(\delta c_j\right) \quad \text{change.} \end{aligned} \tag{7.93}$$

  Based on the analysis of the new differences, two cases are distinguished: all differences $z_j - c_j$ corresponding to the vectors that do not belong to the base B maintain the sign they had before changing the vector C (≤ 0 for the problem of minimum and ≥ 0 for the problem of maximum), which means that the new solution will also be optimal.

  The value of the objective function in the modified problem is:

$$\begin{aligned} \min(\max)\widetilde{C} \cdot X = \widetilde{C}' \cdot B^{-1} &= \left(C' + \delta C'\right)_B \cdot \overline{X}^B \\ &= C' \cdot B^{-1} + \left(\delta C'\right)_B \cdot \overline{X}^B \end{aligned} \tag{7.94}$$

  It results from this relation that the objective function gets another value only if modifying the vector C affects the components corresponding to the basic variables. At least one of the differences $\widetilde{z}_j - \widetilde{c}_j$, corresponding to a vector that does not belong to the base is positive in the case of the problem of minimum and negative in the case of the problem of maximum. In this situation, the optimal solution of the initial (unmodified) problem is no longer optimal and the opti misation is continued also by applying the primal Simplex algorithm by starting from the last Simplex table;

- *choosing some column vectors in matrix A*, if the production program must include new products that have not been taken into account when forming the initial model, re-optimisation consists in adapting the optimal solution found for the initial problem to the increased problem. For this, we shall need to see if the new column vectors inserted satisfy the optimality criterion.

  For this purpose, we need to recalculate the components of the vector $a_l, l \in \widetilde{N}$ (it is the set of newly inserted indices of the vectors) in the optimal base B, afterwards we can calculate the differences $z_l - c_l, l \in \widetilde{N}$.

  Two new situations may appear now: *the conditions of optimality are verified for all vectors* $a_l, l \in \widetilde{N}$ and in this case, the optimal solution of the initial problem also remains for the increased problem; there is at least one vector $a_l, l \in \widetilde{N}$ that does not verify the optimality criterion and, in this case, the Simplex algorithm is continued to determine the optimal solution;

- *modifying a column vector of the matrix A*, in the case where the column vector a_r from matrix A changes and after the optimal solution has been obtained $\left(\overline{X}^B\right)$.

  Obviously, the modified vector a_r can belong or not to the base B and depending on this, we shall consider two situations: the vector a_r does not belong to the base B. In this case, verifying the optimality of the solution $\left(\overline{X}^B\right)$, under the new conditions, comes down to calculating the difference $z_r - c_r$; the vector a_r belongs to the base B, in this case the components of the modified vector $\tilde{a}_r$ in the base B are:

$$y_{ir} = \beta_i \cdot \widetilde{a}_r \tag{7.95}$$

where β_i is the vector the components of which are elements on the line from matrix B^{-1}.

However, $\tilde{a}_r$ can replace a_r in the base if the components of vector $\tilde{a}_r$ corresponding to a_r is different than zero, meaning:

$$y_{rr} = \beta_r \cdot \widetilde{a}_r \neq 0 \tag{7.96}$$

If this condition is met, we shall need to calculate the reverse of the base B obtained from the base by replacing the vector a_r with the vector $\tilde{a}_r$.

For this, we proceed as follows:

We calculate the vector:

$$g = (g_1, g_2, \ldots, g_m) = B^{-1} \cdot \widetilde{a}_r \tag{7.97}$$

and the following vector is formed

$$g^* = \left(-\frac{g_1}{g_r}, -\frac{g_2}{g_r}, \ldots, -\frac{g_{r-1}}{g_r}, \frac{1}{g_r}, \frac{g_{r+1}}{g_r}, \ldots, -\frac{g_m}{g_r} \right) \tag{7.98}$$

The unit matrix of m order is written, where the vector e_r is replaced by g^* and this matrix $E_r^{(m)}$ is noted

With this matrix, we get the wanted reverse.

$$B^{-1} = E_r^{(m)} \cdot B^{-1} \tag{7.99}$$

Having now the reverse of the base $\widetilde{B}$, it is easy to calculate

$$\overline{X}^{\widetilde{B}} = \widetilde{B}^{-1} \cdot b \tag{7.100}$$

and the differences

$$z_j - c_j = C_B' \cdot \widetilde{B}^{-1} \cdot a_j - c_j \tag{7.101}$$

by means of which we test the optimality of this solution.

– *adding some restrictions*, considering the general case in which other r relations of the following type are added to the initial system of restrictions:

$$\sum_{i=1}^{n} a_{m+p,j} \cdot x_j + x_{k+m+p} = b_{m+p} \; (p = 1, 2, \; \ldots \; r) \tag{7.102}$$

Replacing the variables $x_k (k \in B)$ in the above relations, we get linear functions of x variables that do not belong to the base. The free terms in these linear functions noted b_{m+p} can be positive, null or negative numbers.

By completing the vector $\overline{X}$ with the components $\overline{x}_{n+m+p} = b_{m+p}$ $(1 \leq p \leq r)$, vector $\overline{X}$ is obtained, which is a basic solution for the system consisting of the conditions:

$$\begin{aligned} &\sum_{j=1}^{n} a_{ij} \cdot x_j + x_{n+i} = b_i \quad (1 \leq i \leq m) \\ &\sum_{j=1}^{n} a_{m+p,j} \cdot x_j + x_{m+n+p} = b_{m+p} \quad (1 \leq p \leq r) \end{aligned} \tag{7.103}$$

The mathematical model of a linear programming problem where the coefficients of the objective function are linear functions of a parameter α has the following form:

$$\min(\max)[Z(x)] = C'(\alpha) \cdot X$$

in the conditions:

$$\begin{aligned} A \cdot X &= b \\ X &\geq 0 \end{aligned} \tag{7.104}$$

where $C(\alpha) = C^{(0)} + \alpha \cdot C'$ with $\alpha \in \mathfrak{R}$.

The study of the set of optimal solutions requires knowing the optimal solution corresponding to a particular value of the parameter α $(\alpha = \alpha \text{ or } \alpha = 0)$. If $\alpha = 0$ then the above problem is solved for $C(\alpha) = C^{(0)}$ obtaining the optimal base B corresponding to this value.

As it is known, changing the components of the vector C only has effect on the differences Z_j–C_j, which have the form:

$$\begin{aligned} Z_j(\alpha) - C_j(\alpha) &= C'_B(\alpha) \cdot B_a^{-1} - C_j(\alpha) \\ &= \left(C_B^{(0)} + \alpha \cdot C_B^{(1)}\right)' \cdot B^{-1} \cdot a_j - \left(C_j^{(0)} + \alpha \cdot C_j^{(1)}\right) = \\ &= C^{(0)} \cdot B^{-1} \cdot a_j - C_j^{(0)} + \alpha \cdot \left(C_B^{(1)} \cdot B^{-1} \cdot a_j - C_j^{(1)}\right) \\ &= \left(Z_j^{(0)} - C_j^{(0)}\right) + \alpha \cdot \left(Z_j^{(1)} - C_j^{(1)}\right) \end{aligned} \tag{7.105}$$

If we refer to a problem of maximum, the analysis of these differences highlights the following situations:

- $Z_j^{(0)} - C_j^{(0)}$ *for any* $j \in J_s$ *and therefore the optimal solution for* $\alpha = 0$ *was found.*
- *there is* $Z_s^{(0)} - C_s^{(0)} < 0$ *for a subset of vectors* $a_s \in J_s$ *and all components* Y_{is}, $i \in J_s$ *of these vectors in the base B are negative. Then the problem has no finite optimal for* $\alpha = 0$.

If the system of inequations $(Z_s^{(0)} - C_s^{(0)}) + \alpha \cdot (Z_s^{(1)} - C_s^{(1)}) > 0$ for $S \in I_1 \subset J_S$ is not compatible, or i fit is a difference $Z_s^{(1)} - C_s^{(1)} = 0$ for $S \in J_B$, then the problem has no finite optimal for any value of the parameter α.

If the system $\left(Z_j^{(0)} - C_j^{(0)}\right) + \alpha \cdot \left(Z_j^{(1)} - C_j^{(1)}\right) > 0$ is compatible, the lowest value of the parameter α that satisfies all inequations is determined. The base *B* is optimal for $\alpha = \alpha_0$ and the problem has no finite optimal for $\alpha < \alpha_0$.

Let us show that the system:

$$\left(Z_s^{(0)} - C_s^{(0)}\right) + \alpha \cdot \left(Z_s^{(1)} - C_s^{(1)}\right) > 0 \tag{7.106}$$

is incompatible if and only if not all differences $Z_s^{(1)} - C_s^{(1)}$ are of the same sign. Indeed, let us assume that there is an index s_1 for which $Z_{s1}^{(1)} - C_{s1}^{(1)} < 0$ and the condition:

$$\left(Z_{s1}^{(0)} - C_{s1}^{(0)}\right) + \alpha \cdot \left(Z_{s1}^{(1)} - C_{s1}^{(1)}\right) > 0 \tag{7.107}$$

is satisfied, then:

$$\alpha < \frac{Z_{s1}^{(0)} - C_{s1}^{(0)}}{-\left(Z_{s1}^{(1)} - C_{s1}^{(1)}\right)} < 0$$

Because

$$-\left(Z_{s1}^{(1)} - C_{s1}^{(1)}\right) > 0 \tag{7.108}$$

$$Z_{s1}^{(0)} - C_{s1}^{(0)} > 0$$

If there is also an index $s_2 \in I_2 \subset J_s$ for which $\left(Z_{s2}^{(1)} - C_{s2}^{(1)}\right) > 0$ and the following condition is satisfied:

$$\left(Z_{s2}^{(0)} - C_{s2}^{(0)}\right) + \alpha \cdot \left(Z_{s2}^{(1)} - C_{s2}^{(1)}\right) > 0$$

then:

$$\alpha > \frac{Z_{s2}^{(0)} - C_{s2}^{(0)}}{-\left(Z_{s2}^{(1)} - C_{s2}^{(1)}\right)} > 0 \tag{7.109}$$

conditions that cannot be simultaneously satisfied, which demonstrates the statement made.

Therefore, in the parametric programming problems wherein the vector C is linear function of a single parameter, tables corresponding to the simple iterations can be formed, by taking into account the components of the vector $C^{(0)}$ and after a finite number of iterations, one of the following situations is reached:

- *an optimal base B is found for a determined value of the parameter α.*
- *it may be observed that the problem has no optimal solution for any value of the parameter α;*

Therefore, we assume we have determined the base B corresponding to the value $\alpha = \alpha_0$ of the parameter. Without restricting the generality of the problem, we assume that $\alpha = 0$, which can always be done by a convenient change of the origin.

This base remains optimal for all values α for which:

$$\left(Z_j^{(0)} - C_j^{(0)}\right) + \alpha \cdot \left(Z_j^{(1)} - C_j^{(1)}\right) \geq 0 \quad j \in J_s \tag{7.110}$$

As B is optimal for $\alpha = 0$, it results that

$$\left(Z_j^{(0)} - C_j^{(0)}\right) \geq 0, \quad j \in J_s \tag{7.111}$$

Therefore we can determine $[\underline{\alpha}, \overline{\alpha}]$, so that for $\alpha \in [\underline{\alpha}, \overline{\alpha}]$ we would have an optimal base B, where:

$$\underline{\alpha} = \begin{cases} \max\left(-\dfrac{Z_j^{(0)} - C_j^{(0)}}{Z_j^{(1)} - C_j^{(1)}}\right) & \text{if } \left(Z_j^{(0)} - C_j^{(0)}\right) > 0 \text{ for one } j \in J_s \\ -\infty \text{ if } \left(Z_j^{(1)} - C_j^{(1)}\right) \leq 0 & \text{for all } j \in J_s \end{cases} \tag{7.112}$$

and

$$\overline{\alpha} = \begin{cases} \min\left(-\dfrac{Z_j^{(0)} - C_j^{(0)}}{Z_j^{(1)} - C_j^{(1)}}\right) & \text{if } (\exists) \left(x_j^{(0)} - x_j^{(0)}\right) < 0 \text{ for one } j \in J_s \\ -\infty \ \textit{if} \ \left(x_j^{(1)} - x_j^{(1)}\right) \geq 0 & \text{for all } j \in J_s \end{cases} \tag{7.113}$$

It is of interest the case where at least one of the critical values is finite.

If $\overline{\alpha}$ has finite value, then a number of sub-ranges of the range $[\overline{\alpha}, \infty]$ and the corresponding optimal bases are taken into account in the case where $\overline{\alpha}$ is uniquely determined from the relation (7.113), meaning that:

$$\overline{\alpha} = \min\left(-\frac{Z_j^{(0)} - C_j^{(0)}}{Z_j^{(1)} - C_j^{(1)}}\right) = -\frac{Z_k^{(0)} - C_k^{(0)}}{Z_k^{(1)} - C_k^{(1)}} \tag{7.114}$$

the vector a_k shall enter into the new base because $Z_k^{(1)} - C_k^{(1)} < 0$ şi and for a ε, we get:

$$Z_k(\overline{\alpha}+\varepsilon) - C_k \cdot (\overline{\alpha}+\varepsilon) = \left[\left(Z_k^{(0)} - C_k^{(0)}\right) + (\overline{\alpha}+\varepsilon) \cdot \left(Z_k^{(1)} - C_k^{(1)}\right)\right] < 0 \tag{7.115}$$

According to the primal Simplex algorithm, the vector a_k will enter the base B_I (meaning there is $y_{ik}>0$) instead of vector a_l determined based on the base output criterion. By calculating the differences $\Delta Z_j(\overline{\alpha}+\varepsilon)$ corresponding to the base B_I we get:

$$Z_k \cdot (\overline{\alpha}+\varepsilon) - C_k(\overline{\alpha}+\varepsilon) = 0$$

$$\begin{aligned} Z_j \cdot (\overline{\alpha}+\varepsilon) - C_j(\overline{\alpha}+\varepsilon) &= \left(Z_j^{(0)} - C_j^{(0)}\right) + (\overline{\alpha}+\varepsilon) \cdot \left(Z_j^{(1)} - C_j^{(1)}\right) \\ &-\frac{Y_{1j}}{Y_{lk}} \cdot \varepsilon \cdot \left(Z_k^{(0)} - C_k^{(0)}\right) = \\ &= \left(Z_j^{(0)} - C_j^{(0)}\right) + \overline{\alpha} \cdot \left(Z_j^{(1)} - C_j^{(1)}\right) + \varepsilon \cdot \left[\left(Z_j^{(1)} - C_j^{(1)}\right) - \frac{Y_{1j}}{Y_{lk}} \cdot \left(Z_k^{(0)} - C_k^{(0)}\right)\right] \end{aligned} \tag{7.116}$$

If $\left(Z_j^{(1)} - C_j^{(1)}\right) - \frac{Y_{1j}}{Y_{lk}} \cdot \left(Z_k^{(1)} - C_k^{(1)}\right) \geq 0$ for all $j \in J_s - \{k\}$, it results that: $Z_j \cdot (\overline{\alpha}+\varepsilon) - C_j(\overline{\alpha}+\varepsilon) \geq 0$ for any ε and therefore the new optimal base B for all the values of α.

But if $\left(Z_j^{(1)} - C_j^{(1)}\right) - \frac{Y_{1j}}{Y_{lk}} \cdot \left(Z_k^{(0)} - C_k^{(0)}\right) < 0$ for a set of indicators $j \in J_s - \{k\}$, the following value is determined:

$$\varepsilon = \min\left[-\frac{\left(Z_j^{(0)} - C_j^{(0)}\right) + \overline{\alpha}\left(Z_j^{(1)} - C_j^{(1)}\right)}{\left(Z_j^{(1)} - C_j^{(1)}\right) - \frac{Y_{1j}}{Y_{lk}} \cdot \left(Z_k^{(1)} - C_k^{(1)}\right)}\right] \tag{7.117}$$

for $\left(Z_j^{(1)} - C_j^{(1)}\right) - \frac{Y_{1j}}{Y_{lk}} \cdot \left(Z_k^{(1)} - C_k^{(1)}\right) < 0$

It may be seen that $\varepsilon>0$.

It results from here that the base B_I is optimal for

$$\alpha \in [\overline{\alpha}, \alpha_1] \text{ where } \alpha_1 = \overline{\alpha}+\varepsilon \tag{7.118}$$

If α_1 is infinite, the problem is concluded, and if it is not, by further applying the same procedure, the sequence of optimal bases $B_2, B_3, \ldots, B_p$ for $\alpha \in [\alpha_{h-1}, \alpha_h]$ $h = 2, 3 \ldots, p$ with $\alpha_1^{'} = \underline{\alpha}$ (where α_p can be ∞) is determined, until the entire range of the variation of parameter α is covered.

An analogous reasoning enables us to construct the sequence of optimal bases $\widetilde{B}_1, \widetilde{B}_2, \ldots \widetilde{B}_q$ for $\alpha \in \left[\alpha_p^{'}, \alpha_{p-1}^{'}\right]$, $p = 2, 3, \ldots q$ with $\alpha_1^{'} = \underline{\alpha}$ where $\alpha_q^{'}$ can be $-\infty$.

Table 7.3 The supplier-beneficiary relationship

	Beneficiaries				
Suppliers	B1	B2	B3	B4	Quantity available
F1					1,300
F2					1,300
F3					700
Quantity required	1,000	1,200	800	300	3,300

The values $\alpha_1,\alpha_2,\ldots\alpha_p$ si $\alpha_1^{'},\alpha_2^{'},\ldots,\alpha_p^{'}$ are called critical values of the parameter and they divide the set of the values of this parameter into subsets featured by the fact that an optimal base is associated to each of these subsets.

Two optimal bases correspond to each value, therefore an infinity of optimal solutions obtained as linear combinations of two optimal solutions.

If $\overline{\alpha}$ is not uniquely determined, the differences $Z_j(\overline{\alpha}) - C_j\overline{\alpha}$ are cancelled for a subset of indices $S_1 \in S$, and the corresponding differences will be negative for $\alpha = \alpha_1 + \varepsilon \ (\varepsilon > 0)$ and several iterations will be necessary to obtain an optimal base.

The procedure for obtaining them is analogous to the case where $\overline{\alpha}$ is uniquely determined, with the unique difference that the bases corresponding to the values of the parameter $\alpha > \overline{\alpha}$ and $\alpha < \overline{\alpha}$ differ by more than one vector.

An industrial enterprise must supply the raw material it has in three warehouses (*A*, *B* and *C*) to the four production departments it subordinates.

The warehouses *A* and *B* have 1,300 tons of that raw materials, and the warehouse *C* has 700 tons available. According to the provisions of the supply plan, the first department needs a quantity of 1,000 tons, the second department 1,200 tons, the third department 800 tons, and the fourth one 300 tons.

The distances from the warehouses to the four departments and the quantities available and those necessary to the departments are shown in Table 7.3, where the three suppliers (warehouses) have been noted with F1, F2, F3 and the four beneficiary units (departments) have been noted with B1, B2, B3, B4.

Taking into account the data shown in the previous table, an optimal transportation plan must be prepared, having the minimisation of the tons-kilometres as optimisation criterion.

To describe the equations of the problem, the quantity of the given raw material is noted with X_{ij}, which is transported from the supplier (warehouse) i, to the beneficiary (department) j. In our example, i has the values 1, 2, 3, and j the values 1, 2, 3, 4.

The mathematical model of the problem is as follows:

$$minF(x) = min(5X_{11} + 4X_{12} + 2X_{13} + X_{14} + 2X_{21} + 5X_{22} + 4X_{23} + 5X_{24} + 3X_{31} + 3X_{32} + 2X_{33} + 4X_{34})$$

with the restrictions:

$$\begin{aligned}
X_{11} + X_{12} + X_{13} + X_{14} &= 1{,}300 \\
X_{21} + X_{22} + X_{23} + X_{24} &= 1{,}300 \\
X_{31} + X_{32} + X_{33} + X_{34} &= 700 \\
X_{11} + X_{21} + X_{31} &= 1{,}000 \\
X_{12} + X_{22} + X_{32} &= 1{,}200 \\
X_{13} + X_{23} + X_{33} &= 800 \\
X_{14} + X_{24} + X_{34} &= 300
\end{aligned}$$

$$X_{ij} \geq 0$$
$$i = 1, 2, 3;\ j = 1, 2, 3, 4$$

The first equation states the following condition: the quantity transported from the supplier *1* to the beneficiary *1*, plus the quantity transported from the supplier *1* to the beneficiary *2*, plus the quantity transported from the supplier *1* to the beneficiary 3, plus the quantity transported from the supplier 1 to the beneficiary *4* must be equal to *1,300*. The equations *2* and *3* are read similarly.

The fourth equation states the following condition: the quantity of raw material transported from the supplier *1* to the beneficiary *1*, plus the quantity transported from the supplier *2* to the beneficiary *1*, plus the quantity transported from the supplier *3* to the beneficiary *1* must be equal to *1,000*. The equations *5*, *6* and *7* are read similarly.

The eighth equation states the condition that the different quantities transported from the supplier *i* to the beneficiary *j* would be greater than or at least equal to zero.

From the possible solutions of the problem, that which makes the function to optimise minimum is to be found.

A problem of transportation is solved in two stages, and namely:

- *an initial solution of the problem is determined in the first stage;*
- *its optimisation is done during the second stage.*

To determine a basic solution, different procedures may be used, such as the North-West corner process or the main diagonal, the procedure of the maximum differences, the procedure of the minimum element on the column etc.

To optimise the basic solution during the second stage, several methods can also be used, such as: distributive method, the method of potentials, the stepping-stone method (step-scale), etc.

For the first stage, we shall use from these procedures and methods the North-West corner process, and for the second stage the distributive methods, on the actual case of our problem.

It is proceeded by going through the following stages:

- *the use of the North-West corner process or of the main diagonal* (Table 7.4).

  The distances are noted in the right-hand corners. According to the North-West corner process, it is started from the box *A-1* located on the North-West corner of the matrix, whereto the maximum quantity of raw material has been

Table 7.4 The north-west method

Warehouses	Departments				Quantity existing in the warehouses
	1	2	3	4	
A	1,000	300	0	0	1,300
B	0	900	400	0	1,300
C	0		400	300	700
Quantity needed by the departments	1,000	1,200	800	300	3,300

allocated, which can be taken into account from the warehouse *A* to cover its need. After the quantity required on *A-1* (*1,000* tons) is met, the *300* tons still remaining in the warehouse *A* are allocated to the box *A-2*, thereby exhausting the quantity existing in this warehouse. In the department *2*, where *1,200* tons are required, *300* tons were allocated from the warehouse *A* in the box *A-2* and *900* tons in the box *B-2*, from the warehouse *B*, were *400* tons remain available.

In the department *3*, where *800* tons are required, *400* tons from the warehouse *B* in the box *B-3* and *400* tons from the warehouse *C* in the box *C-3*, in warehouse *C* remaining available *300* tons.

In the department *4*, where 300 tons are required, the 300 tons available existing in the warehouse *C* are allocated in the box *C-4*.

By analysing the table shown, it may be observed that, according to this method, it is started from the North-West corner, covering the quantities necessary to the beneficiaries fully, in their order, from the suppliers taken in their sequence, passing from one supplier to another only after the quantity existing at a supplier has been completely allocated by various beneficiaries, ultimately reaching the South-East corner, therefore going in the direction of the main diagonal.

The distribution of the entire quantity existing at the suppliers (on the line) and satisfying the quantities required at different consumers (on columns).

For the problem to be solved by using the algorithm regarding the transportation problem, the number of boxes occupied with quantities must be equal to that given by the expression:

$$m + n - 1,$$

where:

m— the number of suppliers
n— the number of consumers

In our example, $m+n+1=3+4-1=6$

By analysing the basic solution, it results that there are 6 boxes occupied with quantities, which means that the problem can be solved.

After obtaining the basic solution, the total volume of transportation that is to be done will be calculated, by doing the sum of the tons/kilometres for all the boxes of the matrix where quantities have been allocated.

The total volume = *1,000 · 5 + 300 · 4 + 900 · 5 + 400 · 4 + 400 · 2 + 300 · 4 = 14,300 tons/km;*

- *successive improvement of the basic solution until obtaining the optimal variant.*

  In order to improve the basic solution, the distributive method is used, according to which cyclic transfers of some quantities distributed according to some polygonal outlines are performed, with right angles, so that the amounts of the quantities transferred by lines and columns would not modify the total available (on each line) at the supplier and the total needed (on columns) at the consumers.

  Because there are just as many possibilities to improve the basic solution as there are free boxes in the matrix of the transportation plan, the box with the greatest perspective of improvement will be previously determined, by using the process of preparing the cycles of free boxes. In this regard, polygonal outlines will be constructed, so that a corner would be in a free box of the matrix of the transportation plan of the analysed solution, and the remaining corners in boxes where quantities are already allocated. At the polygonal outline thus created, the sign + is noted in the free corner, and after that, alternately, the signs − and + in the other corners. Along with these, the corresponding distances will be done in each corner.

As a rule, a right angle can be formed in each box and only in the case of connected polygons two connected right angles having the same peak of the common right angle.

After creating the polygonal outlines, according to the rules mentioned, the algebraic sum of the distances from the corners is done, taking for each distance the sign of the corner where it is. The box with the greatest improvement perspective will be taken into account, that which by the algebraic sum of the distances will have the greatest negative value.

Starting from Table 7.4, wherein there are six free boxes, six polygonal outlines will be created according to the aforementioned rules, performing the algebraic sum of the distances. Each box will be noted by a symbol consisting of the supplier's (warehouse) initial, according to the line where the box is and the figure corresponding to the consumer (department) from the column where it is. Thus, for example, *A-3* will symbolise the box on the line of the warehouse *A* and the column of the third department. Box *A-3* will have a rectangle with the free corner in *A*-3 and with the other corners *A-2*, *B-2*, *B-3*. The algebraic sum is: *2 − 4 + 5 − 4 = −1*

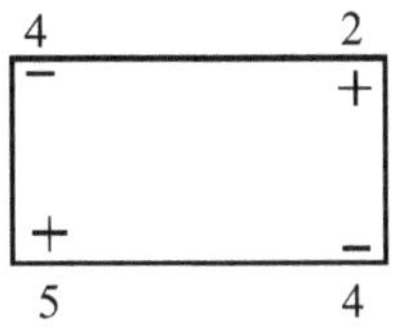

For the box A-*4*, a polygonal outline is formed, with the peaks in the boxes *A-4*, *A-2*, *B-2*, *B-3*, *C-3*, *C-4*. The algebraic sum is: $1-4+5-4+2-4=-4$

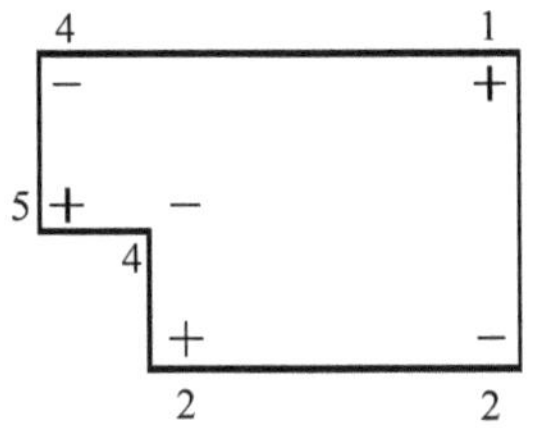

The box *B-1* has a polygonal outline in the corners of the boxes *B-1*, *A-1*, *A-2*, *B-2*. The algebraic sum is: $4-5+2-5=-4$

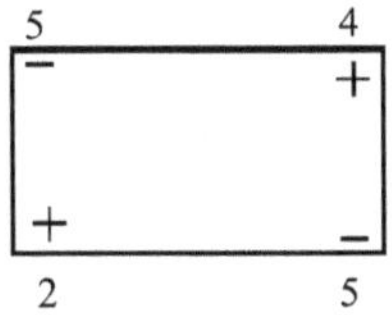

The polygonal outline of the box *B*-4 has the corners in *B-4*, *B-3*, *C-3*, *C-4*. The algebraic sum is: $5-4+2-4=-1$

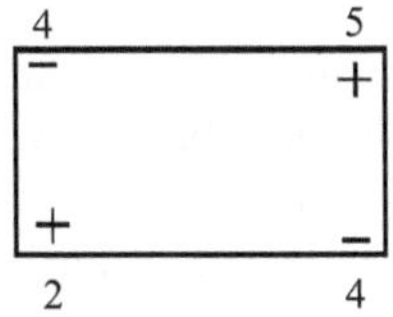

The box *C-1*, the polygonal outline has the corners in the boxes *C-1*, *A-1*, *A-2*, *B-2*, *B-3*, *C-3*. The algebraic sum is: $3-5+4-5+4-2=-1$

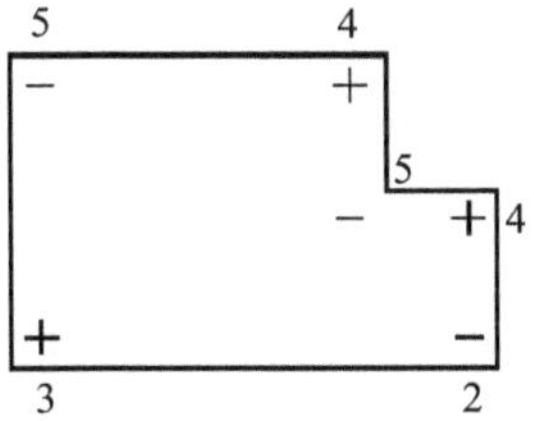

The polygonal outline of the box *C-2* has the corners in *C-2*, *B-2*, *B-3*, *C-3*. The algebraic sum is: $3-5+4-2=0$

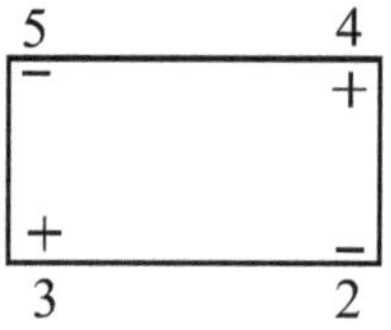

By analysing the algebraic sums obtained for the *6* polygonal outlines, the same maximum negative value results for the boxes *A-4* and *B-1*. It means they are the boxes with the greatest perspective to improve the transportation plan. As both boxes have the same maximum negative value, it is proceeded with the improvement of the basic solution, by performing some cyclic transfers according to the polygonal outline of the box *B-1*. For this purpose, the corresponding quantities are noted in the corners instead of distances, allocated through the basic solution of the transportation plan, which must be improved.

For the cyclic transfer, it is proceeded as follows: the size of the quantities in the corners with the negative sign of the polygonal outline is analysed, by identifying the smallest quantity; the minimum quantity from the corners with the minus sign are added to the quantities existing on the corners with the plus sign, subtracting this quantity from the corners with the minus sign; a new transportation plan is prepared, where the new quantities obtained are noted, by performing the cyclic transfer in the boxes corresponding to the corners of the polygonal outline, all other boxes remaining unchanged as in the basic solution; the new transportation volume is calculated based on the new plan, volume which should be smaller than in the previous variant.

Thus, a new variant for the transportation plan has been obtained, which must be improved in its turn. For this purpose, the same operations performed to improve the basic solution are used. Improving the variants for the transportation plan is done until negative values are no longer obtained when doing the algebraic sum of the distances from the polygonal outline.

For our problem, by using the procedure of free boxes, it results that *B-1* is a box with perspectives to improve the variant for the transportation plan. Its polygonal outline is represented, by noting quantities corresponding to the boxes where the outline corners are, instead of distances. We observe that the smallest quantity is *900* on the corners with the negative sign.

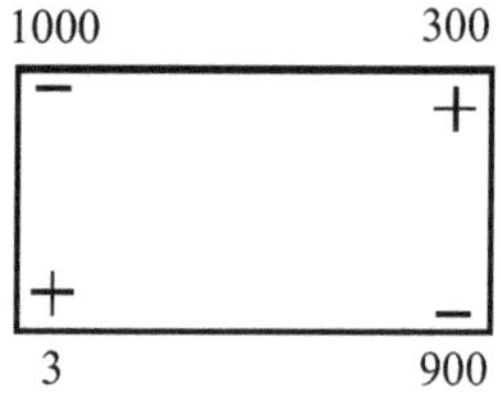

Table 7.5 Transportation plan

Warehouses	Departments				Quantity available
	1	2	3	4	
A	100	1,200	0	0	1,300
B	900	0	400	0	1,300
C	0	0	400	300	700
Quantity needed	1,000	1,200	800	300	3,300

This quantity is added to the corners with the sign+and is subtracted from the corners with the sign −. Thus, a cyclic transfer of quantities is obtained, as the polygonal outline show, which would be represented once more, but with the new quantities allocated on the corners.

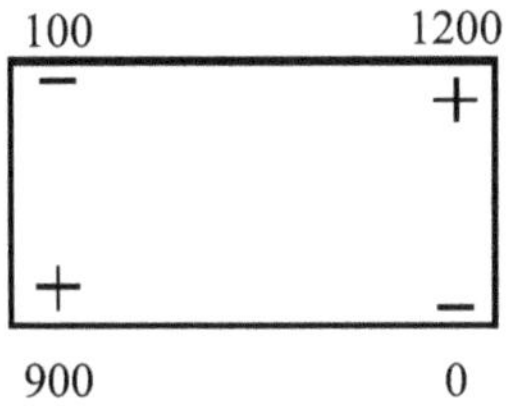

Depending on the new quantities, a transportation plan is prepared, where the quantities obtained are noted, all other boxes remaining unchanged. The transportation plan is represented in Table 7.5.

The transportation volume in the variant is as follows: $100 \cdot 5 + 1{,}200 \cdot 4 + 900 \cdot 2 + 0 \cdot 5 + 400 \cdot 4 + 400 \cdot 2 + 300 \cdot 4 = 10{,}700$ tons/km. In the new variant, the transportation volume has been reduced from *14,300* tons/km to *10,700* tons/km.

A new variant of transportation plan is further searched, the improvement to the existing one. For this purpose, the procedure of the cycles of free boxes is used and based on this, the box with the greatest improvement perspective is determined. The free boxes in the current plan are: *A-3*, *A-4*, *B-4*, *C-1* and *C-2*.

For this, the following polygonal outlines will be obtained.

For *A*-3, the corners are located in the boxes *A-3*, *A-2*, *B-2*, *B-3*. The algebraic sum is: $2 - 4 + 5 - 4 = -1$

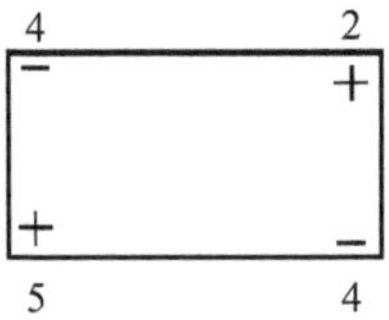

For *A-4*, the corners are located in the boxes *A-4*, *A-2*, *B-2*, *B-3*, *C-3*, *C-4*. The algebraic sum is: $1 - 4 + 5 - 4 + 2 - 4 = -4$

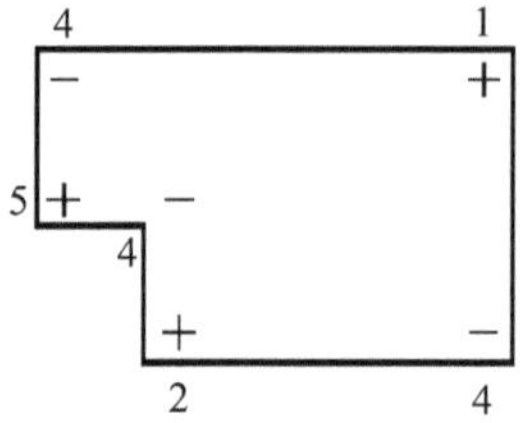

For *B-4*, the corners are located in the boxes *B-3*, *C-3*, *C-4*. The algebraic sum is: $5-4+2-4=-1$

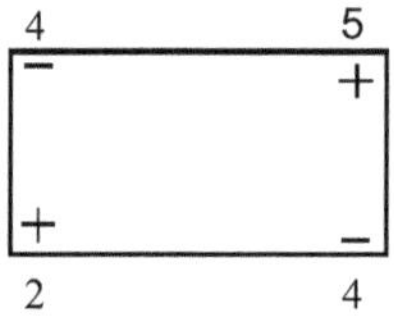

For *C-1*, the corners are located in the boxes *C-1*, *B-1*, *B-3*, *C-3*. The algebraic sum is: $4-2+3-2=3$

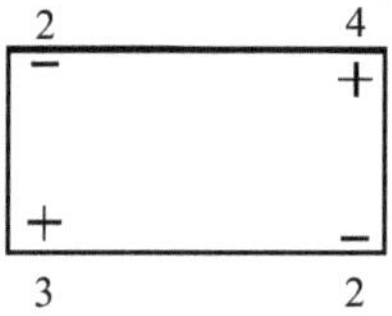

For *C-2*, the corners are located in the boxes *C-2*, *B-2*, *B-3*, *C-3*. The algebraic sum is: $3-5+4-2=0$

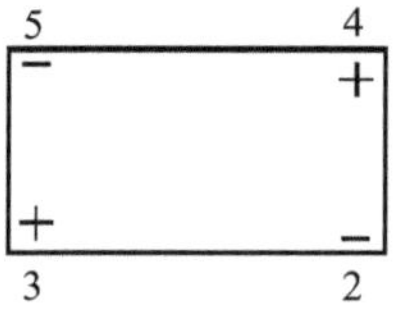

The box with the greatest improvement perspective is *A-4*, which has the algebraic sum with the greatest negative value. Therefore, we are representing the outline of *A-4*, by noting the quantities from the transportation plan that is to be improved in the corners. The quantity will be added and subtracted according to the rule known. Thus, we get the following distribution.

Table 7.6 Variant V_1 of the transportation plan

	Departments				
Warehouses	1	2	3	4	Quantity available
A	100	1,200	0	0	1,300
B	900	0	400	0	1,300
C	0	0	400	300	700
Quantity needed	1,000	1,200	800	300	3,300

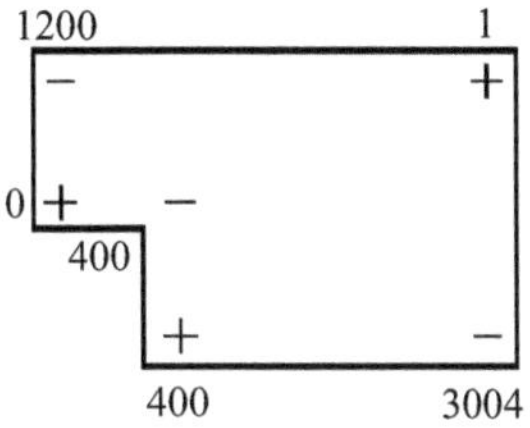

With the new distribution of the quantities, the new variant for the transportation plan is prepared, like in Table 7.6.

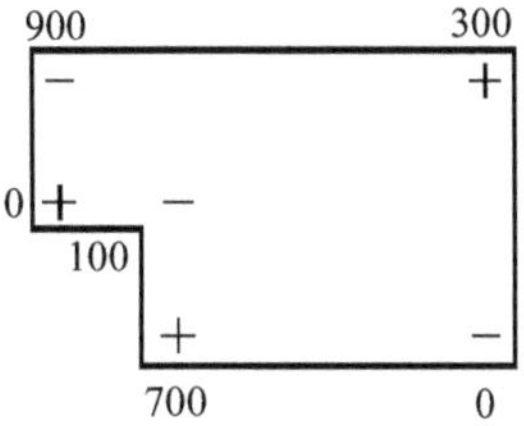

The transportation volume in this variant is as follows:

100 · 5+900 · 4+300 · 1+900 · 2+300 · 5+100 · 4+700 · 2+0 · 4=9,500 tons/km.

In the new variant, the transportation volume has been reduced from 10,700 tons/km to *9,500* tons/km.

It is further proceeded with the improvement of this variant, calculating the cycle of the free boxes *A-3*, *B-4*, *C-1*, *C-2*.

For *A-3*, the corners are located in the boxes *A-3*, *A-2*, *B-2*, *D-3*. The algebraic sum is: *2 − 4+5 − 4 = −1*

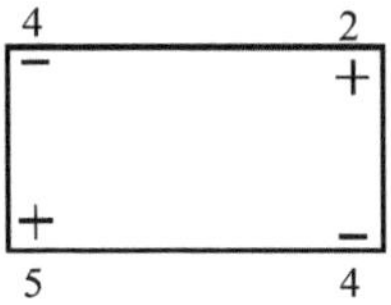

For *B-4*, the corners are located in the boxes *B-4*, *B-3*, *C-3*, *C-4*. The algebraic sum is: $5-4+2=-1$

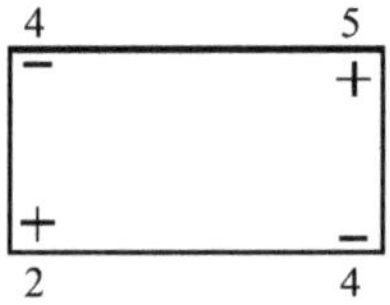

For *C*-1, the corners are located in the boxes *C-1*, *B-1*, *B-3*, *C-3*. The algebraic sum is $4-2+3-2=3$

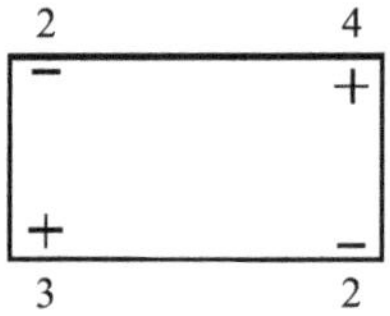

For *C-2*, the corners are located in the boxes *C-2*, *B-2*, *B-3*, *B-4*. The algebraic sum is: $3-5+4-2=0$

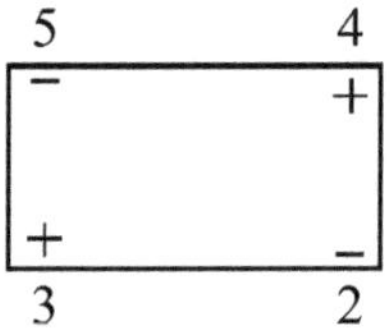

Having two boxes with the same maximum negative value, *A-3* and *B-4*, the box with the greatest improvement perspective *A-3* is taken into account.

The polygonal outline of the box *A-4* is represented with the corresponding quantities from the transportation plan in the corners:

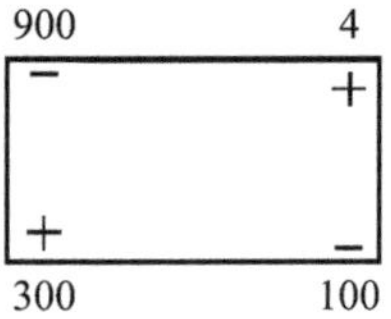

Being the smallest in the corners with the minus sign, the quantity of *100* tons is cyclically transferred. Thus, the following distribution is obtained:

Table 7.7 Variant V_2 of the transportation plan

Warehouses	Departments				Quantity available
	1	2	3	4	
A	100	800	100	300	1,300
B	900	400	0	0	1,300
C	0	0	700	0	700
Quantity needed	1,000	1,200	800	300	3,300

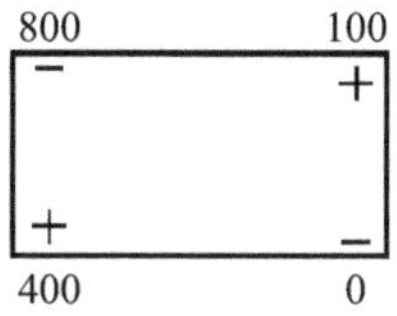

With the new distribution of the quantities, the variant for the transportation plan is prepared, like in Table 7.7.

The transportation volume in the variant is as follows:

$$100 \cdot 5 + 800 \cdot 4 + 100 \cdot 2 + 300 \cdot 1 + 900 \cdot 2 + 400 \cdot 5 + 0 \cdot 4 + 700 \cdot 2 + 0 \cdot 4 = 9400 \text{ tons/kilometres}$$

A new variant of transportation plan is further searched, calculating the cycle of the free boxes (*B-4*, *C-1*, *C-2*).

For *B-4*, the corners are located in the boxes *B-4*, *A-4*, *A-3*, *B-3*. The algebraic sum is: $5-1+2-4=2$

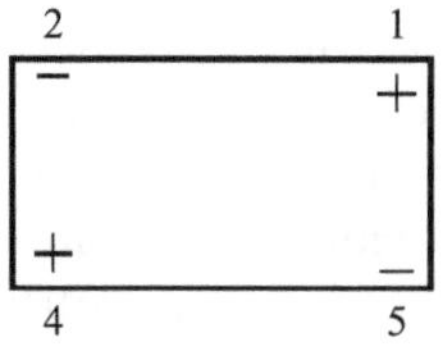

For *C-1*, the corners are located in the boxes *C-1*, *B-1*, *B-3*, *C-3*. The algebraic sum is: $3-2+4-2=3$

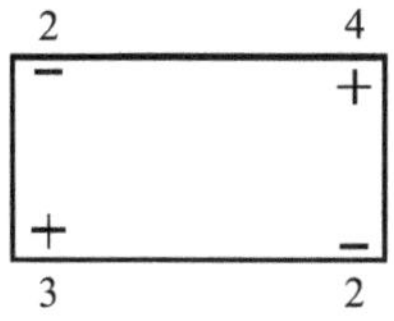

For *C-2*, the corners are located in the boxes *C-2*, *B-2*, *B-3*, *C-4*. The algebraic sum is: $3-5+4-2=0$

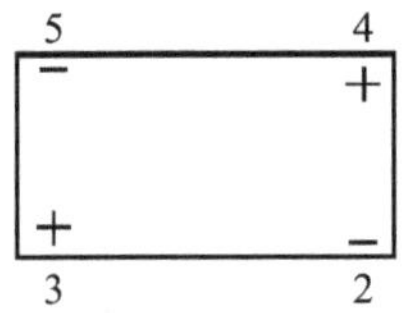

By analysing the cycle of the free boxes, it may be observed that there are no more algebraic sums with the minus sign. This means that the prepared transportation plan can no longer be improved, therefore it is the optimal variant. We observe that against the transportation volume stipulated in the basic solution (*14,300* tons/kilometre), the optimal variant (*9,400* tons/km) has been reached by the improvements made.

The transportation problem solved is part of the category of balanced type problems, where the total volume available at the suppliers is equal to the volume needed at various consumers. On the problem solved, the number of places occupied by the quantities in the transportation plan in all solutions has also been equal to $m+n-1$, where m is equal to the number of suppliers and n to the number of consumers.

In practice, there are situations where the solution for the transportation plan contains less than $m+n-1$ places occupied. In this case, the solution obtained is degenerated. To remove the degeneration and enable the calculation, zero is noted in a free box, considering it to be occupied, provided that the box would be on an even peak in the polygonal outline that is formed for performing the transfer. There are also cases when the volume of total availability of supplies exceeds the volume of the total demand of consumers. In this situation, an additional column is inserted, corresponding to a fictive consumer, where the unit costs are equal to zero, the demand of this column being equal to the difference between the quantity available and the actual demand at teh consumers. For resolution, the method shown previously is used, in the column of the fictive consumer yet highlighting the quantities that remain in stock at the supplier. In the case where the volume of total demand exceeds the volume of the total availability, the resolution is done in two variants: if there are properties, consumers with priorities are satisfied first, using then the development method known; if there are no priorities, a fictive supplier is inserted in the problem, which is to dispatch a quantity equal to the difference between the total volume needed at the consumers and the actual volume available at the suppliers, thus reaching the case of a balanced transportation problem that is solved by the usual methods.

References

Allen RGD (1987) Mathematical analysis for economisis. Mc Millan, London
Allen RGD (1998) Macro-economic theory a mathematical tratament. Mc Millan, London
Boulding WA (2002) La programmation linéaire et la théorie de l'entreprise. Dunod, Paris

Dantzig GB (1993) Linear programming and extension. Princeton University Press, Princeton, NJ
Davis K (2010) Human organizational behaviours. McGraw Hill, New York, NY
Forlan Mc, McKenney V (2008) Corporate information systems. Irwin, Boston.
Kaufmann RF (1993) Initiation a la recherce operationelle. Dunod, Paris
Lange O (1991) Wster do econometrii. PWN, Warszawa
March JG, Simon HA (1993) Organizations, 2nd edn. Wiley, New York, NY
Muller Y (1994) Initiation a l'organisation et a la recherche operationelle. Eyrolles, Paris
Ray B (2007) La theorie de graphes et ses applications en recherce operationelle. Editions d'organisation, Paris
Tinbergen J (1952) Einfiihrung in die Őkonometrie. Humboldt, Wien

Chapter 8
Models Focused on Dynamic Programming

8.1 Time in Econometric Models Using Dynamic Programming

The study of an economic variable enables the clarification of the concept of *probabilistic expectation*. Thus, in the case of one dynamic series, dealt with without any relation to another series of quantitative observations, the *variation* cannot be calculated against the average, but against an "expected value". However, this is itself a variable. For time series, the expected value is a *time function*.

Thus, the time variation of a "y_t" series of data is:

$$\sigma^2 = \frac{1}{n_t}[(y_t - f(t))]^2, \tag{8.1}$$

where:

f(t) is the value expected at each moment "*t*" of *y* and which is different from one moment to another.

Another important characteristic of the dynamic series may also be observed in this context: their elements do not differ from one another merely because they result from different moments in time. This does not make them dynamic yet. For example, if we measure the specific consumption of metal/W in the manufacture of a power machine every year or every month, we might as well get a set of numbers that oscillate very little around any random average. Nothing "dynamic" occurred in this phenomenon. However, if we see—what results from all the statistics of industrially advanced countries—that the set of data for the referred indicator gives us a systematically decreasing value, then we say it proves a trend, a decreasing trend, which in its turn is the indicator of the series dynamics. In this case, time will be explicitly of interest to us as independent variable. If we now assume that a set of data obtained in different times having certain continuity also has a certain tendency, therefore it is a function of time, then our concern will be to establish its

I.C. Dima, M. Man, *Modelling and Simulation in Management*, Contributions to Management Science, DOI 10.1007/978-3-319-16592-9_8

shape in order to predict the future evolution of the set. And we shall choose such a shape for an evaluated $\hat{Y}=f(t)$ that would minimise (1)—the variation to the expected value. Minimising the squares of deviations, the method of least squares, also extends thus over calculating the trend.

However, it is not a matter of the same thing in all respects, for time "does not actually exist", meaning it cannot be dealt with in the same way as the *material variables*, even formulated at a high level of abstraction such as "production", the "national income", "individuals' income", the "investments", the "social raw product", etc. The variable time is a *surrogate factor* we resort to either in case of some primary studies wherein we are only interested in evolution, and not also in the genesis of the values of a variable, or when we simply lack satisfactory information on the "independent" variables that determine the observed sizes of the studied variable; or, finally, when we can explain some independent variables, but others which are not articulate to detail must be replaced with a generalising symbol.

Of what has been presented, we deduce the following question: to what extent can the time study be included in econometrics? By definition, econometrics deals with the techniques to discover or identify the mechanism by which a set "X" of variables is converted into another, "Y", which can be a satisfactory and conclusive model for another mechanism by which, in the "real world" of economy, certain factors (the observation of which the statistics "X" results) convert into certain results (the observation of which the statistics "Y" results). Or, if we calculate for example the trend of the national income, we shall not acquire from there the model of the mechanism that converts time into salaries, benefits, taxes, etc. And yet, we shall observe that in econometrics, time is not at all that ghostly existence as it would appear at first sight and which is suggested by so many bad trend calculations.

Undoubtedly, "pure" time, meaning $y=f(t)$ and nothing more does not always have an economical meaning and sometimes it only serves in preparing some accurate and suggestive graphs. However, this variable is also important for the specialist in econometrics, from several points of view, namely:

- first of all, it helps in revealing some regularities in an evolutionary process, which is a first step towards the precise specification of some variables acting over time;
- second of all, it is the artificial measure of some unquantifiable variables which are however elements of this economic mechanism which we want to discover.

In the analysis of the dynamic series of economic data, normally the following types of regularities in time called dynamic trends, namely:

- secular trends, which characterise the evolution on very long terms;
- cyclic trends, the characteristics of which are suggested even by this name;
- trends, in the narrower meaning of the word, designated by the English term trend and which are the form on a longer (but not "secular") period of time of an evolution;
- seasonal cycles or other fluctuating movements with shorter periods of time.

These forms of "dynamic laws" can also be encountered in series regarding all countries, regardless of the form of government. Only that—of course—their economic content differs essentially. Perhaps certain mathematical forms of trends are more common and of greater importance in the capitalist economy, compared to the socialist economy. All types of trends are however studies in close dependence to the trend itself.

We get a function of *trend* by minimising the function (8.1). *Motivation* is analogous with that for any other statistical function. Things are not the same with the *interpretation* of the time variable in a regression function, for reasons resulting from the nature of the time characteristics.

8.2 Discrete Dynamic Programs

Be S a system the state of which at each moment n, $n \in \{0, 1, 2, \ldots\}$ is defined by means of a state variable x_n. This state variable is defined so as to fully characterise the state of the system, meaning referring to the future evolution of the system, there would be the possibility to distinguish two different evolutions of the system during the periods from 1 to n and which would lead to the same state variable x_n.

A period n of the dynamic program is defined as a couple of moments $(n-1, n)$.

In any period n, there is a decision that must be taken regarding the values of the state variable x_n. In general, the range of variation of the variables x_n is limited to the restrictions that depend on the values of the variable x_{n-1}.

We assume (in a very general way) that the restrictions of the problem define for each value of the moment n and state variable x_{n+1}, a set which we shall note $\Gamma_{n+1} \cdot x_n$.

Thus, we must have:

$$x_{n+1} \in \Gamma_{n+1} \cdot x_n \tag{8.2}$$

Conversely, if the set $\Gamma_{n+1} \cdot x_n$ of the values of the state variable x_{n+1} is given, then the relationship must be satisfied:

$$x_{n+1} \in \Gamma_{n+1}^{-1} \cdot x_{n+1} \tag{8.3}$$

where: $\Gamma_{n+1}^{-1} \cdot x_{n+1}$ is the set of the possible values of x_n, so that

$$x_{n+1} \in \Gamma_{n+1} \cdot x_n \tag{8.4}$$

In mathematical terms, Γ_{n+1} is a generally equivocal application of the set of values of x_n in the set of values of x_{n+1}, and Γ_{n+1}^{-1} is the reverse application of the application Γ_{n+1}.

Then it results that the restrictions on x_n can be written in condensed form:

$$x_n \in \Gamma_n \cdot x_{n-1} \cap \Gamma_{n+1}^{-1} \cdot x_{n+1} \tag{8.5}$$

If it is now started from a given initial state x_0, the range of the possible evolution of the system at the time n, noted $X_n(x_0)$ can be defined step by step by means of the applications Γ_n as follows:

$$\begin{array}{ll} & X_0 = \{x_0\} \\ x_1 \in \Gamma_1 \cdot x_0, & X_1(x_0,.) = \Gamma_1 \cdot X_0 = \Gamma_1 \cdot x_0 \\ x_2 \in \Gamma_2 \cdot x_1, & X_2(x_0,.) = \Gamma_2 \cdot X_1 = \bigcup_{x_1 \in X_1} \cdot \Gamma_2 \cdot x_1, \\ x_3 \in \Gamma_3 \cdot x_2, & X_3(x_0,.) = \Gamma_3 \cdot X_2 = \bigcup_{x_2 \in X_2} \cdot \Gamma_3 \cdot x_2 \\ \cdots\cdots & \cdots\cdots \\ x_n \in \Gamma_n \cdot x_{n-1}, & X_n(x_0,.) = \Gamma_n \cdot X_n = \bigcup_{x_{n-1} \in X_{n-1}} \cdot \Gamma_n \cdot x_{n-1} \end{array} \tag{8.6}$$

If it is required that after N periods a certain state x_N is to be reached, then the sets of possible values shown above must become restrictions, successively using the restrictions $\Gamma_n^{-1} \cdot x_n$ for $n=N, N-1, N-2, \ldots$

The sets $X_n(x_0, x_N)$ are thus obtained, which verify the relation:

$$X_n(x_0, x_N) = \Gamma_n \cdot X_{n-1}(x_0, X_n) \cap \Gamma_{n+1}^{-1} \cdot X_{n+1}(x_0, x_N),\ n = 1,2,\ \ldots, N-1 \tag{8.7}$$

Where $X_0(x_0, x_N)$ and $X_n(x_0, x_N)$ are reduced to sets consisting of one element each.

$$\begin{array}{l} X_0(x_0, x_N) = \{x_0\}; \\ X_n(x_0, x_N) = \{x_n\} \end{array} \tag{8.8}$$

A fundamental set in the study of dynamic programs is the concept of policy to be followed, which we define as follows:

It is called the policy from x_0 to x_N and any succession $(x_0, x_1, \ldots, x_{N-1}, x_N)$ will be noted $\Pi_{0,N}(x_0, x_n)$, so that the following conditions are met:

$$\begin{array}{c} \Pi_{0,N}(x_0, x_n) = (x_0, x_1, \ldots, x_{N-1}, x_N) \\ x_n \in \Gamma_n \cdot x_{n-1} \cap \Gamma_{n+1}^{-1} \cdot x_{n+1},\ n = 1, 2,\ \ldots, N-1. \end{array} \tag{8.9}$$

The problem we intend to solve is the problem of finding the optimal policy Γ^* in relation to a certain criterion we define below.

Firs of all, a determined value $v_n(x_{n-1}, x_n)$ called *immediate value* corresponding to the period n is assigned to each couple (x_{n-1}, x_n).

The economic significance of this value is as follows: if at the time $(n-1)$, the system is in the state x_{n-1}, then the value of the decision x_n is $v_n(x_{n-1}, x_n)$.

Having the immediate values $v_n(x_{n-1}, x_n)$ for any period $n=1, 2, 3, \ldots, N$, a total value $S(\Pi)$ defined by the relation below is assigned to any policy Π:

$$S(\Pi) = \sum_{n=1}^{N} v_n(x_{n-1}, x_n) \tag{8.10}$$

The criterion of choice we shall represent consists in minimisation or maximisation, depending on the actual nature of the values (v_n). We emphasise that the value $S(\Pi)$ is additively defined. There are also situations when the value $S(\Pi)$ is defined multiplicatively or even as convolution product.

If we note by Π the set of all policies and if we suppose that in order to focus our ideas that we want to maximise the value of policy, then the optimal policies Π^* shall be defined by the relationship:

$$S(\Pi^*) = \max_{t \in \Pi} s(\Pi) \tag{8.11}$$

More generally, we can write:

$$S(\Pi^*) = \operatorname{opt}_{t \in \Pi} s(\Pi) \tag{8.12}$$

Depending on the nature of the problem, by *opt*, it is understood one of the *max* or *min* operators.

We can now state and prove the optimality theorem. For this, the concept of subpolicy of a given policy will also be defined.

Definition For any $0 \leq i \leq j \leq N$, we shall name the *subpolicy from* x_i *to* x_j any succession:

$$x_{ij}(x_i, x_j) = (x_i, x_{i+1}, \ldots, x_n, \ldots, x_j) \tag{8.13}$$

So that the following relations are satisfied:

$$x_n \in \Gamma_n \cdot x_{n-1} \cap \Gamma_{n+1}^{-1} \cdot x_{n+1}, n = i+1, i+2, \ldots, j-1. \tag{8.14}$$

Any subpolicy from x_i to x_j will be optimal from x_i to x_j if its value:

$$s_{ij}(\Pi_{ij}) = \sum_{n=i+1}^{j} v_n(x_{n-1}, x_n) \tag{8.15}$$

Is maximum (or minimum, depending on the actual nature of the problem) among all subpolicies from x_i to x_j.

Optimality Theorem any subpolicy $\Pi_{ij}(x_i, x_j)$ extracted from an optimal policy $\Pi^*_{0,N}(x_0, x_N)$ is itself optimal of x_i and x_j.

Demonstration. Be an optimal policy

$$\Pi^* = \left\{x_0, x_1, \ldots, x_{i-1}, x_i^*, x_{i+1}^*, \ldots, x_j^*, x_{j+1}, \ldots, x_N\right\} \tag{8.16}$$

In this case, the subpolicy consisting of the part $\left\{x_i^*, x_{i+1}^*, \ldots, x_j^*\right\}$ of Π^* is optimal from x_i to x_j because otherwise there would be a subpolicy from x_i^* to x_j^* which would have a higher (in the case of the maximum) or smaller (in the case of the minimum) value, which would entail the improvement of the policy Π^* by replacing the section $\{x_i^*,\ldots,x_j^*\}$ with this new subpolicy.

The following *corollary* immediately results from this theorem, namely: in the set of policies containing a given (optimal or not) subpolicy $\Pi \cdot K(x_0, x_K)$, the best one is that which is obtained by completing the optimal given subpolicy: $\Pi_{K,N}^*(x_K, x_N)$

This corollary is formed thus—the so—called *principle of optimality* is due, just like the theorem, to *K*. Bellman and he underlies the method of dynamic programming.

He allows that after successively considering *1, 2, …, N* periods, we would gradually build an optimal policy. For this, one can start either from the first period, or from the last any period.

Let us effectively form a policy by starting from the period 1 towards the period *N*. In this case, we shall say that optimisation is done from the past to the future.

Let us note by

$$f_{0,N}(x_0, x_N) = S(\Pi^*) = \underset{\pi\in\Pi}{\mathrm{opt}}\, S(\Pi) \tag{8.17}$$

and by $f_{0,n}(x_0,x_n)$ the optimal value of the subpolicy from x_0 to x_n.

With these explanations, we proceed as follows:

In period *1*, for any possible decision:

$$x_1 \in X_1(x_{0,.}) = \Gamma_1 \cdot x_0 \tag{8.18}$$

We know the value

$$v_1(x_0, x_1) = f_{0,1}(x_0, x_1) \tag{8.19}$$

We consider the periods *1* and *2* together. For any decision:

$$x_2 \in X_2(x_0, .) = \Gamma_2 \cdot x_1 \tag{8.20}$$

The set of subpolicies from x_0 to x_2 is sought

These subpolicies: $\Pi_{0,2}(x_0, x_2) = \{x_0, x_1, x_2\}$, depend on the value x_1 chosen, a value that would satisfy the condition:

$$x_1 \in \Gamma_1 \cdot x_2 \cap \Gamma_2^{-1} \cdot x_2 = X_1(x_0, x_2) \tag{8.21}$$

The value of such a subpolicy $\Pi_{0,2}(x_0,x_2)$ is given by:

$$S_{0,2}(\Pi_{0,2}) = v_1(x_0, x_1) + v_2(x_1, x_2) \tag{8.22}$$

We can get the amount of optimal subpolicies from x_0 to x_2 by searching the optimal value of $S_{0,2}$:

$$f_{0,2}(x_0, x_2) = \underset{x_1 \in X_1(x_0,x_2)}{\text{opt}} \cdot [v_1(x_0, x_1) + v_2(x_1, x_2)] \tag{8.23}$$

Which enables us to determine x_1^*.

We now consider the set of the periods *1, 2, 3*.

For any:

$$x_3 \in X_3(x_3, .) = \Gamma_3 \cdot X_2(x_0, .) \tag{8.24}$$

The following is determined:

$$X_2(x_0, x_3) = X_0(x_0, .) \cap \Gamma_3^{-1} \cdot x_3 \tag{8.25}$$

According to the optimality theorem, the part (x_0,x_1,x_2) of an optimal subpolicy from x_0 to x_3 is an optimal subpolicy from x_0 to x_2. In order to find out the optimal subpolicies from x_0 to x_3, it is sufficient to consider the subpolicies from x_0 to x_3 which are optimal from x_0 to x_2. The optimal value from x_0 to x_3 will then be:

$$f_{0,3}(x_0, x_3) = \underset{x_2 \in X_2(x_0,x_3)}{\text{opt}} [f_{0,2}(x_0, x_2) + v_3(x_2, x_3)] \tag{8.26}$$

The optimal subpolicies from x_0 to x_3 will be those that pass through the values x_2^* for which the maximum (or minimum) value is reached.

Continuing the process as such in order to find out the value $f_{0,n-1}(x_0,x_{n-1})$ for any $x_{n-1} \in X_{n-1}(x_0,.)$,

$$X_{n-1}(x_0, .) = \Gamma_{n-1} \cdot X_{n-2}(x_0, .) \tag{8.27}$$

is determined

We consider the periods *1, 2, . . ., n* together.

For any $x_n \in X_n(x_0, .)$, the following is determined:

$$X_{n-1}(x_0, x_n) = X_{n-1}(x_0, .) \cap \Gamma_n^{-1} \cdot x_n \tag{8.28}$$

And the optimal value from x_0 to x_n is calculated:

$$f_{0,n}(x_0, x_n) = \underset{x_{n-1} \in X_{n-1}(x_0,x_n)}{\text{opt}} \cdot [f_{0,n-1}(x_0, x_{n-1}) + v_n(x_{n-1}, x_n)] \tag{8.29}$$

If x^*_{n-1} is a value of x_{n-1} which optimises the second member, any subpolicy from x_0 to x_n which is obtained by adding x_n to an optimal subpolicy from x_0 to x^*_{n-1} is, in its turn, optimal from x_0 to x_n:

$$\Pi^*_{0,n}(x_0, x_n) = \{\Pi^*_{0,n-1}(x_0, x^*_{n-1}), x_n\} \tag{8.30}$$

Thus, the optimal subpolicies from x_0 to x_n are obtained. When we reached from $n{=}N$, the problem of finding the optimal policy from the fixed x_N was solved.

In certain problems, the value x_N is not required. Then that optimal policy from x_0 to x_N will be chosen, which has the highest value (when the total value is maximised).

It is clear that we need to drive the optimisation as done above, meaning in the sense of the increasing values of n.

It might happen that x_N would be fixed, and x_0 to have different values. We should then start from $n{=}N$ and advance the optimisation in the decreasing direction of n.

The method is obviously the same, however $f_{0,n}(x_0,x_n)$ and $\Pi^*_{0,n}(x_0,x_n)$ will be replaced by

$$f_{n,N}(x_n, x_N) = \underset{x_{n+1} \in X_{n+1}(x_n,x_N)}{\text{opt}} \cdot [v_{n+1}(x_n, x_{n+1}) + f_{n+1,N}(x_{n+1}, x_N)] \tag{8.31}$$

where: $n{=}N-2, N-3, \ldots, 2, 1, 0$

$$f_{N-1,N}(x_{N-1}, x_N) = v_N(x_{N-1}, x_N) \tag{8.32}$$

We consider an enterprise that must distribute 23 pieces of a certain product *P* in a time interval of *4* months. At the beginning of the month, the enterprise can be supplied with any quantity of that product for a price variable from 1 month to another. The data are those in Table 8.1:

To determine the optimal policy of supply of the product *P* so that the monthly demand would be satisfied, knowing that at the beginning of the first month, there are *4* pieces of the product *P* in the warehouse of the enterprise, and no more than *10* pieces of the product *P* can be stored in the warehouse and at the end of last month (fourth month), all products *P* were sold.

Table 8.1 Data on the product P

Specification	M.U.				
Month		1	2	3	4
Demand	pcs.	5	7	6	5
Unit price	M.U.	12	10	9	10

Be x_i, the number of products P ordered since the beginning of the month i with $i=1, 2, 3, 4$.

The mathematical model is:

$$\min(12 \cdot x_1 + 10 \cdot x_2 + 9 \cdot x_3 + 10 \cdot x_4)$$

with the restrictions:

$$\begin{aligned} &1 \leq x_1 \leq 6 \\ &8 \leq x_1 + x_2 \leq 11 \\ &1 \leq x_4 \leq 5 \\ &x_1 + x_2 + x_3 + x_4 = 19 \\ &x \geq 3 \end{aligned}$$

According to the theory

$4 + x_1 + x_2 + x_3 + x_4 = 23 \Leftrightarrow x_1 + x_2 + x_3 + x_4 = 19$
$4 + x_1 \leq 10 \Leftrightarrow x_1 \leq 6$ and $0 \leq 4 + x_1 - 5 \Leftrightarrow 1 \leq x_1$ then $1 \leq x_1 \leq 6$
$4 + x_1 - 8 + x_2 \leq 10 \Leftrightarrow x_1 + x_2 \leq 11$ and $x_1 + x_2 - 1 - 7 \geq 0 \Leftrightarrow x_1 + x_2 \geq 8$ then $8 \leq x_1 + x_2 \leq 11$
$x_1 + x_2 - 8 + x_3 \leq 10 \Leftrightarrow x_1 + x_2 + x_3 \leq 18$ and $x_1 + x_2 + x_3 - 8 - 6 \geq 0$ then $14 \leq x_1 + x_2 + x_3 \leq 18 \Leftrightarrow 14 \leq 18 - x_4 \leq 18 \Leftrightarrow 1 \leq x_4 \leq 5$

The optimal policy of supply aims to minimise the overall expenses $\min(12 \cdot x_1 + 10 \cdot x_2 + 9 \cdot x_3 + 10 \cdot x_4)$

We shall note by s_i, $i=1, 2, 3, 4$, the stock at the end of the month.

Therefore,

$$s_0 = 4; s_1 = s_0 + s_1 - 5; s_2 = s_1 + s_2 + 7; s_3 = s_2 + s_3 - 6; s_4 = s_3 + s_4 - 5 = 0$$

According to the restrictions, it results:

$s_0 \in S_0 = \{4\}; s_1 = s_0 + x_1 - 5 = s_1 - 1;$ from $1 \leq x_1 \leq 6$ result $s_1 \in S_1 = [0, 5]; s_2 = s_1 + x_2 - 7 = x_1 + x_2 - 8;$ then $8 \leq x_1 + x_2 \leq 11$ result $s_2 \in S_2 > [0, 3];$ $s_3 = s_2 + x_3 - 6 = x_1 + x_2 + x_3 - 14 = 5 - x_4$

Reasoning, similarly it results

$$x_1 \in X_1 \cdot (s_0) = [1, 6]$$

But $0 \leq s_2 \leq 3 \Leftrightarrow 0 \leq s_1 + x_2 - 7 \leq 3 \Leftrightarrow 7 - s_1 \leq x_2 \leq 10 - s_1$

And $x_2 \in X_2 \cdot (s_1) = [7 - s_1, 10 - s_2]$

From $0 \leq s3 \leq 4 \Leftrightarrow 0 \leq s2 + x3 - 6 \leq 4 \Leftrightarrow 6$ $6 - s2 \leq x3 \leq 10 - s2$

It results that $x_3 \in X_3 \cdot (s_2) = [6 - x_2, 10 - s_2]$ from $s_2 + x_4 - 5 = 0$

It results that $x_4 \in X_4 \cdot (s_3) = \{5 - s_3\}$

The transfer functions will be:

$$F_1(s_2, s_1) = s_0 + x_1 - 5; \quad F_2(s_1, x_2) = s_1 + x_2 - 7$$
$$F_3(s_2, x_3) = s_2 + x_3 - 6; \quad F_4(s_3, x_4) = 0$$

The partial efficiency functions and objective functions of the truncated sequential processes will be:

$$\overline{f}_1 = 10 \cdot x_1 + 10 \cdot x_2 + 10 \cdot x_3 + 10 \cdot x_4$$
$$\overline{f}_2 = 10 \cdot x_2 + 9 \cdot x_3 + 10 \cdot x4$$
$$\overline{f}_3 = 9 \cdot x_3 + 10 \cdot x_4$$
$$\overline{f}_4 = 10 \cdot x_4$$

8.3 Stationary Dynamic Programs

We say that a dynamic programs has a secure (deterministic) future and is *stationary* if for all values *n* of the periods which the program performs, possibly except for the extreme values, the following relations are satisfied:

$$\Gamma_n \cdot x_{n-1} = \Gamma \cdot x_{n-1} \tag{8.33}$$

$$v_n(x_{n-1}, x_n) = v(x_{n-1}, x_n) \tag{8.34}$$

From the definition given, it results that for a stationary dynamic program, the applications Γ_n define the restrictions of the program as well as the values assigned to each period $v_n(x_{n-1}, x_n)$ are independent of the period considered.

Based on these, we can write:

$$X_n(x_0, x_N) = \Gamma^n_{(x_0)} \cap \Gamma^{-(N-n)} \cdot x_N \tag{8.35}$$

Where: $\Gamma^{(n)} \cdot x_0 = \Gamma \cdot \left(\Gamma^{(n-1)} \cdot x_0\right)$

and

$$\Gamma^{-(N-n)} \cdot x_N = \Gamma^{-1} \cdot \left(\Gamma^{-(N-n+1)} \cdot x_N\right) \tag{8.36}$$

This leads to the fact that whatever *k* may be, provided that the periods intervening into consideration are part of the periods where the dynamic program is defined, we shall have:

$$X_{n+k}\left(x_k, x_{n'+k}\right) = \Gamma^{(n)} \cdot x_k \cap \Gamma^{-\left(n'-k\right)} \cdot x_{n'+k} \tag{8.37}$$

The following expression results from here:

$$X_{n+k}\left(x_k = x, x_{n'+k} = x'\right) = X_n\left(x_0 = x, x_{n'} = x'\right) \quad (8.38)$$

If, in order to simplify the writing, we insert the notation:

$$X_{n+k}\left(x_k = x, x_{n'+k} = x'\right) = X_{n,n'-n}\left(x, x'\right) \quad (8.39)$$

And:

$$f_k\left(x, x'\right) = f_{n,n+k}\left(x, x'\right) \quad (8.40)$$

Then the systems of recurrence relations by means of which we highlight the optimal policies become:

$$f_n\left(x, x''\right) = \underset{x' \in X_{n-1,1}\left(x,x''\right)}{\text{opt}} \left[f_{n-1}\left(x, x'\right) + v\left(x', x''\right)\right] \quad (8.41)$$

N=1, 2, 3, …, N

$$f_1\left(x, x'\right) = v\left(x, x'\right) \quad (8.42)$$

And respectively:

$$f_n\left(x, x''\right) = \underset{x' \in N_{1,n-1}\left(x,x''\right)}{\text{opt}} \left[v\left(x, x'\right) + f_{n-1}\left(x', x''\right)\right] n = 2, 3, \ldots N. \quad (8.43)$$

$$f_1\left(x_1, x'\right) = v\left(x, x'\right) \quad (8.44)$$

Let us consider the same practical application from the previous paragraph, which is regressively decomposable by

$$F_i(\alpha, \beta) = \alpha + \beta, \quad \text{where} \quad i = 1, 2, 3, 4. \quad (8.45)$$

By using the equations of dynamic programming, the problem of optimum on each phase is solved as follows:

Phase 4:

$\min\{x_4(s_2, x_4) | x_4 \in X_4(s_3)\} \min\{10 \cdot x_4 | x_4 \in \{5 - s_3\}\} = 10 \cdot (5 - s_3) = 50 - 3 \cdot s_3$ obtained for $x_4^*(s_3) = 5 - s_3$

Phase 3:

$$\begin{aligned}
&\min\{\overline{f}_3|x_3 \in X_3(s_2)\} = \min\{9 \cdot x_3 + 50 - 10 \cdot s_3|x_3 \in X_3(s_2)\} = \\
&= \min\{9 \cdot x_3 + 50 - 10 \cdot (s_2 + x_3 - 6)|x_3 \in X_3(s_2)\} \\
&= \min\{9 \cdot x_3 + 50 - 10 \cdot (s_2 + x_3 - 6)|x_3 \in X_3(s_2)\} \\
&= \min\{-x_3 - 10 \cdot s_2 + 110|x_3 \in [6 - s_2, 10 - s_2]\} = 100 - 9 \cdot s_2
\end{aligned}$$

obtained for $x_3^*(s_2) = 10 - s_2$

Phase 2:

$$\begin{aligned}
&\min\{\overline{f}_2|x_2 \in X_2(s_1)\} = \min\{10 \cdot x_2 + 100 - 9 \cdot s_2|x_2 \in X_2(s_1)\} = \\
&= \min\{x_2 - 9 \cdot s_1 + 163|x_2 \in [7 - s_1, 10 - s_1]\} = 170 - 10 \cdot s_1
\end{aligned}$$

obtained for $x_2^*(s_1) = 7 - s_1$

Phase 1:

$$\begin{aligned}
&\min\{\overline{f}_1|x_1 \in X_1(s_0)\} = \min\{12 \cdot x_1 + 170 - 10 \cdot s_1|x_1 \in X_1(s_0)\} = \\
&= \min\{2 \cdot x_1 + 220 - 10 \cdot s_0|x_1 \in [1, 6]\} = 222 - 10s_0 = 182
\end{aligned}$$

obtained for $x_1^*(s_0^*) = 1$ where $s_0^* = s_0 = 4$

$$\begin{aligned}
&s_1^* = s_0^* + x_1^* - 5 = 0 \quad \text{then} \quad x_2^* = x_2^*(s_1^*) = 7 - s_1^* = 7; \\
&s_2^* = s_1^* + s_2^* - 7 = 0 \quad \text{then} \quad x_3^* = x_3^*(s_2^*) = 10 - s_1^* = 10; \\
&s_3^* = s_2^* + x_3^* - 6 = 4 \quad \text{then} \quad x_4^* = x_3^*(s_3^*) = 5 - s_3^* = 1
\end{aligned}$$

Therefore, $\min\{12 \cdot x_1 + 10 \cdot x_2 + 9 \cdot x_3 + 10 \cdot x_4\} = 182$
for $x^* = (x_1^*, x_2^*, x_3^*, x_4^*) = (1, 7, 10, 1)$,
and the trajectory will be:

$$s^*(1) = s_1^* = 0; s^*(2) = 0; s^*(3) = s_3^* = 4; s^*(4) = s_3^* = 0$$

8.4 Interpretation of Dynamic Programs Using Graphs

According to the definition, a graph is called the couple $G(X,\Gamma)$ where X is a set of points called tips, and Γ a multivocal application, generally of X in X. In the context of some dynamic programs with secure future and limited scope, there is the relation:

$$X = \bigcup_{n=0}^{N} \cdot X_N(x_0, x_N) \tag{8.46}$$

And Γ is defined by:

$$\Gamma\widetilde{x}_{n-1} = \Gamma_n \cdot \widetilde{x}_{n-1} \cap X_n(x_0, x_n) \tag{8.47}$$

where $\widetilde{x}_{n-1}$ is a particular value of the state variable x_{n-1} so that:

$$x_{n-1} \in X_{n-1}(x_0, x_N) \tag{8.48}$$

We shall assume that the state variable x_n is a dimensional one and that the sets x_n of the possible values are the most uncountable ones.

Due to the conditions imposed, it results that the elements of the set can be represented by points (meaning the values $\widetilde{x}_n$ of the state variable x_n).

The relation $\widetilde{x}_n \in \Gamma_n \cdot \widetilde{x}_{n-1}$ is represented by an arch that unites the tip $\widetilde{x}_{n-1}$ with the tip $\widetilde{x}_n$ pointing in the direction from $\widetilde{x}_{n-1}$ to $\widetilde{x}_n$.

Taking into account the definition of a transport network, we observe that a dynamic program corresponds to a transport network without circuit, wherein the value related to the arc $(\widetilde{x}_{n-1}, \widetilde{x}_n)$ is $v_n(\widetilde{x}_{n-1}, \widetilde{x}_x)$.

It is particular transport network, because the tips of the graph form $N+1$ sets (X_n) $0 \leq n \leq N$ with the property of starting from one peak $\widetilde{x}_n \in X_n$. It necessarily goes into a peak: $\widetilde{x}_{n+1} \in X_{n+1}$. We shall call such a network a *sequential transport network.*

Let us consider now a finite graph and without circuits $G(X, \Gamma)$ and to define the subsets $X_0, X_1, \ldots, X_n$ so that:

$$\begin{aligned} x_0 &= \left\{x_r : \Gamma_{x_r}^{-1} = \Phi\right\} \\ x_1 &= \left\{x_r : \Gamma_{x_r}^{-1} \subset x_0\right\} \\ x_2 &= \left\{x_r : \Gamma_{x_r}^{-1} \subset x_0 \cup x_1\right\} \\ &\cdots\cdots\cdots\cdots\cdots\cdots \\ x_n &= \left\{x_r : \Gamma_{x_r}^{-1} \subset \bigcup_{n=0}^{N-1} \cdot X_n\right\} \end{aligned} \tag{8.49}$$

Where N is the lowest integer which the following relation is satisfied for:

$$\Gamma \cdot X_n = \Phi. \tag{8.50}$$

The subsets in the peaks $X_0, X_1, \ldots, X_n$ are a partition of the set X, meaning:

$$X_n \cap X_n' = \Phi \text{ if } n \neq n' \text{ and } \bigcup_{n=0}^{N} \cdot X_n = X,\ X_n \neq \Phi \tag{8.51}$$

And are fully strictly ordered by the order relation:

$$X_n < X_n' \text{ if and only if } n < n' \tag{8.52}$$

By definition, the application $O : X \rightarrow \{0, 1, 2, \ldots, N\}$ defined by:

$$x_r \in X_n \Rightarrow O(x_r) = n \tag{8.53}$$

we shall call it *the ordinal function of the graph.*

Several methods to find out the ordinal position of a graph are known. We shall present a method (A. Kaufman) which consists in the following:

- *the Boolean matrix is taken into account* $B = (b_{ij}), 1 \leq i, j \leq M$ attached to the graph, where $M = |X|$ (the number of the elements of the set X) the elements b_{ij} of which are:

$$b_{ij} = \begin{cases} 1 & \text{if } x_j \in \Gamma_{xi} \\ 0 & \text{if } x_j \neq \Gamma_{x_i} \end{cases} \tag{8.54}$$

And then the transposed matrix $B^{'}$ is taken;

- $B^{''}, B^{'} = (V_1, V_2, \ldots, V_M)$ *if we note by* $V_1, V_2, \ldots, V_M$ *the column vectors of the matrix, we consider the vector*

$$V^{(0)} = \sum_{n=1}^{M} V_k \tag{8.55}$$

- *the set of the peaks corresponding to the zero components from the vector* $V^{(0)}$ *is the set X and we also have the value O of the ordinal function*;
- *further, the following is calculated:*

$$V^{(1)} = V^{(0)} - (V_{k_1} + V_{k_2} + \ldots + V_{k_{ro}}) \tag{8.56}$$

Where V_{k_i} are the vectors corresponding to the peaks that are part of the set X_0. From here, we get the value *1* of the ordinal function and the tips that form the set X_1 which consists of the set of the peaks of the components zero from the vector $V^{(1)}$ (others than those obtained in the previous stage). We do the same step by step until all peaks of the graph are finished, when the process ends.

We can summarise in a table the steps of the algorithm in order to determine the ordinal function of a graph (Table 8.2).

Definition A graph $G(X,\Gamma)$ which satisfies the properties: the graph G has an ordinal function $O(x_r)$ with the values *0, 1, 2, …, N*; $\Gamma X_n \subset X_{n+1}$ where $X_n = \{x_r : O(x_r) = n\}$, $n=0, 1, 2, \ldots, N-1$ we shall call *it sequential graph.*

The relation $X_n < X_{n'}$ will be read X_n strictly precedes $X_{n'}$

It results that if $G=(X, \Gamma)$ is a sequential graph, then the inclusions occur:

$$\Gamma^{-1} X_{n+1} \subset x X_n \tag{8.57}$$

Table 8.2 Data to determine the ordinal function of a graph

Specification	x1	x_2	…	x_M	$V^{(0)}$	$V^{(1)}$	…	$V^{(N)}$
x_1	b'_{11}	b'_{12}	…	b_{1M}	$\sum_{j=1}^{M} b'_{1j}$	$\sum_{j=1}^{M} b'_{1j} - \sum_{l=1}^{r_0} b'_{1k_l}$		
x_2 …	b'_{21} …	b'_{22} …	… …	b'_{2M} …	$\sum_{j=1}^{M} b'_{2j}$ …	$\sum_{j=1}^{M} b'_{2j} - \sum_{i=1}^{r_0} b'_{2k_l}$ …	… …	
x_M	b'_{M1}	b'_{M2}	…	b'_{MM}	$\sum_{j=1}^{M} b'_{Mj}$	$\sum_{j=1}^{M} b'_{Mj} - \sum_{i=1}^{r_0} b'_{Mk_l}$	…	
Value of the ordinal function					0	1		N
Peaks					$x_{k1}, x_{k_2}, \ldots, x_{k0}$			
Sets ordered by peaks					X_0	X_1	…	X_n

$$\Gamma \cdot X_n \subset X_{n+1} n = 0, 1, 2, \ldots, N - 1 \tag{8.58}$$

and therefore:

$$\Gamma \cdot X_n = X_{n+1} \tag{8.59}$$

We deduce from here that any sub-graph $G_n\left(X_n \cup X_{n+1}; \Gamma_{X_n \cup X_{n+1}}\right)$ $n=0, 1, 2, \ldots,$ N, of the given graph is a simple graph.

Conversely, if in a graph $G=(X, \Gamma)$ there is a partition $X_0, X_1, \ldots, X_n$ of the set of peaks X so that any sub-graph of the form:

$$G_n = \left(X_n \cup X_{n+1}, \Gamma_{X_n \cup X_{n+1}}\right) n = 0, 1, 2, \ldots, N - 1. \tag{8.60}$$

would be simple, then the graph G is sequential.

The algorithm described above to find out the ordinal function can be successfully used to test whether the given graph is a simple graph.

The previous considerations show that the graph related to a dynamic program is a sequential graph and vice versa. This means, given a system the state of which is characterised by means of a variable and which evolves as a result of the decisions to be chosen using dynamic programming according to the discrete model, in secured future with limited scope, the graph related to the possible evolutions of the system must be sequential.

For such a graph, all peaks of the subset X_n will correspond to a *moment* equal to the value of the ordinal function, and a period (period $n+1$) will correspond to the couple of two successive moments $(n, n+1)$.

Therefore, the period $n+1$ will correspond to the sub-graph:

$$G_n = \left(X_n \cup X_{n+1}, \Gamma_{X_n \cup X_{n+1}}\right) \tag{8.61}$$

References

Baum R (1999) Programing and discrete optimization. Princeton University Press, Princeton, NJ

Bellman ER (1998) Applied dynamic programming. Princeton University Press, Princeton, NJ

Bellman ER (1997) Dynamic programming. Princeton University Press, Princeton, NJ

Blackburn WR (2007) The sustainability handbook. Environmental Law Institute, London

Donald AP (1994) Optimization theory with applications. Wiley, New York, NY

Goldberger A (2001) Econometric theory. Wiley, New York, NY

Hannan EJ (2002) Time series analysis. Methnen, London

Kaufmann RF (1994) La programation dynamique. Dunod, Paris

Lucey T (1991) Management information systems, 6th edn. D.P. Publications, London

Nemhauser LG (1987) Introduction to dinamic programming. Wiley, New York, NY

Sundarasaradula D, Hasan H, Walker DS, Tobias AM (2005) Self-organization, evolutionary and revolutionary change in organizations. Strateg Chang 14(7):367–380

Sundarasaradula D, Hasan H, Walker DS, Tobias AM (2006) Formal organizations: How classical thermodynamics can help us to understand them. Int J Bus Res 6(3):1–14

Teece DJ, Pisano G, Shuen A (1997) Dynamic capabilities and strategic management. Strateg Manag J 18(7):509–533

Teece DJ (2007) Explicating dynamic capabilities: the nature and microfoundations of (sustainable) enterprise performance. Strateg Manag J 28(13):1319–1350

Wiloms JI (2001) Stability theory of dinamical systems. Wiley, New York, NY

Chapter 9
Models Using the Graph Theory

9.1 Elements of Graph Theory

The graph theory was established as an independent chapter in the operational research due to the multiple advantages which it provides to managerial activity. Mathematical models in this class are generally linear, but unlike the linear programming models for example, these ones have structural properties that enable a more complete representation of the analysed phenomena and also the increase of the level of efficiency of the optimisation process. In preparing the production, investment, transportation, marketing programs in the enterprises with highly complex activities, the use of graphs and mathematical models corresponding thereof are a practical necessity.

When applying the graph theory, the concept of graph that uses a specific form of representing the phenomena and activities is used.

By means of graphs, the connections between the components of the economic system taken into account are captured and analysed in detail, the corresponding mathematical model is developed more easily and accurately.

To facilitate the apprehension of the basic concepts of graph theory, of economic significance of the components of a graph and mathematical model attached thereto, it is required to present the following examples:

We consider that in the general problem of transport, c_{ij} is the maximum capacity of transportation on the route (i, j). Therefore, if we exclude the transportation costs, then we can formulate a linear programming problem by which we are to determine the maximum quantity that must be transported on different routes to meet the consumer demand.

I.C. Dima, M. Man, *Modelling and Simulation in Management*, Contributions to Management Science, DOI 10.1007/978-3-319-16592-9_9

The mathematical model corresponding to this problem has the following form:

$$\max\left[Z(x_{ij})\right] = \sum_{i=1}^{m}\sum_{j=1}^{n} x_{ij} \tag{9.1}$$

in the conditions:

$$\sum_{j=1}^{n} x_{ij} \le a_i \quad (i = 1, 2, \ldots\ldots, m) \tag{9.2}$$

$$\sum_{i=1}^{m} x_{ij} \ge b_j \quad (j = 1, 2, \ldots\ldots, n) \tag{9.3}$$

$$x_{ij} \le c_{ij} \quad (i = 1, 2, \ldots, m;\ \ j = 1, 2, \ldots, n) \tag{9.4}$$

$$x_{ij} \ge 0 \tag{9.5}$$

The optimal solution of such a problem can be more easily obtained by means of the graph theory. For this purpose, a graph called transportation network is created, by using the following rules: it is represented in plane through the central producing points $A_1, \ldots, A_m$ and the consuming points $B_1, \ldots B_n$ which are joined through oriented segments (A_i, B_j) called arcs, which we attach the capacity c_{ij} to. Should a producing centre A_i not have means of transportation available to the centre B_j, the capacity of the corresponding arc (A_i, B_j) will be equal to zero. We add to the formed graph an *input* A connected through arcs to each of the points $A_1, \ldots, A_m$ and only to these, and also an *output B* wherein an arc from each of the points $B_1, \ldots B_n$ arrives, and only from these. The capacity of an arc like (A, A_i) will be equal to a_i, while the capacity of an arc like (B_j, B) will be considered to be equal to b_j. In this case, the transportation network shown in Fig. 9.1 has been obtained. Based on a specific algorithm, the maximum flow in the network is determined, which represents the maximum amount of product that starts from the point *A* and arrives in point *B*. By using the same calculation algorithm as in the previous situation, we can solve the so-called transportation problem with the intermediary centres (the transportation problem with linked centres), wherein the warehouses D_i are interposed between the manufacturers A_i and the consumers B_i.

Taking into account the previous explanations, it may be concluded that a graph is defined by the set of peaks $X = (x_1, x_2, \ldots, x_n)$ and the set of the links between them. We note by *Γ* the multivocal application of the set *X* in itself, which emphasises precisely the connections between the peaks x_i of the graph, when the graph *G* is defined by the pair (X, Γ), therefore $G = (X, \Gamma)$.

For clarity, a graph formed as shown below is attached to the graph *G*: each element $x_i \in X$ is represented by a point called peak (node), and the connection between two peaks $x_i \in X$ and $x_j \in X$ are represented by a segment oriented from x_i to x_j if $x_j \in \Gamma(x_i)$. The ordered pair (x_i, x_j) is called arc of the graph *G* and has x_i as initial extremity, and x_j as final extremity. Therefore, the application $\Gamma(x_i)$

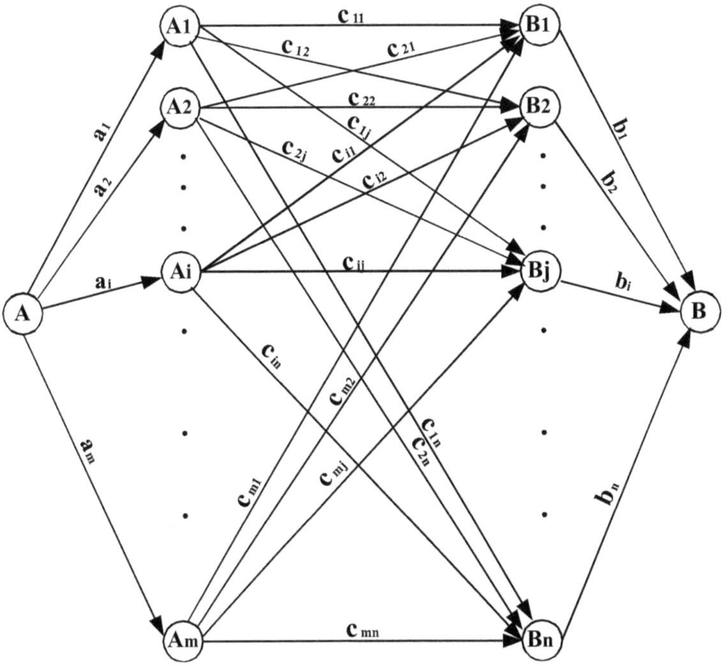

Fig. 9.1 Transport network

emphasises the set of the points x_j linked with x_i through arcs which have the initial extremity in x_i and the final one in x_j.

If the *X* set of elements is finite, then the graph *G* is finite.

To analyse the basic concepts of the graph theory, we use the graph defined by the set $X = \{x_1, x_2, x_3, x_4, x_5, x_6, x_7\}$ and the following applications:

$$\Gamma(x_i) : \Gamma(x_1) = \{x_2, x_3, x_4\}; \quad \Gamma(x_2) = \{x_1, x_2, x_3, x_5\}; \tag{9.6}$$

$$\begin{aligned} &\Gamma(x_3) = \{x_6, x_7\}; \quad \Gamma(x_4) = \{x_2, x_3, x_5\}; \quad \Gamma(x_5) = \{x_6\} \\ &\Gamma(x_6) = \{x_3, x_4, x_7\}; \quad \Gamma(x_7) = \varnothing. \end{aligned} \tag{9.7}$$

The representation shown in Fig. 9.2 corresponds to this application.

The graph in Fig. 9.2 was obtained by joining the points that form the set *X* through arcs defined by the applications $\Gamma(x_i)$. Thus, the application $\Gamma(x_3)$ shows that the peaks x_6 and x_7 are connected through arcs, which have the initial extremity in x_3. We can also use the concept of reverse application on the peak x_j, which is noted with $\Gamma^{-1}(x_j)$ and is defined as follows:

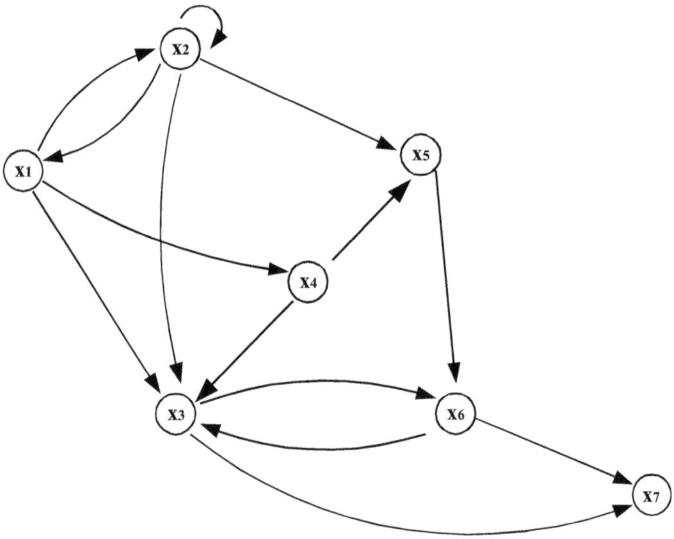

Fig. 9.2 Building a graph defined by the set X

$$\Gamma^{-1}(x_j) = \{x_i : x_j \in \Gamma(x_i)\} \tag{9.8}$$

The application $\Gamma^{-1}(x_j)$ emphasises the set of peaks x_i through arcs that have the final extremity in x_j. Therefore $\Gamma^{-1}(x_3) = \{x_1, x_2, x_4, x_6\}$.

A graph $G = (X, \Gamma)$ is considered, which can be defined by the pair *X* and *U*, meaning $G = (X, U)$.

The set of arcs $u_{ij} = (x_i, x_j)$ of graph *G* was noted with *U*, meaning:

$$U = \{(x_i, x_j)/x_i, x_j \in X,\ \ x_j \in \Gamma(x_i)\} \tag{9.9}$$

Two arcs of the graph *G* are called adjacent if they have a common extremity, and the peaks x_i and x_j are adjacent, if there is an arc joining them.

Be $A \subset X$ a subset of peaks of the graph *G*. An arc $u_j \in U$ is called incident to the outside of the set A, if the initial extremity of u_{ij} is in *A*, and the final extremity is not, therefore $x \in A$, and $x_j \notin A$. The arc u_{ij} is incident to the inside of the set, if the final extremity of u_{ij} is in *A*, and the initial one is not, meaning when $x_i \notin A$ and $x_j \in A$.

In particular, any arc *u* is incident to the outside (inside) of a peak *x*, meaning that the initial (final) extremity of the arc is *u,* and the final (initial) extremity is different from *x*.

The arc that has both extremities in one peak x_i is called a loop.

The set of arcs incident to the outside of the subset *A* (peak *x*) is noted with U_A^+ (respectively U_X^+), and the set of the arcs incident to the inside of the set *A* (peak *x*) is noted U_A^- (respectively U_X^-).

Thus, in the graph shown in Fig. 9.2, the arcs (x_1, x_4) and (x_1, x_3, x_7) are adjacent while the arcs (x_1, x_2) and (x_3, x_6) are not, the peaks x_4 and x_6 are adjacent.

Be $A = \{x_2, x_3, x_6, x_5\}$. For example, the arc (x_3, x_6) is incident to the outside of the set A, as $x_3 \in A$, and $x_6 \notin A$. All arcs incident to the outside of this set form the set U_A^+:

$$U_A^+ = \{(x_1, x_2)(x_4, x_2)(x_5, x_6)(x_3, x_6)(x_3, x_6)\} \tag{9.10}$$

For example, the arc (x_1, x_4) is incident to the inside of the set A, because $x_1 \notin A$, and $x_4 \in A$. The set U_A^- consists of the following arcs:

$$U_A^- = \{(x_1, x_2)(x_1, x_3)(x_1, x_4)(x_6, x_4)(x_6, x_3)\} \tag{9.11}$$

If we consider that $A = \{x_2\}$, then the arc (x_2, x_3) is incident to the outside of the peak x_2, and the arc (x_4, x_2) is incident to the inside thereof. The final and initial extremity x_2 is not incident to the outside or to the inside of x_2.

Therefore:

$$U_{X1}^+ = \{(x_2, x_1)(x_2, x_3)(x_2, x_5)\}; \quad U_{X2}^- = \{(x_1, x_2)(x_4, x_2)\} \tag{9.12}$$

In many rationales in the graph theory, the operation to *delete* (remove) some arcs from a given graph or some peaks and all arcs incident to the outside or inside thereof is frequent. Following these operations, a partial graph or a sub-graph of graph *G* is obtained.

The partial graph of *G* is defined, a graph of the form $G' = (X, \Gamma')$, where the multivocal application Γ' satisfies the condition $\Gamma'(x_i) \subset \Gamma(x_i)$, but $\Gamma'(x_i) \leq \Gamma(x_i)$ for any $x_i \in X$.

Therefore, a partial graph of *G* has the same peaks as *G*, but not less arcs.

A graph of the form $\overline{G} = (\overline{X}, \overline{\Gamma})$ is called sub-graph, wherein $\overline{X} \subset X$, and for any $x_i \in X$, the relation $\overline{\Gamma}\ (x_i) = \Gamma(x_i) \cap X$ is satisfied. Therefore, a sub-graph of the graph *G* is obtained by removing from *G* a number of peaks and arcs incident to the outside and inside thereof.

By combining the two concepts above, a partial sub-graph of a graph will result.

A graph *G* is called complete if any pair of peaks is linked to at least one arc, regardless of its direction. If any pair (x_i, x_j) is linked through arcs in both directions, meaning $(x_i, x_j) \in U$ and $(x_j, x_i) \in U$, then the graph is called symmetric.

A Boolean matrix can be associated to any graph *G*

$$M_G = (m_{ij}) \quad \text{where :}$$

$$m_{ij} \begin{cases} 1 \text{ if there is the arc with initial extremity in } x_i \text{ and the final one in } x_j \\ 0 \text{ if the peaks } x_i \text{ and } x_j \text{ are adjacent} \end{cases} \tag{9.13}$$

The matrix associated to the graph in Fig. 9.2 has the following structure:

$$M_G = \begin{pmatrix} 0 & 1 & 1 & 1 & 0 & 0 & 0 \\ 1 & 1 & 1 & 0 & 1 & 0 & 0 \\ 0 & 0 & 0 & 0 & 0 & 1 & 1 \\ 0 & 1 & 1 & 0 & 1 & 0 & 0 \\ 0 & 0 & 0 & 0 & 0 & 1 & 0 \\ 0 & 0 & 0 & 0 & 0 & 0 & 0 \end{pmatrix} \tag{9.14}$$

It should be noted that a complete graph is determined by the associated Boolean matrix. The various operations performed on a graph are materialised in corresponding operations performed in the matrix M_G. Thus, the matrix associated to a partial graph is deduced from the matrix of the initial graph by replacing certain elements $m_{ij} = 1$ corresponding to the arcs that are removed through elements $m_{ij} = 0$. The matrix associated to a sub-graph is deduced from the initial matrix, by removing the lines and columns corresponding to the removed peaks.

The concept of path is used most commonly in the applications of the graph theory.

A path μ in a graph $G = (X, U)$ is a sequence of arcs $(u_1, u_2, \ldots, u_p)$ with the property that the final extremity of the arc u_i coincides with the initial final extremity of the next arc.

The initial extremity of the path μ is by definition the initial extremity of the arc u_1, while the final extremity of μ is the final extremity of the arc. The path μ is called simple, if its arcs are distinct, otherwise it is composed. The path *V* is called elementary, if it does not pass twice through the same peak, otherwise we say that μ is non-elementary.

The length 1 (μ) of the path μ is, by definition, the number of the component arcs $1\ (\mu) = p$.

A circuit is a path the initial extremity of which coincides with the final one. A circuit or a path that passes once through all the peaks of the graph *G* is called Hamiltonian circuit. A Hamiltonian circuit has the length n, and a Hamiltonian path has the length *n-1*.

A graph is strongly connected if, for any pair of peaks x_i and $x_j\left(x_i \neq x_j\right)$, there is a path from x_i to x_j.

Based on the graph shown in Fig. 9.2 we shall materialise the concepts defined above:

$$\mu_1 = \{(x_1, x_2), (x_2, x_5), (x_5, x_6), (x_6, x_7)\} \quad \text{is simple and elementary path;} \tag{9.15}$$

$$\mu_2 = \{(x_1, x_4), (x_4, x_2), (x_2, x_1), (x_1, x_4), (x_4, x_5)\} \quad \text{is composed path;} \tag{9.16}$$

$$\mu_3 = \{(x_3, x_6), (x_6, x_3), (x_3, x_7)\} \quad \text{is a non-elementary path} \tag{9.17}$$

$$\mu_4 = \{(x_1, x_4), (x_4, x_2), (x_2, x_5), (x_5, x_6), (x_6, x_3), (x_3, x_7)\} \quad \text{is a Hamiltonian path} \tag{9.18}$$

9.2 The Concept of Non-oriented Graph

Oriented graphs are a simple and efficient means of representing many actual phenomena of economic or technical nature.

In the examples analysed, the intuitive idea of orientation translated by conditionings or by subordinations.

If we examine the map of the country's railways, we observe it is very similar to the graphical representation of a graph. We distinguish peaks, major rail centres of the country and arcs, except that they lack the orientation, even a narrow railway could be travelled in both directions.

This example leads us to the notion of non-oriented graph. A non-oriented graph is a pair $G = (X, M)$, consisting in a set *X* and a set *M* of nonempty subsets of *X*.

The elements of the set *X* are called the peaks of the non-oriented graph *G*, and the elements of the set *M* are called edges.

If $m = \{x, y\}$ is an edge, the peaks of the graph non-oriented to the edge *m*. An edge of the form $\{x\}$ is called extremity loop x. To homogenise the language, we agree or say that the loop $\{x\}$ has two extremities confounded in the peak x and we shall note $\{x, x\}$.

The non-oriented graph $G = (X, M)$ is called finite, if the set *X* is finite. We can view a non-oriented graph *G*, randomly setting in plane its peaks and joining through a continuous line those peaks in between which there are edges.

For example, there are the following roads between the localities x_1, x_2, x_3, x_4, x_5: a highway that passes through the localities; x_1, x_3, x_4, an asphalted road that passes through x_2, x_4, x_5; country roads between x_1 and x_2; between, x_1 and x_1; between x_1 and x_3;

We build a non-oriented graph $G = (X, M)$ wherein:

$$X = \{x_1, x_2, x_3, x_4, x_5\} \tag{9.19}$$

$$M = \{(x_1, x_3), (x_3, x_4), (x_2, x_4), (x_4, x_5), (x_1, x_2), (x_1, x_4), (x_2, x_4)\} \tag{9.20}$$

In Fig. 9.3, the graphical representation of this graph is shown.

From an oriented graph $G = (X, \Gamma)$, we can obtain a non-oriented graph *G*, as follows: the non-oriented graph has the same peaks as the non-oriented one; in the non-oriented graph, there is the edge $\{x, y\}$ if and only if in the oriented graph there is the arc (x, y), the arc (y, x) or both.

In a non-oriented graph, we can speak of adjacent peaks, adjacent edges, just like in an oriented graph.

The sequence of edges will be:

$$1 = (m_1, m_2, \ldots, m_p) \; p \geq 3 \text{ of the non-oriented graph } G = (X, M) \tag{9.21}$$

It is called chain if the edge $m_i, 2 \leq i \leq p - 1$ has an extremity coincident with the edge m_{i-1}, and the other extremity coincident with the edge m_{i+1}.

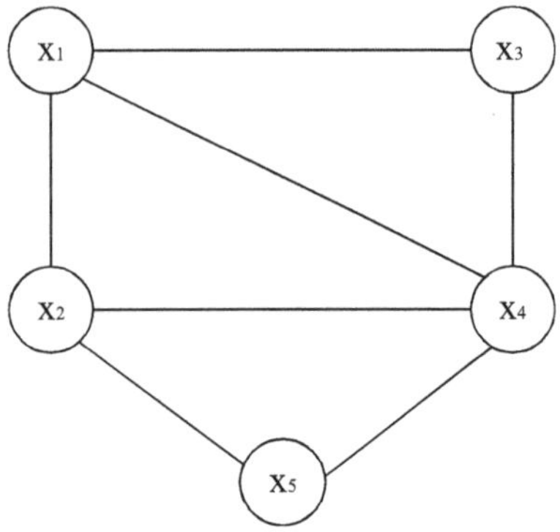

Fig. 9.3 Non-oriented graph

It is necessary to complete this definition by saying that two edges form a chain if they are adjacent.

The extremities of the chain $(m_1, \ldots, m_p)$ are free extremities of the extreme edges m_1 and m_p.

A chain can be given either by the component edges, or by the peaks through which it passes (they join the chain peaks). A chain the component edges of which are different from one another is called simple, otherwise, it is called composed. A chain that passes once through its peaks is called elementary; otherwise, it is called non-elementary.

A chain the extremities of which would coincide is called cycle. The length of a chain is the number of component edges.

9.3 Calculating the Size of the Critical Path in a Graph

One of the applications of the graph theory consists in determining the path of minimum or maximum value between two peaks $x_i \in x$ and $x_j \in x$ of the graph $G(X, \Gamma) = (X, U)$. In this case, a real number noted with $v(u_i) \geq 0$ or $v(x_i, x_j) \geq 0$, called the arc value is assigned to each arc $u_i \in U$ and, depending on the economic problem that is to be solved, it can have one of the following meanings: the cost or duration of the transport on the route (x_i, x_j); the cost to manufacture a product by the workplace represented by the arc (x_i, x_j); the labour time required to make a product (or labour productivity) at the workplace represented by the arc (x_i, x_j), etc.

If we consider the path $\mu = (\mu_1, \mu_2, \ldots, \mu_k)$, then the size $v(\mu)$ defined by the relation:

$$v(\mu) = \sum_{i=1}^{k} v(u_i) \tag{9.22}$$

is called the value of the path μ.

Usually, the optimal value of the road formed by the sequence of arcs $u_i \in U$ connecting the initial node x_i with the final node x_n is of interest.

We shall present below two of the methods to find the path of optimal value in a graph $G = (X, \Gamma)$ without circuits, namely:

- *the Ford algorithm* implies that, in order to find the path of minimum value between two peaks x_1 and x_n, it is necessary to run through the following steps: A variable λ_i is attached to each peak x_i of the graph G. We start with $\lambda_i = 0$ and $\lambda_i = \infty$ for $i = 2, \ldots n$. The variable λ_i has the meaning of value of the path from the peak x_1 to the peak x_n; we seek an arc (x_i, x_j) for which $\lambda_j - \lambda_i > v(x_i, x_j)$. If such an arc has been found, λ_i is replaced with

$$\lambda_i = \lambda_j + v(x_i, x_j) < \lambda_j \tag{9.23}$$

If there are several variants for the relation (9.23) which can decrease the variable λ_{jm}, then we choose the λ_j with the lowest value. We continue in this manner until no arc will enable decreasing the values of the variables λ_j. Because for each peak x_i, the values taken by the variable λ_j form a decreasing string of non-negative numbers, there will be a peak x_{p1}, with the property:

$$\lambda_n - \lambda_{p1} = (x_{p1}, x_n) \tag{9.24}$$

x_p wherein the peak that last contributed in decreasing the value of the variable λ_n.

Analogically, there will be x_{p2} so that:

$$\lambda_{p1}\text{-}\lambda_{p2} = (x_{p1}, x_n)\ \text{etc.} \tag{9.25}$$

The number of peaks being finite, we shall finally get:

$$x_{pk+1} = x_1 \quad \text{and} \quad \lambda_{pk} - \lambda_1 = v(x_1, x_{pk}) \tag{9.26}$$

It can be shown that the minimum value of the path that joins the peak x_1 and x_n is precisely λ_n, and the path μ_0 for which $v(\mu_0) = \lambda_n$ is $\mu_0 = (x_1, x_p, \ldots, x_{p2}, x_{p1}, x_n)$.

To demonstrate this, we consider any path

$$\mu = [x_1, x_{k1}, \ldots, x_{ks+1}] \tag{9.27}$$

for which the following is calculated

$$\lambda_{k1} - 0 \le v(x_1, x_{k1}) \tag{9.28}$$

$$\lambda_{k2} - \lambda_{k1} \le v(x_{k1}, x_{k2}) \tag{9.29}$$

$$\lambda_n - \lambda_{ks} \le v(x_{ks}, x_n) \tag{9.30}$$

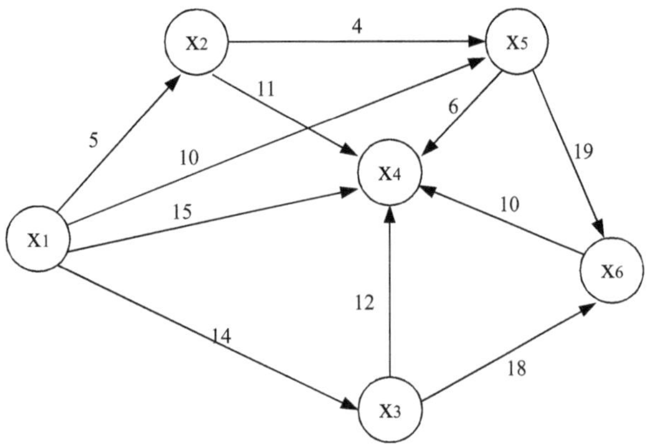

Fig. 9.4 Oriented graph

By separately totalling the terms of these relations, it results that $\lambda_n \leq (\mu)$, which demonstrates that μ_0 is the path with the lowest value.

It can also be shown that the Ford algorithm is equivalent to solving the system:

$$\begin{cases} \lambda_1 = 0 \\ \lambda_j = \min\left[\lambda_i + v(x_i, x_j)\right] \end{cases} \quad (j = 1, 2, \ldots, n); \quad (x_i, x_j) \in U_{xj}^{\infty} \tag{9.31}$$

By using the system (9.31) and the graph shown in Fig. 9.4, the path of minimum value between x_i and x_j is determined, taking into account the path of minimum value between x_1 and x_i and the $v(x_i, x_j)$ for $(x_i, x_j) \in U_{xj}^{\infty}$. Applying this process involves running through the graph algorithm from left to right, and the use of the algorithm defined in the previous paragraphs is equivalent to finding the minimum path starting from the module x_n to the module x_1.

If it is required to find the path of maximum value, the starting values are $\lambda_1 = 0$ and $\lambda_j = -\infty \ (j = 2, \ldots, n)$. When $\lambda_j - \lambda_i < v(x_i, x_j)$, the values λ_j are replaced by $\lambda_j = \lambda_i + v(x_i, x_j)$. If there are several variants that enable decreasing the λ_i, then we choose the indicator λ_j with the maximum value.

Applying this algorithm is equivalent to solving the system:

$$\begin{cases} \lambda_1 = 0 \\ \lambda_j = \max\left[\lambda_i + v(x_i, x_j)\right] \end{cases} \quad (j = 1, 2, \ldots, n); (x_i, x_j) \in U_{xj}^{\infty} \tag{9.32}$$

It should be stated that it is possible that the graph contains several paths of minimum (maximum) value and therefore, to determine them, we should mark all arc sequences (nodes) that lead to the same value.

Thus, two paths of minimum value have been highlighted, namely:

$$\mu = (x_1, x_4, x_6) = 25 \tag{9.33}$$

$$\mu_1 = (x_1, x_2, x_5, x_4, x_6) = 25 \tag{9.34}$$

– *the Bellman–Kalaba algorithm* is based on the general principle of dynamic programming, which in this case acquire the following formulation: if the path of minimum (maximum) value that joins x_h and x_k, then the partial path that joins $-x_h$ with x_k is the path of minimum (maximum) value between these two peaks.

If it is required to determine the path of minimum value, the matrix $C = (x_{ij})$, $i, j = \ldots, n$ where the elements c_{ij} are defined as below is attached to the graph $G(X, \Gamma)$:

$$c_{ij}\begin{cases} v(x_i, x_j) & \text{if} \quad (x_i, x_j) \in U(i \neq j) \\ \infty \quad \text{if} & (x_i, x_j) \notin U(i \neq j) \\ 0 \quad \text{if} \quad i = j \end{cases} \tag{9.35}$$

A variable v_i, which has the meaning of value of the path joining x_i with x_n is assigned to each peak x_i of the graph *G*. The solution of the outlined problem is obtained by solving the system of equations:

$$\begin{cases} v_i = \min\limits_{j \neq i} (v_j + c_{ij}), & i = 1, \ldots, n = 1 \\ v_n = 0 \end{cases} \tag{9.36}$$

Indeed, it can be shown that, if $v_1, v_2, \ldots, v_n$ is the solution of this system, then v_1 is the minimum value of the path joining x_1 and x_n.

To solve the system (9.36), an iterative process is used, which starts from the initial information, defined by:

$$\begin{cases} v_i(0) = c_{in} \\ v_n(0) = 0 \end{cases} \quad i = 1, 2, \ldots, n - 1 \tag{9.37}$$

Each iteration $k(k = 1, 2, \ldots)$ consists in solving the system:

$$\begin{cases} v_i^{(k)} = \min\limits_{j \neq i} \left(v_j^{(k-1)} + c_{ij} \right) \\ v_n^{(k)} = 0 \end{cases} \quad i = 1, \ldots, n\text{-}1, \ j = 1, 2, \ldots n, \ k = 1, 2 \ldots \tag{9.38}$$

The calculation ends when the following is found:

$$v_i^{(k-1)} = v_i^{(k)} \quad i = 1, \ldots, n \tag{9.39}$$

Then $\overset{\infty}{v}_i = v_i^{(k)}$, $(i = 1, \ldots, n)$ and the minimum value of the path that joins x_1 with x_n is

$$v_1^{\infty} = v_i^{(k)}. \tag{9.40}$$

Determining the arcs of the path of minimum value $\overset{\infty}{v}_1 = v_i^{(k)}$ is done as follows:

Be x_{ij} the peak for which:

$$v_1^{(k)} = \min_{j \neq 1} \left(v_j^{k-1} + c_{ij}\right) = v_{j_1}^{(k-1)} + c_{ij} \tag{9.41}$$

The path of minimum length passes through and, according to the principle of dynamic programming $y_{j1}^{(k-1)}$, represents the minimum value of the path joining x_{j1} with x_n.

Further, let us suppose that:

$$v_{j1}^{(k-1)} = \min_{j \neq j_1} \left(v_j^{(k-2)} + c_{ij}\right) = v_{j2}^{(k-2)} + c_{j1\,j2} \tag{9.42}$$

The sought path μ will pass through x_{j_2}. We repeat the procedure by starting from $v_{j_2}^{(k-2)}$ and so on, until we reach a

$$v_{jk}^{(0)} = 0. \tag{9.43}$$

The path of minimum value will be:

$$\mu = \left(x_1, x_{j_1}, x_j, \ldots, x_{jk}, x_n\right) \tag{9.44}$$

It is clear that if one of the intermediary peaks is not uniquely determined, there will be several paths of minimum length.

The calculations can be organised in a table wherein the matrix C, the line vector $v^{(0)} = (c_{1n}, c_{2n}, \ldots c_{n-1}, 0)$ the components of which are precisely the elements of the last column of the matrix C, as well as the line vectors $v^{(k)}$ the elements of which are calculated by the relations (9.38).

In order to apply the Bellman–Kalaba algorithm in order to fiind the path of maximum value, the following changes are inserted: in defining the matrix C, if $\left(x_i, x_j\right) \notin$ then $c_{ij} = -\infty$; in the relations (9.36) and (9.38), the operator of maximum is replaced.

9.4 Graphical Transport Networks

The example shown previously challenged an economic problem that can be represented by a certain type of graph, called transport network.

A finite graph $G = (X, U)$ without loops, which has the following properties, is called *transport network*:

- *an integer* $c(u) \geq 0$ *that is called the capacity of the arc u is attached to each arc* $u \in U$;
- *there is a single peak* x_0 *characterised by the application* $\Gamma^{-1}(x_0) = \phi$, *therefore it is not a final extremity for any arc of the graph G and this is why it is called network input;*
- *there is a single peak* x_n *characterised by applications* $\Gamma(x_n) = \phi$, *therefore it is not the initial extremity for any arc of the graph G and this is why it is called network output.*

The peaks $x_1, \ldots, x_{n-1}$ separate from the input x_0 and output x_n are called intermediary peaks.

A function φ defined on the set of arcs with integer values ($\varphi : U \rightarrow Z$) is called $G(X, U)$ network flow, if:

$$0 \leq \varphi(u) \leq c_v \text{ for any arc } u \in U; \tag{9.45}$$

for any intermediary peak $x_i (1 \leq i \leq n-1)$ the following condition is met:

$$\sum_{u \in U_{x_i}^-} \varphi(u) = \sum_{u \in U_{x_i}^+} \varphi(u) \tag{9.46}$$

By assimilating φ(u) with a quantity of material that runs through the arc *u* in the direction of its orientation, the first condition expresses the natural requirement that this quantity would not exceed the quantity of the arc. The following condition shows that in the intermediary peaks x_i, there are no *losses*, meaning that the sum of quantities arrived in x_i along the arcs incident to inside thereof is equal to the sum of quantities that *exit* from x_i on the arcs incident to the inside thereof.

Totalling the relations (9.46) for all intermediary peaks and reducing the terms shown in both members, it results:

$$\sum_{u \in U_{x_0}^+} \varphi(u) = \sum_{u \in U_{x_n}^-} \varphi(u) = v(\varphi x_n) \tag{9.47}$$

The relation (9.47) shows that in a network without losses, the quantity of material *entered* into the network through x_0 is equal to the quantity arrived in x_n. The size $v(\varphi\, x_n)$ is called the value of the flow φ in the peak x_n. For such issues, we are interested to determine the flow of maximum value in a given transport network. Several methods are known, by means of which we can solve this problem.

The Ford–Fulkerson algorithm is based on the concept of cut in a transport network $G = (X, U)$ and a subset A of its peaks $(A \subset X)$ with the property that $x_0 \notin A$ and $x_n \in A$.

The set U_A^- of the arcs incident to the inside of this subset is called a cut in the network *G*. The capacity of the cut U_A^- is defined as being the sum of the capacities of component arcs.

$$C(U_A^-) = \sum_{u \in U_A^-} c(u) \tag{9.48}$$

It is easy to see that a unit of a material quantity leaving from x_0 necessarily crosses an arc of the cut U_A^-. We immediately deduce that for any flow φ and any cut U_A^- we have:

$$v(\varphi x_n) \leq C(U_A^-) \tag{9.49}$$

The Ford–Fulkerson theorem shows that in a transport network, a flow has the maximum value if and only if there is a cut of equal capacity to the flow value. In this case, the cut has the minimum capacity.

Therefore, in case of equality between the flow and the cut, $v(\varphi x_n) = C(U_A^-)$, then the flow φx_n has the maximum value, while the cut U_A^- has the minimum capacity. This result is the necessary and sufficient condition for the existence of the flow of maximum value and underlies the Ford–Fulkerson algorithm to determine the flow of maximum value.

Applying this algorithm consists in the following:

- a *flow* φ *is propagated in the network, from the peak* x_0 *to* x_n, *so that* $\varphi(u) \leq c(u)$; (9.50)
- *the peak of the network G is marked, according* to *the following rule* : *The input* x_0 *is marked with* $[+]$; (9.51)
- *if the peak* x_j *is not marked and there is* a non-*saturated arc* (x_i, x_j) *the initial extremity* x_i *of which is marked, then we mark* x_j *with* $[+x_i]$. (9.52)

We note that if the arc (x_i, x_j) is saturated, meaning $\varphi(u) = c(u)$, the peak x_j cannot be marked, if the peak x_j is not marked and there is the arc (x_j, x_i) traversed by a nonzero flow the final extremity x_i of which is marked, then we mark x_j with $[-x_i]$, and if the flow is zero, the peak x_j is not marked. If, after applying the marking procedure, the output x_n is not marked, then the flow φ has the maximum value. Indeed, be *A* the set of unmarked peaks; because x_0 is marked and x_n is unmarked, *A* defines a cut U_A^- the arcs of which are saturated by virtue of the previous rule of marking.

Totalling the equalities (9.46) for all intermediary points x_j from A, we get:

$$\sum_{u \in U_A^-} \varphi(u) = \sum_{u \in U_A^+} \varphi(u) + v(\varphi) \tag{9.53}$$

but $\sum_{u \in U_A^-} \varphi(u) = \sum_{u \in U_A^-} c(u) = C(U_A^-)$ because the arcs of the cut are saturated and $\sum_{u \in U_A^+} \varphi(u) = 0$ for any arc and incident to the outside of the set *A*. Therefore:

$$v(\varphi x_n) = C(U_{\bar{A}}^{-}) \tag{9.54}$$

and, according to the Ford–Fulkerson theorem, $\varphi\, x_n$ has the maximum value.

If the output x_n is marked, there will be a chain γ of arcs with the extremities marked, which joins the input x_0 with the output x_n.

Let us note with:

$$d_\gamma^1 = \min_{u \in U_\gamma^{\rightarrow}} [c(u) - \varphi(u)] \tag{9.55}$$

$U_\gamma^{\rightarrow}$ being the set of the arcs of the chain γ, the final extremity of which is marked with $[+]$ (to exclude the peak in relation to which the marking was done), therefore the set $U_\gamma^{\rightarrow}$ consists of the arcs oriented in the *input–output direction.*

Be:

$$d_\gamma^2 = \min_{u \in U_\gamma^{\leftarrow}} \varphi(u) \tag{9.56}$$

$U_\gamma^{\leftarrow}$ being the set of the arcs of the chain γ the initial extremities of which are noted with $[-]$. These are the arcs oriented in the opposite direction of the *input–output* direction.

The indicator $d_\gamma = \min\left(d_\gamma^1, d_\gamma^2\right) > 0$. $\left(\text{If the set is void, } U_\gamma^{\leftarrow} \text{ then } d_\gamma^2 = 0\right)$. (9.57)

By adding the size d_γ to the flows of arcs in $U_\gamma^{\rightarrow}$ subtracting the same size from the flows of arcs of the set $U_\gamma^{\leftarrow}$ and maintaining unchanged the flows of the arcs that are not part of γ, we get a new flow ϕ', *better* than ϕ, because:

$$v\left(\phi'\right) = v(\phi) + d_\gamma > v(\phi) \tag{9.58}$$

In essence, the algorithm to determine the flow of maximum value consists in successively improving an initial flow given by means of the previously described marking procedure. As this procedure is quite laborious, its use is avoided, first seeking a complete flow in all iterations, that is a flow with the property that any path that joins the input with the output from the network would contain at least one saturated arc. If at a certain iteration we have a flow that is not complete, there will be a path γ—which joins the input with the output from the network, consisting only of unsaturated arcs.

If we note:

$$d_\gamma = \min_{u \in \gamma} [c(u) - \varphi(u)] > 0 \tag{9.59}$$

then increasing the flows of the arcs of the path γ with the size d_γ and maintaining unchanged the flows of the other arcs that are not part of γ, we get a flow ϕ' *better* than ϕ, meaning that $v(\phi') = v(\phi) + d_\gamma > v(\phi)$.

Additionally, the path γ will contain at least one saturated arc. At a second stage, we apply the labelling procedure to the complete flow. If the current flow ϕ does not have the maximum value, it can be increased along a chain of arcs that joins the network input with its output, as seen above. The labelling procedure, etc. is applied to the new flow.

9.5 Hamiltonian Paths and Circuits in a Graph

Defining the Hamiltonian paths and circuits implies: in a graph $G = (X, \Gamma)$, a path

$$\mu = (x_{i_1}, x_{i_2}, \ldots, x_{i_n}) \tag{9.60}$$

is called *Hamiltonian* if it passes once and only once through each peak of the graph. If the graph G of order n has Hamiltonian paths, their length is $l(\mu) = n - 1$.

Based on some appropriate mathematical models, the Hamiltonian paths in a graph attached to an economic problem can be determined. Thus, the postal service of a city is responsible to ensure picking up the mailing from all the points where mailboxes are located. An efficient way to solve this problem consists in determining the Hamiltonian paths in a graph *G* defined by the set *X* of the points where the mailboxes are located and by the applications γ that are the network of paths joining the points $x_i \in X$. If there are several Hamiltonian paths, the problem of choosing the path of optimal value arises, using the cost of transportation, duration of transportation etc. as criterion of economic efficiency. To this end, the value of each path μ is determined, by totalling the indicators $v(x_i, x_j)$ attached to the arcs that form that path and finally, the optimal variant is chosen. The range to apply this type of economic-mathematical model can be extended to solving some various management problems.

Another concept characteristic to the aforementioned problem is the Hamiltonian circuit. The circuit $\mu = (x_{i_1}, x_{i_2}, \ldots, x_{i_n})$ is Hamiltonian if it passes once through each peak of the graph, except for the peak x_{i1}. If the graph is of order n, the length of the Hamiltonian circuit is $l(\mu) = n$. Therefore, Hamiltonian circuits are the class of elementary circuits with the length *n*.

A necessary condition to have at least one Hamiltonian circuit is that the graph would be strongly connected. A necessary condition for the existence of a Hamiltonian path is that the graph would be complete.

If the graph is non-oriented, the analogue of the Hamiltonian path or circuit is the chain, respectively the Hamiltonian circuit.

To find the Hamiltonian path, there are several methods, namely:

– *the Lattice method of multiplication* operating with matrix products of special type, which enables the successive enumeration without redundancy, of all paths with the length of $1, 2, \ldots, n-1$.

The matrix $M^{(1)}$ consisting of elements x_{ij} defined as below underlies the calculations that form the multiplication algorithm:

$$m_{ij} = \begin{cases} x_i x_j & \text{if arcs } (x_i x_j) \in U_i \\ 0 & \text{if there is no arcs from } (x_i, x_j) \text{ and for } i = j \end{cases} \tag{9.61}$$

The matrix $\widetilde{M}^{(1)}$ is deduced from this Lattice matrix, suppressing the initial node (the first letter) at each element m_{ij}.

By Lattice multiplication of matrix $M^{(1)}$ by the matrix $\widetilde{M}^{(1)}$, then matrix is obtained $M^{(1)}$. Thus, if we note with *L* the Lattice product, we get:

$$M^{(1)} \ L \ \widetilde{M}^{(1)} = M^{(2)} \tag{9.62}$$

The matrix $M^{(1)}$ provides the lsit of elementary paths with the length *l*, and the matrix $M^{(2)}$ provides the list of elementary paths with the length *2*.

Using the aforementioned rules of Lattice multiplication, the matrix $M^{(3)}$ is calculated:

$$M^{(3)} = M^{(2)} \ L \ \widetilde{M}^{(1)} \tag{9.63}$$

which provides us the list of all elementary paths with the length *3*. The following are calculated below:

$$M^{(3)} \ L \ \widetilde{M}^{(1)} = M^{(4)} \tag{9.64}$$

$$M^{(k)} \ L \ \widetilde{M}^{(1)} = M^{(k+1)} \tag{9.65}$$

We get the list of all elementary paths with the length $(k+1)$ from the last *matrix.*

If in ordinal terms the graph *n* is large, then we have to perform a great volume of *multiplications* of this type.

These calculations can be considerably shortened, because the Lattice multiplication can be extended to the matrix $\widetilde{M}^{(s)}$ $(S > 1)$ as follows:

$$M^{(r)} \ L \ \widetilde{M}^{(s)} = M^{(r+s)} \tag{9.66}$$

where $\widetilde{M}^{(s)}$ is obtained from the matrix $M^{(s)}$ suppressing the first letter from each sequence contained in the matrix.

Therefore, assuming that we are not interested in the elementary paths smaller than n, it will be sufficient to successively calculate:

$$M^{(2)};\ M^{(4)} = M^{(2)}\ L\ \widetilde{M}^{(2)};\ M^{(2^3)} = M^{(4)}\ L\ \widetilde{M}^{(4)}\ \textit{and}\quad M^{(2^k)} = M^{(2^{k-1})}\ L\ \widetilde{M}^{(2^{k-1})} \tag{9.67}$$

with $2^k \leq n$.

By appropriately organising the products that define the matrix $M^{(n)}$, the volume of calculations can be reduced even more.

For example, in order to determine the matrixes $M^{(33)}$ and $M^{(34)}$, the following are calculated: $M^{(2)}$, $M^{(4)}$, $M^{(8)}M^{(16)}$, $M^{(32)}$,

$$M^{(33)} = M^{(32)}\ L\ \widetilde{M}^{(1)} \tag{9.68}$$

$$\text{and } M^{(33)} = M^{(32)}\ L\ \widetilde{M}^{(2)}. \tag{9.69}$$

The *Lattice method of multiplication* can be easily programmed on an electronic computer and if it changes appropriately, it enables us to find paths which additional restrictions have been imposed to.

In order to determine the Hamiltonian circuits (if there are) from the matrix $M^{(n-1)}$, we deduce the matrix $\widetilde{M}^{(n-1)}$ according to the usual rule and calculate:

$$M^{*}_{(n)} = \widetilde{M}^{(n-1)}\ L\ \widetilde{M}^{(1)} \tag{9.70}$$

By adding at the beginning of each Lattice sequence from the matrix $M^{*}_{(n)}$ of the letter that is the index of the line of this matrix, Hamiltonian circuits are obtained (if any).

If the graph is of high order and is not strongly connected, in order to determine the Hamiltonian paths, it is preferable to break it down into strongly connected sub-graphs, by using the Foulkes algorithm;

– *the method of Foulkes* takes into account the fact that a Boolean matrix *M* can be associated to any graph $G = (X, U)$. This matrix underlies the Foulkes algorithm.

X_n and the Boolean matrix *M* associated thereto, then by Boolean multiplication*, we can determine the matrix $M^{(2)}$:

$$M^{(2)} = M \times M = \left\| m_{ij}^{(2)} \right\| \ (ij) = 1, \ldots, n \tag{9.71}$$

where, according to the definition

$$m_{ij}^{(2)} = m_{i1} \times m_{1i} + m_{i2} \times m_{1j} + \ldots + m_{in} \times m_{nj} \tag{9.72}$$

The element $m_{ij}^{(2)}$ will be *1* if at least one of the terms that define it is *l*. Be that $m_{ik} \times m_{kj}$ $(1 \leq k \leq n)$, the product $m_{ik} \times m_{kj} = 1$ if and only if $m_{ik} = 1$, and $m_{kj} = 1$, meaning there is an arc from x_i to x_k and a circle arc from x_k to x_j.

This means there is a path with the length *2* from x_i to x_k. It results that $m_{ij}^{(2)} = 1$ only and only if there is at least one path with the length *2* from x_i to x_j. Therefore, the matrix $M^{(2)}$ provides information on the existence of the paths with the length *2* between the various peaks of the graph *G*. Inductively, the matrix $M^{(r)}$ provides information on the existence of the paths with the length *r*, between the various peaks of the graph.

It immediately results from here that the elements of the matrix $(I+M)^{(r)}$ show if between any two peaks of the graph *G* there is or not a path with a length smaller than or equal to *r*. The calculation of the matrix $(I+M)^{(r)}$ is done by means of the relation:

$$(I+M)^{(r)} = I + M^{(1)} + M^{(2)} + \ldots + M^{(r)} \tag{9.73}$$

The element $d_{ij}^{(r)}$ of this matrix can have the following value:

$$d_{ij}^{(r)} = \begin{cases} 1 & \text{if } x_j \in \{x_j\} U\Gamma(x_i) U \ldots\ldots U\Gamma^{\Gamma}(x_i) \\ 0 & \text{for the rest} \end{cases} \tag{9.74}$$

The set $\Gamma(x_i) = \{x_1\} \cup \Gamma(x_i) \cup \Gamma^2(x_i) \ldots \Gamma^r(x_i)$ is called transitive closure of Γ, therefore $\Gamma(x_i)$ is an application of the set *x* in *x* defined by the previous relation.

Taking into account that $\Gamma^2(x_i) = \Gamma[(x_i)], \Gamma^3(x_i) = \Gamma^2[(x_i)]\,(x_i)$, etc., it results that $x_j \in \hat{\Gamma}(x_i)$ shows that between the peaks x_i and x_j there is a path with a length smaller than or equal to *r*.

For a graph with *n* peaks, any elementary path is of a length at least equal to $n-1$, therefore the matrix $(I+M)^{(n-1)}$ will contain all elementary or non-elementary paths with a length smaller than or equal to $n-1$.

As any path is a collection of elementary paths, the matrix $(I+M)^{(n+p-1)}$ is necessarily equal to $(I+M)^{(n-1)}$, therefore:

$$(I+M)^{(n+p-1)} = (I+M)^{(n-1)} \quad p \geq 1 \tag{9.75}$$

Therefore, it is sufficient to calculate $(I+M)^{(n-1)}$ in order to find out whether there is a path between any peaks x_i and x_j of the graph *G*. To reduce the calculations, it is recommended to successively calculate the matrixes: $(I+M)^{(2)}, (I+M)^{(2^3)}, \ldots, (I+M)^{(2^k)}$.

The operation of Boolean multiplication stops when:

$$(I+M)^{(2^{k+1})} = (I+M)^{(2^k)} \tag{9.76}$$

or when $2^k \geq n-1$.

After obtaining the information on the existence of Hamiltonian paths between any two peaks x_i and x_j, the problem of finding the sequence of arcs that form each path arises. For this purpose, the graph *G* is broken down into classes of equivalence.

A set of elements *C* is a class of equivalence, if its elements satisfy the properties of:

- *reflexivity, that is for any* $x_i \in C$ *there is the relation of equivalence* $x_i \sim x_j$.
- *symmetry, that is if for any two peaks* $x_i, x_j \in C$ *there is the relation of equivalence* $x_j \sim x_i$.
- *transitivity, that is if for the peaks* $x_i, x_j, x_k \in C$ *there are the relations of equivalence* $x_i \sim x_j$ *and* $x_j \sim x_k$, *then there is also the relation of equivalence* $x_i \sim x_k$.

We specify that the relation $x_i \sim x_j$ is interpreted that x_i is equivalent to x_j.

Given a graph G(X, Γ), we consider that between the peaks $x_i \in X$ and $x_j \in X$ there is the relation of equivalence $x_i \sim x_j$ if and only if there is a path from x_i to x_j and vice-versa and, therefore, the following relations must be satisfied:

$$x_j \in \Gamma(x_i) \quad \text{and} \quad (x_i) \in \Gamma'(x_j) \tag{9.77}$$

Therefore, a relation of equivalence so defined will determine a convex sub-graph of the graph:

If the peaks x_i and x_j belong to two classes of equivalence and there is a path from x_i to x_j $(x_j \in \Gamma(x_i))$ then there is no path from x_j to x_i (if it existed, then $x_i \sim x_j$).

We consider that the set *C* is the class of equivalence which x_i belongs to and *C* the class of equivalence of x_j, then there will be a path from each peak of *C* at each peak of C′ and there is no path from any peak of C′ to a peak of C. Thus, a transitive and anti-symmetric relation has been defined.

To easily obtain the peaks that belong to the same class of equivalence, it is sufficient to observe that if two peaks belong to the same class, then in the matrix $(I+M)^{(2^k)}$ the lines corresponding to the two peaks are identical. It results that by ordering the lines (peaks), taking into account the number of elements equal to *1*, the classes of equivalence of the graph *G* are obtained. After this operation, the matrix acquires a semi-triangular aspect. If the matrix ordered so is strictly triangular in relation to the sub-matrixes related to the classes of equivalence, then there is total order and there may be one or several Hamiltonian paths. Otherwise, there is no Hamiltonian path.

Listing the Hamiltonian paths is done first taking into account the Hamiltonian paths existing within each class of equivalence, then they are connected to the arcs that are part of the paths that cross all classes.

References

Berge C (1998) Graphes et hypergraphes. Dunod, Paris
Berge C (1993) Theorie des graphes et applications. Dunod, Paris
Bollobas B (1989) Graph theory. Springer, New York, Heidelberg
Busacker R (2005) Finite graphs and networks and introduction with applications. Mc Graw Hill, New York
Harary F (2005) Introduction to the theory of directed graphs. John Wiley, New York
Kaufmann A, Dezbazeille G (2001) La methode du chemin critique. Dunod, Paris
Nobre FS, Tobias AM, Walker D (2010) A new contingency view of the organization: Managing complexity and uncertainty through cognition. Brazilian Administration Review 7(4):379–396
Ore O (2001) Theory of graphs. Random House, New York
Ore O (1998) Graphs and their uses. Random House, New York
Pacaud P (2001) Chemin critique et coordination. Ed. d'organisations, Paris
Renner A (1965) Der Kritische Weg. VEB Verlagfür Bauwesen, Berlin
Robichaud M (2001) Graphes de fluence. Eyrolles, Paris
Robins S (2001) Management, 3rd edn. Prentice Hall, New York
Schreiter G (1966) Kritischer Weg und PERT. Verlag Die Wirtschaft, Berlin
Siropolis H (2000) Business management. Houghten Hifflin Company, Boston
Wagner G (1992) PERT und CPM als Planingsinstreament der Bauindustrie. Humbold, Wien-Stutgart

Chapter 10
Models that Use the Queuing String Theory

10.1 Fundamentals of the Queuing String Theory

In production processes, an unnecessary and unwanted time-consumption of the production means, resources and performers occurs, due to the impossibility to temporally correlate various activities that are interrelated, thus resulting in the queuing phenomena.

Examples of such queuing phenomena are: The machines waiting unused on a site or in a factory, due to the lack of materials; the queues created in shops or other serving units by purchasers who are waiting to be served; waiting for the free tone on the phone in order to call a subscriber's number or waiting to have a phone conversation on a currently busy number; the situation of a freight train that is waiting to be unloaded in the situation where there is an insufficient number of unloading operators, who cannot unload all freight trains arrived to be unloaded, etc.

A queuing phenomenon is characterised by three main elements:

- *consumers requesting a service;*
- *the waiting string or the queue that is formed should the consumers must wait;*
- *the serving station, the purpose of which is to satisfy the demands.*

The fundamental concepts in the queuing theory may be introduced based on an actual example. Let us suppose that in order to manufacture the concrete, 3 concrete plants are used, and to transport it, 15 dumper trucks. The consumers, meaning the dumper trucks, come before the serving station that consists of 3 concrete plants. If at the serving station there are more than 3 dumper trucks at a given moment, a queuing string is formed. The consumers are placed in the queuing string according to a certain rule, in other words, they have a rate of arrival and similarly, there is also a serving rate.

I.C. Dima, M. Man, *Modelling and Simulation in Management*, Contributions to Management Science, DOI 10.1007/978-3-319-16592-9_10

Thus, the fundamental elements of a queuing model are:

- *the comings (arrivals) into the system, which are generally assumed to be random and independent (however, there are situations—hence also models where the comings are no longer independent)*, and if we consider that the arrivals are Poissonian, meaning the number of arrival into a time unit is the random variable distributed by Poisson, then we demonstrate that the interval between two successive arrivals is a random variable that is negatively exponentially distributed. The incomings can be arrivals from a finite or infinite population;
- *the duration of the service (serving time) is also a random variable, which is usually supposed to be independent from one serving to another and independent from the comings.* Being a random variable, it is assumed it has a determined repartition law that may be, for example, exponentially negative, uniform on an interval $[a, b]{\cdot}\chi$, Gama etc. In each actual model, the repartition of the service duration shall be specified;
- *the service factor or traffic intensity is defined as the relation:* $\rho = \frac{\lambda}{\mu}$ *which indicates the relation between the average number of units that arrive in the system and the average number of units that leave from the system in a chosen unit of time.* The service factor is of particular importance in the queuing string theory, because it shows the distributions of arrivals and departures. All numerical characteristics of the queuing model studied can be expressed with this indicator. It immediately shows it is a matter of a system of unlimited cluster or not, as: $\rho \geq 1$ or $\rho < 1$;
- *the service stations in the system are understood as that mechanism that serves the demand formulated by units.* The role of the station is performed by one or several people, one or several machines, drive lanes in an intersection, etc. There are models with a single service station, or with several stations. In the case of models with several stations, they can be arranged in series in a determined order and the units are required to pass through each station or can be arranged in parallel, each playing the same role in meeting the requests formulated by new units (it is a matter of serving with several service stations);
- *the system discipline is a set of rules specifying how the units will be arranged in the queuing string, as well as the order in which they will be served.* The simplest and also natural discipline is that which briefly states *the first one in is the first one served.* There may also be other disciplines such as the case of models where some units have priority in serving compared to other units or the case of models with undisciplined units;
- *units' way of serving in the system.* Depending on the model, we shall encounter *individual services* where a unit is served once and then the unit leaves the system for good. The station freed by the unit that has been served remains inactive until the arrival of another unit. However, there may also be other types of serving: *bulk services*, where all units waiting up to a preset number are served. When the station finished serving in bulk serves the second bulk, etc.; *mass services*, where the station works continuously on certain time intervals.

In each time interval, all units are served, which by the end of the previous interval were in queue or arrive in this period of time, the number of units entering the station that can not exceed a given number.

In order to perform the analysis of a queuing model, it is necessary to know a number of features of the model and namely:

- *the average number of units in the system (in the queuing string and in course of being served);*
- *the average number of units in the course of being served;*
- *the average number of units in the queuing string;*
- *the average number of unoccupied stations;*
- *the average number of units that arrive in a unit of time;*
- *the average time for serving;*
- *the average queuing time in the system;*
- *the average queuing time in the string;*
- *etc;*

These are only some of the numerical characteristics that will be calculated within the queuing models. One special problem is posed by the models with one or several stations where the comings are Poissonian of the parameter λ and the duration of the services is the random variable that is negatively exponentially distributed by the parameter μ.

10.2 Model with One Service Station and Unlimited Queuing String

To emphasise the model equations, it is necessary to present the working hypotheses, namely: the comings into the system are finite, random, independent of one another and the number of comings by the unit of time is Poisson randomly distributed variable of parameter λ; the services are independent of each other and independent of the comings, and the duration of the service is a random variable that is negatively exponentially distributed by the parameter μ and once served, a unit leaves the system for good; there is a single station that provides the service requested by the units; the discipline of the system is the ordinary one, namely: The first one in is the first one served (the units enter the serving station in the order of their coming into the system, and there are no undisciplined units or units with priority in serving compared to other units).

In these hypotheses of system operation, we shall analyse the models starting from the initial moment $t = 0$.

If we note by $\delta > 0$ the moment when we record a coming and by λ the probability of having a coming at the moment $\delta › 0$, starting from the initial state $t = 0$ then under the conditions we have set, we have:

$$A(\delta) = \lambda \cdot \int_0^{\delta} e^{-\lambda \cdot x} dx = 1 - e^{-\lambda \cdot \delta} \tag{10.1}$$

By developing the function $e^{-\lambda \cdot \delta}$ in series around the origin, we get:

$$A(\delta)1 - \left[1 - \lambda \cdot \delta + \frac{(\lambda \cdot \delta)^2}{2!} + \ldots\right] = \lambda \cdot \lambda + O(\delta) \tag{10.2}$$

where *O(δ)* has the property that: $\lim_{\delta \to 0} \frac{O(\delta)}{\delta} = 0$

If we note by $A(t, t+\delta)$, the probability to record a coming within the time interval $(t, t+\delta)$ then in the hypotheses set we get:

$$A\ (t,\ t+\delta) = \lambda \cdot \int_t^{t+\delta} e^{-\lambda \cdot x} dx = e^{-\lambda \cdot t} - e^{-(t+\delta) \cdot \lambda} = e^{-\lambda \cdot t} \cdot \left(1 - e^{-\lambda \cdot t}\right) \tag{10.3}$$

meaning:

$$A(t,\ t+\delta) = [1 - A(t)]A(t) \tag{10.4}$$

They were expressed in words, the probability to record a coming within the time interval $(t, t+\delta)$ is equal to the probability of not having any coming at the time t multiplied by the probability to record a coming at the time δ. Analogically, the probability for a unit to leave the system at a given time $\delta \rangle 0$ and which we note by $B(\delta)$:

$$B(\delta) \ = \ \mu \cdot \delta \ + \ O(\delta) \tag{10.5}$$

The hypotheses enable us to express the probability that at the time $t+\delta$ to have n units in the system which we note by: $P_n(t+\delta)$.

From the hypothesis that the arrivals are Poissonian, it results that the time between two successive comings into the system is a random variable negatively exponentially distributed by the parameter λ, meaning it has a distribution density of:

$$f(x) = \begin{cases} \lambda \cdot e^{-\lambda \cdot x}, x \rangle 0 \\ 0, x \le 0 \text{ with } \lambda \rangle 0 \end{cases}$$

$$P_n(\delta + t) = P_{n-1}(t) \cdot A(\delta) \cdot [1 - B(\delta)] + P_n(t) \cdot [1 - A(\delta)] \cdot [1 - B(\delta)] + P_{n+1}(t) \cdot [1 - A(\delta)] \cdot B(\delta) + O(\delta) \tag{10.6}$$

Because our probability to be in the state $S(\delta)$ (n units to exist in the system at the time $t+\delta$) is the sum of the following probabilities:

- *our probability that at the time t to be in the state* S_{n-1} *and in the time interval from t to* $t+\delta$ *a unit to come and no unit to leave:*

$$P_{n-1}(t) \cdot A(\delta) \cdot [1 - B(\delta)] \tag{10.7}$$

- *our probability that at the time t to be in the state* S_n *and in the time interval from t to* $t+\delta$ *no unit to come into the system and no unit to leave:*

$$P_n(t) \cdot [1 - A(\delta)] \cdot [1 - B(\delta)] \tag{10.8}$$

- *our probability that at the time t to be in the state* S_{n+1} *and in the time interval from t to* $t+\delta$ *no unit to come and no unit to leave:*

$$P_{n+1}(t) \cdot [1 - A(\delta)] \cdot B(\delta) \tag{10.9}$$

- *the probability that in the time interval from t to* $t+\delta$ *the number of units in the system to vary by more than one:* $O(\delta)$

By replacing $A(\delta)$ and $B(\delta)$ we get:

$$\begin{aligned} P_n(t+\delta) &= P_{n-1} \cdot (t) \cdot [\lambda \cdot \delta + O(\delta)] \cdot [1 - \mu \cdot \delta - O(\delta)] + P_n(t) \cdot \\ &\cdot [1 - \lambda \cdot \delta - O(\delta)] \cdot [1 - \mu \cdot \delta - O(\delta)] + P_{n+1}(t) \cdot [1 - \lambda \cdot \delta - O(\delta)] \cdot \\ &\cdot [\mu \cdot \delta + O(\delta)] + O(\delta) \end{aligned} \tag{10.10}$$

Or by ordering by the powers of δ:

$$\begin{aligned} P_n(t+\delta) = P_{n-1}(t) \cdot \lambda \cdot \delta + P_n(t) \cdot [1 - (\lambda + \mu)\delta] + P_{n-1}(t) \cdot \mu \cdot \delta \\ + O(\delta) \end{aligned} \tag{10.11}$$

From here, we get:

$$\frac{P_n(t+\delta) - P_n(t)}{\delta} = \lambda \cdot P_{n-1}(t) - (\lambda + \mu) \cdot P_n(t) + \mu \cdot P_{n+1}(t) + \frac{O(\delta)}{\delta} \tag{10.12}$$

By making δ tend to zero, the second member has a limit, therefore the first member also has a limit and we get:

$$\frac{dP_n(t)}{dt} = \lambda \cdot P_{n-1}(t) - (\lambda + \mu) \cdot P_n(t) + \mu \cdot P_{n+1}(t)\, n = 1, 2, 3, .. \tag{10.13}$$

For $n = 0$ we get a special equation if we express $P_0(t+\delta)$:

$$P_0(t+\delta) = P_0(t) \cdot [1 - A(\delta)] + P_1(t) \cdot [1 - A(\delta)] \cdot B(\delta) + O(\delta) \tag{10.14}$$

from where by replacing $A(\delta)$ and $B(\delta)$, passing $P_0(t)$ into the first member and dividing by δ we get:

$$\frac{P_0(t+\delta)-P_0(t)}{\delta}=-\lambda\cdot P_0(t)+\mu\cdot P_1(t)+\frac{O(\delta)}{\delta} \tag{10.15}$$

From here, by making δ tend to zero, it results that:

$$\frac{dP_0(t)}{dt}=-\lambda\cdot P_0(t)+\mu\cdot P_1(t) \tag{10.16}$$

Therefore, the model we considered is characterised by the system of differential equations:

$$\frac{dP_n(t)}{dt}=\lambda\cdot P_{n-1}(t)-(\lambda+\mu)\cdot P_n(t)+\mu\cdot P_{n+1}(t)\ n=1,2,3,\ldots$$
$$\frac{dP_0(t)}{dt}=-\lambda\cdot P_0(t)+\mu\cdot P_1(t) \tag{10.17}$$

Solving this system of differential equations enables us to find the probability $P_n(t)$ that at a time t we have n units in the system. We shall not determine these probabilities in the general case, but in the stationary operating regime (or of the statistical balance) characterised by the fact that:

$$\lim_{t\to\infty}\frac{dP_n(t)}{dt}=0,\quad n=1,2,\ldots, \tag{10.18}$$

In this situation, $P_n(t)=p_n, n=0,1,2,\ldots$ and the system of differential equations is reduced to a system of linear algebraic equations:

$$\begin{cases}\lambda\cdot p_{n-1}-(\lambda+\mu)\cdot p_n+\mu\cdot p_{n+1}=0\\ -\lambda\cdot p_0+\mu\cdot p_1=0, n=1,2,3,\ldots\end{cases} \tag{10.19}$$

which are resolved easily.

For this variable relation for $n=1, 2, 3\ldots$, we can write it as:

$$\lambda\cdot p_{n-1}-\mu\cdot p_n=\lambda\cdot p_n-\mu\cdot p_{n+1},\quad n=1,2,\ldots \tag{10.20}$$

By noting:

$$Z_n=\lambda\cdot p_{n-1}-\mu\cdot p_n \tag{10.21}$$

we have:

$$Z_n=Z_{n+1}\quad n=1,2,\ldots \tag{10.22}$$

As $z_1 = \lambda \cdot p_0 - \mu \cdot p_1 = 0$ it results that $z_n = 0, \quad n = 1, 2, \ldots$ and from here:

$$p_n = \frac{\lambda}{\mu} p_{n-1} = \rho \cdot p_{n-1}, \quad n = 1, 2, \ldots \tag{10.23}$$

meaning:

$$p_n = \rho^n \cdot p_o, \quad n = 1, 2, \ldots \tag{10.24}$$

To determine the probability p_0.

If $\rho < 1$, then $\sum_{n=0}^{\infty} \rho^n = \frac{1}{1-\rho}$ and as $\sum_{n=0}^{\infty} p_n = 1$ it results that

$$1 = p_0 \cdot \sum_{n=0}^{\infty} \rho^n = p_0 \cdot \frac{1}{1-\rho} \tag{10.25}$$

and from here:

$$p_0 = 1 - \rho$$

and with this:

$$p_n = \rho^n \cdot (1 - \rho), \quad n = 0, 1, 2, \ldots \tag{10.26}$$

Let us first see what is the maximum value of a probability $p_n(\rho)$. For this, we solve the equation:

$$\frac{d\,p_n(\rho)}{d\,p} = 0 \text{ meaning : } \rho^{n-1} \cdot [n - \rho \cdot (n+1)] = 0 \tag{10.27}$$

which leads us to the solution:

$$\rho = \frac{n}{n+1} \quad \text{and therefore :} \tag{10.28}$$

$$\max p_n(\rho) = \left(\frac{n}{n+1}\right)^n \cdot \frac{1}{n+1} \tag{10.29}$$

In economic calculations, a number of parameters are used, which will be calculated below.

Let Z be the random variable that gives us the number of units in the system. That means Z has the distribution:

$$Z = \begin{pmatrix} 0 & 1 & 2 & \cdot & \cdot & \cdot & n & \cdot & \cdot & \cdot \\ p_0 & p_1 & p_2 & \cdot & \cdot & \cdot & p_n & \cdot & \cdot & \cdot \end{pmatrix} \tag{10.30}$$

The probability that the number of units in the system does not exceed a number n immediately results from here:

$$P(Z \leq n) = \sum_{j=1}^{n} P(Z = j) = \sum_{j=1}^{n} p \cdot j = (1 - \rho) \cdot \sum_{j=1}^{n} \rho^{j} = 1 - \rho^{n+1} \tag{10.31}$$

and also: $P(Z > 0) = \rho^{n+1}$.

$$\text{Particularly}: P\ (Z\ >\ 0)\ = \rho \tag{10.32}$$

$P(Z > 0)$ is the probability that the station is busy and we observe that this probability is equal to the service factor (traffic intensity).

The average number of units in the system:

$$\overline{Z} = M(Z) = \sum_{n=0}^{\infty} n \cdot p_n = \sum_{n=0}^{\infty} n \cdot (1 - \rho) \cdot \rho^n = \frac{\rho}{1 - \rho} \tag{10.33}$$

The average number of units in the queuing string.

If we note by Q the average number of units in the queuing string, then:

$$Q = \begin{pmatrix} 0 & 1 & 2 & . & . & . & n & . & . & . \\ p_0 + p_1 & p_2 & p_3 & . & . & . & p_{n+1} & . & . & . \end{pmatrix} \tag{10.34}$$

Therefore, it results from here that:

$$\overline{Q} = M(Q) = \sum_{n=0}^{\infty} (n - 1) \cdot p_n = (1 - \rho) \cdot \rho^2 \cdot \left(1 + 2 \cdot \rho + 3 \cdot \rho^2 + \ldots\right)$$

$$= \frac{\rho^2}{1 - \rho} \tag{10.35}$$

This can also be calculated in other ways, namely:

Let s be the number of units in the course of being served.

Then:

$$Z = S + Q \tag{10.36}$$

But:

$$S_0 = \begin{pmatrix} 0 & 1 \\ p_0 & 1 - p \end{pmatrix} \tag{10.37}$$

$$\text{so}: \quad \overline{S} = M(S) = 1 - p_0 = \rho \tag{10.38}$$

and therefore:

$$\overline{Q'} = \overline{Z} - \overline{S} = \frac{\rho}{1-\rho} - \rho = \frac{\rho^2}{1-\rho^2} \tag{10.39}$$

One immediately observes that:

$$\overline{Q} = \rho \cdot \overline{Z} = \frac{\lambda}{\mu} \cdot \overline{Z} \tag{10.40}$$

meaning:

$$\frac{\overline{Q}}{\lambda} = \frac{Z}{\mu} \tag{10.41}$$

In practical problems, situations often arise when the average string queuing time (which we note by W) or the average system queuing time (which we note by W*) *is of interest to us.* $\psi(t)$.

The average queuing time in the string is calculated as follows:

$W = M$ [(the number of units in the system)·(the time of a unit service)]

$$W = \overline{Z} \cdot \frac{1}{\rho} = \frac{\rho}{\mu \cdot (1-\rho)} \tag{10.42}$$

The average queuing time in the system immediately results, namely:

$$W^* = W + \frac{1}{\rho} = \frac{\rho}{\mu \cdot (1-\rho)} + \frac{1}{\mu} = \frac{1}{\rho} \cdot \frac{1}{1-\rho} \tag{10.43}$$

The function generating moments for the random variable Z may be immediately calculated:

$$\psi(t) = M \cdot (e^{t \cdot z}) = \sum_{n=0}^{\infty} e^{t \cdot n} \cdot p_n = (1-\rho) \cdot \sum_{n=0}^{\infty} (e^{t + \ln \rho})^n = \frac{1-\rho}{1 - e^{t + \ln \rho}} \tag{10.44}$$

It follows from here:

$$M(Z^2) = \frac{\rho + \rho^2}{(1-\rho)^2} \tag{10.45}$$

and therefore:

$$D^2(Z) = M(Z^2) - M^2(Z) = \frac{\rho}{(1-\rho)^2} \tag{10.46}$$

One may immediately observe that $D^2(Z)$ is an increasing function of ρ and therefore we get the best accuracy for the models where ρ is as close to zero as possible.

An indicator used frequently to analyse the queuing systems is the indicator $P(>\tau)$, which is the probability that a unit would wait in the queue a higher time than a given time τ.

To determine this probability, we shall first determine the density to distribute the string queuing time.

We shall consider a moment t_0 and we shall see what happens with a unit spotted at this moment. Let us calculate the basic probability $f(\tau)d\tau$ as the unit spotted to wait for a time ranging between $\tau + d\tau$.

If the moment t_0 when the specified unit has been spotted to enter into the system, other n units are before it, then the basic probability specified is obtained as the sum of the probabilities $p(n\tau)d\tau$, where $p(n\tau)d\tau$ is the basic probability that at the moment t_0 we have n units, and the spotted unit would wait for a time ranging between τ and $\tau + d\tau$.

As the service time follows a negatively exponential law of parameter μ, the number of departures follows a Poisson law as long as the station is busy.

Therefore the station is busy, the probability to become available within the time range with the length Δt is $\mu\Delta t$ and therefore the distribution of the number of departures as long as the station is busy is given by:

$$p(s) = \frac{(\mu \cdot t)^s \cdot e^{-\mu \cdot t}}{s!}, \quad s = 0, 1, 2, 3, \ldots \tag{10.47}$$

If $n = 0$, then $p(n, \tau)$ which immediately results from the meaning of the probability $p(n, \tau)$.

If we assume that $n > 0$, then:

$$P(n, \tau) \cdot d\tau = p_n \cdot P \cdot \left(\begin{array}{l} \text{leaving s} = \text{n} - 1 \\ \text{units served in the} \\ \text{time interval } \tau \end{array} \middle/ \begin{array}{l} \text{in the system} \\ \text{there are n units} \\ \text{at the moment } t_0 \end{array} \right) \cdot$$

$$\cdot P \left(\begin{array}{l} \text{one unit to} \\ \text{leave in the time} \\ \text{interval } d\tau \end{array} \middle/ \begin{array}{l} \text{at the beginning of the interval} \\ \tau \text{ we have n units;} \\ \text{after elipsing the time} \\ \text{interval } \tau, \text{ s} = \text{n units have left} \end{array} \right)$$

As we assumed that the system is in stationary regime, we have:

$$p_n = (1 - \rho) \cdot \rho^n \tag{10.48}$$

For the two conditioned probabilities, we can write:

$$P\left(\begin{array}{l}\text{leaving s = n-1}\\ \text{units served in the}\\ \text{time interval } \tau\end{array} \middle/ \begin{array}{l}\text{in the system}\\ \text{there are n units}\\ \text{at the moment t}\end{array}\right) = \frac{(\mu \cdot \tau)^{n-1}}{(n-1)}$$

$$P\left(\begin{array}{l}\text{one unit to leave}\\ \text{leave from the system}\\ \text{in the time interval } d\tau\end{array} \middle/ \begin{array}{l}\text{at the beginning of the interval}\\ \tau \text{ we have n units after}\\ \text{elipsing the time interval } \tau,\\ \text{s = n-1 units have left}\end{array}\right) = \mu$$

Therefore:

$$p(n,\tau) \cdot d\tau = \rho^n \cdot (1-\rho) \cdot \frac{(\mu \cdot \tau)^{n-1} \cdot e^{-\mu\tau}}{(n-1)!} \mu \cdot d\tau, \quad n = 1, 2, 3, \ldots \tag{10.49}$$

It follows from here that:

$$f(\tau) \cdot d\tau = \sum_{n=1}^{\infty} p(n.\tau)d\tau = \sum_{n=1}^{\infty} \rho^n \cdot (1-\rho) \cdot \frac{(\mu \cdot \tau)^{n-1} \cdot e^{-\mu \cdot \tau}}{(n-1)!} \cdot \mu \cdot d\tau = \tag{10.50}$$
$$(1-\rho) \cdot \rho \cdot \mu \cdot e^{-\mu \cdot \tau \cdot (1-\rho)} d\tau$$

And:

$$P(>\tau) = \int_{\tau}^{\infty} f(t)dt = (1-\rho) \cdot \rho \cdot \mu \cdot \int_{\tau}^{\infty} e^{-\mu \cdot t \cdot (1-\rho)} dt = \rho \cdot e^{-\tau \cdot \mu \cdot (1-\rho)} \tag{10.51}$$

In particular, the probability for a unit to be waiting is $P(\geq \rho)$ and hence the probability that the unit is not waiting (or in other words, the probability that the station is not busy) is:

$$1 - P(>0) = 1 - \rho \tag{10.52}$$

or

$$P(Z = 0) = p_0 = 1 - \rho \tag{10.53}$$

and thus we reached (in another way) to the result we had already gotten.

10.3 Model with One Service Station and Limited Queuing String

To better understand the phenomenon that leads to such a model, we shall use an example.

In a town, there is a gas station for fuelling the vehicles, equipped with one gas pump (or with several gas pumps served by one person) and we are to admit that this station has a land that allows parking only for a number of N vehicles (at the most). As such, the queuing string can have the maximum length of $N-1$ units, one unit being in the service station.

The capacity of such a system of n units and the vehicles that require fuelling but cannot find place anymore in the waiting line are forced to go elsewhere. We are therefore in the case of a model with a single service station, with coming from an infinite population, and the number n of possible states of the system ranges between 0 and N. We admit that the comings are Poissonian, the duration of the service is an exponentially negatively distributed variable of parameter μ. We also keep unchanged the other elements found in the previous model, including the station discipline.

As such, the differential equations remain valid:

$$\frac{dP_0(t)}{dt} = -\lambda \cdot P_0(t) + \mu \cdot P_1(t) \tag{10.54}$$

$$\frac{dP_n(t)}{dt} = \lambda \cdot P_{n-1}(t) - (\lambda + \mu) \cdot P_n(t) + \mu \cdot P_{n+1}(t), \quad n = 1, 2, 3, \ldots .N-1 \tag{10.55}$$

and we shall obtain the equation for the case where all units are in the system. For this, we express: $P_N(t+\delta)$.

$$P_N(t+\delta) = P_{N-1}(t) \cdot A(\delta) \cdot [1 - B(\delta)] + P_n(t) \cdot [1 - B(\delta)] + O(\delta) \tag{10.56}$$

By replacing $A(\delta)$ and $B(\delta)$, passing $P_N(t)$ into the first member and dividing by δ we get:

$$\frac{P_n(t+\delta) - P_N(t)}{\delta} = \lambda \cdot P_{N-1}(t) - \mu \cdot P_N(t) + \frac{O(\delta)}{\delta} \tag{10.57}$$

and from here, making $\delta \to 0$, we get the differential equation:

$$\frac{dP_N(t)}{dt} = \lambda \cdot P_{N-1}(t) - \mu \cdot P_N(t) \tag{10.58}$$

We assume we are in the case of stationary regime, meaning:

$$\lim_{t\to\infty} \frac{dP_n(t)}{dt} = 0, \quad n = 0, 1, 2, \ldots, N \tag{10.59}$$

in this case also the system of differential equations becomes a system of algebraic equations:

$$\begin{cases} -\lambda \cdot p_0 + \mu \cdot p_1 = 0 \\ \lambda \cdot p_{n-1} - (\lambda + \mu) \cdot p_n + \mu \cdot p_{n+1} = 0, \quad n = 0, 1, 2, \ldots, N \\ \lambda \cdot p_{N-1} - \mu \cdot p_N = 0 \end{cases} \tag{10.60}$$

Noting:

$$Z_n = \lambda \cdot p_{n-1} - \mu \cdot p_n \tag{10.61}$$

we get the relation:

$$Z_n = Z_{n+1}, n = 1, 2, 3, \ldots, N - 1 \text{ and as } Z_1 = 0, \text{ it results that } Z_n = 0 \tag{10.62}$$

so:

$$p_n = \rho \cdot p_{n-1} = \rho^n \cdot p_0, \; n = 1, 2, 3, \ldots, N \tag{10.63}$$

The probability p_0 is immediately determined from the condition: $\sum_{n=0}^{n} p_n = 1$ meaning that $p_0 \cdot \sum_{n=0}^{N} \rho^n = 1$ wherefrom it results that

$$p_0 = \frac{1 - \rho}{1 - \rho^{N+1}}$$

The numerical characteristics of the model result if we note by Z the random variable, the number of units in the system, then:

$$Z = \begin{pmatrix} 0 & 1 & 2 \ldots & n \ldots & N \\ p_0 & p_1 & p_2 \cdots & p_n \cdots & p_N \end{pmatrix} \tag{10.64}$$

and from here the average number of units in the system:

$$\overline{Z} = M(Z) = \sum_{n=0}^{N} n \cdot p_n = \frac{1 - \rho}{1 - \rho^{N+1}} \cdot \rho \cdot \sum_{n=1}^{N} n \cdot \rho^{n-1} \tag{10.65}$$

By performing the calculations, we get:

$$\overline{Z} = \rho \cdot \frac{1 - (n + 1) \cdot \rho^N + N \cdot \rho^{N+1}}{(1 - \rho) \cdot (1 - \rho \cdot N + 1)} \tag{10.66}$$

Let *S* be now the number of units in the course of being served. As there is one station, we have:

$$S = \begin{pmatrix} 0 & 1 \\ p_0 & 1 - p_0 \end{pmatrix} \tag{10.67}$$

and from here:

$$\overline{S} = M(S) = 1 - p_0 = \rho \cdot \frac{1 - \rho^N}{1 - \rho^{N+1}} \tag{10.68}$$

We can now immediately obtain the average number *Q* of units in the queuing string, because:

$$Q = Z - S \tag{10.69}$$

It follows that:

$$\overline{Q} = M(Q) = M(Z) - M(S) = \rho \cdot \frac{1 - (N+1)\rho^N + N \cdot \rho^{N+1}}{(1-\rho) \cdot (1 - \rho^{N+1})} - \rho \cdot \frac{1 - \rho^N}{1 - \rho^{N+1}} = \rho^2 \cdot \frac{1 - N \cdot \rho^N + (N-1) \cdot \rho^N}{(1-\rho) \cdot (1 - \rho^{n+1})} \tag{10.70}$$

We can also calculate the dispersion of the random variable *Z*:

$$\begin{aligned} \sigma_Z^2 &= \sum_{n=0}^{N} n^2 \cdot p_n - \overline{Z}^2 \\ &= \frac{\rho - (N+1)^2 \cdot \rho^{N+1} \cdot (1 + \rho^2) + 2 \cdot N^2 \cdot \rho^{N+2} - \rho^{2 \cdot N+2}}{(1-\rho)^2 \cdot (1 - \rho^{N+1})^2} \end{aligned} \tag{10.71}$$

Often, for the average number of units in the system, we use an approximate formula that is deduced in a relatively simple manner from the exact formula:

$$\overline{Z} \cong \begin{cases} \rho + \rho^2 \text{ if } \rho \langle\langle 1 \\ \frac{N}{2} + \frac{1}{12} \cdot N \cdot (N+2) \cdot (\rho - 1) \text{ if } \rho \to 1 \\ N - \frac{1}{\rho} \text{ if } \rho \rangle\rangle 1 \end{cases} \tag{10.72}$$

A similar approximate formula may also be given for the indicator $\overline{Q}$.

10.4 Model with One Service Station and Arrivals Resulting from a Finite Population

The models of this type are better known as closed models. Actual situations that can be modelled this way occur very frequently.

For example, in a workshop of an enterprise, *N* homogeneous machines operate with the same technological characteristics and work independently of one another. They can get damaged. For a machine, the average number of failures in the time unit is equal to λ. To repair the failures, we assume that the workshop has a qualified mechanic, which means the existence of a single repair stations, and that the duration of a repair is a random variable that follows an exponentially negative distribution of parameter μ.

In this case, the service factor $\rho = \frac{\lambda}{\mu}$ is also called maintenance factor.

Schematically, the operation mode of such a system can be represented as follows: we admit that the machines are repaired as they break down and therefore none of them has priority, which means the discipline of the system is observed: *the first one in, the first one served.*

To emphasise equations that characterise the state of the system, we seek to express the probability that the moment $t+\delta$ there are n units in the system, which we shall note by $P_n(t+\delta)$.

As $1 - A(\delta)$ is the probability that a machine will not fail within a time interval with the length δ and as the failures occur independently of each other, it results that the probability that no machine of the $N - n$ operating will not damage is:

$$[1 - A(\delta)]^{N-n} \tag{10.73}$$

It results from here that the probability for at least one of the $N - n$ machines to fail (which are in operation) is:

$$1- [1-A(\delta)]^{N-n} = (N-n) \cdot \lambda \cdot \delta + O(\delta) \tag{10.74}$$

The probability for a repair to be completed within a time interval with the length δ in the hypotheses formulated is:

$$B(\delta) = \mu \cdot \delta + O(\delta) \tag{10.75}$$

Now, we can express the event that at the moment $t+\delta$ we have units in the system, that the reunion of the following incompatible events takes place two by two: at the moment t, there are n units in the system and in the time interval from t to $t+\delta$ so that we record no coming and no departure; at the moment t, to have n units in the system and in the time interval from t to $t+\delta$ so that we record one coming and no departure; at the moment t, to have $n+1$ units in the system and in the time interval from t to $t+\delta$ so that we record no coming and only one departure; in the time interval from t to $t+\delta$ we are to record a variation of the number of units in the system great than or equal to 2, whatever the number of units in the system at the moment t.

Therefore, in these hypotheses, we can write:

$$P_n(t+\delta) = P_{n-1}(t)\cdot\left[1-(1-A(\delta))^{N-n+1}\right]\cdot[1-B(\delta)] + P_n(t)\cdot[1-A(\delta)]^{N-n}\cdot$$
$$[1-B(\delta)] + P_{n+1}(t)\cdot[1-A(\delta)]^{N-n-1}\cdot B(\delta) + O(\delta) \tag{10.76}$$

By replacing *A(δ)* and *B(δ)*, performing the calculations and dividing by *δ* we get:

$$\frac{P_n(t+\delta)-P_n(t)}{\delta} = (N-n+1)\cdot\lambda\cdot P_{n-1}(t) - [(N-n)\cdot\lambda+\mu]\cdot P_n(t) + \mu\cdot P_{n+1}(t) + \frac{O(\delta)}{\delta} \tag{10.77}$$

By making $\delta\to 0$, the second member has a limit, therefore the first member also has a limit and we have:

$$\frac{d\cdot P_n(t)}{dt} = (N-n+1)\cdot\lambda\cdot P_{n+1}(t) - [(N-n)\cdot\lambda+\mu]\cdot P_n(t) + \mu\cdot P_{n+1}(t);$$
$$n = 1,2,\ldots.,N-1 \tag{10.78}$$

If $n=0$, an analogous reasoning leads us to:

$$P_0(t+\delta) = P_0(t)\cdot[1-A(\delta)]^N + P_1(t)\cdot[1-A(\delta)]^{N-1}\cdot B(\delta) + O(\delta) \tag{10.79}$$

wherefrom we get the equation:

$$\frac{dP_0(t)}{dt} = -N\cdot\lambda\cdot P_0(t) + \mu\cdot P_1(t) \tag{10.80}$$

Finally, if $n=N$ *we have*:

$$P_N(t+\delta) = P_{n-1}(t)\cdot A(\delta)\cdot[1-B(\delta)] + P_N(t)\cdot[1-B(\delta)] + O(\delta) \tag{10.81}$$

wherefrom we get:

$$\frac{dP_N}{dt} = \lambda\cdot P_{N-1}(t) - \mu\cdot P_N(t) \tag{10.82}$$

We assume we are in the case of static balance:

$$\lim_{t\to 0} \frac{dP_n(t)}{dt} = 0,\ n = 0, 1, 2, \ldots, N \tag{10.83}$$

and then the equations of the model probabilities are given in the system of linear algebraic equations:

$$\begin{cases} -N \cdot \lambda \cdot p_0 + \mu \cdot p_1 = 0 \\ (N - n + 1) \cdot \lambda \cdot p_{n-1} - [(N - n) \cdot \lambda + \mu] \cdot p_n + \mu \cdot p_{n+1} = 0 \\ \lambda \cdot p_{N-1} - \mu \cdot p_N = 0 \end{cases} \\ n = 1, 2, \ldots, N - 1 \tag{10.84}$$

The second relation may also be written as follows:

$$(N - n + 1) \cdot \lambda = p_{n-1} - \mu \cdot p_n = (N - n) \cdot \lambda \cdot p_n - \mu \cdot p_{n+1} \\ n = 1, 2, \ldots, N - 1 \tag{10.85}$$

Noting:

$$Z_n = (N - n + 1) \cdot \lambda \cdot p_{n+1} - \mu \cdot p_n \tag{10.86}$$

we have the relation:

$$Z_n = Z_{n+1}, \quad n = 1, 2, \ldots, N - 1 \tag{10.87}$$

As $Z_1 = 0$ it results that $Z_n = 0$, $n = 0, 1, 2, \ldots, N$ and therefore

$$p_n = (N - n + 1) \cdot \rho \cdot p_{n-1}, \quad n = 1, 2, \ldots, N \tag{10.88}$$

where from it follows:

$$p_n = \frac{N!}{(N - n)!} \cdot \rho^n \cdot p_0 \tag{10.89}$$

The probability p_0 is immediately obtained from the relation:

$$\sum_{n=0}^{N} \frac{N!}{(N - n)!} \cdot \rho^n \cdot p_0 = 1 \tag{10.90}$$

Therefore:

$$p_0 = \frac{1}{1 + \sum_{n=0}^{N} \frac{N!}{(N-n)! \cdot \rho^n}} \tag{10.91}$$

We may now immediately get numerical characteristics of the model. From the *Z* random variable distribution, the number of units in the system is:

$$Z = \begin{pmatrix} 0 & 1 & 2 & . & . & . & n & . & . & . & N \\ p_0 & p_1 & p_2 & . & . & . & p_n & . & . & . & p_N \end{pmatrix} \tag{10.92}$$

we get:

$$\overline{Z} = M(Z) = \sum_{n=0}^{n} n \cdot \frac{N!}{(N-n)!} \cdot \rho^n \cdot p_0 \tag{10.93}$$

By replacing p_0 and performing some algebraic calculations, we get the expression:

$$\overline{Z} = N - \frac{1}{\rho} \cdot (1 - p_0) \tag{10.94}$$

Based on this average value, we can get the average number of units in the queuing string:

$$\overline{Q} = M(Q) = \sum_{n=1}^{N} (n-1) p_n = \overline{Z} - (1 - p_0) \tag{10.95}$$

By replacing $\overline{Z}$ by the value determined above, we get:

$$\overline{Q} = N - \frac{\rho + 1}{\rho} \cdot (1 - p_0) \tag{10.96}$$

The average of station's inactivity is:

$$\overline{\beta} = \sum_{n=0}^{1} (1 - n) \cdot p_n = p_0 \tag{10.97}$$

Another feature that is economically important is the average number of units that are not found in the system (in the actual case of the example, this feature is the average number of machines in operation). This average value is also given by:

$$M(N-Z)=\sum_{n=0}^{N}(N-n)\cdot p_n=N-\sum_{n=0}^{N}n\cdot p_n=N-\overline{Z}=\frac{1}{\rho}\cdot(1-p_0) \quad (10.98)$$

The probability for a unit to wait in line, meaning the probability for the station to be busy is:

$$P(>0)=\sum_{n=1}^{N}p_n=1-p_0 \quad (10.99)$$

To calculate the average queuing time we shall first make the observation that in the case of the permanent regime of operation, the average of comings is not longer λ with $\lambda \cdot M \cdot (N-Z)$ meaning $\lambda \cdot (N-\overline{Z})$.

It follows from here that:

$$\overline{Q}=\lambda\cdot\left(N-\overline{Z}\right)\cdot W \quad (10.100)$$

and therefore:

$$W=\frac{1}{\lambda\cdot\left(N-\overline{Z}\right)}\cdot\overline{Q}=\frac{1}{\lambda\cdot\left(N-\overline{Z}\right)}\cdot\left[N-\frac{1+\rho}{\rho}\cdot(1-p_0)\right] \quad (10.101)$$

relation that can also be put in the form:

$$W=\frac{1}{\mu}\cdot\left[\frac{N}{1-p_0}-\frac{1+\rho}{\rho}\right] \quad (10.102)$$

The average queuing time in the system will be:

$$W^{*}=W+\frac{1}{\mu}=\frac{1}{\mu}\cdot\left[\frac{N}{1-p_0}-\frac{1+\rho}{\rho}+1\right]=\frac{\overline{Z}}{\mu\cdot\rho\cdot\left(N-\overline{Z}\right)} \quad (10.103)$$

Based on the statistical methods, it has been established that the comings are Poissonian at the finished product bottling station of a company, with an average number of 120 comings per hour, and a bottling process takes 90 s. To determine the average interval between two consecutive comings, the average number of bottling processes per minute and the probability that no product is bottled every 75 s.

To solve this, we consider the minute as time unit. The average number of comings per minute will be two products. The average interval between two comings will be ½ min, meaning 30 s. The average serving time will be 1/3 min, meaning 20 s. The average bottling rate will be 3 per minute. Because 75 s is 5/4 min, it results that $P_0(5/4)=e^{-0.25}=0.083$.

10.5 Model with Several Service Stations and Arrivals Resulting from an Infinite Population

The models studied previously had the single serving station as common characteristic. In many practical situations, the models with a single station become unsatisfactory, so that we may consider it necessary to study the phenomenon of agglomeration where several service stations are used. In the case of the queuing models with several stations, new problems arise, both in terms of obtaining the system of equations from where the probabilities of the system states are obtained, as well as in terms of the actually economical side. For example, we may pose the problem of determining the minimum number of stations so that the service is conducted in optimal conditions for the applicants and at the lowest maintenance expenses in system operation. The working hypotheses for this model are: the model has s stations arranged in parallel, which operate independently of each other, independently of coming and as duration of the service for each of the s stations, which is a random variable that is negatively exponentially distributed by parameter μ. The comings are random, independent of one another and independent of the departures and are Poissonian of parameter λ. When the station is free, the first unit in the queue enters that station in order to receive the requested service. Therefore, the discipline in the system is the natural one, *the first one in* is *the first one served*, with no preference for a certain station and with no units preferred in serving, in the prejudice of other units. Schematically, such a model is shown in Fig.10.1. The system of equations of the probabilities of system states for the queuing model with s stations will be written in the hypotheses formulated before. For this, we first express the probabilities for a unit to enter the system, respectively

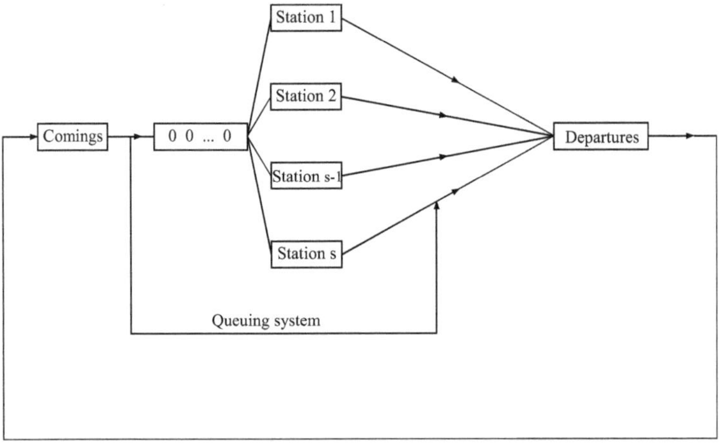

Fig. 10.1 Queuing model with several service stations and arrivals from an infinite population

to leave the system. In the case of models with a single station, our probability $A(\delta)$ to have a coming within a time interval with the length $\delta > 0$ has the expression:

$$A(\delta) = \lambda + \delta + O(\delta) \tag{10.104}$$

And the probability for a unit to leave a station has the expression:

$$B(\delta) = \mu \cdot \delta + O(\delta) \tag{10.105}$$

If we assume that n units are in the system, then in the case of a model with s stations, we shall encounter two situations, namely:

$$\begin{aligned} &a)\ 0 \le n < s; \\ &b)\ n \ge s. \end{aligned} \tag{10.106}$$

If $0 \le n < s$, each of the n units may leave the system in a time interval with the length δ and this probability has the expression:

$$\mathrm{B_n}(\delta) = 1 - [1 - \mathrm{B}(\delta)]^{\mathrm{n}} = \mathrm{n} \cdot \mathrm{B}(\delta) + \mathrm{O}(\delta) \tag{10.107}$$

In the case where all stations are busy, meaning $n \ge s$, the probability for a unit to leave the system will be:

$$\mathrm{B_n}(\delta) = \mathrm{s} \cdot \mathrm{B}(\delta) + \mathrm{O}(\delta), \quad \mathrm{n} = \mathrm{s}, \mathrm{s} + 1 \ldots \tag{10.108}$$

The probability $P_n(t + \delta)$ will be expressed both in the case $0 \le n < s$ and in the case $n \ge s$. For this, the event the probability of which is $P_n(t + \delta)$ will be decomposed into the following incompatible events: at the moment t, there were n units in the system and in the time interval from t to t + δ so no coming and no departure occurred; at the moment t, there were n − 1 units in the system and in the time interval from t to t + δ one coming was produced and no departure occurred; at the moment t, there were n + 1 units in the system and in the time interval from t to t + δ one departure and no coming were recorded; whatever the number of comings into the system at the moment t in the time interval from t to t + δ, the number of units in the system varies by more than two units.

In the previously formulated hypotheses, it results that we can write:

$$\begin{aligned} \mathrm{P_n}(t + \delta) &= \mathrm{P_{n-1}}(t) \cdot \mathrm{A}(\delta) \cdot [1 - \mathrm{B_{n-1}}(\delta)] + \mathrm{P_n}(t) \cdot [1 - \mathrm{A}(\delta)] \cdot [1 - \mathrm{B_n}(\delta)] + \\ &\mathrm{P_{n+1}}(t) \cdot [1 - \mathrm{A}(\delta)] \cdot \mathrm{B_{n+1}}(\delta) + \mathrm{O}(\delta) \end{aligned} \tag{10.109}$$

By particularising depending on the values of n compared to s and by replacing $A(\delta)$ and $B_n(\delta)$, we get:

$$\begin{aligned}&\frac{P_n(t+\delta)-P_n(t)}{\delta}=\lambda\cdot P_{n-1}(t)-(\lambda+n\cdot\mu)\cdot P_n(t)+(n+1)\cdot\mu\cdot P_{n+1}(t)+\frac{O(\delta)}{\delta},\\ &n=1,2,\ldots,s-1\\ &\frac{P_n(t+\delta)-P_n(t)}{\delta}=\lambda\cdot P_{n-1}(t)-(\lambda+n\cdot\mu)\cdot P_n(t)+s\cdot\mu\cdot P_{n+1}(t)+\frac{O(\delta)}{\delta},\\ &n=s,s+1,\ldots\end{aligned} \tag{10.110}$$

In the case $n=0$ we can write:

$$P_0(t+\delta)=P_0(t)\cdot[1-A(\delta)]+P_1(t)\cdot[1-A(\delta)]\cdot B_1(\delta)+O(\delta) \tag{10.111}$$

where from:

$$\frac{P_0(t+\delta)-P_0(t)}{\delta}=-\lambda\cdot P_0(t)+\mu\cdot P_1(t)+\frac{O(\delta)}{\delta} \tag{10.112}$$

By making $\delta\to 0$ we get the system of differential equations:

$$\begin{aligned}&\frac{dP_n(t)}{dt}=-\lambda\cdot P_0(t)+\mu\cdot P_1(t)\\ &\frac{dP_n(t)}{dt}=\lambda\cdot P_{n-1}(t)-(\lambda+n\cdot\mu)\cdot P_n(t)+(n+1)\cdot\mu\cdot P_{n+1}(t),\\ &n=1,2,\ldots,s-1\end{aligned} \tag{10.113}$$

$$\begin{aligned}&\frac{dP_n(t)}{dt}=\lambda\cdot P_{n-1}(t)-(\lambda+s\cdot\mu)\cdot P_n(t)+s\cdot\mu\cdot P_{n+1}(t),\\ &n=s,s+1,\ldots\end{aligned} \tag{10.114}$$

We shall further assume that we are in the case of the stationary regime of operation, meaning:

$$\lim_{t\to\infty}\frac{dP_n(t)}{dt}=0 \tag{10.115}$$

In this case, it results that the probabilities of the states verify the system of algebraic equations:

$$\begin{cases} -\lambda \cdot p_0 + \mu \cdot p_1 = 0 \\ \lambda \cdot p_{n-1} - (\lambda + n \cdot \mu) \cdot p_n + (n+1) \cdot \mu \cdot p_{n+1} = 0, n = 1, 2, \ldots s-1 \\ \lambda \cdot p_{n-1} - (\lambda + s \cdot \mu) \cdot p_n + s \cdot \mu \cdot p_{n+1} = 0, n = s, s+1, \ldots \end{cases} \tag{10.116}$$

From the equations:

$$\lambda \cdot p_{n-1} - (\lambda + n \cdot \mu) \cdot p_n + (n+1) \cdot \mu \cdot p_{n+1} = 0 \tag{10.117}$$

we immediately get:

$$p_n = \frac{\rho}{n} \cdot p_{n-1} = \frac{\rho^n}{n!} \cdot p_0, \quad n = 1, 2, \ldots, s \tag{10.118}$$

If we make $n = s$ in the last group of equations, we get:

$$p_{s+1} = \frac{1}{s \cdot \mu} \cdot [(\lambda + s \cdot \mu) \cdot p_s - \lambda \cdot p_{s-1}] = \frac{\rho^{s+1}}{s \cdot s!} \cdot p_0 \tag{10.119}$$

Then, by making $n = s+1, s+2, \ldots$ we get:

$$\rho_{s+r} = \frac{\rho^{s+r}}{s^r \cdot s!} \cdot p_0 \tag{10.120}$$

or:

$$p_n = \frac{\rho^n}{s! \cdot s^{n-s}} \cdot p_0 \quad n = s, s+1, \ldots \tag{10.121}$$

so:

$$p_n = \begin{cases} \dfrac{\rho^n}{n!} \cdot p_0 \text{ if } 0 \leq n \langle s \\ \dfrac{\rho^n}{s! \cdot s^{n-s}} \cdot p_0 \text{ if } n \geq s \end{cases} \tag{10.122}$$

The probability p_0 is determined making the condition:

$$\sum_{n=0}^{\infty} p_n = 1 \tag{10.123}$$

$$\text{so} : 1 = p_0 \left(\sum_{n=0}^{s-1} \frac{\rho^n}{n!} + \frac{\rho^s}{s!} \cdot \frac{1}{1 - \frac{\rho}{s}} \right) \tag{10.124}$$

or $p_0 = \dfrac{1}{\sum\limits_{n=0}^{s-1} \dfrac{\rho^n}{s!} + \dfrac{\rho^s}{s!(1+\rho^*)}}$ where we put $\rho = \frac{\lambda}{\mu}$ and $\rho^* = \frac{\rho}{s}$ which is also called the system serving factor. Having the probabilities of the states, we can get a number of numerical characteristics useful in economic analyses.

First, the average number of units in the queuing string:

$$\overline{Q} = M(Q) = \sum_{n=s+1}^{\infty} (n-s) \cdot p_n = p_0 \cdot \frac{\rho^s}{s!} \cdot \sum_{n=s+1}^{\infty} (n-s) \cdot \frac{\rho^{n-s}}{s^{n-s}} = p_0 \cdot \frac{\rho^s}{s!} \cdot \frac{\rho^*}{(1-\rho^*)^2} \tag{10.125}$$

If we note by *L* the number of unoccupied (free) stations, we have:

$$\overline{L} = M(L) = \sum_{n=0}^{s-1} (s-n) \cdot p_n = \sum_{n=0}^{s-1} (s-n) \cdot \frac{\rho^n}{n!} \cdot p_0 = p_0 (s-\rho) \cdot \left[\sum_{n=0}^{s-1} \frac{\rho^n}{n!} + \frac{\rho^s}{s!} \cdot \frac{1}{1-\rho^*} \right] \tag{10.126}$$

By taking into account the expression of probabilities p_0 we finally get:

$$\overline{L} = s \cdot \rho \tag{10.127}$$

To calculate the average number of units in the system $\overline{Z}$ (the number of units in the system is the sum of the number of units in the queue and the number of busy stations), we use the immediate relation:

$$\overline{Z} = \overline{Q} + s - \overline{L} \tag{10.128}$$

It follows from here that:

$$\overline{Z} = M(Z) = \overline{Q} + s - \overline{L} = p_0 \cdot \frac{\rho^s}{s!} \cdot \frac{\rho^*}{s!} \cdot \frac{\rho^*}{(1-\rho^*)^2} + \rho \tag{10.129}$$

The average queuing time in the string is:

$$W = \frac{\overline{Q}}{\lambda} = \frac{p_0 \cdot \frac{\rho^s}{s!} \cdot \frac{\rho^*}{(1-\rho^*)^2}}{\rho \cdot \mu} = p_0 \cdot \frac{\rho^s}{1-s!} \cdot \frac{1}{(1-\rho^*)^2} \tag{10.130}$$

10.6 Model with Several Service Stations and Arrivals Resulting from a Finite Population

Due to the many application possibilities, especially in industry, this model is much studied. To better understand how the problem is posed, we shall use a certain actual situation. We assume that it is a matter of a section or a workshop of a particular enterprise where *N* homogeneous (possibly identical) machines operate and that in this workshop *D* mechanics are employed, who intervene when a machine has damaged or no longer work on the parameters specified by the technological process, thus requiring a repair or an adjustment. Schematically, such a model may be shown as in Fig.10.2.

The hypothesis underlying the model are as follows: the duration of service for each station is the random variable that is negatively exponentially distributed of parameter μ; the comings are random, independent of one another and independent of service and that the coming number by the unit of time is a Poisson randomly distributed variable; we admit that the discipline of the system is the usual one, meaning the first one in is the first one served.

By admitting these hypotheses, we can immediately write the probability of passing from a state n to a state $n+k$, as follows:

If at the moment *t* the system was in the state *n*, it can remain in the same state at moment $\delta+t$ with the probability:

$$[1-(\mathrm{N}-\mathrm{n})\cdot\lambda\cdot\delta+\mathrm{O}(\delta)]\cdot[1-\mathrm{n}\cdot\mu\cdot\delta+\mathrm{O}(\delta)] \tag{10.131}$$

if $0<n<p$ and with the probability:

$$[1-(\mathrm{N}-\mathrm{r})\cdot\lambda\cdot\delta+\mathrm{O}(\delta)]\cdot[1-\mathrm{s}\cdot\mu\cdot\delta+\mathrm{O}(\delta)] \tag{10.132}$$

if $s\leq n<N$.

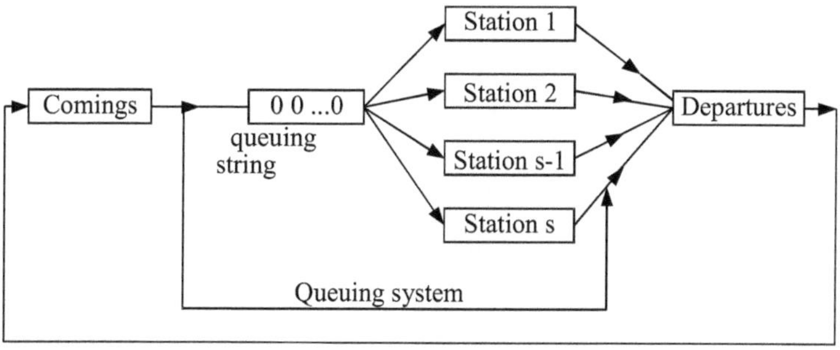

Fig. 10.2 Queuing model with several service stations and arrivals from a finite population

If at the moment t the system was in the state $n+1$, it can pass into the state n at the moment $t+\delta$ with the probability:

$$[1-(N-n-1)\cdot\lambda\cdot\delta+O(\delta)]\cdot[s\cdot\mu\cdot\delta+O(\delta)] \tag{10.133}$$

if $0<n<p$ and with the probability:

$$[1-(N-n-1)\cdot\lambda\cdot\delta+O(\delta)]\cdot[s\cdot\mu\cdot\delta+O(\delta)] \tag{10.134}$$

if $1<n<N$

If at the moment t the system was in the state n - 1, it can pass into the state n at the moment $t+\delta$ with the probability:

$$[(N-n-1)\cdot\lambda\cdot\delta+O(\delta)]\cdot[1-(n-1)\cdot\mu\cdot\delta+O(\delta)] \tag{10.135}$$

if $0<s<n$ and with the probability:

$$[(N-n-1)\cdot\lambda\cdot\delta+O(\delta)]\cdot\left[1-\widetilde{\beta}\cdot\mu\cdot\delta+O(\delta)\right] \tag{10.136}$$

if $s\leq n<N^1$.

From any other state j different from those mentioned above, the system can switch into the state n with the probability $O(\delta)$. Based on this transition probabilities, we can now express the probability $P_n(+\delta)$, the probability that at the time $t+\delta$, the system would be in the state n (these are units in the system) is:

$$\begin{aligned}P_n(t+\delta)&=(N-n+1)\cdot\lambda\cdot\delta\cdot P_{n-1}(t)+\\&[1-\{(N-n)\cdot\lambda+n\cdot\mu\}\cdot\delta]\cdot P_n(t)+(n+1)\cdot\mu\cdot\delta\cdot P_{n+1}(t)+O(\delta)\end{aligned} \tag{10.137}$$

if: $1\leq n\leq s-1$ and:

$$\begin{aligned}P_n(t+\delta)&=(N-n+1)\cdot\lambda\cdot\delta\cdot P_{n+1}(t)+\\&[1-\{(N-n)\cdot\lambda+s\cdot\mu\}\cdot\delta]\cdot P_n(t)+s\cdot\mu\cdot\delta\cdot P_{n+1}(t)+O(\delta)\end{aligned} \tag{10.138}$$

$s\leq r<N.$

If $n=0$, $P_0(t+\delta)$ is expressed as follows:

$$P_0(t+\delta)=(1-N\cdot\lambda\cdot\delta)\cdot P_0(t)+\mu\cdot\delta\cdot P_1(t)+O(\delta) \tag{10.139}$$

and if $n=N$ (meaning all units of the population taken into account are in the system), we can write:

$$\begin{aligned}P_N(t+\delta)&=P_{N-1}(t)\cdot[\lambda\cdot\delta+O(\delta)]\cdot[1-s\cdot\mu\cdot\delta+O(\delta)]+P_N(t)\cdot\\&[1-s\cdot\mu\cdot\delta+O(\delta)]+O(\delta)\end{aligned} \tag{10.140}$$

Passing now $P_n(t)$ into the first member, then dividing by δ in both members and making $\delta \to 0$, we get the following system of differential equations wherefrom the probabilities of the following states are determined:

$$\frac{dP_0(t)}{dt} = -N \cdot \lambda \cdot P_0(t) + \mu \cdot P_1(t)$$

$$\frac{dP_n(t)}{dt} = (N - n + 1) \cdot \lambda \cdot P_{n-1}(t) - [(N - n) \cdot \lambda + n \cdot \mu] \cdot P_n(t) + (n + 1) \cdot \mu \cdot P_{n+1}(t) \tag{10.141}$$

if $1 \leq n < s$

$$\frac{dP_n(t)}{dt} = (N - n + 1) \cdot \lambda \cdot P_{n-1}(t) - [(N - n) \cdot \lambda + s \cdot \mu] \cdot P_n(t) + s \cdot \mu \cdot P_{n+1}(t) \tag{10.142}$$

if $s \leq n < N$

$$\frac{dP_n(t)}{dt} = \lambda \cdot P_{N-1}(t) - s \cdot \mu \cdot P_N(t)$$

We shall determine the probabilities of the states in the case of the stationary regime, meaning when:

$$\lim_{t \to \infty} \frac{dP_n(t)}{dt} = 0 \tag{10.143}$$

In this case also the system of differential equations becomes a system of algebraic equations:

$$\begin{cases} -N \cdot \lambda \cdot p_0 + \mu \cdot p_1 = 0 \\ (N - n + 1) \cdot \lambda_{p_{n-1}} - [(N - n) \cdot \lambda + n \cdot \mu] \cdot p_n + (n + 1) \cdot \mu \cdot p_{n+1} = 0 \quad \text{if} \quad 1 \leq n < s \\ (N - n + 1) \cdot \lambda_{p_{n-1}} - [(N - n) \cdot \lambda + s \cdot \mu] \cdot p_n + s \cdot \mu \cdot p_{n+1} = 0 \quad \text{if} \quad s \leq n < N \\ \lambda \cdot p_{N-1} - s \cdot \mu \cdot p_N = 0 \end{cases} \tag{10.144}$$

It has been noted by s in order to emphasise it is a matter of $p - 1$ if $r = s$ or s if $n > s$.

For $1 \leq n < s$ the relations may also be written as follows:

$$(N - n + 1) \cdot \lambda \cdot p_{n-1} - n \cdot \mu \cdot p_n = (N - n) \cdot p_n - (n + 1) \cdot \mu \cdot p_{n+1} \tag{10.145}$$

$$\text{meaning} \quad Z_n = (N - n + 1) \cdot \lambda \cdot p_{n-1} - n \cdot \mu \cdot p_n \tag{10.146}$$

As $Z_1 = 0$, we get $Z_n = 0$, $n = 1, 2, \ldots, s$ and from here:

$$p_n = \frac{N-n+1}{n} \cdot \rho \cdot p_{n-1} = \rho^n \cdot \frac{N \cdot (N-1) \cdot \ldots (N-n+1)}{n!} \cdot p_0 = C_N^n \cdot \rho^n \cdot p_0 \tag{10.147}$$

For $n = s, s+1, \ldots, N-1$ we get:

$$p_{s+1} = \frac{(N-s) \cdot \rho + s}{s} \cdot p_s - \frac{N-s+1}{p} \cdot \rho \cdot p_{s-1} = \frac{N-s}{s} \cdot \rho \cdot p_s \tag{10.148}$$

....

$$p_{s+r+1} = \left(\frac{\rho}{s}\right)^{r+1} \cdot \rho^s \cdot \frac{N \cdot (N-1) \ldots (N-s-r)}{s!} \cdot p_0; \quad r = 0, 1, \ldots, N-s+1 \tag{10.149}$$

Therefore, it results:

$$p_n = \begin{cases} C_N^n \cdot \rho^n \cdot p_0 & \text{if} \quad 0 \le n \langle s \\ \dfrac{N \cdot (N-1) \ldots (N-n+1)}{s^{n-s} \cdot s!} \cdot \rho^n \cdot p_0 & \text{if} \quad s \le n \le N \end{cases} \tag{10.150}$$

where p_0 is determined from the relation $\sum_{n=0}^{N} p_n = 1$ meaning:

$$p_0 = \frac{1}{\sum_{n=0}^{s-1} C_N^n \cdot \rho^n + \sum_{n=0}^{N} \rho^n \cdot \dfrac{N \cdot (N-1) \ldots (N-n+1)}{s^{n-s} \cdot s!}} \tag{10.151}$$

Having the probabilities of the states, we can calculate the main numerical characteristics of the model. We shall first express the random variables and their distributions and afterwards we aim to actually calculate their average values.

If we note as before by Z the random variable the number of units in the system, then:

$$Z = \begin{pmatrix} 0 & 1 & 2 & \ldots & N \\ p_0 & p_1 & p_2 & \ldots & p_N \end{pmatrix} \tag{10.152}$$

$$\text{where from :} \quad \overline{Z} = M(Z) = \sum_{n=0}^{N} n \cdot p_n \tag{10.153}$$

The number of units in the queuing string is a random variable Q with the distribution:

$$Q = \begin{pmatrix} 0 & 1 & 2 & \dots & N-s \\ \sum_{n=0}^{s} p_n & p_{s+1} & p_{s+2} & \cdots & p_N \end{pmatrix} \tag{10.154}$$

$$\text{and from here :} \quad \overline{Q} = M(Q) = \sum_{n=s+1}^{N} (n-s) \cdot p_n \tag{10.155}$$

The number of inactive stations, L has the distribution:

$$L = \begin{pmatrix} 0 & 1 & 2 & \dots & s \\ \sum_{n=s}^{N} p_n & p_{s-1} & p_{s-2} & \cdots & p_0 \end{pmatrix} \tag{10.156}$$

$$\text{and the average value :} \quad \overline{L} = M(L) = \sum_{n=0}^{s-1} (s-n) \cdot p_n \tag{10.157}$$

The number of busy stations O has the distribution:

$$O = \begin{pmatrix} 0 & 1 & 2 & \dots & s \\ p_0 & p_1 & p_2 & \cdots & \sum_{n=s}^{N} p_n \end{pmatrix} \tag{10.158}$$

$$\overline{O} = M(O) = \sum_{n=0}^{s-1} n \cdot p_n + s \cdot \sum_{n=s}^{N} p_n \tag{10.159}$$

The average queuing time in the string:

$$W = \frac{\overline{Q}}{\mu \cdot (N - \overline{L})} \tag{10.160}$$

Finally, let us also express the probability for a unit to wait to be served:

$$p(>0) = \sum_{n=s}^{N} p_n \tag{10.161}$$

For the actual calculation of these features, as well as of others, we shall use Palm's method.

First, let us express the probability p_0.

The equality:

$$p_0 \cdot \left[\sum_{n=0}^{s-1} C_N^n \cdot \rho^n + \sum_{n=0}^{N} \rho^n \cdot \frac{N!}{(N-n)! \cdot s! \cdot s^{n-s}}\right] = 1 \tag{10.162}$$

may be written:

$$p_0 \cdot \left[\sum_{n=0}^{s-1} C_N^n \cdot \rho^n + \frac{N! \cdot \rho^s}{s! \cdot (N-s)!} \cdot \sum_{m=0}^{N-s} \frac{(N-s)}{(N-m-s)!} \cdot \left(\frac{\rho}{s}\right)^m\right] = 1 \tag{10.163}$$

$$\text{Let us note : } \quad F\left(\frac{\rho}{s}; N-s\right) = \sum_{m=0}^{N-s} \frac{(N-s)!}{(N-m-s)!} \cdot \left(\frac{\rho}{s}\right)^m \tag{10.164}$$

If we now note:

$$P(X=k) = p(k,\theta) = e^{-\theta} \cdot \frac{\theta^k}{k!}, \quad k = 0, 1, 2, \ldots \tag{10.165}$$

and $N = s = k; \quad \theta = \frac{s}{\rho}$ we can express $F\left(\frac{\rho}{s}; N-s\right)$ as follows:

$$F\left(\frac{\rho}{s}; N-s\right) = F\left(\frac{1}{\theta}; k\right) = \frac{\sum_{m=0}^{k} p(k-m;\theta)}{p(k;\theta)} = \frac{1 - P(k+1,\theta)}{p(k,\theta)} \tag{10.166}$$

where:

$$P(k+1;\theta) = \sum_{l=k+1}^{\infty} p(l,\theta) \tag{10.167}$$

With these remarks, we get:

$$\begin{aligned} p_0 &= \frac{1}{\sum_{n=0}^{s-1} C_N^n \cdot \rho^n + C_N^1 \cdot \rho^1 \cdot \frac{1-P(k+1,\theta)}{p(k,\theta)}} = \\ &= \frac{1}{\frac{1}{p(N,\theta)} \cdot \left[\sum_{n=0}^{s-1} \frac{s^n}{n!} \cdot e^{-\theta} \cdot \frac{\theta^{N-n}}{(N-n)!} + \frac{s^s}{s!}\{1 - P(k+1)\cdot\theta\}\right]} \end{aligned} \tag{10.168}$$

or yet:

$$p_0 = \frac{p(N, \theta)}{S(N, s, \theta)} \tag{10.169}$$

where we noted:

$$S(N, s, \theta) = \sum_{n=0}^{s-1} \frac{s^n}{n!} \cdot p(N-n, \theta) + \frac{s^s}{s!} \cdot \{1 - P(k+1, \theta)\} \tag{10.170}$$

We can also express accordingly the probabilities p_n, as follows:

$$p_n = \begin{cases} \frac{s^n}{n!} \cdot \frac{p(N-n, \theta)}{S(N, s, \theta)}, & 0 \leq r\langle s \\ \frac{s^s}{s!} \cdot \frac{p(N-n, \theta)}{S(N, s, \theta)}, & s \leq n \leq N \end{cases} \tag{10.171}$$

Let us first find out:

$$\overline{O} = M(O)$$

According to the definition:

$$\overline{O} = M(O) = \sum_{n=0}^{s-1} n \cdot p_n + s \cdot \sum_{n=0}^{N} p_n = \sum_{n=0}^{s-1} n \cdot \frac{s^n}{n!} \cdot \frac{p \cdot (N-n, \theta)}{S \cdot (N, s, \theta)} + s \cdot \sum_{n=1}^{N} \frac{s^s}{s!} \cdot \frac{p \cdot (N-n, \theta)}{S \cdot (N, s, \theta)} =$$
$$= s \cdot \sum_{n=1}^{N} \frac{s^s}{s!} \cdot \frac{p(N-n, \theta)}{S(N, s, \theta)} = \frac{s}{S(N, s, \theta)} \cdot \left[\sum_{n=1}^{s-1} \frac{s^{n-1}}{(n-1)!} \cdot p(N-n, \theta) + \frac{s^s}{s!} \cdot \{1 - P(N-s+1, \theta)\} \right] =$$
$$= \frac{s \cdot S(N-1, s, \theta)}{S(N, s, \theta)} \tag{10.172}$$

To facilitate the calculations, we shall emphasise the random variable, the number of units existing outside the system *U*.

Then:

$$U = \begin{pmatrix} 0 & 1 & 2 & \dots & N \\ p_N & p_{N-1} & p_{N_Z} & \cdots & p_0 \end{pmatrix} \text{ and } \overline{U} = M(U) = \sum_{n=0}^{N} (N-n) \cdot p_n \tag{10.173}$$

However, we can immediately observes that:

$$\frac{M(U)}{M(O)}=\frac{0\cdot p_N+1\cdot p_{N-1}+\ldots N\cdot p_0}{0\cdot p_0+1\cdot p_1+\ldots+(s-1)\cdot p_{s-1}+s\cdot\sum_{n=s}^{N}p_n}=\frac{1}{\rho}$$

$$\text{so}:\quad M(U)=\frac{M(O)}{\rho}=\frac{s\cdot S(N-1,s,\theta)}{\rho\cdot S(N,s,\theta)}\tag{10.174}$$

As $Z=N-U$, it results that:

$$\overline{Z}=M(Z)=N-M(U)=N-\frac{s\cdot S(N-1,s,\theta)}{\rho\cdot S(N,s,\theta)}\tag{10.175}$$

To calculate the average value $\overline{Q}=M(Q)$ we observe that:
$Q+O+U=N$ and therefore:

$$\overline{Q}=M(Q)=N-M(O)-M(U)=N-\frac{s\cdot S(N-1,s,\theta)}{S(N,s,\theta)}-\frac{s\cdot S(N-1,s,\theta)}{\rho\cdot S(N,s,\theta)}=$$
$$=N-s\cdot\frac{\rho+1}{\rho}\cdot\frac{S(N-1,s,\theta)}{S(N,s,\theta)}\tag{10.176}$$

The average queuing time in the string:

$$W=\frac{\overline{Q}}{\mu\cdot(N-\overline{L})}\tag{10.177}$$

can be calculated as soon as we express: $\overline{L}$
But $L+O=s$ and from here:

$$\overline{L}=s-\overline{O}=s-\frac{s\cdot S(N-1,s,\theta)}{s(N,s,\theta)}=s\cdot\left(1-\frac{S(N-1,s,\theta)}{S(N,s,\theta)}\right)\tag{10.178}$$

$$\text{Therefore}:\quad W=\frac{N-s\cdot\frac{\rho+1}{\rho}\cdot\frac{S(N-1,s,\theta)}{S(N,s,\theta)}}{\mu\cdot\left[N-s\cdot\left(1-\frac{S(N-1,s,\theta)}{S(N,s,\theta)}\right)\right]}\tag{10.179}$$

Finally, the probability for a unit to wait:

$$p(>0)=\sum_{n=s}^{N}p_n=\frac{s^s}{s!}\cdot\sum_{n=s}^{N}\frac{p(N-n,\theta)}{S(N,s,\theta)}=\frac{s^s}{s!}\cdot\frac{1-p(N-s+1,\theta)}{p(N,\theta)\cdot S(N,s,\theta)}\tag{10.180}$$

References

Betbeze JP (2000) Economie de l'enterprise contemporaine. Nathan, Paris

Bharucha RAT (1997) Elements of the theory of Markov processes and their applications. McGraw Hill, New York

Brilman J (1998) Les meilleurs pratiques de management. Éditions d'Organisation, Paris

Dantzig GB (1991) Application of the simplex method to a transportation problem. Wiley, New York

Dantzig GB (1993) Linear programming and extension. Princenton University Press, Princenton

Graenb W (1968) Linear algebra. Springer, Berlin

Harary F (1989) Graph theory. Addison Wesley, Reading, MA

Harary F (1995) Structural models. Wiley, New York

Howard AR (1984) Dynamic programming and Markov processes. The MIT Press, Cambridge

Kaufmann A (1991) Les phenomenes d'attende. Dunod, Paris

Lee AM (1976) Teoria aşteptării cu aplicaţii. Editura Tehnică, Bucureşti

Love C, Zhang Z, Zitron M, Guo R (2000) Theory and methodology: a discrete semi-Markov decision model to determinate the optimal repair/replacement policy under general repairs. Eur J Oper Res 125(2):398–409. doi:10.1016/S0377-2217(99)00009-0

Plane DR (1999) Discrete optimization. Prentice Hall, New Jersey

Chapter 11
Models Based on the Theory of Games

11.1 General considerations on the theory of games

The game is a competitive process that occurs between several participants called players, of which at least one is intelligent and cautious, meaning it can analyse the situation and decide on future actions. The games with two participants are of special importance in modelling the economic processes.

The game means performing players' actions, according to certain rules. Any game has an initial state and a final state, the latter determining a gain or a loss for each player, based on the rules of the games.

The strategy is a collection of sequences of one player's actions, each sequence being prepared as a response to the opponent's strategy (which can sometimes be the kind), in order to achieve the proposed objective, meaning that final state to which the rules of the game relate the maximum possible gain.

A convenient representation of a game with two players is the matrix one (Table 11.1).

In this table, *A* is one of the players, and *B* is the opponent (which can sometimes be the kind);

$A = \{A_1, A_2, \ldots, A_m\}$ is the set of the strategies of *A*;

$B = \{B_1, B_2, \ldots, B_n\}$ the set of the strategies of *B*, and a_{ij} $(i = 1, 2, K, m; \quad j = 1, 2, K\ n)$ is the consequence corresponding to adopting the strategy A_i by *A* and the strategy B_j by *B*.

In the decisional process represented by choosing one or another of the strategies, the utilities $u(a_{ij})$ of each consequence should be taken into account. To simplify, we are to conventionally consider that all consequences are monetary values or even utilities.

A first category of games are the so-called games with *saddle point*, characterised by the fact that a correct reasoning requires each of the two players to choose a certain optimal strategy. The set of the two optimal strategies is a solution of the game. A calculation example will contribute to fix the ideas.

I.C. Dima, M. Man, *Modelling and Simulation in Management*, Contributions to Management Science, DOI 10.1007/978-3-319-16592-9_11

Table 11.1 Game with two players

A	B			
	B_1	B_2	...	B_n
A_1	a_{11}	a_{12}	...	a_{1n}
A_2	a_{21}	a_{22}	...	a_{2n}
.	.	.		.
.	.	.		.
A_m	a_{m1}	a_{m2}	...	a_{mn}

Table 11.2 Game representation matrix

Strategies of A	Strategies of B		
	B_1	B_2	B_3
A_1	1	−1	−1.5
A_2	0.5	−0.5	0

Table 11.3 Amended game representation matrix

Strategies of A	Strategies of B	
	B_2	B_3
A_1	−1	−1.5
A_2	−0.5	0

Table 11.4 Game matrix

Strategies of A	Strategies of B	
	B_2	B_3
A_2	−0.5	0

Be the game represented by the matrix below (Table 11.2).

Table 11.2 is interpreted as follows: if player A chooses the strategy A_1, and player B, the strategy B_1, player A earns *1* point, and B loses *1*; if A chooses strategy A_1, and B the strategy B_2, player A loses *1* point, and B earns *1* point, etc.

What will player A do to choose the optimal strategy?

Choosing the strategy A_1 may lead to the greatest gain for A, in the case where B chooses strategy B_1, but also to the greatest loss, in the case where B chooses strategy B_3. Instead, the strategy A_2 is more prudent, as it cannot bring a maximum gain of *0.5* indeed, but in the worst case, the loss is not higher than *0.5* either. It may also be observed that, both for the strategy B_2 and for B_3, both consequences are more advantageous than the corresponding consequences of the strategy B_1. In the terminology of the theory of games, we can say that the strategies B_2 and B_3 dominate strategy B_1, which can consequently be eliminated as always being disadvantageous for the player B. The amended matrix will have the following appearance (Table 11.3).

In the matrix thus deduced, we may observe that the strategy A_2 dominates A_1 and, consequently, by eliminating the latter, the matrix gets the following final appearance (Table 11.4).

It is obvious that the player B will choose the strategy B_2. Hence, through a series of rationales, both players chose their strategies: the player A the strategy A_2, and player B the strategy B_2.

According to these choices, player A will lose *0.5* points, and player B will gain *0* points. It is important to highlight the fact that these numbers are the minimum numbers which the two players can expect when choosing the two strategies, namely values that result when the opponent *plays* fair. One may easily observe if one of the players makes mistakes, meaning they choose another strategy, the other player gains more than the values above, if they *play* fair.

As it has been observed, for the games as those above, such reasoning requests each player to have an optimal strategy called *pure strategy*. The pair of the two optimal strategies is a solution of the game and determines a so-called *saddle point*. The gain, respectively the loss, the registration by the two players (in the case above *0.5*), as result of applying the pair of optimal strategies, is the *value of the game*.

Determining the optimal strategies for the games with *saddle point* can be done without resuming the entire reasoning, based on the so-called *maximum point*.

Be a game of the $m \times n$ order, with the following associated matrix:

$$A = \begin{bmatrix} a_{11} & . & . & . & a_{1n} \\ . & & & & . \\ . & & & & . \\ . & & & & . \\ a_{m1} & . & . & . & a_{mn} \end{bmatrix} \tag{11.1}$$

According to the maximum principle, the first player will choose that strategy which a minimum gain corresponds to:

$$\mathrm{v_1 = max_i\left(min_j a_{ij}\right); \quad 1 \le i \le m; \ 1 \le j \le n} \tag{11.2}$$

To determine the value $\mathrm{v_1}$ and the corresponding strategy, they will proceed as follows: they will determine all the minimum values by rows ($\mathrm{min\ a_{ij}}$) and will take the maximum value from there ($\mathrm{max\ min\ a_{ij}}$).

The second player will do similarly, choosing all the peaks in the column ($\mathrm{max\ a_{ij}}$) and taking the smallest one of them ($\mathrm{min\ max\ a_{ij}}$):

$$\mathrm{v_2 = min_j\left(max_i a_{ij}\right); 1 \le i \le m; \ 1 \le j \le n} \tag{11.3}$$

In the case of games with *saddle point*, the two values are equal and correspond to the game value:

$$\mathrm{v = v_1 = v_2 = max_i\left(min_j a_{ij}\right); \quad 1 \le i \le m; \ 1 \le j \le n} \tag{11.4}$$

A second category is the *games without saddle point*.

They are characterised by the fact that a player's reasoning, no matter how rigorous it is, it will not necessarily lead them to choosing a certain pair of strategies, as in the case of the *games with saddle point*.

In the case where the economic process of a mathematical model is a game without saddle point and is repeated, under identical conditions, there is a specific solution of the problem, consisting in determining the optimal mixed strategies of the two partners.

A mixed strategy of the player *A*, who has strategies available: $X_1, X_2, K\ X_m$, is a string of numbers $x_1, x_2, K\ x_m$ ($x_1 + x_2 + Kx_m = 1$; x_1, x_2, $Kx_m \geq 0$) representing the probabilities to use each of the m strategies in carrying out a large number of games. The notion of *mixed strategy* of the player *b* has similar meaning. In the theory of games, it is demonstrated that there is a pair of mixed strategies of the two players, which are optimal, ensuring a maximum average gain, respectively a minimum average loss, which are equal to each other.

By means of some games having two opponents that reason, conflicting situations are modelled between two or several parties (the latter are also reduced to games with two participants, by forming the so-called coalitions), each party aiming to choose a strategy that would provide it with the most favourable result to the detriment of the opponent or opponents.

11.2 Decisional Process: Conceptual Approaches

Within the theory of decision, the problems studied can be seen in descriptive terms, when one aims to understand and describe the decisional mechanism, or in normative terms, when one aims to formulate some rational and efficient rules to follow in the decision-making activity.

Often, the two perspectives coexist, complementing each other.

The elements of the decision-making process are: the decision-maker, meaning the individual or the set of individuals that are to make the decision; the formulation (name) that the decision-maker gives to the decisional problem encountered; the set of possible variants (alternatives), which characterise a decisional situation and where an optimal variant must be chosen from; the set of anticipated consequences for each variant taken into account; the set of decision-maker's deciding criteria, meaning the views taken into account when choosing the optimal variant; the decision-maker's objectives (goals), respectively the consequences proposed to be achieved for the chosen decision criteria; the states of nature.

Schematically, the elements of the decision-making process can be represented as in Table 11.5.

In the representation above, the consequences were noted with x_{ijk} ($i = 1, 2, \ldots, m$; $j = 1, 2, \ldots, n$; $k = 1, 2, \ldots, r$), and the decision-maker, the problem formulation and the objectives aimed at must be specified separately.

The concept of utility appears in the theory of decision following the need to compare decisional variants between them, characterised by several consequences.

Table 11.5 The elements of the decision-making process

	State of nature N_1			State of nature N_2				State of nature N_n		
	Crit.	Crit…	Crit.	Crit.	Crit…	Crit.	….	Crit.	Crit….	Crit.
Variants	X_1	X_2	X_n	X1	*X2*	Xn		X1	*X2*	Xn
V_1	x_{111}	$x_{112}\cdots$	x_{11r}	x_{121}	$x_{122}\cdots$	x_{12r}		x_{1n1}	$x_{1n2}\cdots$	x_{1nr}
V_2	x_{211}	$x_{212}\cdots$	x_{21r}	x_{221}	$x_{222}\cdots$	x_{22r}		x_{2n1}	$x_{2n2}\cdots$	x_{2nr}
.	.	.	.	.	.	.		.	.	.
.	.	.	.	.	.	.		.	.	.
.	.	.	.	.	.	.		.	.	.
V_m	x_{m11}	$x_{m12}\cdots$	x_{m1r}	x_{m21}	$x_{m22}\cdots$	x_{m2r}		x_{mn1}	$x_{mn2}\cdots$	x_{mnr}

The *utility* is a subjective amount, depending on the decision-maker's assessment.

To restrict the subjective feature of estimating the utility, five axioms are inserted:

Axiom 1 Two decisional variants V_i and V_j can always be compared to each other, the decision-maker being able to decide on one of the following options:

$$\text{prefers } V_i \text{ for } V_j (V_i < V_j); \tag{11.5}$$

$$\text{prefers } V_j \text{ for } V_i (V_j > V_i); \tag{11.6}$$

$$\text{the two variants are indifferent to them } (V_j \sim V_i). \tag{11.7}$$

Axiom 2 The preference relation is transitive, and the indifference one is both transitive and symmetric.

Axiom 3 Besides $V = \{V_1, V_2, \ldots, V_n\}$ of the simple variants, the decision-maker can take into account a special type of simple variants called *probabilistic mixtures* of the type $V' = [pV_i, (1-p)V_j]$, where *p* is the probability of achieving the variant V_i, and *(1−p)* the variant probability V_j.

Axiom 4 Given three variants V_i, V_j and V_k and one decision-maker expressing the relation $V_i > V_j > V_k$, there is a mixture:

$$V' = [p'V_i, (1-p')V_k], \text{ so that } V' > V_j \tag{11.8}$$

and another mixture

$$V'' = [p''V_i, (1-p'')V_k], \text{ so that } V_j > V'' \tag{11.9}$$

Axiom 5 If a variant (V_i) is preferred for another variant (V_j), then a mixture $V' = [pV_i, (1-p)V_k]$ will always be preferred for the mixture $V' = [pV_j, (1-p)V_k]$.

Based on these axioms, the utility function $u(V_i)$ is inserted, having the set of variants as definition area, and values in the set of real numbers.

Its main properties are:

- *be*V_i*and*V_j*two decisional variants, then* $V_i > V_j$ *if and only if*

$$u(V_i) > u(V_j) \tag{11.10}$$

$$-u[pV_i, (1-p)V_j] = pu(V_i) + (1-p)u(V_j); \tag{11.11}$$

- *if the user function has the previous properties, then it can undergo a positive linear transformation.*

$$u'(V_i) = au(V_i) + b \quad \text{with} \quad a > 0 \quad \text{and} \quad b \geq 0 \tag{11.12}$$

The practical process to estimate the utilities consists in considering the utility of two variants belonging to the set $V = \{V_1, V_2, \ldots, V_m\}$ to be known, the utility of the other variants being determined from calculations.

Classifications of the decision-making processes can be done from several points of view:

- *by the number of possible variants*: decision-making processes with a finite number of variants; decision-making processes with an infinite number of variants;
- *by the number of criteria taken into account*: decision-making processes with a single criterion; decision-making processes with several (multidimensional) criteria;
- *by the number of the states of nature and probability to achieve them*: decision-making processes under conditions of uncertainty (a single state of nature, the probability to achieve 1); decision-making processes under conditions of risk (several states of nature with known achievement probabilities); decision-making processes under conditions of uncertainty (several states of nature, without knowing the probabilities to achieve them);
- *by the number of decision-making processes considered in sequence*: single decision-making process (performed at the time *t*); sequence of decision-making processes performed at different times;
- *by the number of decision-makers*: decision-making processes with single decision-maker; group decisions.

As it has been shown when we estimate the utility of some decisional variants characterised by several consequences, we actually take into account several decisional criteria. The estimation of the utility is however global, meaning it is not analysed separately, consequence by consequence. Unlike this process of comparing the utility of the consequences that originates in the economic theories of the past century, the modern theory of decision felt the need to introduce the estimation of utilities separately by criteria, for the multi-criterion decision-making process. (Table 11.6).

Table 11.6 Multidimensional decisional process

	Criteria			
Variants	X_1	X_2	...	X_n
V_1	x_{11}	x_{12}	...	x_{1n}
V_2	x_{21}	x_{22}	...	x_{2n}
.	.	.		.
.	.	.		.
.	.	.		.
V_m	x_{m1}	x_{m2}	...	x_{mn}

Therefore, be the multidimensional decisional process:

The utility of a consequence V_i will be:

$$u(V_i) = u(x_{i1}) + u(x_{i2}) + K + u(x_{in}) \tag{11.13}$$

The main problems raised by the theory of multidimensional decisions are:

- *how do we estimate the utility of consequences*?
- *under what conditions are the utilities of consequences additive*?

Of the procedures suggested to estimate the utilities of consequences to this type of decisional process, the most advantageous one seems to be that where the set of all consequences

$$X = \{x_{11}, x_{12}, Kx_{m1}, x_{12}, x_{22}, Kx_{m2}, K, x_{1n}, x_{2n}, Kx_{mn}\}$$

is considered and the Neumann-Morgenstern method is applied to all elements of the set. Regarding the multidimensional activity of the utilities, the problem is very tricky, there is no widely accepted operation procedures yet, usually the possibility to gather the utilities when the criteria are independent is accepted. A particular problem is raised by making decisions under risk and uncertainty, namely:

- *risk conditions, meaning the decision is made when many states of nature are known* (Table 11.7).

  Let us assume that for each state of nature we know probabilities of achievement. To determine the optimum variant under conditions of risk, all utilities of the consequences will be estimated according to the methods known.

  The optimal variant will be that which the maximum weighted average utility will correspond to;

$$\max_i \sum_{j=1}^{n} p_i \cdot u(x_{ij}) \qquad i = 1, 2, \ldots, m \qquad p_1 + p_1 + \ldots p_n = 1 \tag{11.14}$$

- *the conditions of uncertainty, when the decision is made under conditions of not*

Table 11.7 Decision-making processes with several states of nature

Variants	States of nature			
	N_1	N_2	...	N_n
	p_1	p_2	...	p_n
V_1	x_{11}	x_{12}	...	x_{1n}
V_2	x_{21}	x_{22}	...	x_{2n}
.	.	.		.
.	.	.		.
V_m	x_{m1}	x_{m2}	...	x_{mn}

knowing the probability $p_j(j = 1, 2, \ldots, n)$ *to achieve the states of nature.* Finding the optimal solution under conditions of uncertainty can be done by using one of the rules below;

– *the prudential rule (Wald)* when we choose the variant which the utility belongs to:

$$\max_i\left[\min{}_j u\left(x_{ij}\right)\right] \quad \begin{array}{l} i = 1, 2, \ldots, m \\ j = 1, 2, \ldots, n \end{array} \tag{11.15}$$

– *the regret rule (Savage)*, when choosing the variant to which the utility belongs to:

$$\min_i\left[\max{}_j\left[\left(\max_i u\left(x_{ij}\right) - u\left(x_{ij}\right)\right]\right] \quad \begin{array}{l} i = 1, 2, \ldots, m \\ j = 1, 2, \ldots, n \end{array} \tag{11.16}$$

The so-called matrix of regrets is created, by subtracting for each state of nature all utilities from the maximum one:

0.1	0.2	0.1
0	0	0.1
0.2	0.3	0

We apply the prudent rule to this matrix, taking into account that the most advantageous are the small *regrets*:

$$min[max(0.1, 0.2, 0.1), max(0, 0, 0.1), max(0.2, 0.3, 0)] = min[0.2, 0.1, 0.3]$$

$$= 0.1 \quad \text{hence, it also results} \sqrt{2} \tag{11.17}$$

– *Laplace's rule*, meaning the problem is considered under conditions of risk with the probabilities to achieve the states of nature equal to each other;

Fig. 11.1 Decision tree

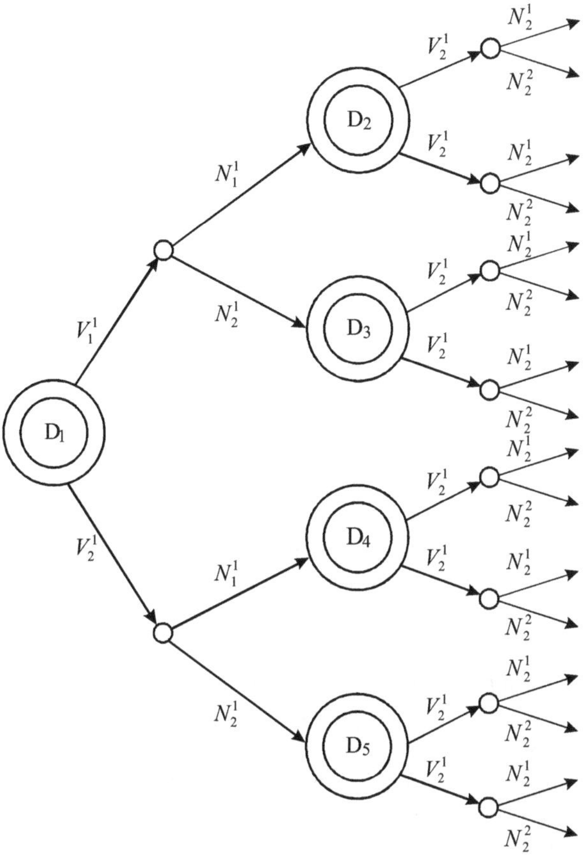

$$\max\left[\frac{1}{3}\cdot\ (1.5+1.3+1.4);\ \frac{1}{3}\cdot\ (1.6+1.5+1.4);\frac{1}{3}\cdot\ (1.4+1.2+1.5)\right]\ =$$
$$\max[1.4;1.5;1.37]=1.5\ \text{hence again}\ \sqrt{2} \tag{11.18}$$

the prudent rule, meaning max [min(1.5, 1.3, 1.4),

$$\min(1.6, 1.5, 1.4) \tag{11.19}$$

$$\min(1.4, 1.2, 1.5)] = \max[1.3, 1.4, 1.2] \ = \ 1.4\ \text{hence}\ \sqrt{2} \tag{11.20}$$

The decision-making process under conditions of risk or uncertainty and having the resolution rules described above is in most practical cases only a stage from a sequence of decisions under conditions of risk or uncertainty. Representing the sequence of the decision processes is done by the so-called *decision tree*. Fig. 11.1 shows the decision tree for the following situation.

An execution variant must be chosen for an investment from two possible variants (V_1 and V_2). The execution of the work can take place in favourable conditions regarding the conditions of import of some machines N_1^1 or in unfavourable conditions N_2^1 influencing the cost. After completing the investment, its exploitation is done in three shifts (V_1^2) or in two (V_2^2), involving, depending on the favourable N_1^2 or unfavourable N_2^1 circumstance of the market, benefits or losses at the end of an exploitation period (for example, for 5 years).

In the decision tree in Fig. 11.1, there are eight possible strategies:

$$
\begin{array}{ll}
1)\ V_1^1 N_1^1 V_2^1 & 5)\ V_2^1 N_1^1 V_1^2 \\
2)\ V_1^1 N_1^1 V_2^2 & 6)\ V_1^2 N_1^1 V_2^2 \\
3)\ V_1^1 N_2^1 V_2^1 & 7)\ V_2^1 N_2^1 V_1^2 \\
4)\ V_1^1 N_2^2 V_2^2 & 8)\ V_2^1 N_2^2 V_2^2
\end{array}
$$

Determining the optimal strategy is done as follows: the optimal variant under conditions of risk or uncertainty, then the probabilities are known or not p (N_1^2) and p(N_2^2) for each of the decisional nodes $D_2 - D_2$ which is equivalent to solving the decisional problems in the second stage; the utility that is obtained for each of the four *optimal* variants thus found will be considered as utility of the consequence related to the corresponding decisional way.

The application of the decision rules under conditions of risk will follow, if they are known p(N_1^1), and p(N_2^1), or under conditions of uncertainty, if the two probabilities are unknown.

In the axiomatic system of von Naumann Morgenstern, as in other systems of underlying the operation with utilities, it is considered that at the level of an individual decision-maker, a choice between two variants *a* and *b* is rational when it can be precisely expressed that *a* is preferable, equivalent or non-preferable of *b* and if it complies with the rule of transitivity.

At the level of a decisional group, the rationality requirements are more complex. J.K. Arrow defines five such conditions:

- *the method of collective decision must be applicable to the set of all possible variants*;
- *if a certain variant goes up the ladder of preferences of each individual, then it must go up the ladder of group's preferences*;
- *if the decision refers to n possible alternatives, the ranking done to them by a group must not be changed by taking into account a new variant.* (for example, if the variants *a* and *b* are compared, the first one being preferred and variant *c* is taken into account, the relation between *a* and *b* must not change);
- *the rule by which the collective decision is extracted must not be independent from the individual opinions and must depend directly on them*;
- *the collective decision must not be identical to the opinion of a certain member of the group, without taking into account the opinions of the others.*

Starting from these conditions, Arrow proves that there is no collective decision method which would satisfy the five conditions of rationality listed and which would always lead to a correct solution when the number of decision-makers is greater than or equal to *2*, and the number of alternatives higher than *2*. This result, called Arrow's paradox, has been greatly debated and analysed, proposing a number of ways to break the impasse.

One of the methods consists in giving up the third condition of Arrow, which is equivalent to the possibility to *grade* the preferences and ultimately to introducing some interpersonal additive utilities. The interpersonal additivity is however disputed by many authors.

Group decisions are taken with great frequency and are of great importance in the management of enterprises, where most of the decisions are taken in teams of specialists. This fully justifies the theoretical analysis of the phenomenon and the attempt of mathematical modelling, even partially for now, which the theory of group decisions provides.

An enterprise has *3* investment variants to increase the turnover shown in Table 11.8, by using the theory of utilities, the Board of Directors of the enterprise must take the optimal decision.

To take an appropriate decision, it is necessary to minimise the value of investments under the conditions of maximising the annual production capacity and the degree of using the production capacity, going through the following stages:

- *setting the problem to be solved, the possible variants and criteria to assess them*;
- *setting the utilities for each criterion and variant*. The utilities are set by interpolation within the range (0.1), 1 for the most favourable level to a criterion and 0 for the most unfavourable one (Table 11.9);
- *setting the coefficients of the criteria importance*. Every decision-maker has available 20 points which they distribute to the criteria as they consider, usually, several points to the more important criteria. (Table 11.10);
- *setting the optimal variant based on the global utility.*

$$\text{UG V1} = 0.6 \cdot 0.375 + 1 \cdot 0.425 + 0 \cdot 0.2 = 0.85$$

$$\text{UG V2} = 1 \cdot 0.375 + 0 \cdot 0.425 + 0.4 \cdot 0.2 = 0.455$$

$$\text{UG V3} = 0 \cdot 0.375 + 0.5 \cdot 0.425 + 1 \cdot 0.2 = 0.412$$

The optimal variant is max UG, meaning in this case V1

An enterprise sells four variants of phones, with production expenses related to the level of sales, shown in Table 11.11. The optimal decision must be taken, by using the pessimistic technique. According to this technique, the optimal variant that involves maximum advantages in the situation where the objective conditions are most unfavourable.

In this case, the optimal variant is that where we have the lowest production expenses for the smallest volume of sales.

Table 11.8 Structure of investment variants

Variants	Investment (m.u.)	Net annual turnover (m.u.)	Degree of using the production capacity (%)
V 1	5.6	3.8	70 %
V 2	5	3.4	73 %
V 3	6	3.6	75 %

Table 11.9 Setting the utilities for each criterion and variant

Variants	Investment (m.u.)	Net annual turnover (m.u.)	Degree of using the production capacity (%)
V1	0.6	1	0
V2	1	0	0.4
V3	0	0.5	1
K i	0.375	0.425	0.2

Table 11.10 Setting the coefficients of importance

Decision-makers	Investment (m.u.)	Net annual turnover (m.u.)	Degree of using the production capacity (%)	Number of points
D_1	8	8	4	20
D_2	7	9	4	20
Number of points	15	17	8	40

Table 11.11 Size of sales and expenses

	Volume of sales (m.u.)				
	500	1,000	1,500	2,000	2,500
Variants	Expenses (m.u.)				
EMTEL 80289	240	1,100	2,400	5,100	14,000
EMTEL 80224	220	900	2,700	4,700	13,800
PHONEM 80062B	250	1,000	2,500	4,600	12,900
PHONEM 80062A	230	1,200	2,800	5,000	12,500

Table 11.12 The minimum level of production expenses related to the production sold

Volume of sales (m.u.)	500	1,000	1,500	2,000	2,500
Minimum expenses	220	900	2,400	4,600	12,500

Two stages are undertaken, namely:

- *setting the lowest production expenses in each column.* (Table 11.12);
- *setting the optimal variant choosing the lowest production expenses for the smallest volume of sales.*

Table 11.13 Regret matrix

Variants	Volume of sales (pcs.)/(m.u.)				
	500	1,000	1,500	2,000	2,500
EMTEL 80289	20	200	0	500	1,500
EMTEL 80224	0	0	300	100	1,300
PHONEM 80062B	30	100	10	0	400
PHONEM 80062A	10	300	400	400	0

Thus, for a volume of *500* pieces sold, the production expenses amounting *220* (m.u.) correspond to the variant *EMTEL 80224*, which is the optimal variant.

By using the previously presented variants and the production expenses related to the volume of sales, it is required to choose the optimal decision variant that ensures the best results for the most favourable objective conditions.

By using the data in the Tables 11.11 and 11.12 and by using the optimistic technique, it results that for a maximum volume of sales equal to 2,500 pieces, the lowest production expenses are recorded, 12,500 (m.u.) corresponding to the variant *PHONEM 80062A*.

By using the method of minimising the regrets, it is required to choose the optimal decisional variant using the data presented in Tables 11.11 and 11.12.

According to this method, the optimum variant is that for which the regret is minimum, respectively the production expenses are minimum.

For this, the following stages are followed:

- *determining the matrix of regrets, where each element is obtained by subtracting the minimum element from its initial value*. (Table 11.13);
- *determining the maximum values of the regrets thus obtained, and the minimum value on each variant from them.*

The optimum variant is *PHONEM 80062B*.

11.3 Models to Optimise the Multiple Criteria Managerial Decisions

In 1965, a group of researchers from *SEMA* founded the well-known *Ranking and selection method in the presence of multiple views*, known as the *ELECTRE* method, applicable in solving many problems of multi-criteria decision. This method enables comparing and ranking the elements of a set of objects, taking into account *m* views in order to find some homogeneous subsets of elements, well as to establish a hierarchy of elements.

Be a set $M = \{M_1, \ldots M_n\}$ the elements of which we will call strategies or variants and *n* criteria or views $X = \{X_1, \ldots X_n\}$, correlated with the *m* objects $M_1, \ldots M_n$. The criteria according to which the objects of the set *M* are calculated can have different importances and meanings, establishing for each individual

Table 11.14 Multiple criteria decision analysis

Specification	x_1	x_2	...	x_n
M_1	a_{11}	a_{12}	...	a_{1n}
M_2	a_{21}	a_{22}	...	a_{2n}
.	.	.		.
.	.	.		.
.	.	.		.
M_m	a_{m1}	a_{m2}	...	a_{mn}

problem: the presence or the absence of some properties; the recognition of some characteristics or a qualitative factor; the assignment of a grade or assessment of a quantitative factor.

The analysis of an element M_i in terms of X_j leads to a result a_{ij} that can be a numerical value, an attributive note of the element M_i or a qualitative assessment (bad, good, very good, etc.).

A note of appreciation can be associated to every element a_{ij}, which can be *normalised* at a certain scale. The elements and criteria, along with the results, can be represented in an array (Table 11.14).

If the elements of the set *M* are a decision-maker's possible ways to act, and the elements of the set *X*—decision criteria, we are facing a typical problem of multidimensional decision.

The *ELECTRE* method enables ordering the alternatives according to complex criteria and therefore choosing the best alternatives, taking into account both the favourable and unfavourable aspects of the various possibilities. The set of results which we will call states are noted for each criterion with $\overline{X}_j = (a_{1j}, a_{2j}, \ldots a_{mj})$, which the analysis can lead us to in terms of X_j of the elements *of M*. Thus, *n* applications can be defined, which reflect this association:

$$\gamma_j : M \to X_j \qquad j = 1, \ldots, n. \tag{11.21}$$

The comparison of the elements of the set *M* by the multidimensional state of $X = \overline{X}_1 \times \overline{X}_2 \times \ldots \times \overline{X}_n$, which is associated by means of the applications γ_j is only possible if any two elements of *M* can be compared in terms of each criterion. This leads us to associating to each criterion X_j a chart $G_j = (M, U_j)$ where: the elements of the set *M* will be the peaks of the chart; between two peaks M_i and M_k we will draw an arc, oriented from M_i towards M_k if M_k exceeds M_i in ordering according to the criterion X_j if in this ordering M_i and M_k are equivalent, an arc will be drawn between them in both directions.

The chart G_i provides a clear representation of the preorder relation defined on *M* by the criterion X_j. This chart has the following properties:

– *it is transitive*, meaning that, if between any two peaks M_i and M_k there is a path oriented from M_i to M_k, then there is also an arc from M_i to M_k;

– *it is complete*, if any two peaks M_i and M_k are unique through an at least in one direction.

Having therefore the possibility to order the elements of the set *M* according to each individual criterion, we must find a procedure to *synthesise* the result of these comparisons in a final ordering. This goes back to obtaining a *synthesis chart* $G_0 = (M, U_0)$ of the n charts G_j from which we can deduce the order of the elements of *M* taking into account all criteria X_j.

By definition, in the chart G_0 we have an arc from one peak M_k to a peak M_0 if and only if there is an arc from M_k to M_i in all $G_j(j = 1, 2, \ldots, n)$. To be able to perform a complete ordering by means of the synthesis chart, it is necessary to introduce the concepts of concordance and discordance which will finally allow its completion G_0 with arcs until a *good* solution is obtained from all points of view.

The indicator of concordance between two strategies M_g and M_h is defined as follows:

$$C(M_g, M_h) = \frac{1}{k_1 + k_2 + \ldots + k_m} \cdot \sum_j k_j \tag{11.22}$$

where the indices $K_i(1, 2, \ldots, n)$ are importance coefficients of the criteria considered, and the sum is done according to those indices *j* for which $a_{gi} \geq a_{hi}$.

From the way it has been defined, it results that this indicator takes values ranging between *0* and *1*. It will give an indication on the level of *exceeding* a strategy M_g by another strategy M_h.

The indicator of discordance between two strategies M_g and M_h is defined as follows:

$$d(M_g, M_h) = 0 \text{ if } a_{hi} < a_{gi} \text{ whatever the } j = 1, \ldots, n; \tag{11.23}$$

$$d(M_g, M_h) = \frac{1}{\alpha} \cdot \max\left|a_{gi} - a_{hi}\right| \tag{11.24}$$

the maximum being taken for those indices *j* for which $a_{hi} \geq a_{gi}$ and α is the maximum gap between the values of the states.

If the concordance indicator provides indications on how a strategy M_h*exceeds* (from the point of view taken into account), the strategy M_g the discordance indicator provides us with a similar information (unless indicated) M_h is exceeded by the strategy M_g.

In the set *M*, an outrunning relation is inserted, which is defined as follows: one strategy M_i outruns a strategy M_k if $c(M_i, M_k) \geq p$ and $d(M_i, M_k) \leq q$ where *p* and *q* are two *threshold values* chosen by the decision-maker and ranging between *0* and *1*, the value of p being close to *1* and that of *q* relatively close to *0*.

A chart is related to this outrunning relation, for each pair of values *p* and *q*:

$$G(p, q) = (M, U(p, q)) \tag{11.25}$$

where

$$[(M_i, M_k) \in U(p,q)] \Leftrightarrow [c(M_i, M_k) \geq p \text{ and } d(M_i, M_k) \leq q] \qquad (11.26)$$

From the definition of the chart G(p, q), it results that if $p \leq p'$ and $q \geq q'$ then G (p′, q′) is a partial sub-chart of G(p, q). In other words, by reducing the concordance threshold *p* and by increasing the discordance threshold *q*, new connections are inserted into the chart G(p, q). In practice, we start from the values *p=l* and *q=0*, we decrease the value of *p* and increase the value of *q*, until we get a variant that outruns all the others. A certain variant M* of the set *M* will outrun all of the others when $c(M^*, M_i) \geq p$ and $d(M^*, M_i) \leq q$ for $j = 1, \ldots, n$, the outrun being so much stronger as *p* is closer to *1*, and *q* closer to *0*. Given the frequency of using the *ELECTRE* method in the most various multidimensional decision problems, let us illustrate that procedure through an example. Before proceeding to calculations, we shall show that the process of assigning he *grades* the method implies, it is insufficiently specified what can be the source of some confusions when calculating the discordance indicators. Indeed, from exposing the method, it seems that in the same problem, the coexistence of some quantitative criteria is possible, for which the values a_{ij} have physical, economical, etc. meanings, along with qualitative criteria for which the values a_{ij} are simple grades of appreciation. There appears an ambiguity on the meaning of the concept of discordance, as the differences $a_{gj} - a_{kj}$ from the expression of $d(M_g, M_k)$ are no longer comparable. This deficiency is in fact the consequence of the fact that the *ELECTRE* method completely ignores the use of utilities. We do not necessarily refer to estimating some utilities through methods which are sometimes complicated, but simply to introducing a common unit of estimation for all elements $d(M_i, M_k) \leq q$, either qualitative or quantitative. To remove this ambiguity, we intended to interpret that in fact the intentions of the method authors were to assign the meaning of other utilities $d(M_i, M_k) \leq q$ to the results, estimated through any method. Therefore, we transcribed in Table 11.15 the utilities of the consequences of a decisional problem with four variants and three decisional criteria, and after that we further proceeded with creating the charts (M, U_i) (Fig. 11.2).

Considering the importance coefficients of the three criteria of the problem, which were estimated as follows: $k_1 = 2$, $k_2 = 2$, $k_3 = 1$, we can proceed with calculating the concordance indicators, which are written in Table 11.16.

Table 11.15 Utilities of the decision problem consequences

Variants	Utilities		
	For the criterion c_1	For the criterion c_2	For the criterion c_3
V_1	1	0	0.8
V_2	0	1	1
V_3	0.7	0.2	0
V_4	0.4	0.8	0.8

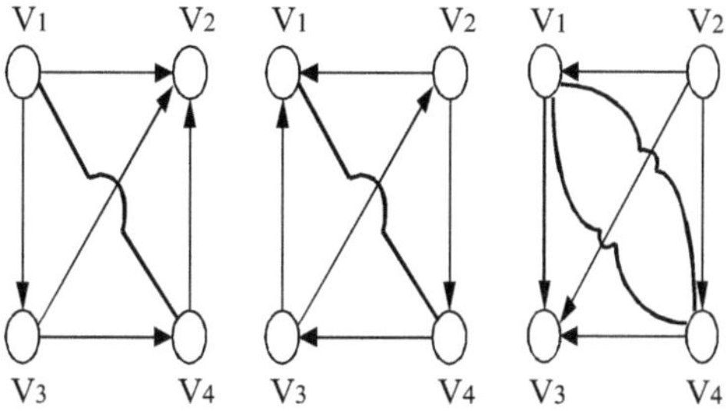

Fig. 11.2 Charts related to Table 11.15

Table 11.16 The calculation of the concordance indicators

V_i	V_j			
	V_1	V_2	V_3	V_4
V_1		0.4	0.6	0.6
V_2	0.6		0.6	0.6
V_3	0.4	0.4		0.4
V_4	0.6	0.4	0.6	

$$c(V_1, V_2) = \frac{1}{5} \cdot 2 = 0.4 \qquad c(V_1, V_3) = \frac{1}{6} \cdot (2 + 1) = 0.6 \tag{11.27}$$

$$c(V_1, V_4) = \frac{1}{5} \cdot (2 + 1) = 0.6 \qquad c(V_2, V_1) = \frac{1}{5} \cdot (2 + 1) = 0.6 \tag{11.28}$$

$$c(V_2, V_3) = \frac{1}{5} \cdot (2 + 1) = 0.6 \qquad c(V_2, V_4) = \frac{1}{5} \cdot (2 - 1) = 0.6 \tag{11.29}$$

$$c(V_3, V_1) = \frac{1}{5} \cdot 2 = 0.4 \qquad c(V_3, V_2) = \frac{1}{5} \cdot 2 = 0.4 \tag{11.30}$$

$$c(V_3, V_4) = \frac{1}{6} \cdot 2 = 0.4 \qquad c(V_4, V_1) = \frac{1}{5} \cdot (2 + 1) = 0.6 \tag{11.31}$$

$$c(V_4, V_2) = \frac{1}{5} \cdot 2 = 0.4 \qquad c(V_4, V_3) = \frac{1}{5} \cdot (2 + 1) = 0.6 \tag{11.32}$$

We further calculate the discordance indicators, which are written in Table 11.17

Table 11.17 The calculation of the discordance indicators

V_k	V_j			
	V_1	V_2	V_3	V_4
V_1		1	0.5	0.8
V_2	1		0.7	0.4
V_3	0.8	0.8		0.8
V_4	0.6	0.2	0.3	

$$d(V_1, V_2) = \frac{1}{1} \cdot 1 = 1 \qquad d(V_1, V_3) = \frac{1}{1} \cdot 0.2 = 0.2 \tag{11.33}$$

$$d(V_1, V_4) = \frac{1}{1} \cdot 0.8 = 0.8 \qquad d(V_2, V_1) = \frac{1}{1} \cdot 1 = 1 \tag{11.34}$$

$$d(V_2, V_3) = \frac{1}{1} \cdot 0.7 = 0.7 \qquad d(V_2, V_4) = \frac{1}{1} \cdot 0.4 = 0.4 \tag{11.35}$$

$$d(V_3, V_1) = \frac{1}{1} \cdot 0.8 = 0.8 \qquad d(V_3, V_2) = \frac{1}{1} \cdot 0.8 = 0.8 \tag{11.36}$$

$$d(V_3, V_4) = \frac{1}{1} \cdot 0.8 = 0.8 \qquad d(V_4, V_1) = \frac{1}{1} \cdot 0.6 = 0.6 \tag{11.37}$$

$$d(V_4, V_2) = \frac{1}{1} \cdot 0.2 = 0.2 \qquad d(V_4, V_3) = \frac{1}{1} \cdot 0.3 = 0.3 \tag{11.38}$$

The strongest outrun will be between V_2 and V_1 for which we have $p(V_1, V_2) = 0.6$ and $q(V_1, V_3) = 0.2$ according to Fig. 11.3a. If we subtract *the level* of outrunning at *p=0.6*; *q=0.4* (Fig. 11.3b) and only at *p=0.4*; *q=0.6* (Fig. 11.3c) the alternative V_4 will outrun all the others, and can be considered *optimal* (according to this method).

One characteristic of the method is its simplicity (particularly compared to the methods of estimating the utility and testing the independence of the criteria suggested by the American school). To mention taking into account the discordance between consequences, which is a new element compared to the classical methods of comparing the utility.

Returning however to critical observations, we shall show that the two coefficients defined by the method have special meanings: $c(M_g, M_h)$ is a ratio of sums of important coefficients, and $d(M_g, M_h)$ is a ratio of gaps between grades. The use of coefficients also increases the degree of procedure subjectivism. We consider that the comparison and classification process would be better to achieve if the two coefficients would have the same size.

Fig. 11.3 Charts related to Table 11.17

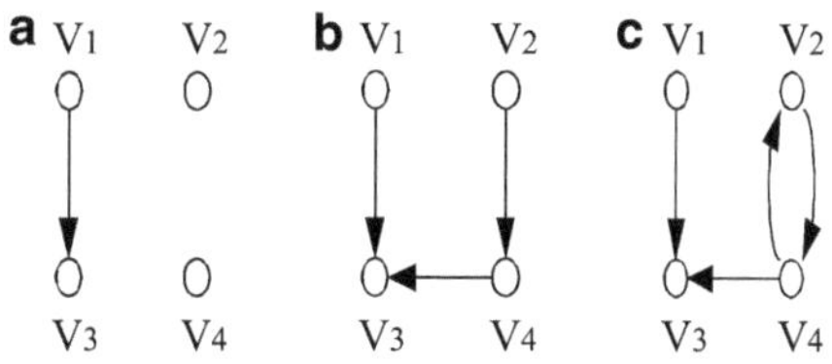

In this sense, the following can be calculated:

– *the maximum normalised coefficient of concordance*:

$$c^*(M_g, M_h) = \sum_j K_j(a_{gi} - a_{hj}) \tag{11.39}$$

where the sum is done according to those indices j for which $a_{gi} > a_{hj}$.

– *the normalised coefficient of discordance*:

$$d^*(M_g, M_h) = \sum_j K_j(a_{hj} - a_{gi}) \tag{11.40}$$

where the sum is done according to those indices j for which $a_{hj} > a_{gi}$.

For the *threshold value p* and *q*, in this case ranging between 0 and 1, the importance coefficients of the criteria are normalised, so that

$$\sum_j K_j = 1 \tag{11.41}$$

as well as the values of the *grades* so that $0 \le a^*_{ij} \le 1$.

The applications performed with these two coefficients have led to the conclusion that they reflect better the phenomenon of similarity and distinction. This may also be observed from the fact that $c^*(M_g, M_k) = d^*(M_k, M_g)$ meaning the concordance between M_k and M_g is equal to the discordance between M_k and M_g which seems natural.

Finally, one last observation is that the *ELECTRE* method does not take into account in any way the dependence, respectively the independence of criteria.

The Board of Directors of a company decides to introduce a new telephone on the market, for subscribers.

After the studies undertaken, four variants of telephones have emerged: *EMTEL 80289, EMTEL 80224, PHONEM 80062B, PHONEM 80062A*.

To take the optimal decision, the *ELECTRE* method is used, which involves going through the following stages:

– *establishing possible variants and criteria to assess these variants* (Table 11.18);

Table 11.18 Structure of possible variants

Variants	Criteria				
	Production expenses (m.u.)	Employees training expenses (m.u.)	Lifespan (years)	Profit (m.u.)	Quality
EMTEL 80289	240	72	20	130	Lux
EMTEL 80224	220	68	15	120	Extra
PHONEM 80062B	250	75	12	140	I
PHONEM 80062A	230	80	10	125	II

Table 11.19 The calculation of the utility coefficients

Variants	Criteria				
	Production expenses (coef)	Employees training expenses (coef)	Lifespan (years)	Profit (coef)	Quality (coef)
EMTEL 80289	0.33	0.66	1	0.5	1
EMTEL 80224	1	1	0.5	0	0.66
PHONEM 80062B	0	0.41	0.2	1	0.33
PHONEM 80062A	0.66	0	0	0.25	0
Importance coefficients (K_i)	0.18	0.28	0.22	0.2	0.12

The criteria used for the assessment are: *minimisation criteria*, meaning production expenses and expenses with employees' training; *maximisation criteria*, meaning the lifespan of machines, profit achieved, quality of telephones;

– *establishing the utilities for each criterion and variant and the importance coefficients of the criteria are calculated* (Table 11.19).

The utilities have been calculated by interpolation within the range *(0,1)*, assigning maximum utility *(1)* to the most favourable level of that criterion and minimum utility *(0)* to the most unfavourable level of that criterion.

$$U_{11} = \frac{250 - 240}{250 - 220} = \frac{10}{30} = 0.33$$

$$U_{14} = \frac{250 - 230}{250 - 220} = \frac{20}{30} = 0.66$$

Table 11.20 The calculation of the importance coefficients

Source	Criteria					
	Production expenses (coef)	Training expenses (coef)	Lifespan (years)	Profit (coef)	Quality (coef)	No. of points
Source 1	5	6	5	6	3	25
Source 2	4	5	7	7	2	25
Source 3	5	7	6	3	4	25
Source 4	4	10	4	4	3	25
No. of points by criteria	18	28	22	20	12	100
Importance coefficients *(K_i)*	0.18	0.28	0.22	0.2	0.12	1

$$U_{21} = \frac{80 - 72}{80 - 68} = \frac{8}{12} = 0.66$$

$$U_{23} = \frac{80 - 75}{80 - 68} = \frac{5}{12} = 0.41$$

$$U_{32} = \frac{15 - 10}{20 - 10} = \frac{5}{10} = 0.5$$

$$U_{33} = \frac{12 - 10}{20 - 10} = \frac{2}{10} = 0.2$$

$$U_{41} = \frac{130 - 120}{140 - 120} = \frac{10}{20} = 0.5$$

$$U_{43} = \frac{125 - 120}{140 - 120} = \frac{5}{20} = 0.25$$

For the criterion *quality*, the utilities are calculated by creating a scale of criteria: *(1)* is assigned to the *lux* quality and *(0)* for the quality *II*; for quality *I 0.33* is assigned, and for the *extra* quality *0.66* is assigned.

The importance coefficients are calculated by choosing several sources that would provide a certain score to each criterion, so that the number of points (*Np*) is equal to 100, and the number of points for each criterion (*Npi*) would be equal to *25* (Table 11.20);

- *determining the concordance and discordance indices*, (Tables 11.21 and 11.22)
- *choosing the optimal variant by outrunning the variants between them, under the conditions of simultaneously meeting two conditions and namely of concordance and discordance*

  $C_{Vg/Vh} \geq p$

  $D_{Vg/Vh} \leq q$, where $p + q = 1$

P—optimism threshold

q—pessimism threshold

Table 11.21 The calculation of the concordance indices

	EMTEL 80289 (V_1)	EMTEL 80224 (V_2)	PHONEM 80062B (V_3)	PHONEM 80062A (V_4)
EMTEL80289 (V_1)		0.46	0.2	0.18
EMTEL80224 (V_2)	0.54		0.2	0.2
PHONEM80062B (V_3)	0.8	0.8		0.18
PHONEM80062A (V_4)	0.82	0.8	0.82	

$$C_{V1/V2} = 0.22 + 0.2 + 0.12 = 0.54$$
$$C_{V1/V3} = 0.18 + 0.28 + 0.22 + 0.12 = 0.8$$
$$C_{V1/V4} = 0.28 + 0.22 + 0.2 + 0.12 = 0.82$$
$$C_{V2/V1} = 0.18 + 0.28 = 0.46$$
$$C_{V2/V3} = 0.18 + 0.28 + 0.22 + 0.12 = 0.8$$
$$C_{V2/V4} = 0.18 + 0.28 + 0.22 + 0.12 = 0.8$$
$$C_{V3/V1} = 0.2$$
$$C_{V3/V2} = 0.2$$
$$C_{V3/V4} = 0.28 + 0.22 + 0.2 + 0.12 = 0.82$$
$$C_{V4/V1} = 0.18$$
$$C_{V4/V2} = 0.2$$
$$C_{V4/V3} = 0.18$$

Table 11.22 The calculation of the discordance indices

	EMTEL 80289 (V_1)	EMTEL 80224 (V_2)	PHONEM 80062B (V_3)	PHONEM 80062A (V_4)
EMTEL80289 (V_1)	–	0.5	0.8	1
EMTEL80224 (V_2)	0.66	–	1	1
PHONEM80062B (V_3)	0.5	1	–	0.75
PHONEM80062A (V_4)	0.33	0.25	0.66	–

$$D_{V1/V2} = \max\{0.66;\ 0.33\} = 0.66$$
$$D_{V1/V3} = \max\{0.5\} = 0.5$$
$$D_{V1/V4} = \max\{0.33\} = 0.33$$
$$D_{V2/V1} = \max\{0.5;\ 0.33\} = 0.5$$
$$D_{V2/V3} = \max\{1\} = 1$$
$$D_{V2/V4} = \max\{0.25\} = 0.25$$
$$D_{V3/V1} = \max\{0.33;\ 0.25;\ 0.8;\ 0.66\} = 0.8$$
$$D_{V3/V2} = \max\{1\} = 1$$
$$D_{V3/V4} = \max\{0.66\} = 0.66$$
$$D_{V4/V1} = \max\{0.66;\ 1;\ 025\} = 1$$
$$D_{V4/V2} = \max\{0.33;\ 1;\ 0.5;\ 0.66\} = 1$$
$$D_{V4/V3} = \max\{0.41;\ 0.2;\ 0.75;\ 0.33\} = 0.75$$

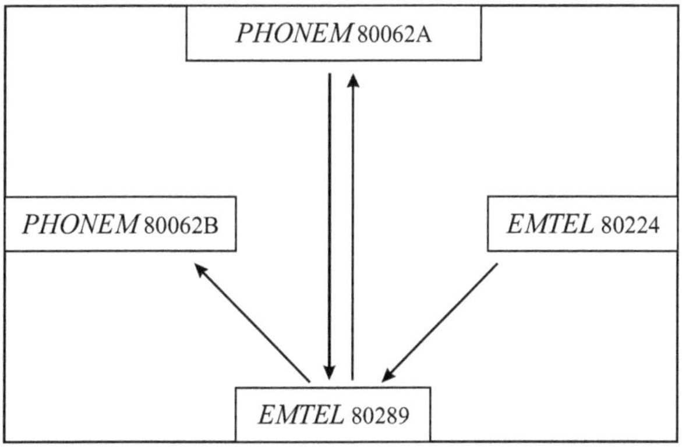

Fig. 11.4 Graphic representation of the optimal variant

Table 11.23 Situation of lens production

Name of Product	Unit duration to use the means of production (hours/machine)	Unit consumption of labour (hours/man)	Unit storage cost (m.u.)	Maximum stock at the end of July (pcs.)
Spherical lens	0.23	0.16	7	2,000
Bifocals	0.76	0.66	9	1,000
Cylindrical lens	0.52	0.78	15	100
Prescription-based lens	1	1.21	25	10

Table 11.24 Calculation data

Months	Production capacity of machines (h)	Consumption of labour (h)	Storage capacity (sqm)
May	2,500	1.000	40
June	2,500	1.000	40
July	2,500	1.000	40

We start from $p=1$, $q=0$, subtracting p and increasing q and performing the outruns until a clear conclusion can be drawn. The optimal variant is that where most arrows start from.

It may be noticed that the *EMTEL 80289* outruns the other variants, this one being the optimal variant (Fig. 11.4). From the records of a company regarding the products it manufactures, spherical lens, bifocals, cylindrical lens and prescription-based ordered lens, the following data are known (Table 11.23):

By using the *Monte Carlo* simulation model and data from the Table 11.24, we are to establish the structure of the offer for the following months: May, June, July.

At the end of April, it has been assessed that there will be no stock for these products. The production in April is of *120,000* pieces of spherical lens, *100,000* pieces of bifocals, *70,000* pieces of cylindrical lens, *8,000* pieces of prescription-based lens.

Based on the data in the records of the company, it has also been assessed that any production increase, regardless of the period, would determine average expenses of *500 m.u./pcs.* and any drop of production determines average expenses of *300 m.u./pcs.*

Based on the data in the previous tables, we can create a Stochastic linear model where both the demand and the profit are random sizes. This model, achieved over a period of 3 months and for four products, contains *30* variables, *28* restrictions and an objective function which becomes itself a random variable.

It is a matter of:

- *the variables of the model*:

X_1—the quantity of spherical lens manufactured in May
X_2—the quantity of spherical lens stored in May
X_3—the quantity of bifocals manufactured in May
X_4—the quantity of bifocals stored in May
X_5—the quantity of cylindrical lens manufactured in May
X_6—the quantity of cylindrical lens stored in May
X_7—the quantity of prescription-based lens manufactured in May
X_8—the quantity of prescription-based lens stored in May
X_9 —the quantity of spherical lens manufactured in May
X_{10}—the quantity of spherical lens stored in June
X_{11}—the quantity of bifocals manufactured in June
X_{12}—the quantity of bifocals stored in June
X_{13}—the quantity of cylindrical lens manufactured in June
X_{14}—the quantity of cylindrical lens stored in June
X_{15}—the quantity of prescription-based lens manufactured in June
X_{16}—the quantity of prescription-based lens stored in June
X_{17}—the quantity of spherical lens manufactured in July
X_{18}—the quantity of spherical lens stored in July
X_{19}—the quantity of bifocals manufactured in July
X_{20}—the quantity of bifocals stored in July
X_{21}—the quantity of cylindrical lens manufactured in July
X_{22}—the quantity of cylindrical lens stored in July
X_{23}—the quantity of prescription-based lens manufactured in July
X_{24}—the quantity of prescription-based lens stored in July
X_{25}—the increase of production in May compared to April
X_{26}—the decrease of production in May compared to April
X_{27}—the increase of production in June compared to May
X_{28}—the decrease of production in June compared to May
X_{29}—the increase of production in July compared to June
X_{30}—the decrease of production in July compared to June

– *the restrictions of the model regarding*:

a) capacity of machines:

C_1—$0.23x_1+0.76x_3+0.52x_5+1x_7 \leq 2{,}500$
C_2—$0.23x_9+0.76x_{11}+0.52x_{13}+1x_{15} \leq 2{,}500$
C_3—$0.23x_{17}+0.76x_{19}+0.52x_{21}+1x_{23} \leq 2{,}500$

b) working time of performers:

C_4—$0.16x_1+0.66x_3+0.78x_5+1.21x_7 \leq 1.000$
C_5—$0.16x_9+0.66x_{11}+0.78x_{13}+1.21x_{15} \leq 1.000$
C_6—$0.16x_{17}+0.66x_{19}+0.78x_{21}+1.21x_{23} \leq 1.000$

c) storage area:

C_7—$0.0001x_2+0.002x_4+0.003x_6+0.002x_8 \leq 40$
C_8—$0.0001x_{10}+0.002x_{12}+0.003x_{14}+0.002x_{16} \leq 40$
C_9—$0.0001x_{18}+0.002x_{20}+0.003x_{22}+0.002x_{24} \leq 40$

d) monthly demand of each product:

C_{10}—x_1-x_2—demand of spherical lens, May
C_{11}—$x_2+x_9-x_{10}$—demand of spherical lens, June
C_{12}—$x_{10}+x_{17}-x_{18}$—demand of spherical lens, July.
C_{13}—$x_{18} \leq 2{,}000$—stock at the end of July.
C_{14}—x_3-x_4—demand of bifocals, May
C_{15}—$x_4+x_{11}-x_{12}$—demand of bifocals, June
C_{16}—$x_{12}+x_{19}-x_{20}$—demand of bifocals, July.
C_{17}—$x_{20} \leq 1{,}000$—stock at the end of July.
C_{18}—x_5-x_6—demand of cylindrical lens, May
C_{19}—$x_6+x_{13}-x_{14}$—demand of cylindrical lens, June
C_{20}—$x_{14}+x_{21}-x_{22}$—demand of cylindrical lens, July.
C_{21}—$1x_{22} \leq 100$—stock at the end of July
C_{22}—x_7-x_8—prescription-based lens demand, May
C_{23}—$x_8+x_{15}-x_{16}$—prescription-based lens demand, June
C_{24}—$x_{16}+x_{23}-x_{24}$—prescription-based lens demand, July
C_{25}—$1x_{24} \leq 10$—stock at the end of July

e) production variation:

C_{26}—$1x_1+1x_3+1x_5+1x_7-1x_{25}+1x_{26}=298$
C_{27}—$-1x_1-1x_3-1x_5-1x_7+1x_9+1x_{11}+1x_{13}+1x_{15}-1x_{27}+1x_{28}=0$
C_{28}—$-1x_9-1x_{11}-1x_{13}-1x_{15}+1x_{17}+1x_{19}+1x_{21}+1x_{23}-1x_{29}+1x_3=0$

To choose the optimal production and storage structure, we use the *Monte Carlo* simulation technique.

Taking into account the what has been shown before, to choose the optimal production and storage structure, the following stages are followed (only two types of spherical and bifocal lens have been taken as example):

Table 11.25 Probability distributions for profit related to spherical lens

Variant	Unit profit with spherical lens (m.u.)	Probability (%)	Cumulated probability (%)
1	(9.6; 9.8; 9.3)	0.35	0.35
2	(10.1; 11; 9.9)	0.40	0.75
3	(10.7; 9.9; 10.1)	0.25	1

Table 11.26 Probability distributions for profit related to bifocals

Variant	Unit profit with bifocals (m.u.)	Probability (%)	Cumulated probability (%)
1	(11; 9; 13)	0.45	0.45
2	(14; 10; 11)	0.23	0.68
3	(12; 13; 9)	0.32	1

Table 11.27 Probability distributions for demand—spherical lens

Variant	Demand of spherical lens (pcs.)	Probability (%)	Cumulated probability (%)
1	(800, 600, 730)	0.20	0.20
2	(750, 820, 900)	0.43	0.63
3	(760, 680, 770)	0.37	1

Table 11.28 Probability distributions for demand—bifocals

Variant	Demand of bifocals (pcs.)	Probability (%)	Cumulated probability (%)
1	(430, 410, 470)	0.22	0.22
2	(430, 450, 485)	0.37	0.59
3	(410, 370, 432)	0.41	1

Table 11.29 Relating the ranges of random numbers for each variable

Variable	Variant	Range
Unit profit with spherical lens	1	(0; 0.35)
Unit profit with spherical lens	2	(0.35; 0.75)
Unit profit with spherical lens	3	(0.75, 1)
Unit profit with bifocals	1	(0; 0.45)
Unit profit with bifocals	2	(0.45; 0.68)
Unit profit with bifocals	3	(0.68; 1)
Demand of spherical lens	1	(0; 0.2)
Demand of spherical lens	2	(0.2; 0.63)
Demand of spherical lens	3	(0.63; 1)
Demand of bifocals	1	(0; 0.22)
Demand of bifocals	2	(0.22; 0.59)
Demand of bifocals	3	(0.59; 1)

- *determining the cumulated probability distribution for each type of lens* (Tables 11.25, 11.26, 11.27, and 11.28);
- *association for each variable, by means of cumulated probability, of a range of random numbers eveny distributed within that range, as follows* (Table 11.29);

Table 11.30 Generating the string of random numbers

No. of variant	Random no.	Variant
1	0.18	1 1 1 1 1 1
2	0.63	2 2 2 3 3 2
1	0.02	1 1 1 1 1 1
3	0.56	2 2 2 2 2 2
1	0.06	1 1 1 1 1 1
4	0.93	3 3 3 3 3 3
1	0.04	1 1 1 1 1 1
5	0.71	2 3 3 3 3 3
5	0.70	2 3 3 3 3 3
2	0.64	2 2 2 3 3 2
4	0.80	3 3 3 3 3 3
6	0.26	1 1 1 2 2 1

Table 11.31 Calculation of optimal solution

No. Variant	Possible variant	Frequency of occurrence	Profit reached (m.u.)
1	1 1 1 1 1 1	7	129,516.8
2	2 2 2 3 3 2	4	131,678.3
3	2 2 2 2 2 2	2	131,652.6
4	3 3 3 3 3 3	5	133,571.8
5	2 3 3 3 3 3	3	132,763.8
6	1 1 1 2 2 1	2	128,368.5
7	1 1 2 2 2 1	1	128,555.7
8	2 1 2 2 2 1	1	129,616.2
Total		25	

- *generating a string of random numbers evenly distributed within the range (0,1)*, (Table 11.30) For each number generated, the range achieved in the previous stage which that number belongs to is searched and the unit profit and related demand are determined. Thus, several possible combinations are obtained for the random variables taken into account (demand and profit).
- *by means of the WINQSB LP/ILP problem, solving the linear model for the variants obtained in the previous stage* (Table 11.31);

The occurrence probability has been calculated as ratio between the frequency of occurrence of each variant and the total number of experiments. From the eight variants obtained, variant 4 has been chosen for presentation, which provides the highest level of profit (122,571.8 m.u.) and which has the occurrence probability 0.2. For this variant, the production programs is as follows: *44,000*, the quantity of spherical lens manufactured in May; *1,207,000*, the quantity of bifocals manufactured in May; *985,000*, the quantity of bifocals manufactured in June; *47,000*, the quantity of spherical lens manufactured in June; *1,105,000*, the quantity of spherical lens manufactured in July; *725,000*, the quantity of bifocals manufactured in July. Manufacturing an additional quantity of prescription-based

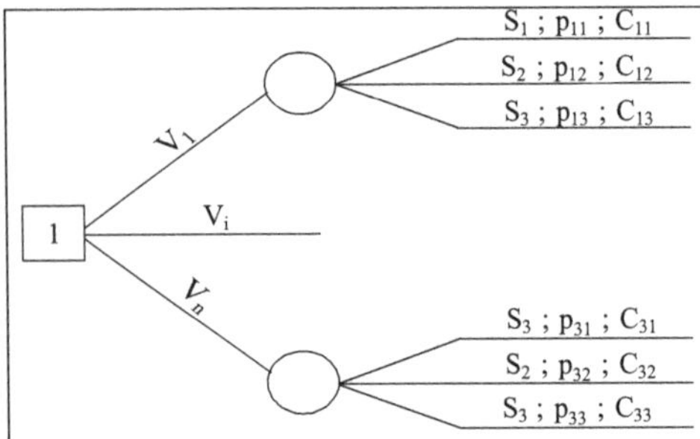

Legend:

○ - decision point or node (PD);

□ - point of separating the chances (nature states) (PS);

V_i - candidate decision variants;

S_{ij} - nature states (probable states of the objective conditions);

p_{ij} - probabilities to cause the "j" state for the variant "i";

C_{ij} - consequences (results) predicted for each state of the "i" nature and decision variant "j";

Fig. 11.5 Graphical representation of the simple decision tree
Legend:
Circle—decision point or node (PD);
Square—point of separating the chances (nature states) (PS);
V_i—candidate decision variants;
S_{ij}—nature states (probable states of the objective conditions);
p_{ij}—probabilities to cause the "j" state for the variant "i";
C_{ij}—consequences (results) predicted for each state of the "i" nature and decision variant "j"

lens is not efficient ($x_8 = 0$), as storing such lens would lead to reducing the total profit by 25 m.u.

11.4 Models Used to Optimise the Decisions Adopted in Strategic Management

The decision tree allows the assessment and comparison of the potential results of a strategic decisions by predicting the future events as a complex diagram (its resemblance to a stylised tree drawn from left to the right is what inspired the name of the method), determining a set of specific values which are related to each of the decisional values taken into account. Therefore, every decision taken at a given moment depends on the result of a random event, which cannot be accurately established when adopting it, but the probability of which can be estimated based on the statistical-mathematical investigations. The structure of a simple decision tree may be analysed based on the graphic representation in Fig. 11.5.

The decision points also called decision nodes are symbolised as a square and represent the moments when managers must choose a course of action (strategic option) from many which are possible that is to be adopted for achieving strategic objectives.

The possible decision variants are represented by arcs or branches that emerge (start from) a decision node. If a certain investment or cost category is associated with any alternative, this must be classified on the arc representing that variant, and if a variant is rejected, this shall be graphically symbolised by the barred sign. A variant (arc) can end with a consequence (result) or continue in a multi-sequential tree with another decision point or chance point.

The chance points represented by circles mark the random events or nature states which occur at a given moment within the strategic decision process.

The nature states or events are also represented as the arcs emerging (stand out) from the chance points. Each branch symbolising a nature state may be followed by a consequence (result), a new decision point or chance point.

The construction of the decision tree is done from left to the right, starting from the original point of the decision, the decision variants of which are represented as the arcs emerging from this original node to the right. Further, new chance points or decision points are or added, according to the events or decision situations predicted to occur after the original decision. When new chance points are drawn on the decision tree representation graph, it is mandatory to note the corresponding nature states, along with the associated probabilities. Thus, the development of the tree is done to the right, to the points where the expected consequences or results are reached. If the tree represented in Fig. 11.5 is a simple mono-sequential one, it must be shown that a complex tree adopted to the strategy development process (involving a series of strategic decisions taken at different moments of the predictable scope) can be interpreted as a reunion of simple trees, each of them representing one period of time. Thus, the complex (multi-sequential) tree may be extended to the limit of the capacities of prediction. Therefore, the essential problem arising when developing the strategy is that of establishing the optimum path of the decisions to take so that at the end of the prediction scope, the maximisation of expected performances in each company is provided.

Contrary to the sequence of developing the decision tree, the resolution process (consisting in comparatively assessing the alternatives) starts from the right extreme of the tree, moving towards the original starting base. The calculation is therefore done from the right to the left, using what specialists in developed countries call it the "roll-back" principle, by assessing the optimal mathematic expectancy at the level of each decision point. The mathematic expectation for the decision node is normally determined by the equation:

$$\mathrm{Sm(Vki)} = \sum_{j=1}^{n} c_{kij}(t) \cdot p_{kij} \tag{11.42}$$

where:

"k" represents the decision point;
"i"—index of the decision variant;
"j"—sequence number of the nature state;
"t"—sequence number of the current year; $t \in [1,T]$;
T—predictable range (5–10–20 years);
$S_m(V_{ki})$—mathematical expectation of the "I" variant of the decision node "k";
$c_{kij}(t)$—consequence (result) for each nature state at the time "t";
p_{kij}—probability to cause the "j" state for the variant "i" in the decision node "k".

However, taking into account that the time range T which a strategy is developed for is normally a long one, it is obvious the cash flow should be taken into account, which is related to the T range, and the consequences (performances) with which it is operated in this range must be updated at the current time of the strategy assessment. For this, the updating techniques based on compound interest are used. Thus, the formula to calculate the mathematical expectations for choosing the optimum variants in the decisional point "k" becomes:

$$Sm(Vki) = \sum_{j=1}^{n} p_{kij} \cdot \sum_{t=t_k}^{T} \frac{c_{kij}(t)}{(1+d)^t} - \frac{i_{ki}}{(1+d)^{t_k}} \tag{11.43}$$

where:

i_{ki}—represents the investment efforts needed to implement the variant "i" of the node D_k;
t_k—sequence number of the year related to the decisional point D_k;
d—interest rate used to update the result.

The most favourable alternative shall decisively correspond to the mathematical expectation with the maximum value:

$$V_k^* = \max\{S_m(V_{ki})\} \tag{11.44}$$

where: V_k^*—the optimal decisional variant in node "k"

Based on what has been shown, it may be concluded that the economic-mathematical models involving decision trees are usually complex models using varied procedures or principles. In the case of using the decision tree to elaborate the strategies, the technique of scenarios, mathematical expectations, graphs, the "roll-back" principle or forecast techniques are involved in the production field. The complexity of such a model to elaborate the strategy by means of the decision trees is the main reason of its appurtenance to the category of heuristic models.

The methodology to solve the heuristic model of the strategic decision tree generally consists of the following stages: creating the scenario of the strategic problem to be solved; the graphical representation of the decision tree as an open graph; determining the decisional consequences of each variant and assessing the investment efforts involved; calculating the probabilities of occurrence and manifestation of random events; assessing the decision tree by determining the mathematical expectations of the variants in each decisional point and applying the "roll-back" procedure; describing the configuration of the chosen strategy, as the sequence of optimal strategic decisions adopted in each decision point.

The effective way to practically implement the described methodology shall be described further on the example of elaborating the strategy of production in the industrial company.

Taking into account the coordinates of the global strategy elaborated at company level, the scenario of reorganising the productive apparatus in the industrial company took into account the following strategic alternatives: V_1—reducing the production of machines and related spare parts and assimilating the manufacture of machines for industrial and civil constructions. If the demand shall have an improvement tendency gradually covering the production capacities maintained in operation, the activity shall continue in the same way. However, if the demand shall remain reduced after diversification, the industrial company shall adopt an extensive orientation to achieve the objective of increasing the market segment. For this purpose, two alternatives are aimed at: the permanent improvement of the quality of the products made or creation of an in-house marketing network, both providing the extension of the market by serving certain categories of new beneficiaries in the country and abroad; V_2—maintaining the current profile for 2 years and disinvesting by involving a considerable part of the company's assets. If the reaction of the market is a favourable one, the activity may continue in the same way on the condition that stable segments correspond to the reduced manufacture, segments mainly requiring spare parts for the mining machines, but in lower quantities and with specific features, adopted to certain categories of mining equipment. If the demand shall stabilise at a very low level, after the second year, it shall turn to diversification by assimilating the spare parts for the electronic and electrical equipment and extension of service provisions; V_3 – the company significantly narrows its manufacturing activity – which would be reduced in this variant only in assembling the spare parts purchased from the country or abroad as mining and/or non-mining machines. In parallel, the service and consultancy services increase for exploiting a wide range of equipment. The surplus fixed assets of the industrial company are placed into preservation by the end of the 4th year, and afterwards, if the company's activity evolves favourably into the mentioned direction, the assets are capitalised by disinvestments. If the industrial company shall encounter difficulties in this variant of manufacture reorganisation (the difficulties primarily derive from the amplitude of the efforts involved in such a process of radical change), one may expect the resumption of manufacture which shall focus this time on manufacturing the spare parts for a wide range of machines, maintaining the option for the extension of related activities of trade, consultancy and service provision.

The assessment of investments for the implementation of strategic variants needs expertise operations or the preparation of some laborious feasibility studies.

The expertise implies the assessment by experts based on the experience gathered in solving some similar situations, on the investment efforts required by each strategic action (without making special calculations, but only using the comparison with the solved cases in past periods). The feasibility studies assess the investment more accurately (by means of the project drawings and cost estimates), but require both significant calculating efforts and great time consumption. The results (like the profits or costs) may be predicted by the same methodologies as the investments. When performing the expertise or preparing the feasibility studies, specialists use databases which include price catalogues, lists of rates for utilities and services, taxes, salaries, duties and other similar variables sized at the time of running the analysis. As time passes however, the listed cost components usually change upwards. At the same time, the change in the foreign exchange rate, potential increase of labour productivity, as well as the decreasing efficiency law are elements which may be taken into account by inserting into the calculation formulas the mathematical expectations of the factors to update money amounts. In the case of the industrial company, both the investments and the incomes from capitalising the disinvested assets and future profits have been forecast based on the financial expertise performed by the specialists of the Research Institute of Mining. In Table 11.32 the estimated values of the parameters of the decision tree have been systematised. Taking into account that the time scope T taken into consideration in the stage of designing the strategic alternatives covers a period of 10 years, it has been deemed that in order to provide the comparability of data the expression is convenient, applicable to investments, profits and costs estimated on variants in US dollars. Under these conditions, the rate adopted for updating the money amounts involved in the opportunity study of the strategic variants has been of 15 %.

In Table 11.32, the estimated results are presented as consequences of year t, symbolised c_{kij} (t) for each strategic variant "i", from each decision point "k" and each state "j" of the non-updated nature. The same can be said about the investments of each year symbolised i_{ki} corresponding to the decision points analysed and strategic variants assessed therein. The consequences c_{kij} (t) may have positive or negative values, as the nature states in each point—chance involve using or decommissioning the production capacities (it has been adopted as working hypothesis—the high demand for those levels ensuring a larger degree of using the capacities than the "threshold point", a case where c_{kij} (t) >0, respectively—the low demand for a level ensuring a use under the "threshold" calculated for the degree of suing the capacity, a case where c_{kij} (t) <0).

Calculating the probabilities of occurrence and manifestation of the nature states (S_{kij}) carries in its turn two distinct methods: the method of simple probabilities and the method of conditioned probabilities. Simple probabilities may be named either objectively (based on the statistical information regarding the occurrence of repetitive phenomena) or subjectively (based on the expertise).

Conditioned probabilities are calculated based on Bayes' theorem, which operates with two types of probabilities: previous (estimated before accumulating any experimental information) and posterior (obtained by reviewing the previous probabilities based on the information provided by statistical experiments).

Taking into account the importance generally given to an as accurate as possible of an evaluation of the probabilities of occurrence of the nature states in solving a

Table 11.32 Variables of the parameters of strategic decision tree

Decision nodes k and deadlines t_k	Variants Vki from the decision points k	Investment efforts by variants		Nature states		Probabilities of nature states		Profits (+)/ Losses (−) in year t	
		Code	mil. $	Code	Specifications	Code	Values	Code	mil. $/ year
0	1	2	3	4	5	6	7	8	9
1 $t_1 = 0$ (2000)	v_{11} Diversification (assimilation of construction machines)	i_{11}	0.4	S_{111}	High demand	p (S_{111})	0.400	$c_{111}(t)$	0.90
				S_{112}	Low demand	p (S_{112})	0.600	$c_{112}(t)$	-0.25
	v_{12} Maintaining the current profit and disinvestment	i_{12}	0	S_{121}	High demand	p (S_{121})	0.800	$c_{121}(t)$	0.35
				S_{122}	Low demand	p (S_{122})	0.200	$c_{122}(t)$	-0.15
	v_{13} Narrowing the manufacturing activities and refocusing on service and consultancy activities	i_{13}	0.15	S_{131}	High demand	p (S_{131})	0.160	$c_{131}(t)$	0.90
				S_{132}	Low demand	p (S_{132})	0.840	$c_{132}(t)$	-0.25
2 $t_2 = 2$ (2002)	v_{21} Specialisation on spare parts adapted to some categories of machines	i_{21}	0.10	S_{211}	High demand	p (S_{211})	0.750	$c_{211}(t)$	1.00
				S_{212}	Low demand	p (S_{212})	0.250	$c_{212}(t)$	-0.20
	v_{22} Diversification by assimilating the parts for electric and electronic equipment	i_{22}	0.08	S_{221}	High demand	p (S_{221})	0.333	$c_{221}(t)$	0.80
				S_{222}	Low demand	p (S_{222})	0.667	$c_{222}(t)$	-0.50

(continued)

Table 11.32 (continued)

Decision nodes k and deadlines t_k	Variants Vki from the decision points k	Investment efforts by variants		Nature states		Probabilities of nature states		Profits (+)/ Losses (−) in year t	
		Code	mil. $	Code	Specifications	Code	Values	Code	mil. $/ year
3 t_3=3 (2003)	v_{31} Quality improvement	i_{31}	0	S_{311}	High demand	p (S_{311})	0.833	$c_{311}(t)$	3.20
				S_{312}	Low demand	p (S_{312})	0.167	$c_{312}(t)$	0.45
	v_{32} In-house trading network	i_{32}	0.05	S_{321}	High demand	p (S_{321})	0.769	$c_{321}(t)$	0.85
				S_{322}	Low demand	p (S_{322})	0.231	$c_{322}(t)$	0.40
4 t_4=5 (2005)	v_{41} "Status—Quo"	i_{41}	-1.8	S_{141}	High demand	p (S_{141})	0.600	$c_{141}(t)$	1.15
5 t_4=5 (2005)	v_{51} "Status—Quo"	i_{51}	3	S_{511}	High demand	p (S_{511})	0.862	$c_{511}(t)$	1.20
				S_{512}	Low demand	p (S_{512})	0.138	$c_{512}(t)$	-0.35
	v_{52} Re-launching the manufacture	i_{52}	5.5	S_{521}	High demand	p (S_{521})	0.400	$c_{521}(t)$	0.60
				S_{522}	Low demand	p (S_{522})	0.600	$c_{522}(t)$	-0.45

Table 11.33 The a priori and conditioned probabilities of the success or failure of the strategic option compared to the demand levels (decision nodes 2, 3 and 5)

Decision node	Nature states	A priori probabilities	Forecasts of the market demand	
			Success	Failure
5	M—High demand	P(M) = 0.7	P(S/M) = 0.8	P(E/M) = 0.2
	m—Low demand	P(m) = 0.3	P(S/m) = 0.3	P(E/m) = 0.7
3	M—High demand	P(M) = 0.8	P(S/M) = 0.5	P(E/M) = 0.5
	m—Low demand	P(m) = 0.2	P(S/m) = 0.4	P(E/m) = 0.6
2	M—High demand	P(M) = 0.6	P(S/M) = 0.8	P(E/M) = 0.2
	m—Low demand	P(m) = 0.4	P(S/m) = 0.4	P(E/m) = 0.6

See footnotes of Table 11.34

complex decision tree, we considered it necessary to get and use the additional information meant to remove the uncertainty in a considerable proportion.

To start with, a set of a priori probabilities is therefore estimated—the option shall be a success or a failure—subjectively determined based on the information gathered from managers and specialists within the industrial company. Using a market research however enables the adoption of a strategic decision based both on the initial performance and on the data acquired from the factual investigation of the demand reactions. In Table 11.33, both the a priori probabilities and those resulted after the forecasts of the marketing research are shown for the decision nodes 2, 3 and 5 (the objective of the market investigations in the three cases was the high levels and low levels of the demand).

The major strategic options emerging from the firs decision node were the topic of a distinct investigation—taking into account the major changes which each of them binds in the structure of the traditional portfolio of activities of the industrial company. The analysis of the market (favourable or unfavourable) reactions has been adapted in this case to the three distinct categories of portfolios—successful, mediocre or losing. The a priori probabilities, as well as those detached from the research have been shown in Table 11.34.

The conditioned probabilities previously explained actually show the level of trust or safety degree that can be assigned to researchers for the forecast of the beneficiary company's evolution. These probabilities which actually describe the experience gathered in market researches of this type are based on the statistics of the successes or failures, the reports of some companies with similar concerns or simply subjective assessments. Normally, it is assumed that the performance of past predictions can also be achieved in the future.

With the two sets of probabilities—a priori and conditioned—the posterior (reviewed) probability may be further determined based on the Bayesian analysis, as a strategic option to register success, given that the market research forecast the success (noted P(M/S) in the case of the decision nodes 2, 3 and 5).

Table 11.34 A priori and conditioned probabilities of the successful, mediocre or losing portfolio compared to the market attitude (the decision node 1)

Decision node	Nature states	A priori probabilities	Forecasts of the portfolio by activities		
			Success	Mediocre	Losing
1	F—favourable attitude	P(F) = 0.40	P(S/F) = 0.60	P(M/F) = 0.20	P(P/F) = 0.20
	N—Unfavourable attitude	P(N) = 0.60	P(S/N) = 0.10	P(M/N) = 0.20	P(P/N) = 0.70

The following notations were sued in both tables
P(M)—a priori probabilities related to a high level of the demand
P(m)—previous probabilities related to the low levels of the demand
P(S/M)—the probability that the marketing research would be a success provided that the demand is actually high
P(S/m)—the probability that the research would be a success provided that a low demand is actually recorded
P(E/M)—the probability of the failure forecast in the research in the situation where the demand was actually at high levels
P(E/m)—the probability of the failure forecast in the research when the level of the demand was indeed low
P(F)—the previous probability related to a favourable attitude of the market
P(N)—the previous probability related to an unfavourable attitude of the market
P(S/F)—the probability that the research would be a success provided that the market attitude has been favourable
P(S/N)—the probability of the success forecast by research in the situation where the market attitude was indeed unfavourable
P(M/F)—the probability of portfolio mediocrity (results from the research) provided that the market reaction is actually a favourable one
P(M/N)—the probability of the portfolio mediocrity forecast in the situation where the market was unfavourable
P(P/F)—the probability of forecasting the losing portfolio when the market attitude is favourable
P(P/N)—the probability of the failure forecast in the research when the portfolio was actually a losing one

This probability is calculated by using the Bayes' formula for two variables:

$$P(M/S) = \frac{P(S/M) \cdot P(M)}{P(S/M) \cdot P(M) + P(S/m) \cdot P(m)} \tag{11.45}$$

where: P(S)—represents the probability of success of the research forecast

In order to generalise the Bayes relation in the case of "n" mutually exhaustive events $S = (S_1 \cup S_2 \cup S_3 \cup \ldots \cup S_n)$ where S_j represents the nature state (the event), we shall note with R the result—event of a particular experience. Bayes' theorem affirms that the posterior probability of a state of the S_j nature in relation to the result R of the empirical investigation is given by the formula:

$$P(S_j/R) = \frac{P(R/S_j) \cdot P(S_j)}{\sum_{j=1}^{m} P(R/S_j) \cdot P(S_j)} \tag{11.46}$$

where:

R—represents the result forecast by the research (or additional information), which in the strategic decision tree in the industrial company is either the success (S), or the failure (E) (in the case of the decision nodes (2, 3 and 5), respectively either the success (S), or the mediocrity (M), or the loss (P) (for the first decision node);

S_j—nature states—high demand (M) or low demand (m), respectively favourable reaction (F) or unfavourable reaction (N) in our case;

$j = 1, 2, \ldots, m$ (the number of nature states – in our example $j = 2$ for each decision node)

Further, the procedure to calculate the conditioned probabilities for the first two decision nodes using the Bayes relation:

– for the decision node 1, the calculations are:

$$P(F/S) = \frac{P(S/F) \cdot P(F)}{P(S/F) \cdot P(F) + P(S/N) \cdot P(N)} = \frac{0.60 \cdot 0.40}{0.60 \cdot 0.40 + 0.10 \cdot 0.60} = 0.800$$

$$P(N/S) = \frac{P(S/N) \cdot P(N)}{P(S/N) \cdot P(N) + P(S/F) \cdot P(F)} = \frac{0.10 \cdot 0.60}{0.10 \cdot 0.60 + 0.60 \cdot 0.40} = 0.200$$

At this moment, we can also determine probability of success of the forecast performed in the research:

$$P(S) = P(S/F) \cdot P(F) + P(S/N) \cdot P(N)$$

As it is immediately observed, the expression of the success probability is the denominator itself of the two previous fractions, namey:

$$P(S) = 0.6 \cdot 0.4 + 0.1 \cdot 0.6 = 0.3000$$

In the case of the mediocrity of the portfolio of activities, we have:

$$P(F/M) = \frac{P(M/F) \cdot P(F)}{P(M/F) \cdot P(F) + P(M/N) \cdot P(N)} = \frac{0.20 \cdot 0.40}{0.20 \cdot 0.40 + 0.20 \cdot 0.60} = 0.400$$

$$P(N/M) = \frac{P(M/N) \cdot P(N)}{P(M/N) \cdot P(N) + P(M/F) \cdot P(F)} = \frac{0.20 \cdot 0.60}{0.20 \cdot 0.60 + 0.20 \cdot 0.40} = 0.600$$

Certainly, for P(N/M) there is also a simpler possibility of calculation based on the complementarity of the two probabilities – P(F/M) and P(N/M). Thus, knowing that the market reaction shall be either a favourable one, or an unfavourable one, we may write:

$$\mathrm{P(F/M)} + \mathrm{P(N/M)} = 1.000$$

where from:

$$\mathrm{P(N/M)} = 1 - \mathrm{P(F/M)} = 1 - 0.400 = 0.600$$

The probability that the portfolio of activities would be a mediocre one results immediately:

$$\mathrm{P(M)} = \mathrm{P(M/F)} \cdot \mathrm{P(F)} + \mathrm{P(M/N)} \cdot \mathrm{P(N)} = 0.200$$

Should the demand show a losing portfolio, based on the Bayes relation, the following probabilities are obtained:

$$\mathrm{P(F/P)} = \frac{\mathrm{P(P/F)} \cdot \mathrm{P(F)}}{\mathrm{P(P/F)} \cdot \mathrm{P(F)} + \mathrm{P(P/N)} \cdot \mathrm{P(N)}} = \frac{0.20 \cdot 0.40}{0.20 \cdot 0.40 + 0.70 \cdot 0.60} = 0.160$$

$$\mathrm{P(N/P)} = \frac{\mathrm{P(P/N)} \cdot \mathrm{P(N)}}{\mathrm{P(P/N)} \cdot \mathrm{P(N)} + \mathrm{P(P/F)} \cdot \mathrm{P(F)}} = \frac{0.70 \cdot 0.60}{0.70 \cdot 0.60 + 0.20 \cdot 0.40} = 0.840$$

The probability of success of the forecast indicating a losing portfolio is:

$$\mathrm{P(P)} = \mathrm{P(P/N)} \cdot \mathrm{P(N)} + \mathrm{P(P/F)} \cdot \mathrm{P(F)} = 0.70 \cdot 0.60 + 0.20 \cdot 0.40 = 0.500$$

Obviously,

$$\mathrm{P(S)} + \mathrm{P(M)} + \mathrm{P(N)} = 1.000;$$

– In the case of the decision node 2, the calculations are done similarly; the only difference is that there are two possible results of the market research for each strategic option: the success (S), respectively the failure (E).

  For the situation where the research forecasts the success, we have:

$$\mathrm{P(M/S)} = \frac{\mathrm{P(S/M)} \cdot \mathrm{P(M)}}{\mathrm{P(S/M)} \cdot \mathrm{P(M)} + \mathrm{P(S/m)} \cdot \mathrm{P(m)}} = \frac{0.8 \cdot 0.6}{0.8 \cdot 0.6 + 0.4 \cdot 0.4} = 0.750$$

$$\mathrm{P(m/S)} = 1 - \mathrm{P(M/S)} = 1 - 0.750 = 0.250$$

The probability of success of the research forecast is:

Table 11.35 The values of the reviewed probabilities according to Bayes and correspondence with the probabilities $p(S_{kij})$ (decision nodes 2, 3 and 5)

Decision node	Nature states	Reviewed probabilities					
		Success	Correspond. to $p(S_{kij})$	Value	Failure	Correspond. To $p(S_{kij})$	Value
2	M—High demand	P(M/S)	$p(S_{211})$	0.750	P (M/E)	$p(S_{221})$	0.333
	m—Low demand	P(m/S)	$p(S_{212})$	0.250	P (m/E)	$p(S_{222})$	0.667
3	M—High demand	P(S/M)	$p(S_{311})$	0.833	P (M/E)	$p(S_{321})$	0.769
	m—Low demand	P(m/S)	$p(S_{312})$	0.167	P (m/E)	$p(S_{322})$	0.231
5	M—High demand	P(M/S)	$p(S_{511})$	0.862	P (M/E)	$p(S_{521})$	0.400
	m—Low demand	P(m/S)	$p(S_{512})$	0.138	P (m/E)	$p(S_{522})$	0.600

$$P(S) = P(S/M) \cdot P(M) + P(S/m) \cdot P(m) = 0.64$$

Should the marketing research show a failure, the probabilities determined according to the Bayes rule are:

$$P(M/E) = \frac{P(E/M) \cdot P(M)}{P(E/M) \cdot P(M) + P(E/m) \cdot P(m)} = \frac{0.2 \cdot 0.6}{0.2 \cdot 0.6 + 0.6 \cdot 0.4} = 0.333$$

$$P(m/E) = 1 - P(M/E) = 1 - 0.333 = 0.667$$

The probability that the research would correctly forecast the failure is:

$$P(E) = P(E/M)\ P(M) + P(E/m)\ P(m) = 0.36$$

This verifies the complementarity with the probability of success:

$$P(S) + P(E) = 1.000$$

Performing the calculations to determine the previous probabilities in the other two decision nodes (with the numbers 3 and 5) is similar.

In Tables 11.35 and 11.36, the result of calculating the posterior probabilities is shown for the four decision nodes and the correspondence with the probabilities of the nature states $p(S_{kij})$ from the decision tree (we mention that the values of the reviewed probabilities are those which have been included directly in Table 11.32 of the values of the parameters of the decision tree).

AS previously discussed, solving the strategic decision tree requires the application of the "roll-back" process.

Therefore, the analysis starts from the last decision point:

Table 11.36 Reviewed Bayes probabilities and correspondences with the probabilities $p(S_{kij})$ (the decision node 1)

Decision node	Nature states	Reviewed probabilities								
		Successful portfolio	Correspond. to $p(S_{kij})$	Val.	Mediocre portf.	Correspond. to $p(S_{kij})$	Val.	Loosing portf.	Correspond. to $p(S_{kij})$	Val.
1	F—favourable attitude	P(F/S)	$p(S_{121})$	0.800	P(F/M)	$p(S_{111})$	0.400	P(F/P)	$p(S_{131})$	0.160
	N—Unfavourable attitude	P(N/S)	$p(S_{122})$	0.200	P(N/M)	$p(S_{112})$	0.600	P(N/P)	$p(S_{132})$	0.840

– decision point 5. We calculate the mathematic expectations of the two variants V_{51} and V_{52}:

$$Sm(V_{51}) = p(S_{511})\sum_{t=6}^{10}\frac{c_{511}(t)}{(1+d)^t} + p(S_{512})\sum_{t=6}^{10}\frac{c_{512}(t)}{(1+d)^t} - \frac{i_{51}}{(1+d)^5} =$$

$$= 0.862\left[\frac{1.2}{(1+0.15)^6} + \frac{1.2}{(1+0.15)^7} + \frac{1.2}{(1+0.15)^8} + \frac{1.2}{(1+0.15)^9} + \frac{1.2}{(1+0.15)^{10}}\right] -$$

$$-0.138\left[\frac{0.35}{(1+0.15)^6} + \frac{0.35}{(1+0.15)^7} + \frac{0.35}{(1+0.15)^8} + \frac{0.35}{(1+0.15)^9} + \frac{0.35}{(1+0.15)^{10}}\right] -$$

$$-\frac{3}{(1+0.15)^5} = 0.862\cdot 1.2\cdot 1.666 - 0.138\cdot 0.35 - 3\cdot 0.497 = 0.152 \text{ (millions\$)}$$

$$S_m(V_{52}) = p(S_{521})\sum_{t=6}^{10}\frac{c_{521}(t)}{(1+d)^t} + p(S_{522})\sum_{t=6}^{10}\frac{c_{522}(t)}{(1+d)^t} - \frac{i_{52}}{(1+d)^5} =$$

$$=0.400\left[\frac{0.60}{(1+0.15)^6} + \frac{0.60}{(1+0.15)^7} + \frac{0.60}{(1+0.15)^8} + \frac{0.60}{(1+0.15)^9} + \frac{0.60}{(1+0.15)^{10}}\right] -$$

$$-0.600\left[\frac{0.45}{(1+0.15)^6} + \frac{0.45}{(1+0.15)^7} + \frac{0.45}{(1+0.15)^8} + \frac{0.45}{(1+0.15)^9} + \frac{0.45}{(1+0.15)^{10}}\right] -$$

$$-\frac{5.5}{(1+0.15)^5} = 0.4\cdot 0.6\cdot 1.666 - 0.6\cdot 0.45\cdot 1.666 - 5.5\cdot 0.497 = -2.783 \text{ (millions\$)}$$

The optimal solution in the decision point 5 is that which satisfies the condition: $\max\{S_m(V_{51});\ S_m(V_{52})\} = \max\{0.152;\ -2.783\} = 0.152 \Rightarrow V_{opt}^* = V_{51}$ meaning "Status—Quo" represents the best option in the decision point 5;

– regarding the decision point 4, at first sight, it does not involve the need to perform any calculation, because V_{41} meaning ("Status—Quo") is the only strategic alternative available in that situation. However, determining the mathematical expectation $S_m(V_{41})$ is indispensable for correctly assessing the alternatives in the first decision node.

$$S_m(V_{41}) = p(S_{141})\sum_{t=6}^{10}\frac{c_{141}(t)}{(1+d)^t} - \frac{i_{41}}{(1+d)^5} =$$

$$=0.6\cdot 1.15\cdot\left[\frac{1}{(1+0.15)^6} + \frac{1}{(1+0.15)^7} + \frac{1}{(1+0.15)^8} + \frac{1}{(1+0.15)^9} + \frac{1}{(1+0.15)^{10}}\right] +$$

$$+\frac{1.8}{(1+0.15)^5} = 1.201 \text{ (millions\$)}$$

– decision point 3. The mathematic expectations of the two variants V_{31} and V_{32} are calculated:

$$S_m(V_{31}) = p(S_{311})\sum_{t=5}^{10}\frac{c_{311}(t)}{(1+d)^t} + p(S_{312})\sum_{t=5}^{10}\frac{c_{312}(t)}{(1+d)^t} - \frac{i_{31}}{(1+d)^4} =$$

$$= 0.833 \cdot 3.2\left[\frac{1}{(1+0.15)^5}+\frac{1}{(1+0.15)^6}+\frac{1}{(1+0.15)^7}+\frac{1}{(1+0.15)^8}+\right.$$

$$\left.+\frac{1}{(1+0.15)^9}+\frac{1}{(1+0.15)^{10}}\right] + 0.167 \cdot 0.45\left[\frac{1}{(1+0.15)^5}+\frac{1}{(1+0.15)^6}+\right.$$

$$\left.+\frac{1}{(1+0.15)^7}+\frac{1}{(1+0.15)^8}+\frac{1}{(1+0.15)^9}+\frac{1}{(1+0.15)^{10}}\right] = 5.931 \text{ (millions \$)}$$

$$S_m(V_{32}) = p(S_{321})\sum_{t=5}^{10}\frac{c_{321}(t)}{(1+d)^t} + p(S_{322})\sum_{t=5}^{10}\frac{c_{322}(t)}{(1+d)^t} - \frac{i_{32}}{(1+d)^4} =$$

$$= 0.769 \cdot 0.85\left[\frac{1}{(1+0.15)^5}+\frac{1}{(1+0.15)^6}+\frac{1}{(1+0.15)^7}+\frac{1}{(1+0.15)^8}+\right.$$

$$\left.+\frac{1}{(1+0.15)^9}+\frac{1}{(1+0.15)^{10}}\right] + 0.231 \cdot 0.40\left[\frac{1}{(1+0.15)^5}+\frac{1}{(1+0.15)^6}+\right.$$

$$\left.+\frac{1}{(1+0.15)^7}+\frac{1}{(1+0.15)^8}+\frac{1}{(1+0.15)^9}+\frac{1}{(1+0.15)^{10}}\right] - \frac{0,05}{(1+0.15)^4} =$$

$$= 1.586 \text{ (millions \$)}$$

$\max\{S_m(V_{31});\ S_m(V_{32})\} = 5.931 \Rightarrow V_{opt}^{*} = V_{31}$, meaning "quality improvement" applied both to the processes and products of the industrial company is the optimal variant in the decision point 3;

– decision point 2. The mathematic expectations of the variables V_{21} and V_{22} are:

$$S_m(V_{21}) = p(S_{211})\sum_{t=3}^{10}\frac{c_{211}(t)}{(1+d)^t} + p(S_{212})\sum_{t=3}^{10}\frac{c_{212}(t)}{(1+d)^t} - \frac{i_{21}}{(1+d)^2} =$$

$$= 0.750 \cdot 1\left[\frac{1}{(1+0.15)^3}+\frac{1}{(1+0.15)^4}+\ldots\ldots+\frac{1}{(1+0.15)^{10}}\right] -$$

$$-0.250 \cdot 0.2\left[\frac{1}{(1+0.15)^3}+\frac{1}{(1+0.15)^4}+\ldots\ldots+\frac{1}{(1+0.15)^{10}}\right] - \frac{0,10}{(1+0.15)^2} =$$

$$= 0.773 \text{ (millions \$)}$$

$$S_m(V_{22}) = p(S_{221})\sum_{t=3}^{10}\frac{c_{221}(t)}{(1+d)^t} + p(S_{222})\sum_{t=3}^{10}\frac{c_{222}(t)}{(1+d)^t} - \frac{i_{22}}{(1+d)^2} =$$

$$= 0.333 \cdot 0.80\left[\frac{1}{(1+0.15)^3} + \frac{1}{(1+0.15)^4} + \ldots\ldots + \frac{1}{(1+0.15)^{10}}\right] -$$

$$-0.667 \cdot 0.50\left[\frac{1}{(1+0.15)^3} + \frac{1}{(1+0.15)^4} + \ldots\ldots + \frac{1}{(1+0.15)^{10}}\right] - 0.08 \cdot 0.756 =$$

$$= -0.288 \ \text{(millions\$)}$$

$$\max\{S_m(V_{21});\ S_m(V_{22})\} = \max\{0.773;\ -0.288\} = 0.773 \text{ (millions \$)}$$

$$\Rightarrow V_{opt}^{\ *} = V_{21};$$

- decision point 1. In this case, it is necessary to calculate 3 mathematic expectations according to the three emerging strategic options: V_{11}—diversification; V_{12}—disinvestment; V_{13}—refocusing on service and consultancy activities. The calculation of the mathematic expectations in the original node must also take into account the mathematical expectations of the strategic alternatives selected in the other decision points:

$$S_m(V_{11}) = p(S_{111})\sum_{t=1}^{10}\frac{c_{111}(t)}{(1+d)^t} + \left[S_m(V_{31}) + p(S_{112})\sum_{t=1}^{3}\frac{c_{112}(t)}{(1+d)^t} - i_{11}\right] =$$

$$= 0.4 \cdot 0.9\left[\frac{1}{(1+0.15)^1} + \frac{1}{(1+0.15)^2} + \ldots\ldots\ldots + \frac{1}{(1+0.15)^{10}}\right] +$$

$$+5.931 - 0.6 \cdot 0.25\left[\frac{1}{(1+0.15)^1} + \frac{1}{(1+0.15)^2} + \frac{1}{(1+0.15)^3}\right] - 0.4 =$$

$$= 6.990 \ \text{(millions\$)}$$

$$S_m(V_{12}) = p(S_{112})\sum_{t=1}^{10}\frac{c_{121}(t)}{(1+d)^t} + \left[S_m(V_{21}) + p(S_{122})\sum_{t=1}^{3}\frac{c_{122}(t)}{(1+d)^t} - i_{12}\right] =$$

$$= 0.8 \cdot 0.35\left[\frac{1}{(1+0.15)^1} + \frac{1}{(1+0.15)^2} + \ldots\ldots\ldots + \frac{1}{(1+0.15)^{10}}\right] +$$

$$+0.773 - 0.2 \cdot 0.15\left[\frac{1}{(1+0.15)^1} + \frac{1}{(1+0.15)^2} + \frac{1}{(1+0.15)^3}\right] - 0 =$$

$$= 2.109 \ \text{(millions \$)}$$

$$S_m(V_{13}) = \left[S_m(V_{41}) + p(S_{131})\sum_{t=1}^{5}\frac{c_{131}(t)}{(1+d)^t}\right] +$$

$$+\left[S_m(V_{51}) + p(S_{132})\sum_{t=1}^{5}\frac{c_{132}(t)}{(1+d)^t} - i_{13}\right] =$$

$$= 1.201 + 0.16 \cdot 0.9\left[\frac{1}{(1+0.15)^1} + \frac{1}{(1+0.15)^2} + \ldots\ldots\ldots + \frac{1}{(1+0.15)^5}\right] +$$

$$+0.152 - 0.84 \cdot 0.25\left[\frac{1}{(1+0.15)^1} + \frac{1}{(1+0.15)^2} + \ldots\ldots\ldots + \frac{1}{(1+0.15)^5}\right] - 0.15 =$$

$$= 0.982 \text{ (millions\$)}$$

$$\max\{S_m(V_{11});\ S_m(V_{12});\ S_m(V_{13})\} = \max\{6.990;\ 2.190;\ 0.982\} =$$
$$= 6.990 \text{ (millions \$)} \Rightarrow V_{opt}{}^* = V_{51}$$

Therefore, the optimal strategy corresponds to the following sequence of strategic decisions: ($V_{11}{}^*$, $V_{31}{}^*$) meaning that it is currently recommended to apply the variant of diversification by assimilating into manufacture the machines for industrial and civil constructions. After 4 years (2007), if the demand is at low levels, the strategic option $V_{31}{}^*$ is chosen, which binds the intervention of company's specialists for the implementation of the total quality management, aiming to achieve both the objective of reinforcing the current market segments and that of expansion on new markets (preferably external markets) by permanently improving the quality. By the special attention given to the quality problems in the same stage, managers shall try to counteract the possible failures which could occur after starting with variant $V_{11}{}^*$ (it should not be omitted that the rapid implementation of diversification is a strategic option accompanied by an inevitable risk margin).

On the contrary, should an increasing tendency of the demand be noticed, the industrial company shall develop on the strategic alternative coordinates which it started in the initial point with.

This is actually the company's most convenient path, which would not guarantee just the overcome of the current critical situation, but also the substantial strengths of the future performances. In any case, the preference for variant V_{11} in the original decision point involved the greatest contribution of net incomes amounting 6.99 millions $ achieved in those 10 years of the period which the strategy has been developed for. Moreover, the mathematical expectation of the greatest incomes may be interpreted as and argument of minimising the risk of reorganising the productive apparatus of the industrial company, by the chosen strategic alternative.

Obviously, solving the strategic decision problems may also be done by means of the computer. Developing a computer software to analyse and assess the strategic decision trees would enable both the manifestation of the sliding feature of the strategy (by regularly examining the validity of the assumptions which determined its adoption and by the possibility to insert into the equation the differences occurred between predictions and result) and the improvement of the computer system attached to the strategic component of the company's management. In the same context, the software packages are not to be neglected either, which determine the so-called "value of perfect information", knowing that the acquisition of additional information involves certain increases of costs (the economic effect of the strategic variant shown by a "traditional" tree with the strategic solution acquired by using the BAYES reviewed probabilities, additionally taking into account the efforts involved in the marketing researches). Further, the computer software for optimising the decision to adopt the optimal variant of the reorganisation strategy is presented, a reorganisation by means of the decision tree. The software has been prepared in the C++ and has a high degree of generality, because it enables the resolution of any decisional situation of choosing the optimal strategy, regardless of the complexity of the actual construction of the decision tree.

Software for determining the optimal variant for the strategic decision tree

```
#include <stdio.h>
#include <conio.h>
#include <stdlib.h>
#include<math.h>
#include<windows.h>
typedef struct node {
      int n, tip,t,pr;
      double c,p,i,vm,sm;
      char name[20];
      node *oo[10],*par;
      };
node *a;
char *dec[20],*sep[20],*cons[20],*re;
int j=0,k=0,h=0,T;
double d;
double put(double x,int y)
{int i;
double p;
p=1;
for(i=1;i<=y;i++)
{p=p*x;printf("put=%d",i);}
return p;
}
void intro(node *x)
{int i;
x->p=0;x->c=0;x->vm=0;x->sm=0;
printf("Insert the node name:");
scanf("%s",x->name);
x->pr=0;
do{
printf("Insert node type(0-decision/1-separation/2-consec):");
scanf("%d",&x->tip);
```

```
}while((x->tip!=1)&&(x->tip!=0)&&(x->tip!=2));
      switch(x->tip)
      {
         case 0:dec[j]=x->name;j++;
            printf("Insert time moment t:");scanf("%d",&x->t);
         break;
         case 1:sep[k]=x->name;k++;
         break;
         case 2:cons[h]=x->name;h++;x->n=0;x->pr=1;
         break;
      };
if(x->par!=NULL)
      {
      switch(x->par->tip)
      {
      case 0:printf("Insert investment effort:");scanf("%s",re);
         x->i=atof(re);
      break;
      case 1:printf("Insert probability:");scanf("%s",re);
         x->p=atof(re);
      printf("Insert the forecast result:");scanf("%s",re);
         x->c=atof(re);
      break;
      }
      }
if(x->tip!=2){
printf("Insert no. of possible decisions:");scanf("%d",&x->n);
for(i=0;i<(x->n);i++)
         {
         x->oo[i]=(nod *)malloc(sizeof(nod));
         x->oo[i]->par=x;
         printf("Insert data for node %d, node %s:\n",i,x->name);
         intro(x->oo[i]);
         }
      }
}
void viz(node *x)
{
int i;
printf("Name:%s, type %d, no. of variants:%d\n, vm=%f, p=%f, sm=%f,
c=%f,pr=%d\n",x->name,x->tip,x->n,x->vm,x->p,x->sm,x->c,x->pr);
for(i=0;i<x->n;i++)
viz(x->oo[i]);
}
```

```
void prel(node *x)
{
int i,ii,kk=0;
double v[20],s,s1;
for(i=0;i<x->n;i++)
   if(x->oo[i]->pr!=1) kk=1;
if(kk==0){
switch(x->tip)
{
case 0: for(i=0;i<x->n;i++)
     {v[i]=x->oo[i]->vm;
     }
     x->sm=v[0];
     for(i=0;i<x->n;i++)
     {if(x->sm<v[i]){x->sm=v[i];};}
break;
case 1:  s=0;
     for(i=0;i<x->n;i++)
     {s1=0;printf("j=%d",i);
     for(ii=x->par->t+1;ii<=T;ii++)
     {s1=s1+x->oo[i]->c/put((1+d),ii);printf("t=%d",ii);}
     s1=s1*x->oo[i]->p;
     s=s+s1;
     }
     x->vm=s-x->i/put((1+d),x->par->t);
break;
}x->pr=1;
}
else {for(i=0;i<x->n;i++)prel(x->oo[i]);}
}
void main()
{
clrscr();
printf("Insert forecast scope T:");scanf("%d",&T);
printf("Insert interest rate:");scanf("%s",re);d=atof(re);
a=(nod *)malloc(sizeof(nod));
a->par=NULL;
//clrscr();
intro(a);
prel(a);prel(a);
viz(a);
}
```

References

Berge C (1992) Programmes, jeux et reseaux de transport. Dunod, Paris
Burgh J (2006) Enterpreneurship. John Wiley, New York
Certo S (2004) Modern management. Allyn & Bacon, Boston
Fischer I (1972) The marking of index numbers. Hougthon Mifflin, Boston
Gelbaum B (1997) Linear and convex programming. Mc Graw Hill, New York
Ghild J (2004) Organization: A guide to problems and practices. Harper & Row, London
Graves R (1994) Parametric linear programming. Mc Graw Hill, New York
Hall RH (2007) Organizations: structures, processes and outcomes. Prentice-Hall, Englewood Cliffs, New Jersey
Kipnis D (1990) Technology and power. Springer, New York
Lawley DN (1993) Factor analysis as a statistical method. Butterwerths, London
Mintzberg H (2004) The risk and fall of strategic planning. Prentice Hall, New York
von Neumann J, Morgenstern O (1984) Theory of games and economic behavior. Prentice-Hall, New York
Owen G (2002) Theory of games. McGraw Hill, New Jersey
Schatteles T (1969) Jocuri strategice şi analiză economică. Editura Ştiinţifică, Bucureşti
Zadeh LA (1997) The roles of fuzzy logic and soft computing in the conception, design and development of intelligent systems. In: Nwana HS, Azarmi N (eds) Software agents and soft computing: Towards enhancing machine intelligence. Springer, Heidelberg, pp 183–190

Chapter 12
Models Used in Stock Management

12.1 Stock Management: Theoretical Approaches

Smoothly performing the activities within the enterprises requires the provision of appropriate quantities of materials, such as: raw materials, fuel, spare parts, semi-finished products of various types, etc.

Because the consumption of resources is basically continuous, and the supply is usually done at certain moments, it is necessary to determine the quantities of material resources that must be stored between two moments of successive resupply, to ensure the continuity of the production process.

Through stock management, it is aimed to substantiate the decisions on the consumption—supply management. Within the stock management, an important role is that to establish the level of stocks in various resources and the times when the resupply is performed, based on economical-mathematical models.

Characteristic of these stock models is that the economic phenomenon analysed is described by a function of the total cost of storage $F(Q_s)$ where Q_s is the volume of raw materials, finished products, etc. that must exist in the enterprise at different times. By determining the extreme value of the function $F(Q_s)$, the stock q_{s0} results, which minimises this function. Models from this class have applications in various fields of activity, such as industrial production, movement of goods, financial operations, etc.

We can say that a stock model is a tool by means of which the volume of funds that is immobilised in the storage process is minimised and at the same time, the continuity of the production or marketing process is ensured. It should be noted that in the applications referring to satisfying consumers' demand there may be concern on maximising the net income resulting from marketing the products.

The main elements intervening in stock management are: the demand for products noted with *C*, which may be fixed or random; the delivery period noted with *t*, which can also be deterministic, can depend on the volume of the supply order or may be random; stock level. Depending on the actual conditions

I.C. Dima, M. Man, *Modelling and Simulation in Management*, Contributions to Management Science, DOI 10.1007/978-3-319-16592-9_12

characterising the phenomenon analysed, the following stock levels can be taken into account: maximum level, limit storage capacity, minimum level, alarm level, resupply (safety) level; the costs incurred in the storage models which are: the storage cost *c* is calculated by the unit of product stored in unit of time and includes the expenses related to storing the materials or products: expenses for storage, maintenance, repairs, the value of perishable products during storage, immobilisation of funds, etc.; the launching cost c_l is the administrative expenses related to the operation of supply; the penalty cost c_p, which is calculated in the case of models that enable the outage and is assessed by the net production achieved due to the absence of stock (losses by reducing the production), fines, additional expenses to satisfy the demand, etc.

It may be that in some cases, the launching and storage costs are negligible in which case we include the following elements: a loss c_1 in stored products when the demand *C* is lower than the stock *S*; an additional stock c_2 for special supply when the demand is higher than the stock *S*; the volume of the supply order n, which can be constant or variable depending on a management law we adopt; the data which the supply is done at noted with *t*, as well as the management periods (the resupply cycle) which we note with *T*.

In their turn, these elements can be constant or variable, their variation following a certain management rule that we adopt.

The evolution of the stock level during a period *T* for each individual product is represented as a function in scale, decreasing over time. For theoretical reasons, it is convenient to replace the chart represented by a straight line (in simple cases) or by a generally descending curve, which would give us the image of the demand variation over time, expressed analytically, which is a more convenient form of expression (Fig. 12.1). Examples of stock variation in time over a period *T* are shown below:

The following cases are distinguished in the case of fixed period management: the demand is constant, the supply occurs instantaneously and in constant quantities *n*; there is no stock outage; the demand is variable, deterministic or random.

The supply is done in variable quantities n_i, so that the stock will reach the maximum level at the end of each period, and the supply will require a certain constant time *t*.

The quantities n_i must be estimated at the times t_i by extrapolating the consumption straight line or curve. In general, in such models, the level coincides with the limit storage capacity (Fig. 12.2).

Figure 12.3 shows that we have a model with outage, where the stock becomes null at some point. The alarm (warning) level is the threshold under which an outage can occur with a negligible probability.

In the case of management with a variable supplying period, we distinguish two situations: the supply is done through fixed quantities Q_i, so that the stock will reach the maximum level at the end of each period, a certain constant time *t* being required (for the supply).

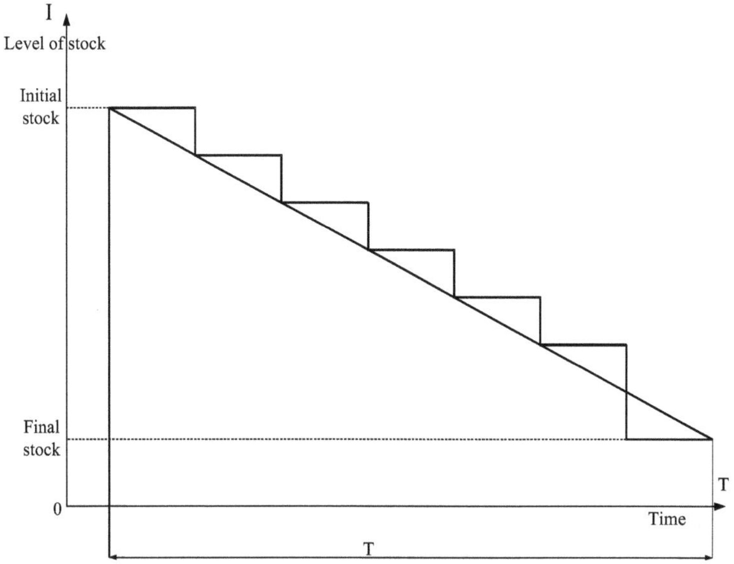

Fig. 12.1 Graphic representation of a stock variation in time

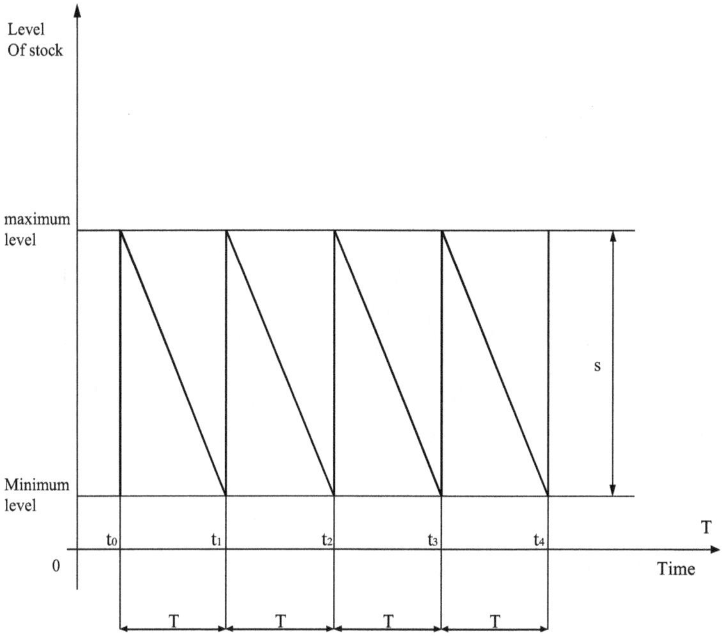

Fig. 12.2 Resupply in fixed quantities at constant time intervals

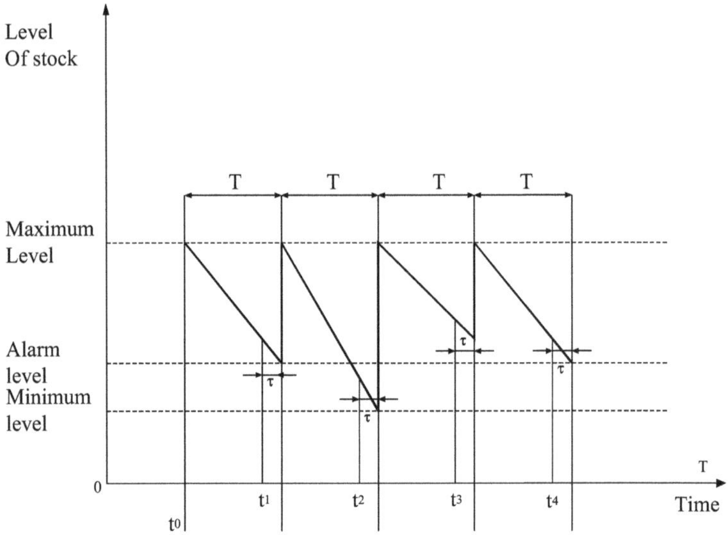

Fig. 12.3 Resupply with outage

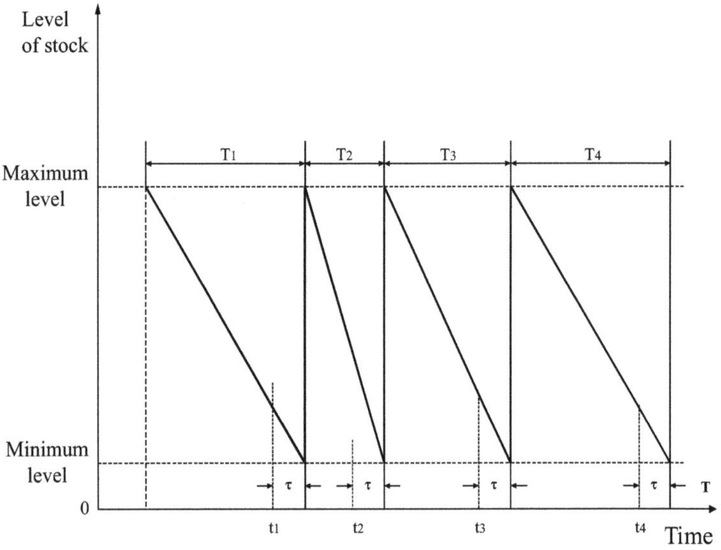

Fig. 12.4 Resupply in a variable period

The dates t_i when the orders are launched must be determined by extrapolating the consumption straight line or curve. Such a model is graphically shown in Fig. 12.4.

When the demand is variable, deterministic or random, the supply is done through fixed quantities and requires a certain constant time since launching the

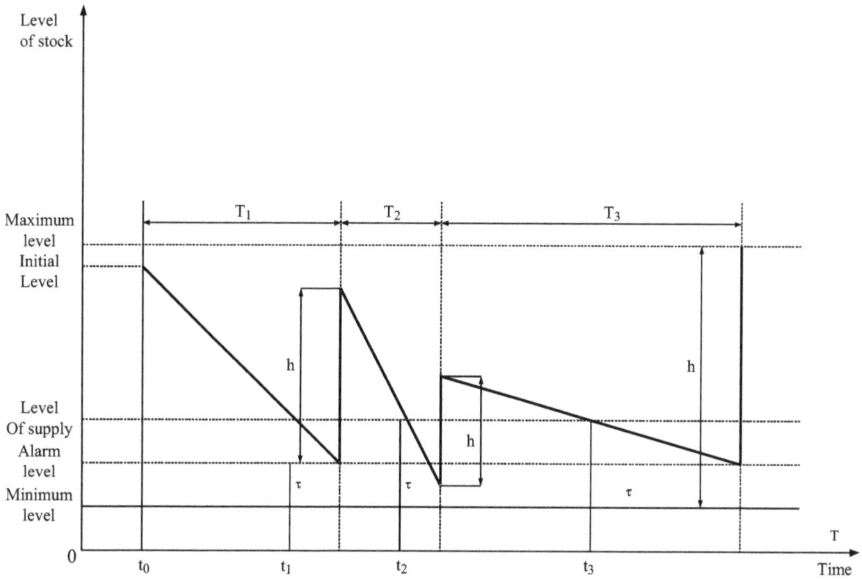

Fig. 12.5 Resupply with variable demand

order. The decision to elaborate the order is taken when the stock reaches a certain conveniently chosen level which we shall call the resupply level, which is above the alarm level. Graphically, this model looks as in Fig. 12.5.

This method of management provides the advantage of a convenient management, but has the disadvantage that it does not guarantee the absence of outages with a sufficient probability.

12.2 The Inversion of a System of Stochastic Equations

In stochastic models, a special problem is that of using the matrix calculation and implicitly the invertible matrix to solve the systems of equations.

Let us take for example a complex model, namely that of Leontief type:

$$(E - A)X - GV = 0, \tag{12.1}$$

where:

G may be considered a matrix that defines way of national income distribution and the structure of consumer goods production;

V is the vector of the national income produced in the "*n*" branches.

So that

$$GV = Y. \tag{12.2}$$

We shall not go into analytically dealing with this problem and we shall only be interested in the mathematical characteristics of the model. We know that in any circumstance the following operations are allowed:

$$X = (E - A)^{-1}GV \tag{12.3}$$

$$V = G^{-1}(E - A)X. \tag{12.4}$$

We now omit that this is a Leontief model and we assume there is another system of variables, which analogous structure relationships are established between (meaning expressible with the same type of equations). By using an established notation, we consider two vectors of "Y" and "Z" variables and we say there is the following structural relationship between them:

$$BY + \Gamma Z = 0, \tag{12.5}$$

which is analogous to the Leontief relationship.

If "Y" includes "*k*" elements and "Z" consists of "*r*" elements, then "B" is a matrix of k*k elements and "Γ" a matrix of k*r elements, then the two matrixes include the system coefficients.

We not admit hypothetically a certain relation of "causality" (just as artificial as most of the causal relations considered by the statistics) between the "k" of "y_i" and the "r" of "z_i". We thus say that the variables "z_i" determine (cause) the sizes of the variables "y_i", which interest us directly. Therefore we shall name the exogenous variables as "z_i", and the endogenous variables of the system (12.5) as "y_i". Thus, the vector "Y" will be "explained" by the vector "Γ" and we can say that:

$$Y = -B^{-1}\Gamma Z. \tag{12.6}$$

This is a perfectly determined causal system.

We are not interested to create an analogous system with (12.6) from statistical data. We want to estimate the matrices "B" and "Γ", but we only have the series of "y" and "z" (however sufficient). At first glance, the simplest solution would be to successively estimate "k" equations $y_i = f(z_1, z_2, \ldots z_i)$ by regression, obtaining as result a matrix

$$G = \begin{vmatrix} g_{01} & g_{11} & g_{21} & \cdots & g_{r1} \\ g_{02} & g_{12} & g_{22} & \cdots & g_{r2} \\ \vdots & \vdots & \vdots & & \vdots \\ g_{0r} & g_{1r} & g_{2r} & \cdots & g_{rr} \end{vmatrix} \tag{12.7}$$

This raises two questions:

Is this really true?

$$-B^{-1}\Gamma = G \tag{12.8}$$

And what if "G" is known, how do we calculate "B" and "Γ" from it.

The answer to the first question is analogous to the one given for the case with a single equation.

In the stochastic case, it is required to change the hypothesis $BY + \Gamma Z = 0$ and we shall say that:

$$BY + \Gamma Z = u, \tag{12.9}$$

where u is a stochastic vector of "k" elements.

That being so, after the "*k*" adjustments, we actually get the following system:

$$Y = GZ + U, \tag{12.10}$$

where we should have

$$G = -B^{-1}\Gamma \, \text{and} \, U = B^{-1}u, \tag{12.11}$$

if the stochastic functions were reversible, but we saw they were not.

As in the case with a single equations, the problem is that questions arise: how big is the deformation caused by reversal?; and what is "endogenous" or "exogenous"? In such cases, we must take for granted certain deformations and leave our additional assessments to the experience and common sense judgement.

At the second question on converting "G" into "Γ" and "B", there are—where there are—several answers, according to some additional characteristics of the system.

All these however involve the clarification of the problem of simultaneously assessing several equations.

12.3 Models Used in the Management of Stocks

In practice, as it happens otherwise in any kind of operational research problem, the studied case is not always reduced to a classical model and therefore, a special study must be done, taking into account the particularities of the restrictions actually intervening in the model considered. Dynamic programming provides a particularly useful mathematical tool in solving the storage problems, which are essentially sequential in their nature.

The following models are known:

– *management model with fixed period and constant demand*, when there is no outage, we have no penalty expenses and therefore, only expenses related to launching the order and storage expenses intervene. We assume the time interval

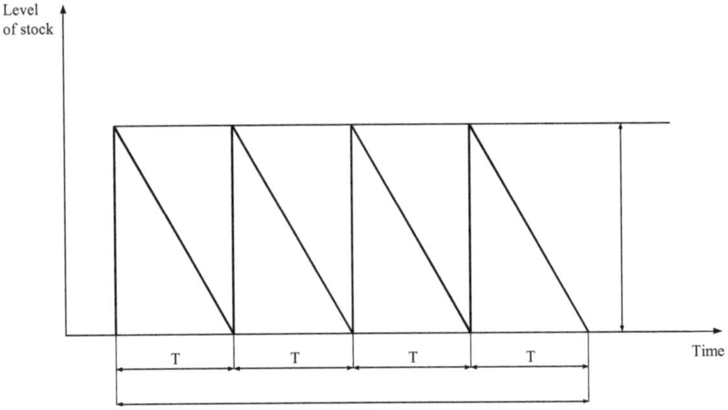

Fig. 12.6 Graphic representation of the resupply at fixed periods with constant demand

θ when the management and the total demand *N* of products is done on this time interval (Fig. 12.6). Under these conditions, it is required to determine the quantity *Qi* with which the periodical supply is done after each period of time *T*, which must be determined so that the total cost for launching the orders and for storage for all *N* products would be minimum (in the absence of penalties). As the demand is constant and the period is fixed, we can write the equality:

$$\frac{N}{n} = \frac{Q}{T} \tag{12.12}$$

where from:

$$T = \frac{n \cdot Q}{N} \tag{12.13}$$

On the other hand, the cost corresponding to a single period (launching expenses, whereto storage expenses are added to) are:

$$c_l + \frac{1}{2} \cdot n \cdot T \cdot c_s \tag{12.14}$$

As there are $\frac{N}{n}$ periods, the following total cost results for the entire interval θ of management, which is:

$$F(n) = \left(c_l + \frac{1}{2} \cdot n \cdot T \cdot c_s\right) \cdot \frac{N}{n} = \frac{N \cdot c_l}{n} + \frac{\theta \cdot c_s}{2} \cdot n \tag{12.15}$$

If we noted with $F_l(n)$ the total launching expenses, with $F_s(n)$ the total storage expenses, with n_0 and with F_0 the optimal amount of an order and

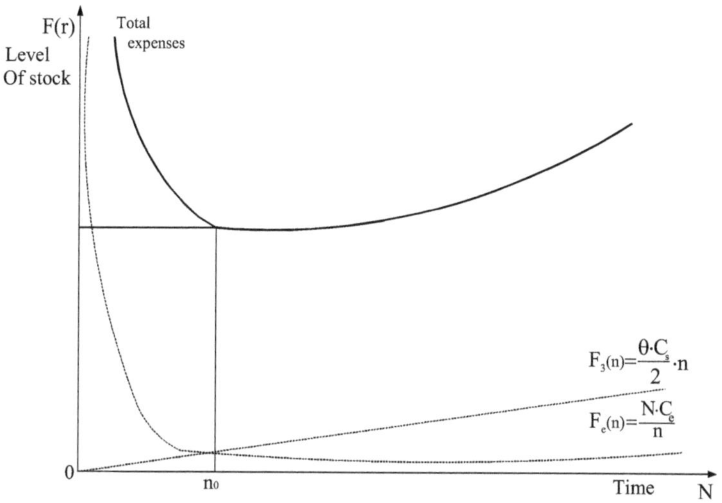

Fig. 12.7 Resupply at fixed period and constant demand

respectively the minimum expenses, then the model considered can be graphically represented as in Fig. 12.7.

As $F_s(n) \cdot F_l(n) =$ is constant, the function F(n) reaches the minimum when $F_l(n) = F_s(n)$ and the following equality results from here:

$$\frac{\theta \cdot c_s}{2} \cdot n = \frac{N \cdot c_l}{n} \text{ meaning } n^2 = \frac{2 \cdot N \cdot c_l}{\theta \cdot c_s} \tag{12.16}$$

And therefore:

$$n_0 = \sqrt{\frac{2 \cdot N \cdot c_l}{\theta \cdot c_s}} \tag{12.17}$$

It is immediately deduced that:

$$T_0 = \frac{n_0 \cdot \theta}{N} = \sqrt{\frac{2 \cdot \theta \cdot c_l}{N \cdot c_s}} \tag{12.18}$$

and:

$$F_0 = F(n_0) = \frac{N \cdot c_l}{\sqrt{\frac{2 \cdot N \cdot c_l}{\theta \cdot c_s}}} + \frac{\theta \cdot c_s}{2} \cdot \sqrt{\frac{2 \cdot N \cdot c_l}{\theta \cdot c_s}} = \sqrt{2 \cdot N \cdot \theta \cdot c_l \cdot c_s} \tag{12.19}$$

An annual (360 days) demand of 200 t of raw materials is considered for an enterprise. The cost for launching an order is of 720 m.u., and the unit cost of

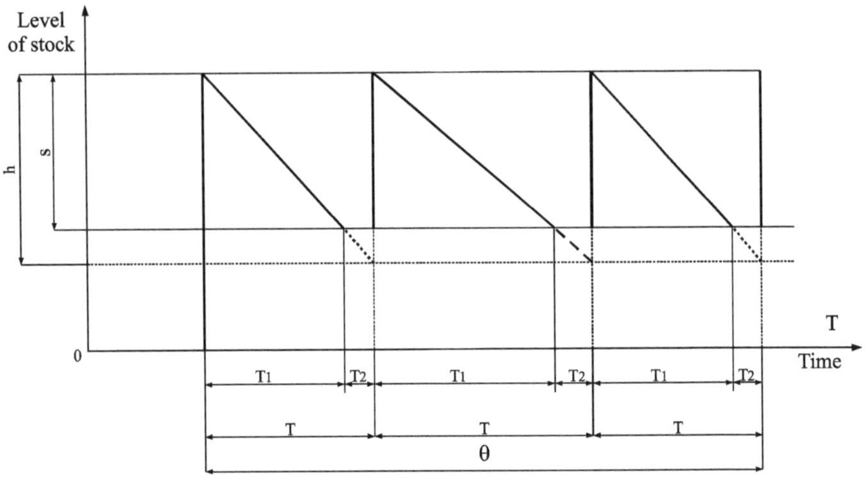

Fig. 12.8 Resupply at fixed periods, constant demand with stock outage possibility

storage for 1 t of raw materials is of 2 m.u. If the consumption is even, the supply is done in equal quantities at equal time intervals and the absence of raw materials in the warehouse is not allowed, the following calculation is required: the optimal volume of an order; the optimal number of supplies; the optimal period and the optimal cost of supply.

By using the previous calculation formulas, it results: the optimal volume of an order 20 t; the optimal number of supplies 10; the optimal period of supply 36 days; the optimal cost of supply will be 14,400 m.u.;

– *model of fixed period management and constant demand with possibilities of outage*, takes into account the fact that the stock outage phenomenon occurs when a demand cannot be satisfied. The penalty cost c_p is attached to this lack of stock and is estimated by the product unit during the unit of time. We shall assume what launching expenses c_l are the same for each period *T*. Schematically, this situation appears as in Fig. 12.8.

Throughout a duration T_1 of each period *T*, the level is sufficient to satisfy the demand, during the duration $T_2 = T - T_1$ we have a shortage of products until the end of the period *T* when a penalty is paid c_p for each item by the unit of time.

In this way, the following expenses corresponding to a period *T* are calculated:

$$\text{storage expenses}: \frac{1}{2} \cdot s \cdot T_1 \cdot c_s; \tag{12.20}$$

$$\text{launching expenses}: c_l; \tag{12.21}$$

$$\text{penalty expenses}: \frac{1}{2} \cdot (n - s) \cdot T_2 \cdot c_p \tag{12.22}$$

The cost per the time interval θ on which the management is considered will be:

$$F(n,s) = \left[\frac{1}{2} \cdot s \cdot T_1 \cdot c_s + c_l + \frac{1}{2} \cdot (n-s) \cdot T_2 \cdot c_p\right] \cdot \frac{N}{n} \tag{12.23}$$

As

$$\frac{N}{n} = \frac{\theta}{T} \tag{12.24}$$

$$\frac{s}{n} = \frac{T_1}{T}; \quad \frac{T_2}{T} = \frac{n-s}{n} \tag{12.25}$$

It results that we can write:

$$\begin{aligned}(n,s) &= \left[\frac{1}{2} \cdot s^2 \cdot \frac{T}{n} \cdot c_s + c_l + \frac{1}{2} \cdot (n-s)^2 \cdot \frac{T}{n} \cdot c_p\right] \cdot \frac{N}{n} = \\ &\frac{1}{2} \cdot \left[\frac{s^2 \cdot \theta \cdot c_s}{n} + \frac{N}{n} \cdot c_l + \frac{(n-s)^2 \cdot \theta \cdot c_p}{2 \cdot n}\right]\end{aligned} \tag{12.26}$$

Thus, the minimum of the function F(n, s) is reached for the values n_0 and s_0, the solutions of equation system (it has been assumed that the demand is continuous):

$$\left\{\begin{aligned}&-\frac{s^2 \cdot \theta \cdot c_s}{2 \cdot n^2} - \frac{N \cdot c_l}{n^2} + \frac{\theta \cdot c_p}{2} \cdot \frac{2 \cdot n \cdot (n-s) - (n-s)^2}{n^2} = 0 \\ &\frac{s \cdot \theta \cdot c_s}{n} - \frac{2 \cdot (n-s) \cdot \theta \cdot c_p}{2 \cdot n} = 0\end{aligned}\right\} \tag{12.27}$$

or

$$\left\{\begin{aligned}&\theta \cdot c_p = 2 \cdot N \cdot c_l + s^2 \cdot \theta \cdot (c_s + c_p) \\ &s \cdot \theta \cdot (c_s + c_p) - n \cdot \theta \cdot c_p\end{aligned}\right\} \tag{12.28}$$

where from it results:

$$s = n \cdot \frac{c_p}{c_s + c_p} \tag{12.29}$$

$$\theta \cdot c_p \cdot n^2 \cdot \left(1 - \frac{c_p}{c_s + c_p}\right) = c \cdot N \cdot c_l \tag{12.30}$$

The quantity

$$\rho = \frac{c_p}{c_s + c_p} \tag{12.31}$$

is called the intensity of the outage or unavailability factor.

meaning:

$$n^2 = \frac{2 \cdot N \cdot c_1}{\theta \cdot c_s} \cdot \frac{c_s + c_p}{c_p} \tag{12.32}$$

and therefore:

$$n_0 = \sqrt{2 \cdot \frac{N \cdot c_1}{\theta \cdot c_s} \cdot \sqrt{\frac{c_s + c_p}{c_p}}} \tag{12.33}$$

and from here it results that:

$$s_0 = n_0 \frac{c_p}{c_s + c_p} = \sqrt{2 \frac{Nc_1}{\theta c_s} \cdot \sqrt{\frac{c_p}{c_s + c_p}}} \tag{12.34}$$

Then we calculate the size of the optimal period:

$$T_0 = n_0 \cdot \frac{\theta}{N} = \frac{\theta}{N} \cdot \sqrt{2 \cdot \frac{N \cdot c_1}{\theta \cdot c_s} \cdot \sqrt{\frac{c_s + c_p}{c_p}}} = \sqrt{2 \cdot \frac{\theta \cdot c_1}{N \cdot c_s} \cdot \sqrt{\frac{c_s + c_p}{c_p}}} \tag{12.35}$$

and

$$\begin{aligned} P_0 &= \frac{1}{2} \cdot \frac{s_0^2 \cdot \theta \cdot c_0^s}{n_0} + \frac{N \cdot c_1}{n_0} + \frac{(n_0 - s_0)^2 \cdot \theta \cdot c_p}{2 \cdot n_0} \\ &= \sqrt{2 \cdot N \cdot \theta \cdot c_s \cdot c_1 \cdot \sqrt{\frac{c_s + c_p}{c_p}}} \end{aligned} \tag{12.36}$$

Let us consider that during 1 year (360 days) the storage of products according to the model above is organised for three products P_1, P_2, P_3 which are products in the quantities 400 t, 2,500 t, 900 t, which incur supply costs of 432 m.u., 675 m.u., 300 m.u. and storage costs of 4.5 m.u., 2 m.u., 8 m.u.

To establish the optimal elements of the previously shown storage model.

By using the formulas above, it results that: the storage of products will be done in the quantities 16 t, 75 t, 15 t; the number of supplies will be 25, 100/3, 60; the duration in which the supply is done 12 days, 9 days, 5 days; the storage cost 21,600 m.u., 45,000 m.u., 3,600 m.u.; total cost 102,600 m.u.;

- *model of determined management for a single product applicable to a production cycle for a given period*, it implies that during a time period *T* the demand *C* of products must be satisfied with a constant intensity

$$c = \frac{C}{T} \tag{12.37}$$

We assume that the production rhythm r is also constant and $r > c$, and the orders which have not been satisfied remain the records to be satisfied subsequently.

Be: c_s, the cost of storage of a product unit in the unit of time; c_p, the penalty cost by unit of product and time; c_1, launching expenses (the expenses of a production cycle); q, the quantity of products made during a production cycle; F, average expenses by the unit of time.

Then, following the production activity and consumption of products manufactured, starting from a given moment, a period of time T_1 the considered product is manufactured and consumed. Given that the production rhythm is higher than the consumption intensity after the period of time T_1, a stock S is achieved, the production stops and the consumption is satisfied for a period of time T_2 from this stock until it is exhausted.

A period of time T_3 begins, when a shortage of products is observed, it is succeeded to resume the production and during the period of time T_4, it is succeeded to satisfy the previously registered and submitted demands, and afterwards we start achieving again the stock S, therefore we start a new production and consumption cycle.

Schematically, this situation is shown in Fig. 12.9.

Therefore, at the beginning the stock is zero and after that it grows as it is produced, until it reaches the level S (the period of time T_1), then the production ceases, and following the consumption, the stock level drops until it reaches the value zero (period of time T_2). Further, the product orders can no longer be satisfied and a shortage is registered (period of time T_3) until the deficit s accumulates, afterwards production starts again, the arrears are gradually eliminated, so that after a period of time T_4, they are completed eliminated and

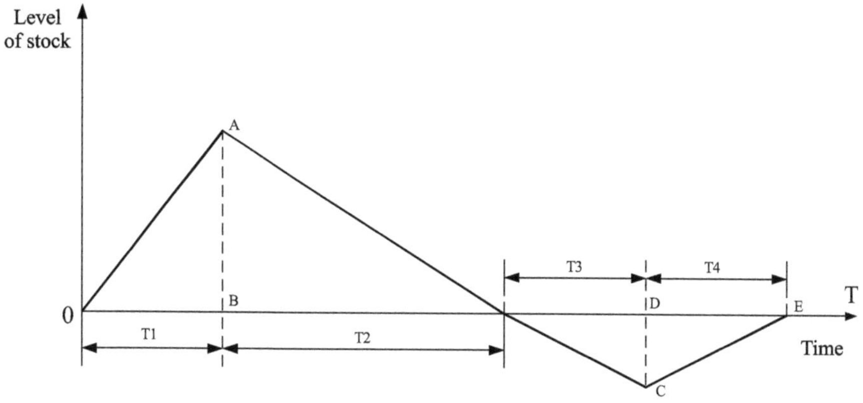

Fig. 12.9 Resupply under the constant intensity conditions

accumulations start to appear again. Therefore, after a period of time $T_1 + T_2 + T_3 + T_4$, the production cycle is resumed again.

Throughout the period of time $T_1 + T_2 + T_3 + T_4$, we have the following expenses:

Storage expenses throughout the period of time $T_1 + T_2$ and they are:

$$c_s = \frac{S \cdot (T_1 + T_2)}{2} \tag{12.38}$$

Penalty expenses throughout the period of time $T_3 + T_4$ and they are:

$$c_p = \frac{S \cdot (T_3 + T_4)}{2} \tag{12.39}$$

Launching expenses are fixed expenses for the entire period, c_1.

Then follows the calculation of average expenses by the unit of time, which are:

$$F(s, S, T_1, T_2, T_3.T_4) = \frac{\frac{1}{2} \cdot c_s \cdot S \cdot (T_1 + T_2) + c_p \cdot s \cdot (T_1 + T_2) + c_1}{T_1 + T_2 + T_3 + T_4} \tag{12.40}$$

The function average expenses by the unit of time depends at a first glance on six variables, but not all variables are independent.

Indeed, during the period of time T_1 the quantity of $r \cdot T_1$ products is produced, so that the maximum stock S is equal to:

$$S = T_2 \cdot (r - u) \tag{12.41}$$

As during the period T_2 all stored products are consumed, it results that $S = T_2 \cdot u$ and therefore we can write:

$$T_1 = \frac{S}{r - u} = \frac{T_2 \cdot u}{r - u} \tag{12.42}$$

During the period T_3 the arrears with the intensity c accumulate, so that $S = T_3 \cdot c$, and during the period T_4 all arrears are liquidated, so that $s = T_4 \cdot (r - c)$ and therefore here:

$$T_4 = \frac{s}{r - c} = \frac{T_3 \cdot c}{r - c} \tag{12.43}$$

By including S, T_1, s, T_4 into $F(s, S, T_1, T_2, T_3, T_4)$ we get:

$$F(T_2, T_3) = \frac{\frac{1}{2} \cdot c \cdot r \cdot \left(c_s \cdot T_3^2 + c_p \cdot T_3^2\right) + c_1 \cdot (r - c)}{r \cdot (T_2 + T_3)} \tag{12.44}$$

To emphasise the quantity of products achieved during the time interval that forms the production cycle, we observe that under the stated conditions, the manufactured quantity is equal to the consumed quantity and from here:

$$q = u \cdot (T_1 + T_2 + T_3 + T_4) = \frac{c \cdot r \cdot (T_2 + T_3)}{r - c} \tag{12.45}$$

Let us determine the minimum of the function of average expenses by the unit of time.

For this, we determine $T_2^{(0)}$ and $T_3^{(0)}$ from the system:

$$\begin{cases} \dfrac{\partial F(T_2, T_3)}{\partial T_2} = 0 & (12.46) \\ \dfrac{\partial F(T_2, T_3)}{\partial T_3} = 0 & (12.47) \end{cases}$$

meaning:

$$\begin{cases} c \cdot r^2 \cdot c_s \cdot T_2 \cdot (T_2 + T_3) - r \cdot \left[\dfrac{1}{2} \cdot c \cdot r \cdot \left(c_s \cdot T_2^2 + c_p \cdot T_3^2\right) + c_1 \cdot (r - c)\right] = 0 & (12.48) \\ c \cdot r^2 \cdot c_p \cdot T_3 \cdot (T_2 + T_3) - r \cdot \left[\dfrac{1}{2} \cdot c \cdot r \cdot \left(c_s \cdot T_2^2 + c_p \cdot T_3^2\right) + c_1 \cdot (r - c)\right] = 0 & (12.49) \end{cases}$$

By solving, we get the optimum periods $T_2^{(0)}$ and $T_3^{(0)}$ (12.50)

$$T_2^{(0)} = \sqrt{\frac{2 \cdot c_p \cdot c_1 \cdot (r - c)}{c \cdot r \cdot c_s \cdot \left(c_s + c_p\right)}} = \sqrt{\frac{2 \cdot c_p \cdot c_1 \cdot \left(1 - \frac{c}{r}\right)}{c \cdot c_s \cdot \left(c_s + c_p\right)}} \tag{12.51}$$

$$T_3^{(0)} = \sqrt{\frac{2 \cdot c_s \cdot c_1 \cdot (r - c)}{c \cdot r \cdot c_p \cdot \left(c_s + c_p\right)}} = \sqrt{\frac{2 \cdot c_s \cdot c_1 \cdot \left(1 - \frac{c}{r}\right)}{c \cdot c_p \cdot \left(c_s + c_p\right)}} \tag{12.52}$$

It results from here: the optimum batch

$$F^{(0)} = \left(\frac{2 \cdot u \cdot c_s \cdot c_p \cdot c_1 \cdot \left(1 - \frac{c}{r}\right)}{\left(c_s + c_p\right)}\right)^{\frac{1}{2}} \tag{12.53}$$

the optimum stock:

$$S^{(0)} = \sqrt{\frac{2 \cdot c \cdot c_p \cdot c_1 \cdot \left(1 - \frac{c}{r}\right)}{c_s\left(c_s + c_p\right)}} \tag{12.54}$$

and the nominal value of average expenses by the unit of time:

$$F^{(0)} = \left(\frac{2 \cdot u \cdot c_s \cdot c_p \cdot c_1 \cdot \left(1 - \frac{c}{r}\right)}{\left(c_s + c_p\right)} \right)^{\frac{1}{2}} \tag{12.55}$$

Let us not do some additional assumptions which will lead us to particular management problems, namely:

- *let us assume that the production rhythm r is very high compared to the intensity of the demand.* In this case, the total production time $T_1 + T_4$ can be neglected, which is equivalent to $\frac{r-c}{r} \approx 1$, meaning it is a matter of *instantaneous production.*

  With these clarifications, the average expenses by the unit of time become:

$$P(T_2, T_3) = \frac{\frac{1}{2} \cdot c \cdot \left(c_s \cdot T_2^2 + c_p \cdot T_3^2\right) + c_1}{T_2 + T_3} \tag{12.56}$$

And $T_2^{(0)}$, $T_3^{(0)}$, $q^{(0)}$, $S^{(0)}$, $F^{(0)}$ are respectively:

$$T_2^{(0)} = \sqrt{\frac{2 \cdot c_p \cdot c_1}{c \cdot c_s \cdot \left(c_s + c_p\right)}}; \quad T_3^{(0)} = \sqrt{\frac{2 \cdot c_s \cdot c_1}{c \cdot c_p \cdot \left(c_s + c_p\right)}} \tag{12.57}$$

$$q^{(0)} = \sqrt{\frac{2 \cdot c \cdot c_1 \cdot \left(c_s + c_p\right)}{c_s \cdot c_p}}; \quad S^{(0)} = \sqrt{\frac{2 \cdot c \cdot c_1 \cdot c_p}{c_s \cdot \left(c_s + c_p\right)}} \tag{12.58}$$

$$s^{(0)} = \sqrt{\frac{2 \cdot c \cdot c_s \cdot c_1}{c_p\left(c_s + c_p\right)}}; \quad F^{(0)} = \sqrt{\frac{2 \cdot c \cdot c_p \cdot c_s \cdot c_1}{c_s + c_p}} \tag{12.59}$$

- *another simplifying assumption is achieved when product shortage is not admitted.* This is equivalent to the fact that the penalty expenses are however great, meaning we can make $c_p \to \infty$ in which case $T_3 \to 0$.

  In this case, we get the following values for $T_2^{(0)}$, $q^{(0)}$, $S^{(0)}$, $F^{(0)}$:

$$T_2^{(0)} = \sqrt{\frac{2 \cdot c_1}{c \cdot c_s}}; \quad q^{(0)} = \sqrt{\frac{2 \cdot c_1 \cdot c}{c_s}}; \quad S^{(0)} = 0; \quad F^{(0)} = \sqrt{2 \cdot c \cdot c_s \cdot c_1}; \tag{12.60}$$

- *management models with variable purchase prices or production expenses,* highlights the fact that in the previously shown deterministic model, except for the (supposedly fixed) launching expenses, production expenses were ignored. This is valid if the production expenses per unit of product does not vary along with the production output, and the demand is satisfied in full (or in the supply models by the product unit it does not vary with the volume of the order).

However, in general the production expenses depend on the production volume noted with q and namely a nondecreasing function $f(q)$ with $f(0) = 0$. For the launching expenses $c_l \neq 0$, the function $f(q)$ also has a jump equal to $c_l \cdot C_0$ or the function $f(q)$ also has other jumps that must be taken into account when determining the optimal quantity q that must be purchased (manufactured).

Let us suppose that the intensity of the demand for products is C and let us note as before with c_s the storage expenses by the unit of product in the unit of time, and with c_l the (fixed) launching expenses of an order. Be p the unit price of the product when the volume is smaller than a quantity Q and p' when the volume of the order is greater than or equal to Q, with $p' < p$.

Then $f(q)$ has the expression:

$$f(q) = \begin{cases} 0 & q = 0 \\ c_l + q \cdot p & 0 < q < Q \\ c_l + q \cdot p' & q > Q \end{cases} \tag{12.61}$$

If we assume no shortage of items is admitted and that the supply is done instantaneously, then the average expenses by the unit of time are achieved based on the relation $F(T_2) = \frac{1}{2} \cdot c \cdot c_s \cdot T_2 + \frac{c_l}{T_2}$ by replacing

$$T_2 = \frac{q}{c} \tag{12.62}$$

$$F(q) = \begin{cases} \dfrac{c_l^u}{q} + p \cdot c + \dfrac{1}{2} \cdot c_s \cdot q & \text{if } 0 < q < Q \\ \dfrac{c_l^u}{q} + p' \cdot c + \dfrac{1}{2} \cdot c_s \cdot q & \text{if } q \geq Q \end{cases} \tag{12.63}$$

The function $f(q)$ has a discontinuity in q and its minimum is achieved either in Q or in q, the root of the equation $\frac{dF}{dq} = 0$

$$\text{As } \frac{dF}{dq} = -\frac{c_l \cdot c}{q^2} + \frac{c_s}{2} \quad \text{if } q \neq Q \tag{12.64}$$

$$\text{It results } q^{(0)} = \sqrt{\frac{2 \cdot c \cdot c_l}{c_s}} \tag{12.65}$$

(The minimum can be possibly be achieved also in the point $q = Q$ which is discontinuity point of the function F).

Let us analyse what happens for $q^{(0)} < Q$ and for $q^{(0)} \geq Q$. If $Q \leq q^{(0)}$ the minimum of the function F is achieved for $q = q^{(0)}$ and we get:

$$F^{(0)} = p' \cdot c + \sqrt{2 \cdot c_s \cdot c_l \cdot c} \tag{12.66}$$

If $Q > q^{(0)}$ and $q^{(0)}$ product units are driven, the expenses will be

$$p \cdot c + \sqrt{2 \cdot c_s \cdot c_1 \cdot c} \tag{12.67}$$

On the other hand, if it is decided to drive Q product units at a lower price, the expenses will be

$$p' \cdot c + \frac{c_1 \cdot c}{Q} + \frac{1}{2} \cdot c_s \cdot Q. \tag{12.68}$$

For these reasons, it follows that we decide on solving Q product units if:

$$p - p' \geq \frac{1}{c} \cdot \left[\frac{c_1 \cdot c}{Q} + \frac{1}{2} \cdot c_s \cdot Q - \sqrt{2 \cdot c_s \cdot c_1 \cdot c}\right] \tag{12.69}$$

Of course, the reasoning used may be also extended when there are several price changes, the function F having in this case several points of discontinuity and the analysis is to be according to these points.

Let us analyse a solution analogous to the described one and which appears in the production process.

Certainly, producing a greater quantity of products requires additional working time and therefore the unit production expenses could increase. Let us suppose that when the volume of products made $q \leq Q$, each product unit cost p units and if $q > Q$ the cost of a product unit is $p' > p$.

In this case, the production expenses f(q) will be:

$$f(q) = \begin{cases} 0 & q = 0 \\ c_1 + q \cdot p & 0 < q < Q \\ c_1 + Q \cdot p + p' \cdot (q - Q) & q \geq Q \end{cases} \tag{12.70}$$

Placing for the period of time when there is stock $T_2 = \frac{q}{c}$ and expressing the total expenses by the unit of time by:

$$\frac{1}{2} \cdot c \cdot c_s \cdot T + \frac{c_1}{T_2} \tag{12.71}$$

It results that, in our case, the total expenses in the unit of time will be:

$$F(q) = \begin{cases} \dfrac{c_1 \cdot c}{q} + p \cdot c + \dfrac{1}{2} \cdot c_s \cdot q & \text{if } 0 < q < Q \\ \dfrac{c_1 - (p' - p) \cdot Q \cdot c}{q} + p' \cdot c + \dfrac{1}{2} \cdot c_s \cdot q & \text{if } q \geq Q \end{cases} \tag{12.72}$$

It appears that the function F(q) is continuous for $q > 0$ and derivable in any point $q > 0, q \neq Q$. For such a function, the minimum is done either in the point $q = Q$, or in the point where the derivative $F'(q)$ is cancelled.

From this condition, it results $q^{(0)}$ for which we get the minimum expenses, $\min F(q) = F(q^{(0)})$;

- *Deterministic storage model for several products*, is used because in the activity of an enterprise, the most frequent case intervening is when the stock is simultaneously assessed for several products.

  The problem of optimal stock management can be solved, taking into account each product separately. And if the storage capacities or production possibilities are limited, the problem for each individual product can no longer be considered. Then things get complicated and such a problem must be dealt with separately.

  Below, a simple case will be taken, which will be dealt with by means of Lagrange multipliers. Let us consider the case of *n* products, when the production can be considered instantaneous and when product shortage is not allowed.

  Let us note with c_i the intensity of the demand of the product *i*, with c_{li} the launching expenses and with c_{si} the storage expenses, where $i = 1, 2, \ldots, n$.

  Then, by replacing $T_{2i} = \frac{q_i}{c_i}$, the total expenses by the unit of time will be:

$$F(q_1, q_2, \ldots q_n) = \sum_{i=1}^{n} \left[\frac{1}{2} \cdot c'_{si} \cdot q_1 + \frac{c_{li} \cdot c_i}{q_i} \right] \tag{12.73}$$

q_i is the quantity of the product *i* that comes into stock.

If we do not impose limitations on the storage capacities or on production, to determine the minimum expenses, we need to solve the system of equations:

$$\frac{\partial F(q_1, \ldots\ldots, q_n)}{\partial q_1} = \frac{1}{2} \cdot c_{si} - \frac{c_{li} \cdot c_i}{q_1^2} \tag{12.74}$$

which leads to optimal values:

$$q^{(0)} = \sqrt{\frac{2 \cdot c_i \cdot c_{li}}{c_{si}}} \tag{12.75}$$

(it is shown that it is indeed a matter of a minimum).

If there is a restriction imposed by the storage capacity, then we need to take into account a problem of minimum with restrictions.

Thus, for example, if we impose that in average the stored quantity should not increase a certain value *K*, then $F(q_1, q_2, \ldots, q_n)$ will need to be minimised provided that:

$$\frac{1}{2} \cdot \sum_{i=1}^{n} q_j \leq K \tag{12.76}$$

and the quantities $q_i^{(0)}$ $(i = 1, 2, \ldots, n)$ are determined.

$$\text{If } \sum_{i=1}^{n} q_i^{(0)} \leq 2 \cdot K, \text{ no problems arise:} \tag{12.77}$$

$$\text{butmspace width} = \}0.5\text{em}\}/ > \text{if} \sum_{i=1}^{n} q_i^{(0)} > 2 \cdot K \tag{12.78}$$

then the values found must be reduced $q^{(0)}$.

The factor ½ appears following the fact that the average stock is taken into account, and the intensities c_i are constant.

The resolution of the problem is as follows:

In we insert:

$$G(q_1, q_2, \ldots q_n; \lambda) = \sum_{i=1}^{n} \left[\frac{1}{2} \cdot c_{si} \cdot q_i + \frac{c_{li} \cdot c_i}{q_i}\right] + \lambda \cdot \left[\sum_{i=1}^{n} q_i - 2 \cdot K\right] \tag{12.79}$$

from the system of equations

$$\frac{\partial G}{\partial q_i} = \frac{1}{2} \cdot c_{si} - \frac{c_{li} \cdot c_i}{q_1^2} + \lambda = 0 \quad i = 1, 2, \ldots, n \tag{12.80}$$

we immediately get:

$$q_i^{(0)} = \sqrt{\frac{2 \cdot c_i \cdot c_{li}}{c_{si} + 2}} \qquad i = 1, 2, \ldots, n \tag{12.81}$$

and we determine λ so that

$$\sum_{i=1}^{n} q_i^{(0)} = 2 \cdot K \tag{12.82}$$

assuming therefore that we have the relation $\frac{1}{2} \cdot \sum_{i=1}^{n} q_i = K$ and therefore

$$F(q_1, \ldots, q_n) = G(q_1, \ldots, q_n). \tag{12.83}$$

We can proceed in several ways to find out λ, but the simplest way is for λ to be determined with an approximation based on trials.

We can also observe that from the relations:

$$\frac{\partial G}{\partial q_i} = 0 \quad i = 1, 2, \ldots, n \quad \text{it immediately results} \tag{12.84}$$

$$\frac{\partial F}{\partial q_i} = -\lambda \quad i = 1, 2, \ldots, n \tag{12.85}$$

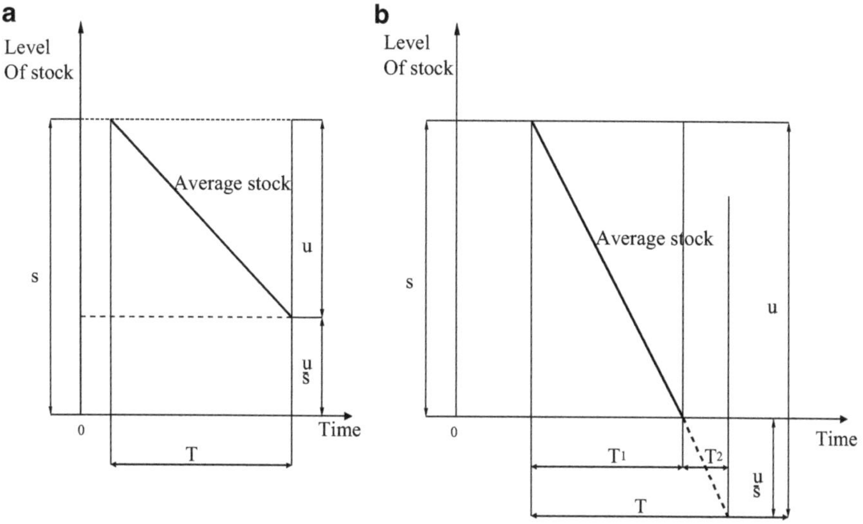

Fig. 12.10 Resupply at fixed periods under the conditions of a random demand with the stock outage possibility

And it results from here that $q_i^{(0)}$ are chosen so that most of the quantities q_i the variation of expenses by the product unit would be the same whichever the product $i = 1, 2, \ldots, n$;

– *Model of fixed period management and random demand with the possibility of outage*, because in reality there appear problems very often, which this hypothesis is no longer satisfied for and therefore we shall now consider a fixed management model and random demand.

Because the demand is random, it may happen that the stock is depleted during a period of time, so that we shall also take into account this possibility. Therefore, during a period *T* one of the situations shown in Fig. 12.10 may occur.

In Fig. 12.10a, we may observe that the total demand is lower than the stock $s \geq c$, and in Fig. 12.10b, the total demand exceeds the stock $s \leq c$.

We want to determine the average management expenses during the period *T*. For this, we shall assume that the random *U* variable repartition law is known (demand for products).

That is the probabilities $P(C = c) = p(c), c = 0, 1, 2, \ldots, n$ in a time interval of size *T* are known. The average management expenses will consist of the average storage expenses and the average penalty expenses (to neglect the launching expenses shown in Fig. 12.10).

The average storage corresponding to the situation in Fig. 12.10a is given by the relation:

$$\frac{[s + (s - c)] \cdot T}{2T} = [s] - \frac{c}{2} \tag{12.86}$$

In the situation in Fig. 12.10b we have storage expenses only on the time interval T_1. The average stock is in this case $\frac{s \cdot T_1}{2T}$.

However, as:

$$\frac{T_1}{T} = \frac{s}{c} \tag{12.87}$$

$$\text{The average stock results} : \frac{s^2}{2c} \tag{12.88}$$

During the time interval T_2, penalties are paid for the average quantity of missing items, which is given by:

$$\frac{(c - s) \cdot T_2}{2T} = \frac{(c - s)^2}{2c} \tag{12.89}$$

Hence, it results that the average management expenses during the period *T* are given by:

$$F(s) = c_s \cdot \sum_{n=0}^{s} \left(s - \frac{c}{2}\right) \cdot p_u + c_s \cdot \sum_{c=s+1}^{\infty} \frac{s^2}{2 \cdot c} \cdot p(c) + c_p \cdot \sum_{u=s+1}^{\infty} \frac{(c-s)^2}{2 \cdot c} \cdot p(c) \tag{12.90}$$

(if we assume that *U* is the continuous random variable, the amounts are replaced with integrals). The optimum level of the stock is given by that value s_0 at s for which:

$$F(s - 1) > F(s) < F(s + 1) \tag{12.91}$$

Let us determine the value of s_0 which meets this double inequality:

$$F(s+1) = c_s \cdot \sum_{c=0}^{s+1} \left(s + 1 - \frac{c}{2}\right) \cdot p(c) + c_s \cdot \sum_{c=s+2}^{\infty} \frac{(s+1)^2}{2 \cdot c} \cdot p(c) + c_p \cdot \sum_{c=s+2}^{\infty} \frac{(c-s-1)^2}{2 \cdot c} \cdot$$
$$\cdot p(c) = F(s) + (c_s + c_p) \cdot \left[P(C \le s) + \left(s - \frac{1}{2}\right) \cdot \sum_{c=s-1}^{\infty} \frac{p(c)}{c}\right] - c_p \tag{12.92}$$

Or if we note:

$$L(s) = P(C \le s) + (s + 1/2) \cdot \sum_{u=s+1}^{\infty} \frac{p(c)}{c} \tag{12.93}$$

The condition $F(s) < F(s + 1)$ returns to:

$$c_p < (c_s + c_p) \cdot L(s) \tag{12.94}$$

$$\text{And from here: } \rho = \frac{c_p}{c_s + c_p} < L(s) \tag{12.95}$$

Proceeding analogously with F(s – 1) we can write:

$$F(s-1) = c_s \cdot \sum_{c=0}^{s-1} \left(s - 1 - \frac{c}{2}\right) \cdot p(c) + c_s \cdot \sum_{c=s}^{\infty} \frac{(s-1)^2}{2 \cdot c} \cdot p(c) + c_p \cdot \sum_{c=s}^{\infty} \frac{(c-s+1)^2}{2 \cdot c} \cdot$$
$$p(c) = F(s) - (c_s + c_p) \cdot \left[P(C \leq s-1) + (s - 1/2) \cdot \sum_{u=s}^{\infty} \frac{p(c)}{c}\right] + c_p \tag{12.96}$$

And the inequality $F(s-1) > F(s)$ becomes:

$$c_p > (c_s + c_p) \cdot L(s-1) \tag{12.97}$$

Or:

$$\rho = \frac{c_p}{c_s + c_p} < L(s-1) \tag{12.98}$$

Therefore, there is a value s_0 so that:

$$L(s_0 - 1) < \frac{c_p}{c_s + c_p} < L(s_0) \tag{12.99}$$

Or explicitly written:

$$P(C \leq s_0 - 1) + \left(s_0 - \frac{1}{2}\right) \cdot \sum_{c=s_0}^{\infty} \frac{p(c)}{c} < \frac{c_p}{c_s + c_p} < P(C \leq s_0)$$
$$+ \left(s_0 + \frac{1}{2}\right) \cdot \sum_{c=s_0+1}^{\infty} \frac{p(c)}{c} \tag{12.100}$$

And the practical rule to determine the value s_0 also results from here, which is the optimal stock.

12.4 Heuristic Models Used in the Management of Stocks

In many enterprises, the number of products entering and leaving the warehouse is very big. For this reason, it is not practically possible to follow the storage phenomenon for all products. To master however the process broadly, a selective control method called the *ABS method* has been imagined, which originates from the USA, where the researches performed within the *General Electric* group approximately in 1960, have emphasised the need to review the procedures of treating the management of stocks. Subsequently, in the '80's, in a number of published articles, the Americans R.S. Kaplan, H.T. Johnson and R. Cooper have drawn the attention on the limits of the traditional methods used by the management of stocks. Their criticisms were particularly related to the procedures of distributing the expenses incurred by the process of storing the materials.

R.S. Kaplan and R. Cooper have developed a much more exact method to distribute the expenses incurred by the storage processes, called the ABC method.

Since the early '90s, many companies have studied the implementation of this method. A study performed in 1995 shows that 20 % of the British companies have adopted the *ABC method*. The acceptance of the *ABC method* by an increasingly more important number of companies seems to have its roots in the deep discontents, first of all of managers to the traditional methods used in the management of stocks.

Using the *ABC method* in enterprises consists in choosing a corresponding criterion based on which the division of materials into three groups *A*. *B*. *C*. is done. Such a criterion can be the value of the material, the way of using it in production or its origin from import.

Each product has a certain annual consumption and correspondingly a value, which enables the division of products from the stocks into three groups, namely:

- *group A*, which expensive products are part of and quantitatively represent 10 % of the stock and 70 % in value;
- *group B* contains the products representing 20 % in quantity and 20 % in value;
- *group C* refers to the products that represent 70 % in quantity and 10 % in value.

Because in *group A* there are few products, the level of stocks can be controlled daily, recording the variation of the demand and it is also closely supervised whether the suppliers comply with the deadlines. Therefore, part of the buffer stock of expensive products is replaced by a closer management control. This decision is efficient because it leads to a considerable reduction of the funds blocked in stocks.

For the products in *group C* which are cheaper, it is more efficient to bear storage costs than to pay the personnel who would be indispensable, in order to increase the control.

For the products in *group B*, the control is done only on the buffer stock.

The ABC method enables practising a different policy in the three groups, with a more intense control on the products from *group A*.

The management methods based on using the mathematical models involve great accuracy in determining the costs that are part of the calculations. Unfortunately, it is often that this cannot be done, the management of stocks being resumed to simply recording the movement of resources and applying a resupply policy based on intuition and experience.

It must also be shown that in practice, the management of stocks is determined by the existence of some normative acts regarding the limitation of immobilising current assets.

However, we consider that the advantages the application of some scientific methods would bring into the management of stocks would justify the expenses necessary for a more analytical record of costs, as well as the efforts to re-examine and recalculate the regulations on immobilising current assets.

References

Barney J, Ketchen D, Wright M (2011) The future of resource-based theory: revitalization or decline? J Manag 37(5):1299–1315

Daft R (2004) Management. The Dryden Press, New York

Dima IC (2011) Operational management systems of the production achieved in flexible manufacturing cells. Technical University of Kosice, FMT-Presov

Geoffrion A (1996) Stochastic programming with aspiration or fractile criteria. Prentice Hall, New Jersey

Kelejean H (1996) Introduction to econometrics. Harper, New York

Kotter J (2002) The general manages. Free Press, New York

Lesca N (1996) Gestion de l'information. Litec, Paris

Schroeder RG (2007) Operations management. McGraw-Hill, New York

Sinha SM (2004) Stochastic programming. McGraw Hill, New York

Stoner I, Freeman E (2009) Management. Prentice Hall, New Jersey

Wagner MH (1989) Principles of operations researches with applications to managerial decisions. Prentice Hall, New Jersey

Wren DA (2007) Evolution of management thought. Wiley, New York

Zadeh LA, Polak E (1969) System theory. McGraw-Hill, New York

Zadeh LA (1999) From computing with numbers to computing with words – from manipulation of measurements to manipulation of perceptions. IEEE Trans Circuits Syst 45(1):105–119

Chapter 13
Models Used in the Management of Replacing Fixed Assets

13.1 Theoretical Considerations

The technological innovation is that process of creating and implementing the new technologies, products or services, in conditions of economical, social and ergonomic efficiency instead of the existing ones. Specialised literature suggests the level of labour productivity as well as the quality level of goods and services produced by an enterprise are decisively influenced by the technological exchange rate and by the type of technologies used in production in time.

In their works, authors Abernathy and Clark deem that innovation leads to changes in: *conception of products; production systems; knowledge and skills base; nature of the material resources used; the technical level of the equipments, machines and work installations.*

Porter deems the technological change as being one of the main forces of competition. It plays a decisive role in the occurrence of some structural changes at the level of industry and it can also lead to creating new industries. The technological change may be a balancing factor, scouring the competitive advantage of some strong enterprises and impelling other enterprises to the top. Frohman recommends enterprises to use the technology as a means of protecting the competitive advantage they have. Those enterprises which formed an effective system of encouraging and managing the technological innovations are in a much better position to develop and manufacture quality products and services. The products and services obtained after the technological innovation will determine the increase of the work environment quality, as well as the social one.

In order to get out of the vicious circle of lacking the technology, as shown in Fig. 13.1 it is necessary to clearly understand the problems, restrictions and opportunities related to the technological progress management. At an enterprise

I.C. Dima, M. Man, *Modelling and Simulation in Management*, Contributions to Management Science, DOI 10.1007/978-3-319-16592-9_13

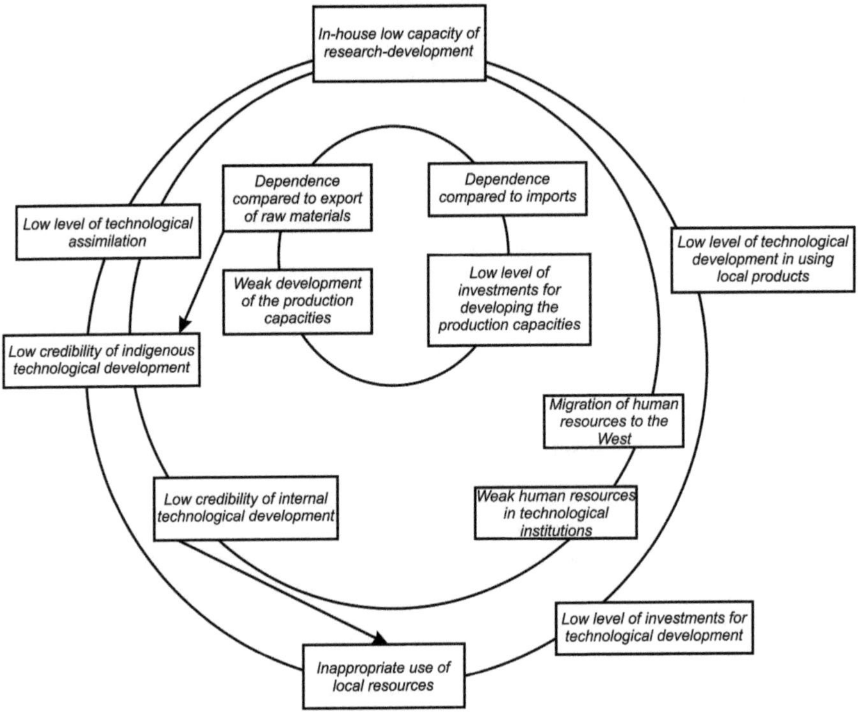

Fig. 13.1 The structure of lacking the technology

level, the technological factor is much more important than at a national level, as enterprises face the following problems:

- *the life cycle of products is much lower than during the period of state-owned economy;*
- *the existence of technological discrepancies, compared to countries in Western Europe;*
- *the limited feature of resources;*
- *the occurrence and development of international competition.*

Western specialists assess that, in principle, 40 % of the increase in the per capita income is due to the technological progress, which is not an independent phenomenon, but it has an impact on the economical, social and ergonomic efficiency.

The impacts of lacking technology are very apparent in the domain of replacing fixed assets.

These impacts can be: *impacts of the technological progress onto the social efficiency, as well as impacts of the technological progress onto the ergonomic efficiency.*

Woodward analyses in detail the negative social consequences of the new equipments and technologies. Thusly, due to the technological innovation, workers are separated from the product of their work, a separation leading to various forms of alienation, boredom, apathy and loss of self-confidence.

Thusly:

- *due to the technological progress, labour becomes more productive, but less independent (workers do not have total control anymore over the product of their work);*
- *labour becomes more formalised as there will be more procedures and rules to be followed;*
- *less workers are needed for the same production task, which leads to reorganisations and layoffs and, consequently, to a drop in workers' moral;*
- *the education system must keep up the pace with the new requirements imposed by the technological progress, and those who are not capable of accepting this change in mentality will have less chances on the labour market;*

The new equipments will have consequences over the ergonomic labour organisation conditions, as the replacement of the equipments is integral part of the technological progress.

The management of replacing the equipments, machines and work installations represents a modality of justifying the new equipments and consists in:

- *identifying and evaluating the new equipments;*
- *the maintenance management of old equipments;*
- *the management of research and development, as well as determining the technological feasibility of new equipments;*
- *integrating new equipments into technical overall operations of the enterprise;*
- *commissioning the new equipments.*

New equipments, not only they directly contribute to accomplishing the strategic and tactical aims of the enterprise, but they also have a decisive impact onto the organisational culture, which is defined as the totality of the social norms, aptitudes and behaviours within the enterprise.

First of all, the new technology will affect the managerial team, taking into account the fact that in Western countries, the managerial teams do not have a technical orientation, which determines the delegation of technical decisions at the level of specialists in production.

The new machines will have an impact onto workers and foremen, as the formal and informal relations between them will be affected, meaning that some of them will be promoted, and others will be laid off. Thusly, the new machines will have many effects onto the enterprise.

Edosomwan suggests a template, referred to as *the multifunctional template of the effects of the new machines onto the enterprise*, shown in Fig. 13.2.

Justifying a new machine implies taking into account certain tangible factors, as well as some less tangible ones. The Romanian specialized literature focuses on tangible factors, whereas Western literature offers a more ample perspective regarding less tangible factors.

Structure of the factors to be optimised, namely:

Factor 1 **Productivity**	**Factor 2** **Personnel**	**Factor 3** **Quality of production**	**Factor 4** **Accomplishing the work**	**Factor 5** **Psychological stress**	**Factor 6** **Labour protection**	**Factor 7** **System results**	**Factor 8** **Ergonomy**
Productivity total partial	Need of personnel	Need of faults	Worker's perception regarding their own satisfaction	Worker's perception regarding stress	Work conditions Machine-equipments labour environment	Easiness in operation; flexibility easiness which the production tasks are understood with	Organising the work place conception of the system Dividing the activities

Fig. 13.2 Multifunctional template of the effects of new machines and installations onto the enterprise

Hunter suggests that the decision of replacing machines is more easily substantiated in the following conditions:

- *when the management team is the one initiating this decision;*
- *when the project manager is properly trained in technical terms;*
- *when the level of current overheads is exactly known;*
- *when the investment financing department has a cautionary orientation.*

The replacement of machines is based on certain mathematical methods for explaining such replacement, but these methods do not consider tangible factors.

The issues related to the machine's replacement, considering the degree of knowledge thereof may be: determinist issues, probabilistic ~ stochastic issues.

Determinist issues are those when the time and implications of the replacement action may be certainly determined (known). For instance, the situation of a machine whose operating costs increase in direct proportion to the duration of use. In order to reduce this cost, the machine must be replaced, so that the operating cost shall tend to increase, as shown in Fig. 13.3.

Probabilistic situations are those when the time and implications of the replacement action cannot be exactly determined. Let us consider that the machine has two states: proper operating state (F) and non-operating state (N). The probabilistic law,

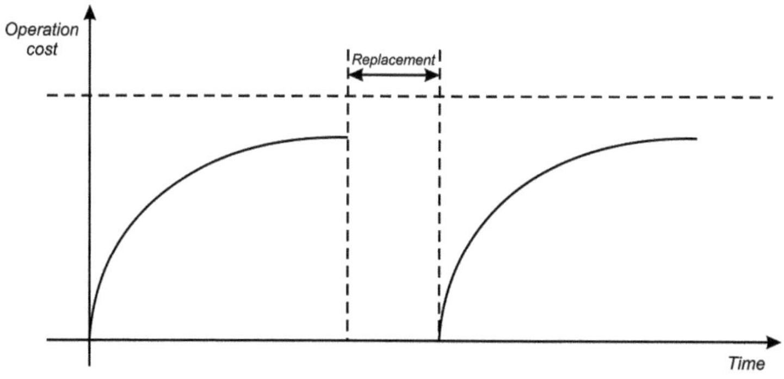

Fig. 13.3 Operating cost–time relation

describing the transition from state F to state N may be described by the distribution of time between the end of the replacement action and the fall of the equipment.

The decisions to replace machines in case the fall of machines follows a probabilistic law are those decisions where the risk is given by the impossibility to exactly determine the moment when such machine falls or the transition moment from state F to state N. Another source of risk is given by the impossibility to determine the state of the equipment when no inspection or other maintenance activity occurs. We consider that there are only two states of the equipment F and N, which are always known. We have to determine the times when the action of replacement of machines should occur. This is called machine replacement policy. In this case, we are interested in the optimal replacement policy, i.e. the one maximising or minimising certain economic criteria, such as: profit, total cost, non-operating time.

Let us consider that the activity of replacement of the equipment results in the further production, at the same quality level, of the same products and services previously produced by the replaced machine. Hence, fall distributions and related costs are the same for all models (except for the model which considers the technological improvement of the machine).

Preventive replacement for fixed assets implies two conditions: *the total replacement cost shall be higher after the fall itself at the moment when the preventive replacement is made; the fall rate of the equipment increases instead of remaining constant. In order to prove this, let us consider than an equipment has a constant fall rate and follows a negative exponential law. In this case, the replacement of the machine before the fall itself does not affect the chance that the equipment may fall at the following moment. In the case of negative exponential distribution, preventive replacement represents a loss of money and other resources.*

Therefore, preventive replacement is only justified when the rate of replacement grows. In case the machine is damaged, the specialist in the department should increase the preventive replacement activity. This may be a mistake, as the preventive replacement of machines (or machine components) is not always justified.

13.2 Econometric Methods Used in Analysing Technological Innovations

For the analysis of technological innovations, we shall use several mathematical methods regarding the decision of replacement of tools, which shall be presented in the following.

Methods used in analysing technological innovations are:

– The Method of Replacing the Equipments Based on the Operation Cost-Replacement Cost Interdependence

It implies that, at the beginning of every year, data is collected on a certain machine, regarding operation and replacement costs. The data shows an increase in the operation cost, because of the damages in certain components of the machine. Some of these components may be replaced, reducing thus the equipment operating cost. The replacement thereof implies costs with materials and salaries and, hence, such costs have to be compensated through the savings which may be obtained pursuant to the reduction of operating costs. Thus, we want to determine an optimal replacement policy, able to minimize the sum of operating and replacement expenses during the period between two successive data collections.

Figure 13.4 outlines the conflict between the two costs.

Consider: $c(t)$, the operating cost per time unit at the moment t, after replacement and c_r, the cost of a replacement. Then, the relation between the operating cost, replacement cost and time is that in Fig. 13.4.

The replacement policy is presented in Fig. 13.5, with the following notations: $[0, T]$, the time interval regarding the collection of data on the machine and t_r, intervals when n replacements shall occur.

The proposed goal is the determination of the optimal interval between replacements, so that the sum of the operating and replacement cost $C(t_r)$ is minimal.

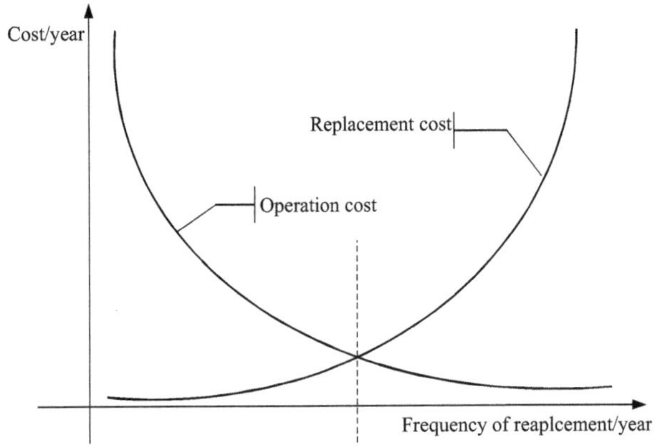

Fig. 13.4 Relation between operation cost, replacement cost–time

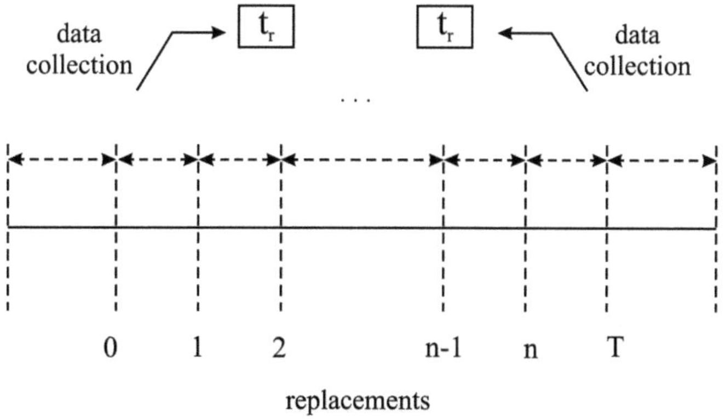

Fig. 13.5 Graphical representation of the replacement policy

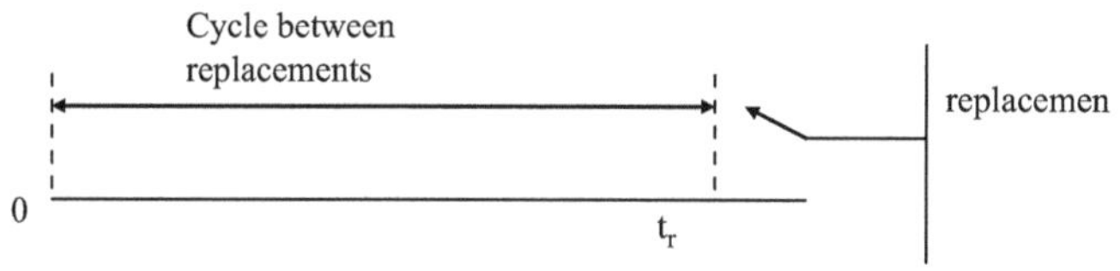

Fig. 13.6 Machine replacement policy

$C(t_r)$ is the replacement cost during the period $[0, T]$, plus operating cost during the period $[0, T]$.

$$\text{Replacement cost by period } [0, T] = n \cdot C_r \tag{13.1}$$

Thus, n is the name of replacements by period $[0, T]$ and C_r, the cost of one replacement.

The proposed goal is the determination of the optimal interval between successive replacements, so that the operating and replacement cost per time unit is minimal.

The total cost per time unit $C(t_r)$, for the replacement performed at the moment t_r is: $C(t_r)$ i.e. total cost in the interval $(0, t_r)$ related to the length of the interval (Fig. 13.6).

The total cost in the interval $(0, t_r)$ is the operating cost plus replacement cost.

$$\int_0^{t_r} c(t)dt + C_r = \left[\frac{\int_0^{t_r} c(t)dt + C_r}{t_r} \right] \tag{13.2}$$

As we may see, the two methods are similar, because the minimization of $C(t_r)$ is desired, depending on t_r. Neither of the two methods considers the time required for performing a replacement (Fig. 13.7).

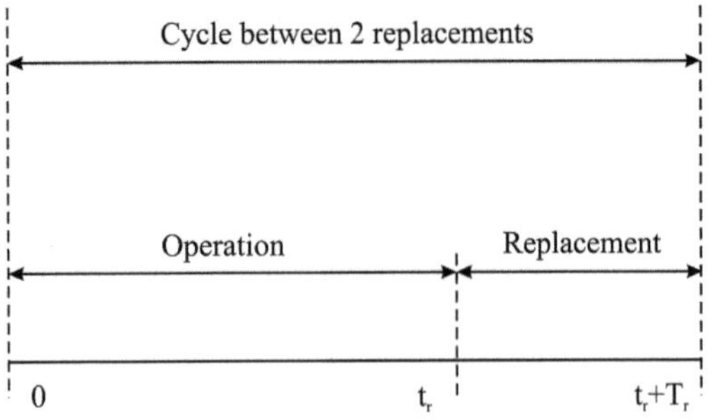

Fig. 13.7 Graphic representation of the comparison of methods

If the time required for performing a replacement is considered, Eq. (13.2) becomes:

$$C(t_r) = \frac{\int_0^{t_r} c(t)dt + C_r}{t_r + T_r} \quad (13.3)$$

– The Method of Replacing the Equipment at a Certain Age

We consider that the machine shall be used for a certain number of years. This situation is possible when a certain machine manufactures certain products, according to the production plan. In this case, the goal consists in the determination of the optimal replacement policy, establishing whether, at a certain age of the machine, the latter should be replaced or left to operate continuously, in order to minimize the total operating and replacement cost for a fixed time period.

Consider: I, the age of the equipment (from the last replacement, with n time periods of proper operation, until the end of the production plan); $c(a)$, the cost of operating the equipment for a time period, when the equipment has age a; J, the age of the equipment from the moment of the last replacement, having $(n - 1)$ operating time periods until the end of the production plan; C_r, replacement cost; $C(I,J)$, total cost during the period when the equipment develops from age I to age J. The proposed goal consists in the determination of a replacement policy, so that the cost of operating and replacing the machine $C_n(i)$, along the following n time periods is minimal.

When $C_n(i)$ has a minimal value, the smallest cost is defined as $f_n(i)$.

Figure 13.8 presents the replacement policy for a machine whose life is: $I = 3$ weeks, and $n = 10$ weeks.

10 weeks before the end of the production plan, two decisions may be made: continuous use or replacement of the machine. If it is decided that the machine should operate further, the equipment shall have age 4 when a new decision may be made (Fig. 13.9).

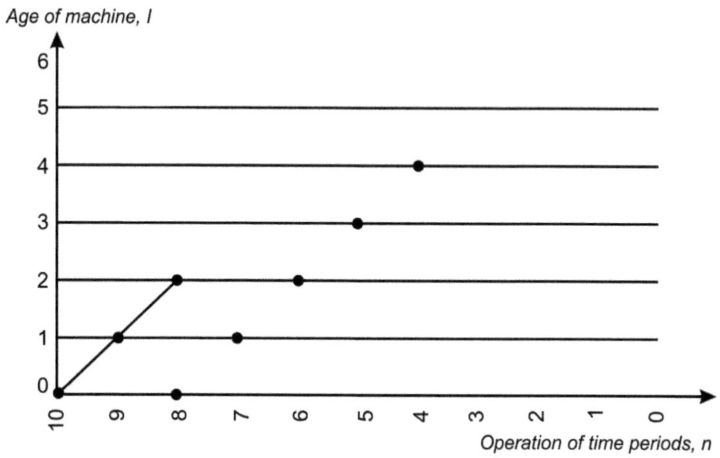

Fig. 13.8 Replacement policy for a machine with a 3-week life

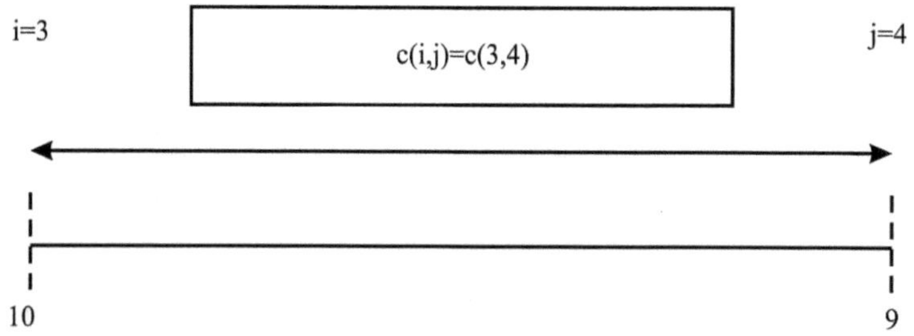

Fig. 13.9 Replacement policy for the machine with age "4"

The total operating cost for the period (10, 9) is:

$$C(3,4) = C(3) \tag{13.4}$$

If the decision to replace the machine is made (Fig. 13.10), then the total cost for the period (10, 9) shall be:

$$C(3,1) = C_r + C(0) \tag{13.5}$$

Thus, C_r is the replacement cost, and $c(0)$, the operating cost for a period, when the machine has age *0*.

The optimal replacement policy is graphically presented in Fig. 13.11.

The mathematical model used for identifying this optimal policy has the following form:

Consider: $f_n(i)$, the minimal cost resulting from taking the best decision at the beginning of the period n plus the cost of the best decision taken on the remaining

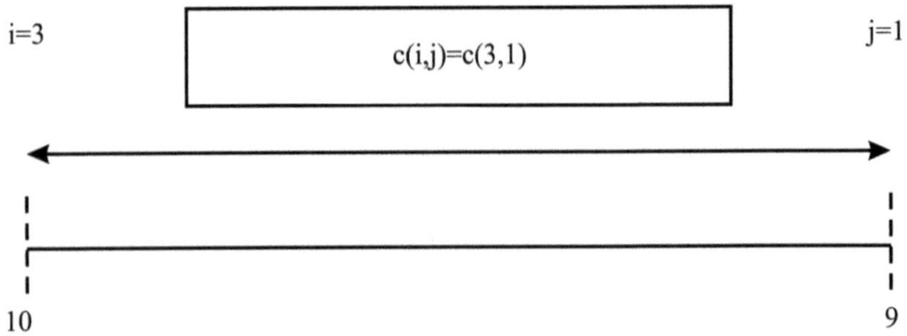

Fig. 13.10 Cost of the decision of replacement of the machine

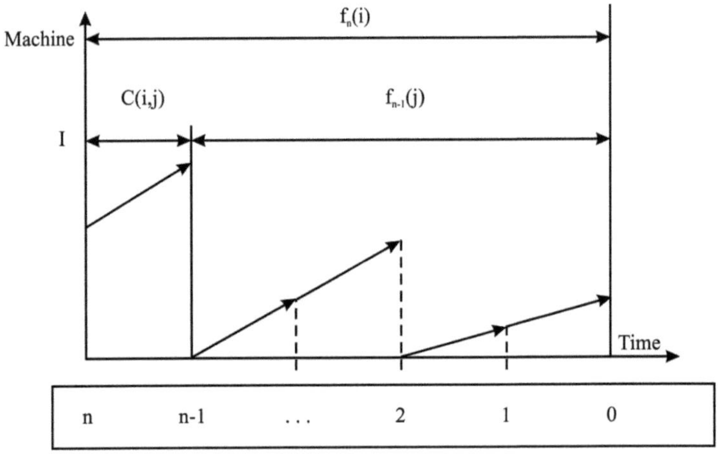

Fig. 13.11 Optimal replacement policy

periods $(n - 1)$; $C(i,j)$, the cost resulting from taking the decision at the beginning of the period n; $f_{n-1}(j)$, minimal cost by periods $(n - 1)$ remaining at the moment when the machine has the age J.

The cost by the n periods is:

$$C(i, j) + f_{n-1}(j), \tag{13.6}$$

so:

$$f_n(i) = min[C(i, j) + f_{n-1}(j)] \tag{13.7}$$

with:

$$f_0(i) = 0$$

$$j = i + 1 \quad \text{or } 0$$

This equation may be solved by means of dynamic programming methods;

– The Method of Replacement Based on the Existence of an Equipment in Standby

It implies the replacement of assets provided that the manufacturing flow contains a spare asset, and the operating cost increases with the use of the asset existing in production.

In this case, an optimal replacement policy must be determined, combined for the two assets, which shall minimize the total replacement and operating cost for a fixed time period.

The state of the production system at the beginning of a period shall be noted with I, where I is equivalent to the pair of numbers (x, y), where x refers to the asset (A or B) which is generally used, and y, to the age of the asset.

Consider: $C_x(y)$, the operating cost for a period; j, the state of the production system at the end of a period, where j is equivalent to (x, y); $C_r =$ replacement cost, considered equal for both assets $C(i, j)$, total cost of the system between the states of the system i and j. The time required for the replacement of an asset is a period when the replacement decision is made, then the *stand by* asset becomes operative. The proposed goal is the determination of an optimal combined policy for replacement/operation, so that the operating and replacement cost for the following n time periods is minimal. Figure 13.12 shows such a policy, where $n = 10$, the system is in state $I = (B, 2)$. At the beginning of period 10, a decision is made to go on with asset B.

At the beginning of period 9, a decision is made to replace asset B etc. The total minimal cost for replacement and operation, for the n periods is $f_n(i)$.

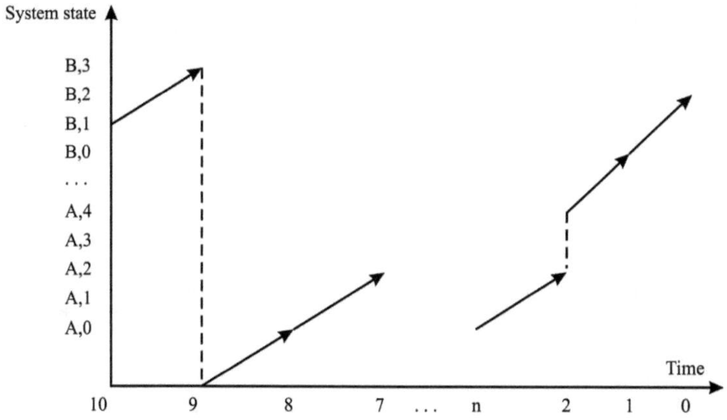

Fig. 13.12 Replacement policy given the existence of the standby asset

The cost of the first decision taken at the beginning of the period n is $C(i, J)$. At the end of this period, the system is in state j, having $(n - 1)$ operating periods. The minimal cost for the remaining period is $f_{n-1}(j)$:

$$\text{Total cost} = C(i, j) + f_{n-1}(j) \tag{13.8}$$

$$f_n(i) = min[C(i, j) + f_{n-1}(j)] \tag{13.9}$$

This equation can also be solved by means of dynamic programming;

– The Method of Replacing Equipments Based on Maximising the Net Updated Benefit

It aims to maximise the net updated benefit, in the case of fixed capital assets. Pursuant to damages in the equipment, the benefit resulting from the obtained production decreases, so that, at a certain moment, a replacement of the equipment is more efficient than continuing to operate the existing fixed asset.

Consider: $b(t)$, the net benefit obtained from using the equipment at the moment t, and $c(t)$, the net cost of replacement of the equipment with age t (Fig. 13.13).

This cost includes the purchase price, plus the installation cost, plus the production cost, which is lost pursuant to such replacement.

Consider: T, the time required for the replacement of the equipment; t_r, the age of the equipment when the replacement occurs; $t_r + T_r$, the replacement cycle; $B(t_r)$, the total net updated benefit, pursuant to the operation of the equipment for a period t_r (Fig 13.14).

The proposed goal consists in determining the optimal interval between two replacements, which maximises the total updated net benefit for an infinite period of time.

Let us consider the first operating cycle, as follows: $B_1(t_r + T_r)$, the benefit for the period $(0, t_r)$ updated at its current value minus the replacement cost for the

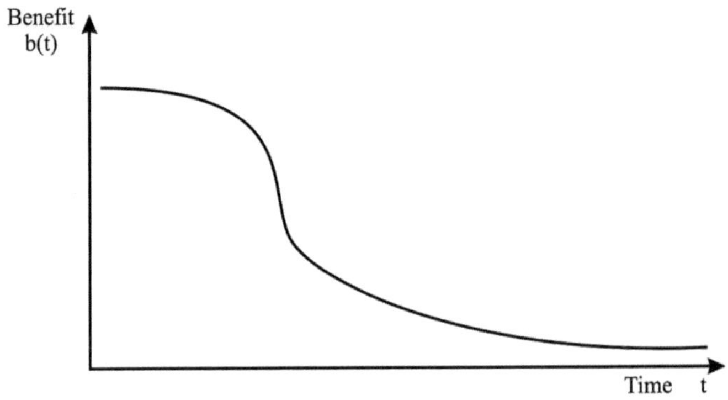

Fig. 13.13 Benefit–time correlation

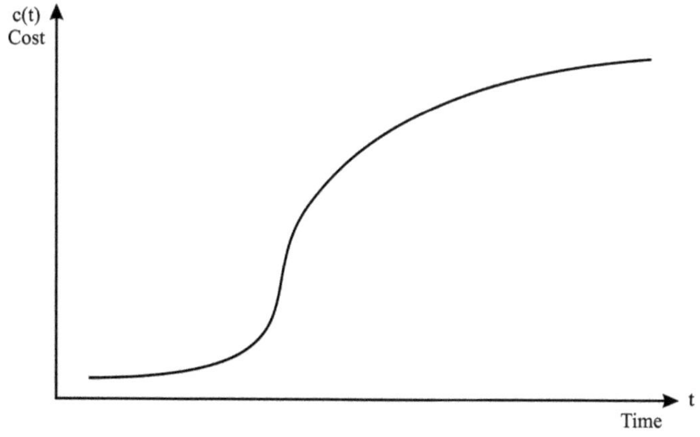

Fig. 13.14 Replacement cost–time correlation

equipment of age t_r updated to the current value; i, the update factor, then: the updated benefit for the first cycle is:

$$\int_0^{t_r} b(t) \cdot exp[-it]dt, \tag{13.10}$$

and the updated replacement cost, $C(t_r) \cdot exp[-it_r]$ will be:

$$B_1(t_r + T_r) = \int_0^{t_r} b(t) \cdot exp[-it]dt - C(t_r) \cdot exp[-it_r] \tag{13.11}$$

Let us consider now the second operating cycle:

$$B_2(t_r + T_r) = \int_0^{t_r} b(t) \cdot exp[-it]dt - C(t_r) \cdot exp[-it_r] \tag{13.12}$$

$B_2(t_r + T_r)$ is the total net updated benefit at the moment of beginning the second cycle.

For updating it at the moment of beginning the first cycle, we use the formula:

$$B_2(t_r + T_r) \cdot exp[-i \cdot (t_r + T_r)] \tag{13.13}$$

Similarly, we calculate the following:

$$B_3(t_r + T_r) \cdot exp[-i \cdot 2 \cdot (t_r + T_r)] \tag{13.14}$$

$$\dots$$

$$B_n(t_r + T_r) \cdot exp[-i \cdot (n - 1) \cdot (t_r + T_r)] \tag{13.15}$$

The total net updated benefit will be given by the sum of the expressions above:

$$\begin{aligned} B(t_r) &= B_1(t_r + T_r) + B_2(t_r + T_r) \cdot exp[-i \cdot (t_r + T_r)] + B_3(t_r + T_r) \\ &\cdot exp[-i \cdot 2 \cdot (t_r + T_r)] + \dots + B_n(t_r + T_r) \cdot exp[-i \cdot (n - 1) \cdot (t_r + T_r)] \end{aligned} \tag{13.16}$$

because:

$$B_1(t_r + T_r) = B_2(t_r + T_r) = \dots = B_n(t_r + T_r) \tag{13.17}$$

$$B(t_r) = B_1(t_r + T_r) \cdot \{1 + exp[-i \cdot (t_r + T_r)] + \dots + [-i \cdot (n - 1) \cdot (t_r + T_r)]\} \tag{13.18}$$

the expression in the accolades is a geometrical progression, tending to infinite. The expression becomes:

$$B(t_r) = \frac{B_1(t_r + T_r)}{\{1 - exp[-i \cdot (t_r + T_r)]\}} = \left\{ \frac{\int_0^{t_r} b(t) \cdot exp[-it]dt - C(t_r) \cdot exp[-it_r]}{\{1 - exp[-i \cdot (t_r + T_r)]\}} \right\} \tag{13.19}$$

With mathematical processing, the formula becomes:

$$\begin{aligned} B(t_r) = &\left(\int_0^{t_r} b(t) \cdot exp[-it]dt - C(t_r) \cdot exp[-it] \right) \\ &\cdot \left\{ \frac{\{1 - exp[-n \cdot i \cdot (t_r + T_r)]\}}{\{1 - exp[-i \cdot (t_r + T_r)]\}} \right\} \end{aligned} \tag{13.20}$$

As the expression in the second brackets is constant, by solving the first equation, we will obtain the optimal value t_r, for which $B(t_r)$ is maximum (Fig. 13.15);

– **The Method of Replacing the Equipments Based on Minimising the Total Cost**

It aims to determine the optimal replacement interval for fixed capital assets, provided that the total cost is minimised.

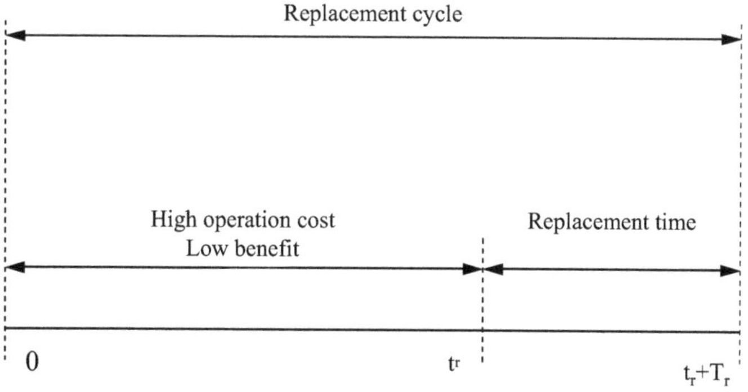

Fig. 13.15 Operating cost, benefit–time correlation

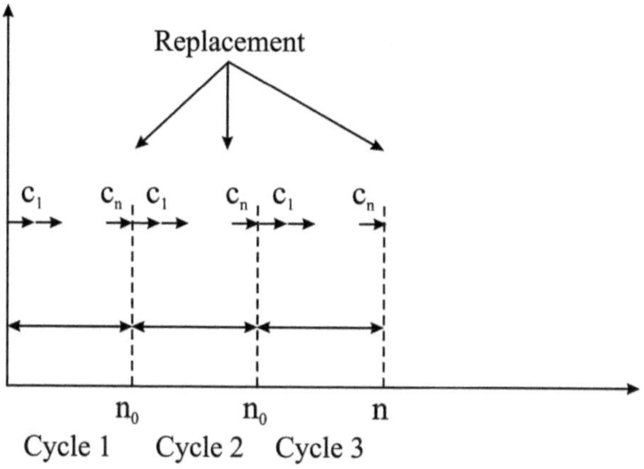

Fig. 13.16 Replacement policy

The data of the problem are similar to those of the previous method, with the difference that, by this method, we try to minimise the maintenance and replacement cost for a long period of time, and the cost is considered to be a discrete variable (not continuous).

Consider: A, cost of purchase of the equipment; C_i, maintenance cost in the period i (to be paid at the end of the period); $i = 1, 2, \ldots n$; S_i, remaining value of the equipment at the end of period I; r, update factor; n, the age (no. of periods) of the equipment, at the moment of replacement thereof; $C(n)$, the total updated maintenance and repair cost for a long period of time, considering that replacements occur after n periods of use.

The proposed goal is the determination of the optimal interval between replacements, so that $C(n)$ is minimal.

We present the replacement policy in Fig. 13.16.

Let us consider the first operating cycle.

The total cost for this first cycle, considering that the equipment is already installed, is:

$$\begin{aligned} C_I(n) &= C_I \cdot r + C_I \cdot r^2 + \ldots + C_n \cdot r^n + A \cdot r^n - S_n \cdot r^n \\ &= \sum_{i=1}^{n} C_i \cdot r^i + r^n \cdot (A - S_n) \end{aligned} \tag{13.21}$$

For the second cycle, the total updated cost at the beginning of the cycle is:

$$C_I(n) = \sum_{i=1}^{n} C_i \cdot r^i + r^n \cdot (A - S_n) \tag{13.22}$$

After the update of such costs at the beginning of cycle 1, the formula for the total updated cost becomes:

$$C(n) = C_I(n) + C_2(n) \cdot r^n + C_3(n) \cdot r^{2n} + \ldots + +C_n(n) \cdot r^{(n-1)n} \tag{13.23}$$

as:

$$C_I(n) = C_2(n) = \ldots = C_n(n) \tag{13.24}$$

is a geometrical progression, which results in the following formula, for an infinite period:

$$C(n) = \frac{C_I(n)}{1 - r^n} = \frac{\sum_{i=1}^{n} C_i \cdot r^i + r^n \cdot (A - S_n)}{1 - r^n} \tag{13.25}$$

The issue was again reduced to a quite simple equation, which may be solved by means of a simple mathematical calculation;

– The Method of Replacing the Equipments Based on Technological Improvement in Finished Time Horizon

Considers that the replacement of an old machine by a new one not always is an exact copy of the old one, but that the latter is better, so that operating and maintenance costs are smaller, efficiency is higher etc. The following model aims at determining the way how the new available machines may be used with a successful purpose, considering that the time period is fixed and finite.

Consider: n, the number of operating periods (periods when the machine must operate); $C_{p,i}$, maintenance cost of the current equipment in the period I ($i = 1, 2, \ldots n$); $S_{p,i}$, sales value of the current equipment at the end of the time period; A, purchase cost for the new, better equipment; $C_{t,j}$, maintenance cost of the new machine in the dj period after installation ($j = 1, 2, \ldots n$); $S_{t,j}$, sale value of the new equipment at the end of the operating period j; r—update factor.

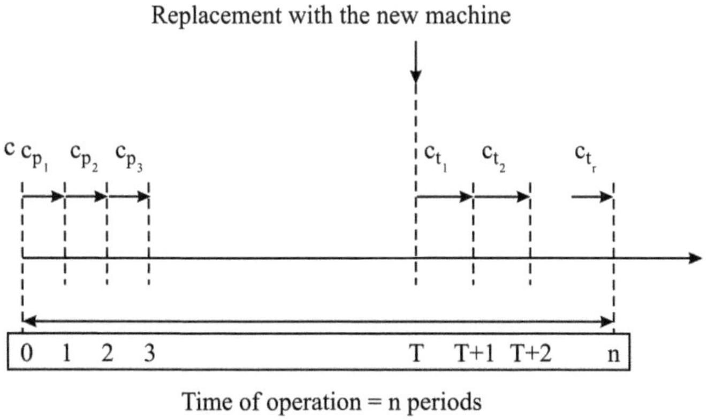

Fig. 13.17 Graphical calculation of T value

The method aims at determining the value T when replacement should be made with the new, better machine (Fig. 13.17) $T = 0, 1, 2, \ldots, n$.

The total updated cost for the n periods when replacement occurs at the end of the T period is: $C(T)$, updated cost for the maintenance of the current machine in the period $(0, T)$, plus the updated maintenance cost of the new machine in the period (T, n), plus the updated purchase cost of the new machine, minus the updated sale value of the current equipment at the end of the T time period, minus the updated sale value of the new equipment at the end of period n:

$$\begin{aligned} C(T) &= \left(C_{p,1} \cdot r^1 + C_{p,2} \cdot r^2 + \ldots + C_{p,T} \cdot r^T\right) \\ &+ \left(C_{t,1} \cdot r^{T+1} + C_{t,2} \cdot r^{T+2} + \ldots + C_{t,n-T} \cdot r^n\right) + A \cdot r^T - \left(S_{p,T} \cdot r^T + C_{t,n-T} \cdot r^n\right) \end{aligned} \tag{13.26}$$

Hence

$$C(T) = \sum_{i=1}^{T} C_{p,i} \cdot r^i + \sum_{j=1}^{n-T} C_{t,j} \cdot r^{T+j} + A \cdot r^T - \left(S_{p,T} \cdot r^T + C_{t,n-T} \cdot r^n\right) \tag{13.27}$$

As the sole unknown variable is T, the minimisation of $C(T)$ depending on T does not raise special issues.

13.3 Econometric Patterns Used for Adopting the Decision of Replacing the Equipments and Machine-Tools

The models used for the replacement of fixed assets include both tangible and intangible factors and generally proceed from Western literature. We talk about the models to be approached in the following paragraphs.

Table 13.1 The pattern of simple score

No.	Decisional factors	Machines 1	2	3
1	Net value	1	1	0
2	Increased productivity	0	1	1
3	Increased flexibility	1	1	0
4	Increased quality and reliability	1	1	1
5	Compatibility	1	0	0
Total score		3	4	3

Table 13.2 The pattern of balanced score

No.	Decisional factors	Ponderosity of the decisional factor	Machines 1	2	3
1	Current net value	1.0	1.0	0.9	0.4
2	Increased productivity	0.9	0.4	1.0	0.8
3	Increased flexibility	0.8	0.4	0.7	1.0
4	Increased quality and reliability	0.8	0.7	0.7	1.0
5	Compatibility	0.6	1.0	0.6	0.5
Total score			2.84	3.28	3.02

The models used for the replacement are:

– The Pattern of Simple Score

It implies taking the following steps: assessment of each machine on basis of a set of factors (*1*—if the machine complies with such factors, *0*—if the machine does not comply with such factors); summing up the value attached to these factors for each type of machine; selecting the machine with the highest score.

Table 13.1 presents this pattern, which is easily applied, but there are certain disadvantages regarding the selection of these criteria and their importance;

– The Pattern of Balanced Score

It considers the importance of the two criteria presented in the previous model. Thus, the most important criterion shall have value *1*, the following *0.9*, and as follows. Table 13.2 presents the application of this model.

$$S_i = \sum_{j=1}^{n} w_{ij} \cdot x_{ij} \tag{13.28}$$

Thus, S_i is the total score for machine i; w_j, the weight of factor j; x_{ij}, the place of machine i depending on the factor j; n, the number of decisional factors; $j = 1, \ldots n$.

This model also considers intangible factors, such as: safety of workers, the impact of machines on social relations, ergonomic issues, psychological state of workers pursuant to the use of machines, life quality and the workers' easiness to understand new technologies;

– Patterns for Optimising the Assignment of Resources

It was conceived by Saad, who developed a linear programming model, trying to optimise the assignment of resources for the purchase of various machines.

Consider: *j*, the index for the new machines to be bought; $j = 1, 2, \ldots n$; *i*, index for financing sources, $i = 1, 2, \ldots m$; π_j, average income for the machine *j*; C_i, capital cost under *I* financing conditions (it also includes the interest for the borrowed funds and the profit reinvested by the company); U_{ij}, the risk associated to the use of the financing source *I* for purchasing machine *j*; $V_{ij} = (\pi_j - C_j) \cdot U_{ij}$, integrated variable of probability $(\pi_j - C_j)$ and risk (U_{ij}); x_{ij}, capital from source *I* used for machine *j*; A_i, accessible capital from source *I*; R_j, required capital for purchasing the equipment *j*.

We have to maximise:

$$Z = \sum_i \sum_j V_{ij} \cdot x_{ij} \tag{13.29}$$

provided that:

$$\sum_i x_{ij} = R_j\,;\ \mathrm{j} = 1, 2, \ldots, \mathrm{n} \tag{13.30}$$

$$\sum_j x_{ij} < A_i;\ \mathrm{j} = 1, 2, \ldots, \mathrm{n} \tag{13.31}$$

$$x_{ij} > 0, \quad for\,any\ i, j$$

Table 13.3 represents the matrix equality between available funds $\left(\sum F_i\right)$ equal to the funds required for purchasing the machine $\left(\sum R_j\right)$.

The implementation of new machines is difficult because of problems such as:

- *workers' resistance, as they are used to the old machine;*
- *lack of will to change the workstyle;*
- *fear of the unknown, i.e. workers are scared that they will lose their jobs pursuant to the introduction of new technologies or that they won't be able to adjust to the new working requirements;*
- *lack of support regarding specialized documentation;*
- *difference of opinions regarding the operation of the equipment;*
- *complexity of the machine.*

The Western literature contains various management models, providing solutions for this issue. These are only valuable in certain economic and cultural contexts, which is why the Romanian manager must use them selectively.

The first model proposed by Western literature is the ***model of the 9 steps***.

Table 13.3 Pattern for optimising the assignment of resources

Specifications			Using the financial resources for the period				Available funds
			T_1	T_2	T_j	T_n	
Source of financing	Internal financing	Profit retained for investments P1	P_{11}	P_{12}	P_{1j}	P_{1n}	F_1
Source of financing	Internal financing	Attracted capital P2	P_{21}	P_{22}	P_{2j}	P_{2n}	F_2
Source of financing	Internal financing	Total	$P_{11}+P_{21}$	$P_{12}+P_{22}$	$P_{1j}+P_{2j}$	$P_{1n}+P_{2n}$	$P=F_1+F_2$
Source of financing	External financing	Long-term credit C_1	C_{11}	C_{12}	C_{1j}	C_{1n}	F_3
Source of financing	External financing	Short-term credit C_2	C_{21}	C_{22}	C_{2j}	C_{2n}	F_4
Source of financing	External financing	Total	C_1	C_2	C_j	C_n	$C=F_3+F_4$
Capital necessary for purchasing the equipment			R_1	R_2	R_j	R_n	$\sum R_j$ \ $\sum_{i=1}^{n} F_i$

These steps are:

- *analysis of the machine's impact on workers and work management;*
- *pheasibility analysis of the machine's goals;*
- *analysis of the machine's relevance;*
- *collective training of all the persons who shall use the machine after commissioning and education thereof regarding calibration and proper use;*
- *analysis of the machine's variability;*
- *proving the machine's value not only in economic, but also in social terms;*
- *changing some features of the machine, depending on the requirements of workers;*
- *implementation of systems which will control the variables related to the technological process.*

The second model proceeds from the researches of Meredith and Green, who elaborated the ***model of the 4 steps*** applied in the implementation of new machines, which includes the following steps:

- *the management team must try to change the organisational enterprise culture, simultaneously with the new technology;*

- *the management team must accept that the new machines can also have negative effects;*
- *a higher degree of oral communication between the manager and performers regarding the new machines;*
- *a change in the company's strategy, as the new machines are used.*

Graynor proposes another model, known as the ***model of the 3 steps***, which implies:

- *all the workers who will work with the new equipment must understand the tasks they must fulfil, as well as their contribution at the enterprise level;*
- *higher attention to key factors and problem factors which may prevent the success of the new tool;*
- *critical and continuous evaluation of the issues which arise and the solutions thereof.*

The success of implementation of the new machines, using any of the presented models, implies teamwork and dedication from all those involved in the process.

References

Askin RM, Standridge CR (1993) Modeling and analysis of manufacturing systems, 1st edn. Wiley, New York

Bean JC, Lohmann JR, Smith RL (1994) Equipment replacement under technological change. Nav Res Log 41:117–128. doi:10.1002/1520-6750(199402)41:1 < 117::AIDNAV3220410108 > 3.0.CO; 2-U.

Dehayem Nodem FI, Kenné JP, Gharbi A (2009) Hierarchical decision making in production and repair/replacement planning with imperfect repairs under uncertainties. Eur J Oper Res 198(1):173–189. doi:10.1016/j.ejor.2008.09.001

Dima IC (2013a) Industrial production management in flexible manufacturing systems. IGI Global, Hersey

Dima IC (2013b) Organisational strategies – a systemic approach – on the example of the automotive industry. Lambert Academic, Saarbrucken

Grifiin R (2008) Management. Houghton Mifflin Company, Boston

Groover MP (2001) Automation, production systems, and computer integrated manufacturing. Prentice Hall, New Jersey

Kmenta J (1991) Elements of econometrics. Macmillan, New York

Kreitner R (2008) Management. Houghten Hifflin Company, Boston

Landon K, Landon Price J (2004) Management information systems. Macmillan, New York

Pindyck K (1986) Econometric models and economic forecasts. McGraw Hill, New York

Samuelson PA (1967) Economics. McGraw Hill, New York

Scarf PA (1997) On the application of mathematical models in maintenance. Eur J Oper Res 99:493–506. doi:10.1016/S0377-2217(96)00316-5

Spirey W (1997) Econometric models. McGraw Hill, New York

Tanchoco JMA, Leung LC (1987) An input-output model for equipment replacement decisions. Eng Cost Prod Econ 11:69–78

Walters AA (1998) An introduction to econometrics. Macmillan, London

Chapter 14
Econometric Models Used in the Management of Production Costs

14.1 Using the Matrix Calculus to Determine the Structure of Primary Production Expenses by Product

The expenses incurred for achieving a certain production volume have a complex feature and knowing their structure in a given period is practically special interest. In order to establish which place the problem of the structure of production expenses occupies in the enterprise's economy, we shall start from the concept of cybernetic system in economy.

In order to elaborate an econometric model of production costs, it is necessary to follow two stages:

Stage 1

Determining the matrix of the structure of primary production costs, by products

Be,

X_j^i—the consumption at the input E_i into the process (*S*), determined by the achievement of a product in the group P_j—unitary primary consumption by product;

Y_j^i—the expense corresponding to consumption X_j^i—the unitary primary expense by product;

p_i—the price of a unit in the primary input E_i, so that,

$$Y_j^i = p_i X_j^i \; (i = 1, 2, \ldots, I; \; j = 1, 2, \ldots, J) \tag{14.1}$$

I.C. Dima, M. Man, *Modelling and Simulation in Management*, Contributions to Management Science, DOI 10.1007/978-3-319-16592-9_14

If we note with:

$$X_*^* = \begin{pmatrix} X_1^1 & X_2^1 & \cdots & X_j^1 & \cdots & X_J^1 \\ X_1^2 & X_2^2 & \cdots & X_j^2 & \cdots & X_J^2 \\ \vdots & \vdots & & \vdots & & \vdots \\ X_1^I & X_2^I & \cdots & X_j^I & \cdots & X_J^I \end{pmatrix} \tag{14.2}$$

the matrix of the unitary primary consumptions, by products,

$$Y_*^* = \begin{pmatrix} Y_1^1 & Y_2^1 & \cdots & Y_j^1 & \cdots & Y_J^1 \\ Y_1^2 & Y_2^2 & \cdots & Y_j^2 & \cdots & Y_J^2 \\ \vdots & \vdots & & \vdots & & \vdots \\ Y_1^I & Y_2^I & \cdots & Y_j^I & \cdots & Y_J^I \end{pmatrix} \tag{14.3}$$

the matrix of the unitary primary expenses, by products,

$$P_* = \begin{pmatrix} p_1 & 0 & \cdots & 0 & \cdots & 0 \\ 0 & p_2 & \cdots & 0 & \cdots & 0 \\ \vdots & \vdots & & \vdots & & \vdots \\ 0 & 0 & \cdots & 0 & \cdots & p_I \end{pmatrix} \tag{14.4}$$

then, in a matrix form, (14.1) we can write:

$$Y_*^* = P_* X_*^* \tag{14.5}$$

While for fixed i and j p_i is a constant, the sizes X_j^i and Y_j^i are variables and the variable X_j^i can respectively receive the values $a_{j1}^i, a_{j2}^i, \ldots, a_{jN_j}^i$ in a number of N_j, as many units there are in the group of products P_j.

If we insert the average value of the variable X_j^i,

$$\overline{X_j^i} = \frac{1}{N_j}\left(a_{j1}^i + a_{j2}^i + \ldots + a_{jN_j}^i\right) \tag{14.6}$$

then, from (14.1), it results that

$$\overline{Y_j^i} = p_i \overline{X_j^i} \; (i = 1, 2, \ldots, I; \; j = 1, 2, \ldots, J) \tag{14.7}$$

or, by using the matrix writing,

$$\overline{Y_*^*} = P_* \overline{X_*^*} \tag{14.8}$$

where,

$$\overline{X_*^*} = \begin{pmatrix} \overline{X_1^1} & \overline{X_2^1} & \cdots & \overline{X_j^1} & \cdots & \overline{X_J^1} \\ \overline{X_1^2} & \overline{X_2^2} & \cdots & \overline{X_j^2} & \cdots & \overline{X_J^2} \\ \vdots & \vdots & & \vdots & & \vdots \\ \overline{X_1^I} & \overline{X_2^I} & \cdots & \overline{X_j^I} & \cdots & \overline{X_J^I} \end{pmatrix} \tag{14.9}$$

and

$$\overline{Y_*^*} = \begin{pmatrix} \overline{Y_1^1} & \overline{Y_2^1} & \cdots & \overline{Y_j^1} & \cdots & \overline{Y_J^1} \\ \overline{Y_1^2} & \overline{Y_2^2} & \cdots & \overline{Y_j^2} & \cdots & \overline{Y_J^2} \\ \vdots & \vdots & & \vdots & & \vdots \\ \overline{Y_1^I} & \overline{Y_2^I} & \cdots & \overline{Y_j^I} & \cdots & \overline{Y_J^I} \end{pmatrix} \tag{14.10}$$

For a given period, the elements of matrix (14.10) are constant. These constants achieve a connection between the components of the input and output of the process (S). Thus, on the line i ($i = 1, 2, \ldots, I$) of the matrix, we can read how much was spent on average during that period of the element E_i per product unit, respectively in the group P1, group P2 ..., group P_j. In column j ($j = 1, 2, \ldots, J$) we also read the average expense, respectively from the components of primary input $E_1, E_2, \ldots, E_I$, which returns on a product unit from group P_J. This means that the matrix (14.10) synthetically characterises the structure of the production expenses by primary elements of expense and products. For this reason, this matrix will be called *the matrix of the structure of primary production costs, by products*, and matrix (14.9) will be called the *matrix of the structure of primary consumptions, by products.*

Knowing the elements of the matrix (14.10) is indispensable in calculating the price by product unit, in assessing the efficiency of the production process, by comparing the actual structure to the planned one, the profitability of the various products and of the process as a whole. In other words, knowing the matrix of the structure of production expenses by products would enable a deeper and thorough analysis of the production cost, by using some appropriate mathematical methods or programming models where the function to be optimised is a production expense. The prediction of the elements of the matrix of primary production costs structure would also enable the controller of the system to adjust the behaviour of the driven process, by comparing the probable structure to the controlled structure.

Stage 2

Analysis of the current way of determining the matrix of the structure of primary production costs, by products

Starting from the importance of the elements of the matrix of primary production costs structure—by products, in conducting the production process, the need to calculate them during any period becomes obvious. But it results from (14.8) that the possibility to calculate the elements of the matrix (14.10) is conditioned by knowing the elements of matrices (14.4) and (14.9).

Regarding the matrix (14.4), based on the current system of record, only those elements corresponding to the primary input components from outside the system are known. For the other elements of the matrix (14.4), their calculation method is prepared. From (14.6), it results that the elements of the matrix (14.10) depend on the results of the measurements concerning the variables that form the matrix (14.2). Or the measurements $a^i_{j1}, a^i_{j2}, \ldots, a^i_{jN_j}$ obtained in relation to the variable X^i_j are not generally noted in the existing informational documents, either due to the large volume of data and therefore of work, or due to the impossibility for some of them to be obtained. In the documents existing at the manufacturing units, only the following results are noted down:

$$X^i_j = \sum_J X^i_j = \sum_J \left(a^i_{j1} + a^i_{j2} + \ldots + a^i_{jN_j}\right) \tag{14.11}$$

for some of the values $i = 1, 2, \ldots, I$. In other words, in the existing informational documents, the complete consumptions are found to be recorded for one part of the components of primary input $E_1, E_2, \ldots, E_I$.

If we insert the notation:

$$X^i_\bullet = C^i_\bullet \; (i = 1, 2, \ldots, I) \tag{14.12}$$

then the following system results:

$$\begin{cases} N_1\overline{X^1_1} + N_2\overline{X^1_2} + \ldots + N_J\overline{X^1_J} = C^1_\bullet \\ N_1\overline{X^2_1} + N_2\overline{X^2_2} + \ldots + N_J\overline{X^2_J} = C^2_\bullet \\ \cdots\cdots\cdots\cdots\cdots\cdots\cdots\cdots\cdots\cdots \\ N_1\overline{X^I_1} + N_2\overline{X^I_2} + \ldots + N_J\overline{X^I_J} = C^I_\bullet \end{cases} \tag{14.13}$$

or the matrix one,

$$\overline{X^*_*}N_* = C^*_\bullet \tag{14.14}$$

where, the transpositions of the vectors N_* and $C^*_\bullet$ respectively have the following components:

$$N^T_* = (N_1 \quad N_2 \quad \ldots \quad N_J) \tag{14.15}$$

and

$$C^*_* T = (C^1_\bullet \quad C^2_\bullet \quad \ldots \quad C^I_\bullet) \tag{14.16}$$

In general $I \geq 1, J \geq 1$.

If J is equal to 1, the output from the process is reduced to a single group of products and we say in this case that the process is with *homogeneous output*.

Assuming that in the case of J = 1, the output from the process is mistaken for example to the group of products P_1, and the system of equations (14.13) becomes:

$$N_1\overline{X_1^i} = C_\bullet^i \ (i = 1, 2, \ldots, I)$$

where from,

$$\overline{X_1^i} = \frac{C_\bullet^i}{N_1} = \frac{1}{N_1}\left(a_{11}^i + a_{12}^i + \ldots + a_{1N_1}^i\right) \ i = \overline{1,I} \tag{14.17}$$

Therefore, if the output from the process is age homogeneous, the elements of the matrix (14.10), reduced to a vector-column is uniquely determined, namely:

$$\begin{pmatrix} \overline{Y_1^1} \\ \overline{Y_1^2} \\ \vdots \\ \overline{Y_1^I} \end{pmatrix} = \begin{pmatrix} p_1 & 0 & \ldots & 0 \\ 0 & p_2 & \ldots & 0 \\ \vdots & \vdots & & \vdots \\ 0 & 0 & \ldots & p_I \end{pmatrix} \begin{pmatrix} \overline{X_1^1} \\ \overline{X_1^2} \\ \vdots \\ \overline{X_1^I} \end{pmatrix} \tag{14.18}$$

where, the elements of the last vector are calculated according to formula (14.17).

However, in reality such cybernetic systems with homogeneous output from the process are encountered relatively rarely. The most common case encountered is that where the output from the process is heterogeneous.

If the cybernetic system taken into account has *the output from the process heterogeneous*, meaning $J > 1$, then because I is over-unitary, it results that the product IJ will be strictly greater than 1. The problem in this case is not determined, the restrictions established are not sufficient, as it is necessary to find some additional information on the elements of the matrix (14.9).

Due to the fact that the number of unknowns in the system of equations (14.13) generally exceeds the number of equations, in economic practice, with all of the great importance knowing the elements of the matrix (14.9) has and finally the elements of the matrix (14.10), starting from the known components of the vector (14.16), only the components of the following vector are calculated:

$$P_*C_\bullet^* = \begin{pmatrix} p_1C_\bullet^1 \\ p_2C_\bullet^2 \\ \vdots \\ p_IC_\bullet^I \end{pmatrix} \tag{14.19}$$

In order to yet achieve a connection between the input and output from the production process—as the only way to be able to assess its efficiency—in the economic theory and practice, another decomposition of the input into the process was used. Decomposition starts from the following two considerations: The production process is carried out by production departments; part of the inputs into the process are found or can be found entirely in the outputs from the production and therefore they can be actually measured, quantified.

Such a classification of the inputs into the process includes: raw materials and direct materials, direct labour force, input intended for the maintenance and operation of machines, inputs intended to manage the activity of the departments, inputs intended to manage the process as a whole, etc. and is encountered under the name of *grouping the inputs by calculation items*.

A similar *grouping* of the *production costs by calculation items* corresponds to grouping the input into the process, respectively the production means and labour force by calculation items, namely: expenses with the raw materials and direct materials; direct wages; expenses with the maintenance and operation of the machine; overheads of departments; overheads of the enterprise; expenses with losses from waste; marketing expenses; expenses for introducing new techniques, etc.

The components of production expenses resulted as such are divided in their turn into two groups, namely: components of direct expenses and components of indirect expenses.

In order to explain the meaning in which the concept of direct and indirect expense is used, let us analyse for example the expense with the labour force, respectively the remunerations, which can also be direct or indirect.

Direct remunerations includes the basic remunerations for workers' basic wage, respectively for the remuneration of workers working directly to achieve the products.

Indirect remunerations are those remunerations partially included into the *expenses with the maintenance and operation of the machine* (the remuneration of the personnel directly involved in the maintenance and performance of current repairs for the production machines and means of transportation, as well as the remunerations also representing expenses with the maintenance and operation of the machine of a department included in the prices of delivered energy and fuel and of other works performed or services provided by the other production departments), into the *general expenses of the production departments* (basic and additional remunerations with the technical and administrative personnel, as well as remunerations also representing general expenses of the production departments, included in the price of the delivered energy and fuel and of other works performed by the other production departments) and into the *general expenses of the enterprise* (basic and additional remunerations of the management and administrative personnel, as well as the remunerations included in the prices of the delivered energy and fuel and of other works performed or services provided at the level of the enterprise by its production departments).

Starting from this example, we can define the concept of the direct expense and indirect expense in general.

The expense Y_j^i is called *indirect expense*, if the variable of the consumption X_j^i cannot be subject to a direct statistical observation, meaning it cannot be measured. The expense Y_j^i is called *direct expense*, if the variable of the consumption X_j^i can be subject to a direct statistical observation, meaning it can be measured. This means that by decomposing the input into the process by calculation items, in relation to the components of direct expense, there is the possibility to have an additional information outside the system of equations (14.13), which would consist in the results of measuring the variables of matrix (14.2) of primary unitary consumptions by products. In other words, if X_j^i is an element of the matrix (14.2), then we have the following measurements regarding it:

$$a_{j1}^i,\ a_{j2}^i,\ \ldots,\ a_{jN_j}^i \tag{14.20}$$

for $j = 1, 2, \ldots, J$ and part of the values $i = 1, 2, \ldots, I$.

In the economic practice, due to the high volume of work required to octane the measurements (14.20), these are not done and thus, in order to establish the elements of the matrix of primary production costs structure, we use empirical methods.

Such a method, frequently used in the economic practice is that of distributing the direct production expenses by products, in proportion to the production volume.

If we note with:

v_j—the value volume of production in group P_j;
v—the value volume of the entire production;
z_j^i—the direct expense with the input E_i necessary to make a N_j units in the group of products P_j;
$p_j{}'$—the price which the production in group P_j is assessed at.

Then, the method of distributing direct production expenses by products, in proportion to the value volume of production, leads to the following equalities:

$$\frac{z_1^i}{v_1} = \frac{z_2^i}{v_2} = \ldots = \frac{z_J^i}{v_J} = \frac{p_i C_\bullet^i}{v}\ (i = 1, 2, \ldots, I)$$

$$z_j^i = \frac{p_i C_\bullet^i}{v} v_j = c_\bullet^i p_i{}' N_j\ \left(i = 1, 2, \ldots, I;\ j = \overline{1, i}\right) \tag{14.21}$$

On the other hand,

$$\overline{Y_j^i} N_j = p_i \overline{X_j^i} N_j\ \left(i = \overline{1, I};\ j = \overline{1, J}\right) \tag{14.22}$$

By comparing the result (14.21) to (14.22), we can conclude that the current way of distributing the direct expenses by products is accurate to the extent where the average unitary consumptions and the prices which the achieved production is assessed at are respectively proportional, meaning:

$$\frac{p_1{}'}{\overline{\overline{X_1^i}}} = \frac{p_2{}'}{\overline{\overline{X_2^i}}} = \ldots = \frac{p_J{}'}{\overline{\overline{X_J^i}}} \tag{14.23}$$

But it is difficult to assume that the equalities (14.23) can be practically achieved, so that the method described above and used in the economic practice does not have a scientific background and any other method that would disregard the information contained in the result of the direct measurements of the variables of matrix (14.2).

Another method of empirical feature and used in the economic practice is that which approximates the elements of matrix (14.9) of the structure of primary consumptions during a period t with the corresponding matrix from the previous period or with the matrix of the structure of consumptions planned during the period t. The empirical feature of this method results from the fact that both the planned and actual structure from the period $t-1$ may essentially differ from the actual structure of the average primary consumptions in the period t. Starting from this situation, we tried and achieved some results regarding the distribution of direct expenses by items.

Still remaining at the considered case of the heterogeneous output from the production process (S), let us analyse the problem of determining the structure of indirect production expenses.

If the methods used did not take into account the potential information (14.20) in order to determine the structure of direct expenses, being based exclusively on the conditions (14.13), the methods to determine the structure of indirect expenses cannot take into account such an information because it does not exist in reality. Practically, being a matter of indirect expenses, the variables of matrix (14.2) cannot be measured. For example, by means of direct measurements, it is impossible to know the share of the remuneration of the manager, engineer, guardian, etc., which corresponds to the various products of group P_j $(j=1, J)$, their activity serving the process as a whole. As a result, the methods used in the economic practice also have in this case—in a somewhat justified way—a conventional nature, as they take into account only the conditions (14.13).

Among the methods used in the economic practice for this purpose, we recall the following: the method of equivalence indices and the method of supplementation.

For example, the method of supplementation consists in distributing the indirect production expenses on the basic production of a supplementation coefficient established by relating the indirect expenses to an element from direct expenses (raw materials, remunerations, etc.) to several elements or to the total expenses which contributed to the production achieved.

In such situations, the matrix thus obtained for the structure of indirect production expenses does not reflect the actual structure of the production expenses, with all consequences resulting from here, including: determining the cost by product unit, the production price, the delivery price, etc.

To summarise the observations regarding the problem of determining the matrix of the primary production costs structure, it is required to consider and separately study the following two cases:

- if the output from the production process is homogeneous, then the restrictions (14.13) on the elements of matrix (14.9) and components of vectors (14.15) and (14.16), being given, uniquely determine the matrix of the structure of primary consumptions by product and finally the matrix of the primary production costs structure by products. In this case, the problem of distributing the production expenses by elements and products can be considered as solved;
- even the output from the production process is heterogeneous, the unknown matrix of the structure of primary production costs, by products, and can be decomposed into the amount of the following two matrices: the expenses that, they given problem decomposes in its turn into two problems: matrix of the structure of direct primary expenses and the matrix of the structure of indirect primary expenses.

Thus, the given problem also decomposes into two problems. Both the unknown elements of the matrix of the direct primary consumptions and those of the matrix of indirect primary consumptions satisfy a certain number of linear equations of the type (14.13), in both cases being smaller than the number of unknowns, with the difference that: in the case of the structure of direct primary consumptions, the variables of matrix (14.2) can be—theoretically and practically—subject to a direct observation, while in the case of the structure of indirect expenses, the variables of matrix (14.2) cannot be subject to such an observation, however not excluding the possibility of some direct measurable factors, which the variables of matrix (14.2) depend upon.

If in the case of components of direct expense, the elements of the collectivity of products distributed in the groups P_1, P_2, ..., P_J we subject them to a total observation, by the variables of matrix (14.2), we get as a result (14.20), based on which, by means of the relations (14.6) we get the matrix (14.9) and then the wanted matrix from (14.8).

This process is not efficient (this can become efficient by using the IT technique), because: the volume of work it requires, the total observation of the $N = N_1 + N_2 + \ldots + N_J$ elements of the collectivity of products is very big, practically almost impossible to achieve. It is therefore required to find a way to solve the problem which would be based on the results of observation by the variables of matrix (14.2), and not of the entire collectivity of products, but only of a sub-collectivity of selection, having the volume $n = n_1 + \ldots + n_J$. Thus, this problem translates into a problem of assessment, which could be formulated more accurately as follows: *the assessment of some parameters*—the elements of the matrix of the structure of primary consumptions (14.9) and then the elements of the matrix of the structure of direct expenses (14.10)—*subject to connections*—the system of linear equations (14.3)—based on a *sample of direct observations*.

For the case of indirect expense components, assuming that those directly observable factors which the variables of matrix (14.2) depend upon can be emphasised and that we start from a random sample of measurements, performed on the factors, the given problem also becomes a problem of assessment, which would be formulated more generally as follows: *the assessment of some parameters—the elements of the matrix of the structure of indirect primary expenses* (14.10)—*subject to connections*—the system of linear equations (14.13)—*based on a random sample of indirect observations*.

In conclusion, the economic problem of distributing the production expenses by products is in reality a problem of mathematical statistics, more exactly of estimation theory. Furthermore, both the model of estimating the structure of direct production expenses and especially that of estimating the structure of indirect expenses are a new models to estimate the parameters, which leads to the development of the estimation theory.

14.2 Addressing the Organisational Entities by Using the Systems Theory

Making the finished and semi-finished products within an enterprise is conditioned by a certain organisation of the production process. In general, organising the production process occurs by production departments, and it is decomposed by operations within the departments. By the role they have in making the products of the enterprise, the production departments can be main (basic) or auxiliary.

The main or basic departments are the headquarters of basic activities of an enterprise, the main production places. All operations required to make a product are performed in the basic departments. The activity in the basic departments is completed and served by an entire range of auxiliary activities performed by auxiliary departments. The auxiliary departments (the power plant, the water unit, the steam plant, maintenance and repair unit, modelling facility, etc.) mainly aim to provide the conditions necessary to perform various production operations that occur in the main departments. The auxiliary departments also provide mutual services.

Therefore, it results that both the basic activity performed in the main production departments and the secondary activities performed within the auxiliary departments contribute in obtaining the finished products of an enterprise. Certain connections are established between them, wherein changes of activities and information occur. They influence each other, eventually tending to achieve a self-adjustment process. As a result, the enterprise may be conceived as a complex macroeconomic cybernetic system and the subsystems it is made of can be the departments where the production process is performed.

(P1)—main production department
(*P2*)—main production department
(*P3*)—main production department
(D_{P1}), (D_{P2}), (D_{P3})—the places for storing the products of the main departments P1, P2, P3
(D_{Pf})—the warehouse of finished products of the enterprise
(R)—controller of the conducted process

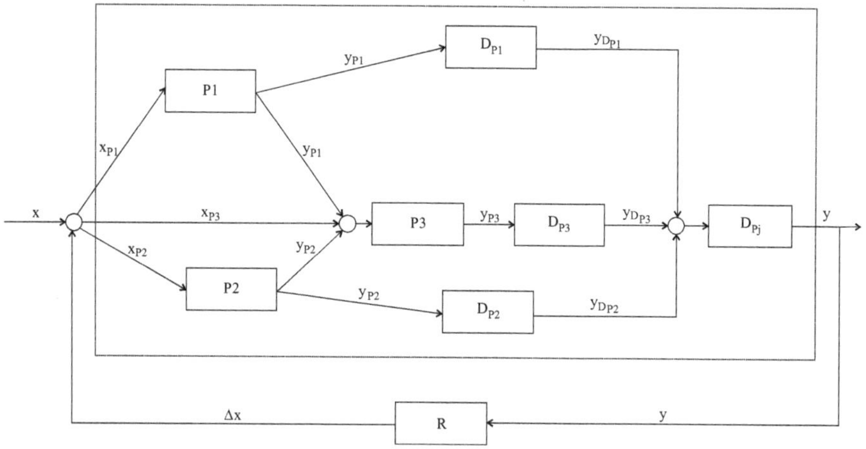

Fig. 14.1 Diagram of an industrial enterprise

P1, *P2*, *P3*, D_{P1}, D_{P2}, D_{P3}—operators of the processes corresponding to those workstations
R—operator of the controller of conducted process
X—the vector of the input into the conducted process
Y—the vector of the output from the process
ΔX—input correction

As example, in Fig. 14.1, we present the block diagram of an industrial enterprise.

Obviously, in the given diagram, as in general, the connection of the departments is mixed.

To enter the production process (S) of the system decomposed by departments, the classification by primary elements is maintained:

$$\mathrm{E}_1,\ \mathrm{E}_2,\ \ldots,\ \mathrm{E}_\mathrm{I}\left(\mathrm{i}=\overline{1,\ \mathrm{I}}\right) \tag{14.24}$$

where E_i can represent: raw materials, basic and auxiliary materials, fuel, energy, fixed means, labour force, etc. The entry thus decomposed is also an input for the subsystems of the system taken into account, respectively for the main departments and auxiliary departments of the enterprise. Due to the role the auxiliary departments have, that of serving the main departments in performing the production process, the input into a main department can also include components representing outputs of the auxiliary departments. This means that the entrance into a main department of a certain primary element $E_i\left(\mathrm{i}=\overline{1,\ \mathrm{I}}\right)$ consists of:

- the share of the input into the system of element E_i intended to that department;
- the share of the input into the system of element E_i intended to auxiliary departments and included in their output to that department.

If the name of *own primary input* is inserted for the first component of the input from the element E_i and of *primary transferred input* for the second component, then the input from the primary element $E_i\left(i = \overline{1, I}\right)$ in any main department consists of the own input and its transferred input. Obviously, this decomposition is also maintained if the input $E_i\left(i = \overline{1, I}\right)$ occurs in an auxiliary department.

The own or transferred primary input E_i in a certain main production department is subject to some transformation operations in order to achieve the controlled output from the process (S).

If the output from the process (S) is considered to consist of a collectivity of products distributed into J groups, by kinds:

$$P_1,\ P_2,\ \ldots,\ P_J\left(j = \overline{1, J}\right) \tag{14.25}$$

then achieving any product of the group P_j involves the performance of the following on the primary own input components:

M_{j1} operations in the main department 1
M_{j2} operations in the main department 2
……………………………………………
M_{JS^*} operations in the main department S*
(S*—the number of main departments).

The operations required to be done on the own primary input components in the first $S^* < S$ production departments, respectively in the main departments, so that the output from the process (S) would be part of the group of products P_j, can be shown in the following table:

$$\begin{vmatrix} O_{j11} & O_{j12} & \cdots & O_{j1M_{j1}} \\ O_{j21} & O_{j22} & \cdots & O_{j2M_{j2}} \\ \vdots & \vdots & & \vdots \\ O_{jS^*1} & O_{jS^*2} & \cdots & O_{jS^*M_{jS^*}} \end{vmatrix} \tag{14.26}$$

where, by $O_{jsu_{js}}$ we noted the operation $u_{js}\left(u_{js} = \overline{1, M_{js}}\right)$ performed in the main department $s\left(s = \overline{1, S^*}\right)$ in connection with any of the products of group $P_j\left(j = \overline{1, J}\right)$.

If the output from the process (S) is heterogeneous and made of J groups of products, then the number of the tables of the type (14.26) is equal to J and reflects the difference between the technologies of the products located in different groups. Those J tables are identical if the output is homogeneous.

While the primary input components, which occur in the main departments, are the object of the transformations shown in table (14.26), the primary input components transferred in the same departments aim to ensure the conditions necessary to perform these operations and therefore to achieve the final purpose—the controlled output from the system, consisting of J groups of products.

Part of the own primary input components, such as some raw materials and basic materials, are directly consumed when manufacturing the products forming their substance, which facilitates the identification and measurement of their consumption by various operations. Some auxiliary materials are also included in this category. The work consumption related to various operations and products of workers directly working to achieve the production can also be measured.

The primary input into a main department the consumption of which can be measured by operations and products is called *directly measurable primary input*, otherwise referred to as *non-directly measurable primary input.*

Obviously, part of the own primary input component is directly measurable, while part of it is non-directly measurable. Any directly measurable primary input into a section is necessarily own; whereas a non-directly measurable primary input can be both own or transferred.

Considering the primary input $E_i \left(i = \overline{1, I}\right)$ it's directly measurable component will be noted with E_{i0} and the non-directly measurable component with E_{i1}. In its turn, the non-directly measurable primary input E_{i1} from any main department is decomposed into the following components: E_{i10} and E_{i11} where:

E_{i10}—own component;
E_{i11}—transferred component;

For the directly measurable primary input E_{i0}, it is not necessary to use a third index, as this is not always own.

Starting from the destination which an owner or transferred component of non-directly measurable primary input, in relation to the production process of a department for E_{i10} and E_{i11} the following classification occurs:

E_{i101}, respectively E_{i111}—component of the primary input E_{i10} and E_{i11} intended for the maintenance and operation of the machine in the department;
E_{i102}, respectively E_{i112}—component of the primary input E_{i10} and E_{i11} intended for conducting the process in a main department;
E_{i103}, respectively E_{i113}—component of the input E_{i10} and E_{i11} in a main department intended to conduct the process as a whole;

Following these classifications, the primary input $E_i \left(i = \overline{1, I}\right)$ in a main production department consists of the following seven components:

E_{i0}—component of the primary input E_i, which is directly measurable;
E_{i101}—component of the primary input E_i, which is non-directly measurable, own, intended for the maintenance and operation of the machine in the a main department;
E_{i102}—component of the primary input E_i, non-directly measurable, own, intended to conduct the activity in a main department, meaning the component of the primary input E_{i10}, which is the control information of the controller (R_S) to the process (S_S) in that department $s = \overline{1, S^*}$—*own local control information*;
E_{i103}—component of the primary input E_i non-directly measurable, intended to conduct the process as a whole, which lies in a main production department,

meaning that component of the primary input E_{i10} in a main section, representing the control information of the controller (R) of the process (S), to a main production department $s = \overline{1, S^*}$—*own central control information*;

E_{i111}—component of the primary input E_i, which is non-directly measurable, transferred, intended for the maintenance and operation of the machine in the department where it comes from;

E_{i112}—component from the primary input E_i, non-directly measurable, transferred and intended to manage the department where it comes from, meaning that component of the input E_{i11} into a main department, representing the control information of the controller of an auxiliary department $s = S^*, S^* + 1, \ldots, S$ to the own process—*transferred local control information*;

E_{i113}—component from the primary input E_i, non-directly measurable, transferred, intended to manage the process as a hole, meaning that component of the input E_{i11} in a main department, representing the control information of the controller (S) if the process (S) to an auxiliary department $s = S^*, S^* + 1, \ldots, S$—*transferred central control information.*

In conclusion, the enterprise can be seen as a complex microeconomic cybernetic system, wherein:

- the process (S) is the result of serial, parallel or mixed connection of the production departments and, in their turn, cybernetic subsystems with reverse connection;
- the controller of the process (S) is the element (R)—the management of the enterprise along with the managements of its departments and divisions;
- the input into the process (S) consists of the primary elements (14.24);
- the input E_i into each department—is characterised by the components,

$$E_{i0},\ E_{i101},\ E_{i102},\ E_{i103},\ E_{i111},\ E_{i112},\ E_{i113}\left(\mathrm{i} = \overline{1, \mathrm{I}}\right) \tag{14.27}$$

and by the operations (14.26) which it is subject to in order to achieve the output (14.25).

Starting from the sense of the enterprise as complex microeconomic cybernetic system, we can proceed to creating the econometric model of assessing the parameters characterising the structure of production expenses, but creating this model involves the prior introduction of some preparatory elements;

14.3 Developing an Econometric Model of the Production Cost

Elaborating such a model is a complex process that involves going through several stages, namely:

(a) *the variables of primary consumptions are established by production departments and technological operations*

If we consider (W) the microeconomic cybernetic system of the enterprise and consider the output from the production process **(S), then** achieving N_j units from the output P_j within a certain period involves performing the operations of the table (14.26) and their repetition of N_j times on the primary input E_i—in each of the S* main department. Along with performing this process, a consumption from each primary input E_i $\left(i = \overline{1, I}\right)$ occurs by departments and operations, a consumption that can vary from one group of products to another $P_j\left(j = \overline{1, J}\right)$.

Given the primary input E_i, the output P_j and the table of operations (14.26), the following table of variables will be attached:

$$\begin{vmatrix} X^i_{j11} & X^i_{j12} & \cdots & X^i_{j1M_{j1}} \\ X^i_{j21} & X^i_{j22} & \cdots & X^i_{j2M_{j2}} \\ \vdots & \vdots & & \vdots \\ X^i_{jS^*1} & X^i_{jS^*2} & \cdots & X^i_{jS^*M_{jS^*}} \end{vmatrix} \tag{14.28}$$

where, $X^i_{jsu_{js}}$ is the consumption from the primary input E_i $\left(i = \overline{1, I}\right)$ determined by the achievement of the operation $O_{jsu_{js}}$.

Starting from the meaning of the table elements, of inserted the variables, they will further be called *variables of the primary consumptions by departments and operations*. Table (14.28) is therefore a table of the variables of primary consumptions E_i intended to the output P_j—by departments and operations.

Let us consider now the seven components of the primary input E_i and inserted the following notation:

$A_{jsu_{js}}$—the consumption from the primary input E_{i0} determined by the achievement of the operation $O_{jsu_{js}}$—*variable of the direct primary consumption*;

$X^{i101}_{jsu_{js}}$—the consumption from the primary input E_{i101}, in the operation $O_{jsu_{js}}$—*own indirect primary consumption intended for the maintenance and operation of the machine in a main department*;

$X^{i102}_{jsu_{js}}$—the consumption from the input E_{i102} into the operation $O_{jsu_{js}}$—variable of the primary, indirect, own consumption intended to conduct the activity in a main department or variable of the primary (indirect, own) consumption *of own local control information*;

$X^{i103}_{jsu_{js}}$—consumption from the input E_{i103} into the operation $O_{jsu_{js}}$—*variable of the indirect, own consumption from the central control information*;

$X^{i111}_{jsu_{js}}$—the consumption from the input E_{i111}, into the operation $O_{jsu_{js}}$—*variable of the indirect primary transferred consumption intended for the maintenance and operation of the machine* in the department where it comes from;

$X^{i112}_{jsu_{js}}$—consumption from the input E_{i112} into the operation $O_{jsu_{js}}$—*variable of the indirect, primary transferred consumption of the local control information*;

$X^{i113}_{jsu_{js}}$—consumption from the input E_{i113} into the operation $O_{jsu_{js}}$—*variable of the indirect, primary transferred consumption from the central control information.*

Based on the meaning of the notations inserted, whatever the variable of the primary consumption $X^{i}_{jsu_{js}}$, would be, the following decomposition occurs:

$$X^{i}_{jsu_{js}} = X^{i0}_{jsu_{js}} + \sum_{k=0}^{1} X^{i1k1}_{jsu_{js}} + \sum_{k=0}^{1} X^{i1k2}_{jsu_{js}} + \sum_{k=0}^{1} X^{i1k3}_{jsu_{js}} \quad (14.29)$$

The size $X^{i0}_{jsu_{js}}$ being a variable of the direct primary consumption, it means that the assumption of repeating the operation $O_{jsu_{js}}$ on the input E_{i0} of $N^{i0}_{jsu_{js}}$ times, the values

$$\left(a^{i0}_{jsu_{js}1},\ a^{i0}_{jsu_{js}2},\ \ldots,\ a^{i0}_{jsu_{js}N^{i0}_{jsu_{js}}} \right) \quad (14.30)$$

can be known by a direct statistical observation, what ever would be $i = \overline{1, I}$; $j = \overline{1, J}$; $s = \overline{1, S^*}$, $u_{js} = \overline{1, M_{js}}$. In this way, the vector of the measurements (14.1)–(14.3) can be associated to each of the $\sum_{(j)} S^*(M_{j1} + M_{j2} + \ldots + M_{jS^*})$ variables of the direct primary consumptions. Moreover, in relation to these variables, the integral consumptions from the primary input E_{i0} into any main production department are also known, independent of the individual consumptions (14.1)–(14.3). In other words, for a fixed period, whatever the primary component E_{i0}, in the record documents, the following vector is noted:

$$X^{i0^T}_{\bullet*\bullet} = \left(X^{i0}_{\bullet1\bullet}\ \ X^{i0}_{\bullet2\bullet}\ \ \ldots\ \ X^{i0}_{\bullet S\bullet} \right) \quad (14.31)$$

where,

$$X^{i0}_{\bullet S\bullet} = \sum_{j} \sum_{u_{js}} \left(a^{i0}_{jsu_{js1}} + a^{i0}_{jsu_{js2}} + \ldots + a^{i0}_{jsu_{js}N^{i0}_{jsu_{js}}} \right)$$

If we insert the notation,

$$X^{i0}_{\bullet S\bullet} = C^{i0}_{\bullet S\bullet} \quad (14.32)$$

then the vector of integral direct primary consumptions is written as follows:

$$C^{i0^T}_{\bullet*\bullet} = \left(C^{i0}_{\bullet1\bullet}\ \ C^{i0}_{\bullet2\bullet}\ \ \ldots\ \ C^{i0}_{\bullet S*\bullet} \right) \quad (14.33)$$

While for the variables of the direct primary consumptions, the results (14.30) can be obtained by a direct, statistical observation, this is not possible for the variables of the indirect primary consumptions. However, for these, it is possible that whatever may be the primary input E_{i1kr} into the operation $O_{jsu_{js}}$, the cause factors determining its consumption, factors which can also be subject to a direct statistical observation.

Taking this into account, let us concede that the variable $X^{i1kr}_{jsu_{js}}$ and note with:

$$\left(X^{i1kr}_{jsu_{js}}\right)_1, \left(X^{i1kr}_{jsu_{js}}\right)_2, \ldots, \left(X^{i1kr}_{jsu_{js}}\right)_{H^{i1kr}_{jsu_{js}}} \tag{14.34}$$

the cause factors determining the consumption $X^{i1kr}_{jsu_{js}}$. For the cause factors that inserted, we shall use the name of *factorial variables*, while for $X^{i1kr}_{jsu_{js}}$ we shall use the name of *resultant variable*, whatever may be $i = \overline{1, I}$; $j = \overline{1, J}$; $k = 0, 1$; $r = 1, 2, 3$; $s = \overline{1, S^*}$; $u_{js} = \overline{1, M_{js}}$.

We suppose now that the dependence between the resultant variable $X^{i1kr}_{jsu_{js}}$ and the factorial variables (34) are expressed as follows:

$$X^{i1kr}_{jsu_{js}} = G^{i1kr}_{jsu_{js}}\left[\left(X^{i1kr}_{jsu_{js}}\right)_1, \left(X^{i1kr}_{jsu_{js}}\right)_2, \ldots, \left(X^{i1kr}_{jsu_{js}}\right)_{H^{i1kr}_{jsu_{js}}}\right] \tag{14.35}$$

for any $i = \overline{1, I}$; $j = \overline{1, J}$; $k = 0, 1$; $r = 1, 2, 3$; $s = \overline{1, S^*}$; $u_{js} = \overline{1, M_{js}}$, on the functions (14.35) doing for now only the specification that the independent variables are directly measurable. Taking into account the meaning of the inserted functions, the name of *functions of consumption* can also be used for them.

Just as for the variables of direct primary consumptions, for the resultant variables of indirect primary consumptions, there is also the possibility to know, independent of the results of the observation of their factorial variables, the *integral consumption* by each main production department and in any period. In other words, for any department, we can know the integral consumptions from the primary input E_{i10r} and E_{i11r}, meaning the vectors:

$$X^{i10r}_{\bullet *\bullet} = \begin{pmatrix} X^{i10r}_{\bullet 1\bullet} \\ X^{i10r}_{\bullet 2\bullet} \\ \vdots \\ X^{i10r}_{\bullet S^*\bullet} \end{pmatrix} \text{ and } X^{i11r}_{\bullet *\bullet} = \begin{pmatrix} X^{i11r}_{\bullet 1\bullet} \\ X^{i11r}_{\bullet 2\bullet} \\ \vdots \\ X^{i11r}_{\bullet S^*\bullet} \end{pmatrix} \tag{14.36}$$

where,

$$X^{i1kr}_{\bullet s\bullet} = \sum_j \sum_{u_{js}} \left(a^{i1kr}_{jsu_{js}1} + a^{i1kr}_{jsu_{js}2} + \ldots + a^{i1kr}_{jsu_{js}N^{i1kr}_{jsu_{js}}}\right)$$

for any $s = \overline{1, S^*}$; $i = \overline{1, I}$; $k = 0, 1$; $r = 1, 2, 3$.

It is worth mentioning that in the economic practice none of the inequalities (14.31) or (14.36) is a means to calculate the integral consumptions: the first ones, because the volume of statistical observation is the so large that becomes practically impossible to be done, and those corresponding to the indirect primary consumptions because such an observation is practically not possible. The following paragraph will be devoted to exposing the way of establishing the direct and particularly indirect primary consumptions.

If we insert the notation: $X^{i10r}_{\bullet s \bullet} = C^{ilkr}_{\bullet s \bullet}$ and $X^{i11r}_{\bullet s \bullet} = C^{ilkr}_{\bullet * \bullet}$, for any $s = \overline{1,\ S^*}$, then the vectors of the indirect integral primary consumptions are written as follows:

$$C^{i10r}_{\bullet * \bullet}T = \left(C^{i10r}_{\bullet 1 \bullet},\ \ldots,\ C^{i10r}_{\bullet S^* \bullet}\right) \tag{14.37}$$

$$\text{and } C^{i11r}_{\bullet * \bullet}T = \left(C^{i11r}_{\bullet 1 \bullet},\ \ldots,\ C^{i11r}_{\bullet S^* \bullet}\right) \tag{14.38}$$

Taking the values 1, 2, 3 into (14.37) and (14.38) for *r*, in order, we get six vectors of the integral primary consumptions of the input E_{i1} into the process.

In summary, for the variable $X^{i}_{jsu_{js}}$ of the primary consumption from the input E_i into the operation $O_{jsu_{js}}$, the following composition results:

$$X^{i}_{jsu_{js}} = X^{i0}_{jsu_{js}} + \sum_{k}\sum_{r} G^{ilkr}_{jsu_{js}}\left[\left(X^{ilkr}_{jsu_{js}}\right)\right] \tag{14.39}$$

where, $\left(X^{ilkr}_{jsu_{js}}\right)_* = \left[\left(X^{ilkr}_{jsu_{js}}\right)_1, \left(X^{ilkr}_{jsu_{js}}\right)_2, \ \ldots,\ \left(X^{ilkr}_{jsu_{js}}\right)_{H_{jsu_{js}}}\right]$ whatever may be $i = \overline{1,\ I};\ j = \overline{1,\ J};\ s = \overline{1,\ S^*};\ u_{js} = \overline{1,\ M_{js}}$.

In this decomposition, both the variables of the direct primary consumptions and the factorial variables of the indirect primary consumptions can be the object of statistical observation. Moreover, from the documents specially intended for this purpose, we can directly read the components of the direct integral primary consumptions, as well as the components of the vectors of own indirect integral primary consumptions.

(b) *The primary integral consumptions are established by production departments*

Be,

$$q_{**} = \begin{pmatrix} q_{11} & \cdots & q_{1S^*} & q_{1S^*+1} & \cdots & q_{1S} \\ \vdots & & \vdots & \vdots & & \vdots \\ q_{S^*1} & \cdots & q_{S^*S^*} & q_{S^*S^*+1} & \cdots & q_{S^*S} \\ q_{S^*+1,1} & \cdots & q_{S^*+1,S^*} & q_{S^*+1,S^*+1} & \cdots & q_{S^*+1,S} \\ \vdots & & \vdots & \vdots & & \vdots \\ q_{S1} & \cdots & q_{SS^*} & q_{S,S^*+1} & \cdots & q_{SS} \end{pmatrix} \tag{14.40}$$

the dimensional matrix (S, S)—of the flows between the departments wherein the process (S) occurs, where q_{ls} is for $l \neq s$, the part from the department output

$l = \overline{1,\ S}$ intended to the productive consumption in the department s—*productive consumption transferred* from section *l* into the department s.

If $s = 1$, then q_{1s} becomes q_{11} and is the total own total productive consumption of the department 1. The own total productive consumption of the departments is emphasised on the diagonal of matrix (14.40) of the flows between departments, the remaining elements in each column indicating the transferred productive consumptions, respectively in each department. In terms of the supplying department, $l = \overline{1,\ S}$, the quantity q_{ls} is part of this volume of activity (fuel, energy, amount of information, of management in the case where department 1 is a management and administration division of the enterprise are over department, etc.) and namely that part of the production achieved, which has been transferred as service to the department $l = \overline{1,\ S}$.

Typically, the auxiliary departments are primarily in the position of service providing department, their purpose being to provide the conditions to perform the process in the main departments through the services they perform. Such connections can also occur in a reverse direction, or even between pairs of main departments or pairs of auxiliary departments. The matrix (14.40) of the flows between departments can be decomposed into four sub-matrices (blocks), each corresponding to a certain kind of connections between departments. Thus,

$$q_{(S^*,S^*)} = \begin{pmatrix} q_{11} & \cdots & q_{1S^*} \\ \vdots & & \vdots \\ q_{S^*1} & \cdots & q_{S^*S^*} \end{pmatrix} \tag{14.41}$$

representing the first block of the matrix (14.40), characterises the mutual connections between the main departments—the sub-matrix of the flows between the main departments.

The sub-matrix,

$$q_{(S^*,S-S^*)} = \begin{pmatrix} q_{1,S^*+1} & \cdots & q_{1S} \\ \vdots & & \vdots \\ q_{S^*,S^*+1} & \cdots & q_{S^*S} \end{pmatrix} \tag{14.42}$$

characterises the services of the main departments to the auxiliary departments, the sub-matrix of the services transferred from the main departments to the auxiliary departments.

The sub-matrix,

$$q_{(S-S^*,S^*)} = \begin{pmatrix} q_{S^*+1,1} & \cdots & q_{S^*+1,S^*} \\ \vdots & & \vdots \\ q_{S1} & \cdots & q_{SS} \end{pmatrix} \tag{14.43}$$

characterises the services provided by the auxiliary departments to the main departments—the sub-matrix of the services transferred from the auxiliary departments to the main departments.

Finally, the last sub matrix,

$$q_{(S-S^*,S-S^*)} = \begin{pmatrix} q_{S^*+1,S^*+1} & \cdots & q_{S^*+1,S} \\ \vdots & & \vdots \\ q_{S,S^*+1} & \cdots & q_{SS} \end{pmatrix} \tag{14.44}$$

made of the last S—S* lines and columns, expresses the mutual connections between the auxiliary departments—the sub-matrix of the flows between the auxiliary departments.

By using the notations inserted for the four blocks, the matrix (14.40) can be written as follows:

$$q_{**} = \begin{pmatrix} q_{S^*,S^*} & \cdots & q_{S^*,S-S^*} \\ \vdots & & \vdots \\ q_{S-S^*,S^*} & \cdots & q_{S-S^*,S-S^*} \end{pmatrix} \tag{14.45}$$

By analysing the quantity q_{1S} from the point of view of the supplying department 1, it easily results that its achievement occurs simultaneously with a specific consumption, in the department 1, by means of production and labour force. If the input of means of production and labour force into the department l, intended to achieve the output of volume q_{lS} we assume it as decomposed on the elements E_1, $E_2, \ldots, E_{\mathrm{I}}$ and we also assume that each primary element $E_i\left(\mathrm{i} = \overline{1,\ \mathrm{I}}\right)$ consists of the components $E_{i0}\left(i = \overline{1,\ \mathrm{I}}\right), E_{il0r}$ $(\mathrm{i} = \overline{1,\ \mathrm{I}};\ \mathrm{r} = 1, 2, 3)$ and E_{il1r} $(\mathrm{i} = \overline{1,\ \mathrm{I}};\ \mathrm{r} = 1, 2, 3)$ as in the following diagram:

Then, for any $\mathrm{i} = \overline{1,\ \mathrm{I}};\ r = 1, 2, 3$, the consumption of production means and labour force in the process of achieving the output of volume q_{1S}, actually means a certain consumption from each primary input and its components.

In the case where l is one of the auxiliary departments, meaning $l = S^* + 1, \ldots, S$, then the input into it does not contain any of the components E_{i0} $(\mathrm{i} = \overline{1,\ \mathrm{I}})$, their presence having sense only for the main departments.

Therefore, the primary input into any auxiliary department consists of—as it results from Fig. 14.2—the following two categories of components:

- the components E_{i10r} $(\mathrm{i} = \overline{1,\ \mathrm{I}};\ \mathrm{r} = 1, 2, 3)$ of own indirect primary input;
- the components E_{il1r} $(\mathrm{i} = \overline{1,\ \mathrm{I}};\ r = 1, 2, 3)$ of primary transferred input and included into the services of volume $(q_{11} + q_{21} + \ldots + q_{S1})$.

An essential difference between the two groups of components is$q_{11}, \ldots, q_{pl}, \ldots, q_{Sl}$ transferred from the other departments.

The output from an auxiliary department l necessarily has at least the following elements: $q_{l1}, \ldots, q_{ls}, \ldots, q_{lS}$ representing the services to the other departments. some auxiliary departments could also contain other elements in the output, such as: services to third parties, semi-finished products intended for delivery, etc.

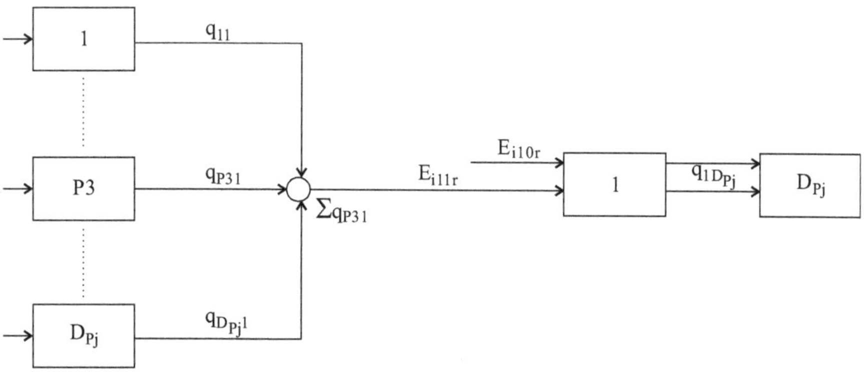

Fig. 14.2 Diagram the consumption of production

From the elements of the output of the—auxiliary or main—department l—we note the quantity q_{ls}, as mandatory element of the input into the department s for any $l = \overline{1,\ S}$.

If the department s is a main department, meaning $s = \overline{1,\ S^*}$ then the input thereto includes:

- the components E_{i0} ($i = \overline{1,\ I}$) of direct primary input,
- the components E_{i10r} ($i = \overline{1,\ I}$; r = 1, 2, 3) of own indirect primary input and
- the components E_{i10r} ($i = \overline{1,\ I}$; r = 1, 2, 3) of transferred indirect primary input.

By stating that the output from the main department $s = \overline{1,\ S^*}$ consists of J groups of products, $P_1, P_2, \ldots, P_j$ which the services to the other departments are added to, respectively of volume: $q_{s1}, \ldots, q_{sh}, \ldots, q_{sS}$, the corresponding diagram is as follows:

The input of the direct primary components, $E_{10}, E_{20}, \ldots, E_{I0}$ into the department s does not occur by groups, but individually, which enables their corresponding emphasis. Moreover, the integral consumption from any department $s = \overline{1,\ S}$ is also noted in special primary documents, for any of the components E_{i0}. This means that the elements of the matrix:

$$C^{*0}_{\bullet*\bullet} = \begin{pmatrix} C^{10}_{\bullet1\bullet} & \cdots & C^{i0}_{\bullet1\bullet} & \cdots & C^{I0}_{\bullet1\bullet} \\ \vdots & & \vdots & & \vdots \\ C^{10}_{\bullet s\bullet} & \cdots & C^{i0}_{\bullet s\bullet} & \cdots & C^{I0}_{\bullet s\bullet} \\ \vdots & & \vdots & & \vdots \\ C^{10}_{\bullet S\bullet} & \cdots & C^{i0}_{\bullet S\bullet} & \cdots & C^{I0}_{\bullet S\bullet} \end{pmatrix} \tag{14.46}$$

made of the direct primary integral conception—by departments—are known from the primary documents specially intended for this purpose, that is by means of a direct statistical observation.

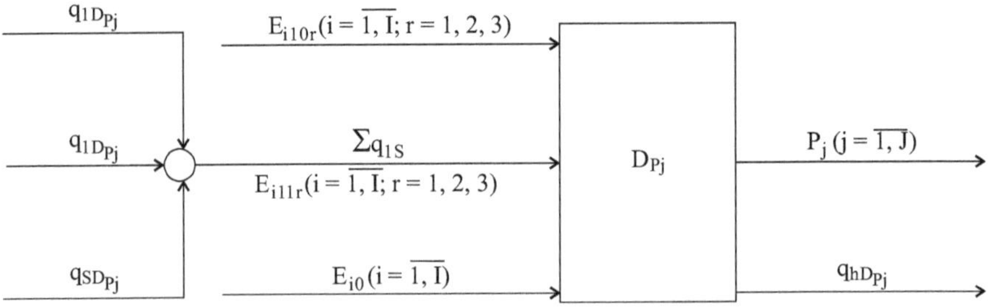

Fig. 14.3 Output from groups of products, $P_1, P_2, \ldots, P_j$

Obviously, as the primary input components $E_{i0}\left(\mathrm{i}=\overline{1,\ \mathrm{I}}\right)$ are inputs only in the main departments, $C^{i0}_{\bullet s\bullet}=0$ for $\mathrm{s}=\mathrm{S}^*+1, \ldots, S$ and whatever $\mathrm{i}=\overline{1,\ \mathrm{I}}$ may be.

As it also results from Fig. 14.3, nor the input consisting of own indirect primary components $E_{110r}, E_{210r}, \ldots, E_{I10r}$ (r = 1, 2, 3) into the department s occurs by groups, but also individually, which makes it possible to directly measure the integral consumptions in each department. Therefore, for any r = 1, 2, 3, the elements of the matrix

$$C^{*10r}_{\bullet*\bullet}=\begin{pmatrix} C^{110r}_{\bullet1\bullet} & \cdots & C^{i10r}_{\bullet1\bullet} & \cdots & C^{I10r}_{\bullet1\bullet} \\ \vdots & & \vdots & & \vdots \\ C^{110r}_{\bullet s\bullet} & \cdots & C^{i10r}_{\bullet s\bullet} & \cdots & C^{I10r}_{\bullet s\bullet} \\ \vdots & & \vdots & & \vdots \\ C^{110r}_{\bullet S\bullet} & \cdots & C^{i10r}_{\bullet S\bullet} & \cdots & C^{I10r}_{\bullet S\bullet} \end{pmatrix} \tag{14.47}$$

are or can be known in primary documents intended for this purpose, by means of a direct statistical observation. Of course, for $r=2$ and 3 knowing the corresponding matrices that result from (14.47) is conditioned by the issue of measuring the local or central management information, for the purpose of which the indicator "informational energy" could be used.

If the input of own direct and indirect primary components into the department s occurs individually and as such, the integral consumption from each of them can be obtained based on a direct statistical observation, it does not happen the same for the transferred—indirect primary input components. As it also results from Fig. 14.3, the input of the transferred indirect components occurs within the group, by means of the services which each auxiliary department $l=S^*+1, \ldots, S$ it provides to a main department $s=\overline{1,\ S^*}$. In general the indirect primary input components, transferred into a random department $s=\overline{1,\ S}$ are included into the services of the other departments $1=1, 2, \ldots, s-1, s+1, \ldots$, S, destined to that department. Because of this, for such inputs, obtaining the consumption is not possible in department $s=\overline{1,\ S}$, by means of a direct statistical observation. This time, the object of direct statistical observation is the volume of services inputted into a department and where the transferred indirect components are included. Therefore, it remains to establish another way—by calculation—to obtain the elements of the matrix,

$$C^{*11r}_{\bullet*\bullet} = \begin{pmatrix} C^{111r}_{\bullet1\bullet} & \cdots & C^{i11r}_{\bullet1\bullet} & \cdots & C^{I11r}_{\bullet1\bullet} \\ \vdots & & \vdots & & \vdots \\ C^{111r}_{\bullet s\bullet} & \cdots & C^{i11r}_{\bullet s\bullet} & \cdots & C^{I11r}_{\bullet s\bullet} \\ \vdots & & \vdots & & \vdots \\ C^{111r}_{\bullet S\bullet} & \cdots & C^{i11r}_{\bullet S\bullet} & \cdots & C^{I11r}_{\bullet S\bullet} \end{pmatrix} \quad (14.48)$$

r = 1, 2, 3.

Whatever would be the method to determine the elements of matrices (14.48) by calculation, it is necessary to take into account that in any department $s = \overline{1,\ S}$, based on a direct observation, we know the quantities $q_{1s}, \ldots, q_{ls}, \ldots, q_{Ss}$, respectively the elements of matrix (14.40) of the flows between departments.

In order to establish such a method, let us consider the vector Q, the transposition of which is: $Q^T_* = (Q_1 \quad \ldots \quad Q_s \quad \ldots \quad Q_S)$ consisting of the total volume of production of each department $s = \overline{1,\ S}$.

If the output from the department s is homogeneous, then the calculation of the indicator Qs does not include any difficulty, as it is a simple sum of partial results, corresponding to the various time intervals of the period taken into account.

Special problems arise in the case of the heterogeneous output. In this case, to assess the volume of the entire activity of the department, it is necessary to insert a commensuration unit (hours-workload, comparable price, etc.), so that the results of different kinds can be summed.

Both in the case of homogeneous output, and of heterogeneous output, there appears a difficulty in relation to how the unfinished production is assessed, as component of the volume of production activity of a department.

Now be the matrix:

$$a_{**} = \begin{pmatrix} a_{11} & \cdots & a_{aS^*} & a_{1S^*+1} & \cdots & a_{1S} \\ \vdots & & \vdots & \vdots & & \vdots \\ a_{S^*1} & \cdots & a_{S^*S^*} & a_{S^*,S^*+1} & \cdots & a_{S^*S} \\ a_{S^*+1,1} & \cdots & a_{S^*+1,S^*} & a_{S^*+1,S^*+1} & \cdots & a_{S^*+1,S} \\ \vdots & & \vdots & \vdots & & \vdots \\ a_{S1} & \cdots & a_{SS^*} & a_{S,S^*+1} & \cdots & a_{SS} \end{pmatrix} \quad (14.49)$$

where,

$$a_{ls} = \frac{q_{ls}}{Q_s}(l = \overline{1,\ S};\ s = \overline{1,\ S}) \quad (14.50)$$

is the consumption of the service of department $l = \overline{1,\ S}$, necessary to achieve in the department $s = \overline{1,\ S}$ a production with the volume equal to the unit and is called coefficient of the technological consumption or technological coefficient, and (14.49)—the matrix of the technological coefficients.

If in (14.50) we take l = 1, 2, . . ., S and we maintain the index s fixed, then we get the coefficients a_{1s}, a_{2s}, a_{Ss} which in matrix (14.49) are in column s and represent the volume of the inputs from the departments 1, 2, . . ., S, consumed in the department s and necessary to achieve a volume of production equal to the unit.

If we divide the line s of the matrix (14.46) by Q_s and make $s = \overline{1,\ S}$, then we get

$$c_{**} = \begin{pmatrix} c_{\bullet 1\bullet}^{10} & \cdots & c_{\bullet 1\bullet}^{i0} & \cdots & c_{\bullet 1\bullet}^{I0} \\ \vdots & & \vdots & & \vdots \\ c_{\bullet s\bullet}^{10} & \cdots & c_{\bullet s\bullet}^{i0} & \cdots & c_{\bullet s\bullet}^{I0} \\ \vdots & & \vdots & & \vdots \\ c_{\bullet S\bullet}^{10} & \cdots & c_{\bullet S\bullet}^{i0} & \cdots & c_{\bullet S\bullet}^{I0} \end{pmatrix} \tag{14.51}$$

where, $c_{\bullet s\bullet}^{i0} = \frac{C_{\bullet s\bullet}^{i0}}{Q_s}$ for any $i = \overline{1,\ I}$ and $s = \overline{1,\ S}$ is the integral consumption from the primary input E_{i0}, necessary to achieve in department s a volume of production equal to the unit.

By operating similarly also on the matrices (14.47) and (14.48), its results:

$$c_{\bullet *\bullet}^{*1kr} = \begin{pmatrix} c_{\bullet *\bullet}^{11kr} & \cdots & c_{\bullet 1\bullet}^{i1kr} & \cdots & c_{\bullet 1\bullet}^{I1kr} \\ \vdots & & \vdots & & \vdots \\ c_{\bullet s\bullet}^{11kr} & \cdots & c_{\bullet s\bullet}^{i1kr} & \cdots & c_{\bullet s\bullet}^{I1kr} \\ \vdots & & \vdots & & \vdots \\ c_{\bullet S\bullet}^{I1kr} & \cdots & c_{\bullet S\bullet}^{i1kr} & \cdots & c_{\bullet S\bullet}^{I1kr} \end{pmatrix} \tag{14.52}$$

where, $c_{\bullet s\bullet}^{i1kr} = \frac{C_{\bullet s\bullet}^{i1kr}}{Q_s}$ for any i $= \overline{1,\ I}$ and $s = \overline{1,\ S}$; $k = 0, 1$; $r = 1, 2, 3$ are the integral consumption from the primary input E_{i1kr}, necessary to achieve in department s a volume of production equal to the unit.

Therefore, achieving in the department s a production with a volume equal to the unit implies the following consumption, by components, of the primary input E_i:

- $c_{\bullet s\bullet}^{i0}$ units from the component of primary input E_{i0}
- $c_{\bullet s\bullet}^{i10r}$ units from the component of primary input E_{i10r}
- $c_{\bullet s\bullet}^{i11r}$ units from the component of primary input E_{i11r} by means of the services of the other departments, respectively of volume: $a_{1s}, \ldots, a_{ls}, \ldots, a_{Ss}$.

Inserting the notation,

$$c_{\bullet s\bullet}^{i1\bullet r} = c_{\bullet s\bullet}^{i10r} + c_{\bullet s\bullet}^{i11r} \tag{14.53}$$

then for the integral consumption $c_{\bullet s\bullet}^{i0} + c_{\bullet s\bullet}^{i1\bullet r}$ from the primary input E_i, necessary to achieve in the department s a production with a volume equal to the unit, based on its significance, the following equality results:

$$c_{\bullet s\bullet}^{i0} + c_{\bullet s\bullet}^{i1\bullet r} = \left(c_{\bullet s\bullet}^{i0} + c_{\bullet s\bullet}^{i10r}\right) + \sum_{l=1}^{S}\left(c_{\bullet l\bullet}^{i0} + c_{\bullet l\bullet}^{i1\bullet r}\right)a_{ls} \quad \text{s} = 1,\ 2,\ \ldots,\ \text{S} \qquad (14.54)$$

forming the so-called system of equations of the integral consumptions by departments.

If we note $c_{\bullet *\bullet}^{i0} = \begin{pmatrix} c_{\bullet 1\bullet}^{i0} \\ \vdots \\ c_{\bullet s\bullet}^{i0} \\ \vdots \\ c_{\bullet S\bullet}^{i0} \end{pmatrix}$, $c_{\bullet *\bullet}^{i10r} = \begin{pmatrix} c_{\bullet 1\bullet}^{i10r} \\ \vdots \\ c_{\bullet s\bullet}^{i10r} \\ \vdots \\ c_{\bullet S\bullet}^{i10r} \end{pmatrix}$, $c_{\bullet *\bullet}^{i11r} = \begin{pmatrix} c_{\bullet 1\bullet}^{i11r} \\ \vdots \\ c_{\bullet s\bullet}^{i11r} \\ \vdots \\ c_{\bullet S\bullet}^{i11r} \end{pmatrix}$ for any $i = \overline{1,\ \text{I}}$; r = 1, 2, 3 and

$$c_{\bullet *\bullet}^{i1\bullet r} = c_{\bullet *\bullet}^{i10r} + c_{\bullet *\bullet}^{i11r} \qquad (14.55)$$

then, in a matrix form, the established system of equations (14.54) can be written as follows: $c_{\bullet *\bullet}^{i0} + c_{\bullet 1\bullet}^{i1\bullet r} = c_{\bullet *\bullet}^{i0} + c_{\bullet *\bullet}^{i10r} + a_{**}^{T} c_{\bullet *\bullet}^{i0} + a_{**}^{T} c_{\bullet *\bullet}^{i1\bullet r}$ or $c_{\bullet *\bullet}^{i1\bullet 1} = c_{\bullet *\bullet}^{i10r} + a_{**}^{T} c_{\bullet *\bullet}^{i0} + a_{**}^{T} c_{\bullet *\bullet}^{i1\bullet r}$ where,

$c_{\bullet *\bullet}^{i0}$—the vector of unitary integral consumptions from the direct primary input component E_{i0},
$c_{\bullet *\bullet}^{i10r}$—the vector of unitary integral consumptions from the own primary input component E_{i10r},
$c_{\bullet *\bullet}^{i11r}$—the unknown vector of unitary integral consumptions from the component E_{i10r}

If we also take into account (14.50), the system of equations deducted in relation to the unknown vector $c_{\bullet *\bullet}^{i11r}$ can also be written:

$$c_{\bullet *\bullet}^{i10r} + c_{\bullet *\bullet}^{i11r} = c_{\bullet *\bullet}^{i10r} + a_{**}^{T} c_{\bullet *\bullet}^{i0} + a_{**}^{T}\left(c_{\bullet *\bullet}^{i10r} + c_{\bullet *\bullet}^{i11r}\right)$$

or

$$\left(E_{**} - a_{**}^{T}\right) c_{\bullet *\bullet}^{i11r} = a_{**}^{T}\left(c_{\bullet *\bullet}^{i0} + c_{\bullet *\bullet}^{i10r}\right) \qquad (14.56)$$

where, E_{**} is the unit matrix of the same size as matrix a_{**}.

By assuming that the quadratic matrix a_{**} admits the reverse, it results from (14.56) for the unknown vector $c_{\bullet *\bullet}^{i11r}$ that

$$c_{\bullet *\bullet}^{i11r} = b_{**}^{T} a_{**}^{T}\left(c_{\bullet *\bullet}^{i0} + c_{\bullet *\bullet}^{i11r}\right) \qquad (14.57)$$

where, $b_{**} = (E_{**} — a_{**})^{-1}$

In this way, the components of the vector $c_{\bullet *\bullet}^{i11r}$ and at the same time the elements from the column "i" of matrix (14.52) result from (14.57) for $k = 1$.

If, in (14.57) we successively take for the index i the values 1, 2,. . ., I, then we get all the columns of the matrix (14.52) corresponding to the case k = 1.

Inserting the notation, $Q_{**} = \begin{pmatrix} Q_1 & \cdots & 0 & \cdots & 0 \\ \vdots & & \vdots & & \vdots \\ 0 & \cdots & Q_s & \cdots & 0 \\ \vdots & & \vdots & & \vdots \\ 0 & \cdots & 0 & \cdots & Q_S \end{pmatrix}$ and taking into account that $c^{i1kr}_{\bullet s \bullet} = \frac{C^{i1kr}_{\bullet s \bullet}}{Q_s}$, whatever may be i = $\overline{1,\ I}$, $s = \overline{1,\ S}$; k = 0, 1; r = 1, 2, 3.

Then the three sought matrices (14.48) are obtained as follows:

$$C^{*11r}_{\bullet * \bullet} = Q_{**} c^{*11r}_{\bullet * \bullet} \ (\mathrm{r} = 1,\ 2,\ 3) \tag{14.58}$$

Along with this last result, we can say that whatever the studied period would be, the seven matrices of the integral consumptions by primary input components and departments, respectively $C^{*0}_{\bullet * \bullet}$, $C^{*10r}_{\bullet * \bullet}$ and $C^{*11r}_{\bullet * \bullet}$ for $r = 1, 2, 3$ can be effectively determined as follows: the first four by means of a direct statistical observation, and the last three by means of the described method.

(c) We assess the unfinished production

Be,

$$\mathrm{O} = \begin{vmatrix} \mathrm{O}_{j11} & \cdots & \mathrm{O}_{j1u_{j1}} & \cdots & \mathrm{O}_{j1M_{j1}} \\ \vdots & & \vdots & & \vdots \\ \mathrm{O}_{js1} & \cdots & \mathrm{O}_{jsu_{js}} & \cdots & \mathrm{O}_{jsM_{js}} \\ \vdots & & \vdots & & \vdots \\ \mathrm{O}_{jS^*1} & \cdots & \mathrm{O}_{jS^*u_{jS^*}} & \cdots & \mathrm{O}_{jS^*M_{jS^*}} \end{vmatrix} \tag{14.59}$$

the table of operations performed in the S* main departments in relation to the products of group P_j.

Making a product of group P_j means performing each of the operations in table (14.59) by a certain number of times and in a certain sequence—by means of the primary inputs from the main departments. To simplify the writing, let us assume that the frequency of using the operations in this table, to make any of the products of group $P_j(j = \overline{1,\ J})$ is the same and therefore can be considered as equal to the unit.

In order to establish the unfinished production, we shall clarify the following:

- a product from the group $P_j(j = \overline{1,\ J})$ is called finished product in relation to the process (S), if all operations of table (14.59) have been performed in relation to it;
- a product from the group P_j is called unfinished product in relation to the process (S), if at least one operation of table (14.59) has not been entirely performed. The unfinished product in relation to a certain process of production (S) appears to us as a product the manufacturing process of which has not been finished, with an

intermediary situation between the primary input called raw material and finished product, or between the semi-finished and the finished product under processing, assembly or pending. The existence of unfinished products at any time is an element inherent to any process (S), given that the duration of manufacturing cycle does not usually coincide with the calendar periods which the production volume is determined for;
- any product from the group $P_j\,(j = \overline{1,\ J})$ is called finished product in relation to the process in the department s, if all operations $O_{js1} \ldots O_{jsu_{js}} \ldots O_{jsM_{js}}$ have been performed in relation to it;
- a product from the group P_j is called unfinished product in relation to the process in any department s, if at least one of the operations $O_{js1} \ldots O_{jsu_{js}} \ldots O_{jsM_{js}}$ has not been performed.

A finished product in relation to the process of each department is a finished product in relation to the production process (S), and an unfinished product in relation to at least one of the processes of the main departments is an unfinished product in relation to the production process (S).

The calculation of the unfinished production as component of the volume of the entire production achieved during a period is required both at the level of department and at the level of enterprise. Currently, establishing the unfinished production is done by using either the indirect method of accounting feature, or one of the direct methods, such as inventorying, by determining the degree of technical finish.

It has been thoroughly shown in literature that neither the indirect methods nor the direct ones have a rigorous scientific background and, as such, their use does not lead to the actual volume of the unfinished production.

The need to remove the deficiencies of the methods used in practice, in order to assess the unfinished production, has led to preparing a method of assessing an unfinished production based on the normed time.

It is necessary to establish a method to assess the unfinished production in relation to the production process (S), the way of assessing the unfinished production in relation to the process in a department, resulting then customisation.

For this purpose, let us note by $t_{jsu_{js}}$ the normed time to achieve an operation u_{js} in the department s, in relation to any product from the group P_j and form the following table:

$$\begin{vmatrix} t_{j11} & \cdots & t_{j1u_{j1}} & \cdots & t_{j1M_{j1}} \\ \vdots & & \vdots & & \vdots \\ t_{js1} & \cdots & t_{jsu_{js}} & \cdots & t_{jsM_{js}} \\ \vdots & & \vdots & & \vdots \\ t_{jS^*1} & \cdots & t_{jS^*u_{jS^*}} & \cdots & t_{jS^*M_{jS^*}} \end{vmatrix} \tag{14.60}$$

Any product P_j consists of a certain number of components, respectively a certain number of parts that can be divided into the following two groups:

- G_I is the group of parts whereon all operations in table (14.59) should be done;

- G_2 is the group of parts, components of any product P_j for which only part of the operations in table (14.59) are done.

Obviously, for the parts in group G_2, part of the elements of people (14.60) are null.

To assess the volume of unfinished production in each department and as a whole, we shall do the following notations:

- $a_{jsu_{js}}(t)$ is the number of parts G_1 of the products P_j, which at the end of the period t were finished in relation to the operation $O_{jsu_{js}}$;
- $b_{jsu_{js}}(t)$ is the number of parts G_2 of the unfinished products P_j, which at the end of the period t were finished in relation to the operation $O_{jsu_{js}}$.

The production unfinished at the end of the period t will be assessed by the number of workload hours contained in the parts G_1 and G_2—constituents of the unfinished production.

For this, we shall do the following notations:

- $A_j(t)$—the volume of the unfinished production P_j, at the end of the period t, relatively to the parts G_1;
- $B_j(t)$—the volume of the unfinished production P_j,—at the end of the period t—relatively to the group of parts G_2;
- $A_{js}(t)$—the value of the workload hours of the parts G_1, which at end of the period t were outputs of the process from the department s;
- $B_{js}(t)$—the value of the workload hours of the parts G_2,—outputs of the process from the department s at the end of the period t.

Based on these notations, the volume of unfinished production P_j, at the end of the period t is:

$$A_j(t) + B_j(t) = \sum_s A_{js}(t) + \sum_s B_{js}(t) \qquad (14.61)$$

where the second sum extends only to those departments that contributed in making the parts G_2 during the period t.

On the other hand, from the definition given to the indicator $A_{js}(t)$, the following calculation expression results for this:

$$\begin{aligned} A_{js}(t) &= a_{js1}(t)\left(\sum_{u_{j1}}^{M_{j1}} t_{j1u_{j1}} + \ldots + \sum_{u_{js-1}}^{M_{js-1}} t_{js-1u_{js-1}} + t_{js1}\right) + \\ &+ a_{js2}(t)\left(\sum_{u_{j1}}^{M_{j1}} t_{j1u_{j1}} + \ldots + \sum_{u_{js-1}}^{M_{js-1}} t_{js-1u_{js-1}} + \sum_{u_{js}}^{2} t_{jsu_{js}}\right) + \ldots + \\ &+ a_{jsM_{js}}(t)\left(\sum_{u_{j1}}^{M_{j1}} t_{j1u_{j1}} + \ldots + \sum_{u_{js-1}}^{M_{js-1}} t_{js-1u_{js-1}} + \sum_{u_{js}}^{M_{js}} t_{jsu_{js}}\right) \end{aligned} \tag{14.62}$$

whatever $s = \overline{1,\ S^*}$ may be.

In this context, $A_{js}(t)$ can also be written as follows:

$$\begin{aligned} A_{js}(t) &= t_{js1}\left(\sum_{u_{js}=1} a_{jsu_{js}}(t) + \ldots + \sum_{u_{jS^*}=1} a_{jS^*u_{jS^*}}(t)\right) + \\ &+ t_{js2}\left(\sum_{u_{js}=2} a_{jsu_{js}}(t) + \ldots + \sum_{u_{jS^*}=1} a_{jS^*u_{jS^*}}(t)\right) + \ldots + \\ &+ t_{jsM_{js}}\left(a_{jsM_{js}}(t) + \ldots + \sum_{u_{jS^*}=1} a_{jS^*u_{jS^*}}(t)\right) \end{aligned} \tag{14.63}$$

for any $s = \overline{1,\ S^*}$.

For the indicator $B_{jS}(t)$, we also have the following expression:

$$\begin{aligned} B_{js}(t) &= b_{js1}(t)\left(\sum_{u_{j1}}{}' t_{j1u_{j1}} + \ldots + \sum_{u_{js-1}}{}' t_{js-1u_{js-1}} + t_{js1}\right) + \\ &+ b_{js2}(t)\left(\sum_{u_{j1}}{}' t_{j1u_{j1}} + \ldots + \sum_{u_{js-1}}{}' t_{js-1u_{js-1}} + t_{js1} + t_{js2}\right) + \ldots + \\ &+ b_{jsM}(t)\left(\sum_{u_{j1}}{}' t_{j1u_{j1}} + \ldots + \sum_{u_{js}}{}' t_{jsM_{js}}\right) \end{aligned} \tag{14.64}$$

where $\sum{}'$ extends only to those departments that contributed in making the parts G_2 during the period t.

The expression (14.61) is an assessment of the unfinished production, corresponding to the output P_j, however summing in relation to the index j, we get the entire unfinished production at the end of the period t, namely:

$$\sum_j A_j(t) + \sum_j B_j(t) = \sum_j \sum_s A_{js}(t) + \sum_j \sum_s B_{js}(t) \tag{14.65}$$

By a reasoning similar to that done at the level of the production process (S), we can establish a way to assess the unfinished production for any department.

If we note by p_j the current production price, comparable or restored by work-load hours into the group of products P_j, then the value of the unfinished production will be:

$$V(t) = \sum_j p_j A_j(t) + \sum_j p_j B_j(t) \tag{14.66}$$

(d) The matrix of the primary consumptions by products is established

In the introductory section of the chapter, for matrix (14.2) we used the name of matrix of primary unitary consumptions by products. As the elements of this matrix are variable sizes, in the same sense, we shall also use further the name of matrix of the variables of primary consumptions—by products.

The consumption from the input into the process of production (S) occurring on various workstations and on the occasion of performing the various operations, we shall consider the enterprise as a complex microeconomic, cybernetic system, consisting of the main production departments with all of the existing interdependencies. This enabled the insertion of the variables of primary consumptions into the calculation—by departments and operations and also the decomposition (14.29) thereof by components.

We shall formulate the following problem:

If

- the input into the process (S) of the system (W) is decomposed by primary elements $E_1, E_2, \ldots, E_I$
- the output from the process (S) is heterogeneous and consists of the kinds $P_1, P_2, \ldots, P_J$
- the process (S) occurs by departments and operations, so that any primary input $E_i\left(i = \overline{1,\ I}\right)$ destined to the output $\mathrm{P_j}\left(j = \overline{1,\ J}\right)$ is subject to the operations in table (14.26).

Then,

$$X_j^i = X_{j\bullet\bullet}^i = \sum_s \sum_{u_{js}} X_{jsu_{js}}^i \left(i = \overline{1,\ \mathrm{I}};\ j = \overline{1,\ J}\right) \tag{14.67}$$

The demonstration immediately results from the very content of the variables that appear in (14.67). Ultimately, whatever may be the primary input $E_i\left(i = \overline{1,\ \mathrm{I}}\right)$ into the process (S)—intended to achieve the output P_j—on the one hand the variable X_j^i corresponds to it, and on the other hand the table of variables (14.28), a table which through its elements reflects the consumption from E_i by departments and operations. This means that by summing all elements of this table, we get the consumption X_j^i from the input E_i by the unit of product P_j. If we insert the notation,

$$X_{*\bullet\bullet}^{*} = \begin{pmatrix} X_{1\bullet\bullet}^{1} & \dots & X_{j\bullet\bullet}^{1} & \dots & X_{J\bullet\bullet}^{1} \\ \vdots & & \vdots & & \vdots \\ X_{1\bullet\bullet}^{i} & \dots & X_{j\bullet\bullet}^{i} & \dots & X_{J\bullet\bullet}^{i} \\ \vdots & & \vdots & & \vdots \\ X_{1\bullet\bullet}^{I} & \dots & X_{j\bullet\bullet}^{I} & \dots & X_{J\bullet\bullet}^{I} \end{pmatrix} \tag{14.68}$$

then the equalities (14.67) can be written as follows:

$$X_*^* = X_{*\bullet\bullet}^* \tag{14.69}$$

where,

$$X_{j\bullet\bullet}^{i} = \sum_{s}\sum_{u_{js}} X_{jsu_{js'}}^{i} \ \left(\mathrm{i} = \overline{1,\ \mathrm{I}};\ j = \overline{1,\ J}\right) \tag{14.70}$$

We shall formulate the following problem:
If,

- any primary input $E_i\left(\mathrm{i} = \overline{1,\ \mathrm{I}}\right)$ into the process (S) of the system (W) is decomposed by the components $\mathrm{E_{i0}}$, $\mathrm{E_{i10r}}$, $\mathrm{E_{i102}}$, $\mathrm{E_{i103}}$, $\mathrm{E_{i111}}$, $\mathrm{E_{i112}}$, $\mathrm{E_{i113}}$;
- the output from the process (S) is heterogeneous and consists of the kinds P_1, P_2, ..., P_J;
- the process (S) occurs by departments and operations, so that any primary input $E_i\left(\mathrm{i} = \overline{1,\ \mathrm{I}}\right)$ decomposed on the seven components is subject to the operations in table (14.26).

Then,

$$X_*^* = X_{*\bullet\bullet}^* = X_{*\bullet\bullet}^{*0} + \sum_{k}\sum_{r} X_{*\bullet\bullet}^{*1kr} \tag{14.71}$$

where,

$$X_{*\bullet\bullet}^{*0} = \begin{pmatrix} X_{1\bullet\bullet}^{10} & \dots & X_{j\bullet\bullet}^{10} & \dots & X_{J\bullet\bullet}^{10} \\ \vdots & & \vdots & & \vdots \\ X_{1\bullet\bullet}^{i0} & \dots & X_{j\bullet\bullet}^{i0} & \dots & X_{J\bullet\bullet}^{i0} \\ \vdots & & \vdots & & \vdots \\ X_{1\bullet\bullet}^{I0} & \dots & X_{j\bullet\bullet}^{I0} & \dots & X_{J\bullet\bullet}^{I0} \end{pmatrix},\ (\mathrm{k} = 0,\ 1;\ r = \overline{1,\ 3}) \tag{14.72}$$

$$X^{*1kr}_{*\bullet\bullet} = \begin{pmatrix} X^{11kr}_{1\bullet\bullet} & \dots & X^{11kr}_{j\bullet\bullet} & \dots & X^{11kr}_{J\bullet\bullet} \\ \vdots & & \vdots & & \vdots \\ X^{i1kr}_{1\bullet\bullet} & \dots & X^{i1kr}_{j\bullet\bullet} & \dots & X^{i1kr}_{J\bullet\bullet} \\ \vdots & & \vdots & & \vdots \\ X^{I1kr}_{1\bullet\bullet} & \dots & X^{I1kr}_{j\bullet\bullet} & \dots & X^{I1kr}_{J\bullet\bullet} \end{pmatrix}, \left(\mathrm{k} = 0, 1; r = \overline{1, 3}\right) \quad (14.73)$$

$$X^{i0}_{j\bullet\bullet} = \sum_s \sum_{u_{js}} X^{i0}_{jsu_{js}}, \left(\mathrm{i} = \overline{1, \mathrm{I}}; j = \overline{1, J}\right) \quad (14.74)$$

$$X^{i1kr}_{j\bullet\bullet} = \sum_s \sum_{u_{js}} X^{i1kr}_{jsu_{js}} \left(\mathrm{i} = \overline{1, \mathrm{I}};\ j = \overline{1, J};\ k = \overline{0, 1};\ r = \overline{1, 3}\right) \quad (14.75)$$

The demonstration of theorem is immediate. For this, it is sufficient to apply the form (14.69) of the previously formulated problem to each term of the equality (14.71).

(e) The matrix of the variables of primary expenses by products is established

The matrix of the variables of primary expenses by products has been inserted in the introductory part of the chapter (paragraph) and noted with (14.3).

On the other hand, according to (14.29), a connection between the variable of the primary consumption $X^{i}_{jsu_{js}}$ and its seven components was established, a connection extended in the previous paragraph also to the variables of primary consumption by products.

This connection is expressed as follows:

$$X^{i}_{j} = X^{i0}_{j} + \sum_r \sum_k X^{i1kr}_{j}, \left(\mathrm{i} = \overline{1, \mathrm{I}}; j = \overline{1, J}\right) \quad (14.76)$$

In order to achieve a similar decomposition of the variables of primary production costs, the following notations are inserted:

- Y^{i0}_{j}—the expense related to the consumption X^{i0}_{j};
- Y^{i1kr}_{j}—the expense related to the consumption X^{i1kr}_{j};
- p_{i0}—the price of a unit in the primary input E_{i0};
- p_{i1kr}—the price of a unit in the primary input E_{i1kr}.

Based on the inserted notations, the following equalities can be written:

$$Y^{i0}_{j} = p_{i0}X^{i0}_{j}, \left(\mathrm{i} = \overline{1, \mathrm{I}}; j = \overline{1, J}\right) \quad (14.77)$$

and

$$Y^{i1kr}_{j} = p_{i1kr}X^{i1kr}_{j}, \left(\mathrm{i} = \overline{1, \mathrm{I}}; j = \overline{1, J}; \mathrm{k} = 0, 1; \mathrm{r} = 1, 2, 3\right) \quad (14.78)$$

$$Y_j^i = Y_j^{i0} + \sum_k \sum_r Y_j^{i1kr},\ \left(\mathrm{i} = \overline{1,\mathrm{I}};\, j = \overline{1, J}\right) \tag{14.79}$$

We shall formulate the following notations:

- the variable Y_j^{i0} determined by the equality (14.77) is called direct primary expense;
- the variable Y_j^{i1kr} defined by (14.78) is called indirect primary expense, which is own or transferred (as k = 0 or k = 1), with the destination r (if r = 1, the expense is intended for the maintenance and operation of the machine, if r = 2, this is an expense with the local conducting information and if r = 3, this is an expense with the central conducting information).

Taking into account the inserted definitions and (14.79), we can formulate the following problem:

Any primary expense $Y_j^i\left(\mathrm{i} = \overline{1,\mathrm{I}};\, j = \overline{1, J}\right)$ incurred by the consumption X_j^i in the process (S) can be obtained by summing the following components:

- a component Y_j^{i0} of direct primary expense;
- six components Y_j^{i1kr} $(k = 0, 1;\, r = 1, 2, 3)$ of indirect primary expense, respectively with the following meaning;

Y_j^{i101}—components of own indirect expense, incurred by the maintenance and operation of the machine;
Y_j^{i102}—component of own indirect expense, incurred by the local conducting information;
Y_j^{i103}—component of own indirect expense, with central conducting information;
Y_j^{i111}—component of transferred indirect expense, incurred by the maintenance and operation of the machine;
Y_j^{i112}—component of transferred indirect expense, incurred by the local conducting information;
Y_j^{i113}—component of transferred indirect expense, incurred by the central conducting information;

If we note with:

$$P_{*0}^r = \begin{pmatrix} p_{10} & \cdots & 0 & \cdots & 0 \\ \vdots & & \vdots & & \vdots \\ 0 & \cdots & p_{i0} & \cdots & 0 \\ \vdots & & \vdots & & \vdots \\ 0 & \cdots & 0 & \cdots & p_{I0} \end{pmatrix} \tag{14.80}$$

and

$$P_{*1kr} = \begin{pmatrix} p_{11kr} & \cdots & 0 & \cdots & 0 \\ \vdots & & \vdots & & \vdots \\ 0 & \cdots & p_{i1kr} & \cdots & 0 \\ \vdots & & \vdots & & \vdots \\ 0 & \cdots & 0 & \cdots & p_{I1kr} \end{pmatrix} \tag{14.81}$$

$(k = 0, 1; r = \overline{1, 3})$, respectively the matrix of unit prices of the direct primary input components and the matrices of unit prices of the indirect primary input components.

Then the equalities (14.77) and (14.78) can be written in a matrix form,

$$Y_*^{*0} = P_{*0} X_*^{*0} \tag{14.82}$$

and

$$Y_*^{*1kr} = P_{*1kr} X_*^{*1kr}, \; (k = 0, 1; r = 1, 2, 3) \tag{14.83}$$

The equalities (14.79) can also be written in a matrix form as follows

$$Y_*^* = Y_*^{*0} + \sum_k \sum_r Y^{*1kr} \tag{14.84}$$

We note:

- The matrix Y_*^{*0} consisting of the IJ variables of the direct primary expenses, which is called the matrix of direct primary expenses;
- The matrices Y_*^{*1kr} $(k = 0, 1; r = 1, 2, 3)$ consisting of variables of indirect expense by elements and products, which are called the matrices of indirect primary expenses;
- The matrix Y_*^* consisting of the IJ variables of the unit primary expenses, by elements and products, which is called the matrix of the variables of production expenses.

The equality (14.84) can now be formulated as follows:
If,

- any component of primary input E_i $(i = \overline{1, I})$ into the process (S) of the system (W) consists of the components $E_{i0}, E_{i111}, E_{i102}, E_{i103}, E_{i111}, E_{i112}, E_{i113}$,
- the output from the process is heterogeneous and consists the group J of products,

then, the dimensional matrix (I, J)—of the variables of production expenses Y_*^* is decomposed into the sum of the following components:

- one dimensional matrix (I, J) of the direct primary expenses Y_*^{*0};

– six matrices—each dimensional (I, J)—of primary indirect expenses, respectively with the following name,

$Y_*^{*\,101}$—the matrix of own indirect expenses, for the maintenance and operation of the machine;
$Y_*^{*\,102}$—the matrix of own indirect primary expenses, with the central conducting information;
$Y_*^{*\,103}$—the matrix of own primary indirect expenses, with the central conducting information;
$Y_*^{*\,111}$—the matrix of transferred indirect expenses, for the maintenance and operation of the machine;
$Y_*^{*\,112}$—the matrix of transferred indirect expenses, with the local conducting information;
$Y_*^{*\,113}$—the matrix of transferred indirect primary expenses, with the central conducting information;

Starting from the decomposition achieved for the matrix of primary production expenses and taking into account the essential differences between the two groups of expenses in terms of the difficulties to distribute them buy products, we shall successively define and study the matrix of the structure of direct primary expenses, then the matrix of the structure of indirect primary expenses, after we first clarify the problem of how to establish the elements of the matrices of unit prices, respectively (14.80) and (14.81).

(f) The unit prices of primary input components are determined

Be, P_{*0} and P_{*1kr}, ($k=0, 1$; $r=1, 2, 3$) the matrices of unit prices of the inputs into a department $s=\overline{1,\ S}$, decomposed by primary components. By means thereof, the dependence between the matrices Y_*^{*0} and X_*^{*0} on the one hand, respectively between $Y_*^{*\,1kr}$ and $X_*^{*\,1kr}$ on the other hand are expressed in the previous paragraph. Therefore, knowing the elements of matrices (14.80) and (14.81) is directly related to the possibility to actually determine the matrices of the variables of direct and indirect primary expenses.

In order to establish a way to calculate the elements of the matrices of unit prices, let us consider any department $s=\overline{1,\ S}$ and the three groups of inputs thereto, as in the diagram Fig. 14.4., and let us observe that:

- P_{*0}—is the matrix of the prices of inputs E_{i0} $\left(\mathrm{i}=\overline{1,\ \mathrm{I}}\right)$;
- P_{*10r}—is the matrix of the prices of inputs E_{i10r} $\left(\mathrm{i}=\overline{1,\ \mathrm{I}};\ \mathrm{r}=1, 2, 3\right)$;
- P_{*11r}—is the matrix of the prices of inputs E_{i11r} $\left(\mathrm{i}=\overline{1,\ \mathrm{I}};\ \mathrm{r}=1, 2, 3\right)$.

The input of direct primary components E_{i0} $\left(\mathrm{i}=\overline{1,\ \mathrm{I}}\right)$ into a department s, as well as of components E_{i10r} $\left(\mathrm{i}=\overline{1,\ I};\ r=\overline{1,\ 3}\right)$ of own primary indirect input, being individual, the unit price of each exists and can be extracted for some of the so-called price catalogues. Therefore, the elements of the matrices,

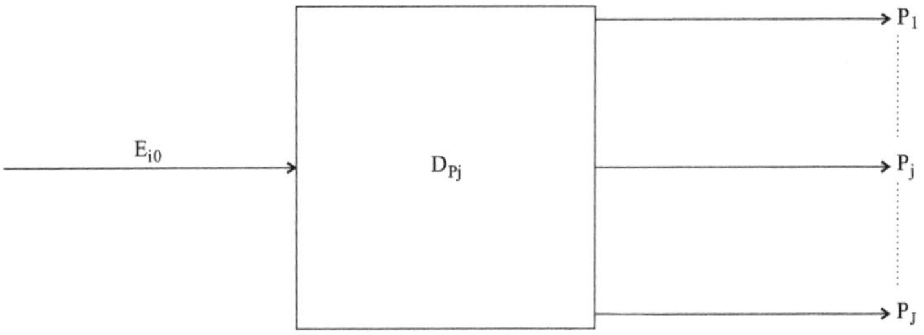

Fig. 14.4 Diagram of inputs from three groups of products

$$P_{*0} = \begin{pmatrix} p_{10} & \cdots & 0 & \cdots & 0 \\ \vdots & & \vdots & & \vdots \\ 0 & \cdots & p_{i0} & \cdots & 0 \\ \vdots & & \vdots & & \vdots \\ 0 & \cdots & 0 & \cdots & p_{I0} \end{pmatrix} \tag{14.85}$$

and

$$P_{*10r} = \begin{pmatrix} p_{110r} & \cdots & 0 & \cdots & 0 \\ \vdots & & \vdots & & \vdots \\ 0 & \cdots & p_{i10r} & \cdots & 0 \\ \vdots & & \vdots & & \vdots \\ 0 & \cdots & 0 & \cdots & p_{I10r} \end{pmatrix} (\mathrm{r} = 1, 2, 3) \tag{14.86}$$

are actually determined based on the price catalogues valid during that period, respectively on other sources.

Regarding the elements of the matrices $P_{*l l r}\left(r = \overline{1,\ 3}\right)$ corresponding to the primary inputs $E_{i1Ir}\left(\mathrm{i} = \overline{1,\ \mathrm{I}};\ r = 1,\ 2,\ 3\right)$ into the department $s = \overline{1,\ S}$, we do not find them in the aforementioned price catalogues. Therefore, the problem of establishing a process to determine them by calculation arises.

In order to establish such a process, let us first define and second determine the unit prices the departments use to supply their services.

We define an note with λ_s the unit price based on which the department s recovers all expenses incurred by achieving the production of volume Q_s, if it provides services to the other departments.

The vector consisting of these prices, we shall use the notation:

$$\lambda_* = \begin{pmatrix} \lambda_1 \\ \vdots \\ \lambda_s \\ \vdots \\ \lambda_S \end{pmatrix} \tag{14.87}$$

and it will be called the vector of unit prices of the outputs to departments.

Then, we can formulate the following problem:

Be,

$$w_{\bullet s \bullet}^{\bullet 0} = \sum_i p_{i0} c_{\bullet s \bullet}^{i0} \tag{14.88}$$

– the direct total (and also own) expense corresponding to achieving a production in the department s, with a volume equal to the unit and

$$w_{\bullet s \bullet}^{\bullet 10 \bullet} = \sum_i \sum_r p_{i10r} c_{\bullet s \bullet}^{i10r} \tag{14.89}$$

– the indirect total—own—expense corresponding to achieving a production in the department s, with a volume equal to the unit.

If,

$$\mathrm{w}_{\bullet * \bullet}^{\bullet 0} = \begin{pmatrix} \mathrm{w}_{\bullet 1 \bullet}^{\bullet 0} \\ \vdots \\ \mathrm{w}_{\bullet s \bullet}^{\bullet 0} \\ \vdots \\ \mathrm{w}_{\bullet S \bullet}^{\bullet 0} \end{pmatrix} \; and \; \mathrm{w}_{\bullet * \bullet}^{\bullet 10 \bullet} = \begin{pmatrix} \mathrm{w}_{\bullet 1 \bullet}^{\bullet 10 \bullet} \\ \vdots \\ \mathrm{w}_{\bullet s \bullet}^{\bullet 10 \bullet} \\ \vdots \\ \mathrm{w}_{\bullet S \bullet}^{\bullet 10 \bullet} \end{pmatrix} \tag{14.90}$$

are respectively the vector of total direct expenses at the product unit and the vector of indirect total—own—expenses by product unit, then the vector λ_* of unit prices of the outputs to the departments verified the following equation:

$$\left(\mathrm{E} - \mathrm{a}_{**}^{\mathrm{T}}\right)\lambda_* = \mathrm{w}_{\bullet * \bullet}^{\bullet 0} + \mathrm{w}_{\bullet * \bullet}^{\bullet 10 \bullet} \tag{14.91}$$

where E is the—dimensional—unit matrix (S, S)

Indeed, from the definition (14.88), the following equality results

$$\mathrm{Q_s}\lambda_\mathrm{s} = \sum_\mathrm{i} \left(\mathrm{p_{i0}} \mathrm{C}_{\bullet \mathrm{s} \bullet}^{\mathrm{i0}} + \sum_\mathrm{r} \mathrm{p_{i10r}} \mathrm{C}_{\bullet \mathrm{s} \bullet}^{\mathrm{i10r}} \right) + \mathrm{q_{1s}}\lambda_1 + \ldots + \mathrm{q_{Ss}}\lambda_{\mathrm{Ss}} \tag{14.92}$$

for any $s = \overline{1,\ S}$.

If in both members of the equality, we divide by Q_s, then we get

$$\lambda_s = \sum_i \left(p_{i0} c^{i0}_{\bullet s \bullet} + \sum_r p_{i10r} c^{i10r}_{\bullet s \bullet} \right) + a_{1s}\lambda_1 + \ldots + a_{Ss}\lambda_{Ss} = w^{\bullet 0}_{\bullet s \bullet} + w^{\bullet 10 \bullet}_{\bullet s \bullet} + \sum_l a_{ls}\lambda_s,\ (s = \overline{1,\ S}) \tag{14.93}$$

a result which, if written in matrix for, identifies with (14.91), which demonstrates the stated theorem.

Consequently, as the components of the vectors $w^{\bullet 0}_{\bullet * \bullet}$ şi $w^{\bullet 10 \bullet}_{\bullet * \bullet}$ are given by (14.88) şi (14.89), and the elements of the matrix a_{**} are also known, then to the extent where a_{**} admits the reverse, for λ_* it results that

$$\lambda_* = b^T_{**}\left(w^{\bullet 0}_{\bullet * \bullet} + w^{\bullet 10 \bullet}_{\bullet * \bullet}\right) \tag{14.94}$$

In relation to the result obtained, it is worth mentioning that in the economic practice the methods to determine the components of the vector λ_* do not have a rigorous background, are empirical, with many conventional elements.

We shall now do a decomposition of the integral consumption $C^{i11r}_{\bullet s \bullet}$, so that the contribution of each supplying department will result.

For this, we shall formulate two problems:

- whatever would be the primary input $E_{i11r}\left(i = \overline{1,\ I};\ r = 1, 2, 3\right)$, for its integral consumption $C^{i11r}_{\bullet s \bullet}$ in the department s, the following decomposition occurs:

$$C^{i11r}_{\bullet s \bullet} = C^{i11r}_{\bullet (1s) \bullet} + C^{i11r}_{\bullet (2s) \bullet} + \ldots + C^{i11r}_{\bullet (Ss) \bullet} \tag{14.95}$$

where

$C^{i11r}_{\bullet (ls) \bullet}$—is the part of the consumption in the department s of the primary input E_{i11r}, transferred into the department l by means of the service of volume q_{ls} and

$$C^{i11r}_{\bullet (ls) \bullet} = \left(c^{i0}_{\bullet l \bullet} + c^{i10r}_{\bullet l \bullet} + c^{i11r}_{\bullet l \bullet}\right) q_{ls};\ \left(l = \overline{1,\ S}\right) \tag{14.96}$$

if the integral consumption from any primary input into a department is directly proportional to the volume of production achieved in that department;

- whatever would be the primary input $E_{i11r}\left(i = \overline{1,\ I};\ r = 1, 2, 3\right)$, its unit price p_{i11r} is obtained as a weighted arithmetic average of the unit prices, $\lambda_1, \lambda_2, \ldots, \lambda_S$ of the outputs to the departments, the weights consisting of the quantities $C^{i11r}_{\bullet (1s) \bullet}$, $C^{i11r}_{\bullet (2s) \bullet}$, …, $C^{i11r}_{\bullet (Ss) \bullet}$, respectively consumed in the S departments and then transferred into the department s meaning:

$$p_{i11r} = \frac{\sum_l \lambda_l C_{\bullet (ls) \bullet}}{\sum_l C^{i11r}_{\bullet (ls) \bullet}},\ \left(i = \overline{1,\ I};\ r = 1,\ 2,\ 3\right) \tag{14.97}$$

Starting from the content of the price p_{i11r}, it results that this must leave the following expression invariant,

$$C^{i11r}_{\bullet(1s)\bullet}\lambda_1 + C^{i11r}_{\bullet(2s)\bullet}\lambda_2 + \ldots + C^{i11r}_{\bullet(Ss)\bullet}\lambda_S, \tag{14.98}$$

so that we have:

$$\sum_{l} C^{i1lr}_{\bullet(ls)\bullet}\lambda_l = p_{i1lr}\sum_{l} C^{i1lr}_{\bullet(ls)\bullet} \tag{14.99}$$

and (14.97) it immediately results.

If in (14.97) we successively take, $i = \overline{1,\ I}$ and $r = 1, 2, 3$ then, after performing the calculations, the elements of matrix P_{*11r} (r = 1, 2, 3) are obtained and, along with them, any of the matrices P_{*0}, P_{*10r} and P_{*11r} (r = 1, 2, 3) can be considered to be actually determined.

(g) The mathematical model of the structure of direct primary expenses is done

Be,

$$X^{*0}_{*} = \begin{pmatrix} X^{10}_{1} & \ldots & X^{10}_{j} & \ldots & X^{10}_{J} \\ \vdots & & \vdots & & \vdots \\ X^{i0}_{1} & \ldots & X^{i0}_{j} & \ldots & X^{i0}_{J} \\ \vdots & & \vdots & & \vdots \\ X^{I0}_{1} & \ldots & X^{I0}_{j} & \ldots & X^{I0}_{J} \end{pmatrix} \tag{14.100}$$

the matrix of the variables of primary—direct consumptions, attached to the process (S) of the system (W). As the process (S) occurs by departments and operations, it means that whatever the primary input $E_i\ (i = \overline{1,\ I})$ would be, destined to the output $P_j\ (j = \overline{1,\ J})$, it is subject to the transformations in table (14.26). In this way, the table of the variables shown below corresponds to any variable X^{i0}_{j} of the matrix (14.72),

$$\begin{pmatrix} X^{i0}_{j11} & \ldots & X^{i0}_{j1u_{j1}} & \ldots & X^{i0}_{j1M_{j1}} \\ \vdots & & \vdots & & \vdots \\ X^{i0}_{js1} & \ldots & X^{i0}_{jsu_{js}} & \ldots & X^{i0}_{jsM_{js}} \\ \vdots & & \vdots & & \vdots \\ X^{i0}_{lS*1} & \ldots & X^{i0}_{jS*u_{jS*}} & \ldots & X^{i0}_{jS*M_{jS*}} \end{pmatrix} \tag{14.101}$$

and not only one, so that if we sampled its elements, the consumption in E_{i0} results, which returns on a product in the group P_j, namely

$$\sum_{s}\sum_{u_{js}} X^{i0}_{jsu_{js}} = X^{i0}_{j\bullet\bullet} = X^{i0}_{j}, \ \left(i=\overline{1,\ I};\ \ j=\overline{1,\ J}\right) \tag{14.102}$$

If on the input E_{i0}, the operation $O_{jsu_{js}}$, was repeated $N^{i0}_{jsu_{js}}$ times, this means that whatever the variable $X^{i0}_{jsu_{js}}$ of the table (14.101) would be, directly measurable, it registers the following number of the values:

$$X^{i0}_{jsu_{js}} : \left(a^{i0}_{jsu_{js}1} \ldots a^{i0}_{jsu_{js}v^{i0}_{jsu_{js}}} \ldots a^{i0}_{jsu_{js}N^{i0}_{jsu_{js}}}\right) \tag{14.103}$$

so that its average value is

$$\overline{X}^{i0}_{jsu_{js}} = \frac{1}{N^{i0}_{jsu_{js}}}\sum a^{i0}_{jsu_{js}v^{i0}_{jsu_{js}}} \tag{14.104}$$

$\left(i=\overline{1,\ I};\ j=\overline{1,\ J};\ s=\overline{1,\ S^*};\ u_{js}=\overline{1,\ M_{js}}\right)$, the summation being performed in relation to the index $v^{i0}_{jsu_{js}}$.

If in both members of the equalities (14.102), we apply the medium operator, then we get

$$\overline{X}^{i0}_{j} = \sum_{s}\sum_{u_{js}} \overline{X}^{i0}_{jsu_{js}} = \overline{X}^{i0}_{j\bullet\bullet}, \ \left(i=\overline{1,\ I};\ \ j=\overline{1,\ J}\right) \tag{14.105}$$

or in matrix form,

$$\overline{X}^{*0}_{*} = \overline{X}^{*0}_{*\bullet\bullet} \tag{14.106}$$

In this context, we shall formulate the following problems:

- If the production process (S) of the system (W) is performed by departments and operations, then between the elements of the matrix of primary direct expenses structure

$$\overline{X}^{*0}_{*} = \begin{pmatrix} \overline{X}^{10}_{1} & \ldots & \overline{X}^{i0}_{j} & \ldots & \overline{X}^{10}_{J} \\ \vdots & & \vdots & & \vdots \\ \overline{X}^{i0}_{1} & \ldots & \overline{X}^{i0}_{j} & \ldots & \overline{X}^{i0}_{J} \\ \vdots & & \vdots & & \vdots \\ \overline{X}^{i0}_{1} & \ldots & \overline{X}^{i0}_{j} & \ldots & \overline{X}^{i0}_{J} \end{pmatrix} \tag{14.107}$$

and the elements of the matrix

$$\overline{X}_*^{*0} = \begin{pmatrix} \overline{X}_{1\bullet\bullet}^{10} & \cdots & \overline{X}_{j\bullet\bullet}^{10} & \cdots & \overline{X}_{J\bullet\bullet}^{10} \\ \vdots & & \vdots & & \vdots \\ \overline{X}_{1\bullet\bullet}^{i0} & \cdots & \overline{X}_{j\bullet\bullet}^{i0} & \cdots & \overline{X}_{J\bullet\bullet}^{i0} \\ \vdots & & \vdots & & \vdots \\ \overline{X}_{1\bullet\bullet}^{I0} & \cdots & \overline{X}_{j\bullet\bullet}^{I0} & \cdots & \overline{X}_{J\bullet\bullet}^{I0} \end{pmatrix} \tag{14.108}$$

also (I, J)—dimensional, there is a biunique correspondence, so that

$$\overline{X}_j^{i0} = \overline{X}_{j\bullet\bullet}^{i0}, \ \left(i = \overline{1,\ I};\ j = \overline{1,\ J}\right) \tag{14.109}$$

where, the averages from the second member are defined by (14.105)

The matrix

$$Y_*^{*0} = \begin{pmatrix} Y_1^{10} & \cdots & Y_j^{10} & \cdots & Y_J^{10} \\ \vdots & & \vdots & & \vdots \\ Y_j^{i0} & \cdots & Y_J^{i0} & \cdots & Y_J^{i0} \\ \vdots & & \vdots & & \vdots \\ Y_1^{I0} & \cdots & Y_j^{I0} & \cdots & Y_J^{I0} \end{pmatrix} \tag{14.110}$$

by analogy with the name of matrix of the structure of direct primary consumptions used for (14.107) it is called the matrix of the structure of direct primary expenses, and its elements—the parameters of the structure of the direct primary expenses;

- If,

$\overline{X}_*^{*0}$ Is the dimensional matrix (I, J) of the structure of direct primary expenses;
P_{*0} is the matrix of the prices defined by (14.80) and
$\overline{Y}_*^{*0}$ is the dimensional matrix (I, J) of the structure of direct primary expenses.

Then,

$$\overline{Y}_*^{*0} = P_{*0}\overline{X}_*^{*0} \tag{14.111}$$

The equality (14.111), it immediately results if we apply the medium operator to both members of the equality (14.82).

If in a certain period, the operations of table (14.26) have the following frequencies:

$$\begin{matrix} N_{j11}^{i0} \cdots N_{j1u_{j1}}^{i0} \cdots N_{j1M_{j1}}^{i0} \\ \cdots\cdots\cdots\cdots\cdots\cdots \\ N_{js1}^{i0} \cdots N_{jsu_{js}}^{i0} \cdots N_{jsM_{js}}^{i0} \\ \cdots\cdots\cdots\cdots\cdots\cdots \\ N_{1S^*1}^{i0} \cdots N_{1S^*u_{1S^*}}^{i0} \cdots N_{1S^*M_{1S^*}}^{i0} \end{matrix} \tag{14.112}$$

then, whatever may be the variable $X^{i0}_{jsu_{js}}\left(s=\overline{1,\ S^*};\ u_{js}=\overline{1,\ M_{js}}\right)$ of the table (14.101), this registers $N^{i0}_{jsu_{js}}$ numerical values, (14.103), values that can be obtained through a direct statistical observation, along with performing the process (*S*). Then, based on the relations (14.104), the elements intervening in creating the table can be calculated

$$\begin{array}{l} \overline{X}^{i0}_{j11}\ldots\overline{X}^{i0}_{j1u_{j1}}\ldots\overline{X}^{i0}_{j1M_{j1}} \\ \ldots\ldots\ldots\ldots\ldots\ldots\ldots\ldots \\ \overline{X}^{i0}_{js1}\ldots\overline{X}^{i0}_{jsu_{js}}\ldots\overline{X}^{i0}_{jsM_{js}} \\ \ldots\ldots\ldots\ldots\ldots\ldots\ldots\ldots \\ \overline{X}^{i0}_{JS^*1}\ldots\overline{X}^{i0}_{JS^*u_{JS^*}}\ldots\overline{X}^{i0}_{JS^*M_{JS^*}} \end{array} \tag{14.113}$$

and by using (14.105), the elements of matrix (14.107) of the structure of direct primary consumptions result immediately.

If the described process is applied IJ times, therefore for any $i=\overline{1,\ I}$ and $j=\overline{1,\ J}$ we ultimately get all the elements of the matrix of direct primary consumptions $\overline{X}^{*0}_{*}$.

Given the matrix P_{*0}, based on (14.102), it results that the matrix of the structure of direct primary expenses $\overline{Y}^{*0}_{*}$ is uniquely determined.

This way of establishing the matrix of the structure, direct primary expenses, in practice can not be followed because the numerical values (14.103) which the variable $X^{i0}_{jsu_{js}}$ (for any values of the indices it depends on) registers them, as it was also highlighted in the introductory chapter, practically they are not noted—in their entirety—in the existing information documents, due to the too large volume of data and therefore of labour which this operation would require.

If a total observation of the values of variables in tables (14.101), $\left(i=\overline{1,\ I};\ j=\overline{1,\ J}\right)$ is not efficient and practically almost impossible, we can obtain a random sample of their observations in a relatively easy way and with a low volume of work.

In this way, for any variable $X^{i0}_{jsu_{js}}$ of the table (14.101), we shall have instead of the $N^{i0}_{jsu_{js}}$ values (14.101) a random sample of observations, respectively

$$x^{i0}_{jsu_{js}1},\ x^{i0}_{jsu_{js}2},\ \ldots,\ x^{i0}_{jsu_{js}n^{i0}_{jsu_{js}}} \tag{14.114}$$

of volume $n^{i0}_{jsu_{js}}$.

Using the results (14.114) instead of (14.101) as starting point, we get estimations of the parameters of the structure of direct primary expenses and not their true values;

– Be E_{i0} the primary input into a main department s of the process (S), intended to achieve the heterogeneous output consisting of the kinds $P_1, P_2, \ldots, P_J$ is in the diagram (Fig. 14.4). The of the input E_{i0} on the operations of the products $P_1, P_2, \ldots, P_J$, performed in the department s can be characterised by the table of variables

$$\begin{vmatrix} X^{i0}_{1s1} \ldots X^{i0}_{1su_{js}} \ldots X^{i0}_{1sM_{1s}} \\ \ldots\ldots\ldots\ldots\ldots\ldots \\ X^{i0}_{js1} \ldots X^{i0}_{jsu_{js}} \ldots X^{i0}_{jsM_{js}} \\ \ldots\ldots\ldots\ldots\ldots\ldots \\ X^{i0}_{Js1} \ldots X^{i0}_{Jsu_{Js}} \ldots X^{i0}_{JsM_{Js}} \end{vmatrix} \tag{14.115}$$

A synthetic characterisation of this consumption during the entire period taken into account is given by the average value of the variables in the previous table,

$$\begin{vmatrix} \overline{X}^{i0}_{1s1} \ldots \overline{X}^{i0}_{1su_{1s}} \ldots \overline{X}^{i0}_{1sM_{1s}} \\ \ldots\ldots\ldots\ldots\ldots\ldots \\ \overline{X}^{i0}_{js1} \ldots \overline{X}^{i0}_{jsu_{js}} \ldots \overline{X}^{i0}_{jsM_{js}} \\ \ldots\ldots\ldots\ldots\ldots\ldots \\ \overline{X}^{i0}_{Js1} \ldots \overline{X}^{i0}_{Jsu_{Js}} \ldots \overline{X}^{i0}_{JsM_{Js}} \end{vmatrix} \tag{14.116}$$

If in the period taken into account the operations

$$\begin{vmatrix} O_{1s1} \ldots O_{1su_{1s}} \ldots O_{1sM_{1s}} \\ \ldots\ldots\ldots\ldots\ldots\ldots \\ O_{js1} \ldots O_{jsu_{js}} \ldots O_{jsM_{js}} \\ \ldots\ldots\ldots\ldots\ldots\ldots \\ O_{Js1} \ldots O_{Jsu_{Js}} \ldots O_{JsM_{Js}} \end{vmatrix} \tag{14.117}$$

performed on the input E_{i0} in the main department s were repeated respectively with the frequencies

$$\begin{vmatrix} N^{i0}_{1s1} \ldots N^{i0}_{1su_{1s}} \ldots N^{i0}_{1sM_{1s}} \\ \ldots\ldots\ldots\ldots\ldots\ldots \\ N^{i0}_{js1} \ldots N^{i0}_{jsu_{js}} \ldots N^{i0}_{jsM_{js}} \\ \ldots\ldots\ldots\ldots\ldots\ldots \\ N^{i0}_{Js1} \ldots N^{i0}_{Jsu_{Js}} \ldots N^{i0}_{JsM_{Js}} \end{vmatrix} \tag{14.118}$$

then the $M_{1s}+\ldots+M_{js}+\ldots+M_{Js}$ average direct primary consumptions by departments and operations from the table (14.115) verify the following equation:

$$\sum_{j}\left(\overline{X}^{i0}_{js1}N^{i0}_{js1}+\ldots+\overline{X}^{i0}_{jsu_{js}}N^{i0}_{jsu_{js}}+\ldots+\overline{X}^{i0}_{jsM_{js}}N^{i0}_{jsM_{js}}\right)=C^{i0}_{\bullet s\bullet}\qquad(14.119)$$

The demonstration of the theorem results from the very content of the elements that appear in the first and second member of the equalities (14.118).

Consequently, if we amplify both members of the equation corresponding to the input E_{i0} into the equation s, with the price p_{i0}, we get:

$$\sum_{j}\sum_{u_{js}}\left(p_{i0}\overline{X}_{jsu_{js}}N_{jsu_{js}}\right)=p_{i0}C^{i0}_{\bullet s\bullet}\qquad(14.120)$$

or $\sum_{j}\left(\overline{Y}_{js1}N_{js1}+\ldots+\overline{Y}_{jsu_{js}}N_{jsu_{js}}+\ldots+\overline{Y}_{jsM_{js}}N_{jsM_{js}}\right)=p_{i0}C^{i0}_{\bullet s\bullet}$

One and only one equation of the type (14.119) corresponds to each table (14.115), expressing the structure of the integral consumption $C^{i0}_{\bullet s\bullet}$ of the input E_{i0} into the main department s, on the outputs P_1, P_2, …, Pj, …, P_J. For this reason, an equation of the type (14.119) will be called—the equation of the structure of direct primary integral consumption by product and operations, or in short forum the structural equation. In our case, the structural equation of the direct primary consumption $C^{i0}_{\bullet s\bullet}$ is written.

The number of structural equations of the direct primary consumptions that can be attached to the process (S) depends on the number of main departments wherein it occurs, as well as on the number of primary components wherein the input is decomposed. If the number of direct primary input components is I, and the number of main department is S*, then the number of corresponding structural equations IS*. These equations are independent between them, each expressing the structure of a consumption of a certain kind and in a well determined department.

While the equation (14.119) expresses the structure of the consumption $C^{i0}_{\bullet s\bullet}$, the equation (14.22) expresses the structure of integral expenses $p_{i0}C^{i0}_{\bullet s\bullet}$, therefore such an equation will be called—the equation of the structure of direct integral primary expenses, by product and operations, or in short form—the structural equation of the expenses $C^{i0}_{\bullet s\bullet}$. The number of these equations is also $IS*$, and the total number of parameters characterising the structure of integral consumptions or of direct integral expenses is

$$I\sum_{j}\sum_{s}M_{js}\qquad(14.121)$$

If the output from the process (S) is heterogeneous ($J > 1$) and is in relation to each kind P_1, P_2, …, P_J in the department s at least one operation is performed, then

$$\sum_{j}M_{js}>1\text{ si }\sum\sum M_{js}>IS*\qquad(14.122)$$

The first inequality shows that the number of parameters characterising the structure of the integral consumption in the department $s = \overline{1,\ S^*}$—if the output from the process (S) and the department s is heterogeneous—is strictly greater than the unit, meaning than the number of structural equations. The second inequality shows that this is generally valid.

Returning to the problem of establishing the mathematical model for assessing the parameters of the structure of direct primary expenses, the last established theorem shows that by starting from the random sample of observations (14.114), the sought mathematical model must also include the structural equation (14.119) for any $i = 1, 2, \ldots, I$ and $s = 1, 2, \ldots S^*$.

In order to formulate the mathematical model for estimating the parameters of the structure of direct primary expenses, be

$1, 2, \ldots, S^*$—the main production departments,
$E_{10}, E_{20}, \ldots, E_{I0}$—the input into each main department decomposed by primaryelements and
$P_1, P_2, \ldots, P_J$—the output from each department consisting of J groups of products

In relation to each main department, bearing in mind the input, output and production processes, let us consider the following diagram (Fig. 14.5):

and associate thereto for any $i = \overline{1,\ I}$, respectively the tables of variables

$$\left| \begin{array}{ccccc}
X^{i0}_{111} & \cdots & X^{i0}_{11u_{11}} & \cdots & X^{i0}_{11M_{11}} \\
\vdots & & \vdots & & \vdots \\
X^{i0}_{j11} & \cdots & X^{i0}_{j1u_{j1}} & \cdots & X^{i0}_{j1M_{j1}} \\
\vdots & & \vdots & & \vdots \\
X^{i0}_{J11} & \cdots & X^{i0}_{J1u_{J1}} & \cdots & X^{i0}_{J1M_{J1}} \\
\cdots & \cdots & \cdots & \cdots & \cdots \\
\cdots & \cdots & \cdots & \cdots & \cdots \\
\cdots & \cdots & \cdots & \cdots & \cdots \\
X^{i0}_{1s1} & \cdots & X^{i0}_{1su_{1s}} & \cdots & X^{i0}_{1sM_{1s}} \\
\vdots & & \vdots & & \vdots \\
X^{i0}_{js1} & \cdots & X^{i0}_{jsu_{js}} & \cdots & X^{i0}_{jsM_{js}} \\
\vdots & & \vdots & & \vdots \\
X^{i0}_{Js1} & \cdots & X^{i0}_{Jsu_{Js}} & \cdots & X^{i0}_{JsM_{Js}} \\
\cdots & \cdots & \cdots & \cdots & \cdots \\
\cdots & \cdots & \cdots & \cdots & \cdots \\
\cdots & \cdots & \cdots & \cdots & \cdots \\
X^{i0}_{1S^*1} & \cdots & X^{i0}_{1S^*u_{1S^*}} & \cdots & X^{i0}_{1S^*M_{1S^*}} \\
\vdots & & \vdots & & \vdots \\
X^{i0}_{jS^*1} & \cdots & X^{i0}_{jS^*u_{jS^*}} & \cdots & X^{i0}_{jS^*M_{jS^*}} \\
\vdots & & \vdots & & \vdots \\
X^{i0}_{JS^*1} & \cdots & X^{i0}_{JS^*u_{JS^*}} & \cdots & X^{i0}_{JS^*M_{JS^*}}
\end{array} \right| \qquad (14.123)$$

Fig. 14.5 Diagram input-output in production processes

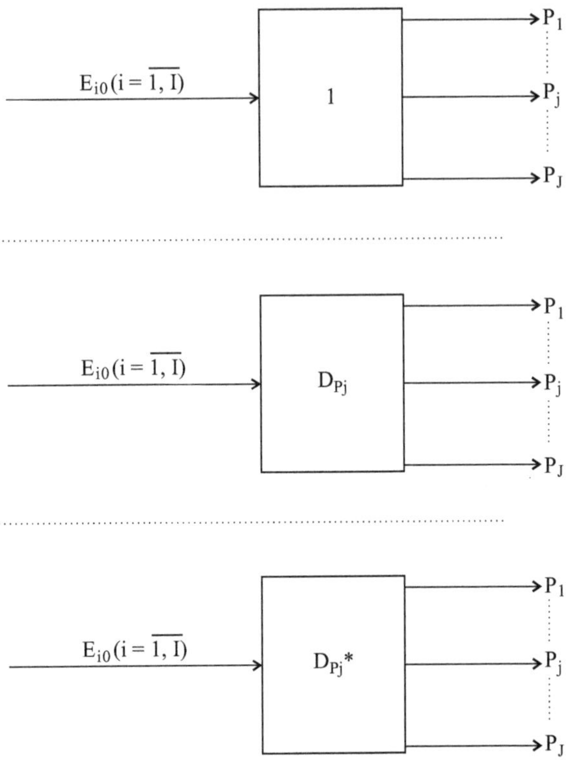

characterising the consumptions from the primary input $E_{i0}\left(i = \overline{1, I}\right)$ into each main department—by products and operations—and satisfying the relations (14.102), respectively

$$\sum_{s}\sum_{u_{1s}} X^{i0}_{1su_{1s}} = X^{i0}_{1},\ \ldots,\ \sum_{s}\sum_{u_{Js}} X^{i0}_{Jsu_{Js}} = X^{i0}_{J},\ \left(i = \overline{1, I}\right) \tag{14.124}$$

Assuming that whatever the variable $X^{i0}_{jsu_{js}}$ from (14.123) would be, there is the random sample (14.114) then the problem of distributing direct expenses—by elements and products—becomes a problem of estimating the parameters of the structure of direct primary expenses, respectively of the matrix,

$$\overline{Y}^{*0}_{*} = \begin{pmatrix} \overline{Y}^{10}_{1} & \ldots & \overline{Y}^{10}_{j} & \ldots & \overline{Y}^{10}_{J} \\ \vdots & & \vdots & & \vdots \\ \overline{Y}^{i0}_{1} & \ldots & \overline{Y}^{i0}_{j} & \ldots & \overline{Y}^{i0}_{J} \\ \vdots & & \vdots & & \vdots \\ \overline{Y}^{I0}_{1} & \ldots & \overline{Y}^{I0}_{j} & \ldots & \overline{Y}^{I0}_{J} \end{pmatrix}$$ knowing that:

$$\begin{pmatrix} \overline{Y}_1^{i0} & \cdots & \overline{Y}_J^{i0} \\ \vdots & & \vdots \\ \overline{Y}_1^{I0} & \cdots & \overline{Y}_J^{I0} \end{pmatrix} = \begin{pmatrix} p_{10} & \cdots & 0 \\ \vdots & & \vdots \\ 0 & \cdots & p_{I0} \end{pmatrix} \begin{pmatrix} \overline{X}_1^{10} & \cdots & \overline{X}_J^{10} \\ \vdots & & \vdots \\ \overline{X}_1^{I0} & \cdots & \overline{X}_J^{I0} \end{pmatrix} \tag{14.125}$$

$$\overline{X}_1^{i0} = \sum_s \sum_{u_{1s}} \overline{X}_{1su_{1s}}^{i0} \ldots \overline{X}_J^{i0} = \sum_s \sum_{u_{Js}} \overline{X}_{Jsu_{Js}}^{i0} \; \left(i = \overline{1, I}\right) \tag{14.126}$$

$$(K_0) \sum_j \left(\overline{X}_{js1}^{i0} N_{js1}^{i0} + \ldots + \overline{X}_{jsu_{js}}^{i0} N_{jsu_{js}}^{i0} + \ldots + \overline{X}_{jsM_{js}}^{i0} N_{jsM_{js}}^{i0} \right) = C_{\bullet s \bullet}^{i0}$$

$$(s = 1, 2, \ldots, S^*; \; i = 1, 2, .., I)$$

The mathematical model established shows that the process of estimating the parameters of the structure of direct primary expenses must begin—once the formed sample of measurements (14.114) by estimating the parameters intervening in the equations of structure (K_0). In the second stage, we can proceed to estimate the parameters of the structure, the direct primary consumptions, parameters which appear as linear combinations of the parameters estimated in the first stage, as it results from (14.126). Only in the third stage it is possible to estimate the parameters of the structure of direct primary expenses, by using for this purpose the inequality (14.125), where the unknown parameters also appear as linear combinations of some parameters already estimated in the previous stage.

Therefore, the mathematical model to estimate the parameters of the structure of direct primary expenses appears as consisting of the following three types of models: a linear model to estimate the connected parameters based on the samples of direct measurements, consisting of the samples of measurements (14.114) and the structural equations ($\boldsymbol{K_0}$) and two models to estimate the linear combinations of parameters, respectively (14.126) and (14.125).

(h) The mathematical model of the structure of indirect primary expenses is done

Be,

$$X_*^{*1kr} = \begin{pmatrix} X_1^{11kr} & \cdots & X_j^{11kr} & \cdots & X_J^{11kr} \\ \vdots & & \vdots & & \vdots \\ X_1^{i1kr} & \cdots & X_j^{i1kr} & \cdots & X_J^{i1kr} \\ \vdots & & \vdots & & \vdots \\ X_1^{I1kr} & \cdots & X_j^{I1kr} & \cdots & X_J^{I1kr} \end{pmatrix}, \; \left(k = 0, \; 1; \; r = \overline{1, \; 3}\right) \tag{14.127}$$

the dimensional matrices (I, J) of the indirect primary consumptions attached to the process (S) of the system (W)

$$\begin{pmatrix} a_{1\,j1} & \cdots & a_{1su_{1s}} & \cdots & a_{1sM_{js}} \\ \vdots & & \vdots & & \vdots \\ a_{js1} & \cdots & a_{jsu_{js}} & \cdots & a_{jsM_{js}} \\ \vdots & & \vdots & & \vdots \\ a_{Js^*1} & \cdots & a_{Js^*u_{Js^*}} & \cdots & a_{Js^*M_{Js^*}} \end{pmatrix} \tag{14.128}$$

indicating the input E_{i1k} intended for the output P_j and the operations it is subject to. Such a diagram can be attached to any of the variables X_j^{i1kr} of matrix (14.127).

Corresponding to the table (14.128), let us consider the table of variables

$$\begin{pmatrix} X_{j11}^{i1kr} & \cdots & X_{j1u_{j1}}^{i1kr} & \cdots & X_{j1M_{j1}}^{i1kr} \\ \vdots & & \vdots & & \vdots \\ X_{js1}^{i1kr} & \cdots & X_{jsu_{js}}^{i1kr} & \cdots & X_{jsM_{js}}^{i1kr} \\ \vdots & & \vdots & & \vdots \\ X_{jS^*1}^{i1kr} & \cdots & X_{jS^*u_{jS^*}}^{i1kr} & \cdots & X_{jS^*M_{jS^*}}^{i1kr} \end{pmatrix} \tag{14.129}$$

representing the consumption X_j^{i1kr} from the input E_{i1kr} decomposed by departments and the operations contributing to achieve the output P_j.

The variables in table (14.129) forming a decomposition of the consumption X_j^{i1kr} by departments and operations, we have:

$$\sum_{s}\sum_{u_{js}} X_{jsu_{js}}^{i1kr} = X_{j\bullet\bullet}^{i1kr} = X_j^{i1kr} \tag{14.130}$$

for any $i = \overline{1,\ I}$; $j = \overline{1,\ J}$; $k = 0,\ 1$; $r = 1,\ 2,\ 3$.

If during the period taken into account, the operation $O_{jsu_{js}}$—on the input E_{i1kr}—was repeated by $N_{jsu_{js}}^{i1kr}$ times, it means that the variable $X_{jsu_{js}}^{i1kr}$ from the table (14.129), non-directly measurable is characterised by the following series of numerical values

$$X_{jsu_{js}}^{i1kr} : \left(a_{jsu_{js}1}^{i1kr},\ a_{jsu_{js}2}^{i1kr},\ \ldots,\ a_{jsu_{js}N_{jsu_{js}}^{i1kr}}^{i1kr} \right) \tag{14.131}$$

Practically however, the values (14.131) cannot be obtained, a statistical observation in this regard is possible.

In the introductory chapter, it was however mentioned that, whatever the result of the variable $X_{jsu_{js}}^{i1kr}$ would be from the table (14.129), the factorial variables (14.34) can be emphasised theoretically and especially practically and subject to a direct statistical observation.

Let us assume now that in the period studied, the frequency of using the operation $O_{jsu_{js}}$ on the input E_{i1kr} was $N_{jsu_{js}}^{i1kr}$ and that for the factorial variables (14.34), the following numerical values were registered after a direct statistical observation:

$$\begin{array}{l} \left(a^{ilkr}_{jsu_{js}}\right)_{11}, \ \ldots, \ \left(a^{ilkr}_{jsu_{js}}\right)_{H^{ilkr}_{jsu_{js}1}} \quad N^{ilkr}_{jsu_{js}1} \ \textit{times}, \\ \ldots\ldots\ldots\ldots\ldots\ldots\ldots\ldots\ldots\ldots\ldots \\ \left(a^{ilkr}_{jsu_{js}}\right)_{1g}, \ \ldots, \ \left(a^{ilkr}_{jsu_{js}}\right)_{H^{ilkr}_{jsu_{js}g}} \quad N^{ilkr}_{jsu_{js}g} \ \textit{times}, \\ \ldots\ldots\ldots\ldots\ldots\ldots\ldots\ldots\ldots\ldots\ldots \\ \left(a^{ilkr}_{jsu_{js}}\right)_{1G}, \ \ldots, \ \left(a^{ilkr}_{jsu_{js}}\right)_{H^{ilkr}_{jsu_{js}G}} \quad N^{ilkr}_{jsu_{js}G} \ \textit{times}, \end{array} \tag{14.132}$$

so that,

$$N^{ilkr}_{jsu_{js}1} + \ldots + N^{ilkr}_{jsu_{js}g} + \ldots + N^{ilkr}_{jsu_{js}G} = N^{ilkr}_{jsu_{js}} \tag{14.133}$$

If the dependence between the resultant variable $X^{ilkr}_{jsu_{js}}$ and the factorial variables (14.34) would be functional, this would mean that in each of the G groups of observations, $X^{ilkr}_{jsu_{js}}$ would be constant, which is difficult to assume, because besides the mentioned factors, in each group, are the non-quantifiable factors can also act and which make the resultant variable have some variations on both sides of the average value. Therefore, while between the resultant variable $X^{ilkr}_{jsu_{js}}$ and the factorial variables (14.34) the dependence is statistical, between the conditional average of the resultant variable and the factorial variables mentioned, the dependence is functional.

As such:

$$\begin{aligned} & E\left[X^{ilkr}_{jsu_{js}} / \left(X^{ilkr}_{jsu_{js}}\right)_1, \ \ldots, \ \left(X^{ilkr}_{jsu_{js}}\right)_{H^{ilkr}_{jsu_{js}}}\right] \\ & \quad = G^{ilkr}_{jsu_{js}}\left[\left(X^{ilkr}_{jsu_{js}}\right)_1, \ \ldots, \ \left(X^{ilkr}_{jsu_{js}}\right)_{H^{ilkr}_{jsu_{js}}}\right] \end{aligned} \tag{14.134}$$

for any $i = \overline{1, I}$; $j = \overline{1, J}$; $k = 0, 1$; $r = 1, 2, 3$; $s = \overline{1, S^*}$; $u_{js} = \overline{1, M_{js}}$.

If we take into account the results of statistical observation (14.132) of the factorial variables that intervene in the regressions (14.134), then we can get the average value of each of them, namely:

$$\begin{array}{l} \left(\overline{X}^{ilkr}_{jsu_{js}}\right)_1 = \dfrac{1}{N^{ilkr}_{jsu_{js}}} \sum\limits_g \left(a^{ilkr}_{jsu_{js}}\right)_{1g} N^{ilkr}_{jsu_{js}g} \\ \ldots\ldots\ldots\ldots\ldots\ldots\ldots\ldots\ldots\ldots\ldots \\ \left(\overline{X}^{ilkr}_{jsu_{js}}\right)_{H^{ilkr}_{jsu_{js}}} = \dfrac{1}{N^{ilkr}_{jsu_{js}}} \sum\limits_g \left(a^{ilkr}_{jsu_{js}}\right)_{H^{ilkr}_{jsu_{js}g}} N^{ilkr}_{jsu_{js}g} \end{array} \tag{14.135}$$

If in (14.134), for the factorial variables their average values thus obtained are taken and it is assumed that the regressions are completely determined, then for the average value of the resultant variable $X^{i1kr}_{jsu_{js}}$, it results

$$\begin{aligned}\overline{X}^{i1kr}_{jsu_{js}} &= E\left[X^{i1kr}_{jsu_{js}}/\left(\overline{X}^{i1kr}_{jsu_{js}}\right)_1, \ldots, \left(\overline{X}^{i1kr}_{jsu_{js}}\right)_{H^{i1kr}_{jsu_{js}}}\right] = \\ &= G^{i1kr}_{jsu_{js}}\left[\left(\overline{X}^{i1kr}_{jsu_{js}}\right)_1, \ldots, \left(\overline{X}^{i1kr}_{jsu_{js}}\right)_{H^{i1kr}_{jsu_{js}}}\right]\end{aligned} \tag{14.136}$$

By doing in this way for all the values $u_{js} = \overline{1,\ M_{js}}$ and $s = \overline{1,\ S^*}$, we finally get the average value of each of the variables of table (14.129), so that we have the table

$$\begin{pmatrix} \overline{X}^{i1kr}_{j11} & \cdots & \overline{X}^{i1kr}_{j1u_{j1}} & \cdots & \overline{X}^{i1kr}_{j1M_{j1}} \\ \vdots & & \vdots & & \vdots \\ \overline{X}^{i1kr}_{js1} & \cdots & \overline{X}^{i1kr}_{jsu_{js}} & \cdots & \overline{X}^{i1kr}_{jsM_{js}} \\ \vdots & & \vdots & & \vdots \\ \overline{X}^{i1kr}_{jS^*1} & \cdots & \overline{X}^{i1kr}_{jS^*u_{jS^*}} & \cdots & \overline{X}^{i1kr}_{jS^*M_{jS^*}} \end{pmatrix} \tag{14.137}$$

But, from (14.130), it results that ($k = 0, 1; r = 1, 2, 3$)

$$\sum_{s}\sum_{u_{js}} \overline{X}^{i1kr}_{jsu_{js}} = \overline{X}^{i1kr}_{j\bullet\bullet} = \overline{X}^{i1kr}_{j},\ (k = 0,\ 1;\ r = 1,\ 2,\ 3) \tag{14.138}$$

by this obtaining the average value of the variable X^{i1kr}_{j}, component of the matrix (14.127).

By ding this for any $i = \overline{1,\ I}$ and $j = \overline{1,\ J}$, we get the following matrix,

$$\overline{X}^{*1kr}_{*} = \begin{pmatrix} \overline{X}^{11kr}_{1} & \cdots & \overline{X}^{11kr}_{j} & \cdots & \overline{X}^{11kr}_{J} \\ \vdots & & \vdots & & \vdots \\ \overline{X}^{i1kr}_{1} & \cdots & \overline{X}^{i1kr}_{j} & \cdots & \overline{X}^{i1kr}_{J} \\ \vdots & & \vdots & & \vdots \\ \overline{X}^{I1kr}_{1} & \cdots & \overline{X}^{I1kr}_{j} & \cdots & \overline{X}^{I1kr}_{J} \end{pmatrix} \tag{14.139}$$

for any $k = 0$, 1 and $r = 1$, 2, 3.

In this context, the matrices (14.139) the elements of which are defined by the equalities (14.138), (14.136) and (14.135) are called matrices of the indirect primary consumptions, and their elements—parameters of the structure of indirect primary expenses.

The six matrices of the structure of indirect primary consumptions have different significances for various values of the indices $k = 0$, 1 and $r = 1$, 2, 3.

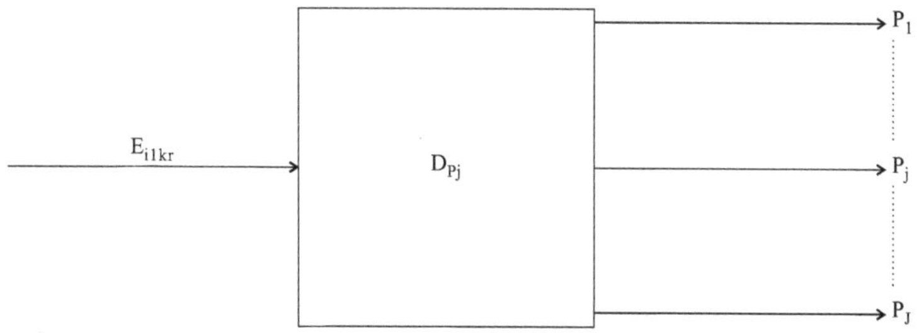

Fig. 14.6 Diagram of primary input from heterogeneous output $P_1, P_2, \ldots, P_J$

And the matrices:

$$\overline{Y}_*^{*1kr} = \begin{pmatrix} \overline{Y}_1^{11kr} & \cdots & \overline{Y}_j^{11kr} & \cdots & \overline{Y}_J^{11kr} \\ \vdots & & \vdots & & \vdots \\ \overline{Y}_1^{i1kr} & \cdots & \overline{Y}_j^{i1kr} & \cdots & \overline{Y}_J^{i1kr} \\ \vdots & & \vdots & & \vdots \\ \overline{Y}_1^{I1kr} & \cdots & \overline{Y}_j^{I1kr} & \cdots & \overline{Y}_J^{I1kr} \end{pmatrix} \quad (k = 0,\ 1;\ r = 1,\ 2,\ 3) \qquad (14.140)$$

made of the average values of the indirect primary expenses, they are called matrices of the structure of indirect primary expenses, and their elements—the parameters of the structure of indirect primary expenses.

We formulate the following problems:

- Whatever may be the matrix $X_*^{*\,1kr}$ (k = 0, 1; r = 1, 2, 3) (I, J)—dimensional—the matrix P_{*1kr} of the prices and the matrix $\overline{Y}_*^{*1kr}$, (I, J)—dimensional—of the structure of indirect primary expenses, the following equality occurs,

$$\overline{Y}_*^{*1kr} = P_{*1kr}\overline{X}_*^{*1kr} \qquad \text{for any } k = 0,\ 1 \text{ and } r = 1,\ 2,\ 3. \qquad (14.141)$$

The theorem results immediately from the equality (14.83), after applying the medium operator to both its members;

- Be E_{i1kr} the primary input into any main department s of the process (s), intended to achieve the heterogeneous output $P_1, P_2, \ldots, P_J$ and the following diagram (Fig. 14.6):

  If the table of the variables of the consumption attached to the previous diagram is:

$$\begin{pmatrix} X_{1s1}^{i1kr} & \cdots & X_{1su_{1s}}^{i1kr} & \cdots & X_{1sM_{1s}}^{i1kr} \\ \vdots & & \vdots & & \vdots \\ X_{js1}^{i1kr} & \cdots & X_{jsu_{js}}^{i1kr} & \cdots & X_{jsM_{js}}^{i1kr} \\ \vdots & & \vdots & & \vdots \\ X_{Js1}^{i1kr} & \cdots & X_{Jsu_{Js}}^{i1kr} & \cdots & X_{JsM_{Js}}^{i1kr} \end{pmatrix} \qquad (14.142)$$

then, the synthetic characterisation of the consumption in the period taken into account can be done by means of the average values of the variables (14.142), respectively with:

$$\begin{pmatrix} \overline{X}_{1s1}^{i1kr} & \dots & \overline{X}_{1su_{1s}}^{i1kr} & \dots & \overline{X}_{1sM_{1s}}^{i1kr} \\ \vdots & & \vdots & & \vdots \\ \overline{X}_{js1}^{i1kr} & \dots & \overline{X}_{jsu_{js}}^{i1kr} & \dots & \overline{X}_{jsM_{js}}^{i1kr} \\ \vdots & & \vdots & & \vdots \\ \overline{X}_{Js1}^{i1kr} & \dots & \overline{X}_{Jsu_{Js}}^{i1kr} & \dots & \underline{X}_{JsM_{Js}}^{i1kr} \end{pmatrix} \tag{14.143}$$

Assuming that—in the studied period—the operations (14.117) performed on the primary input E_{i1kr} into the main department s were repeated respectively with the frequencies,

$$\begin{pmatrix} N_{1s1}^{i1kr} & \dots & N_{1su_{1s}}^{i1kr} & \dots & N_{1sM_{1s}}^{i1kr} \\ \vdots & & \vdots & & \vdots \\ N_{js1}^{i1kr} & \dots & N_{jsu_{js}}^{i1kr} & \dots & N_{jsM_{js}}^{i1kr} \\ \vdots & & \vdots & & \vdots \\ N_{Js1}^{i1kr} & \dots & N_{Jsu_{Js}}^{i1kr} & \dots & N_{JsM_{Js}}^{i1kr} \end{pmatrix} \tag{14.144}$$

then, the indirect primary consumptions from the table (14.143) verify the following equation:

$$\sum_j \left(\overline{X}_{js1}^{i1kr} N_{js1}^{i1kr} + \dots + \overline{X}_{jsu_{js}}^{i1kr} N_{jsu_{js}}^{i1kr} + \dots + \overline{X}_{jsM_{js}}^{i1kr} N_{jsM_{js}}^{i1kr} \right) = C_{\bullet s \bullet}^{i1kr}$$

for any s = 1, 2, . . ., S*, or if (14.136) is taken into account, the equation can also be written as follows:

$$\sum_j \sum_{u_{js}} \left\{ G_{jsu_{js}}^{i1kr} \left[\left(\overline{X}_{jsu_{js}}^{i1kr} \right)_1, \ \dots, \ \left(\overline{X}_{jsu_{js}}^{i1kr} \right)_{H_{jsu_{js}}^{i1kr}} \right] \right\} N_{jsu_{js}}^{i1kr}$$
$$= C_{\bullet s \bullet}^{i1kr} \ (k = 0, \ 1; \ r = 1, \ 2, \ 3) \tag{14.145}$$

If we amplify by p_{i1kr} both members of the equation corresponding to the input E_{i1kr} into the department s, then we get:

$$\sum_j \left(\overline{Y}_{js1}^{i1kr} N_{js1}^{i1kr} + \dots + \overline{Y}_{jsM}^{i1kr} N_{jsM}^{i1kr} \right) = p_{i1kr} G_{\bullet s \bullet}^{i1kr} \tag{14.146}$$

for any $k = 0, 1$ and $r = 1, 2, 3$.

The equation (14.145) that connects the elements of the table (14.143) between them, expresses the structure of the integral consumption $C_{\bullet s \bullet}^{i1kr}$ of the input E_{i1kr} into the main department s, by operations and products, and this is why an equation of the type (14.145) will be called—the equation of the structure of the primary—indirect—integral consumption. In our case, it is a matter of the equation of the structure of indirect primary integral consumption $C_{\bullet s \bullet}^{i1kr}$ in the department s.

For a department s and a fixed indirect primary input E_{il} we have, if we make k = 0, 1 and r = 1, 2, 3, six such equations of the structure of indirect integral consumption. The total number of the equations of the indirect primary integral consumptions coincides for a—fixed—period t with the number of the tables of type (14.143) and is equal to *6IS**.

These equations are independent between them, each expressing the structure of an—indirect—integral consumption of a certain kind and in a certain department.

Analogously, the equation (14.146) expresses the structure of the integral expense $p_{i1kr}C^{i1kr}_{\bullet s \bullet}$ in the main department s, by operations and products.

We shall call such an equation—the equation of the structure of the—indirect—primary integral expense.

In (14.146) we are given the structure of the integral expense $C^{i1kr}_{\bullet s \bullet}$ corresponding to the main department s. As in the previous case, the number of these equations is *6IS**, however the number of parameters of the structure of consumptions respective of indirect expenses is

$$6I\sum_{j}\sum_{s} M_{js} \tag{14.147}$$

If the output from the process (S) is heterogeneous (J > 1) and the output from each department $s = \overline{1,\ S^*}$ is also heterogeneous, then

$$\sum_{j} M_{js} > 1 \textit{ and } 6I\sum_{j}\sum_{s} M_{js} > 6IS^* \tag{14.148}$$

This shows that both the parameters of the structure by departments and products, as well as the parameters of the structure by primary elements and products exceed the number of the corresponding structure equations, thus creating a high degree of freedom in their assessment.

In order to formulate the mathematical model to assess the parameters of the structure of—indirect—production primary expenses, we shall follow the same reasoning as for the mathematical model for assessing the parameters of the structure of—direct—primary expenses.

For this purpose, let us consider the following diagram (Fig. 14.7):

and associate thereto, for any $i = \overline{1,\ I}$; k = 0, 1; r = 1, 2, 3, respectively the following tables of resultant variables:

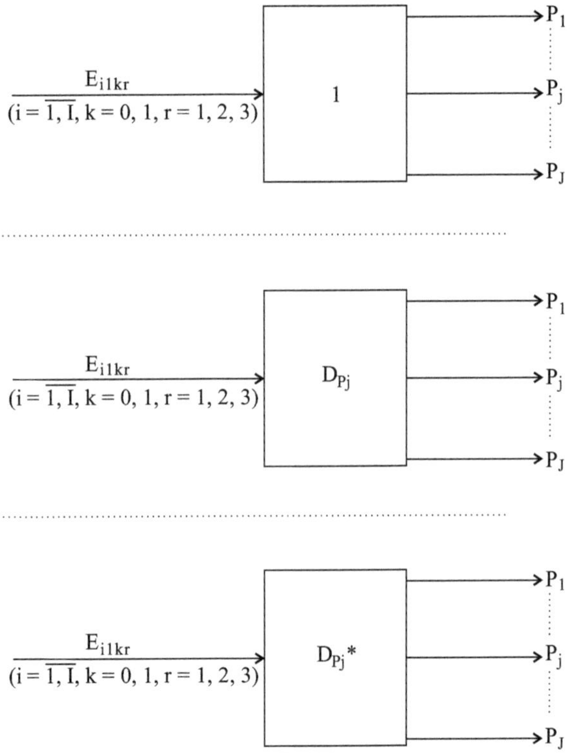

Fig. 14.7 Diagram of indirect expenses from production primary

$$\begin{vmatrix}
X^{i1kr}_{111} & \cdots & X^{i1kr}_{11u_{11}} & \cdots & X^{i1kr}_{11M_{11}} \\
\vdots & & \vdots & & \vdots \\
X^{i1kr}_{j11} & \cdots & X^{i1kr}_{j1u_{j1}} & \cdots & X^{i1kr}_{j1M_{j1}} \\
\vdots & & \vdots & & \vdots \\
X^{i1kr}_{J11} & \cdots & X^{i1kr}_{J1u_{J1}} & \cdots & X^{i1kr}_{J1M_{J1}} \\
\cdots & \cdots & \cdots & \cdots & \cdots \\
\cdots & \cdots & \cdots & \cdots & \cdots \\
\cdots & \cdots & \cdots & \cdots & \cdots \\
X^{i1kr}_{1s1} & \cdots & X^{i1kr}_{1su_{1s}} & \cdots & X^{i1kr}_{1sM_{1s}} \\
\vdots & & \vdots & & \vdots \\
X^{i1kr}_{js1} & \cdots & X^{i1kr}_{jsu_{js}} & \cdots & X^{i1kr}_{jsM_{js}} \\
\vdots & & \vdots & & \vdots \\
X^{i1kr}_{Js1} & \cdots & X^{i1kr}_{Jsu_{Js}} & \cdots & X^{i1kr}_{JsM_{Js}} \\
\cdots & \cdots & \cdots & \cdots & \cdots \\
\cdots & \cdots & \cdots & \cdots & \cdots \\
\cdots & \cdots & \cdots & \cdots & \cdots \\
X^{i1kr}_{1S^*1} & \cdots & X^{i1kr}_{1S^*u_{1S^*}} & \cdots & X^{i1kr}_{1S^*M_{1S^*}} \\
\vdots & & \vdots & & \vdots \\
X^{i1kr}_{jS^*1} & \cdots & X^{i1kr}_{jS^*u_{jS^*}} & \cdots & X^{i1kr}_{jS^*M_{jS^*}} \\
\vdots & & \vdots & & \vdots \\
X^{i1kr}_{JS^*1} & \cdots & X^{i1kr}_{JS^*u_{JS^*}} & \cdots & X^{i1kr}_{JS^*M_{JS^*}}
\end{vmatrix} \tag{14.149}$$

characterising the unitary consumptions from the primary input E_{i1kr} ($i=\overline{1,\ I}$; $k=0,\ 1$; $r=1,\ 2,\ 3$) into each main department, by products and operations, and satisfying the relations

$$\sum_{s}\sum_{u_{js}} X^{i1kr}_{1su_{1s}} = X^{i1kr}_{1} \ldots \sum_{s}\sum_{u_{js}} X^{i1kr}_{jsu_{js}} = X^{i1kr}_{j} \ldots \sum_{s}\sum_{u_{Js}} X^{i1kr}_{Jsu_{Js}} = X^{i1kr}_{J} \tag{14.150}$$

for any $i=\overline{1,\ I}$; $k=0,\ 1$; $r=1,\ 2,\ 3$.

By assuming that whatever the resultant variable $X^{i1kr}_{jsu_{js}}$ from the table (14.149) may be, for the factorial variables (14.34) from the $N^{i1kr}_{jsu_{js}}$ values (14.132) registered during the period taken into account, the following sample is selected:

$$\begin{array}{l}\left(x^{iukr}_{jsu_{js}}\right)_{11}, \ \ldots, \ \left(x^{i1kr}_{jsu_{js}}\right)_{1n^{i1kr}_{jsu_{js}}}\\ \cdots\cdots\cdots\cdots\cdots\cdots\cdots\cdots\cdots\\ \left(x^{i1kr}_{jsu_{js}}\right)_{H^{i1kr}_{jsu_{js}}1}, \ \ldots, \ \left(x^{i1kr}_{jsu_{js}}\right)_{H^{i1kr}_{jsu_{js}}n^{i1kr}_{jsu_{js}}}\end{array} \tag{14.151}$$

respectively of the volume $n^{i1kr}_{jsu_{js}}$, then the problem of distributing the indirect expenses by elements and products becomes a problem of assessing the parameters of the structure of indirect primary expenses, meaning of the elements of matrices:

$$\overline{Y}^{i1kr}_{*} = \begin{pmatrix} \overline{Y}^{11kr}_{1} & \ldots & \overline{Y}^{11kr}_{J} \\ \vdots & & \vdots \\ \overline{Y}^{I1kr}_{1} & \ldots & \overline{Y}^{I1kr}_{J} \end{pmatrix}, \ (k=0,\ 1;\ r=1,\ 2,\ 3) \tag{14.152}$$

knowing that for any $k=0,\ 1$ and $r=1,\ 2,\ 3$;

$$\begin{pmatrix} \overline{Y}^{11kr}_{1} & \ldots & \overline{Y}^{11kr}_{J} \\ \vdots & & \vdots \\ \overline{Y}^{I1kr}_{1} & \ldots & \overline{Y}^{I1kr}_{J} \end{pmatrix} = \begin{pmatrix} p_{11kr} & \ldots & 0 \\ \vdots & & \vdots \\ 0 & \ldots & p_{I1kr} \end{pmatrix} \begin{pmatrix} \overline{X}^{I1kr}_{1} & \ldots & \overline{X}^{I1kr}_{J} \\ \vdots & & \vdots \\ \overline{X}^{I1kr}_{1} & \ldots & \overline{X}^{I1kr}_{J} \end{pmatrix} \tag{14.153}$$

$$\overline{X}^{i1kr}_{j} = \sum_{s}\sum_{u_{js}} \overline{X}^{i1kr}_{jsu_{js}}, \ \left(i=\overline{1,\ I};\ j=\overline{1,\ J}\right), \tag{14.154}$$

$$\begin{aligned}\overline{X}^{i1kr}_{jsu_{js}} &= E\left[X^{i1kr}_{jsu_{js}} / \left(\overline{X}^{i1kr}_{jsu_{js}}\right)_{1}, \ \ldots, \ \left(\overline{X}^{i1kr}_{jsu_{js}}\right)_{H^{i1kr}_{jsu_{js}}}\right] = \\ &= G^{i1kr}_{jsu_{js}}\left[\left(\overline{X}^{i1kr}_{jsu_{js}}\right)_{1}, \ \ldots, \ \left(\overline{X}^{i1kr}_{jsu_{js}}\right)_{H^{i1kr}_{jsu_{js}}}\right]\end{aligned} \tag{14.155}$$

for any $i = \overline{1,\ I}$; $j = \overline{1,\ J}$; $s = \overline{1,\ S^*}$; $u_{js} = \overline{1,\ M_{js}}$ and

$$(K_1)\sum_{j}\sum_{u_{js}} G^{i1kr}_{jsu_{js}}\left[\left(\overline{X}^{i1kr}_{jsu_{js}}\right)_1, \ \ldots, \ \left(\overline{X}^{i1kr}_{jsu_{js}}\right)_{H^{i1kr}_{jsu_{js}}}\right] N^{i1kr}_{jsu_{js}}$$
$$= C^{i1kr}_{\bullet s \bullet}, \ \left(s = \overline{1,\ S^*};\ i = \overline{1,\ I}\right) \qquad (14.156)$$

The mathematical model established shows that the process of assessing the parameters of the structure of indirect primary expenses must also begin—once the random sample of the measurements (14.151) is formed—by assessing the parameters intervening into the corresponding structure equation, respectively (K_1). The model (K_1) is however much more complex than the model (K_0), and it also contains as unknown parameters, besides the averages (14.135) of the factorial variables, coefficients of the factorial variables, of their powers, in a small or greater number, by the degree of the polynomials by which the regressions are approximated (14.134).

In the second stage, if the parameters stated in the first stage have been removed, we can estimate the averages of the variables (14.14914.145), by using the relations (14.155) for this purpose. In the second stage, the parameters to be estimated appear as functions of parameters already estimated in the first stage, the form of these functions being determined by the form of the regressions (14.134).

In the third stage, once first two once are completed, based on the relations (14.154), we can estimate the parameters of the structure of indirect primary consumptions, by using the model (14.155) for this purpose.

The last two stages of the described estimating process are identical to the last two stages of the process of estimating the parameters of the structure of direct primary expenses.

By analysing the process of distributing the indirect expenses—by elements and products—in terms of the estimation theory, the following types of estimation models result: one model, which is generally a non-linear model for estimating the connected parameters, based on samples of measurements, for some direct and for others indirect, consisting of the structural equations (K_1) and the random samples (14.151); one regressive model of estimation (14.155) and two models to estimate the linear combinations of parameters, respectively (14.154) and (14.153) also encountered for estimating the structure of the direct primary expenses.

(i) The mathematical model of the structure of total production expenses is done

Taking into the mathematical model of the structure of direct and indirect primary expenses stated previously, as well as the rules of calculation in a matrix form, we can create the mathematical model of the structure of total production expenses, a model materialised in the matrix of the structure of total production expenses.

To do it, we take into account the following: the matrix of the variables of direct primary consumptions attached to the process (S) of the system (W) for the state of output P_j $\left(j = \overline{1,\ J}\right)$, meaning the finished product which completed all operations of the manufacturing technology, a matrix noted with X_*^{*0} (14.100); the matrices (I, J)—dimensional—of the indirect primary consumptions attached to the same process and system noted with X_*^{*1kr} (14.127); the distribution of ll indirect input son the state of output P_j; the prices in the price catalogues; the matrix of unit prices of the components of direct primary input noted with P_{*0} (14.80); the matrix of the unit prices of the components of indirect primary input noted with P_{*1kr} (14.81).

Taking into account the previously shown matrixes, afterwards the matrix of the structure of direct primary expenses noted with Y_*^{*0} (14.110) and the matrix of the structure of indirect primary expenses noted with $\overline{Y}_*^{*1kr}$ (14.140) were drawn.

Because the matrices Y_*^{*0} (14.110) and $\overline{Y}_*^{*1kr}$ (14.140) are of the same type (i, j) and taking into account that achieving a state of output P_j requires direct and indirect expenses, by summing the two aforementioned matrices, we get the matrix of total expenses related to the state of output P_j.

This is:

$$Y_*^{*CT} = \begin{pmatrix} Y_1^{CT} & \cdots & Y_j^{CT} & \cdots & Y_J^{CT} \\ \vdots & & \vdots & & \vdots \\ Y_1^{CT} & \cdots & Y_j^{CT} & \cdots & Y_J^{CT} \\ \vdots & & \vdots & & \vdots \\ Y_1^{CT} & \cdots & Y_j^{CT} & \cdots & Y_J^{CT} \end{pmatrix} \tag{14.157}$$

a matrix of the type (i, j), where $i = \overline{1,\ I}$; $j = \overline{1,\ J}$.

The elements of the matrix Y_*^{*CT} (14.157) are of the following type

$$Y_j^{CT} = Y_j^{i0} + \overline{Y}_j^{i1kr} \tag{14.158}$$

where$Y_j^{CT} \in Y_*^{*CT}$

$$Y_j^{i0} \in Y_*^{*0}$$

$$\overline{Y}_j^{i1kr} \in Y_*^{*1kr}$$

All these elements are expressed in monetary units, which makes the total production expenses to be also expressed in monetary units.

References

Arrow KJ (1994) Studies in the mathematical theory of inventary and production. Stanford University Press, Stanford

Charreaux G (2005) Synthese, economie et comptabilité. Editions Litec, Paris

Cheney EW (1996) Introduction to approximation theory. McGraw Hill, New York

Collatz L, Wetterling W (1966) Optimie rungsanfgaben. Springer, Berlin

Courtois A, Pillet M, Martin C (2006) Gestion de productions. Les Editions D'organisation, Paris
Danskin JM (1967) The theory of Max-Min. Springer, Berlin
Dima IC, Grabara J (2009) Budzetowanie. Wydawnictwa Wydzialu Zarzadzania Politechniki Czestochowskiej, Czestochowa
Kaufmann RF (1992) Methodes et modeles de la recherche operationelle. Dunod, Paris
Kosiol E (1956) Plankostenrechung als Instrument moderner Unternenhmungsfiihrung, Berlin
Kunzi HP (1967) Numerische Methoden der mathematischen optimierung. B.G. Tenbner, Stuttgart
Kupfernagel P (1968) Kostenrechnung det Industrie, 2nd edn. Die Wirtschaft, Berlin
Mellerowicz K (1968) Kosten und Kostenrehnung, vol 11, 4th edn. Theorie der Kosten, Springer, Berlin
Tucher SA (1962) Cost estimating and pricing with machine-hour rates. Ed. Prentice-Hall, New York
Waerden V (1957) Der Mathematiche Statistik. Springer, Berlin
Wilde DJ (1997) Foundations of optimization. Prentice Hall, New Jersey

Chapter 15
Using Budgets Modeling Unit Cost of Production

15.1 Budget Cost of Production: Theoretical Approaches

The main stages of drawing up expenditure budgets are the following: the establishment of responsibilities on different levels of organization; the establishment, on each center, of the costs that must be controlled by the responsible of the center, as a decisional factor on that hierarchical level; the forecasting of the coordinates of that center taking into account the forecasted level of the center's activity and the prices and tariffs negotiated by the supplying and beneficiary units; the sizing of costs really registered; the comparison of the achievements with the forecasts for that period, the identification of the deviation and the evaluation of the tendency of the respective center; the drawing up of expenditures budget at the center level; the negotiation at the superior level of decision, regarding the dimension of the required budget; the agreement upon the revised budget and the assumption of responsibility of the expenditure centers for the administration and achievement of the desired profit.

The drawing up of expenditure budget starts with communicating the details related to the forecasting policy of coal mining and the actions, which must be taken by the ones responsible for the preparation of partial budgets. The main data sources used for drawing up the annual expenditure budget are the forecasts of the management regarding the possible levels of the different actions and the book-keeping that contain the indicators specific to past and present operations.

The sizing of budgets focuses not only on the hierarchical relations between the subsystems of mine working but also on the functional relations, which imply the dependency of one budget upon another, according to the relation inputs-outputs (Fig. 15.1)

The holders of the expenditure centers prepare the basic data of sizing the budget and they are responsible for its achievement. Thus, budgetary technique implies the development of the attributes of forecasting, organization, coordination and control of the management through expenditures. Moreover, the management through

I.C. Dima, M. Man, *Modelling and Simulation in Management*, Contributions to Management Science, DOI 10.1007/978-3-319-16592-9_15

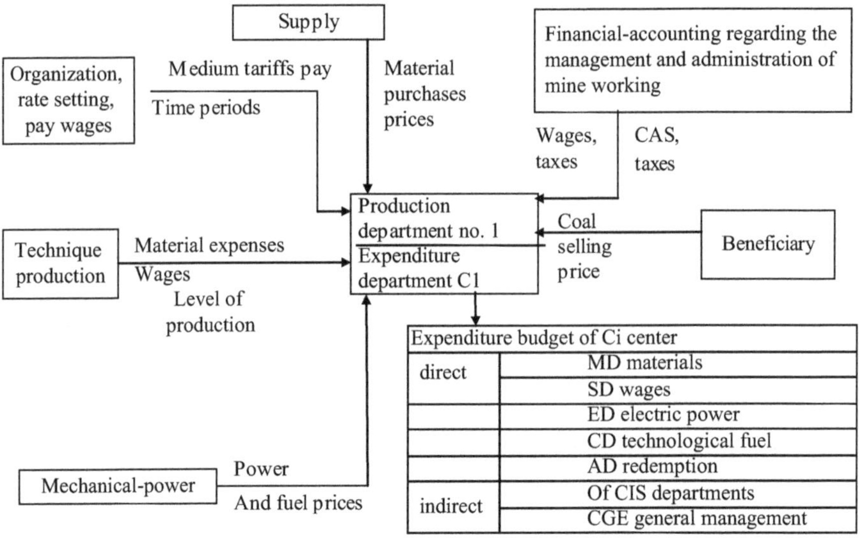

Fig. 15.1 Drawing up expenditure budget, at the level of a production center on the basis of the informational system and the functional relationships between departments

expenditure budgets is of great help to communication and to drawing up the tactical and strategically decisions in order to regulate the coal mining activity.

The model of the expenditure budget (*BC*) of coal mining can be based on a relation made up of several terms, respectively more partial expenditures budget, as it follows:

$$\mathrm{BC} = \mathrm{MD} + \mathrm{SD} + \mathrm{ED} + \mathrm{CD} + \mathrm{AD} + \mathrm{CIS} + \mathrm{CGE} \tag{15.1}$$

where:

MD—represents raw materials and direct materials expenditures budget
SD—direct wages expenditure budget (including the contributions to these)
ED—budget of power direct expenses for technological purposes
CD—direct expenses budget of technological fuel
AD—direct expenditures budget of fixed means redemption
CIS—indirect expenditures budget of departments
CGE—general management expenditure budget

It must be mentioned that coal-mining activities do not lead to sale costs and this is the reason why in the above relation the sale costs budget was not present. This happens because coal sale is ensured by the preparation operations of the coal that takes place as distinct units.

In what follows the expenditure center is considered as a production sector within a mine working. The production sector represents a structural subdivision well defined from the point of view of its management. All the stages of coal mining take place in this subdivision and they start with the preparation of the working grounds and end with bringing to surface the extracted quantity of coal. The representation from Fig. 15.1 will be used in order to understand the structure of an expenditures budget of the specific center marked with C1.

15.2 Budget Structure Model of Unit Cost of Production

The drawing up of production costs budgets, for e.g. in the mining carboniferous industry, implies drawing up the following budgets:

– *raw materials and direct materials expenditures budget*
The drawing up of raw materials and direct materials expenditure budget at the level of the production department of coal mining implies the knowledge of the following data:

1. the account of the production volume that is forecasted to be achieved in the year for which the budget (N) is drawn up, is a document that reflects both the account existing when it was drawn up (the forecasted volume of coal production/the achieved volume of coal production/subtractions (+/−) as well as the forecasted level of coal production for the next year together with its division on the four quarters of the year. At the same time, the production volume calculated in tones of coal per month and in tons of coal per day, is forecasted both for the overall level of coal mining and for each production sector. The model of such an account is rendered in Table 15.1;
2. the specific usage (quantitative standards) forecasted for the year N, afferent to the raw materials and to the direct materials used in the coal mining process. It is the document that allows the establishment of the quantitative standards of raw materials and direct materials on the basis of a careful analysis of each material that must be used in the technological process, taking into account the necessary quantity, the quality, the procurement possibilities, the further manufacturing operations etc. Quantitative standards of materials are written down in the technical documents and further on they are placed in the "List of quantitative standards of materials" which comprises data referring to the current number, name of material, unit of measure, standard usage, observations (Table 15.2).

   For drawing up the account of specific usage of raw materials and materials forecasted for the budgetary year there must be known the direct materials consumed during production, the unit of measure and the specific usage when this account was drawn up, respectively the specific forecasted usage, the specific achieved usage and the subtractions (+/−). The forecasts for the next year are established on the following accounts: the knowledge of the resulted subtractions and the causes that led to them (non-observance of the established standards, the use of some materials of a different quality, some situations which were not predicted when drawing up the standards etc.) correlated with the

Table 15.1 Account of production volume forecasted on production departments for the year N

Department	U.M.	Cumulated 10 months year N−1			Forecasts year N							
					Month			Quarter				
		Forecasted	Achieved	Subtraction +/−	I	II	III	I	II	III	IV	Total
1	t/month	72,500	69,407	−3,093	7,770	7,400	7,770	22,940	23,310	20,460	22,050	88,760
	t/day	337	323	−14	370	370	370	370	370	310	361	350
2	t/month	114,530	114,985	455	19,020	10,400	10,920	32,240	32,760	30,360	30,500	125,860
	t/day	533	535	2	520	520	520	520	520	460	500	500
3	t/month	88,580	82,077	−6,503	8,400	8,000	8,400	24,800	26,460	25,080	24,400	100,740
	t/day	412	382	−30	400	400	400	400	420	380	400	400
4	t/month	211,850	215,448	3,598	22,470	21,400	22,470	66,340	66,150	64,020	62,830	259,340
	t/day	985	1,002	17	1,070	1,070	1,070	1,070	1,050	970	1,030	1,030
5	t/month	77,780	72,458	−5,322	11,340	10,800	11,340	33,480	34,020	31,680	31,720	130,900
	t/day	362	337	−25	540	540	540	540	540	480	520	520
6	t/month	6,960	–	−6,960	–	–	–	–	–	–	–	–
	t/day	32		32								
Total mine	t/month	572,200	554,375	−17,825	60,900	58,000	60,900	17,980	182,700	171,600	171,500	705,600
	t/day	2,661	2,579	−82	2,900	2,900	2,900	2,900	2,900	2,600	2,811	2,800

Table 15.2 List of quantitative standards of materials

Name of material	U. M.	Quantitative standard	Observations
Mine wood	mc/t	0.017	
Metallic net	kg/t	2,500	
T. H. profile	kg/t	1,300	
Explosive	kg/t	0.300	
Staples	bc/t	0.750	

managers' desire of diminishing manufacturing costs in order to bring them closer to the forecasted level of the returns.

For exempla, for the "mine wood" material that has a specific usage, forecasted in the year N−1, of 17.00 mc/1,000 t of coal it can be noticed when drawing up the budget for the next year that the achieved level of usage is of 17.70 mc/1,000 t of coal. Thus an exceeding is registered, respectively a subtraction of +0.70 mc/1,000 t. In this case, the specialized technical staff, who takes part in the drawing up of the budget, analyze the causes that led to the exceeding of the forecasted specific usage. If the exceeding of this level cannot be justified, then the forecasted specific usage for the next year is lowered or it is kept at the same level as in the previous year. Or, for the "profile T.H." material it can be noticed that at the date when the budget was drawn up, the achieved specific usage was a lot under the level of the forecasted specific usage. Savings are registered, namely a negative subtraction of 304 kg/1,000 t. If, when the causes that led to this subtraction were analyzed, it were noticed that for this material the forecasted specific usage was too high, the level of the forecasted specific usage for the next year could be diminished.

The account of the specific usage of materials and the account of the unitary standard purchase prices forecasted for the budgetary year N is presented in Table 15.3;

3. standard purchase prices, forecasted for the year N, afferent to the director materials will be purchased from the suppliers. They are established starting from the level of the purchases prices afferent to direct materials, registered in the book-keeping when the budget was drawn up. At the same time it will be taken into account the present tendency in Romanian economy. This tendency is one of increasing the prices, reason for which for the year N, the prices actual when drawing up the budget is not used. They are multiplied according to the inflation index of the year N, as far as this one can be established at that time.

   Once established, the standard purchase prices are registered in the "List of standard prices" (Table 15.4).

   The quantitative standards of materials can have quite a long validity in time (2–3 years), their change being produced only by the appearance of some modifications in the technology of power coal mining or of some situations by comparison with those taken into account when drawing up standards. In contrast to these, the standard supply prices have a less stability in time because of the frequent changes in prices.

Table 15.3 Account of specific usage of raw materials and materials and the account of the unitary standard purchase prices forecasted for the year N

	Specific usage					Unitary prices		
		Cumulated 10 months year N						
Name of material	UM	Forecasted	Achieved	Subtractions	Forecasts year N	UM	Achieved month 10 year N−1	Forecasts year N
Mine wood	mc/1,000 t	17.00	17.70	0.70	17.00	u.m./mc	101,000	121,200
Metallic net	kg/1,000 t	2,500.00	2,559.00	59.00	2,500.00	u.m./kg	1,925	2,310
T. H. profile	kg/1,000 t	1,311.00	1,007.00	−304.00	1,300.00	u.m./kg	1,054	1,265
Explosive	kg/1,000 t	300.00	299.00	−1.00	300.00	u.m./kb	3,913	4,696
Staples	bc/1,000 t	689.00	749.00	60.00	750.00	u.m./bc	1,836	2,203
Casing	kg/1,000 t	60.00	55.00	−5.00	60.00	u.m./kg	1,054	1,265

Table 15.4 List of standard prices

Name of material	U. M.	Standard supply price	Observations
Mine wood	u.m./mc	121,200	
Metallic net	u.m./kg	2,310	
T. H. profile	u.m./kg	1,265	
Explosive	u.m./kg	4,696	
Staples	u.m./bc	2,203	

Further on, using these data, it can be drawn up the raw materials and direct materials expenditure budget for a specific expenditure center, respectively the no. 1 production department of the mine working by using the following mathematical relations:

$$MD^1 = \sum_{k=1}^{6} q^1 \times CS_k \times p_k \tag{15.2}$$

where:

q^1—is the volume of coal production forecasted to be obtained in the production department no. 1.
CS_k—the standard usage of the material k
p_k—standard purchase price of the material k
k—the nature of the material.

Starting from this mathematical relation, it is determined, as a first stage, the level of afferent expenditures to the specific usage of raw materials and direct materials forecasted in the year N at a specific production department.

For example the material "mine wood" is chosen, about which the following data, from Table 15.3, are known:

1. Specific usage
   - level achieved in the first 10 months in the year N−1:

$$CS^r{}_1 = 17.70\ \text{mc}/1{,}000\ \text{t}$$

   - level forecasted for the year N:

$$CS^P{}_1 = 17.00\ \text{mc}/1{,}000\ \text{t}$$

2. Purchase prices
   - level achieved in the first 10 months of the year N−1

$$p^r{}_1 = 101{,}000\ \text{u.m./mc}$$

   - level forecasted for the year N

$$p^P{}_1 = 121{,}200\ \text{u.m./mc}$$

The calculus relation of standard purchases with the "mine wood material":

- for standard purchases with "mine wood" achieved in the first 10 months of the year N−1:

$$\begin{aligned} ChS^{r}{}_{1} &= CS^{r}{}_{1} \times p^{r}{}_{1} = 17.70\,\text{mc}/1{,}000\,\text{t} \times 101{,}000\,\text{u.m.}/\text{mc} \\ &= 1{,}787.7\,\text{u.m.}/\text{t} \end{aligned}$$

- for the standard purchases with the mine wood forecasted for the year N

$$\begin{aligned} ChS^{p}{}_{1} &= CS^{p}{}_{1} \times p^{p}{}_{1} = 17.00\,\text{mc}/1{,}000\,\text{t} \times 121{,}200\,\text{u.m.}/\text{mc} \\ &= 2{,}060.40\,\text{u.m.}/\text{t} \end{aligned}$$

It is done the same for other direct materials (metallic net, TH profile, explosive etc.). By summing up the obtained values the total of standard expenditures with direct materials of the production department can be obtained:

$$ChS^{1}{}_{m} = \sum_{k=1}^{6} Ch \times S_{k} \tag{15.3}$$

where:

$ChS^{1}{}_{m}$—represents standard expenditures with the direct materials of production department no. 1

ChS_{k}—standard expenditures with the direct material k

k—the nature of the material

By substituting the data from Table 15.3 in the above relation, it is obtained:

- the level of standard expenditures with direct materials of the production department no. 1, accomplished in the first 10 months of the year N−1

$$\begin{aligned} ChS^{1r} &= 17.70 \times 101{,}000 + 2{,}559 \times 1.925 + \ldots + 55 \times 1{,}054 \\ &= 10{,}378.29\,\text{u.m.}/\text{t} \end{aligned}$$

- the level of standard purchases with direct materials of production department no. 1 forecasted in the year N;

$$\begin{aligned} ChS^{1p} &= 17 \times 121{,}200 + 2{,}500 \times 2.310 + \ldots + 60 \times 1.265 \\ &= 12{,}616.85\,\text{u.m.}/\text{t} \end{aligned}$$

For example the account of direct materials expenditures afferent to the specific usage forecasted for the year N, by contrast to the achievements obtained in the first months of the year N−1 is presented in Table 15.5.

Table 15.5 Account of direct materials expenditures afferent to the specific usage forecasted for the year N, in contrast to the achievements in the first 10 months N−1 (Production department no. 1.)

Name of material	Specific usage			Purchase prices			Standard material expenditures u.m./t	
	U.M.	Achievements cumulated in 10 months of year N−1	Forecasts year N	U.M.	Achievements on year N−1	Forecasts year N	Achievements on year N−1	Forecasts year N
Wood mine	mc/1,000 t	17.70	17.00	u.m./mc	101,000	121,200	1,787.70	2,060.40
Metallic net	kg/1,000 t	2,559.00	2,500.00	u.m./kg	1,925	2,310	4,926.08	5,775.00
T. H Profile	kg/1,000 t	1,007.00	1,300.00	u.m./kg	1,054	1,265	1,061.38	1,644.50
Explosive	kg/1,000 t	299.00	300.00	u.m./kg	3,913	4,696	1,169.99	1,408.80
Staples	bc/1,000 t	749.00	750.00	u.m./bc	1,836	2,203	1,375.17	1,652.25
Casings	kg/1,000 t	55.00	60.00	u.m./kg	1,054	1,265	57.97	75.90
Total standard material expenditures							10,378.29	12,616.85

Table 15.6 Direct expenditures budget with materials forecasted for the year N (*Production department no. 1*)

Pit-coal production (t)		Direct material expenses (u.m./t)		Direct material expenditures budget (mii u.m.)	
Achievements on year N–	Forecasts year N	Achievements on year N–	Forecasts year N	Achievements on year N–	Forecasts year N
69,407	88,760	10,378.29	12,616.85	720,325.97	1,119,871.61

Further on, the raw materials and direct materials expenditures budget of the production department can be drawn up as all the necessary data are available (Table 15.6).

– the production volume forecasted for the year N:

$$q^p = 88,760 \text{ t coal}$$

– the production volume achieved in the first 10 months of the N−1 year:

$$q^r = 69,407 \text{ t coal}$$

– standard expenditures with direct materials forecasted for the year N

$$ChS^{1p} = 12,616.85 \text{ u.m./t}$$

– standard expenditures with direct materials met in the first 10 months of the N−1 year

$$ChS^{1r} = 10,378.29 \text{ u.m./t}$$

By substituting the data in the relation (15.2) it is obtained:

$$MD^1 = \sum_{k=1}^{6} q^1 \times CS_k \times p_k = \sum_{k=1}^{6} q^1 \times ChS \qquad (15.4.)$$

It can be therefore noticed that the raw materials and direct materials expenditures budget afferent to the production department no. 1 from the mine carboniferous working is of 1,119,871.61 thousands u.m. It is done the same for other production departments of mine working.

By analyzing the obtained results it can be noticed that the raw materials and direct materials expenditures budget of production department no. 1 drawn up for the year N is larger in contrast to the N−1 year. The main causes are: the level of production department no. 1 forecasted for the year N is of 887,607 being higher than the forecasted level of the previous year (87,000 t) and therefore higher than the achievements in the first 10 months of the N−1 year (69,407 t) which anyway

Table 15.7 Structure of the working staff on production departments and on categories of skilled and unskilled workers forecasted for the year N (no. of employees)

	Production departments					
Working staff	1	2	3	4	5	Total
Total workers from whom:	350	630	450	1,100	670	3,200
– Skilled	300	450	360	746	480	2,336
– Unskilled	50	180	90	354	190	864

are under the forecasted level of production in that period (72,500 t); purchase prices of direct materials forecasted for the year N are established at their maximum peak. They are negotiated with the suppliers and are changed with every indexation.

– *expenditure budget of direct wages, the contribution to the social insurances and the afferent social protection*

The direct charges budget for wages at the level of a single mine carboniferous working and at the level of a production department considered as an expenditures center (place) supposes the knowledge of the following data: the account on trades of the workers from the mine working, in which it is mentioned the number of workers on the staff, on trade categories, achieved in the N−1 year as well as the forecasted number to be accomplished in the year N, the structure of the working staff on production departments, on total mine working and on categories of skilled and unskilled workers forecasted for the year N (Table 15.7); the account of mining activities and of exploitation methods on production departments and on labor teams forecasted to be done in the year N; the organizational structure of labor teams; "labor rules and regulations" in which these ones are expressed through the quantity of products and activities that have to be done by a worker during a shift or through the labor quantity (hours) necessary for doing an activity; the account "Standardized labor teams and average wages in order to charge the underground activities in the mining sections" in which, for each type of activity (frontal coal-face with a mechanic complex; frontal coal-face with individual support; digging galleries etc.) The number of necessary workers is established, their skill (front miner, front miner helper, front haulage man, shotsman) and the average wage on shifts of that team.

Drawing up the budget of expenditures with direct wages of the production department no. 1 implies two stages: in the first stage the budget of each team from the production department is drawn up; in the second stage the centralizing budget is drawn up at the level of the production department. In this way, the drawing up of the "Sheet for establishing the technical standards and the tariff" can start. It is filled in separately for each production department, exploitation method and labor team. In this sheet there are filled in a series of data referring to: the technical characteristics of the activity; the name of the activity or operation; labor conditions and calculus elements; total quantity; standard (U.M., number-chart, value); standard jobs; establishing the labor team; wage tariff of the labor team; value.

For a labor team the level of direct expenditures met for the wages can be determined by using the sheet for establishing the technical standard of the tariff, using the relation:

$$sd_i = \sum_{j=1}^{m} PN_j \times TF_j \tag{15.5}$$

where:

sd_i—represents the expenditures met for the direct wages of the labor team i
PN_j—standard jobs for doing the activity or operation j
TF_j—average tariff of pay wage of the labor team for the activity or operation j
J—type of activity or operation.

Time standards represent the necessary times for accomplishing the production, which are established according to the characteristics of the technological process. The following aspects must stand at the basis of determining time standards: the knowledge of the technical operation chain (perforating rock, cutting with explosives, loading face-coal, separating walls etc.), the labor conditions (length of the face-coal, the thickness of the coal layer, the number of holes on m^2 front etc.), the workers' skills (miner, miner helper, haulage man etc.) etc.

Thus, in order to determine the standard time of the "perforating rock" activity, firstly it must be determined, through measurements, the length of face-coal, the thickness of the coal layer, the height of the face-coal. According to the obtained values there can be determined: the quantity in m^2 of perforated hole, the standard of perforating and the number of standard jobs.

For example, the following data are considered:

- length of face-coal: 17.83 m
- thickness of coal layer: 1.65 m
- number of holes on m^2 front at the height of the face-coal = 1.34

The quantity of perforated rock is determined:

$$K = \frac{L \times g}{n} \tag{15.6}$$

where:

K—quantity in m^2 of perforated rock
L—length of face-coal
g—thickness of face-coal
n—number of holes on m^2 front.

$$K = \frac{17.83 \times 1.65}{1.34} = 21.96 \text{ m.l.}$$

The number of standard jobs (time standard) is determined:

Table 15.8 List of standard operation times

Name of work	U. M.	Standard time	Observations
Perforation	Standard working places	1,702	
Explosive cutting		11,320	
Coal-face loading		8,910	
Assembled partition wall		2,122	
Supporting		3,544	
Moves		1,184	
Transport		1,562	

$$t_S = \frac{K}{N} \tag{15.7.}$$

where: t_s is the time standard
N = perforation standard

$$t_S = \frac{21.96}{12.90} = 1.702 \text{ standard posts}$$

Using the same method, the time standard can also be determined for the other activities of the technological process (Table 15.8)

The tariffs of standard pay wage are established on the basis of the standard skills of the workers, of the data regarding the paid salaries in the previous period, of the labor conditions in the following period and of the actual legislation. Therefore, the account "standard labor teams and average wages in order to charge the activities", which is done underground, in the mining departments, is extremely useful.

Pay wage tariffs, established on the data presented in the above accounts are noted in the "List of standard pay wage tariffs on types of works" (Table 15.9).

Thus for determining the standard pay wage tariff afferent to the "perforation" work the following data are known: the coal mining method frontal coal-face with individual supporting; number of workers on levels of skills established for the "perforation" work and the coal mining method "frontal coal-face with individual supporting" = 2 workers, out of whom: 1 front miner and 1 miner helper; workers' average salary per working place: miner 3,500 u.m./working place; miner helper 3,660 u.m./working place; the coal production extracted through the frontal coal-face with individual supporting = 100 t of coal.

Thus the average pay wage tariff of the working team is determined:

$$\frac{35,000 \text{ u.m./post} + 30,660 \text{ u.m./post}}{2} = 32,830 \text{ u.m./post}$$

Then, the standard pay wage tariff of the working team per ton of coal extracted from the coal-face is extracted:

Table 15.9 Lists of standard pay wage tariffs on types of work

Name of work	U. M.	Standard pay wage tariffs	Observations
Perforation	u.m./working place/t	328.30	
Explosive cutting		320.14	
Coal-face loading		306.18	
Assembled partition wall		306.18	
Supporting		328.30	
Transport		318.21	
Moves		320.14	

$$\frac{32,830\ \text{u.m./post}}{100\ \text{t}} = 328.30\ \text{u.m./post/t}$$

Multiplying the time standards with the standard pay wage tariff, standard costs of the manual work can be determined. Mathematically, the mathematical relation is:

$$\text{Ch}_{\text{SM}} = \text{t}_{\text{S}} \times \text{T}_{\text{S}} \tag{15.8}$$

where:

Ch_{SM}—represents standard manual work expenditures (costs)
t_s—time standard
T_s—the standard pay wage tariff.

Replacing with data in relation (15.8), for the "perforation" work, standard cost is:

Ch_{SM} = 1,702 standard working places × 328.3 u.m./post/t = 558,76 u.m./t

Through the centralization of direct wages expenses with the direct wages determined for each operation (perforation, explosive cutting, loading in coal-face etc.) performed by a working team for a total number of 47.911 standardized working places, the level of these costs is of 1,531,831.596 u.m. Moreover on the basis of the data supplied by this form, the average expenses for miners' salaries per ton of coal are determined. Several stages must be observed. The following calculations are done:

- the transformation of the norms through applying the decrease coefficient from 8 to 6 working hours, because the present norms were established many years ago, when the working schedule in mining was of 8 h, the following mathematical relation is used:

$$\text{PN}_6 = \text{K} \times \text{PN}_8 \tag{15.9}$$

where:

PN_6—represents the number of standardized working places for a working schedule of 6 h
k—decrease coefficient = 1.21
PN_8—number of standardized working places for a working schedule of 8 h
$PN_6 = 1.21 \times 47.911 = 57.97$ standardized working places.

- determining the volume of extracted rock for a promotion step, on the basis of the following relation:

$$V = L \times h \times P \tag{15.10}$$

where:

V—represents the volume of extracted rock (mc)
L—length of the coal-face (m)
H—maximum height of the coal-face (m)
P—promotion step (m).
$V = 45 \times 3.20 \times 1.25 = 180$ mc

- determining the quantity of extracted rock and its transformation from cubic meters in tons:

$$CRE = \frac{V}{PN_6} \times GV \tag{15.11}$$

where:

CRE—represents the quantity of extracted rock (t/working place)
V—the volume of extracted rock (mc)
PN_6—number of standardized working places for a working schedule of 6 h
GV—volumetric weight of the coal = 1.45 t/mc

Replacing with data the relation, the following is obtained:

$$CRE = \frac{180\ \text{mc}}{57.97\ \text{normate posts}} \times 1.45\ \text{t/mc} = 4.5\ \text{t/post}$$

- determining the average expenses per working place for the direct wages met for the activity of the team:

$$\overline{C_{SD}^{P}} = \frac{CSD}{PN_8} \tag{15.12}$$

where:

$\overline{C_{SD}^{P}}$—represents the average expenses per working place for the direct wages
CSD—direct wages expenses
PN_8—number of standardized working places.

$$\overline{C_{SD}^{P}} = \frac{1,531,831.596}{47.911} = 31,972.44 \text{ u.m./post}$$

– determining the average expenses per ton of coal for the direct wages met for the activity of the team:

$$\overline{C_{SD}^{T}} = \frac{\overline{C_{SD}^{P}}}{CRE} \tag{15.13}$$

$$\overline{C_{SD}^{T}} = \frac{31,972.44 \text{ u.m./post}}{4.5 \text{ t/post}} = 7,104.98 \text{ u.m./t}$$

Then, after determining the expenses for the team's direct wages, through summing up these expenses met for the activity of all working teams from the sector, we can determine the level of expenses for that sector. Thus, for the no. 1 production department of the mine carboniferous working, the mathematical relation of determining these expenses is the following:

$$SD^1 = \sum_{i=1}^{n} sd_i^1 + CAS^1 + FS^1 + Fs^1 \tag{15.14}$$

where:

SD^1—represents the direct wages expenditure budget regarding the production department no. 1
$sd_i{}^1$—expenses for the direct wages of the team I within the production department no. 1, including the afferent increases
CAS^1—the tax share to the social insurances of the production department no. 1
FS^1—the tax share to the unemployment fund of the production department no. 1
Fs^1—the tax share to the health fund of the production department no. 1
n—number of teams within the production department no. 1.

In order to determine the sum of the direct wages expenses regarding the team of the production department (sd_i), the following is done: the summing up of the expenses calculated in the sheets of establishing the technical norm and the tariff (drawn up for each team) correlated with the production that these teams in the budgetary year (N) is drawn up. To these sums there are added the miners' increases, for example: fidelity increase, danger increase, length in service increase, leadership increase.

If to the sum of the expenses met for the direct wages afferent to the teams of the department, there are added the above increases, the fund of gross direct wages of that department, is obtained.

Thus, for example, let's assume that the level of these expenses met for the direct wages of the production department no. 1, achieved at the date when the budget was drawn up, is of 4,095,000 thousands u.m. It corresponds to number of 325 productive workers (miners, miner helpers, haulage man etc.) from the production department no. 1. Whose annual average of the expenses met for the direct wages per worker is that date of 12,600,000 u.m.

For the forecast of the level of these expenses for the next year it will be taken into account that the production of the department will raise from 72,500 to 87,000 t, the number of the working staff will, raise reaching 350 miners and miner helpers, as well as the fact that some wages indexations may appear. These ones will increase the gross salaries fund.

The percentage of 33 % representing the tax to social insurance of the production department no. 1 will be applied to the gross salary fund:

$$CAS^1 = \sum_{i=1}^{n} sd_i \times 33\,\% \qquad (15.15)$$

$$CAS.^1 = 4{,}095{,}000 \times 33\,\% = 1{,}351{,}350 \text{ thousands u.m.}$$

The tax to the unemployment fund is determined through applying the 5 % to the salary fund:

$$FS^1 = \sum_{i=1}^{n} sd_i \times 5\,\% \qquad (15.16)$$

$$FS^1 = 4{,}095{,}000 \times 5\,\% = 204{,}750 \text{ thousands u.m.}$$

The tax to the health fund is determined through applying the 2 % to the gross salary fund:

$$Fs^1 = \sum_{i=1}^{n} sd_i \times 2\,\% \qquad (15.17)$$

$$Fs^1 = 4{,}095{,}000 \times 2\,\% = 81{,}900 \text{ thousands u.m.}$$

The model of the direct wages expenditure budget forecasted for the year N for the production department no. 1 is presented in Table 15.10.

Table 15.10 Direct wages expenditure budget and their taxes forecasted for the year N (Production department no. 1)

Indicators	Achievement cumulated 10 months year N−1	Forecasted year N
No. of working staff (no. of employees)	325	350
Annual average of direct wages expenses (u.m./worker)	12,600,000	13,200,000
Annual gross salary fund (thousands u.m.)	4,095,000	4,620,000
Tax to social insurance (thousands u.m./year)	1,351,350	1,524,600
Tax to unemployment fund (thousands u.m./year)	204,750	231,000
Tax to health fund (thousands u.m./year)	81,900	92,400
Total direct wages expenses (thousands u.m./year)	5,733,000	6,468,000

– *direct expenses budget for electric power in motor purposes*
Direct expenses budget for electric power can be drawn up by using the same method as in the case of raw materials and direct materials expenditure budget. For budgeting the direct expenses met for electric power, it is necessary to know the specific usage of existing electric power at the date when the budget was drawn up, the unitary purchase price and real usage of electric power. Thus, at the date of drawing up the budget for the year N for the production department no. 1, the following are known; the specific usage of electric power 76.00 kWh/t, the real usage of electric power 76.36 kWh/t and real purchase price 146.6 lei/kWh. From the analysis of the causes that lead to the exceeding of the specific usage with 0.36 kWh/t, it is noticed that the exceeding of the established level is not justified. That is why it is maintained at the same level as the one of the year for which the budget is drawn up. The standard purchase price is determined by taking into account the purchase price existing at the date of drawing up the multiplied budget corresponding to the inflation index afferent to the year N and by taking into consideration the possible price increases for electric power.

Then, the direct expenses budget for electric power can be drawn up at the level of no. 1 production department, using the mathematical relation:

$$ED^1 = q^1 \times CS_e \times p_e \tag{15.18}$$

where:

ED^1—represents the direct expenses for electric power at the level of the production department no. 1
q^1—volume of coal production forecasted to be achieved in no. 1 production department
CS_e—standard usage of electric power
p_e—standard purchase price for electric power.

For example, the account of direct expenses for electric power, afferent to the specific usage forecasted for the year N, comparatively with the achievements of the first 10 months of the year N−1, is presented in Table 15.11.

Then the direct expenses budget for electric power can be drawn up for the production department no. 1 (Table 15.12)

– volume of production forecasted for the year N

$$q^1 = 88{,}760 \text{ t coal}$$

– standard usage of electric power forecasted for the year N

$$CS_e = 76.00 \text{ kWh/t}$$

– standard purchase price of electric power, forecasted for the year N:

Table 15.11 Account of direct expenses for electric power afferent to the specific usage forecasted for the year N comparatively with the achievements on the first 10 months of the year N−1 (Production department no. 1)

Name of item	Specific usage			Purchase price			Standard expenses u.m./t	
	U. M.	Achievement cumulated 10 months year N−1	Forecasts year N	U. M.	Achieved year N−1	Forecasts year N	Achieved 10 months year N−1	Forecasts year N
Electric power	kWh/t	76.36	76	u.m./kWh	146.6	176	11,194.38	13,376
Total standard expenses for electric power							11,194.38	13,376.00

Table 15.12 Electric power expenditures budget forecasted for the year N (Production department no. 1)

Pit-coal production (t)		Electric power direct expenditures (u.m./t)		Direct expenditures budget (thousands u.m.)	
Achieved cumulated 10 months year N−1	Forecasted for year N	Achieved cumulated 10 months year N−1	Forecasted for year N	Achieved cumulated 10 months year N−1	Forecasted for year N
69,407	88,760	11,194.38	13,376.00	776,968.33	1,187,253.76

$$ED^1 = q^1 \times CS_e \times p_e = 88,760 \times 76 \times 176 = 1,187,253.76 \text{ thounsed u.m.}$$

Replacing the data in the relation (15.18) it is obtained:

$$p_e = 176 \text{ u.m./kWh.}$$

It can be noticed that the electric power direct expenditures budget, afferent to the production department no. 1 is of 1,187,253.76 thousands u.m. The same can be done for the other production departments from the mine-working field.

– *technological fuel direct expenditures budget*
Using the same means as in the case of the previous budget can draw up the technological fuel direct expenditures budget. On the basis of the data presented in the previous paragraph, at the level of the production department no. 1, the technological fuel direct expenditures budget can be drawn up using the following relation:

$$CD^1 = \sum_{i=1}^{3} q^1 \times CS_i \times p_i \tag{15.19}$$

where:

CD^1—represents the technological fuel direct expenditures budget at the level of production department no. 1
q^1—the volume of coal production forecasted to be achieved in production department no. 1
CS_i—standard usage of fuel I
p_i—standard purchase price of fuel I
$i = 1, 3$—type of fuel.

In order to drawn up the technological fuel direct expenditures budget, there is necessary to know the account of the technological fuel direct expenditures forecasted for the year N in contrast with the achievements in the first 10 months of the year N−1 (Table 15.13).

Starting from the previous mathematical relation in the first stage the level of the standard expenditures afferent to the technological fuel specific usage forecasted for year N, that are afferent to production department no. 1, were determined. For

Table 15.13 The account of the technological fuel direct expenditures afferent to the specific usage forecasted for the year N in contrast to the achievements in the first 10 months of the year N−1

Item's name	Specific usage			Purchasing price			Standard expenditures u.m./t	
	U. M.	Achieved 10 months year N−1	Forecasted for year N	U. M.	Achieved 10 months year N−1	Forecasted for year N	Achieved 10 months year N−1	Forecasted for year N
Gasoline	l/1,000 t	494.89	566.25	u.m./l	625	750	309.31	424.69
Gas	l/1,000 t	7.52	4.25	u.m./l	1,000	1,200	7.52	5.10
Petroleum	l/1,000 t	–	2.82	u.m./l	–	679	–	1.92
Total technological fuel standard expenditures							316.83	431.71

example, it is chosen the technological fuel gasoline and the following data are known:

- specific usage (level achieved in the first 10 months of year N−1–494.89 l/1,000 t; forecasted level for year N–566,25 l/1,000 t);
- purchasing prices (level achieved in the first 10 months of year N−1–625 lei/l; forecasted level for year N–750 u.m/l).

Therefore the gasoline expenditures done in the first 10 month of year N−1 were of 309.31 u.m/t (494.89 l/1,000 t × 750 u.m/l).In the same way calculations for other items can be done.

By summing up the obtained values the total technological fuel standard expenditures afferent to the production department no. 1 can be obtained, thus:

$$\mathrm{ChS}^1{}_\mathrm{c} = \sum_{\mathrm{i}=1}^{3} \mathrm{ChS}_\mathrm{i} \tag{15.20}$$

where:

$ChS^1{}_c$—represents the technological standard expenditures afferent to production department no. 1
ChS_i—technological fuel i standard expenditures
i—type of technological fuel.

By substituting the data from Table 15.13 in the (15.20) relation it is obtained:

- the level of technological fuel standard expenditures afferent to production department no. 1, achieved in the first 10 months of year N−1:

$$\mathrm{ChS}^{1\mathrm{r}}{}_\mathrm{c} = 494.89 \times 625 + 7.52 \times 1,000 = 316.83 \text{ u.m./t}$$

- the level of technological fuel standard expenditures afferent to production department no. 1 forecasted for year N:

$$\mathrm{ChS}^{1\mathrm{p}}{}_\mathrm{c} = 566.25 \times 750 + 4.25 \times 1,200 + 2.82 \times 679 = 431.71 \text{ u.m./t}$$

Further on the technological fuel expenditures budget afferent to production department no. 1 can be drawn up as we have all the necessary data (Table 15.14).

Substituting with the data from Table 15.13 the present relation it results that the level of technological fuel direct expenditures budget afferent to production department no. 1 for the year N is of 38,318.58 thousands u.m.

$$\begin{aligned}\mathrm{CD}^1 &= 88,760 \times (566.25 \times 750 + 4.25 \times 1,200 + 2.82 \times 679) = \\ &= 88,760 \times 431.71 = 38,318.58 \text{ thousands u.m.}\end{aligned}$$

– the budget of direct expenditures with the fixed means' redemption

The budget of direct expenditures with the fixed means redemption from the production department no. 1 is drawn up using the data obtained from the "Program

Table 15.14 Technological fuel direct expenditures budget (Production department no. 1)

Pit-coal production (t)		Technological fuel direct expenditures (u. m./t)		Direct expenditures budget (thousands u. m.)	
Achieved 10 months year N−1	Forecasted for year N	Achieved 10 months year N−1	Forecasted for year N	Achieved 10 months year N−1	Forecasted for year N
69,407	88,760	316.83	431.71	21,990.22	38,318.58

of fixed means' redemption" which is elaborated at the mine working level. From this program there are obtained the following information referring to: actual number, name, code, unit of measure, quantity, unitary price, value, data of setting to work and data of integral redemption (Table 15.15).

Also it is had in view "the program of purchasing new fixed means" drawn up for the following year which comprises information referring to: name of fixed mean; unit of measure, quantity, estimate purchasing price, value, standardized functioning period, estimate data at which the purchase of the fixed mean will take place (Table 15.16).

Using this data, for each fixed mean it will be calculated the annuity afferent to budgetary year N.

Thus, about the fixed mean "TR3 transporter" the following data are known: code—500268; unit of measure-pieces; quantity—1; unitary price—12,251,130 u. m.; value—12,251,130 u.m.; data of setting to work—March 2, 1990; data of integral redemption—March 1, 2010.

The rate of linear redemption (t) is calculated:

$$t = \frac{100}{n} \qquad (15.21)$$

where: $t = \frac{100}{20} = 5\ \%$; n is the number of years of the fixed mean life span.

The annuity for the complete exercise (a) is determined:

$$a = V \times t \qquad (15.22)$$

where: V is the input value of the fixed mean

$$a = 12,251,130 \times 5\ \% = 612,556.50\ \text{u.m.}$$

For the fixed means that will be set to work during the budgetary year the first annuity will be calculated. The calculus is done on the basis of the estimate data at which it is purchased or set to work the fixed mean and the estimate purchasing price. Thus, the fixed mean "Scrapers transporter" has an estimate purchasing price of 10 millions u.m. a piece and the estimate purchasing data is August 20, year N. Substituting with data in the presented relations it is obtained:

Table 15.15 Fixed means redemption program (Production department no. 1)

Name	Code	U. M	Quantity	Unitary price	Value	Data	
						Set working	Integral redemption
TR 3 transporter	500,268	Pieces	1	12,251,130	12,251,130	3/1990	2/2010
72 kW cells	300,303	Pieces	1	3,591,369	3,591,369	8/1987	7/2002
KSM pump	300,475	Pieces	2	19,881,007	39,762,013	5/1990	4/2005
Hydraulic central aggregate	300,718	Pieces	1	4,526,000	4,526,000	2/1995	1/2001
TAP winch	500,294	Pieces	2	1,816,544	3,633,087	11/1990	10/2005
Total	–	–	–	–	7,147,798,355	–	–

Table 15.16 Fixed means purchasing program (Production department no. 1)

	U. M.	Quantity	Unitary estimate price	Value	Standard functioning period	Input data
Scrapers transporter	Pieces	1	10,000,000	10,000,000	10 years	8/N
P90 perforator	Pieces	1	700,000	700,000	9 years	4/N
Electro-pump	Pieces	2	5,500,000	10,100,000	12 years	7/N
VEP ventilator	Pieces	1	4,250,000	4,250,000	8 years	4/N
Total	–	–	–	87,550,000	–	–

$$t = 100/10 = 10\,\%$$
$$a = 10,000,000 \times 10\,\% = 1,000,000 \text{ u.m}$$

Further on, we can determine the first annuity, the number of days comprised in the interval August 20, N—December 31, N being of 130.

$$a_p = a \times \frac{n_z}{360} \tag{15.23}$$

where:

a_p—is the first annuity;
a—the annuity for a complete exercise;
n_z—the number of days from the data of setting to work till the end of the year;
360—the number of days in a year.

$$a_p = 1,000,000 \times \frac{130}{360} = 361,111.11 \text{ u.m.}$$

In the opposite case, respectively in the case in which a fixed mean is completely redeemed during the budgetary year, the first annuity must be calculated. Using the data from the previous example in order to calculate the last annuity (au) it is obtained:

$$a_u = 1,000,000 \times \frac{230}{360} = 638,888.89 \text{ u.m.}$$

or

$$a_u = 1,000,000 - 361,111.11 = 638,888.89 \text{ u.m.}$$

Thus, knowing every fixed mean's annuity from the production department no. 1 it can be filled in the budget of direct expenditures with the fixed means of this sector. The model of such a budget is presented in Table 15.17.

Table 15.17 The budget of direct expenditures with the fixed means redemption

Name	UM	Quantity	Unitary price (u.m.)	Value (u.m.)	Standard redemption	
					Achieved cumulated 10 months year N−1 (u.m.)	Forecasted for year N (u.m.)
TR 3 transporter	Pieces	1	12,251,130	12,251,130	510,463.75	612,556.50
72 kW cells	Pieces	1	3,591,369	3,591,369	199,520.50	239,424.60
KSM pump	Pieces	2	19,881,007	39,762,014	2,209,000.78	2,650,800.94
Hydraulic central aggregate	Pieces	1	4,526,000	4,526,000	942,916.67	1,131,500.00
TAP winch	Pieces	2	1,816,544	3,633,087	201,838.17	242,205.80
Scrapers transporter	Pieces	1	10,000,000	10,000,000	–	361,111.11
P90 perforator	Pieces	1	700,000	700,000	–	58,333.33
Electro-pump	Pieces	2	5,500,000	10,100,000	–	420,833.33
VEP ventilator	Pieces	1	4,250,000	4,250,000	–	398,437.50
Total	–	–	–	7,235,348,355	–	12,578,640

Synthesizing, it can be noticed that the budget of direct expenditures with the fixed means redemption from production department no. 1 (AD1) can be determined using the mathematical relation:

$$AD = \sum_{i=1}^{m} a_i + \sum_{j=1}^{n} a_{pj} \tag{15.24}$$

where:

a_i—is the annuity calculated for a complete exercise

i—the type of fixed means whose functioning duration integrally covers the budgetary year; $i = 1, m$

a_{pj}—partial (first/last) calculated annuity

j—type of fixed mean that is managed during the budgetary year or that is to be completely redeemed during the budgetary year; $j = 1, n$.

Coming back to the previous data, the budget of direct expenditures with the fixed means redemption from the production department no. 1 will be:

$$AD^1 = (612,556.50 + 239,424.60 + 2,650,800.94 + 1,131,500 + 242,205.80 + \ldots) + (361,111.11 + 58,333.33 + 420,833.33 + 398,437.50 + \ldots) == 125,178,640.00 \text{ u.m}$$

As the level of the standard production of coal for the year N of the no. 1 production department is of 88,760 t, it derives that the level of standard redemption expenses of the fixed means per tone of coal will be of 1,410.30 u.m.

– *indirect manufacturing costs budget*

This one comprises:

1. the indirect (common) manufacturing costs budget of the departments, which will be detailed for mine carboniferous workings, case in which these budgets of the departments can be drawn up for each production department. Their main goal is the sizing of the expenses met for the activity of the departments.

   Within this type of budget the expenses can be grouped in three categories, as it follows: maintenance charges and equipment running costs (expenses for technical revision, running revisions and maintenance of the means of transport); expenses for general overhauling of the equipment and of the means of transport (redemption of the equipment and of the means of transport); general expenses of the department (wages of the leading, technical, economic and administrative staff including the taxes to the social insurance and to the unemployment fund; redemption of buildings and of the other fixed means of the department; labor protection expenses); administrative—housekeeping expenses (for the telephone exchange; materials for the maintenance and the cleaning up of buildings and other fixed means; transport of the materials produced by third parties; heat and power expenses etc.).

For budgeting indirect (common) manufacturing costs of the department, it can be chosen the analytical procedure known in the specialized literature as "individual standards procedure". The basis of calculating the indirect standard manufacturing costs, through the analytical procedure, is either the annual average of the costs from the last 3–5 years or the data from the period previous to that for which the budget is drawn up.

The budgeting of the indirect (common) manufacturing costs of the departments can be done by taking into account their content as well as the different behavior that they have towards the volume of production. The used methodology differs in relation to the fact that if the standard volume of production is equal or not with the average volume of production in the last years, respectively in the previous year. Thus, if the standard production is equal with the average production, respectively with the one from the previous year, there are adopted as standard the average (common) manufacturing costs or the ones from the previous period, correlated with the value of the stimulation factor. In the case when standard production differs from the average production, respectively from the one of the previous year, when establishing the individual standards it is taken into consideration the behavior of the different types of costs against the physical volume of production, applying different methods for: establishment charges, variable expenses and mixed expenses.

Practically, for drawing up the indirect manufacturing (common) costs budget afferent to a production department within a mine carboniferous working, it is made out the "Account of the indirect manufacturing costs" of that department (Table 15.18) on the basis of the accounting data regarding the level of these expenses in the last years. At the same time, the expenses are divided from the beginning in three categories, mentioned above, namely: establishment charges, variable expenses and mixed (semi-variable) expenses.

When drawing up the indirect manufacturing costs budget of the no. 1 production department for the year N, it is no problem to determine the standards for the establishment charges because their unchanged nature against the modifications of the volume of production allows the adoption as standard of their level from the previous year without making any change.

For the variable overheads, the establishment of the standards implies the following stages:

2. *the correlation of the average expenses from one period (or of the ones from the previous year) with the standard volume of the activity,* is based on the following relations:

$$\overline{ch_v} = \frac{\overline{Ch_v}}{\overline{Q}} \tag{15.25}$$

and

$$\mathrm{Ch_c} = \mathrm{Q_S} \times \overline{\mathrm{ch_v}} \tag{15.26}$$

3. *the taking into consideration of the stimulation factor if it is considered that the new level of expenses does not imply enough efforts on the part of the staff from the production department for observing it;* this is done using the relation:

$$\mathrm{Ch_S} = \mathrm{Ch_C} - \frac{\mathrm{Ch_C} \times \mathrm{P_S}}{100} \tag{15.27}$$

where:

$\overline{\mathrm{ch_v}}$—represents the average variable costs per unit of product;
$\overline{\mathrm{Ch_v}}$—average variable total costs;
$\overline{\mathrm{Q}}$—average volume of production;
$\mathrm{Ch_c}$—total variable costs correlated with the volume of production;
$\mathrm{Q_S}$—standard volume of production;
Ch_s—standard total variable costs;
Ps—percentage corresponding to the stimulation factor.

The above mentioned relations are used when determining the standards for the indirect variable manufacturing costs. Knowing that for the year N the standard production is of 88,760 t of coal and that it has at its basis the average of the expenses and of the prediction calculated according to the data from the last 5 years (Table 15.18), it can be determined the standard for each type of variable expenses.

Thus:

- *for the expenses with technical previsions, running repairs and maintenance of the means of transport of the department:*

$$\begin{aligned}\overline{\mathrm{ch_v}} &= \frac{98,520,000}{84,560} = 1,165.08 \text{ u.m./t}\\ \mathrm{Ch_c} &= 88,760 \times 1,165.08 = 103,412,500.8 \text{ u.m.}\\ \mathrm{Ch_s} &= 103,412,500.8 - \frac{103,412,500.8 \times 2}{100} = 101,344,250.78 \text{ u.m.}\end{aligned}$$

- *for the expenses with general overhauling of the equipment and the means of transport of the department:*

$$\begin{aligned}\overline{\mathrm{ch_v}} &= \frac{65,680,000}{84,560} = 776.73 \text{ u.m/t}\\ \mathrm{Ch_c} &= 88,760 \times 776.73 = 68,942,554.8 \text{ u.m.}\end{aligned}$$

Table 15.18 Account of indirect manufacturing costs of the department (Production department no. 1, thousands u.m.)

Type of costs	Year					Average
	N−5	N−4	N−3	N−2	N−1	
Volume of activity (in tones)	83,250	84,000	84,700	85,100	85,750	84,560
I. Establishment charges	188,975	188,980	189,000	189,305	189,550	189,162
– Wages of the leading staff, TESA, taxes to social insurance and to the unemployment fund	117,700	117,750	117,800	117,900	118,000	117,830
– Redemption of buildings and other fixed means	18,000	18,000	18,000	18,000	18,000	18,000
– Wear and tear of inventory objects	12,100	12,100	12,100	12,100	12,100	12,100
– Heat expenses	18,500	18,400	18,350	18,500	18,650	18,480
– Electric power for lighting	10,000	10,050	10,050	10,100	10,100	10,060
– Expenses for the ventilation of the department	500	505	505	510	510	506
– Materials for maintenance and cleaning up of the buildings and other fixed means	1,225	1,225	1,235	1,235	1,240	1,232
– Water, sewer, sanity for administrative and housekeeping needs	1,050	1,050	1,060	1,060	1,050	1,054
– Other establishment charges	9,900	9,900	9,900	9,900	9,900	9,900
II. Variable expenses	172,300	178,250	187,800	193,600	200,000	186,390
– Expenses for technical revisions, running repairs and maintenance of the means of transport of the department	92,100	94,800	99,000	101,700	105,000	98,520
– Expenses for general overhauling of the equipment and the means of transport of the department	61,400	63,200	66,000	67,800	70,000	65,680
– Electric power for motor purposes	12,400	13,350	14,900	15,500	16,000	14,430
– Expenses for environment protection	6,400	6,900	7,900	8,600	9,000	7,760
III. Mixed expenses	31,500	31,600	31,750	31,900	32,000	31,750
– Labor protection	31,500	31,600	31,750	31,900	32,000	31,750
Total	392,775	398,830	408,550	414,805	421,550	407,302

$$\text{Ch}_\text{s} = 68{,}942{,}554.8 - \frac{68{,}942{,}554.8 \times 2}{100} = 67{,}563{,}703.70 \text{ u.m.}$$

– *for the electric power in motor purposes:*

$$\overline{\text{ch}_\text{v}} = \frac{14{,}430{,}000}{84{,}560} = 170.64 \text{ u.m./t}$$

$$\text{Ch}_\text{c} = 88{,}760 \times 170.64 = 15{,}146{,}006.4 \text{ u.m.}$$

$$\text{Ch}_\text{s} = 15{,}146{,}006.4 - \frac{15{,}146{,}006.4 \times 2}{100} = 14{,}843{,}086.27 \text{ u.m.}$$

– *for the expenses with environment protection:*

$$\overline{\text{ch}_\text{v}} = \frac{7{,}760{,}000}{84{,}560} = 91{,}760 \text{ u.m./t}$$

$$\text{Ch}_\text{c} = 88{,}760 \times 91.76 = 8{,}144{,}617.6 \text{ u.m.}$$

$$\text{Ch}_\text{s} = 8{,}144{,}617.6 - \frac{8{,}144{,}617.6 \times 2}{100} = 7{,}981{,}725.24 \text{ u.m.}$$

In what regards the mixed overheads, the determination of standards implies the separation of the variable part from the fixed one in the case of each cost and the individual treatment of each of them according to the methodology specific to the establishment charges, respectively the variable expenses. For these, the procedure of maximum and minimum points will be used.

Replacing with data, the determination of the standards for the "labor protection expenses" implies the following stages:

– the average variable unitary expenses are determined:

$$\overline{\text{ch}_\text{v}} = \frac{\text{chm}_\text{max} - \text{chm}_\text{min}}{\text{Vol}_\text{prod. max} - \text{Vol}_\text{prod. min}} \tag{15.28}$$

$$\overline{\text{ch}_\text{v}} = \frac{32{,}000{,}000 - 31{,}500{,}000}{85{,}750 - 83{,}250} = \frac{500{,}000}{2{,}500} = 200 \text{ u.m./t}$$

– the variable part of labor protection expenses is determined:

$$\text{Ch}_\text{v} = \text{Q}_\text{max} \times \overline{\text{ch}_\text{v}}$$

$$\text{Ch}_\text{v} = 85{,}750 \times 200 = 17{,}150{,}000 \text{ u.m.} \tag{15.29}$$

– the fixed part of labor protection expenses is determined:

$$Ch_f = Ch_\text{max} - Ch_v \tag{15.30}$$

$$Ch_f = 32,000,000 - 17,150,000 = 14,850,000 \text{ u.m.}$$

– average variable expenses are correlated with the standard volume of production for the year N:

$$Ch_c = Q_s \times \overline{ch_v} \tag{15.31}$$

$$Ch_c = 88,760 \times 200 = 17,752,000 \text{ u.m.}$$

– it is taken into account a stimulation factor of 2 %:

$$Ch_{vS} = 17,752,000 - 17,752,000 \times 2\,\% = 17,396,960 \text{ u.m.}$$

– the standard labor protection expenses for the year N are determined:

$$Ch_S = Ch_{vS} + Ch_f \tag{15.32}$$

$$Ch_S = 17,396,960 + 14,850,000 = 32,246.60 \text{ u.m.}$$

With the help of these data the indirect (common) costs budget can be completed. Its model, drawn up on a production department within a mine carboniferous working, is presented in Table 15.19.

Knowing the expenditure budgets drawn up for no. 1 production department as well as the general administration costs of the mine working of the respective department, it can be drawn up a centralizing manufacturing costs budget of the production activity of that department.

This budget will comprise: raw materials and direct materials expenditure budget of the department (Tables 15.5 and 15.6), direct wages expenditure budget and the taxes afferent to these expenses of the department (Table 15.10), direct expenses budget for electric power afferent to the department (Table 15.12), direct expenses budget for the technological fuel afferent to the department (Table 15.14), direct expenses budget for the redemption of the fixed means of the department (Table 15.17), indirect (common) manufacturing costs budget of the department (Table 15.19) and the share from the general administration expenditure budget of the mine working of that department.

These centralizing manufacturing cost budgets of the activity of each production department must be related to the responsibility of the manager of that department (departmental manager). This fact will make it easy to watch, to control and to analyze the model of costs' framing in the limit established by budgets.

The model of such a centralizing budget drawn up for no. 1 production department within the mine working is represented in Table 15.20.

It must be mentioned the fact that expenditures budget can also be drawn up for the auxiliary departments. These budgets have only an informative role as the expenses from these are taken over in the budgeting stage by the beneficiary places of the works that are to be done. In other words, the expenses of the

Table 15.19 Indirect (common) manufacturing costs budget of the department (Production department no. 1, thousands u.m.)

Name of expenditures	Expenditures	
	The average on the last years	Forecasted year N (standard)
Volume of activity (in tones)	84,560	88,760
I. Establishment charges	189,162	189,162
– Wages of the leading staff, TESA, taxes to social insurance and to the unemployment fund	117,830	117,830
– Redemption of buildings and other fixed means	18,000	18,000
– Wear and tear of inventory objects	12,100	12,100
– Heat expenses	18,480	18,480
– Electric power for lighting	10,060	10,060
– Expenses for the ventilation of the department	506	506
– Materials for maintenance and cleaning up of the buildings and other fixed means	1,232	1,232
– Water, sewer, sanity for administrative and house-keeping needs	1,054	1,054
– Other establishment charges	9,900	9,900
II. Variable expenses	186,390	191,733
– Expenses for technical revisions, running repairs and maintenance of the means of transport of the department	98,520	101,344
– Expenses for general overhauling of the equipment and the means of transport of the department	65,680	67,564
– Electric power for motor purposes	14,430	14,843
– Expenses for environment protection	7,760	7,982
III. Mixed expenses	31,750	32,247
– Labor protection	31,750	32,247
Overall total	407,302	413,142

Table 15.20 Manufacturing costs centralizing (standard) budget of the department (Production department no. 1, thousands u.m.)

Name of component budgets	Preliminary year N−1	Forecasted year N (standard)
Raw materials and direct materials budget	865,400	1,119,871.61
Direct wages expenditures budget and their afferent taxes	6,250,000	6,468,000.00
Electric power direct expenditures budget	933,500	1,187,253.76
Technological fuel direct expenditures budget	27,550	38,318.50
Budget of direct expenses with the fixed means redemption	114,150	125,178.64
Indirect (common) manufacturing costs budget of the department	452,000	413,142.00
The share of the mine carboniferous working general manufacturing expenditures budget	407,302	475,296.84
Total	9,049,902	9,827,061.35

auxiliary departments are to be indirectly found within the budgets of the production departments and within the general administration budget of mine working.

4. *the budget of the mine working general manufacturing costs* does not rise problems regarding the sizing as the necessary data are given by the partial budgets drawn up separately for every department by summing up all indirect usage of general interest. For example, as it follows, there is presented the model of the budget of the expenditures of financial-accounting departments.

In order to draw up the expenditures budget of the financial-accounting department the following aspects were taken into account: the indexation with 20 % of wages in the budgetary year N, according to the legislative expectations; the increase of the carriage expenses at and from the working place as a result of the increase of tariffs used by transport companies; the cutting of mail charges with 10 % as it is estimated that until the end of the N−1 year the achieved expenditures will be under the level of preliminary expenditures meaning that the establishment of these expenditures was not exact; the increase of shifting, detachments, transfers, expenditures with 20 % as a consequence of the increase of carriage tariffs; maintaining at the same level with the one forecasted for the year N−1 of the expenditures forecasted for the year N in the case of the other expenditures comprised by this budget. In the mine carboniferous industry, the general administration expenses of the mine carboniferous working can be divided into four large categories of expenses: general interest expenses (leading staff wages and TESA including the taxes to the social insurance and the unemployment fund; redemption of fixed means of general interest etc.); general expenditures regarding the exceptions from payment (coal allocation; rents; electric power price differences; introduction of distinct heating plans taxes etc.); management-housekeeping expenditures (office supplies; subscriptions for books, magazines, publications; shifts; detachments; transfers etc.); direct departmental expenses (materials for the maintenance and cleaning up of buildings, water, salubrity etc.). The expenditures comprised in the general administration expenditure budget are establishment charges as they are not dependent on the achieved volume of coal production. Therefore, in order to draw up this budget, the preliminary level of the general administration expenditures of the previous year, the level of the achieved expenditures at the data when the budget was drawn up and the expenditures of the budgetary year increase or decrease tendencies were take into account.

Thus, there were taken into account the increases of the prices at the electric and thermic power, the increase of wages as a result of their indexation, the increase of tariffs used by the transport companies; the increase of carriage tariffs of the railroads; the decrease of the expenditures of the wear and tear of some inventory objects as a result of their getting out of gear etc. (Table 15.21).

The model of the general administration expenditures drawn up for a mine carboniferous working is presented in Table 15.22.

The general administration expenses can be distributed over the manufacturing establishment charges of a certain production department by taking into

Table 15.21 The expenditure budget of the financial-accounting department (thousands u.m.)

Name of expenditures	Preliminary year N−1	Achieved cumulated Month X year N−1	Forecasted Year N
Wages of leading and TESA staff, including C.A.S, F.S	25,000	20,000	30,000
Automatic electronic data processing	10,000	8,000	10,000
Staff training	5,000	5,000	5,000
Transport at and from the working place	700	600	840
Office supplies	800	750	800
Subscriptions, books, magazines, publications	500	500	500
Mail expenditures	650	400	585
Shifts, detachments, transfers	500	480	600
Other office expenses	200	195	200
Total	43,350	35,925	48,525

account the share value of achieved production of a certain production department in the total production of the mine working.

Thus, it is known that for the budgetary year, the volume of the standard production of the mine carboniferous working is of 705,600 t, the volume of the standard production of no. 1 productison department is of 88,760 t and the unitary selling price is of 60,000 u.m./t.

The distribution key for the general administration expenses is:

$$\mathrm{K} = \frac{\mathrm{Val}_{\text{prod.carb. sec t.}}}{\mathrm{Val}_{\text{prod.exp.min e}}} \times 100 \tag{15.33}$$

$$\mathrm{K} = \frac{5,325,600 \text{ thousands u.m}}{42,336,000 \text{ thousands u.m.}} \times 100 = 12.57\,\%$$

and the share of general administration expenses of that production department is:

$$share = CGA \times K \tag{15.34}$$

where:

CGA—represents the total of general administration expenses of the mine working forecasted in the budget;

K—distribution key;

share = 3,781,200 thousands u.m. × 12.57 % = 475,296.84 thousands u.m

Table 15.22 General administration expenditure budget (thousands u.m.)

Name of expenditures	Preliminary year N−1	Forecasted year N (standard)
General interest expenditures	470,000	510,000
Wages of leading and TESA staff, including C.A.S, F.S	200,000	240,000
Redemption of fixed means of general interest	6,000	6,000
Automatic electronic data processing	72,000	72,000
Field taxes	72,000	72,000
Buildings taxes	120,000	120,000
General expenditures regarding the exceptions from payments	2,830,200	2,917,200
Coal grants	1,200,000	1,200,000
Rents	48,000	48,000
Differences of electric power prices	400,000	480,000
Thermic taxes	100,000	120,000
Staff training	36,000	36,000
Kindergartens and nurseries	1,200	1,200
Medical dispensary	240,000	240,000
Tickets for rest and treatment	800,000	840,000
Transport at and from the working place	5,000	6,000
Administrative-housekeeping expenditures	25,400	26,400
Office supplies	2,400	2,400
Subscriptions, books, magazines, publications	6,000	6,000
Mail expenditures	12,000	12,000
Other office expenses	2,000	2,400
Shifts, detachments, transfers	3,000	3,600
Heating expenses	239,500	240,000
Electric power for lighting and motive power	6,000	6,000
Materials for the maintenance and cleaning of buildings	6,000	6,000
Wear and tear, maintenance, repairs of inventory objects	3,750	3,600
Water, sewer, sanitation	12,500	12,000
Other expenditures for maintenance and household	6,000	6,000
Total general administration expenses	3,599,350	3,781,200

– *the general budget of manufacturing costs*

The general budget of manufacturing costs of mine carboniferous working can be drawn up by summing up the seven types of partial budgets presented in above: the raw materials and direct materials expenditure budget, direct wages expenditure budget and their afferent taxes; electric power direct expenditure budget; technological fuel direct expenditure budget; budget of direct expenses with redemption; manufacturing (common) indirect costs budget of the departments and the general administrative expenditure budget.

The model of the general administration expenditure budget drawn up for a mine carboniferous working is presented in Table 15.23.

Table 15.23 General administration expenditure budget (thousands u.m.)

Name of component budgets	Preliminary year N−1	Forecasted year N
Raw materials and direct materials budget	6,856,541.83	8,902,449.36
Direct wages expenditures budget and their afferent taxes	45,450,902.95	51,417,489.88
Electric power direct expenditures budget	7,395,701.48	9,438,105.60
Technological fuel direct expenditures budget	209,317.54	304,614.57
Budget of direct expenses with the fixed means redemption	982,004.00	995,111.00
Indirect (common) manufacturing costs budget of the department	3,200,000.00	3,200,000.00
General administration expenditures budget	3,599,350.00	3,781,200.00
Total	67,693,817.80	78,038,970.41

– *unitary costs budget per product*

A judicious sizing of the unitary price per product represents a necessity that stands at the basis of an efficient strategy in the field of manufacturing costs. In this purpose, at the level of a mine carboniferous working the unitary costs budget per product can be drawn up by grouping the expenditures on calculation items. In this way it is ensured the exact knowledge of the size of every calculation item and of the way in which this one contributes to the drawing up of the unitary cost of the product.

The substantiation of the budget of the unitary price per ton of coal is done on the basis of the data comprised in the expenditures partial budgets, components of the general budget of the mine working manufacturing price presented above. The expenditures comprised in the already drawn up budgets are taken over by the unitary price budget and regrouped according to the classification of the calculation items. For the calculation item "raw materials and direct materials" the calculus of the unitary price is simple as it is already known, being determined in the stage of budgeting the raw materials and direct materials expenditures (Table 15.5). Thus, in the "Account of the raw materials and direct materials expenditures, afferent to the specific usage forecasted for the year N, in contrast with the achievements on the first 10 months of the N−1 year" drawn up at the level of the no. 1 production department, the unitary cost was determined. Its level was of 12,616.85 u.m./t. Mathematically, the calculus relation can be written:

$$\mathrm{cmd} = \frac{\sum_{i=1}^{m} \mathrm{cs_i} \times \mathrm{p_i}}{1{,}000} \tag{15.35}$$

where:

cmd—represents the unitary expenditures of raw materials and direct materials;
cs_i—the specific usage from material i (at 1,000 t of extracted coal);

p_i—unitary supply price of material i;
i—type of material;
1,000—transformation of 1,000 kg into 1 t.

Replacing with data from (15.35) it is obtained:

$$\begin{aligned} \text{cmd} = & \left(17\ \text{mc}/1{,}000\text{t} \times\ 121{,}200\ \text{u.m.}/\text{mc}\ + 2{,}500\ \text{kg}/1{,}000\ \text{t} \times 310\ \text{u.m.}/\text{kg} + \right. \\ & + 1{,}300\ \text{kg}/1{,}000\ \text{t} \times 1{,}265\ \text{u.m.}/\text{kg}\ +\ 300\ \text{kg}/1{,}000\ \text{t} \times 4{,}696\ \text{u.m.}/\text{kg}+ \\ & \left. + 750\ \text{bc}/1{,}000\ \times\ 2{,}203\ \text{u.m.}/\text{bc}\ +\ 60\ \text{kg}/1{,}000\ \text{t} \times 1{,}265\ \text{u.m.}/\text{kg}\right) /1{,}000 \\ = & \ 12{,}616.85\ \text{u.m.}/\text{t} \end{aligned}$$

In order to determine the unitary expenditures with the mine working direct wages the following stages are necessary:

determining the expenditures with the mine carboniferous working direct wages afferent to the budgetary year N:

$$\text{CSD} = \frac{\text{css} \times \text{Q}}{\text{q}} \tag{15.36}$$

where:

CSD—represents the expenses with the mine carboniferous working direct wages afferent to the budgetary year;
css—forecasted direct wages expenditures of production department no. 1 afferent to the achieved coal manufacture = 4,620,000 thousands u.m. (Table 15.26)
Q—forecasted volume of physical production afferent to the mine working for the budgetary year = 705,600 t (Table 15.7)
q—forecasted volume of the physical production of production department no. 1 = 88,760 t (Table 15.7).

$$\text{CSD} = \frac{4{,}620{,}000\ \times\ 705{,}600}{88{,}760} = 36{,}726{,}813.88\ \text{thousands u.m.}$$

the calculus of unitary expenses with mine carboniferous working direct wages afferent to the budgetary year N:

$$\text{csd} = \frac{\text{CSD}}{\text{Q}} \tag{15.37}$$

where:

csd—represents the unitary expenses with the mine working direct wages afferent to the budgetary year

$$\text{csd} = \frac{36,726,813.88}{705,600} = 52,050.47\ \text{u.m./t}$$

For the substantiation of the level of indirect manufacturing expenses and of the general administration expenses the drawn up financial regulations are taken into account.

Thus, in order to establish the expenditures determined by the consumption of compressed air at the level of a mine working, two factors must be taken into account: the price of a m^3 of compressed air and the consumption of compressed air.

The consumption of compressed air or the debit of compressed air (m^3 24 h) is calculated according to the relation:

$$Q_{ac} = K_1 \times K_2 \times \sum_{i=1}^{n} q_i \tag{15.38}$$

where:

Q_{ac}—represents the consumption of compressed air of the mine carboniferous working;
K_1—the correction coefficient of the compressed air losses in the ventilation pipes;
K_2—the simultaneity coefficient of compressed air consumers which depends on the number of working points of the mine working that are simultaneously connected;
q_1—compressed air consumption in 24 h per working point of the mine carboniferous working;
$i = 1,n$—number of working points of the mine carboniferous working (coal-face; gallery)

The size of the simultaneity coefficient is presented in Table 15.24.

The size of the correction coefficient of the pipe losses, as it results from the normative regulations, is estimated to be optimum for losses between 10 % and 18 %. The compressed air consumption for a working point is established in average of normative at 60 m^3/24 h. The price of a m^3 of compressed air is estimated at 80,000 u.m.

Table 15.24 The size of the simultaneity coefficient

No. of working points simultaneously supplied	Simultaneity coefficient
1	1
2–3	0.9
4–6	0.83–0.80
7–10	0.78–0.71
11–20	0.69–0.59

So, the size of the expenditures with the compressed air consumption of the mine carboniferous working, comprising five working points simultaneously supplied will be:

$$\mathrm{Ch_{ac}} = \mathrm{p_{ua}} \times \mathrm{Q_{ac}} = \mathrm{p_{ua}} \times \mathrm{K_1} \times \mathrm{K_2} \times \sum_{i=1}^{5} \mathrm{q_i} \tag{15.39}$$

where:

Ch_{ac}—represents the compressed air expenditures;
p_{ua}—the price of a m^3 of compresses air;
Q_{ac}—compressed air consumption.

Substituting the data in formula (15.39) it is obtained:

$Ch_{ac}{}^{min} = 80{,}000 \times 0.80 \times 0.1 \times 5 \times 60 = 1{,}920{,}000$ u.m./24 h
(The variant of the smallest losses in the compressed air network)
$Ch_{ac}{}^{max} = 80{,}000 \times 0.83 \times 0.18 \times 5 \times 60 = 3{,}456{,}000$ u.m./24 h
(The variant of the biggest losses in the compressed air network)

In order to determine the expenditures with the compressed air, their level is considered as the arithmetic mean of the expenses in the cases of the smallest and biggest losses in the compressed air network:

$$\mathrm{Ch_{ac}}^{\mathrm{med}} = \frac{1{,}920{,}000 + 3{,}456{,}000}{2} = 2{,}688{,}000 \text{ u.m./24h}$$

Knowing that for the budgetary year the achievement of a coal production of 705,600 t is forecasted and the number of working days is of 240, the level of the compressed air unitary expenditures will be of 914.28 u.m/t, calculated by using the relation:

$$\mathrm{c_{aer}} = \frac{\mathrm{Ch_{ac}}^{\mathrm{med}} \times \mathrm{T}}{\mathrm{Q_c}} \tag{15.40}$$

where:

c_{air}—represents the compressed air unitary expenditures afferent to the budgetary year;
$Ch_{ac}{}^{med}$—average expenditures with the compressed air (u.m/day);
T—number of working days of the budgetary year;
Q_c—forecasted coal production of the mine working (t/year).

$$\mathrm{c_{aer}} = \frac{2{,}688{,}000 \times 240}{705{,}600} = 914.28 \text{ u.m./t}$$

The calculus of the expenditures for the electric power consumption for lighting refers to the consumption for the interior and exterior lighting established according to: number of lighting objects and of their unitary power, the simultaneity coefficients of the consumption of electric power for the interior and exterior lighting, the power factor and the coefficient of the network losses. The calculus relation is:

$$Q_{ee} = \frac{1.10}{\cos\ \varphi} \times (K_1 \times P_i + K_2 \times P_e) \quad (15.41)$$

where:

Q_{ee}—represents the electric power consumption for lighting (kWh);
1,10—the coefficient that takes into account the loss of power from the network;
$cos\ \Phi$—the power factor of the network which depends on the number and type of duties (in average of 0.75);
P_i—the nominal power of the interior lighting installation (kW);
P_e—the nominal power of the exterior lighting installation (kW);
K_1,K_2—simultaneity coefficient of the electric power consumption in the network, which in average are: k1 of 0.7 for less than 100 lighting objects used for interior lighting and of 0.65 for more than 100 lighting objects; k2 of 0.74 for less than 100 lighting objects used for exterior lighting and of 0.68 for more than 100 lighting objects.

The nominal power of the lighting installation both for interior and exterior is calculated by taking into account the number of lighting objects, the unitary power of a lighting object and the number of functioning hours.

$$Q_{ee} = \frac{1.10}{\cos\ \phi} \times (K_1 \times P_i + K_2 \times P_e) \quad (15.42)$$

where:

$N_{i,e}$—represents the number of interior and exterior lighting objects;
$Pu_{i,e}$—the power of a interior, exterior lighting objective;
t—the time the lighting object functions in a year (hours);
1,000—transformation of W into kW.

It is assumed that the number of lighting objects used for interior spaces is of 75, each with a power of 75 W, and the time fond that each lighting object functions in a year is of 1,900 h, and the lighting objects used for exterior spaces is of 100, each with a power of 100 W, and the time fond that each lighting object functions in a year is of 3,600 h. By substituting with data in the relation (15.42) it is obtained:

$$P_i = \frac{75 \times 75 \times 1{,}900}{1{,}000} = 10{,}687.50\ \text{kW/year}$$

$$P_e = \frac{100 \times 100 \times 3{,}600}{1{,}000} = 36{,}000\ \text{kW/year}$$

The size of the electric lighting expenditures will be:

$$Ch_{ee} = P \times Q_{ee} = p_{ue} \times \frac{1.10}{\cos\phi} \times (K_1 \times P_i + K_2 \times P_e) \tag{15.43}$$

Knowing that the estimate price of a kWh (pue) is of 450 u.m., by substituting with data the (15.43) relation it is obtained:

$$Ch_{ee} = 450 \times \frac{1.10}{0.75}(0.70 \times 10{,}687.50 + 0.68 \times 36{,}000) = \frac{15{,}820{,}818.75}{0.75} = \\ = 21{,}094{,}425\ \text{u.m./year}$$

Further on the unitary expenditures for the electric power for lighting afferent for the budgetary year can be determined:

$$C_{ee} = \frac{Ch_{ee}}{Q_c} \tag{15.44}$$

By substituting with data the (15.44) relation it is obtained:

$$C_{ee} = \frac{21{,}094{,}425}{705{,}600} = 29.89\ \text{u.m./}t_{carb}$$

The establishment of the level of expenditures for the thermic power consumption used for heating up the administrative-housekeeping spaces has in view the heat consumption for the heating up of that spaces and the cost of a Gcalory.

This heat consumption can be calculated using the following relation:

$$Q_{et} = (\bar{t}_i - \bar{t}_e) \times V_i + P_i \tag{15.45}$$

where:

Q_{et}—represents the consumption of thermic power for heating;
$\bar{t}_i$—average interior temperature to achieve (°C)
$\bar{t}_e$—average exterior temperature considered (°C)
V_i—the interior volumes of buildings that are to be heated (m^3)
P_i—the loss of global heat for the temperature's increase with a degree per 1 m^3 of interior volume considering the nature of the construction (kcal/m^3 degree) and is presented in Table 15.25.

The level of expenditures determined by the heating up of the administrative-housekeeping spaces will be:

Table 15.25 The size of the heat losses coefficient

Type of construction	Value of the coefficient kcal/m^3
Buildings of brickwood or of finished reinforced concrete	40
Buildings of brickwood or of closed unfinished reinforced concrete	45
Temporary wood buildings	50

$$Ch_{et} = p_{ue} \times Q_{et} = p_{uet} \times (\overline{t_i} - \overline{t_e}) \times V_i \times P_i \times T \tag{15.46}$$

where:

p_{uet}—represents the price of a kcalory;
T—number of days in a year as the spaces heating takes place.

Knowing that the average exterior temperature is of –5 °C, the average interior temperature is of 18 °C, the interior volume of the spaces that are to be heated 500 m^3, the heat losses coefficient 40 kcal/m^3, the estimate tariff of a kcal is of 21.8 u.m./kcal and the number of days that the spaces heating is necessary is of 150 days a year, it can be determined the level of expenditures determined by the heating of administrative-housekeeping spaces:

$$Ch_{et} = 21,\ 8 \times [18 - (-5)] \times 500 \times 40 \times 150 = 1{,}504{,}200{,}000 \text{ u.m./year}$$

Further on, the unitary expenses with thermic power afferent to the budgetary year can be determined by using the relation:

$$C_{et} = \frac{Ch_{et}}{Q_c} \tag{15.47}$$

$$C_{et} = \frac{1{,}504{,}200{,}000}{705{,}600} = 2{,}131.80 \text{ u.m./t}$$

The expenditures, determined by the drinking water consumption and the consumption for special purposes, focus on the existence of an uniformity of the water consumption during the working program, the number of employees who consume water, the consumption of water par employee during a shift, the consumption of water for special purposes (maid, showers etc.) and the price of a m^3 of water.

The water consumption is calculated according to the relation:

$$Q_{apa} = K_1 \times (N_s \times A_m + A_{sp}) \tag{15.48}$$

where:

Q_{water}—represents the drinking water consumption for special purposes;
K_1—uniformity coefficient of water consumption during a day (for the mine carboniferous industry = 1.4);
N_s—no. of employees of the mine working;
A_m—water consumption per employee during a day;
A_{sp}—water consumption for special purposes (maid, showers) 1/day.

The size of the expenditures determined by the water consumption will be:

$$\mathrm{Ch_{apa}} = \mathrm{p_{ua}} \times \mathrm{Q_{apa}} = \mathrm{p_{ua}} \times \frac{1}{1,000} \times \mathrm{K_1}\left(\mathrm{N_s} \times \mathrm{A_m} + \mathrm{A_{sp}}\right) \times \mathrm{T} \quad (15.49)$$

where:

Ch_{water}—represents the water consumption expenses;
p_{ua}—tariff per 1 m^3 water;
1,000—transformation from l in m^3;
T—no. of working days in a year.

Knowing that the estimated tariff for a m^3 of water is of 1,100 u.m., the no. of employees of the mine working is of 3,400, the water consumption per employee in a day is of 3 l water, the water consumption for special purposes is of 90,000 l/day, the number of working days is of 240. Then the level of water consumption expenditures can be determined:

$$\begin{aligned}\mathrm{Ch_{water}} &= 1,100 \times \frac{1}{1,000} \times 1.4 \times (3,400 \times 3 + 90,000) \times 240 \\ &= 37,033,920 \text{ u.m./year}\end{aligned}$$

For the budgetary year, the unitary costs are determined by using the formula:

$$\mathrm{C_{water}} = \frac{\mathrm{Ch_{water}}}{\mathrm{Q_c}} \quad (15.50)$$

$$\mathrm{C_{water}} = \frac{37,033,920}{705,600} = 52.48 \text{ u.m./t}$$

Using similar means and also the financial elaborated normative, the four categories of establishment charges (materials for cleaning up, general overhauling of buildings, office supplies etc.) their level per unit of product can be determined.

The model of the unitary manufacturing costs budget drawn up at the level of a mine working for the year N is presented in Table 15.26.

Table 15.26 The unitary costs budget afferent to the "extracted coal" product

Specification	Preliminary year N−1 (thousands u.m.)	Preliminary year N−1 (u.m./t)	Forecasted year N (thousands u.m.)	Forecasted year N (u.m./t)
Quantity (t)	660.62		705.60	
Raw materials and direct materials	6,856,541.83	10,378.29	8,902,449.36	12,616.85
Direct wages	32,464,930.68	49,140.00	36,726,813.88	52,050.47
Taxes for social insurance, unemployment fund afferent to the direct wages	12,985,972.27	19,655.99	14,690,676.00	20,820.11
Electric power	7,395,701.48	11,194.38	9,438,105.60	13,376.00
Technological fuel	209,317.54	316.83	304,614.57	431.71
Fixed means redemption	982,004.00	1,486.39	995,111.00	1,410.30
Total of direct expenses	60,894,467.80	92,171.90	71,057,770.41	100,705.46
Maintenance and running equipment expenses	1,350,000.00	2,043.40	1,350,000.00	1,913.26
Overheads of the department	1,850,000.00	2,800.22	1,850,000.00	2,621.88
General administration expenses	3,599,350.00	5,448.09	3,781,200.00	5,358.84
Total complete cost	67,693,817.80	102,463.62	78,038,970.41	110,599.45

References

Baranger P (2003) Management et techniques de gestion. Editions Sirey, Paris

Bouquin H (2006) Le contrôle de gestion. PUF, Paris

Burlaud A, Simion C (2003) Comptabilité de gestion. Editions Collection Vuibert, Paris

Charreaux G (2001) Gestion financiére. Editions Litec, Paris

Charreaux G (2005) Synthese, economie et comptabilité. Editions Litec, Paris

Courtois A, Pillet M, Martin C (2006) Gestion de productions. Les Editions D'organisation, Paris

Cuyaubére T (2001) Contrôle de gestion. Édition La Villeguérin, Paris

Decoster D (2000) Management accounting: a decision emphasis. Irwin Editions, Homewood, IL/Boston, MA

Dima IC (2013a) Organisational strategies—a systemic approach—on the example of the automotive industry. Lambert Academic Publishing, Saarbrucken

Dima IC (2013b) Industrial production management in flexible manufacturing systems. IGI Global, Hersey

Dima IC, Grabara J (2009) Budzetowanie. Wydawnictwa Wydzialu Zarzadzania Politechniki Czestochowskiej, Czestochowa

Dima IC, Man M (2013) Budgeting and management control in industrial companies. Lambert Academic Publishing, Saarbrucken

Dupuy Y (2001) Manuel de contrôle de gestion. Dunod, Paris

Gervais M (2001) Contrôle de gestion et stratégie de l'entreprise. Éditions Economic, Paris

Lanzel P (2005) Controle de gestion et budgets. Éditions Litec, Paris

Chapter 16
Models Used in Production Quality Management

16.1 The Concept of Quality Management

The perspective generalising the advanced production systems that use modern managerial methods for the manufacturing process requires that certain new demands are met in the continuous improvement of the production quality and products in automotive companies. Thus, reaching some high quality standards becomes the primary goal that conditions the smooth performance of the companies' activities in the branch. The importance of the approach to develop and implement the quality strategy is in this context more than obvious. Organically integrated into the overall strategy of the company, the strategy in the field of quality provides the materialisation of the directions concerning the size of the company's future performances, the abilities to build and exploit the competitive advantages and to determine the behavioural procedures on different markets.

The ISO quality standards of the 9000 series require the precise definition of the policy in the field of quality, which means a set of rules and medium-term targets set forth based on the major goals guiding the quality strategy. J. Juran identified four distinct theories, based on which the company's strategies and policies can be formulated in the field of quality: the theory of capability, according to which the emphasis is placed on the appropriate performance of the production process; the theory of competitiveness, which focuses on the goals of attracting the customers and providing their loyalty; the theory of use, which gives importance to satisfying the consumers' variable needs, by diversifying the offer of goods and services; the theory of maximum performance, according to which the company seeks to become leader through the quality of products and services provided.

Therefore, the process to prepare the quality strategy in the automotive companies should be subordinated to the following requirements: the integration into the strategic vision and company's mission; meeting the social needs and customers' demands (by removing the possibilities of occurrence and perpetuation of defects); the establishment of the optimum levels for the quality characteristics (in agreement

I.C. Dima, M. Man, *Modelling and Simulation in Management*, Contributions to Management Science, DOI 10.1007/978-3-319-16592-9_16

with the requirements related to the competitiveness of products on the markets); stimulating the employees' involvement in the processes of continuous quality improvement, etc.

The main components of the quality strategy—goals, options, resources and achievement deadlines show particularities that are specific to the field which they adapt to.

If the strategic goals related to quality must respond to the same requirements as the goals of the overall strategy—realism, comprehensibility, stimulating character, feasibility—the specific materialising way is based on the principle of satisfying the customer. This idea originally emerged in some marketing studies (its promoter being Robert Wood), but it imposed as strategic goal in the quality field in the original form of Theodore Levitte. He considers that one is to seek the customer's satisfaction and not the production of goods, which is done by creating excellent products, by improving their quality and efficiently using the resources.

In the process of establishing the goals, a series of methods can be used, of which the most common ones are: Hoshin method, management through goals or the "goal deployment" method.

The Hoshin method was introduced in Japan in the sixth decade by Bridgestone Tire Company and is a "a cascade process" by means of which the strategy translates into goals. Unlike the classical method of management through goals popularised in the USA, this method—based on the Japanese Hoshin Kanri principle—has the meaning of a "management of objectives" or a policy management (which explains its spreading under the English name of "policy deployment"). The goals of quality are originally based at the top-management level, within the overall strategy, following to develop vertically in the next stage by applying the so-called "catch-ball" principle. This involves providing the feedback both in the process of adjusting the goals and in that of preparing the action plans. The main advantages of this method are: ensuring the involvement of all employees from any hierarchic level in designing the goals of quality; the ability to achieve the goals based on the analysis of performances during the previous period; providing the realism and palpable character of objectives by materialisation in the Hoshin action plans; the inter-department approach provides the possibility to "mix" the desiderata of various participants in the company's processes.

Those companies where the authoritarian management style is predominant achieve a diffusion of the goals "from the top to the bottom". This approach gave rise to the method of management through goals based on the thorough determination of goals to the level of performers and by correlating the rewards with the degree of fulfilling the set targets. A horizontal development of the goals occurs in the participating companies, starting from the customers' needs. Basically, the management through goals requires the exact knowledge of both the own goals, and of the abilities to detail and combine the subordinates' goals (optimisation of quality parameters is however uncertain in singularly using this approach).

The "goal deployment" method allows taking into account customers' requirements in the field of quality on the one hand, and the correlation of fundamental goals with those corresponding to some different hierarchic levels on the other hand, through some consultations performed in both directions. Unlike the management through goals, by "goal deployment", one aims to reinforce some strategies to achieve the goals before completing them, requiring the removal of the unrealistic goals. The success of using the method is conditioned by promoting the participatory style of management, by the ability to trans-functionally achieve the orientation towards the customer and by keeping all company's processes under control.

Japanese companies also implement other methodologies to prepare the goals and appropriate action plans. For example, in the Komatsu company—which manufactures machine-tools—at the beginning of the year, every employee receives a book containing: the chairman's annual goals (making some quality products under the conditions of using some modern technologies); the factory manager's goals (details the chairman's goals—assimilation of the new technologies to achieve the competitive products, for example); the department manager's goals (materialises the goals on the higher level such as the optimisation of logistical flows related to the introduction of the new technique by the "production" department); foreman's goals (they are established by every foreman in collaboration with their subordinates, being materialised in specific actions to achieve the objectives established by the department manager).

The options to put into practice the quality strategies covers a wide range of possibilities to achieve the goals such as: improvement of the constructive and technological design of products; compliance with the content of standards, rules, legislative regulations; preparation of updated technical and technological documentations to define, release and make the products and services; inspection of how to perform the production process in its various stages and determining the level of the technical features of the parts and subassemblies; performance of tests to check the compliance in various stages of manufacturing the products; achievement of quality classes in relation to the demands and requirements specific to the segments of consumers; the analysis of the behaviour of products in operation and improvement of technical support services and post-sale repairs; preparation and distribution of the instructions on the assembly, commissioning and operation of the complex products; qualification and continuous adaptation of the company's staff training to the requirements imposed by the target-levels of the activity and product quality, etc. These elements, along with others the importance of which is different in relation to the concept of managerial teams concerning the quality actually represent just as many ways to improve the quality of products and services.

Finally, the deadlines and resources assigned to achieve the strategic alternatives vary from one company to another in connection with the typological classification and level of complexity of the adopted quality strategies. If we refer to the first aspect, one can observe that the quality strategies are often addressed in literature from different angles. Thus, in the first concept, the strategies of this field are classified in the large family of competitive strategies, because the mission of quality is nowadays that of building solid competitive advantages—as it has been shown. The configuration of the quality strategies therefore derives from the provisions of the company's overall strategy. Thus, those managers who adopt

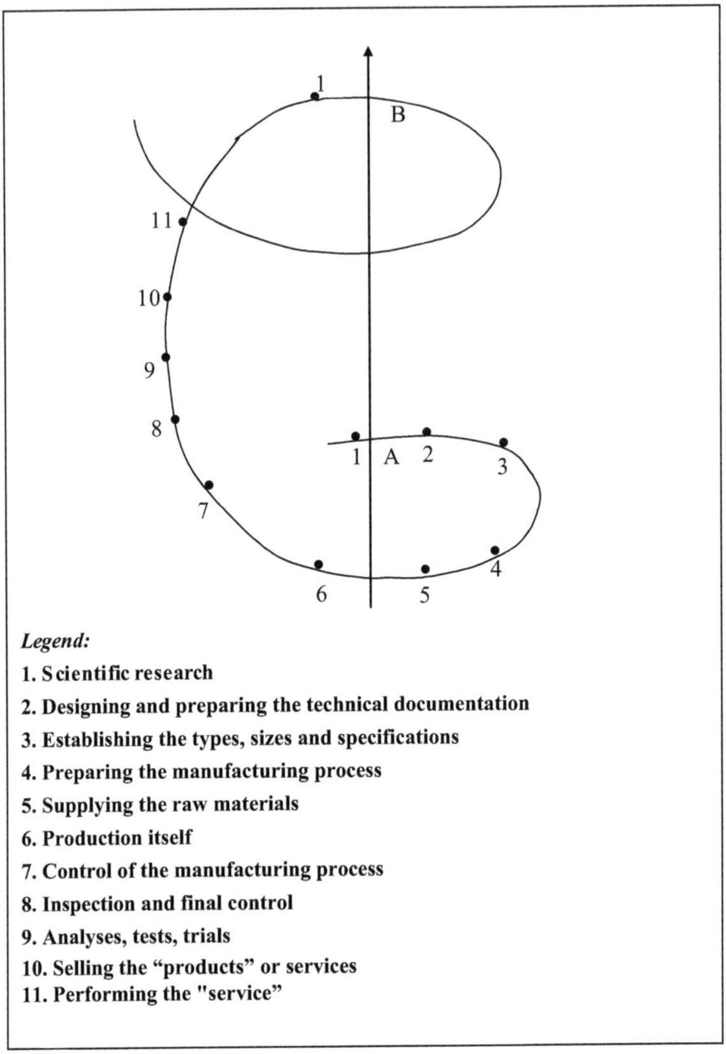

Fig. 16.1 Spiral of quality

aggressive strategies to penetrate some new market segments focus on the high quality as a guarantee of competitiveness, by using a global approach covering the range of all activities located on the "spiral of quality" (Fig. 16.1).

Considering the qualitative level of products as a distinct strategic variable that dictates the orientation of the product policy within the marketing mixture, the specialists in this field associate the quality strategies to the strategic alternatives regarding the product ranges and renewal degree, resulting the following systematisation: strategies to adapt the quality of products to the requirements of the market segments (also often called "crenel" or "niche" strategies); the strategies of differentiation by quality from the offers of the other competitors; strategy of diversification by quality, assuming the addition of new fields of activity oriented by quality classes or located at higher quality levels compared to the competitors; the strategy of quality improvement usually adopted in the situations where those companies have solid positions on the market.

In the same context, referring to the product strategy, the American authors Kotler and Dubois delimit the alternatives of quality improvement through the intensive way (by the favourable variation of the characteristics of products) and through the extensive way (by increasing the number of characteristics of the quality of products to achieve, for example, an increased safety in operation). Deepening this systematisation, Phillip Kotler underlies within another reference paper in the field of marketing a third way of improvement—"the strategy of searching a style" through quality wherein the focus drifts from the operational properties of products to the aesthetic ones (for example, releasing some more attractive models of the basic products).

The analysis of the typology of quality strategies from the perspective of the coverage area allows the delimitation of the following three large categories: the overall strategy of quality is based on the precepts of the "total quality management" and assumes the manifestation of some sustained preoccupations to achieve the quality in all phases of a product, including that of the operation by the beneficiary (a mandatory condition of applying the overall quality strategy is to write the "manual of quality" and the documentation related to the quality system"); the procedural quality strategy which, in agreement with the available resources and specific goals, it focuses on the quality levels in the scope of some actions or activities, such as: technological design, marketing-supply, production of analyses and tests, storage and delivery of products, etc. (in this case it is a matter about gradually going through the so-called "spiral of quality"—Fig. 16.1); the strategy focused on the costs of quality, which is based on the principle of maximising the company's profit by reducing the expenses imputable to the non-quality of products and allocation of additional financial resources to the activities of improving it (the strategy involves the thorough management of costs regarding the quality—the structure of costs, analysis of expenses for each category of cost, the correlations between the costs of quality and the indicators of economic efficiency).

The recent history of quality management (1980–1990s) marks the increase in the concerns to underlie some functional, interrogative quality strategies. According to certain authors, the total quality would be such a strategy. Thus, according to the definition formulated by AFCERQ, "the total quality is a set of principles and methods organised in an overall strategy aiming to mobilise the entire enterprise in order to get a better customer satisfaction at the lowest possible cost." In a similar concept, for a company, the total quality would be a policy subordinated to the overall strategy by means of which it is aimed to improve the products and services, as well as the company's quality of operation and goals, in relation to the competitive environment.

Another integrating strategy is considered to be the excellence, the coordinates of which would the quality, efficiency and time saving. The concept of excellence was introduced by the management consultants Thomas J. Peters and Robert H. Waterman jr., authors of the paper "In Search of Excellence", where the causes of the success of the best managed companies in the USA are analysed (they were selected based on some indicators, such as the average recovery of capitals, growth in the share capital and rate of innovations). In the financial environments, the concept of excellence was approached both in relation to the principles of the total quality management ("the forefront quality" is the fundamental principle associated with excellence) and distinctly as a quality strategy. In this vision, excellence is synonymous to the success in competition, by making certain higher quality products under the conditions of efficiency which would be provided to customers in the shortest possible time. The American Institute for Management establishes a set of recommendations to achieve the excellence, namely: the development of the process improvement strategy, reduction of the production costs and manufacturing cycle time, satisfaction of consumers' exigencies by using the techniques of improving the processes (JIT, "zero defects" total quality), implementation of the "quality system" by taking into account all stages to make the products, establishing the partnership relations with sub-suppliers in order to increase the quality of delivered products, formulating the quality policy, etc. The specialists in quality consider it is only natural that the focus of strategic objectives is on excellence: "excellence is part of the aspirations of each of us. Who accepts today the idea of products or services as excellence does not have an understandable behaviour…".

Last but not least, one should not omit the special interest shown lately both theoretically and especially pragmatically to conceptualise and implement the KAIZEN strategy. For this purpose, it is necessary to specify the place of the concerns for quality within each of the three dimensions of KAIZEN. Thus, regarding the perception of global strategy, it may be shown that in spite of the trans-functional character, the major object aimed at through KAIZEN is the permanent improvement of the managerial system quality. On the other hand, relative to the operational dimension, it is obvious that the KAIZEN strategy circumscribes a set of methods and techniques borrowed from the quality management and addressed in an innovative vision, systematically integral (KANBAN, "zero defects", the total quality control—"Company Wide Quality Control", the circles of quality, customer orientation, total productive maintenance, etc.). If we refer to the third dimension of KAIZEN—the human side, then the overlap with the goals of any quality strategy is almost complete, because the quality improvement cannot ignore this component and aims to create the favourable premises of an organisational climate appropriate to the active participation of employees in the process of increasing the performances achieved by the company.

Regardless of the volume of the action to prepare the strategy that underlies the option for an overall trans-functional approach or by a simple procedural strategy, it is mentioned that the quality strategy represents the essential component of the total quality management.

According to J. Kelda, the total quality management is a three-dimensional concept, a management philosophy based on a certain logic and involves the use of a set of methods and specific techniques. Although it is the most difficult to perceive, the philosophical dimension of TQM involves a series of principles that set out the achievement of quality objectives (in relation to this aspect, Kelada identifies four elements: recognition of the customer's essential role, orientation towards the workers and processes that condition the overall quality, concern for increasing the profitability, engaging the external partners to the achievement of total quality).

The logic of TQM involves a systemic vision in that field in compliance with which the quality concept does not exclusively relate to the characteristics of the products/services, but to a larger extent, it aims at the activity and processes performed by the company. Therefore, every activity or worker brings its or their own contribution in achieving the total quality, each representing a "ring" that can strengthen or weaken the "spiral of quality" (Fig. 16.1).

The technical dimension of TQM refers to the operational side, amounting a set of specific methods and techniques investigating the practical achievement of strategies to improve the quality. The literature abounds with classifications of the methods used in the field of quality. However, the most important systematisation takes into account the nature of the problems to be solved (quality diagnosis, prevention of the occurrence of defects, quality improvement, quality prediction, etc.). Of all methods and techniques used in the quality strategies, we list only a few of the most commonly used, namely: statistical techniques of production control, value analysis, graphical representations (the cause-effect diagram, the Pareto diagram, histograms, control graphs, etc.), the FMECA method (failure modes, effects and criticality analysis), total productive maintenance, the "zero defects" programs, QFS (Quality Function Department), the Deming cycle, the Taguchi method to improve the product manufacturing concepts and processes, etc.

The implementation of the evolved methods to improve the quality in a broader framework set by the content of the KAIZEN strategy must not be a temporary step (the parallel between the continuous quality improvement and a "marathon" race the performance of which differs from the "100 m dash" race is suggestive in this regard). In automotive companies, a special problem is the need to get some high compliance quality levels, a process conditioned by a set of factors, such as: the quality of raw matters and materials, technologies used, the level of employees' qualification, performance of fitted equipment, organisation of production, etc. By its definition, the compliance is probably the most important quality attribute that reflects the degree of concordance between the product properties and specifications of the projects or standards.

The key to solving any problem related to the compliance quality lies in correctly determining the tolerances allowed to the theoretical values determined by calculations, taking into account that the tolerances that are too "narrow" attract the considerable increase of costs, while the tolerances that are too "wide" allow the reduction of the product quality levels. The compromise solution was determined by the specialist Genichi Taguchi, who developed the statistical tools to substantiate the tolerance limits that are equally distributed in relation to the nominal-value. Using the Taguchi method in the quality improvement strategy has enabled the Japanese manufacturers to reach some compliance levels of over 95 %. In line with

Taguchi's thinking, Japanese managers consider that, even after a labour process has corresponded to the prescribed specifications, the costs of quality can be further reduced by fading the variations registered at the level of the relevant characteristics.

16.2 Model of Production Quality Based on the Taguchi Technique

Since 1973, the propagation of Taguchi's original concept regarding the quality improvement has determined significant progresses in the field. Taguchi's name is increasingly mentioned alongside those of the "titans" Edward Deming, Kaoru Ishikawa or Joseph M. Juran. Although it initially recorded remarkable successes within the Japanese and American companies, the use of the Taguchi method becomes more familiar in countries like the United Kingdom and Canada, followed by another group of developed countries of Western Europe. Specifying the place occupied by Taguchi's approach in the panoply of the means used for the quality control and improvement requires the more or less chronological approach of the evolution of concepts regarding quality (Fig. 16.2).

As it results from the graphical representation, Taguchi's contribution is quartered at the levels five and six. The final quantity of products and necessary costs to acquire it are conditioned by the values defined in the design stage, as well as by the manufacturing process adjustment parameters (temperatures, electric power supplies, compression forces, etc.).

Taguchi's idea exceeds the concept of guaranteeing the quality in a narrow sense in that it states that the combined efforts of quality insurance and inspection lead in the field of concept to mastering the "off-line" quality, and in that of performance, to an "online" control in itself. Thus, it is shown that achieving the quality starting from the design stage requires efforts to design the parameters of the manufacturing processes that aim to establish the optimum level of each parameter, so that the product would be desensitised in relation to the action of disturbing factors. In other words, the originality of Taguchi's strategy consists in that it does not want to remove these parasite factors (called by Taguchi "noise factors"), but only to minimise their impact on quality, by determining that combination of parameters mitigating the effects of some undesirable causes.

In these circumstances, it is obvious that when the production quality proves to be robust (meaning insensitive to environmental influences), the premises of improving the manufacturing processes are ensured, through specific KAIZEN-type developments (in small steps), meaning: suppressing the products under manufacturing and safety stocks for the finished products; decrease of the serial number changing times (SMED method); assimilation of the "JIT" system, introduction of computer aided manufacturing, etc.

	Level	Concept	Targets
	7	Quality Function Deployment (QFD) • Step by step disclaimer of the customer's wish in terms of specifications and actions	Customer
Taguchi's Contribution	6	"Quality loss" function • Quantifying the quality in financial terms	Economic efficiency
Taguchi's Contribution	5	Quality starting with the design stage • Optimising the parameters to reach robustness • Functionality acquired with minimum costs	Company
	4	Training all collaborators • Changing the individual attitudes and behaviours	Employees
	3	Ensuring the quality involved in all functions • Design, manufacture and suppliers, sales, service	Functional entities and the relations between them
	2	Ensuring the quality in production • Statistical process control (SPC) • Warning devices (Poka yoke)	Manufacturing processes
	1	Final inspection • Sampling from finished products • Problem solving activities	The product

Fig. 16.2 The evolution of concepts on quality

In essence, the Taguchi concept has two distinct sides: the first once concerning the "function—loss" of quality and quantification of non-quality costs; the second one states the actual way to solve the quality problems, by using special statistical methods. The philosophy inspiring the mathematical calculations of underlying the "function—loss" is based on relating the quality to that feature that avoids the financial losses not just for the manufacturer while performing the manufacturing process, but also for the user and even for the company as a whole. Should the non-quality costs usually mean additional manufacturing costs (scraps, remedies,

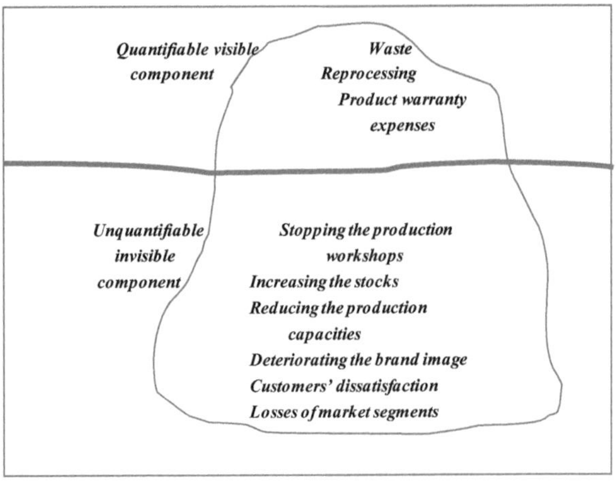

Fig. 16.3 The iceberg of non-quality costs

etc.), according to Taguchi's concept, non-quality is the "loss induced to the society as of shipping the product" and also includes a series of more or less quantifiable collateral components, such as: stopping the production workshops, increasing the stocks, degrading the brand image, pollution and related harmful effects, losses of materials, power and labour resulting from making some unusable products, etc. (Fig. 16.3).

Therefore, any deviation from the objective results in a loss, even though that deviation is within the limits set by the tolerance range. Therefore, the authentic way to minimise the quality losses does not lie in establishing certain "compliant/incompliant" limits for the specifications of products or processes, but in reducing their variation in relation to the nominal values. Assessing the performances of the products or manufacturing processes must take into account both the degree of achieving the set objectives, as well as the undesirable outputs to be avoided. For this purpose, Taguchi introduces a synthetic indicator of performance, which he calls the Signal/Noise ratio (S/N) and simultaneously takes into account the unreachable desired value (the average of the features to optimise) and the variability of the values of the measured characteristics (dispersion) that must be minimised.

The higher the algebraic value of the S/N ratio is, the lower the losses are, and therefore the performance of the product performance or process that must be optimised shall be higher.

The mathematical expressions given by Taguchi for the "quality loss function" and the Signal/Noise ratio differ in relation to the categories of criteria regarding the quality which are subject to optimisation: target-criteria (for which the optimum corresponds to the nominal value); criteria to be minimised (for example the wear of a product, aspect defects, contribution of cast parts, etc.); criteria that must be maximised (hourly yield, reliability, resistance of a material to rupture, lifespan of a product, etc.).

The "quality loss" for a target—criterion is:

$$L(y) = k \cdot (y - y_N)^2 \tag{16.1}$$

where:

$L(y)$ represents the unit loss (stated in monetary units)
y the value of the measured feature
y_N rated value (meaning the target value)
k the constant of the loss (which can be determined based on the information arising from the retails market).

If the loss due to a deviation A_0 compared to the target value is P_0, then k can be calculated with the formula:

$$k = \frac{P_0}{{A_0}^2} \tag{16.2}$$

The function (16.1) is a simple approximation and not a rule. In this respect, it is useful to remember that J. Tinbergen analysed the loss on another occasion (related to the variation of unemployment and prices), by using a similar equation:

where:

$$L = a \cdot (u - u^*)^2 \tag{16.3}$$

a is the unit loss
u^* rated value
u existing level.

By means of the loss function, Taguchi shows that loss is a continuous function of the deviation in relation to the target-value, thus proving that loss is not caused by simply exceeding certain tolerance limits, which are often established empirically. The converted expression of the "loss function" for a batch of parts (or sample of products) is:

$$L(y) = k \cdot \left[s^2 + (\overline{y} - y_N)^2\right] \tag{16.4}$$

where:

$L(y)$ represents the unit loss, stated in monetary units
s standard deviation of the measured values (y_1, y_2 ,...., y_n)
$\overline{y}$ the arithmetic average of the measured values (y_1, y_2 ,...., y_n)
y_N the measured value
k constant of loss.

This transformed form of the expression $L(y)$ is the advantage that it highlights very clearly the variables that intervene in minimising the loss and namely the dispersion (s^2) of the values measured around the averages and $(\overline{y} - y_N)^2$ deviations of averages compared to the rated value.

Regarding this ratio of Signal/Noise (measured in decibels) for the target—criterion, Taguchi performs a number of statistical-mathematical calculations and afterwards he proposes the formula:

$$S/N = 10\ \log\ \left[\left(\overline{y}^2/s^2\right) - 1/n\right]\quad [\mathrm{dB}] \tag{16.5}$$

where:

S/N represents the Signal/Noise ratio
n the number of measurements done.

For the particular case of a target-criterion with positive and negative values, the calculation of the ratio of Signal/Noise uses the relation:

$$S/N = -10 \log s^2 \quad [\mathrm{dB}] \tag{16.6}$$

The calculation of the dispersion around the average is meaningless in this case, as both positive and negative values can be assigned to the measured characteristics. The "minus" sign preceding the logarithm in the relation (16.6) proves again that the algebraic value of the S/N ratio shall be even greater as the variance (s^2) shall be lower.

For a criterion that needs to be minimised, the function of quality loss has the following transformed form:

$$L(y) = k \cdot \left(s^2 + \overline{y}^2\right) \tag{16.7}$$

It is the case of zero nominal value features. Graphically, "the loss function" is shaped like a half of a parable that is far more sensitive to the average value than to the scatter of measured values (under the conditions of such criteria, it is preferable to work with the smallest average value and a significant standard deviation rather than adopt the reverse solution). The requirements of loss minimisation translates by minimising the amount $s^2 + \overline{y}^2$.

The ratio of Signal/Noise for the criteria to be minimised is also expressed in decibels and is determined based on the relationship:

$$S/N = -10 \log \left(s^2 + \overline{y}^2\right) \quad [\mathrm{dB}] \tag{16.8}$$

The case of a quality criterion that must be maximised is assimilated to the features to be optimised with the (theoretically) infinite target. In this case, the graphical representation of the "loss-function" takes the form of a hyperbole, and the simplified mathematical formula for calculating the unitary loss is:

$$L(y) = k \cdot \frac{1}{\overline{y}^2}\left[1 + 3\left(s^2/\overline{y}^2\right)\right] \quad (16.9)$$

The sensitivity of the "loss-function" in the case of criteria to be maximised is higher for the averages of the measured values compared to their dispersion (the situation where high average values are registered is therefore preferred, even though the standard deviation is important). Therefore, the requirement to minimise the loss requires in this case the minimisation of the expression: $(1/\overline{y})\left(1 + 3s^2/\overline{y}^2\right)$.

The expression used to calculate the ratio of Signal/Noise takes the following form:

$$S/N = -10\log\left[\left(1/\overline{y}^2\right)\left(1 + 3s^2/\overline{y}^2\right)\right] \quad [\text{dB}] \quad (16.10)$$

Since the mathematical substantiation of the Signal/Noise ratio derives for any type of quality criterion from the "loss function", that indicator can be interpreted as a "bridge" between the technical approach and economic approach of quality. Taguchi's major contribution is located exactly on the border between the two approaches. The Japanese specialist combines the engineering techniques with the statistical ones, in order to reach a rapid improvement of the quality costs under the conditions of establishing the optimal configurations at the level of designing the products and manufacturing processes. The concept of "designing the parameters" actually consists in searching the most appropriate combinations of the controllable factors able to minimise the influence of the disturbance factors.

The Taguchi method is actually a remarkable improvement of the classical method of the plans of experiences, which at the beginning of the century were grounded by the statisticians Ronald Fisher and Jacques Hadamard. According to their view, a plan of experiences is defined as sequences of organised tests intended to quantify with maximum precision the possible influences exerted by different parameters on the performances of the analysed system. As it shall be shown, a plan of experiences can be rapidly transposed into an array format. Although with a high potential of practical utility, the statistical techniques developed by Fisher and Hadamard have experienced a low industrial spread, mainly determined by the extreme complexity of their implementation. Taguchi's great merit lies in the effort to develop some standard tools that simplify the experimental approach and both equipped with a very wide range of application, meaning "a collection" of orthogonal fractional experience arrays and a set of "accessories"—triangular tables and linear graphs (that facilitate the study of possible interactions between factors or make it possible to adapt the standard arrays to specific situations). The familiarisation with Taguchi's tools requires the appeal to a few simple notions of the industrial statistics.

Table 16.1 Standard orthogonal experience array (seven factors with two levels)

	Tested factors							
No. of test	A	B	C	D	E	F	G	The result of the test
1	1	1	1	1	1	1	1	R1
2	1	1	1	2	2	2	2	R2
3	1	2	2	1	1	2	2	R3
4	1	2	2	2	2	1	1	R4
5	2	1	2	1	2	1	2	R5
6	2	1	2	2	1	2	1	R6
7	2	2	1	1	2	2	1	R7
8	2	2	1	2	1	1	2	R8

Thus, a full plan of experiences analyses all the possible combinations of the levels of tested factors. The factorial plans of experiences allow the extraction of a volume of information that is almost of equal relevance to those obtained based on an equivalent complete plan, under the considerable reduction in the number of tests performed (and therefore of the time consumption and costs related to the experimentation). The orthogonality of a fractioned factorial plan is that feature allowing the isolation of individual effects caused by the simultaneously tested factors, in various conditions. Basically, in order to meet the orthogonality condition, each level of a factor included into the experience plan must combine with each level corresponding to the other factors and this within an equal number of times (Table 16.1).

The array of experiences in the table above includes a column for each of the seven factors (A, B, C, D, E, F, G), which shall be successively analysed and a line each for the tests performed. The two levels of each factor are symbolised by the numbers "1" and "2". During the first test, all factors are adjusted at level "1", and the result measured is R1.

The orthogonality of this array can be easily proved if the actual way to combine the first two factors (A and B) are analysed, to start with. When A is adjusted at level "1" (the tests with the numbers 1, 2, 3, 4), B is located twice at level "1" (tests 1 and 2) and twice at level "2" (tests 3 and 4); also when A is switched to level "2" (the tests 5, 6, 7 and 8), B is yet adjusted twice at level 1 (the tests 5 and 6) and twice at level "2" (the tests 7 and 8). Consequently, when the average results for A level "1" (meaning $A_1 = \frac{1}{4}(R1 + R2 + R3 + R4)$) respectively for A at level "2" (meaning $A_2 = \frac{1}{4}(R5 + R6 + R7 + R8)$), it is clear that the effect of B intervenes with the same weight between A_1 and A_2.

In an orthogonal array, this method of combination persists for any couple consisting of two factors.

As an example, Table 16.2 represents an array with four factors and three levels that are part of Taguchi's standard "collection" and meets the orthogonality condition.

To the extent wherein a plan of experience all possible combinations of factors meets the orthogonality property, it may be deemed that their effects are

Table 16.2 Orthogonal Taguchi array (four factors with three levels)

No. of test	Controlled factors			
	A	B	C	D
1	1	1	1	1
2	1	2	2	2
3	1	3	3	3
4	2	1	2	3
5	2	2	3	1
6	2	3	1	2
7	3	1	3	2
8	3	2	1	3
9	3	3	2	1

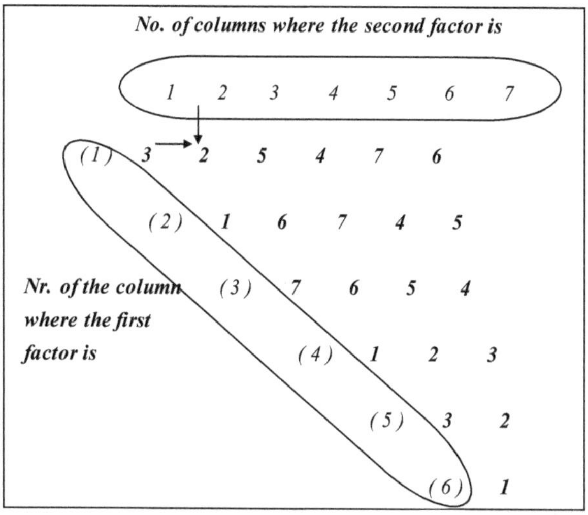

Fig. 16.4 Taguchi's triangular table

independent. However, there are sometimes situations where the interactions between factors are obvious, meaning the effect of a factor depends on the level of another factor subject to the analysis. In this case, a separate column is reserved in the array of experiences to calculate the interactions (this column is not randomly chosen, but it is chosen by means of the triangular tables prepared by Taguchi for each standard array).

Such a table is represented in Fig. 16.4 and serves for determining the interactions for a matrix with seven factors and eight tests (Table 16.1). Because factor A has the first column in the experience matrix, while B has column 2, then we find the column to be reserved to for the interaction "AB" (column 3) at the intersection of line (1) (corresponding to column 1 distributed to factor A) and column 2 (of factor B).

Taguchi however shows that "we must sufficiently reflect in order to determine whether the interaction is considered important enough to be provided with a column in the experience array used". The authors balances the large number of tests required to accurately quantify the interactions with the relevance of the results that must effectively contribute to improving the process under the conditions of a limited budget. The industrial practice comes to support Taguchi's conclusion that it is often more advantageous to increase the number of the studied factors than to stress on the problem of the interactions (which sometimes register "tolerable" values).

A symbol is assigned to each standard experience array. For example, L_8 (2^7) describes an array of eight tests (lines) and seven factors (columns) for two levels which belong to each factor. Similarly, another array shall be symbolised L_9 (3^4), meaning it contains four factors with three levels and nine tests. Moreover, composite symbols can be created for the arrays which contain factors with a variable number of levels. L_{18} ($2^1 \times 3^7$) means a plan of experiences with 18 tests (lines), a column (a factor) for two levels and seven columns (factors) with three levels. Although it is not at the reach of non-specialists, the effort to substantiate the standard arrays of experiences would have probably not been as worthy if it had been deprived of the practical devices that allow the extension of the scope of Taguchi's method to the quasi-totality of actual situations encountered in industrial practice. Thus, besides the triangular tables which we have already mentioned, the author creates the linear graphs the purpose of which is to facilitate the use of standard arrays. A linear graph is actually the graphical representation of a triangular table. Each standard array is provided with just as many linear graphs as potential combinations of the distributions may occur. In Fig. 16.5, the linear graphs related to the array L_8 are represented.

The use of linear graphs is based on a few simple rules, such as: the analysed factors are related to the circles; the number of the column reserved for the calculation of the interaction of factors corresponds to the segment of connection between circles; the number next to the circles and those on the segments joining them are related to the columns in the experience array. For example, if factors A and B in the array of experiences L_8 are provided to the columns with the numbers 2 and 4 (represented by the circles 2 and 4 on graph (1) in Fig. 16.5), the number of the column assigned for measuring the interaction AB—column 6—originates from the connection segment joining the circles 2 and 4.

However, the industrial practice proves that using the triangular tables for the same purpose (quantification of the interactions between factors) allows a higher generality level and an increased safety. The major reason of the call to "Taguchi accessories"—triangular tables and linear graphs—is however linked to the need to

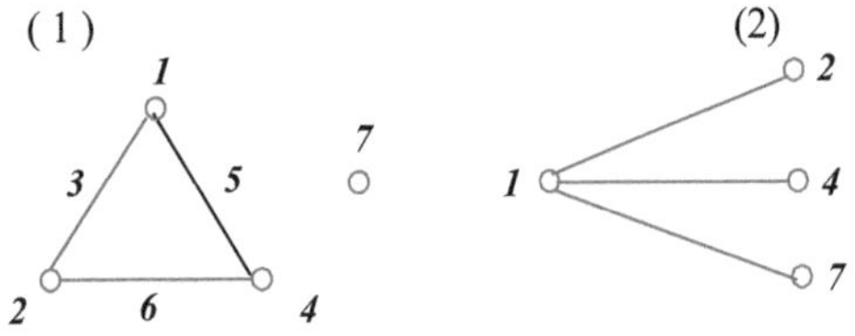

Fig. 16.5 The linear graphs related to the array L_8

deal with particular situations where the standard arrays cannot be used without operating some additional processes. The insertion of four-level factors into the two-level arrays or the integration of two-level factors into the three-level arrays represent only two of the examples of the procedures to adapt the standard plans of experiences to specific needs. The development of the possibilities of adequacy of the standard arrays was what allowed Taguchi to trivialise the classical techniques of the plans of experiences, transforming the latter into statistical tools available to all non-specialist engineers or technicians. The familiarisation with the "mechanisms" and principles of operating the practical devices represents the "ABC" of the Taguchi method. Assimilating the pragmatic methods to efficiently conduct an experiment is the major prerequisite to exploit the entire power of the Taguchi plans of experiences.

Using the Taguchi method to optimise a product/manufacturing process therefore requires the following steps to be taken: to define the goal of the experiment and choose the features to be optimised. Setting the goals actually involves determining the subjects to be optimised and, at this stage, the literature recommends a series of techniques—Ishikawa diagram, the diagram of major causes, comparison in pairs—in order to select a small group of influential factors containing the "guilty ones", from a number of possible and often important causes. Regarding the features to be optimised, it is important to specify the desired values (target criterion to be minimised or maximised), measurement methods (size of the sample, number of tests, number of measurements for testing, etc.), as well as the prioritisation should simultaneous optimisation be searched for more than one features, etc. Choosing the criteria that should be optimised represents the sine-qua-non condition to design a reliable experiment. As a general rule, it is recommended to select those criteria that are directly related with the energy—whichever this would be and in any possible form—used in the system studied. If such a direct connection is not obvious, the need to quantify the possible interactions between the effects of the modified factors shall be taken into account; to choose the factors and establish the levels which are subject to testing. The condition that should have been followed in the process of selecting the quality criteria is encountered at this stage, and namely the detention of those factors that are related to the energy used in the system. To better understand such a rule, we believe it is useful to exemplify a few of the "possible forms of energy". Mechanical energy: The force to drive the wheels, the step depth, feed rate, lubricating method, etc. (in a machining process), the deformation depth, thickness of the processed material (in a stamping process), etc.; the chemical energy of the processed materials—chemical composition, crystalline structure, etc.; the thermal energy—cooling or heating the processed areas, acceleration or deceleration of chemical reactions, etc.; electrical, hydraulic, thermodynamic energy, etc. Therefore, those forms of energy shall be analysed, which are relevant to the manufacturing process of a product for its operation. Regarding the number of controlled factors, it is obvious that increasing them is directly related to the reliability of the experiment. However, the size of the budget allocated to the measurements must be taken into account when adopting this decision. In any case, when a first experiment is performed to select the factors, it is preferable to limit the number of levels to two for each factor, without proceeding to testing the possible interactions so that the size of the plan of experiences would be a reasonable one, as far as possible. Several considerations are required regarding the choice of the levels of factors to be tested. They must be far enough from each other in order to avoid the risks to record the effects which differ very little and interpret the results incorrectly. During the performance of an experiment, it is sometimes very difficult to proceed with changing the levels of some different factors (for example, in a heat treatment furnace, it is necessary to wait for the stabilisation of the temperature exchanger in order to vary this latter factor). For these reasons, it is advantageous to provide those factors presenting difficulties in changing the levels with the three columns from the left in the Taguchi experience plans, knowing that they are provided with less variations of the levels for all the tests that are performed; to select the experience array corresponding to the goal of the experiment. The lowest plan of experiences that is most consistent with the goals of the experiment shall be chosen. For this purpose, the total number of the freedom levels is calculated, which is related to the array of experiences as the sum between the freedom levels related to factors (established in relation to their levels) and freedom levels of the interactions to be analysed. In connection with this last point, we recall Taguchi's opinion which is also confirmed by the industrial practice, according to which it is more advantageous—under the conditions of a given budget—to boost the number of the controlled factors than to unjustifiably detail the problem of measuring the interactions between factors (which most often record negligible values). In this context, Taguchi recommends the following approach: The performance of an experiment to select the influential factors, followed when needed by one or more experiments for purification; to perform the selection experiment. This starts from the hypothesis according to which the values of the potential interactions are negligible in relation to the analysed factors (the interactions are dealt with as "noise" factors). Under these conditions, all available columns of the array of selected experiences shall be reserved to the controlled factors, in order to highlight the most influential factors (main effects and potential overlapped interactions); the purifying experimentation. After performing the prior experiment of selection, a number of 2–4 factors considered to be the most influential has resulted, along with the most favourable values related to them. The experiment of purifying the results shall therefore focus on the most influential factors. Should the new levels which these factors are tested at be close to those already known to be favourable, it becomes possible to quantify the interactions between a low number of factors at a reasonable cost based on the Taguchi experience plans. Confirming the utility of these steps (performing the experiments of selection, respectively those of purification) intervenes when performing the test to validate the configuration chosen for the levels of the factors optimising the process/product; to perform the tests and measure the results. At this stage, where the actual performance of the experiment itself occurs. In order to improve the quality of the process/product, the following formalised aspects must be taken into account, to the extent of the possibilities, based on some technical documents: The means used to perform the tests, possibilities to adjust the levels of the tested factors, taking and identifying the measured samples, the target-values specified and the measurement conditions (temperature, humidity, injection pressure, cutting angle, etc.), explicit identification of the controlled factors and "noise" factors tested during the tests, etc.

To process and statistically analyse the results. This involves to successively go through certain stages wherein the following calculations are done:

1) Determining the average answer Signal/Noise for each of the levels of the analysed factors. This corresponds to the average of the results acquired through the tests where the factor has been adjusted at that level. For example, for factor A of the array of experiences $L_8(2^7)$ (Table 16.1), the following can be written:

$$\overline{A_1} = \frac{R_1 + R_2 + R_3 + R_4}{4} \tag{16.11}$$

$$\overline{A_2} = \frac{R_5 + R_6 + R_7 + R_8}{4} \tag{16.12}$$

By generalising, the average answer Signal/Noise for the level n of any factor F is calculated based on the fraction:

$$\overline{F_n} = \frac{R_{1n} + R_{2n} + \ldots + R_{Nn}}{N} \tag{16.13}$$

where:

$\overline{F_n}$—represents the average answer Signal/Noise for the level "n" of the factor "F";

$R_{1n}, R_{2n}, \ldots R_{Nn}$—The values of the results acquired through the tests where the factor "F" has been maintained at level "n".

N—the number of tests where "F" is at level "n";

2) The average effect of S/N of each level of the factors is calculated as the difference between the average answer S/N and general average of the answers S/N (symbolised as $\overline{T}$):

$$E_{Fn} = \overline{F_n} - \overline{T} \tag{16.14}$$

where:

E_{Fn}—represents the average effect S/N of the factor F at level "n"

Similarly, the relation of the average effect S/N can be written for another level "m" of the same factor "F":

$$E_{Fm} = \overline{F_m} - \overline{T} \tag{16.15}$$

where $\overline{F_n}$ has been determined based on a relation like (16.11), taking into account those results provided by the tests where factor "F" has been adjusted at level "m".

Obviously, if factor "F" has two levels (n = 1 and m = 2), the following equality is checked:

$$E_{Fn} = -E_{Fm}, \text{ meaning } E_{F1} = -E_{F2} \quad (16.16)$$

3) The potential interactions taken into account are quantified. To exemplify the calculation relation used in this case, the singular interaction between two any factors F and G is taken into account. If F and G have two levels each, the possible combinations that should be analysed are symbolised: F1G1, F1G2, F2G1 and F2G2. The average effect of the first combination F1G1 includes the very effects of the levels F1 and G1 plus the value of the interaction I_{F1G1} (if it exists):

$$E_{F1G1} = E_{F1} + E_{G1} + I_{F1G1} \quad (16.17)$$

(Just as in position 2)) the average effect of this answer can be analysed by reference to the overall average $\overline{T}$ of all the answers:

$$E_{F1G1} = \overline{F_1 G_1} - \overline{T} = \left(\overline{F_1} - \overline{T}\right) + \left(\overline{G_1} - \overline{T}\right) + i_{F1G1} \quad (16.18)$$

where from:

$$i_{F1G1} = \overline{F_1 G_1} - \left(\overline{F_1} - \overline{T}\right) - \left(\overline{G_1} - \overline{T}\right) \quad (16.19)$$

$$i_{F1G1} = \overline{F_1 G_1} - \overline{T} - E_{F1} - E_{G1} \quad (16.20)$$

Therefore, the interaction I_{F1G1} achieved when both factors are at level is equal to the mean answer of the system in the configuration $\overline{F1}\,\overline{G1}$ minus the overall average and the sum of the effects of each of the two factors. Similarly, the relations related to the other interactions can be written as follows:

$$i_{F1G2} = \overline{F_1 G_2} - \overline{T} - E_{F1} - E_{G2} \quad (16.21)$$

$$i_{F2G1} = \overline{F_2 G_1} - \overline{T} - E_{F2} - E_{G1} \quad (16.22)$$

$$i_{F2G2} = \overline{F_2 G_2} - \overline{T} - E_{F2} - E_{G2} \quad (16.23)$$

4) Plotting the graphs of the answers based on the results summarised in the table of answers (to create it, it is necessary to determine the effects of all factors and interaction taken into account). The graphs use the systems of coordinates representing on the abscissa the factors and the analysed interactions, and on the ordinate the effects on the measured values or the effects on the S/N ratio. Plotting the graphs of answers allows both the visualisation of factors exercising considerable influences on the quality features, as well as easing the effort to create a configuration to improve the process/product.
5) Choosing the level of the factors to improve the quality criteria.

This involves selecting those levels of the controlled factors minimising the dispersion of the features of the manufacturing process. The theoretical result shall be determined based on the hypothesis of the effects of the factors (and interactions) compared with the overall average of all tests. For an experiment with four factors (F, G, H, I) and an interaction (FG), the theoretical result is calculated as the sum of:

$$R\ theoretic = \overline{T} + E_{Fo} + E_{Go} + E_{Ho} + E_{io} + i_{FGo} \qquad (16.24)$$

where "o" means the level withheld for each factor, in order to optimise the quality criterion taken into account.

If the classical method of the plans of experiences enables the determination of the combination of factors optimising the quality of the processes/products, the Taguchi approach additionally allows the assessment of the theoretical robustness of the optimised manufacturing process. Similarly to the previous process used to calculate the theoretical result (the equation (16.24)), one is to begin from the hypotheses according to which the individual effects S/N of the controlled factors are additive if the factors are maintained at optimal levels:

The S/N ratio

$$\hat{r} = \overline{T} + E_{Fo} + E_{Go} + E_{Ho} + E_{io} + i_{FGo} \quad [\mathrm{dB}] \qquad (16.25)$$

where E_{Fo}, E_{Go}, E_{io}, E_{Ho} and I_{Fgo} represent the average effects of Signal/Noise and the interactions with major impact on the S/N ratio at the level chosen to be optimised.

The resulted theoretical deviation (s), exponent of the robustness of the manufacturing process can be easily determined if the size of μ is known. For example, for a quality target-criterion (such as the thickness of the protective layer in the metal covers), it can be written:

$$\mu = 10\log\left(\overline{y}/s^2\right) \quad [\mathrm{dB}] \qquad (16.26)$$

(if the ratio 1/n is neglected), where it results from that the calculation relation of the standard deviation is:

$$s = \sqrt{\frac{\overline{y^2}}{10^{(\mu/10)}}} \qquad (16.27)$$

The analyses performed to define the optimal configuration needs a two-stage approach. The combination of factors is firstly done, which determines the highest algebraic value for the S/N ratio and the criterion to be optimised, following to adjust the resulting value of the feature in the next stage (weight, size, viscosity, etc.) at the predefined target value (maximum, minimum or nominal value (based on the factors with great influence on the measured value. Therefore, determining the optimal configuration often requires the purification of the initial configuration that results from the calculations by analysing some technical or economical additional considerations. In this process, compromises are knowingly made sometimes between performance and a convenient S/N ratio.

Taguchi's approach enables the simultaneous optimisation of several quality criteria. In this case, difficulties frequently occur related to achieving the most reasonable compromise which balances the improvements made on all the quality criteria to be optimised (conflicts occur often regarding the favourable or less favourable influence of the levels of controlled factors on some different quality criteria). To relativize the influence that a factor exercises on the analysed features, they often have very different natures—sizes, temperatures, yields-and disparate orders of magnitude), it shall be proceeded with calculating the percentage of the S/N contribution for each factor:

$$\%Contribution\ S/N\ of\ factor\ F\ at\ level\ 1 = \frac{E_{F1}}{|\overline{T}|}100 \tag{16.28}$$

where E_F is the effect of factor F at level 1

The relation for calculating the ratio S/N in the case of the previous example (for factors F-I and an interaction FG) shall be:

$$\hat{r} = \overline{T} + [\%\ Contribution\ Fo, Go, Ho, I_o, FGo]\ \frac{|\overline{T}|}{100}[\mathrm{dB}] \tag{16.29}$$

The optimising process shall involve in this case the sequence of the following phases: To determine the levels of the factors optimising each feature; to regroup in a tabular form the preliminary results in order to highlight the potential conflicts regarding the influence of the levels of factors on certain different quality criteria; to achieve an initial "sorting" to optimise and indicate the level of each factors that leads to the greatest sum of the S/N contribution percentage for all the features; to purify the configuration of the retained factors so that after a few iterations where the levels of some different factors are varied, that combination ensuring the global improvement of all quality criteria would be reached.

The validation test represents the mandatory confirmation of any experiment undertaken with the Taguchi method. The purpose of the validation test is to verify the additivity hypothesis of the levels of the controlled factors (this hypothesis was the starting point for calculating the expected theoretical results). It is sometimes possible that this test would use an combination of factors that is identical to another one already performed during the experiment. In this case, the validation aims at the simple physical verification of achieving the expected results.

Should the result of the validation test prove to be close to the value expected by the calculation, it is obvious that the interactions of the tested factors are negligible. Any step to conduct certain complementary investigations for the study of the interactions is useless (the practical experience supports this conclusion for a number of contemporary industrial activities). Conversely, should the additivity of the effects of the factors levels be compromised, then the presence of the interactions after other possible causes have been removed should be taken into account. In this case, an additional experiment to purify the results should be run followed by the appropriate adaptation of the array of experiences used to the requirements imposed by the correct determination of the interactions between factors.

The success of the Taguchi experiment essentially depends on the actual method to implement the sequential process of preparing and performing the statistical operations it involves. This task is subject to the reflection group formed for this purpose. The efficiency of the Taguchi method is proven by rapidly reaching a proportion of 70–90 % of the desired optimisation with minimum costs (the additional 10–30 % can be achieved with one or two further experiments limited at 2–4 parameters judged to be the most influential).

This pragmatic approach in successive stages calls for knowing the phenomena and experience acquired during a long period by the interested technicians and specialists (actually the experience is the variable allowing the future limitation of the number of statistical tests). It is therefore obvious that the already mentioned reflection group, formed to implement the method, must include only individuals who have an important background of theoretical, technological and especially practical knowledge regarding the subject that is to be solved. Besides the immediate interest to perform the experiment and improve the quality, the unitary coordination of the efforts of individuals from various organisational departments allows the enhancement of the employees' cohesion and is a strong link between the strategies of human and quality resources.

For example, in the electric field, the problem of optimising the parameters of a manufacturing process can be addressed from many points of view. In manufacturing mining machines, it presents a number of difficulties: thus, if a machine-tool or an electronic item operates under certain conditions, it cannot be said the same about a complex mining machine the operation of which organically depends on the ore conditions (layer, block, slab, panel, etc.). Moreover, it is obvious that the underground environment operating the mining machines can be characterised as a highly corrosive environment.

Corrosion is practically present in all industrial sectors of a national economy, causing the most harmful effects, as because of this, large quantities of materials are lost every year. The losses caused by corrosion may be assimilated to some costs of the machines and are classified into direct and consequential losses. An example of direct loss could be the opportunity cost of a metal mining machine which replaces another identical machine damaged by corrosion. Consequential losses are generally higher and it is more difficult to assess their actual value. For example, the expenses needed to oversize the machines are included into this category, so that in case of corrosion, their mechanical strength and normal operation would be ensured for a given period of time. The drop in production caused by water, gas losses or by losses of various technological fluids, interruptions, yield drops caused by a faulty heat exchange or large power consumptions is also a consequential loss, all of them being based on corrosion. Certain specialists deem that about 30 % of the total steel quantity annually produced worldwide generally turns into rust as consequence of the corrosion processes. In other words, of three blast furnaces, one shall only produce the steel needed to replace the one destroyed by corrosion. This is why the combined efforts of some researchers from various countries have turned to elaborating and applying several methods of anticorrosion protection at industrial scale. The difficult conditions in which the technological processes are currently performed in different branches (high pressures, temperatures, humidities, varied loads, etc.) still deman outstanding efforts in order to obtain new protective materials and methods of maximum efficiency.

Returning to the mining machines and highly corrosive underground environment where they operate, the galvanic covers of metal components by chroming, nickel or electrolytic plating processes can be specified among the anticorrosive protective methods.

In the case study presented, electrochemical cadmium plating in the drum achieved to protect the representative benchmarks of the mining hydraulic gear. The experiments performed aimed at obtaining some even layers, adherent both on the inner surfaces and on the outer ones, taking into account the complex geometrical configuration of the parts.

The quality criterion that must be analysed is the thickness of the cadmium layer (the target-criterion); in compliance with the stipulations of the standards in force, the allowable cadmium layer thickness must fall within the tolerance range of 20 ± 2 μm. Following a preliminary selection experiment, a number of seven relevant factors have been identified (the first three factors shall be tested on two levels, and the next four factors are detailed on a number of four levels). In Table 16.3, all controlled factors and levels related to each of them are presented.

The experiment was performed with an L_{16} experience matrix (Table 16.4) modified for accepting the factors with four levels. For each of the 16 tests, 10 parts have been loaded on the drum, of which five samples have been taken, the cadmium layer thickness being measured for a part of two, in the sequence in which they have been inserted into the cadmium plating bath. The values of the measured thicknesses are shown in Table 16.5.

For each test, the average of the answers ($\overline{y}$), standard deviation (s) and Signal/Noise (S/N) ratio have been calculated in decibels.

For calculating the standard deviation (s), the following relation has been used:

$$s = \sqrt{\sum_{i=1}^{n} \frac{(y_i - \overline{y})^2}{n-1}} \tag{16.30}$$

where:

y_i represents the measured values ($y_1, y_2, \ldots, y_5$)
y the arithmetic average of the measured values
n number of measured values ($n = 5$).

Table 16.3 Factors controlled within the Taguchi experiment

No.	Symbol of factor	Name of factor	Levels of factors Level 1	Level 2	Level 3	Level 4
1	A	Chemical composition of the cadmium bath	R1	R2	–	–
2	B	Electric voltage	3; 5 V	5 V	–	–
3	C	Ratio between the anodic surface in the bath and the cathode surface SA/SK	1.5/1	2/1	–	–
4	D	Temperature of the cadmium plating bath	18 °C	20 °C	30 °C	35 °C
5	E	Drum speed	11 rpm	10 rpm	9 rpm	8 rpm
6	F	Cathode current density	1 A/dm^2	1.3 A/dm^2	1.6 A/dm^2	2 A/dm^2
7	G	Working time	40 min	44 min	47 min	50 min

Table 16.4 L_{16} experience matrix (three factors with two levels and four factors with four levels)

Test no.	Controlled factors A	B	C	D	E	F	G
1	1	1	1	1	1	1	1
2	1	2	2	2	2	1	2
3	1	1	1	3	4	4	2
4	1	2	2	4	3	4	1
5	1	2	2	3	1	2	4
6	1	1	1	4	2	2	3
7	1	2	2	1	4	3	3
8	1	1	1	2	3	3	4
9	2	1	2	4	1	3	2
10	2	2	1	3	2	3	1
11	2	1	2	2	4	2	1
12	2	2	1	1	3	2	2
13	2	2	1	2	1	4	3
14	2	1	2	1	2	4	4
15	2	2	1	4	4	1	4
16	2	1	2	3	3	1	3

For example, how to calculate the standard deviation in the case of test no. 1 shall be given in detail:

$$s = \sqrt{\frac{(21.01-20.85)^2}{4} + \frac{(20.82-20.85)^2}{4} + \frac{(20.77-20.85)^2}{4} + \frac{(20.79-20.85)^2}{4}}$$
$$= 0.095$$

The standard deviations related to the tests 2–16 are shown in Table 16.5. The results of the calculations to determine the Signal/Noise ratios relative to each of the

Table 16.5 The results of tests: averages, standard deviations and signal/noise ratios

Test no.	Part					Average (m)	Standard deviation (s)	S/N ratio
	1	2	3	4	5			
1	21.01	20.82	20.77	20.85	20.79	20.85	0.095	46.82
2	20.64	20.65	20.56	20.55	20.45	20.57	0.081	48.09
3	19.8	19.75	19.82	20.02	19.9	19.86	0.105	45.54
4	18.88	18.9	18.5	18.81	18.91	18.8	0.208	39.12
5	19.55	19.5	19.58	19.52	19.61	19.55	0.044	52.95
6	19.9	19.82	19.85	19.84	19.83	19.85	0.031	56.13
7	20.12	20.2	20.1	20.22	20.3	20.18	0.081	47.93
8	19.65	19.72	19.84	19.82	19.64	19.73	0.093	46.53
9	18.95	19.02	19.15	18.89	19.12	19.03	0.11	44.76
10	19.83	19.92	19.79	19.85	19.9	19.86	0.052	51.64
11	20.44	20.38	20.5	20.32	20.48	20.42	0.074	48.82
12	19.97	20.1	20.18	20.2	20.09	20.11	0.091	46.88
13	18.52	18.93	19.05	18.87	19.12	18.9	0.233	38.18
14	19.65	19.92	19.51	19.78	19.83	19.74	0.16	41.82
15	20.12	20.03	20.25	20.18	20.21	20.16	0.086	47.4
16	20.44	20.23	20.35	20.19	20.1	20.26	0.134	43.59

16 tests are included into the same table. We recall that, the criterion regarding the quality that must be optimised—the cadmium layer thickness—is a target type criterion. In this situation, the Signal/Noise ratios have been calculated with the formula:

$$S/N = 10\log\left[\left(\overline{y/s}\right) - 1/n\right] \quad [\text{dB}] \tag{16.31}$$

For the test no. 1 we have:

$$S/N = 10\log\left[\left(\overline{20.85}/0.095\right)^2 - 1/5\right] = 46.82 \quad [\text{dB}]$$

For the other 15 tests, the calculation procedure is similar; and the results are shown in the last column of Table 16.5.

The average answers for the levels of controlled factors are determined as some simple arithmetic averages of the results obtained for the tests where the factor is encountered at that level. For factor A with two levels, the averages are:

$$\overline{A}_1 = \frac{20.85 + 20.57 + 19.86 + 18.8 + 19.55 + 19.85 + 20.18 + 19.73}{8}$$
$$= 19.92 \quad (\mu m)$$

$$\overline{A}_2 = \frac{19.03 + 19.86 + 20.42 + 20.11 + 18.9 + 19.74 + 20.16 + 20.26}{8}$$
$$= 19.8 \quad (\mu m)$$

Similarly, the average answers Signal/Noise are determined:

$$\overline{A}_1^{S/N} = \frac{46.82 + 48.09 + 45.54 + 39.12 + 52.95 + 56.13 + 47.93 + 46.53}{8}$$
$$= 47.89 \quad [\text{dB}]$$
$$\overline{A}_2^{S/N} = \frac{44.76 + 51.64 + 48.82 + 46.88 + 38.18 + 41.82 + 47.4 + 43.59}{8}$$
$$= 43.59 \quad [\text{dB}]$$

The general average $\overline{T}$ of all tests shall correspond to the central point of the average answers for the levels of each factor:

$$\frac{\overline{A_1} + \overline{A_2}}{2} = \frac{19.92 + 19.8}{2} = 19.86 \quad (\mu\text{m})$$

respectively:

$$\frac{\overline{A}_1^{S/N} + \overline{A}_2^{S/N}}{2} = \frac{47.89 + 43.59}{2} = 46.64 \quad [\text{dB}]$$

The average effect of each level of the factor is assessed by relating to the overall average. For the measured values, the average effect of the factor A at level 1 is:

$$E_{A1} = \overline{A}_1 - \overline{T} = 19.92 - 19.86 = +0.06 \ \ (\mu\text{m})$$

The effect at level 2 shall be determined as the difference:

$$E_{A2} = \overline{A}_2 - \overline{T} = 19.8 - 19.86 = -0.06 \ \ (\mu\text{m})$$

The average effects for the S/N answers are calculated similarly:

$$E_{A1}^{S/N} = \overline{A}_1^{S/N} - \overline{T}^{S/N} = 47.89 - 46.64 = 1.25 \quad [\text{dB}]$$

respectively:

$$E_{A2}^{S/N} = \overline{A}_2^{S/N} - \overline{T}^{S/N} = 45.39 - 46.64 = -1.25 \quad [\text{dB}]$$

It is obvious that $E_{A1} = -E_{A2}$ and $E_{A1}^{S/N} = -E_{A2}^{S/N}$ (the equalities are valid for any factor with two levels).

The calculation of the answers and average effects in the case of a factor with four levels for the two situations—the measured values of the cadmium layer thickness and Signal/Noise ratios—is similar.

For example, for factor D with four levels (temperature of the cadmium plating bath), the average answers are:

$$\overline{D}_1 = \frac{20.85 + 20.18 + 20.11 + 19.74}{4} = 20.21 \quad (\mu\text{m})$$

$$\overline{D}_2 = \frac{20.57 + 19.73 + 20.42 + 18.90}{4} = 19.89 \quad (\mu\text{m})$$

$$\overline{D}_3 = \frac{19.86 + 19.55 + 19.86 + 20.26}{4} = 19.88 \quad (\mu\text{m})$$

$$\overline{D}_4 = \frac{18.8 + 19.85 + 19.03 + 20.16}{4} = 19.46 \quad (\mu\text{m})$$

$$\overline{D}_1^{S/N} = \frac{46.82 + 47.93 + 46.88 + 41.82}{4} = 45.87 \quad [\text{dB}]$$

$$\overline{D}_2^{S/N} = \frac{48.09 + 46.53 + 48.82 + 38.18}{4} = 45.41 \quad [\text{dB}]$$

$$\overline{D}_3^{S/N} = \frac{45.54 + 52.95 + 51.64 + 43.59}{4} = 48.43 \quad [\text{dB}]$$

$$\overline{D}_4^{S/N} = \frac{39.12 + 56.13 + 44.76 + 47.4}{4} = 46.85 \quad [\text{dB}]$$

Accordingly, the average effects shall be determined by relating to the general averages ($\overline{T}$ and $\overline{T}^{S/N}$):

$$E_{D1} = \overline{D}_1 - \overline{T} = 20.21 - 19.86 = 0.35 \ (\mu\text{m})$$

$$E_{D2} = \overline{D}_2 - \overline{T} = 19.89 - 19.86 = 0.03 \ (\mu\text{m})$$

$$E_{D3} = \overline{D}_3 - \overline{T} = 19.88 - 19.86 = 0.02 \ (\mu\text{m})$$

$$E_{D4} = \overline{D}_4 - \overline{T} = 19.46 - 19.86 = -0.40 \ (\mu\text{m})$$

$$E_{D1}^{S/N} = \overline{D}_1^{S/N} - \overline{T}^{S/N} = 45.87 - 46.64 = -0.77 \ [\text{dB}]$$

$$E_{D2}^{S/N} = \overline{D}_2^{S/N} - \overline{T}^{S/N} = 45.41 - 46.64 = -1.23 \ [\text{dB}]$$

$$E_{D3}^{S/N} = \overline{D}_3^{S/N} - \overline{T}^{S/N} = 48.43 - 46.64 = 1.79 \ [\text{dB}]$$

$$E_{D4}^{S/N} = \overline{D}_4^{S/N} - \overline{T}^{S/N} = 46.85 - 46.64 = 0.21 \ [\text{dB}]$$

In the case of factor D with four levels, the following equalities are verified: $E_{D1} + E_{D2} + E_{D3} + E_{D4} = 0$; respectively $E_{D1}^{S/N} + E_{D2}^{S/N} + E_{D3}^{S/N} + E_{D4}^{S/N} = 0$

Table 16.6 Table of answers

Effect on S/N in dB					Effect on the measured values (μm)			
Level 1	Level 2	Level 3	Level 4	Factors	Level 1	Level 2	Level 3	Level 4
1.25	−1.25	–	–	A	+0.06	−0.06	–	–
0.11	−0.11	–	–	B	0.10	−0.10	–	–
0.75	−0.75	–	–	C	0.05	−0.05	–	–
−0.77	−1.23	1.79	0.21	D	0.35	0.03	0.02	−0.40
−0.95	2.78	−2.61	0.78	E	−0.28	0.14	−0.14	0.29
−0.17	4.56	1.08	−5.47	F	0.60	0.11	−0.16	−0.55
−0.04	−0.32	−0.18	0.54	G	0.11	0.03	−0.06	−0.08

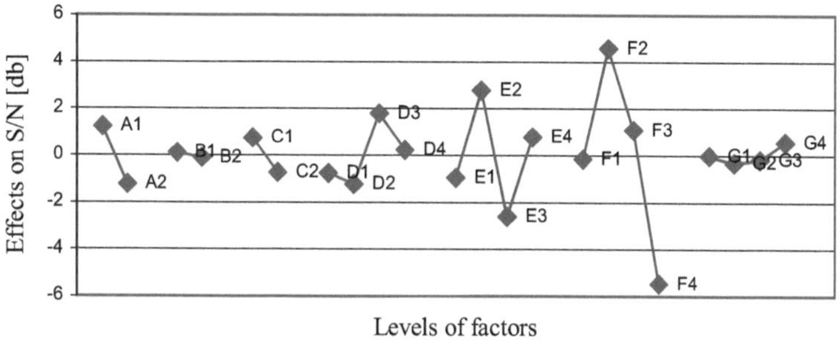

Fig. 16.6 Effects on the S/N ratios

For the other factors tested—B and C with two levels, respectively E, F, G with four levels—the procedure to perform the calculations is identical. The results are summarised as the table with answers (Table 16.6).

It is therefore observed that there are certain differences between the effects registered on the values measured and effects on the S/N ratios. We must remember in this context that if only the average values of the cadmium layer thickness are included in the first case, then the variation of results additionally intervenes in the case of S/N ratios. The higher the S/N algebraic values are, the lower the registered losses are, therefore the performance of the electrochemical cadmium plating process is improved.

The Signal/Noise ratio must be primarily used in order to appropriately choose the levels of factors.

In order to compare the effects exercised by each of the seven controlled factors, the graphical representation of the data in the recapitulative table of answers is highly useful and suggestive (Figs. 16.6 and 16.7).

Based on the table with answers and graphs, it is observed that the factors D, E, F appear as having the most significant effects on the cadmium layer. However, choosing the optimum configuration of the manufacturing process requires the arbitration between the levels of the factors for achieving the double objective: minimising the variance and developing an average thickness as close to the target—value of 20 μm.

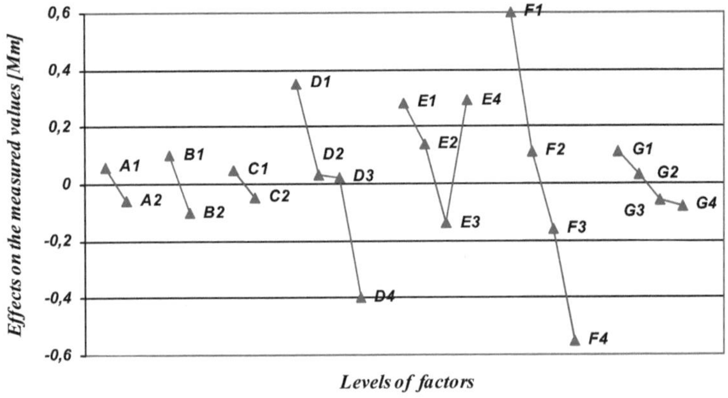

Fig. 16.7 Effects on the measured values

Table 16.7 The first optimisation in relation to S/N

Symbol of factor	Description of factor	Suggested level	Effect on S/N dB	Effect on the value μ
A	Chemical composition of the cadmium plating bath	1	1.25	0.06
B	Electric voltage	1	0.11	0.10
C	SA/SK ratio	1	0.75	0.05
D	Temperature of the cadmium plating bath	3	1.79	0.02
E	Drum speed	2	2.78	0.14
F	Cathode current density	2	4.56	0.11
G	Working time	4	0.54	0.08
The theoretic S/N ratio resulted [dB]			57.77	
Average S/N [dB]			46.64	
Average thickness of the cadmium layer (μm)				19.86
Theoretically resulting measured value (μm)				20.26

In Table 16.7, a first configuration to optimise the manufacturing process is given, depending on the objective to improve the Signal/Noise ratio.

The assessment of the theoretically resulting S/N ratio was based on the hypothesis that, if all factors are adjusted at their optimum levels, then their individual S/N effects must meet the additivity property. Calculating the theoretic S/N ratio has taken into account only the major effects (because the experimental error is found in each of the established averages) for the configuration chosen A1B1C1D3E2F2G4:

$$\mu(\text{The theoretic S/N ratio}) = T + E_{A1} + E_{C1} + E_{D3} + E_{E2} + E_{F2} =$$
$$= 46.64 + 1.25 + 0.75 + 1.79 + 2.78 + 4.56 = 57.77 \qquad [\text{dB}]$$

The theoretic thickness of the cadmium layer resulted from the configuration suggested in Table 16.6 is as follows, taking into account the additivity of the influencing factors:

$$\hat{g} = T + E_{A1} + E_{B1} + E_{C1} + E_{D3} + E_{E2} + E_{F2} + E_{G4} =$$
$$= 19.86 + 0.06 + 0.10 + 0.05 + 0.02 + 0.14 - 0.16 + 0.08 = 20.26\,(\mu m)$$

The configuration A1B1C1D3E2F2G4 enables the significant reduction of the dispersion of the manufacturing process, because it interferes in the transition from an average value S/N of 46.64 dB which is constant during the 16 tests, to a higher value of 57.77 dB.

Moreover, the suggested configuration does not optimise the resulting thickness for the cadmium layer, because it exceeds the maximum limit of the allowable tolerance range [−20,20] μm. It is therefore necessary to proceed with adjusting the resulting value of the layer thickness with the levels of some factors with determining influence on the measured value, but which decrease as little as possible the S/N ratio.

The analysis of the table of answers shows that the most appropriate one is factor F—the cathode current density. At level 3, factor F practically brings the correction desired because it is a transition from the effect +0.11 μm to −0.16 μm, which means −0.27 μm in relation to the previously withheld level. Furthermore, the correction is simple, practically acting on the adjustment of the current density (the value of 1.3 A/dm^2 shall be retained). The final suggested configuration is shown in Table 16.8.

The final configuration in the aforementioned table differs from that resulted after the first optimisation only concerning the factor F which the level 3 has been chosen for. Therefore, for the formula A1B1C1D3E2F3G4, the S/N ratio is still better than the average one resulted after the 16 experiments:

Table 16.8 Final optimum configuration

Symbol of factor	Description of factor	Suggested level	Effect on S/N dB	Effect on the value μm
A	Chemical composition of the cadmium plating bath	1	1.25	0.06
B	Electric voltage	1	0.11	0.10
C	SA/SK ratio	1	0.75	0.05
D	Temperature of the cadmium plating bath	3	1.79	0.02
E	Drum speed	2	2.78	0.14
F	Cathode current density	3	1.08	−0.16
G	Working time	4	0.54	−0.08
The resulting theoretic S/N ratio [dB]			54.29	
Average S/N [dB]			46.64	
Average thickness of the cadmium layer (μm)				19.86
Theoretically resulting measured value (μm)				19.99

$$\mu_o(\text{Theoretic S/N ratio}) = T + E_{A1} + E_{C1} + E_{D3} + E_{E2} + E_{F3} = \\ = 46.64 + 1.25 + 0.75 + 1.79 + 2.78 + 1.08 = 54.29 \quad [\text{dB}]$$

The configuration chosen however leads to a theoretically measured value for the cadmium layer thickness very close to the nominal value of 20 μm:

$$\hat{g} = T + E_{A1} + E_{B1} + E_{C1} + E_{D3} + E_{E2} + E_{F3} + E_{G4} = \\ = 19.86 + 0.06 + 0.10 + 0.05 + 0.02 + 0.14 - 0.16 + 0.08 = 19.99\ (\mu\text{m})$$

Based on this cadmium layer thickness theoretic value, the theoretic standard deviation can be predicted. Thus, if the 1/n ratio is neglected (with a very low value) of the formula for calculating the Signal/Noise ratio, the following can be written:

$$\hat{y} \approx 10 \log (\mu/s)^2 \tag{16.32}$$

$$\frac{\mu}{10} = \log(\bar{y}/s)^2 \tag{16.33}$$

$$10^{\frac{\mu}{10}} = \frac{y^2}{s^2} \tag{16.34}$$

It results that:

$$s = \sqrt{\frac{y^2}{10^{(\mu/10)}}} \tag{16.35}$$

By replacement in the aforementioned relation, we get:

$$s = \sqrt{\frac{19.99^2}{10^{\frac{54.29}{10}}}} = 19.99\sqrt{10^{-5.429}} = 0.0385$$

This value predicted for the standard deviation is the witness of a robust process of electrochemical cadmium plating for the mining hydraulic gear.

As it has been previously stated, any statistical experiment performed with the Taguchi method must be completed by an attempt to validate the theoretic results obtained.

In the case of electrochemical cadmium plating in the industrial company, the validation attempt used the combination of levels of the factors in Table 16.9.

The purpose of the validation attempt is to verify the effective achievement of the level of the predicted result. The value achieved for the cadmium layer thickness was of 19.97 μm, which shows a result close to the expected one. The small difference between the two values—suggested and achieved—can be explained either by the presence of some light interactions between the controlled factors, or by a non-linear variation of the current density effect. Overall, it may be

Table 16.9 Levels to adjust the factors tested by the validation attempt

No.	Symbol of factor	Description of factor	Adjusted level
1	A	Chemical composition of the cadmium plating bath	R1
2	B	Electric voltage	3 V
3	C	Ratio between the anodic surface in the bath and the cathode surface	1.5/1
4	D	Temperature of the cadmium plating bath	30 °C
5	E	Drum speed	10 rpm
6	F	Cathode current density	1.3 A/dm^2
7	G	Working time	50 min

said that the reproducibility of the experiment is good (the adjustment of the amperage operates as intended).

Taking into account the large volume of calculations to establish the configuration of factors optimising the production process, the electronic technique of calculation may be used, which based on an elaborated program, it enables the calculations to be done within a very short time range, thus increasing the efficiency of applying this method.

16.3 Model Used to Measure the Quality and of Poor Quality Products in View of Their Life Cycle

Taking into account the limitation of the life cycle of products and strategic investments that require the use of certain technologies, the decision of setting forth a new product on the market should rely upon the costs of its life cycle. Each setting forth of a new product determines: research and development costs, equipment costs, pre-industrialization costs and implementing costs, production costs, marketing costs, logistics costs (that is costs with storage, distribution and transport), administration costs, and costs of the customer focused services, etc.

The success of such a setting forth should be based on optimizing the global cost of the product life cycle. Such an optimisation consists in choosing between the decrease of development costs in case subsequently it will be necessary to operate several changes of the product due to industrialization problems or due to a poor adaptation to the customer's demand or the decrease of production costs that might determine a series of quality find guarantee term drawbacks, and the increase of post- selling service costs (guarantee term).

The stages of conceiving the product, of choosing its fabrication procedure are difficult, having consequences upon the evolution of future costs, and making useless the optimization of a single stage without taking into account the impact upon the others.

Accordingly, it is necessary to determine a cost that has in view most of the problems of the life cycle of the product (that is a global cost), and to optimize the product's conception by using the target costing technique (that is an objective costs).

In order to determine the global cost of the product's life cycle it is necessary to have in view both the drawbacks of the traditional methods as the traditional ways of determining it lead to an answer which is not adapted to the demands of the life cycle of the product as they divide time into annual exercises, connecting the costs to the period in which they have been done (research and development costs, pre-exploitation, industrial and commercial setting forth costs, as well as the other movement costs having a general character are usually registered during the period in which they have been done) and the consideration of the costs of the product's life cycle as real costs, depending on the product's success, as all the costs that are investments from an economic point of view (research, development, new technology costs) represent immobilizations and are the object of a paying off depending on the wear of the whole life cycle of the product (the costs of cycle ending are covered and the initial research costs may remain uncovered without determining incomes).

In case the product is not viable, its "life" stops at the conception stage. As the costs determined by this already dead product do not generate any income, they can be assimilated to the general costs that must be covered by the profitableness of certain products.

When the product prematurely dies, at the beginning of the exploitation stage, a cover from incomes is already present; nevertheless it is not sufficient to cover all the costs engaged (especially those that are paid off during the envisaged life cycle). The real annual cost will be superior to the estimated cost and the loss will be sustained by the product itself.

In case the product's life is prolonged (the product having a sequence with double cycle or a cycle comprising the resuming of the activity), the real costs of conceiving it as well as those included within rejects are already covered by the sales that took place during the envisaged cycle. The only costs that should be taken into account during the supplementary period are accordingly those that come out of the extension of the cycle, namely marginal costs.

The correct estimation of the life cycle (services associated to the product) is based upon its prevision calculation that requires the determination of both technological risk and of commercial risk.

Technological risk manifests itself either during the product's conception, in case the product seems to be too complex, or after the product's conception in case a new technology makes it look obsolete. The immediate consequence is that the product dies before being born, that is before being marketed.

Commercial risk appears when, despite technological success, the product does not encounter any demand or only an insignificant one. The product dies during the planning stage or, in case it has already been marketed, it dies before the envisaged date.

Once having evaluated these two types of risk, the estimation of quality costs during the life cycle of the product may be done taking into account the two possibilities of conceiving the new product:

- *the optimization of the global cost of the product's life cycle by comparing estimated cost to target cost.*

  In order to do such an optimization it is necessary to take into account the reasoning that starts with a market research (the evolution of the needs and technologies) and with an analysis of the competitors, defining the characteristics of the product that respond the demands of the customer and determining accordingly a target price that should let the company be competitive (to conquer a certain market share).

  Then, taking into account the unitary profit estimated by the company, a unitary target cost is to be determined, according to the formula:

$$C_{ut} = P_{usc} - P_{ue\,p}, \tag{16.36}$$

where:

C_{ut} represents the unitary target cost
P_{usc} the unitary target sales cost
P_{uep} the estimated unitary target profit

The unitary target sales cost for this product can be determined as follows:

$$P_{usc} = P_{us} + (f_1 + f_2 + f_3 + \ldots + f_n) \tag{16.37}$$

where

P_{us}—represents the unitary sales cost of the already existent product that resembles the best the new product;
$f_1, \ldots, f_n$—the unitary value of the functioning changes added to the new product and accepted on the market.

If the new product will be set forth on the market in a Q amount of units corresponding to a cautious prevision, then the target business figures will be determined as follows:

$$C_{tf} = P_{usc} \times Q \tag{16.38}$$

where:

C_{tf} represents the target business figures
Q the product's retail amount

The target total estimated profit will be determined as follows:

$$P_{tt} = C_{tf} \times p \tag{16.39}$$

or

$$P_{tt} = P_{usc} \times Q \tag{16.40}$$

where:

P_{tt} represents the target total profit
p the percent of the target profit in target business figures.

The target total cost is determined as follows:

$$C_{tt} = C_{tf} - P_t \tag{16.41}$$

or

$$C_{tt} = C_{ut} \times Q \tag{16.42}$$

where:

C_{tt} represents the target total cost.

The target total cost may also be determined as follows:

$$C_{ut} = C_{tt}/Q \tag{16.43}$$

At the same time, in order to check at the beginning whether the target cost is achievable, an estimated cost is going to be determined; it shows the whole amount of the company's costs (including its common procedures and operational abilities); it also shows whether the company is capable to set forth on the market and observe a certain conception scheme.

The target unitary cost of the new product may be determined as follows:

$$C_{ues} = C_{ues0} + / - A + \ldots m_i \tag{16.44}$$

where:

C_{ues} represents the target unitary estimated cost of the new product
C_{ues0} the unitary cost of the existent product that mostly resembles the new product
A the variation of the cost due to the difference in the retail volume between the existent product and the new product (Q_0–Q)

m_i the change of the cost that accompanies the change in design or in the level of comfort of the "i" part of the product.

Once this first evaluation is accomplished, we generally get only a rough sketch of the new model. The evaluation is done by conception engineers depending on the technical problems that such an achievement implies.

Then, as the sketch evolves, the calculus will be progressively adjusted. Beginning with the conception stage an opinion on the supplementary investments should be formulated in order to evaluate during the first stage the supplementary debts to be included in the cost.

The comparison between the target cost (an outer point of view) and the estimated cost (an inner point of view) allows the noticing of a deviation that can be eliminated, either by acting upon the conception parameters or upon the product's functionality.

In order to watch over such technical adjustments upon subsequent commercial aspects and at the level of future quality, various stages of the estimated cost can be determined.

And, in order to assure the profitableness of the new product during its entire life cycle, one should: attach target costs to its main components; identify the administration conditions that do not accept the exceed of such target costs; establish a commonly agreed reference which guarantees that during the stages subsequent to production the real cost is going to be inferior to the target cost.

The model of evaluating the estimated cost is, at the beginning, quite approximate, taking into account the lack of experience and the necessity of not getting an excessive complexity.

Accordingly, as any other instrument of simulation, it will enrich itself while gaining in experience and integrating o deeper knowledge of the companies' economic mechanisms; it will ultimately become better.

Let's take into consideration a P product that would determine during its life cycle the following costs and incomes (Table 16.10).

In case the traditional method is being used, the level of the estimations according to the data in Table no. l is that contained by Table 16.11.

- *The calculus of amortization has been done according to the method of linear repartition for 5 years* (600/5 = 120).

In case the method of the global costs during the product's life cycle is employed, then the results are those specified in Table 16.12.

The use of the global cost exhibits the company's activity in a realistic vision. The positive profitableness of the company obtained in year N + 2 is due to the re-employment of provisions; in case they lack, profitableness would be (235 – 80)/600 = 26 %.

The re-employment of provisions determines the re-compensation of the assumed risk; the profitableness of 38 % of year N + 4 is the effect of a performance superior to previsions as if real sales would have the envisaged level, then profitableness could maintain its 26 %.

Table 16.10 The structure of the costs and incomes of the P product (M.U.: million lei)

No.	Year	Specification	Total
1.	N	Costs with the conception of the new product	80
2.	N+1	Cost of the market research Research and development costs The market research shows that 3,000 tons of the product (successively 500 tons, 2,000 tons, 500 tons) can be sold at a price of 1.2 million lei/ton; direct costs with materials and labor should increase to 0.5 million lei The prevision of sales costs for 3 years The amortization of technical equipment (for 5 years)	30 10 450 600
3.	N+2	Setting forth commercial costs 500 tons of P products manufactured and sold	200 600
4.	N+3	2,000 tons of P products manufactured and sold Sales costs	2,400 200
5.	N+4	1,000 tons of P products manufactured and sold (either 500 tons in addition to the estimated previsions) Sales costs (45 million lei in addition to the planned level due to the sales increase)	1,200 95

Table 16.11 The influence of the P product cost upon the results of the financial exercise according to the traditional method of estimation during the product's life cycle (M.U.: million lei)

No.	Specification years	N	N+1	N+2	N+3	N+4
1.	Sales incomes			600	2,400	1,200
2.	Conception, research and development costs	80	10			
3.	Materials and labor costs			250	1,000	500
4.	Amortization of technical equipment*			120	120	120
5.	Product's abandoning costs (uncovered amortization)					240
6.	Commercial costs		30	200	200	95
7.	Financial result	−80	−40	30	1,080	245
8.	Coefficient financially resulted/incomes from sales			5 %	45 %	20 %

And the optimization of the global cost of the life cycle of the product starting from its utility cost for consumers, as quite useful could be the appreciation of the costs the buyer has to pay during the use of the product; also the question regarding the acceptability of such costs for the buyer may be asked.

Such estimations are going to direct conception towards products that are easily disassembled and fixed, that are rapidly adjusted, having a long life cycle, with drawbacks that comprise few components and whose elements are interchangeable with common elements, etc.

By calculating the costs of non-quality and those regarding the quality of the product's life cycle, accounting is not only a means of analyzing but it becomes a control instrument. In such a case we propose the method for the calculus of the costs of dissatisfied customers, employed by Original Research, a counseling company in Chicago, specialized in measuring the degree of fidelity.

Table 16.12 The influence of P product cost upon the results of the financial exercise according to the method of the global costs during the life cycle of the product (M.U.: million lei)

No.	Specification years	N	N+1	N+2	N+3	N+4
1.	Sales incomes			600	2,400	1,200
2.	Differentiated costs[a,c]			15	60	15
3.	Materials and labor costs			250	1,000	500
4.	Amortization of technical equipment[b,c]			100	400	100
5.	Provisions[d]	80		−80		
6.	Commercial costs[e]			800	320	125
7.	Financial results	−80		235	620	460
8.	Coefficient financially resulted/incomes from sales			39 %	26 %	32 %

[a]They correspond to the whole of research and development costs (80 + 10) million lei amortized by the 3,000 tons of P products envisaged to be sold according to an established plan
[b]The amortization of technical equipment is done according to the estimated quantity of P products sold (500 tons, 2,000 tons, 500 tons)
[c]In N + 4 the plans regarding the amortization of technical equipment and the delayed costs do not modify due to the fact that, in case the intensive production rhythm (500 tons P product in addition to the initial level) justifies a revise, it nevertheless does not affect the level of amortization previously established
[d]They regard the first research costs as the establishment of provisions is done at the beginning as it is not sure that research generates incomes. In year N + 1 a supplemental endowment is not necessary as the market research shows product's viability; in year N + 2 the endowment is in fact a taking over when the first incomes effectively show
[e]The estimated commercial costs (30 + 450) million lei are included in the costs to be distributed; later they are distributed according to financial exercises that generate incomes according to the envisaged level of P product (500 tons, 2,000 tons, 500 tons). In year N + 4 the marginal cost is being added (45 million lei) determining a sale of P product higher than the prefigured level

Concerning the commensuration of the costs incurred by the non-quality of products, two methods may be used, and namely:

– *the calculation of the costs incurred by non-quality in J. Harrington's view.*

  According to this concept, the expenses are dissociated into two categories: *the direct non-quality costs* (which the company bears immediately for avoiding the deficiencies or for repairing them); *the indirect non-quality costs* (those measuring the effects by comparison, which the deficiencies trigger for the client).

  The category of *direct non-quality costs* (defined as being those which a company bears, because the company's management deems that people may also make mistakes and perform them for training people for being better and for meeting precisely their production tasks) includes: *the prevention costs* (which correspond to the efforts which the company engage for preventing the occurrence of some errors in the future and consist in costs for personnel training, prior investigations at suppliers, actions aiming to prevent the reoccurrence of some error, etc.); *the evaluation costs* (including the expenses engaged for verifying the situation where an action has been correctly fulfilled and refers to the inspection cost and tests aiming to determine the compliance of products with the specifications, the cost of receptions, etc.); *the costs of internal errors* (corresponding to the costs of damages found out before the product would be delivered to the client and aims the costs of discards, declassifications, corrections, unused purchases, etc.); *the costs of external errors* (are the costs which a company bears for damages noticed after delivery, meaning the costs with complaints, costs of the post-sale service, costs of the warranty management, etc.); *costs with equipment* (it is a matter about the cost of investments in materials used for approving or controlling the products, being itself increased by the cost of the space occupied by these materials, etc.)

Costs of indirect non-quality is divided into three large categories: *the costs the client bears for having been delivered a damaged product* (it drops the productivity in case the equipment is damaged, additional hours for exceeding the production delay due to the failure of the equipment, transportation costs and time consumed for resending a damaged product to the supplier, etc.); *costs due to client's dissatisfaction regarding a certain product* (the client's expectation and satisfaction level progresses in time, clients request today a much better product which would meet their expectations); *the costs due to loss of fame* (they reflect the client's attitude towards the company as a whole and not to a certain product, therefore they have effects on the assembly of products realised).

It may be stated in this conception concerning the *behaviour of non-quality costs* that prevention and evaluation costs are controllable by the company, being low if the number of errors is high (medium quality) and high when the number of errors is low (increased quality). The costs of internal errors and those of external errors may be deemed as being resulting costs, being important when there are many errors and the low controllable and less important costs when the expense with errors is modest and controllable costs high (Fig. 16.8).

By summing up the curves representing the controllable costs and resulting costs, it is possible to obtain the lowest price point (cost) (or of the greatest efficiency) from the company's point of view.

The costs the client bears, as well as those related to the client's dissatisfactions progress in the same manner as the resulting costs. By summing up the curves representing these costs with those of the resulting costs (which the company bears), the best efficiency point is moved upwards and to the right.

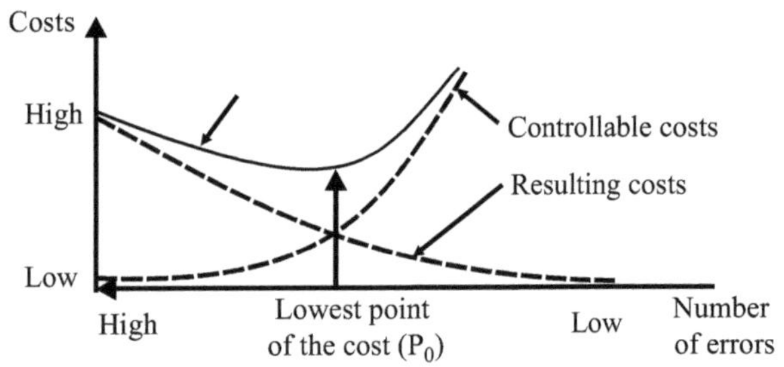

Fig. 16.8 Optimisation of direct non-quality costs

It is worth noting that when the indirect costs are integrated into ratiocination (let us suppose the client's exigency is high), the best efficiency point moves continuously to the right, and the curve of the costs related to client's dissatisfaction also moves to the right.

- *the calculation of the non-quality costs (hidden costs) in H. Savall's view.*

  In this situation, it is tried to estimate the cost of a weak quality of company's operation (the cost of a bad internal operation by privileging the human aspect, because the hidden costs represent indeed the financial impact of disturbances undergone and activities of rectifying and adjusting these problems. Although H. Savall groups the errors and company's poor operation around five malfunction indicators (*absenteeism, labour accidents, personnel's circulation, lack of direct productivity, non-quality of products*), he however considers that the level of costs incurred by the non-quality (hidden) is influenced by: *additional expenses* (he refers to the additional consumptions of materials or services); *additional times* (due to the additional activities which the malfunctions and their remedy involve); *additional salaries* (which occur when an activity is performed by one of the performers in charge of a better paid position than the one who should assume it when the remuneration does not correspond to a counterparty at work); *expenses related to the production defects* (it refers to the fact that quality defects need time for correcting or for resuming the items already manufactured, which reduces the merchantable production for the period taken into account); *expenses related to non-creating the potential* (or *strategic hidden cost)* is the cost in time of human's actions of immaterial investment which the company cannot achieved during a given period, as its *actors* were engaged with adjusting the malfunctions and a sufficient time could not be freed for certain longer-term actions).

Henri Savall's method is based on a pattern for assessing the costs related to non-quality (the hidden costs), which associates five types of costs to each malfunction indicator (Table 16.13).

The first four types of costs have a direct impact onto the account of results of the exercise in progress, the expenses related to non-creating the potential mainly influence the results of future exercises, the additional salaries, additional times and additional expenses being costs diluted into the existing accounting system, also called historical costs, included into the visible costs. The costs related to manufacturing defects and expenses related to non-creating the potential correspond to some costs of opportunity.

The level of costs related to non-quality (hidden costs) of a company mainly depends on two factors: *number of malfunctions* that occur, *the adjustment actions* needed (along with the quantities of matters and time consumed that follow one after another) in order to remedy each malfunction.

The calculation of costs incurred by the production non-quality represents a special interest because: *the non-quality cost may be deemed as motivation instrument*, because the calculation of this cost allows the manager's motivation, by supplying the information in a language that he/she understands better (financial

Table 16.13 The general pattern of calculating the costs related to non-quality (hidden costs)

No.	Malfunction indicators	Costs related to non-quality (hidden costs)					
		Additional expenses	Additional times	Additional salaries	Expenses related to production defects	Expenses related to non-creating the potential	Total (7) = (2) + (3) + (4) + (5) + (6)
0.	1.	2.	3.	4.	5.	6.	7.
1.	Absenteeism						
2.	Labour accidents						
3.	Circulation of personnel						
4.	Insufficiency of direct productivity						
5.	Non-quality of products						
6.	Total						
7.	Types of costs	Historical costs			Opportunity costs		Total costs

language), determining one to be more sensitive to quality problems; *the non-quality cost may help in underlying the managerial decision*, as the financial assessment enables knowing the malfunctions that occur and employees' orientation towards quality improving actions.

References

Abelgglen JC, Stalk G Jr (1985) Kaisha – La strategie des entreprises japonaise. Les Edition d'Organization, Paris
Brown M (2006) On the theory and measurement of technological change. Cambridge University Press, Cambridge
Courtois A, Pillet M, Martin C (2006) Gestion de productions. Les Editions D'organisation, Paris
Daft R (2004) Management. The Dryden Press, New York, NY
Dima IC (2010) Elements of industrial operational management. Prace Naukowe Wydzialu Zarzadzania, Czestochowa
Dima IC (2013) Industrial production management in flexible manufacturing systems. IGI Global, Hershey
Masaaki I (1994) La cle'de la competitivité japonaise. Ed. Eyrolles, Paris
Masaaki I (2006) Kaizen the key to Japoan's competitive success. McGraw-Hill, New York, NY
Milgrom P, Roberts J (1992) Economics, organizations & management. Prentice-Hall, New York, NY
Miner J (2008) The management process. McMillan, New York, NY
Pugh DS, Hickson DJ (1997) Writers on organizations. McGraw-Hill, New York, NY
Robins St (2001) Management, 3rd edn. Prentice Hall, New York, NY
Shingo S (1990) Le système Shingo. Les cles de l'améliorition de la production. Les Editions d'Organization, Paris
Taguchi G (1989) Quality engineering in production systems. McGraw-Hill, New York, NY
Vachette JL (1990) Amélioration continue de la qualité. Les Editions d'Organization, Paris

MIX
Papier aus verantwortungsvollen Quellen
Paper from responsible sources
FSC® C105338

If you have any concerns about our products,
you can contact us on
ProductSafety@springernature.com

In case Publisher is established outside the EU,
the EU authorized representative is:
Springer Nature Customer Service Center GmbH
Europaplatz 3, 69115 Heidelberg, Germany

Printed by Libri Plureos GmbH
in Hamburg, Germany